Communications
in Computer and Information Science   365

W0225788

Juan M. Corchado   Javier Bajo
Jaroslaw Kozlak   Pawel Pawlewski
Jose M. Molina   Vicente Julian
Ricardo Azambuja Silvcira
Rainer Unland   Sylvain Giroux (Eds.)

Highlights on Practical Applications of Agents and Multi-Agent Systems

International Workshops of PAAMS 2013
Salamanca, Spain, May 22-24, 2013
Proceedings

 Springer

Volume Editors

Juan M. Corchado
University of Salamanca, Spain
E-mail: corchado@usal.es

Javier Bajo
Universidad Politécnica de Madrid, Spain
E-mail: javier.bajo@upm.es

Jaroslaw Kozlak
AGH University of Science and Technology
Krakow, Poland
E-mail: kozlak@agh.edu.pl

Pawel Pawlewski
Poznan University of Technology, Poland
E-mail: pawel.pawlewski@put.poznan.pl

Jose M. Molina
Universidad Carlos III de Madrid, Spain
E-mail: molina@ia.uc3m.es

Vicente Julian
Universidad Politécnica de Valencia, Spain
E-mail: vinglada@dsic.upv.es

Ricardo Azambuja Silveira
Universidade Federal de Santa Catarina
Florianópolis S.C., Brazil
E-mail: ricardo.silveira@ufsc.br

Rainer Unland
Universität Duisburg-Essen, Germany
E-mail: rainer.unland@icb.uni-due.de

Sylvain Giroux
Université de Sherbrooke, QC, Canada
E-mail: sylvain.giroux@usherbrooke.ca

ISSN 1865-0929   e-ISSN 1865-0937
ISBN 978-3-642-38060-0   e-ISBN 978-3-642-38061-7
DOI 10.1007/978-3-642-38061-7
Springer Heidelberg Dordrecht London New York

Library of Congress Control Number: Applied for

CR Subject Classification (1998): I.2.11, I.2, K.3, K.4, H.3, J.1, J.2, J.7, I.6, H.4, G.3

Typesetting: Camera-ready by author, data conversion by Scientific Publishing Services, Chennai, India

Printed on acid-free paper

Springer is part of Springer Science+Business Media (www.springer.com)

Preface

PAAMS, the International Conference on Practical Applications of Agents and Multi-Agent Systems, is an evolution of the International Workshop on Practical Applications of Agents and Multi-Agent Systems. PAAMS is an international yearly event with a platform to present, to discuss, and to disseminate the latest developments and the most important outcomes related to real-world applications. It provides a unique opportunity to bring multi-disciplinary experts, academics, and practitioners together to exchange their experience in the development of agents and multi-agent systems.

The PAAMS Workshops complement the regular program with new or emerging trends of particular interest connected to multi-agent systems.

This volume presents the papers that were accepted for the 2013 workshops: Workshop on Agent-based Approaches for the Transportation Modeling and Optimization, Workshop on Agent-Based Solutions for Manufacturing and Supply Chain, Workshop on User Centric Technologies and Applications, Workshop on Conflict Resolution in Decision Making, Workshop on Multi-Agent System-Based Learning Environments, Workshop on Multi-Agent-Based Applications for Sustainable Energy Systems, Workshop on Agents and Multi-Agent Systems for AAL and e-HEALTH.

We would like to thank all the contributing authors as well as the members of the Program Committees of the workshops and the Organizing Committee for their hard and highly valuable work. Their work contributed to the success of the PAAMS 2013 event. Thank you for your help – PAAMS 2013 would not have been possible without your contribution.

Juan Manuel Corchado
Javier Bajo

Organization

Workshops

Invited Talks

W1 – Workshop on Agent-Based Approaches for the Transportation Modeling and Optimization.

W2 – Workshop on Agent-Based Solutions for Manufacturing and Supply Chain.

W3 – Workshop on User-Centric Technologies and Applications.

W4 – Workshop on Conflict Resolution in Decision Making.

W5 – Workshop on Multi-Agent System-Based Learning Environments.

W6 – Workshop on Multi-Agent-Based Applications for Sustainable Energy Systems.

W7 – Workshop on Agents and Multi-Agent Systems for AAL and e-HEALTH.

Invited Talks

Michael Huhns
Sascha Ossowski
Juan M. Corchado

Workshop on Agent-Based Approaches for the Transportation Modeling and Optimization Committee

Organizing Committee

Jean-Michel Auberlet (Co-chair)	iIFSTTAR, France
Flavien Balbo (Co-chair)	Université Paris-Dauphine, France
Jaroslaw Kozlak (Co-chair)	AGH-UST, Poland

Program Committee

Jean-Michel Auberlet	IFSTTAR, France
Flavien Balbo	Université Paris-Dauphine, France
Didac Busquets	Imperial College of London, UK
Paul Davidsson	Malmo University, Sweden
Emmanuelle Grislin-Le Strugeon	University of Valenciennes, France
Otthein Herzog	University of Bremen, Germany

Abder Koukam	UTBM, France
Jaroslaw Kozlak	AGH-UST, Poland
Jörg P. Müller	Clausthal University of Technology, Germany
Rudy Negenborn	Delft University of Technology, The Netherlands
Sascha Ossowski	University Rey Juan Carlos, Spain
Rosaldo Rossetti	University of Porto-LIACC/FEUP, Portugal
Nicolas Saunier	Polytechnique Montreal, Canada
Bartlomiej Sniezynski	AGH-UST, Poland
Janusz Wojtusiak	George Mason University, USA
Mahdi Zargayouna	IFSTTAR, France

Workshop on Agent-Based Solutions for Manufacturing and Supply Chain Committee

Organizing Committee

Pawel Pawlewski	Poznan University of Technology, Poland
Zbigniew J. Pasek	IMSE/University of Windsor, Canada

Program Committee

Paul-Eric Dossou	ICAM Vendee, France
Grzegorz Bocewicz	Koszalin University of Technology, Poland
Izabela E. Nielsen	Aalborg University, Denmark
Joanna Kolodziej	Cracow University of Technology, Poland
Peter Nielsen	Aalborg University, Denmark

Workshop on User-Centric Technologies and Applications Committee

Organizing Committee

José Manuel Molina López (Co-chair)	University Carlos III of Madrid, Spain
José Ramón Casar Corredera (Co-chair)	Polytechnic University of Madrid, Spain
Manuel Felipe Cátedra Pérez (Co-chair)	University of Alcalá, Spain
Javier Ortega-García (Co-chair)	Autonomous University of Madrid, Spain

Program Committee

Álvaro Luis Bustamante	Carlos III University of Madrid, Spain
Ana Bernardos	Polytechnic University of Madrid, Spain
Ana Cristina Bicharra	University Federal Fluminense, Brazil
Antonio Berlanga	Carlos III University of Madrid, Spain
Antonio Ortega	University of Southern California, USA
Carlos Delgado	University of Alcalá, Spain
Changjiu Zhou	Singapore Polytechnic, Singapore
Daniel Ramos Castro	Autonomous University of Madrid, Spain
David Griol	Carlos III University of Madrid, Spain
Doroteo Torre Toledano	Autonomous University of Madrid, Spain
Eleni Mangina	University College Dublin, Ireland
Eliseo García	University of Alcalá, Spain
Enrique Martí Muñoz	Carlos III University of Madrid, Spain
George Cybenko	Dartmouth College, USA
Gonzalo de Miguel	Polytechnic University of Madrid, Spain
Gonzalo Blazquez Gil	Carlos III University of Madrid, Spain
Gregori Vázquez	Polytechnic University of Cataluña, Spain
James Llinas	State University of N.Y. at Buffalo, USA
Javier Carbó	Carlos III University of Madrid, Spain
Javier Galbally Herrero	Autonomous University of Madrid, Spain
Javier Portillo	Polytechnic University of Madrid, Spain
Jesús García-Herrero	Carlos III University of Madrid, Spain
Joaquín González Rodríguez	Autonomous University of Madrid, Spain
Jørgen Bach Andersen	Aalborg University, Denmark
José Luis Guerrero	Carlos III University of Madrid, Spain
Jose Manuel Gómez	University of Alcalá, Spain
Juan Besada	Polytechnic University of Madrid, Spain
Juan M. Corchado	University of Salamanca, Spain
Juan Pavón	Complutense University of Madrid, Spain
Julián Fiérrez Aguilar	Autonomous University of Madrid, Spain
Juan Gómez Romero	Carlos III University of Madrid, Spain
Luis Correia	Lisbon University, Portugal
Luis Vergara	Polytechnic University of Valencia, Spain
Miguel Ángel Patricio	Carlos III University of Madrid, Spain
Miguel Serrano Mateos	Carlos III University of Madrid, Spain
Nayat Sánchez	Carlos III University of Madrid, Spain
Oscar Gutiérrez	University of Alcalá, Spain
Paula Tarrío	Polytechnic University of Madrid, Spain
Raj Mitra	Pennsylvania State University, USA
Rodrigo Cilla Ugarte	Carlos III University of Madrid, Spain
Rubén Vera Rodríguez	Autonomous University of Madrid, Spain
Virginia Fuentes	Carlos III University of Madrid, Spain

Workshop on Conflict Resolution in Decision Making Committee

Organizing Committee

Reyhan Aydogan (Co-chair)	Delft University of Technology, The Netherlands
Joost Broekens (Co-chair)	Delft University of Technology, The Netherlands
Carlos Chesñevar (Co-chair)	Universidad Nacional del Sur, Argentina
Catholijn M. Jonker (Co-chair)	Delft University of Technology, The Netherlands
Stella Heras (Co-chair)	Universitat Politècnica de València, Spain
Vicente Julián (Co-chair)	Universitat Politècnica de València, Spain
Michael Rovatsos (Co-chair)	University of Edinburgh, UK
Victor Sanchez-Anguix (Co-chair)	Universitat Politècnica de Valencia, Spain

Program Committee

Javier Bajo	Universidad Politécnica de Madrid, Spain
Elizabeth Black	King's College London, UK
Anais Garrell	Universitat Politècnica de Catalunya, Spain
Koen Hindriks	Delft University of Technology, The Netherlands
Gert Jan Hofstede	Wageningen University, The Netherlands
Mark Klein	MIT, USA
Minyi Li	Swinburne University of Technology, Australia
Ivan Marsa-Maestre	Universidad de Alcalá, Spain
Eva Onaindia	Universitat Politècnica de València, Spain
Miguel Rebollo	Universidad Politécnica de Valencia
Valentin Robu	University of Southampton, UK
Sara Rodriguez	Universidad de Salamanca, Spain
Juan Antonio Rodríguez-Aguilar	CSIC-IIIA, Spain
Carles Sierra	CSIC-IIIA, Spain
Andreas L. Symeonidis	Aristotle University of Thessaloniki, Greece
Michael Ignaz Schumacher	University of Applied Sciences Western Switzerland, Switzerland
Serena Villata	WIMMICS Research Team

Workshop on Multi-Agent System-Based Learning Environments Committee

Organizing Committee

Ricardo Azambuja Silveira
(Co-chair)   Universidade Federal de Santa Catarina, Brazil
Rosa Vicari (Co-chair)   Universidade Federal do Rio Grande do
                                    Sul – UGRGS, Brazil

Néstor Darío Duque
Méndez (Co-chair)   Universidad Nacional de Colombia, Colombia

Program Committee

Cesar Alberto Collazos
Ordoñez   Universidad del Cauca Colombia, Colombia
Demetrio A Ovalle
Carranza   Universidad Nacional de Colombia, Colombia
Ramon Fabregat   Universidad de Girona, Spain
Maria Moreno Garcia   Universidad de Salamanca, Spain
Ana Belén Gil   Universidad de Salamanca, Spain
Martín Llamas Nistal   Universidad de Vigo, Spain
Carlos Vaz de Carvalho   Instituto Politécnico do Porto, Portugal
Helder Manuel
Ferreira Coelho   Universidade de Lisboa, Portugal
José Cascalho   Universidade dos Açores, Portugal

Workshop on Multi-agent based Applications for Sustainable Energy Systems Committee

Organizing Committee

Giancarlo Fortino
(Co-chair)   Università della Calabria, Italy
Ryszard Kowalczyk
(Co-chair)   Swinburne University of Technology, Australia
Rainer Unland
(Co-chair)   University of Duisburg-Essen, Germany

Program Committee

Alexander Pokahr   University of Hamburg, Germany
Andreas Symeonidis   University of Thessaloniki, Greece
Anke Weidlich   Hochschule Offenburg, Germany
Bao Vo   Swinburne University of Technology, Australia
Benjamin Hirsch   EBTIC, UAE
Bernhard Bauer   Universität Augsburg, Germany

Bo Nørregaard Jørgensen   Mærsk Mc-Kinney Møller Instituttet, Denmark
Christian Derksen   Universität Duisburg-Essen, Germany
Christoph Weber   Universität Duisburg-Essen, Germany
Costin Bădică   University of Craiova, Romania
Cristina Baroglio   Università degli Studi di Torino, Italy
David Sislak   Gerstner Laboratory, Czech Republic
Fabrice Saffre   Etisalat BT Innovation Centre, UAE
Frank Allgöwer   Universität Stuttgart, Germany
Georg Frey   Universität des Saarlandes, Germany
Hanno Hildmann   Khalifa University, UAE
Huaglory Tianfield   Glasgow Caledonian University, UK
Huib Aldewereld   Universiteit Utrecht, The Netherlands
Ingo J. Timm   J.W. Goethe-University Frankfurt, Germany
Jan Sudeikat   Hamburg Energie GmbH, Germany
John Collins   University of Minnesota, USA
Lars Braubach   University of Hamburg, Germany
Lars Mönch   Fernuniversität Hagen, Germany
Marcin Paprzycki   Polish Academy of Sciences, Poland
Maria Ganzha   Polish Academy of Sciences, Poland
Martin Tröschel   OFFIS - Institut für Informatik, Germany
Mathijs de Weerdt   TU Delft, The Netherlands
Matthias Klusch   DFKI GmbH, Germany
Ori Marom   Rotterdam School of Management,
   The Netherlands
Peter Palensky   AIT Austrian Institute of Technology, Austria
Sascha Ossowski   Universidad Rey Juan Carlos, Spain
Stamatis Karnouskos   SAP, Germany
Steven Guan   Xian Jiatong-Liverpool University, China
Wolfgang Ketter   Rotterdam School of Management,
   The Netherlands
Zakaria Maamar   Zayed University, UAE

Workshop on Agents and Multi-Agent Systems for AAL and e-HEALTH Committee

Organizing Committee

Kasper Hallenborg
  (Co-chair)   University of Southern Denmark, Denmark
Sylvain Giroux (Co-chair)   University of Sherbrooke, Canada

Program Committee

Juan M. Corchado   University of Salamanca, Spain
Javier Bajo   Technical University of Madrid, Spain
Juan F. De Paz   University of Salamanca, Spain

Sara Rodríguez	University of Salamanca, Spain
Dante I. Tapia	University of Salamanca, Spain
Fernando de la Prieta Pintado	University of Salamanca, Spain
Davinia Carolina Zato Domínguez	University of Salamanca, Spain
Gabriel Villarrubia González	University of Salamanca, Spain
Alejandro Sánchez Yuste	University of Salamanca, Spain
Antonio Juan Sánchez Martín	University of Salamanca, Spain
Cristian I. Pinzón	University of Salamanca, Spain
Rosa Cano	University of Salamanca, Spain
Emilio S. Corchado	University of Salamanca, Spain
Eugenio Aguirre	University of Granada, Spain
Manuel P. Rubio	University of Salamanca, Spain
Belén Pérez Lancho	University of Salamanca, Spain
Angélica González Arrieta	University of Salamanca, Spain
Vivian F. López	University of Salamanca, Spain
Ana de Luís	University of Salamanca, Spain
Ana B. Gil	University of Salamanca, Spain
Mª Dolores Muñoz Vicente	University of Salamanca, Spain
Jesús García Herrero	Carlos III University of Madrid, Spain

PAAMS 2013 Workshops Organizing Committee

Juan M. Corchado (Chair)	University of Salamanca, Spain
Javier Bajo (Co-chair)	Technical University of Madrid, Spain
Juan F. De Paz	University of Salamanca, Spain
Sara Rodríguez	University of Salamanca, Spain
Dante I. Tapia	University of Salamanca, Spain
Alejandro Sánchez	Pontifical University of Salamanca, Spain
Gabriel Villarrubia	University of Salamanca, Spain
Fernando de la Prieta Pintado	University of Salamanca, Spain
Davinia Carolina Zato Domínguez	University of Salamanca, Spain
Elena García	University of Salamanca, Spain
Roberto González	University of Salamanca, Spain

Table of Contents

Workshop on User-Centric Technologies and Applications

Workshop on Conflict Resolution in Decision Making

Workshop on Multi-Agent System Based Learning Environments

Workshop on Multi-Agent Based Applications for Sustainable Energy Systems

Workshop on Agents and Multi-Agent Systems for AAL and e-HEALTH

Social Control of Power System Demand
Based on Local Collaborative Preferences

Michael N. Huhns

University of South Carolina, Dept. of Computer Science and Engineering,
Columbia, SC USA
huhns@sc.edu

Abstract. This paper describes a computational approach to energy use that assigns importance to human psychology and social interactions. Specifically, this paper describes our investigations into computational mechanisms that encourage prosocial behavior on the part of consumers. Examples of prosocial behavior in the context of electrical energy use are reducing average aggregate consumption and peak total consumption. We consider an approach that combines minority games and cake-cutting that includes elements of human decision-making in situations that are hybrids of competitive and cooperative settings. For example, people may be motivated to reduce their consumption if that were posed as a competition wherein they would win a game, possibly by collaborating with their neighbors. And, people may be motivated to behave in a prosocial manner if selfish behaviors were shunned in their social group. Previous approaches disregard such dynamics from technical studies, relegating them to psychological analyses; yet the interrelationship of the human and the technical aspects is crucial in a complex sociotechnical system such as the power grid.

Keywords: Multiagent systems, electric power, demand-side control, social computing.

1 Introduction

There are many facets to the world-wide electric power problem, concerning how electric power can be generated in an environmentally sound way, how it can be stored and distributed efficiently, and how it can be used wisely. Although energy resources can be viewed strategically as an advantage for geopolitical entities that own the resources, we prefer to view them broadly as societal resources to be shared among the members of a society. The *control* of energy resources is *not* societal, however: it is centralized at the energy provider, where preferences of the members of the society are generally not considered.

We are investigating the modulation of electric power demand via socially intelligent computing. We seek to develop efficient consensus and incentive-based computational mechanisms for decentralized control of demand that respects system-wide objectives and individual preferences. Our mechanisms will influence consumer decisions regarding local energy usage, generation, and storage, as well as overall energy

J.M. Corchado et al. (Eds.): PAAMS 2013 Workshops, CCIS 365, pp. 1–12, 2013.

supply and demand, according to local consumption preferences and global supply objectives of grid operators. The societal benefits are lowered peak demand, improved operating efficiency, and lowered capital expenses.

1.1   Current Situation

In general terms, our problem involves the allocation of electric power (treated as a scarce societal resource) among independent consumers (households and small businesses). Recent approaches collected under the term "smart grid" enable consumer devices to be controlled by electric power utilities. The objective is to shed demand when it exceeds supply. For example, household air conditioners can be turned on or off easily from a central controller. However, deciding *whether* and *when* to turn them on or off based on consumer preferences is nontrivial. The smart grid is smart only from the viewpoint of the electric power utilities. Because consumers typically want their preferences to remain private, centralized approaches that allocate resources by fiat are not acceptable. How can consumers with diverse preferences make local decisions about the allocation and management of electric power that are globally effective? The problem is exacerbated by large consumer communities and frequently changing preferences.

Two forms of demand-side management are being used to solve energy resource allocation problems. In one, a central control form, a utility enters into agreements with customers, for a rebate incentive, under which the utility can directly control appliances, usually for load shedding when needed [1]. Central control does not address customer comfort and exception requests. In the other form, home management systems monitor and manage appliances. Some utilities are considering providing real-time pricing signals to improve the effectiveness of such systems. Home management systems suffer from customer reluctance to participate and lack of clear benefits [2]. Utilities have begun to realize that pure technical or economic approaches are not effective, so they are investigating alternatives to better engage their customers [3, 4].

Here is an example of the problem we are trying to address. Charging an electric vehicle is equivalent to approximately four houses using all of their appliances. The transformers in a neighborhood (the ones you might typically see on a pole) are sized for approximately ten houses. If 3 or 4 people in a neighborhood buy an electric vehicle and try to recharge it at the same time, the transformer will fail. To prevent this, the power company could double or quadruple the capacity of their lines and transformers, which would be very expensive, or the power company could take control of when people can recharge their vehicle, OR the neighbors could cooperate with each other in staggering when they recharge. We believe that the last is the best solution, but it requires the neighbors to be cooperative and possibly altruistic, and it must be done with local consumer cognizance of the global context.

1.2 Investigation Framework and Research Hypotheses

Our investigations are being conducted in a framework of realistic premises designed to make this large problem manageable. The premises are

Premise 1. Current pricing incentives are insufficient, because they are based on a history of past aggregate behavior and have little predictive value.

Premise 2. The community of consumers exhibits rich social relationships and energy usage dependencies that can be handled better through peer-to-peer interactions rather than through centralized control.

With these as a basis, the key is fostering peer-to-peer interactions among consumers to guide their individual control decisions and, by aggregating the decisions, produce effective system-level control. Individual demands are coordinated to reduce peak demand, flatten overall demand, and yield a power factor closer to 1.0. We believe that two levels of peer-to-peer interactions will be needed. At the macro-level, interactions create consensus on the overall goals and trade-offs, producing the equivalent of supply-and-demand curves. At the micro-level, interactions cause individual control decisions to be as dissimilar as possible, so as to spread demand as uniformly as possible.[1] To investigate this foundation for a demand-side approach, we have formulated the following hypotheses:

Hypothesis 1: Participation. A sufficient number of people in a society can be motivated to participate either directly or indirectly via their intelligent software agents in the management of an essential and limited resource (electric power).

Subhypothesis 1.1: Influence. Consumers' decisions can be influenced to promote prosocial behavior, if such behavior does not detract from their personal preferences.

Subhypothesis 1.2: Privacy. Consumers will share some private information (indirectly via their agents) so as to cooperate in promoting prosocial behavior.

Subhypothesis 1.3: Cooperation. Consumers are more amenable to promoting prosocial behavior if they can cooperate with known parties, not with anonymous strangers. Consumers who cooperate will achieve better outcomes.

Subhypothesis 1.4: Competition. A game environment offering competition among consumer groups can motivate consumers to exhibit prosocial behavior.

Subhypothesis 1.5: Trust. Consumers will trust software agents to represent their interests in negotiating for resources.

Hypothesis 2: Stability. A system of interacting agents cooperating and competing for resources on behalf of a community of users will produce a controllable, stable, and prosocial allocation of resources.

---

[1] We also recognize that at times it is important to develop "herd behavior." For example, if power is largely solar, then it is preferable to use that energy as it is being produced. Or, if industry needs large power during working hours, then it is desirable to push all residential demand into the nighttime so that the net consumption becomes flatter.

The scientific results will be improved understanding of how the macro-level and micro-level aspects of control come together and how users remain in control while engaging in socially desired behaviors. There will be three interdependent types of macro-level and micro-level interaction among providers, consumers, and the software agents representing individual interests (see Figure):

1. Expressing preferences: software agents interact with consumers to acquire their preferences and provide incentive-based feedback to influence their behavior.
2. Reaching consensus: macro-level interactions among agents to optimize their distributed demand decisions based on computational collective intelligence and consensus-based optimization, resulting in supply-demand curves based on local preferences and system objectives.
3. Achieving objectives: micro-level interactions between groups of consumer agents and resource provider agents to minimize impact on resources (i.e., reduce peak demand) based on field theory from particle physics, cake-cutting algorithms from studies on negotiation among multiple agents, and incentive-based optimization mechanisms.

The problem of allocating shared resources matches naturally with socially intelligent computing—the intersection of social behavior and distributed computational systems—and multiagent systems. Multiagent systems can apply social computing to investigate the technical problem of how to allocate, distribute, and govern scarce societal resources in a sustainable manner across a sufficiently coherent community of users, each potentially having different preferences for the resources and when to consume them. This is difficult, because communities are large and preferences will change frequently and, from a centralized viewpoint, unpredictably. The sharing should accommodate member preferences, yet provide fair and envy-free incentives to those whose preferences most promote sustainability. Because preferences are mostly personal and private, centralized approaches that allocate such resources by fiat are usually not acceptable in a free society. The key to this is fostering peer-to-peer interactions among the participants so as to accommodate both the personal and the interpersonal dimensions of decision making by rational, social participants.

The two complementary strategies we have investigated for the interactions are based on: (1) control systems and (2) a negotiation approach that combines minority games, particle physics, and cake-cutting algorithms. Multiagent negotiation is one of the decision-making mechanisms that can be used to provide for the allocation of resources. The results of such negotiations, from the viewpoint of the consumers, should be fair and envy-free, which motivates the investigation of "cake-cutting" approaches.

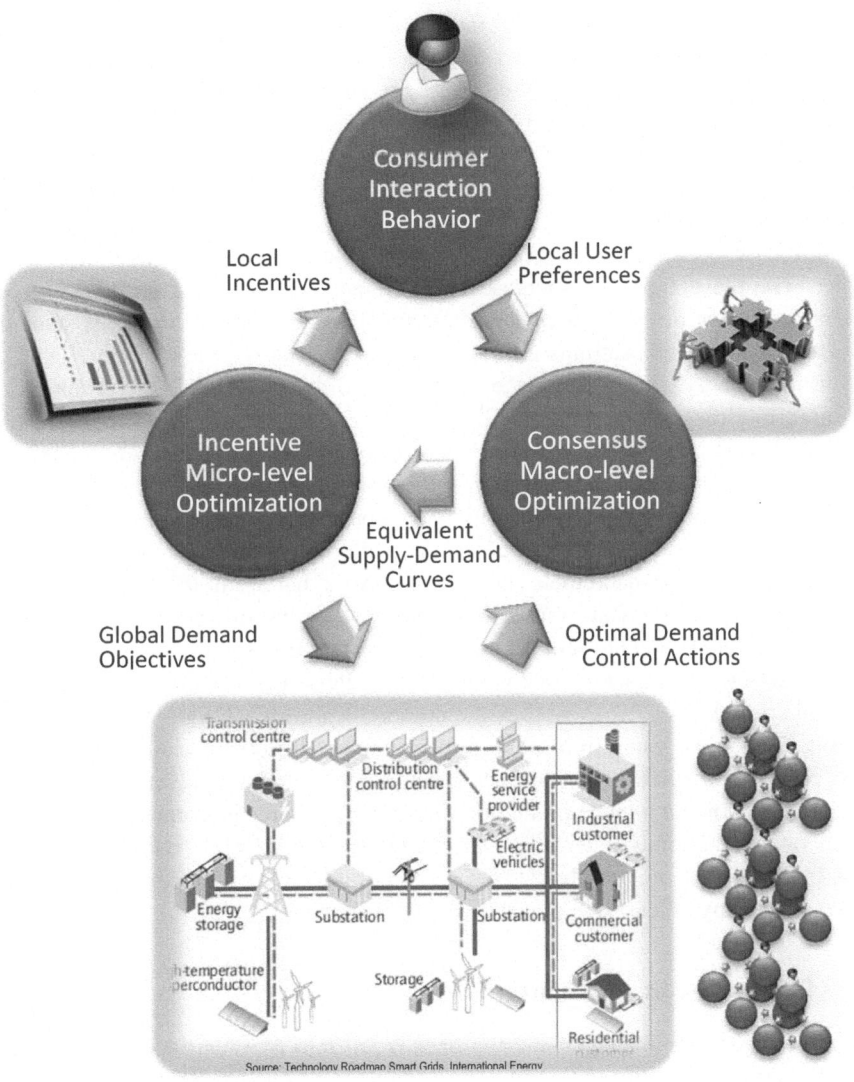

2 Background and Significance

Crowdsourcing [5] has drawn a lot of interest lately. Crowdsourcing involves (usually implicit) collaboration between users to solve a problem. However, crowdsourcing approaches are fundamentally limited to solving centrally allocated problems where the mode or median or individual solutions converge to the ideal solution. We refer to such central tendencies loosely as the majority. In majority problems, a statistical aggregation of individual solutions proves effective. To follow Galton's example from 1907 of the wisdom of crowds, if 800 people estimate the weight of an ox by just looking at it, their individual estimates may vary a lot, but in a Gaussian manner: their majority estimate (the median) could be close to the actual weight of the ox. So much so that when we have no other means to determine the weight of an ox, we might rely solely on the majority estimate, which is what crowdsourcing pursues. Such solutions can be promoted by giving users an incentive to be nearest to the majority. Notice that if we gave users an incentive to be far from the majority, the result would be meaningless.

In the case of resource usage, however, the participants' interests are not well aligned with the majority. If increased peak demand causes the price to go up, consumers are better off spreading their individual loads to lower the peak and, thus, lower the price. In such settings we are not seeking a majority view of the "right" time to consume energy, but to influence consumers to distribute their consumption. The consumer in effect has an incentive to be in a minority. Minority settings in general are highly volatile. Are there social mechanisms that can motivate behavior to produce effective solutions in minority settings?

The *minority game* [7][9] is defined as a game with a large number of players, N, with each player making a choice between two alternatives at each round of the game. After all players have made their choice, the players that are in the minority each win one point. This is relevant for electric power distribution, because the preferred solution is for consumers to request power at different times.

A variant of the minority game is the Kolkata Paise Restaurant Problem [8] where the number of choices (n) as well as the number of players (N) are relatively large. It is a repetitive game where information regarding the history of choices made by different players is available to everyone. Assuming that n = N, a player ϵ N wins a point by making a choice ϵ n made by no other player. If a choice is made by more than one player, one is randomly selected to earn a point. Hence, while each player gains a point for making a unique choice, the resource utilization is maximized when each choice is made by at least one player.

2.1   Power Systems and Control Theory

Current demand-side management approaches fall into two main categories. First, in central control, the utility enters into agreements with customers, for a rebate incentive, under which the utility can directly control appliances, usually for load shedding when needed [1]. Central control does not address customer comfort and exception requests. Thus, customers are reluctant to participate and only a few do. Second, home management systems monitor and manage appliances (e.g., by turning them on and off, or adjusting temperature settings). The consumer is expected to play a major role in (paying for) installing and configuring such systems. Utilities can provide realtime pricing signals to improve the effectiveness of such systems. Walker and Meier [2] observe that home management systems suffer from customer reluctance to participate, and lack of clear benefits. They also observe that some kind of automation is essential: as they found, in settings where consumers sought to control their air conditioner usage manually, they would turn on their respective air conditioners precisely at peak times thus exacerbating peak demand.

As support for the significance of our proposed approach, Berst [3] points out that pure technical or economic approaches are not proving effective and utilities are investigating alternatives to better enlist their customers' support. Similarly, the Federal Energy Regulatory Commission [12] acknowledges the challenge of communicating the importance of demand response and engaging consumers effectively.

In recent influential works, Sean Meyn [4] has articulated well some of the challenges of relying purely on pricing mechanisms for system control. At the macro-level, such approaches have led to well-known problems though they have demonstrated that consumers can change their demand in response to severe price signals. However, this doesn't mean that the resulting allocations are equitable or that consumption is smoothed in the process. Mathieu et al. [14] study different types of industrial and commercial consumers and observe challenges in prediction, specifically, that variation may often be dominated by model error rather than due to explicit response. Shao et al. [15][16] study residential load profiles, including the charging of electrical vehicles, which creates heavy loads. Shao et al. are concerned with capturing consumer priorities regarding various appliances and being able to control them as a way to shape the overall load.

Japan's Digital Grid Consortium envisions large-scale energy grids that can handle power the way the Internet handles data, using routers and service providers to efficiently direct the flow of electricity [17]. The consortium seeks to develop technology that can track units of energy across an entire grid, tagging them with their source and destination similar to the way Internet packets are handled. The consortium plans for inputs to include existing power plants, solar facilities, and other alternative sources. The grid will include local power storage systems, such as large-scale batteries in homes. The units of energy will be managed by service providers, tracing and charging for them like a currency exchange. The energy "messages" are intended for *supply-side management*, but could be adapted to serve *demand-side management*.

Because power systems are inherently distributed, agent-based approaches apply naturally therein to support local control. They contrast with extant approaches, which develop centralized solutions, placing all the intelligence in central controllers. Baran and El-Markabi [18] show how to characterize a multiagent protocol that facilitates control in the presence of local sensitivities as long as appropriate communication assumptions are met. Hernández et al. [19] study the modeling of power sources in smart grids. Pipattanasomporn et al. [20] apply multiagent systems from the utility standpoint. They show how their approach can isolate a local system from the grid adaptively as needed. Pipattanasomporn et al. [21] motivate a home power network architecture, which accords with our conception. Their proposed home management system corresponds to an agent that controls local loads on behalf of a consumer and responds to signals from the grid.

2.2   Multiagent Negotiation for Multiplayer Resource Allocation

An important feature of multiagent systems is that the agents can behave autonomously considering the interest of the people they represent. Fairness and envy-freedom are criteria used to judge the effectiveness of allocation procedures. Assume the resource being allocated is measurable. An allocation procedure is called fair if it distributes a resource among n agents such that every agent values its portion as exactly $1/n$ of the total value of the resource. An allocation procedure is called envy-free if every agent values its portion at least as much as the portions allocated to other agents. Thus, envy-freedom is stricter than fairness. When a mediator is involved in resource allocation, an additional desirable criterion is that the mediator is unbiased. In addition, the procedure should be efficient in time and space complexity, strategy-proof, and constructive.

In open multiagent systems there is generally no global control, no globally consistent knowledge, and no globally shared goals or success criteria [22]. So the agents compete to maximize their own utilities. We assume each agent's utility function is private. A negotiation protocol should be immune to information hiding and lying by the agents. In addition, protocols can be evaluated on various criteria such as fairness, envy-freedom, equitability, and efficiency. Brams and Taylor [23] discuss various procedures for allocating resources. They show that it is generally difficult for any given procedure to fulfill more than two of the above mentioned criteria. These criteria are by no means exhaustive, but may be taken as an initial test of the allocation procedure that is being proposed. For example, other criteria that can used to evaluate protocols are: simplicity, computational complexity, and verifiability.

A protocol for negotiated resource allocation—the basis for the multiplayer game envisioned here—is said to be verifiable if the allocation of the resource is invariant to the bias of the mediator (game engine). Iyer and Huhns [10][11] address verifiability in a resource allocation procedure for one or two-dimensional resources, proving that if the agents follow a specified multiagent negotiation protocol, it is possible to have a fair and unbiased allocation of the resource. At the end of the negotiation, one of the agents volunteers to act as a mediator and executes the procedure. Based on the computation of agent preferences, there are two outcomes: the procedure (i) finds a solution and all agents get a fair deal; or (ii) fails to find a solution and all agents receive the conflict deal, i.e., no agent receives any part of the resource. The salient point is that the agents can detect if the mediator attempts to manipulate the results. Hence the results of this method are verifiable to any agent who wants to check them and the mediator need not be a trusted outsider. Importantly, the utility functions of the agents are not compared and therefore are unconstrained: all that matters is how the agents' preferences relate to one another.

3   Analysis

Let us consider one concrete scenario of how sustainable energy use can be treated as a societal problem. This scenario seeks to reduce peak demand but does not address reducing total demand. That is, we would like consumers to shift their individual demands in time so that the peak aggregate demand at any time is reduced. Doing so has benefits in yielding a more stable load and reducing the need for capital expenses.

The most traditional approach would be to determine the popular times of the day or week for demand and to set the price higher for such times, so as to encourage consumers to move away from such times. Such an approach works from historical data and lacks knowledge of and flexibility in addressing changing situations.

A more modern approach is to apply real-time pricing. However, real-time pricing is difficult from a practical standpoint because of characteristics of power systems that cannot match production to demand instantaneously. Further, real-time pricing is difficult for consumers to deal with, and often leads to chaotic outcomes [5].

We now describe the interactions between a consumer, a power supplier, and our proposed system, which could be thought of as a mapping to an energy service provider (ESP) [13]. Let's begin with a variant wherein the consumers act independently of each other.

As the Figure shows, a consumer assisted by an agent submits constraints on an expected future load profile. A local broker/manager considers all the submitted profiles and determines a nonbinding allocation for each consumer that reduces the peak demand and demand variations. The allocation is guaranteed to satisfy each consumer's stated constraints. A simple way to find such an allocation is to order the consumers randomly and, for each consumer in turn, allocate power usage timeslots to that consumer in a way that greedily minimizes the peak consumption. Each consumer may or may not act according to the allocation.

A consumer who follows the recommended consumption profile pays the average price for the current total demand in each time slot. A consumer who consumes power arbitrarily either by never participating in our approach or by participating but deviating from the recommendation pays the usual marginal rate.

The price for power increases with the instantaneous demand at the time of consumption. With some key assumptions, this scenario provides a way to address some important properties:

- **Prosociality.** The local broker/manager charges a higher price to ad hoc consumers than for plan-ahead consumers, which creates an overall incentive to reduce peak demand.
- **Individual rationality.** Those who submit a profile and follow the resulting allocation benefit by paying a smaller price for the power they draw. Thus participants pay a lower price for power in a given slot than someone who consumes the same amount of power in the same slot but without a prior submission. Thus consumers are motivated to participate in the brokering and management.
- **No coercion.** Those who submit a profile are free to ignore the suggested allocation. They pay the same price for that consumption as if they had never participated.
- **Budget balance.** When consumers as a group create more expensive demand on the power source, they pay more for the privilege.

However, this approach assumes the consumers have NO knowledge of the constraints (preferences) of other consumers or of the constraints of the power generation and distribution system. That is, a consumer might be willing to shift its need for power to a slightly different time interval if it would result in a major savings in cost, but has no way of discovering this. This approach forms an imperfect information game.

Our approach combines pricing with social mechanisms. Consumers join cooperatives, which we assume are small, such as neighborhood blocks. Each cooperative seeks to minimize its overall cost in terms of financial units or in terms of environmental impact. Thus the members of each cooperative, must negotiate with each other with respect to their individual preferences as such preferences are affected by important externalities such as the changing price of energy, changing weather, and social factors such as whether it is a holiday season.

We are investigating some key challenges that arise from our vision, such as power system models, social interaction models, design models of agents, user models, and economic models. In addition to formal models and simulations, we are using games to explore how consumers interact in different circumstances and how we may effectively promote prosocial behavior. The interactions among power consumers might take the form of

1. Auctions, with the following features:

   — Individuals base their bids on their own preferences
   — Individuals do not reveal their preferences
   — Individuals could maintain and use a history of interactions. Based on this, individuals could learn the strategies of others, although the auctions might be designed to reduce or eliminate the need for this
   — The auctions do not allow any future considerations

2. Round-robin power scheduling, where individuals take turns having first preference for power use, in an endless cycle.
3. Direct negotiating among consumers, involving promises / commitments for future use, and which might be multiparty.

Particle physics provides both a metaphor and a mathematical basis for solving the resource allocation problem. Particle physics dictate that particles tend to occupy the most energetically favorable states, while certain other particles cannot occupy the same state together. This translates into an analogy of electric power resources that either any number of consumers can share or that only one consumer can have.

4   Research Agenda

The goal of the power company (maximize profit) is different than the consensus goals of its customers (minimize cost, maximize comfort, protect environment). Although the proposed project studies household electrical power consumption, its results could be applied to a broader class of societal resources, such as fresh water, thus promoting sustainability in such settings as well. Our approach applies social computing to sustainability problems. We treat consumers and providers as important participants and rely upon their mutual interactions—mediated by computational agents—as a basis for arriving at high-quality solutions. Each user delegates some authority to an agent, which then acts on the user's behalf. Traditional social computing approaches are limited to information problems where consensus is important. In contrast, our approach applies to allocation problems where the *dissimilarity* of the participants' decisions improves social welfare and helps capture each participant's local preferences. There are two main considerations:

1. Can a sufficient number of people in a society be motivated to participate either directly or indirectly via their intelligent software agents in the prosocial management of an essential and limited resource (electric power)?
2. Will a power distribution system managed from the edge by consumers be controllable and stable in a control system theory sense?

4.1   Uninvestigated Hypotheses

The following hypotheses are relevant and deserving of investigation, but this has not yet been done:

- Bottom-up preferences negotiated among users in a neighborhood are more secure than top-down control of appliances by power companies, as is envisioned for various "smart grids."
- Being cognizant of global warming and climate change, people will act altruistically towards their neighbors in allocating electric power resources.
- It remains to be shown that the grid will be more efficient and more fair if consumer preferences are considered.
- Because they have only local information and minimal global information, consumers have been shown to act suboptimally when the global grid is considered and not even in their own best interests locally when allowed to participate in decisions about the distribution and usage of electric power.
- Agents expressing local preferences and exchanging information with providers and other consumers can obtain a global view and can act optimally in both an individual and global sense.

References

1. Rahman, S.: Integration of demand response with renewable energy for efficient power system operation. In: IEEE PES ISGT Middle East Conference and Exhibition (2011)
2. Walker, I.S., Meier, A.K.: Residential thermostats: Comfort controls in California homes. Project Report LBNL-938E, Lawrence Berkeley National Laboratory (March 2008)
3. Berst, J.: How cities (and their utilities) are blowing it: New research reveals three failures. Smart Grid News (December 2011), http://www.smartgridnews.com
4. Meyn, S.P., Negrete-Pincetic, M., Wang, G., Kowli, A., Shafieepoorfard, E.: The value of volatile resources in electricity markets. In: Proc. 49th IEEE Conference on Decision and Control (CDC), Atlanta, pp. 1029–1036. IEEE (December 2010)

5. Howe, J.: The rise of crowdsourcing. Wired 14(6) (June 2006), http://www.wired.com/wired/archive/14.06/crowds.html
6. Rahman, S.: Integration of demand response with renewable energy for efficient power system operation. In: IEEE PES ISGT Middle East Conf. and Exhibition (2011)
7. Challet, D., Marsili, M., Zhang, Y.-C.: Minority Games: Interacting Agents in Financial Markets. Oxford University Press, Oxford (2005)
8. Gualdi, S., Medo, M., Zhang, Y.-C.: Crowd Avoidance and Diversity in Socio-Economic Systems and Recommendation (January 2013), arXiv:1301.1887
9. Tarko, V.: Minority Games (2012), http://news.softpedia.com/news/Minority-Games-38625.shtml
10. Iyer, K., Huhns, M.N.: Multiagent negotiation for fair and unbiased resource allocation. In: Meersman, R., Tari, Z. (eds.) OTM 2005. LNCS, vol. 3760, pp. 453–465. Springer, Heidelberg (2005)
11. Iyer, K., Huhns, M.N.: A procedure for the allocation of two-dimensional resources in a multiagent system. International Journal of Cooperative Information Systems 18(3-4), 381–422 (2009)
12. FERC. National action plan on demand response. Docket AD09-10, Federal Energy Regulatory Commission, Washington, DC (June 2010), http://www.ferc.gov/legal/staff-reports/06-17-10-demand-response.pdf
13. ESP. Energy service providers (2012), http://www.csd.ca.gov/Programs/Energy
14. Mathieu, J.L., Callaway, D.S., Kiliccote, S.: Variability in automated responses of commercial buildings and industrial facilities to dynamic electricity prices. Energy and Buildings 43(12), 3322–3330 (2011)
15. Shao, S., Pipattanasomporn, M., Rahman, S.: Demand response as a load shaping tool in an intelligent grid with electric vehicles. IEEE Transactions on Smart Grid 2(4), 624–631 (2011)
16. Shao, S., Pipattanasomporn, M., Rahman, S.: Grid integration of electric vehicles and demand response with customer choice. IEEE Transactions on Smart Grid 3(1), 543–550 (2012)
17. Alabaster, J.: Japan group to build smart power grids that treat energy like network data (December 2011), http://www.computerworld.com/s/article/9222580
18. Baran, M.E., El-Markabi, I.M.: A multiagent-based dispatching scheme for distributed generators for voltage support on distribution feeders. IEEE Transactions on Power Systems 22(1), 52–59 (2007)
19. Hernández, L., Zorita, C.B., Aguiar, J., Carro, B., Sánchez-Esguevillas, A., Lloret, J., Chinarro, D., Gómez-Sanz, J.J., Cook, D.: A multi-agent system architecture for smart grid management and forecasting of energy demand in virtual power plants. IEEE Communications Magazine 51(1), 106–113 (2013)
20. Pipattanasomporn, M., Feroze, H., Rahman, S.: Multi-agent systems in a distributed smart grid: Design and implementation. In: IEEE PES Power Systems Conference and Exposition (PSCE), pp. 1–8 (March 2009)
21. Pipattanasomporn, M., Kuzlu, M., Rahman, S.: Demand response implementation in a home area network: A conceptual hardware architecture. In: Procedings of the 2nd IEEE PES Conference on Innovative Smart Grid Technologies (ISGT), Anaheim, California, pp. 1–8. IEEE Power & Energy Society (January 2012)
22. Rosenschein, J.S., Zlotkin, G.: Rules of Encounter. MIT Press, Cambridge (1994)
23. Brams, S.J., Taylor, A.D.: Fair Division: From Cake-Cutting to Dispute Resolution. Cambridge University Press, Cambridge (1996)

Agent-Based Applications for the Smart Grid: A Playground for Agreement Technologies

Sascha Ossowski[1] and Matteo Vasirani[2]

[1] CETINIA, University Rey Juan Carlos, Móstoles (Madrid), Spain
sascha.ossowski@urjc.es
[2] LSIR, École Polytechnique Fédérale de Lausanne (EPFL), Lausanne, Switzerland
matteo.vasirani@epfl.ch

Abstract. This paper summarises an invited talk given at the Multi-agent based Applications for Sustainable Energy Systems (MASSES) workshop, as part of the 11th Conference on Practical Applications of Agents and Multi-Agent Systems (PAAMS). It first delineates the emerging field of Agreement Technologies (AT) and then points to several case studies showing how findings from the field of AT can be used for building advanced applications for the Smart Grid.

1 Agreement Technologies

Agreement Technologies (AT) refer to computer systems in which autonomous software agents negotiate with one another, typically on behalf of humans, in order to come to mutually acceptable agreements [1]. Autonomy, interaction, mobility and openness are the characteristics that the AT paradigm covers from a theoretical and practical perspective. Semantic alignment, negotiation, argumentation, virtual organizations, learning, real time, and several other technologies are in the sandbox to define, specify and verify such systems.

The key research fields of AT can be conceived of in a tower structure, where each level provides functionality to the levels above [4]. *Semantic technologies* provide solutions to semantic mismatches through the alignment of ontologies, so agents can reach a common understanding on the elements of agreements. In this manner, a shared multi-faceted "space" of agreements can be conceived, providing essential information to the remaining layers. The next level is concerned with the definition of *norms* determining constraints that the agreements, and the processes leading to them, should satisfy. Thus, norms can be conceived of as a means of "shaping" the space of valid agreements. *Organisations* further restrict the way agreements are reached by imposing organisational structures on the agents. They thus provide a way to efficiently design and evolve the space of valid agreements, possibly based on normative concepts. The *argumentation and negotiation* layer provides methods for reaching agreements that respect the constraints that norms and organisations impose over the agents. This can be seen as choosing certain points in the space of valid agreements. Finally, the *trust and reputation* layer keeps track of as to how far the agreements reached

J.M. Corchado et al. (Eds.): PAAMS 2013 Workshops, CCIS 365, pp. 13–16, 2013.
© Springer-Verlag Berlin Heidelberg 2013

respect the constraints put forward by norms and organisations. So, it complements the other techniques that shape the "agreement space", by relying on social mechanisms that interpret the behaviour of agents.

Even though one can clearly see the main flow of information from the bottom towards the top layers, results of upper layers can also produce useful feedback that can be exploited at lower levels. For instance, norms and trust can be conceived as a priori and a posteriori approaches, respectively, to security [4]. Therefore, in an open and dynamic world it will certainly make sense for the results of trust models to have a certain impact on the evolution of norms. As a result, it has been proposed to conceive the key research fields of AT as a circle rather than a tower structure [3].

2   AT for the Smart Grid

There is no limitation *per se* regarding the domains where AT can be successfully applied. Still, some domains are particularly attractive as a playground for AT: firstly, because the problems and challenges in these areas are of significant socio-economic relevance, so that applications based on AT can actually make a difference; and secondly because applications in these fields usually require the simultaneous use of several of the AT building blocks. As argued in [3], the field of *traffic and transportation* is certainly one of those key applications areas for AT. Another high-profile application domain is the field of *Smart Grids*, as we will argue in the sequel.

The basis of an efficient functioning of a power grid is an accurate balancing of the electricity demand, of all consumers and at any instant, with supply. Nowadays, this task involves only the grid operator and retail electricity providers. One of the facets of the Smart Grid vision is that consumers may have a more active role in the problem of balancing demand with supply. With the deployment of intelligent information and communication technologies in domestic environments, homes are becoming smarter and able to play a more active role in the management of energy. We use the term Smart Consumer Load Balancing to refer to algorithms that are run by energy management systems of homes in order to optimise the electricity consumption, to minimise costs and/or meet supply constraints. In [7], we analyse different approaches to Smart Consumer Load Balancing based on AT. We put forward a new model of Smart Consumer Load Balancing, where consumers actively participate in the balancing of demand with supply by forming groups that agree on a joint demand profile to be contracted in the market with the mediation of an aggregator. A business model as well as the optimisation model for load balancing is put forward, showing the economic benefits for the consumers in a realistic scenario based on the Spanish electricity market.

Another important challenge refers to the integration of renewable sources of clean energy into the power grid. To this respect, wind power is certainly gaining significance. Still, due to their inherent uncertainty, wind generators are often unable to participate in the forward electricity markets like the more predictable and controllable conventional generators. Given this, virtual power plants (VPPs) are being advocated as a solution for increasing the reliability of such intermittent renewable sources. In [5,8] we take this idea further by considering VPPs as coalitions of wind generators and electric vehicles, where wind generators seek to use electric vehicles (EVs) as a storage medium to overcome the vagaries of generation. Using electric vehicles in this manner has the advantage that, since the number of EVs is increasing rapidly, no initial investment in dedicated storage is needed. In more detail, we first formally model the VPP and then, through an operational model based on linear programming, we show how the supply to the Grid and storage in the EV batteries can be scheduled to increase the profit of the VPP, while also paying for the storage using a novel scheme. The feasibility of our approach is examined through a realistic case study, using real wind power generation data, corresponding electricity market prices and electric vehicles characteristics.

Another case study is related to the near-future penetration of plug-in electric vehicles, which is expected to be large enough to have a significant impact on the power grid. If EVs were allowed to charge simultaneously at the maximum power rate, the distribution grid would face serious problems of stability. Therefore, mechanisms are needed to coordinate various EVs that charge simultaneously. We propose an allocation mechanism based on AT that allows for balancing allocative efficiency and fairness, providing preferential treatment to the EVs that have a high valuation of the available power, while guaranteeing a fair share of this power to all the EVs [6].

3   Conclusions

This paper provided a short overview of the novel and vibrant field of Agreement Technologies. Setting out from the work of Sierra et al. [4], and drawing upon [1], the key technological areas of AT were described and related to each other. Furthermore, the domain of Smart Grids was identified as a playground for models and mechanisms originating from the field of AT, and several examples were sketched.

While the domain of Smart Grids is certainly of foremost importance for AT, other fields of socio-economic relevance are candidates for game-changing applications of AT as well. Traffic and transportation as well as mobile healthcare applications are likely to be among them [1].

Acknowledgements. This work was partially supported by the Spanish Ministry of Science and Innovation through the projects *OVAMAH* (grant TIN2009-13839-C03-02; co-funded by Plan E) and *Agreement Technologies* (grant CSD2007-0022; CONSOLIDER-INGENIO 2010), as well as by the Spanish Ministry of Economy and Competitiveness through the project *iHAS* (grant TIN2012-36586-C03-02), and by the COST office through Action IC0801 on Agreement Technologies.

References

1. Ossowski, S., Sierra, C., Botti, V.: Agreement Technologies – A Computing Perspective. In: Chapter 1 of [2], pp. 5–18 (2013)
2. Ossowski, S., et al. (eds.): Agreement Technologies. Law, Governance and Technology Series, vol. 8. Springer (2013),
   http://dx.doi.org/10.1007/978-94-007-5583-3
3. Ossowski, S.: Enabling Distributed Intelligent Systems in Open Environments through Agreement Technologies. In: Proceedings of the 14th International Symposium on Symbolic and Numeric Algorithms for Scientific Computing, pp. 3–7. IEEE (2013)
4. Sierra, C., Botti, V., Ossowski, S.: Agreement Computing. Künstliche Intelligenz 25(1), 57–61 (2011)
5. Vasirani, M., Ossowski, S., Kota, R., Cavalcante, R., Jennings, N.: Using coalitions of wind generators and electric vehicles for effective energy market participation. In: Proceedings of the 10th International Conference on Autonomous Agents and Multiagent Systems (AAMAS 2011), pp. 1099–1100. IFAAMAS (2011)
6. Vasirani, M., Ossowski, S.: A proportional share allocation mechanism for coordination of plug-in electric vehicle charging. Engineering Applications of Artificial Intelligence (2013), http://dx.doi.org/10.1016/j.engappai.2012.10.008
7. Vasirani, M., Ossowski, S.: Smart Consumer Load Balancing – State of the Art and an Empirical Evaluation in the Spanish Electricity Market. Artificial Intelligence Review 39(1), 81–95 (2013)
8. Vasirani, M., Kota, R., Cavalcante, R., Ossowski, S., Jennings, N.: An Agent-Based Approach to Virtual Power Plants of Wind Power Generators and Electric Vehicles. Submitted to: IEEE Transactions on Smart Grid (2013)

Practical Applications of Virtual Organizations and Agent Technology

Juan M. Corchado[1], Gabriel Villarrubia[1], Juan F. De Paz[1], Sara Rodríguez[1],
Carolina Zato[1], Fernando de la Prieta[1], and Javier Bajo[2]

[1] Departamento Informática y Automática Universidad de Salamanca
Plaza de la Merced s/n, 37008, Salamanca, Spain
{corchado,gvg,fcofds,srg,carol_zato,fer}@usal.es
[2] Departamento de Inteligencia Artificial, Universidad Politécnica de Madrid
Campus Montegancedo s/n, 28660, Madrid, Spain
jbajo@fi.upm.es

Abstract. Computation as interaction paradigm can be considered the most promising technological evolution in the areas of Computer Science and Communication in the last few years. Recent tendencies have conducted to the use of Virtual Organizations (VOs), which can be considered as a set of individuals and institutions that need to coordinate resources and services across institutional boundaries. Multi-agent systems (MAS) technology, which allows forming dynamic agent organizations, is particularly well suited as a support for the development of these open systems. PANGEA is an agent platform to develop open multi-agent systems, specifically those including organizational aspects such as virtual agent organizations. The platform allows the integral management of organizations and offers tools to the end user. Additionally, it includes a communication protocol based on the IRC standard, which facilitates implementation and remains robust even with a large number of connections.

Keywords: Multi-agent systems, Virtual Organizations, Dynamic architectures, Adaptive Environments.

1 Introduction

Open MAS should allow the participation of heterogeneous agents with different architectures and even different languages [2][1]. The development of open MAS is still a campo muy investigado field of the multi-agent system paradigm and its development will allow applying the agent technology in new and more complex application domains. However, this makes it impossible to trust agent behavior unless certain controls based on norms or social rules are imposed. To this end, developers have focused on the organizational aspects of agent societies, using the concepts of organization, norms, roles, etc. to guide the development process of the system.

There are several agent frameworks and platforms [3] [16] [17] that provide a wide range of tools for developing distributed multi-agent systems, however those that allow for the creation of VOs number much fewer, and it is difficult to find one single

J.M. Corchado et al. (Eds.): PAAMS 2013 Workshops, CCIS 365, pp. 17–23, 2013.

platform containing all of the requirements for a VO. In conclusion, it could be said that when dealing with all aspects of complex multiagent systems such as VOs, it is also necessary to deal with multiple levels of abstractions and openness, which is not the case for most solutions.

The remainder of the paper is structured as follows: the next section introduces the paradigm of VOs. Section 3 presents an overview of the main characteristics of the platform. Section 4 explains some applications and finally, some conclusions are presented in section 5.

2   Virtual Organizations Perspective

The usefulness of any technology, including multi-agent systems (MAS), can be judged by two criteria: (i) its ability to solve new types of problems and (ii) its ability to improve the efficiency of existing solutions [5]. With this in mind, agents and multi-agent systems provide a natural method of characterizing intelligent systems. Intelligence and interaction are two concepts that are inextricably joined, a fact that is well established in agent technology. When discussing MAS, the idea of a single agent is expanded to include an infrastructure for interaction and communication. Ideally, MAS include the following characteristics [4]: (i) they are typically open with a non-centralized design; (ii) they contain agents that are autonomous, heterogeneous and distributed, each with its own "personality" (cooperative, selfish, honest, etc.). They provide an infrastructure specifically for communication and interaction protocols. Open MAS should allow the participation of heterogeneous agents with different architectures and even different languages [2]. MAS agents based on organizational concepts coordinate and exchange services and information; they are capable of negotiating and coming to an agreement; and they can carry out other more complex social actions. At present, research focusing on the design of MAS from an organizational perspective seems to be gaining most ground. The emergent thought is that modeling the interactions in a MAS cannot be related exclusively to the actual agent and its communication capabilities; instead, organizational engineering is necessary as well. The concepts of rules [7], norms and institutions [8] and social structures [9] are rooted in the idea of needing a higher level of abstraction, independent from the agent, that explicitly defines the organizations in which the agents reside.

Virtual organizations [10] are a means of understanding system models from a sociological perspective. A VO is an open system formed by the grouping and collaboration of heterogeneous entities and there is a separation between form and function that requires defining how a behaviour will take place. The dynamics of open environments is one of the reasons that have encouraged the use of Virtual Organizations of Agents (VOs).

Agent organizations depend on the type of coordination and communication among agents, as well as the type of agents that comprise the group. There are several different organizational approaches [14] [13] [12][2][11][15].

From our perspective, an open platform has been created and allows any type of configuration, adaptation mechanisms, reorganization, search services, etc. All the artifacts that make up a virtual organization can be developed with PANGEA platform.

3   PANGEA

PANGEA (Platform for Automatic coNstruction of orGanizations of intElligents Agents) [22] is an agent platform to develop open multi-agent systems, it can manages roles, norms, organizations and suborganizations that facilitate the inclusion of organizational aspects. The services offered by the agents are included completely separate from the agent, facilitating their flexibility and adaption. PANGEA incorporates a CBR-BDI reasoning mechanism available for the agents. The basic agent types defined in PANGEA can be seen in Figure 1, they are:

- OrganizationManager: the agent responsible for the actual management of organizations and suborganizations. It is responsible for verifying the entry and exit of agents, and for assigning roles. To carry out these tasks, it works with the OrganizationAgent, which is a specialized version of this agent.
- InformationAgent: the agent responsible for accessing the database containing all pertinent system information.
- ServiceAgent: the agent responsible for recording and controlling the operation of services offered by the agents. It works as the Directory Facilitator defined in the FIPA standar.
- NormAgent: the agent that ensures compliance with all the refined norms in the organization.
- CommunicationAgent: the agent responsible for controlling communication among agents, and for recording the interaction between agents and organizations.
- Sniffer: manages the message history and filters information by controlling communication initiated by queries.
- DiscoveryAgent: implements an intelligent mechanism to discover services.
- MonitorAgent: interacts with the platform to show the information to the end user.

PANGEA is a service-oriented platform that can take maximum advantage of the distribution of resources. To this end, all services are implemented as Web Services. This makes it possible for the platform to include both a service provider agent and a consumer agent, thus emulating a client-server architecture. The provider agent (a general agent that provide a service) knows how to contact the web service, the rest of the agents know how to contact with the provider agent due to their communication with the ServiceAgent, which contains this informacion about services.

Using Web Services also allows the platform to introduce the SOA architecture (Service-Oriented Arquitecture) into MAS systems. SOA is an architectural style for building applications that use services available in a network such as the web. It promotes loose coupling between software components so that they can be reused. Applications in SOA are built based on services. A service is an implementation of a well-defined functionality, and such services can then be consumed by clients in different applications or processes. SOA allows for the reuse of existing services and a level of flexibility that was not possible before in the sense.

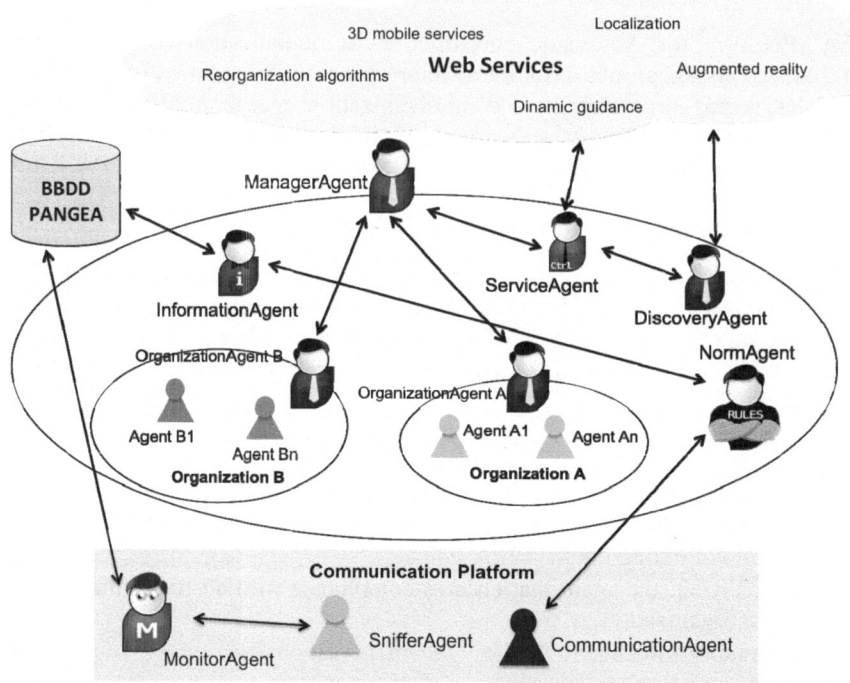

Fig. 1. First-person training view

One of the most important features that characterize the platform is the use of the IRC protocol for communication among agents. The IRC protocol was used to implement communication. Internet Relay Chat (IRC) is a Real Time Internet Protocol for simultaneous text messaging or conferencing. This protocol is regulated by 5 standards: RFC1459, RFC2810, RFC2811, RFC2812 y RFC2813 [18][19]. The use oh the protocol facilitates the implementation process and provides a flexible and robust communication, already tested by many users. Using IRC involves the ease in implementing communication. The platform's code generating tool makes it possible to easily create an outline of an agent, with the communication code requiring few lines of code. Moreover, it is an open standard protocol that is continuously evolving. There are also IRC clients for all operating systems, including mobile devices. Then, it is important to remark that PANGEA admits mobile agents deployed in Smartphones or tablets and agents in any programming language, it is not necessary to learn a new language in order to use it.

4   Applications

Given the advantages provided by the unique characteristics found in the development of open MAS from an organizational perspective, PANGEA as a VO platform can be use in many different domains.

It has been successfully used to develop many tools and systems. Some examples are: a powerful tool to regulate the elasticity of a Cloud Computing system, different intelligent guidance systems installed in shopping centres or public buildings, management of smart grids, many mobile applications with Augmented Reality for education contexts, a localization and guidance system for planning touristic routes and PANGEA is the main skeleton of all the tools that formed the integral system created in the AZTECA project and the Elderly People Online project.

The AZTECA project [21][23][24] aims to develop new technologies that contribute to the employment of groups of people with visual, hearing or motor disabilities in office environments. Some of these tools are a head mouse to control the mouse with the eyes, a vibrator bracelet to send Morse messages, an avatar for the deaf people, a localization system, etc. The different tools for the disabled people have been modelled with intelligent agents that consume Web services. These agents are implemented and deployed within the PANGEA platform so they form an integral system that can be use regardless of their physical location or implementation.

The Elderly People Online project [25] intends to develop an intelligent multi-agent system aimed at improving healthcare and assistance to elderly and dependent people in geriatric residences and their homes. The system is implemented using the PANGEA platform and integrates a set of autonomous deliberative agents and planning mechanisms designed to support the caregivers' activities and to guarantee that the patients are given the right care.

5   Conclusions

PANGEA facilitates the development of open MAS in an organizational paradigm and has great potential to create open systems highly dynamics. This architecture includes various tools that make it easy for the end user to create, manage and control these systems in aspects such as structural organizations (supporting groups, assuming roles, topology, interactions, and social rules) and the dynamic part of the organization (entry and exit of external agents, creating roles, life cycle of the agents, controlling behaviours, adaption and coordination).

One of the greatest advantages of this system is the communication platform that, by using the IRC standard, offers a robust and widely tested system that can handle a large number of connections, and that additionally facilitates the implementation for other potential extensions. The model used to design PANGEA is very general but without presenting particular restrictions to allow its application to many domains. Its ability to adapt to specific problems does not imply a diminished efficiency in many different applications.

References

[1] Corchado, E., Pellicer, M.A., Borrajo, M.L.: A MLHL Based Method to an Agent-Based Architecture. International Journal of Computer Mathematics 86(10&11), 1760–1768 (2008); ISI JCR Impact Factor: 0.423

[2] Zambonelli, F., Jennings, N.R., Wooldridge, M.: Developing Multiagent Systems: The Gaia Methodology. ACM Transactions on Software Engineering and Methodology 12, 317–370 (2003)

[3] Bravo, J., Hervas, R., Chavira, G., Nava, S.: Modeling contexts by RFID-sensor fusión. In: Fourth Annual IEEE International Conference on Pervasive Computing and Communications Workshops, Pisa, Italy, pp. 30–34 (2006) ISBN: 076952520-2

[4] Huhns, M., Stephens, L.: Multiagent Systems and Societies of Agents. In: Weiss, G. (ed.) Multi-agent Systems: A Modern Approach to Distributed Artificial Intelligence. MIT (1999)

[5] Jennings, N., Wooldridge, M. (eds.): Agent Technology: Foundations, Applications and Markets. Springer (1998)

[6] Zambonelli, F., Jennings, N.R., Wooldridge, M.: Developing Multiagent Systems: The Gaia Methodology. ACM Transactions on Software Engineering and Methodology 12, 317–370 (2003)

[7] Zambonelli, F.: Abstractions and Infrastructures for the Design and Development of Mobile Agent Organizations. In: Wooldridge, M.J., Weiß, G., Ciancarini, P. (eds.) AOSE 2001. LNCS, vol. 2222, pp. 245–262. Springer, Heidelberg (2002)

[8] Esteva, M.: Electronic Institutions: from specification to development. Ph. D. Thesis, Technical University of Catalonia (2003)

[9] Van Dyke Parunak, H., Odell, J.J.: Representing Social Structures in UML. In: Wooldridge, M.J., Weiß, G., Ciancarini, P. (eds.) AOSE 2001. LNCS, vol. 2222, pp. 1–16. Springer, Heidelberg (2002)

[10] Ferber, J., Gutknecht, O., Michel, F.: From Agents to Organizations: An Organizational View of Multi-agent Systems. In: Giorgini, P., Müller, J.P., Odell, J. (eds.) AOSE 2003. LNCS, vol. 2935, pp. 214–230. Springer, Heidelberg (2004)

[11] Omicini, A., Ricci, A., Viroli, M.: Coordination artifacts: Environment-based coordination for intelligent agents. In: Proceedings of 3rd International Joint Conference on Autonomous Agents and Multiagent Systems (AAMAS 2004), pp. 286–293 (2004)

[12] Pavón, J., Gómez-Sanz, J.J.: Agent oriented software engineering with INGENIAS. In: Mařík, V., Müller, J.P., Pěchouček, M. (eds.) CEEMAS 2003. LNCS (LNAI), vol. 2691, pp. 394–403. Springer, Heidelberg (2003)

[13] Dignum, V.: A model for organizational interaction: based on agents, founded in logic, Ph.D. Thesis (2004)

[14] Boissier, O., Gateau, B.: Normative multi-agent organizations: Modeling, support and control. Normative Multiagent Systems (2007)

[15] Hübner, J.F., Sichman, J.S., Boissier, O.: Using the $\mathcal{M}$OISE$^+$ for a cooperative framework of MAS reorganisation. In: Bazzan, A.L.C., Labidi, S. (eds.) SBIA 2004. LNCS (LNAI), vol. 3171, pp. 506–515. Springer, Heidelberg (2004)

[16] Galland, S.: JANUS: Another Yet General-Purpose Multiagent Platform. Seventh AOSE Technical Forum, Paris (2010)

[17] Bordini, R.H., Hübner, J.F., Vieira, R.: Jason and the Golden Fleece of agent-oriented programming. In: Bordini, R.H., Dastani, M., Dix, J., El Fallah Seghrouchni, A. (eds.) Multi-Agent Programming: Languages, Platforms and Applications, ch. 1, pp. 3–37. Springer (2005)

[18] Oikarinen, J., Reed, D.: Internet Relay Chat Protocol, RFC 1459 (May 1993)

[19] Kalt, C.: Internet Relay Chat: Client Protocol, RFC 2810, 2811, 2812, 2813 (April 2000)

[20] Chen, M., Kwon, T., Yuan, Y., Choi, Y., Leung, V.C.M.: Mobile agent-based directed diffusion in wireless sensor networks. EURASIP J. Appl. Signal Process., 219 (2007)

[21] AZTECA Project, http://www.tecnologiasaccesibles.com/es/azteca_
      index.htm
[22] Zato, C., Villarrubia, G., Sánchez, A., Barri, I., Rubión, E., Fernández, A., Rebate, C.,
      Cabo, J.A., Álamos, T., Sanz, J., Seco, J., Bajo, J., Corchado, J.M.: PANGEA – Platform
      for Automatic coNstruction of orGanizations of intElligent Agents. In: Omatu, S., De Paz
      Santana, J.F., González, S.R., Molina, J.M., Bernardos, A.M., Rodríguez, J.M.C. (eds.)
      Distributed Computing and Artificial Intelligence. AISC, vol. 151, pp. 229–239.
      Springer, Heidelberg (2012)
[23] Sánchez, A., Villarrubia, G., Macarro, A., Jiménez, A., Zato, C., Bajo, J., Rodríguez, S.,
      Hallenborg, K., Corchado, J.M.: Learning languages using the mobile devices'
      accelerometer. In: Vittorini, P., Gennari, R., Marenzi, I., De la Prieta, F., Corchado, J.M.
      (eds.) International Workshop on Evidenced-based Technology Enhanced Learning
      (2012)
[24] Villarrubia, G., Sánchez, A., Barri, I., Rubión, E., Fernández, A., Rebate, C., Cabo, J.A.,
      Álamos, T., Sanz, J., Seco, J., Zato, C., Bajo, J., Rodríguez, S., Corchado, J.M.:
      Proximity detection prototype adapted to a work environment. In: Novais, P.,
      Hallenborg, K., Tapia, D.I., Rodríguez, J.M.C. (eds.) Ambient Intelligence - Software
      and Applications. AISC, vol. 153, pp. 51–58. Springer, Heidelberg (2012)
[25] Zato, C., Sánchez, A., Villarrubia, G., de la Prieta, F., Rodríguez, S., Bajo, J., Corchado,
      J.M.: New Agent Platform with a Communication System based on the IRC Protocol. In:
      European Agent Systems Summer School (EASSS 2012), pp. 1–8 (2012)

Agent-Driven Variable Pricing in Flexible Rural Transport Services

C. David Emele, Nir Oren, Cheng Zeng, Steve Wright, Nagendra Velaga, John Nelson,
Timothy J. Norman, and John Farrington

RCUK dot.rural Digital Economy Research Hub, University of Aberdeen, UK
{c.emele,n.oren,c.zeng,s.d.wright,n.velaga,j.d.nelson,
t.j.norman,j.farrington}@abdn.ac.uk

Abstract. The fares that passengers are asked to pay for their journey have implications on such things as passenger transport choice, demand, cost recovery and
revenue generation for the transport provider. Designing an efficient fare structure
is therefore a fundamental problem, which can influence the type of transport options passengers utilise, and may determine whether or not a transport provider
makes profit. Fixed pricing mechanisms (e.g., zonal based fares) are rigid and
have generally been used to support flexible transport services; however, they do
not reflect the cost of provision or quality of service offered. In this paper, we
present a novel approach that incorporates variable pricing mechanisms into fare
planning for flexible transport services in rural areas. Our model allows intelligent agents to vary the fares that passengers pay for their journeys on the basis of
a number of constraints and externalities. We empirically evaluate our approach
to demonstrate that variable pricing mechanisms can significantly improve the efficiency of transport systems in general, and rural transport in particular. Furthermore, we show that variable pricing significantly outperforms more rigid fixed
price regimes.

Keywords: rural transport, flexible transport, agents, fares, variable pricing.

1 Introduction

There are particular transport challenges in rural areas, which are characterised by limited transport service provision, low population density, sometimes inappropriate and
rigid fare structures, and highly uncertain transport demands [1]. The adoption of flexible transport services is seen as a promising option to mitigate some of the challenges
faced by travellers in rural areas. Many previous attempts to encourage advances in
flexible and demand responsive transport service design in rural areas have been problematic [2]. This is partly, because many flexible transport services in rural areas are
standalone, small scale, and offer passengers limited travel options [3].

One important aspect of flexible transport service (FTS) design that appears
neglected is the design of appropriate fare structures to facilitate flexible transport provision in rural areas. Public transport fares are well investigated in the economic literature. Many researchers approach them from a macro-economic perspective in terms
of elasticities, equilibrium conditions, and marginal cost analyses with a view to deriv-
ing qualitative insights (e.g., [4–8]). Glaister and Collings [4] and Nash [9] proposed

J.M. Corchado et al. (Eds.): PAAMS 2013 Workshops, CCIS 365, pp. 24–35, 2013.

to treat the setting of fares as an optimisation problem, namely, to maximise objectives such as revenue, passenger miles, or social welfare subject to a budget constraint. They also considered issues such as different transport modes, peak and off-peak times, etc.

FTS in rural areas rely on subsidies from Local Authorities in order to be viable for transport providers. A recent review of 48 FTS schemes in England and Wales ([9]) found that in rural areas, 16 out of 25 FTS required more than £5 subsidy per passenger trip. Brake et al. [2] note that fare setting is often constrained by the need to make a certain level of revenue, or rather to limit the subsidy payments required. This is a delicate issue since the number of passengers multiplied by the fare will provide the fare-box revenue. The cost side of the equation can present more problems and it is necessary to identify the cost elements of a flexible service – these are normally divided into administrative, capital and operating (including dispatching) costs. Total fare revenue often doesn't even cover drivers wages and the bulk of the revenue to providers comes from subsidy payments. Wright [10] offers a new approach to identify realistic acceptable levels of subsidy for rural transport services which are density-related and therefore flexible in this dimension. However, to date, no work (to our knowledge) has looked at designing a flexible fare structure for rural transport.

In this paper, we argue for a more flexible fare structure, which reflects the quality of service, and the externalities of the environment, and takes into account the characteristics and constraints of the transport provider and/or passenger to more adequately reflect the cost of service provision. Given that fixed pricing mechanisms (for example, zonal based or even flat fares) are rigid and inefficient (in the sense that it is insensitive to factors like quality of service, passenger constraints, etc.), we advocate the use of variable pricing and present a framework that utilises agents to represent the actors in the system. Our model allows intelligent agents to vary the fares that passengers pay for their journeys on the basis of a number of constraints and variables (see Section 3).

In the research presented in this paper, we intend to validate the following hypothesis: utilising variable pricing can significantly improve the performance of rural transport in at least two dimensions, namely: (i) increased number of passenger requests met; and (ii) increased average passenger benefit. This may promote the sustainable implementation of FTS in rural areas, particularly where higher and more predictable demand for transport is desirable.

The remainder of this paper is organised as follows: Section 2 discusses the theoretical background to this work and Section 3 describes our approach. Section 4 reports the results of our empirical evaluation and Section 5 presents discussion and conclusions.

2 Background

Economists and transport researchers have long recognised the need for efficient pricing policy for transport services [5, 6, 11–13]. Irrespective of whether the transport service is provided in a rural or urban context, the level of fares charged should be such that the total revenue earned by a service provider is sufficient to cover the total cost of providing the service and, possibly, some profit. Thus, one of the greatest challenges for transport providers is the design of a fare structure that reconciles the passenger's need for an affordable transport service with the business objectives of the provider. It must be recognised that this is further complicated in rural areas where many services require additional financial support, in the form of subsidies provided by local authorities, in order to return a profit for the transport provider. In general, there are two major pricing categories, namely: (1) Journey-based; and (2) Passenger-based [11].

2.1 Journey-Based Pricing

In journey-based pricing, the fare is determined by the characteristics of the journey (for example, distance travelled, transport mode, time of travel, etc.), and can be broken down into the following categories:

- Flat fare: This system is the simplest and most rigid. All passengers are charged uniform fares irrespective of distance, type of passenger, route, etc.
- Route fare: Here, different routes are charged differently similar to some bus fare models that calculate fares based on approximate route length.
- Zonal fare: In this category, the route or network is divided into zones - with a flat fare set for each zone. A passenger's fare is determined by the number of zones visited by the passenger.
- Distance-based fare: This type of fare applies a price per km travelled. Typically, each network or route is divided into fare stages, with a clearly identifiable boundary point for each stage. The interval between fare stages may be varied to consider different demand characteristics, segments of a route, and different operating costs. Taxi pricing is a variation of this fare, which is based on distance and time, and includes an initial flat minimum fare.

2.2 Passenger-Based Pricing

Passenger-based pricing considers the situation where the fare is influenced by the characteristics of the passenger (for example, income, age, requirements for group travel, etc.). Some social groups that may be entitled to concessionary fares include: (1) Members of the armed forces; (2) Elderly people and pensioners; (3) Unemployed people; (4) Pupils and students; (5) Disabled; (6) Children.

In both journey-based and passenger-based categories, a time-based fare can be implemented to reflect the time of day the journey was undertaken (i.e., peak or off-peak). Usually, fares are higher at peak periods and lower otherwise.

3 Approach

Most prior work on fare planning has adopted fixed pricing because it is easier to implement and manage. In many domains, there is significant evidence about the benefits of flexible pricing mechanisms (e.g., auctions), and it seems counterproductive to ignore it. For example, in many auction applications, researchers have often reported higher revenue for the seller, and in some cases cheaper deals for the buyer [14].

In our setting, the fare planning problem considers a transportation network represented as a directed graph $G = (V, E)$, where the nodes V represent the pickup and drop-off points in the network, while edges E are routes/paths that can be followed to complete a journey from one node to another. We define a relation $D : V \times V$ of *origin-destination pairs* (OD-pairs) representing possible journeys within the system. Further, we define a path, $P_{o \to d}$ as a set of routes that link nodes o and d in the network such that an agent can travel from o to d. We assume that there is at least one path (i.e., $P_{o \to d} \neq \emptyset$) through the network that transport providers can follow when transporting a passenger between each OD-pair (o, d). We utilise A-star algorithm [15] to generate the shortest path, and we assume that transport providers will follow the optimal shortest path covering requested pick-up and drop-off points between any two nodes in the network. Furthermore, we consider n nonnegative fare variables $x_1, \cdots, x_n$, which is used to determine what the fare for each journey is. Examples of fare variables include: the driver's hourly pay, the distance to be travelled to pickup and drop-off the passenger, time of travel (peak or off-peak), discount for sharing the vehicle with another passenger, and so on.

In our approach, *variable pricing* is defined as the use of both journey and passenger characteristics/constraints to determine the fare to be charged for a journey. Such characteristics may include distance, time of the trip, passenger preferences and requirements, other operator variables such as vehicle occupancy, vehicle operating cost, and so on, whereas *fixed pricing* uses flat, route-based, zone-based or distance-based fares, which is generally based on the approximate route length, time of day and passenger type (in terms of concessionary fares).

Let $\mathcal{A}$ be the set of transport providers. A fare vector is a vector $x \in \mathbb{R}_+^n$ containing the fare variables. We define our fare function as follows:

Definition 1. *The fare function is given as* $\mathcal{F}_{o \to d}^a : \mathbb{R}_+^n \to \mathbb{R}_+$ *for each OD-pair* (o, d) $\in D$ *and each transport provider* $a \in \mathcal{A}$ *such that*

$$\mathcal{F}_{o \to d}^a(x) = \sum_{i=1..n} x_i . k_i \tag{1}$$

where k_i is the weighting for each variable (and we assume linearity).

The fare function $\mathcal{F}_{o \to d}^a(x)$ determines the fare that a passenger will pay for travelling with transport provider a from o to d depending on the constituents of the fare vector x.

Table 1. A table showing some of the variables in the fare vector

Hourly wage (£)	Distance (miles)	Time of travel	$\cdots$	Occupancy
5.50	5.7	off-peak	...	single
6.00	7.2	peak	...	shared
5.80	3.6	off-peak	...	single
7.55	6.4	off-peak	...	shared
...	...	...	...	...
5.85	9.3	off-peak	...	shared

3.1   Preferences and Requirements

We consider a finite set C of travel constraints that passengers possess. These constraints may be *hard constraints* or *soft constraints*. Hard constraints are requirements, which must be met for a given passenger to travel. For example, a *wheelchair* user needs a vehicle that is *wheelchair-friendly*. Another passenger may require assistance to move and so may need an escort in order to travel – that is a hard constraint. Yet another hard constraint may be in the form of an upper limit for a given journey (which we refer to as a *threshold*) beyond which a passenger would rather not travel. On the other hand, soft constraints can be conceived as preferences that passengers express regarding their journeys. Examples of journey attributes that passengers may express preferences about include (i) single or shared vehicle occupancy; (ii) number of changes; (iii) overall journey time, and so on. The hard constraints help to shortlist the transport providers that have the capability and capacity to provide the services requested by the passenger. In other words, it helps to filter who may be approached for a bid to deliver on the passenger's request. Similarly, soft constraints aid decision making with regards to which transport provider to select for the journey. We present the following definition.

Definition 2.   *Given a set of soft constraints, S, we define a preference ordering $\succ$ on S such that $x \succ y$ means that x is preferred to y, where $x, y \in S$.*

3.2   Contract Net Protocol

We utilise the Contract Net Protocol (CNP) to support the interaction between distributed agents (passengers and transport providers - see Section 4) engaging in automated negotiation through the use of agreements called contracts. The protocol enables tasks to be distributed among a collection of agents [16]. The Contract Net allows the creation of an electronic marketplace to support buying and selling. An underlying assumption in this protocol is that agents are self-interested and will act in their best interests. However, this means that the final solution may not necessarily be globally optimal. In a CNP setting, a passenger could specify the journey they want to make together with any hard and soft constraints they may have. Such constraints could include pricing limits, seating preferences and the like. In general, the interaction protocol for CNP involves five steps, which agents must go through to conclude each contract:

1. The initiating agent sends out a request to a broker (see Section 4 for details).
2. The broker sends out a Call for Proposals (CFPs).
3. Each participating agent reviews the CFP and sends in a bid, if feasible.
4. The broker then chooses the best bid (using some utility metric) and awards the task to the chosen agent.
5. The broker rejects the other bids.

3.3   Bids

Each passenger sends his/her request to the marketplace agent (see Figure 1) who then sends out a call for bids to all registered transport providers taking into account the requirements of the passenger (e.g., assistance to get on/off vehicles is required for the journey). Interested transport providers will send in their bids to the marketplace agent. It is worth noting that transport providers may have made certain information on those service characteristics, constraints and limitations they can influence (e.g., eligibility criteria, vehicle capacity, price structure, locations covered and boundaries) available to the marketplace agent during registration. Such information does not constitute a bid because it does not specify real-time availabilities of such service nor does it constitute a commitment to make the required resources available when requested. However, such information could be utilised by the marketplace agent in shortlisting the provider agents to approach for a bid. The bid may specify things like tentative pickup (and drop-off) time (or window), the route, the journey time, cost (if appropriate), and so on.

Definition 3. *A passenger's request $\mathcal{R}$ is a tuple $\langle D, T_p, T_d, H, S \rangle$, where D is an OD-pair (o, d), T_p is the pickup time, T_d is the drop-off time, and H and S are hard and soft constraints respectively.*

For example, a passenger may send the following request: $\langle (Peterhead, Fraserburgh),$ *08.30, 11.00,* $\{\}$, $\{Cost\ of\ journey \succ Overall\ journey\ time\} \rangle$.

Definition 4. *A bid $\mathcal{B}$ is a tuple $\langle D, T_{ap}, T_{ad}, \mathcal{F}^a_{o \to d}, O \rangle$, where D is an OD-pair (o, d), T_{ap} is an approximate pickup time, T_{ad} is an approximate drop-off time, $\mathcal{F}^a_{o \to d}$ is the fare for the journey, and O is the set of other details about the journey (e.g., whether or not the vehicle would be shared with others).*

For example, a transport provider may return the following bid: $\langle (Peterhead, Fraserburgh), 09.35, 10.50, 12.60, \{single\} \rangle$.

The bidding system can be instrumented to support the automation of the bidding process such that the level of information provided initially by transport providers on service design characteristics, eligibility criteria and preferences can be utilised to enable bids to be automatically generated by transport providers.

3.4 Utility of Bids

After transport providers send bids in response to the call for bids (see Figure 1) then the marketplace agent computes the *utility score* of each bid received (in terms of how closely it matches the request of the passenger) while taking into account the preferences and requirements of the passenger. In computing the *utility score*, the marketplace agent utilises the following function:

Definition 5. *The utility score of a bid is given as $\mathcal{U}_{o \to d} : \mathcal{R} \times \mathcal{B}_a \to \mathbb{R}$ such that OD-pair $(o, d) \in D$, and transport provider $a \in \mathcal{A}$ responded to a request $\mathcal{R}$ from a given passenger with a bid $\mathcal{B}_a$.*

3.5 Passengers' Provider Choice

This aspect of the bidding process allows the passenger to decide which of the available transport options best meet his needs and preferences. There might be scenarios where the passenger may be willing to stick to certain aspects of the service that are most

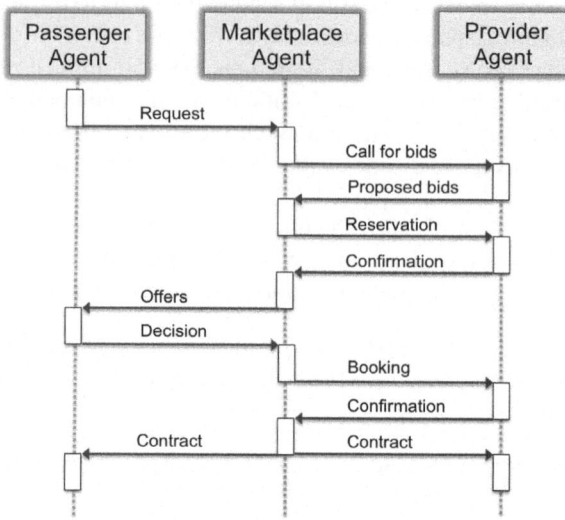

Fig. 1. Contract Net Protocol (CNP)

important to him, and some other times where he is willing to make compromises based on the options available. In the initial request, a passenger might have stated that the cost of the journey is more important to them than the overall journey time. However, if there is little difference in price but a huge difference in drop-off times then a passenger may want to temporarily relax his preference for cost and, therefore, choose the slightly more expensive journey with shorter overall journey time. For example, suppose passenger $P1$'s request for transport service is as follows:

- Origin: x
- Destination: y
- Pickup time: 7.00
- Drop-off time: 12.00
- Hard Constraints: None
- Soft Constraints: cost of journey $\succ$ overall journey time $\succ$ window seat

Let us assume that the following bids from transport providers $T1$ and $T2$ (respectively) were shortlisted.

- **Bid 1:** $T1$ offers to pickup passenger $P1$ from x at about 10.00 and drop-off at y at about 11.35, window seat is available, and the fare will be £20.10, while
- **Bid 2:** $T2$ offers to pickup passenger $P1$ from x at about 8.30 and drop-off at y at about 11.05, no window seat is available, and the fare will be £15.80.

In real life scenarios, some passengers may prefer Bid 1 over Bid 2, while some others may prefer Bid 2 over Bid 1. The decision to choose one over the other lies with the passenger, and can be simulated using a number of heuristics. In our implementation, we assume that passengers will stick to their preferences for that journey and will choose the option that best suits their specified preferences, irrespective of whether there is another option that is similar or may be better in some other respects. Thus, in our system passenger *P1* will select Bid 2 if the threshold set by *P1* for that journey is not less than £15.80.

4   Evaluation

In order to evaluate our approach, we developed a simulated flexible transport system where a set of passenger agents interact with a set of transport provider agents in a marketplace. The interactions are mediated by a brokering agent (called the marketplace agent). The rest of this section will present our system architecture, describe the experimental setup and report initial results of our empirical evaluation.

4.1   System Architecture

The framework developed to evaluate the ideas in this paper (illustrated in Figure 2) is a multi-agent system involving passengers ("*P agents*"), transport providers ("*T agents*"), and a marketplace agent ("*M agent*"), which acts as a broker in the system. The framework enables passengers to send their transport requests to a broker who then sends out a call for bids and transport providers can assess these requests and send in bids.

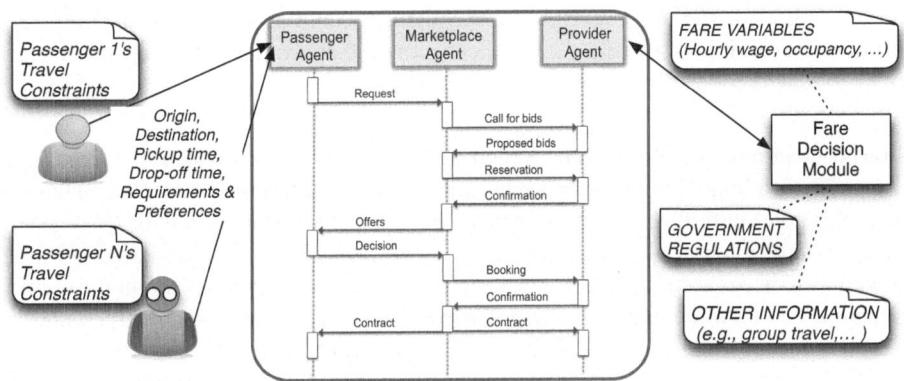

Fig. 2. System Architecture

P agents: In our system, these agents are provided with a map (i.e., a directed graph with nodes and edges that link the nodes) and a built-in journey generator, which generates feasible journeys for passengers. For example, each journey generated must lie within the map and the *origin* must not be the same as the *destination*. A number of other checks are made, such as the difference in time between pickup and drop-off cannot be less than the time it will take to travel at constant speed limit between the two points on the map. For example, if the distance by road connecting points x and y is 20 miles and the speed limit for that road is $30mph$ then the difference between pickup and drop-off times for any journey going from x to y is not allowed to be less than 40 mins.

Each *P agent* has a number of constraints for each journey generated. The journey details and the preferences/requirements form passengers' travel constraints and they are communicated to the *M agent* in the form of a request for transport.

M agent: This agent mediates between *P agents* and *T agents*. When *M agent* receives requests from *P agents*, it sends out a call for bids to *T agents*. When *T agents* send in their bids, the *M agent* computes the *utility score* of each bid and those that exceed a certain *threshold* are shortlisted for reservation. The *utility score* is used to determine how closely a bid matches a passenger's request. The *M agent* then sends shortlisted bids to the *P agent* to choose from. Upon receipt of a decision from a given *P agent*, the *M agent* confirms the reservation that has been selected with the *T agent*. Thereafter, a contract is created between that *P agent* and the appropriate *T agent*.

T agents: When a call for bids is received, *T agents* check whether they can fit the request into their current schedule. If yes, then they send in a bid. A bid contains the fare to be paid for the journey, approximate pickup and drop-off times, and so on. In order to compute the fare for a journey, *T agents* have built-in fare generator called a *fare decision module* (see Figure 2). The fare decision module takes as input a number of fare variables (such as occupancy, hourly wage, etc.) and other information (for example, traffic information) and recommends a fare that the transport provider should charge the passenger for the journey. Based on availability, current commitments and traffic information (or time of travel), *T agents* can generate approximate pickup and drop-off times for each request they receive.

Shared Occupancy Negotiation. When a *T agent*, say *T1*, already has at least a passenger (*P1*) on board but receives a new call for bids for a journey that can be shared in part (or whole) with the current journey *T1* engages in a negotiation with *P1* regarding changes in the journey plan. *T1* may want to negotiate about pickup and drop-off times, as well as a discount in the fare for sharing the vehicle/journey with another (potential) passenger (*P2*). At the end of the negotiation if *T1* and *P1* come to an agreement then *T1* sends a bid to the *M agent*. If *T1*'s bid is shortlisted and then chosen by the new passenger, then a new contract is established between *T1* and *P1*. In the same vein, a contract is then established between *T1* and *P2*.

4.2   Experimental Setup

In evaluating the contributions of our approach, we test the following hypothesis:

> *Hypothesis:* Utilising *variable pricing* can significantly allow more passenger requests to be met as well as increase the average passenger benefit when compared to *fixed pricing*.

In our experimental scenario, there are 5 passengers that wish to travel from different points on the map to another. We have 32 flexible transport providers in the system who can carry passengers from any point on the map to another. Each transport vehicle can carry up to 5 passengers (i.e., capacity).

We consider two experimental conditions, namely: Fixed Pricing and Variable Pricing. The operating cost for each transport provider is fixed throughout the experiment, and is set at $5 \leq y \leq 10$. In order to simplify the computation, we assume that the price of fuel (be it diesel or petrol) is identical and all vehicle have the same fuel consumption rate. We also assume that fuel consumption depends only on distance travelled and the journey time such that the cost of fuel for a journey can be computed as $C_F = d \times k_d + t \times k_t$, where C_F is the cost of fuel, d and t are distance and time respectively while k_d and k_t are their respective weightings.

We conducted 10 runs of the experiment, and in each run each of the five passengers randomly generates 10 (feasible) journeys sequentially (every 30 minutes) and seeks transport options to use in making the journeys. For each journey generated, a *threshold* (i.e., upper limit) is also generated. In total, each passenger generates 100 journeys throughout the experiment. In the *variable pricing* scenario, each of the 32 providers receives the call for bids for each of the passengers' journey requests. In the *fixed pricing* scenario, providers utilise distance-based pricing and so the fare that a passenger pays is determined by how many zones they travel across and the time of day.

4.3   Results

Figure 3 illustrates the performance of the two *pricing* categories that we considered in this paper. The results show that *variable pricing* constantly outperforms the *fixed pricing* approach throughout the experiment. The total number of passenger requests met by transport providers in *variable pricing* scenarios was consistently and significantly higher than those recorded in *fixed pricing*. For example, in the sixth run of the experiment, while the total number of requests met by transport providers that utilised *variable pricing* was 47, the value recorded by their counterparts was about 41. It is worth noting that in as few as 50 journeys (since each of 5 passengers generate 10 journeys per experiment) there is a significant difference in the total number of journey requests met in the two scenarios. The reason for this is simply because *variable pricing* allows more passenger requests to be met because there is flexibility in providers meeting passenger thresholds when setting the fares - this is not possible in fixed pricing.

Furthermore, in Figure 3 we plot the average passenger fare per journey in the two experimental conditions. Results show that, as expected, the average passenger fare recorded by *variable pricing* was consistently and significantly lower than that recorded using *fixed pricing* approach. For instance, in the sixth run of the experiment, the average passenger fare dropped to as low as 12.00 as compared to 13.40 recorded by *fixed pricing*. Again, the reason for this is simply because using variable pricing enables providers to adapt the fares to reflect the externalities and characteristics of the journey.

Tests of significance were applied to the results of our evaluation, and they were found to be statistically significant by t-test with $p < 0.05$. Overall, scenarios where *variable pricing* was used consistently yielded higher total revenue for transport providers as well as lower average passenger fare. These results confirm our hypothesis that exploiting *variable pricing* means that the average cost of travel to passengers can be significantly reduced while providers have the potential to meet more passenger requests.

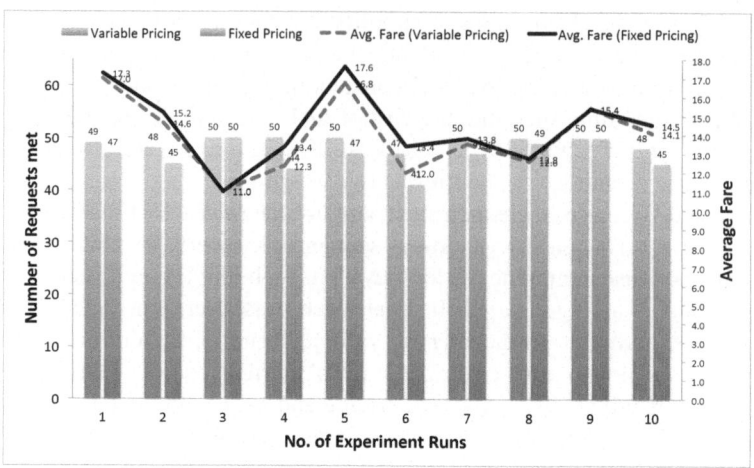

Fig. 3. Variable pricing vs. Fixed pricing

5   Discussion and Conclusions

This work has advocated for a variable pricing approach, and has shown some of the potential benefits. In Section 3, we discussed one possible way in which passengers' requests can be matched with bids from transport providers – utility assessment. Utilising utility assessment of bids (i.e., *utility score*) means that the platform can accommodate free and discounted travel entitlements since the utility function can assess other variables such as time of travel, pickup and drop-off times, number of changes, etc., which could be computed to give a utility score. In the same vein, in many cases where fares are regulated (distance-based or stage-based fare structure) and are not negotiable, utilising bid utility assessment is useful. Interestingly, in regimes that allow for variable pricing the utility function can be instrumented to allow the bidding system to be free and fair by employing a second-price sealed bid auction [17], which encourages bidders to bid their true values. In a second-price sealed bid auction, each bidder submits a sealed bid to the marketplace agent and the highest bidder wins but pays the amount offered by the second-highest bidder.

As future work, we plan to extend the framework to allow the integration of different modes of transport. Furthermore, we plan to investigate opportunistic seat sharing (e.g., going slightly out of ones way to pick up an additional passenger), and enable providers to place requests on the market place in order to further optimise their service provision.

In conlusion, we have explored in this paper mechanisms for variable pricing in rural transport where transport providers can present bids to passengers' transport requests. The question addressed in this research is how may we utilise variable pricing in the rural context? In an attempt to answer this question, we propose a virtual transport market scenario, which utilises CNP to enable transport providers to bid for transport requests that they intend to deliver on. We have empirically evaluated our approach and the results of our investigations show that exploiting *variable pricing* means that the average cost of travel to passengers can be significantly reduced while transport providers have the potential to meet more passenger requests. We believe that the research reported here will provide useful insight into numerous issues regarding optimising flexible transport services in rural areas.

Acknowledgements. The research described here is supported by the award made by the RCUK Digital Economy programme to the dot.rural Digital Economy Hub; award reference: EP/G066051/1.

References

1. Velaga, N.R., Beecroft, M., Nelson, J.D., Corsar, D., Edwards, P.: Transport poverty meets the digital divide: accessibility and connectivity in rural communities. Journal of Transport Geography 21, 102–112 (2012)
2. Brake, J., Mulley, C., Nelson, J.D., Wright, S.D.: Key lessons learned from recent experience with flexible transport services. Transport Policy 14, 458–466 (2007)
3. Mulley, C., Nelson, J.D., Teal, R., Wright, S.D., Daniels, R.: Barriers to implementing flexible transport services: an international comparison of the experiences in Australia, Europe and USA. Research in Transportation and Business Management 3, 3–11 (2012)
4. Curtin, J.F.: Effect of fares on transit riding. Highway Research Record 213, 8–20 (1968)
5. Goodwin, P.B.: A review of new demand elasticities with special reference to short and long run effects of price changes. Journal of Transport Economics and Policy 26, 155–169 (1992)
6. Oum, T.H., Waters II, W.G., Yong, J.: Concepts of price elasticities of transport demand and recent empirical estimates. Journal of Transport Economics and Policy 26, 139–154 (1992)
7. Pedersen, P.A.: On the optimal fare policies in urban transportation. Transportation Research Part B: Methodological 37(5), 423–435 (2003)
8. Samuelson, P.A.: Economics, 12th edn. MacGraw-Hill, NY (1986)
9. Laws, R., Enoch, M., Ison, S., Potter, S.: Demand responsive transport: A review of schemes in England and Wales. Journal of Public Transportation 12, 19–37 (2009)
10. Wright, S.: Designing flexible transport services: guidelines for choosing the vehicle type. Transportation Planning and Technology 36, 76–92 (2013)
11. Borndörfer, R., Karbstein, M., Pfetsch, M.E.: Models for fare planning in public transport. Discrete Appl. Math. 160(18), 2591–2605 (2012)
12. Lam, W.H.K., Zhou, J.: Models for optimizing transit fares. In: Lam, W.H.K., Bell, M.G.H. (eds.) Advanced Modeling for Transit Operations and Service Planning, pp. 315–345. Pergamon Press, Oxford (2003)
13. Nash, C.A.: Management objectives, fares and service levels in bus transport. Journal of Transport Economics and Policy 12, 70–85 (1978)
14. Likhodedov, A., Sandholm, T.: Approximating revenue-maximizing combinatorial auctions. In: Proceedings of the 20th National Conference on Artificial Intelligence, AAAI 2005, vol. 1, pp. 267–273. AAAI Press (2005)
15. Hart, P., Nilsson, N., Raphael, B.: A formal basis for the heuristic determination of minimum cost paths. IEEE Transactions on Systems Science and Cybernetics 4(2), 100–107 (1968)
16. Smith, R.G.: The contract net protocol: High-level communication and control in a distributed problem solver. IEEE Trans. Comput. 29(12), 1104–1113 (1980)
17. Vickrey, W.: Counterspeculation, auctions, and competitive sealed tenders. The Journal of Finance 16, 8–37 (1961)

Solving Road-Network Congestion Problems by a Multi-objective Optimization Algorithm with Brownian Agent Model

Bin Jiang[1,2], Xiao Xu[1], Chao Yang[1,2], Renfa Li[1], and Takao Terano[2]

[1] College of Information Science and Engineering, Hunan University, Changsha, Hunan, China
tearxuxiao@gmail.com, lirenfa@vip.sina.com
[2] Department of Computational Intelligence and Systems Science,
Interdisciplinary Graduate School of Science and Engineering, Tokyo Institute of Technology,
Yokohama, Kanagawa, Japan
{jiangbin,yangchao}@trn.dis.titech.ac.jp,
terano@dis.titech.ac.jp

Abstract. The past decades witnessed a big effort in solving road-network congestion problem through routing optimization approaches. With a multi-objective optimization perspective, this paper proposed a new method which solved the road-network congestion problem by combining two objectives of shortest routing and congestion avoidance. Especially, we applied the approach of Brownian agents to find the next intersection of road network to avoid congestion. Vehicles were simulated as Brownian agents with automatic movements in the road-network, and the entire network congestion distribution were optimized at the same time. We tried to find out the relationship between the moving strategies of the vehicles and the network congestion. By means of computer simulation, we implemented our proposed method with a predefined road-network topological structure. We tested the parameters sensitivity by scaling the proportion of agent with two moving strategies: the shortest path strategy and a mix strategy combining two objectives of shortest routing and congestion avoidance. Furthermore, we analyzed the various network congestions under a mix strategy by changing the weights to represent different focus on two moving strategies. The simulation results proved the applicability and efficiency of our proposed method for alleviating the network congestion distribution, and the intersections within a higher vehicle density were observed decreased.

Keywords: road-network congestion, multi-objective optimization, Brownian agent.

1 Introduction

Road-network congestion becomes a more and more serious problem in our daily life. Facing the traffic problems, ITS (intelligent transportation system) was proposed to handle it. There lots of agent-based traffic applications and systems among the ITS. In the early year, Nagel introduce a stochastic discrete automaton model to simulate

J.M. Corchado et al. (Eds.): PAAMS 2013 Workshops, CCIS 365, pp. 36–48, 2013.
© Springer-Verlag Berlin Heidelberg 2013

freeway traffic [1], and lots of traffic application using CA (Cellular Automata) in the later years were proposed [2][3][4]. Wang also summarized the multi-agent system used for traffic management systems, and rethink control systems and reinvestigate the use of simple task-oriented agents for traffic control and management of transportation systems in 2005[5]. Later, more and more researchers focus on this area. Du proposed an urban traffic coordination control system based on Multi Agent-Game, the system uses the coordination control of each agent to coordinate the urban traffic signal for elimination the congestion of traffic network [6]. Chin introduced a Q-Learning algorithm acts as the learning mechanism for traffic light intersections to release itself from traffic congestions situation in 2012[7].

Based on the above mentioned works, the conventional traffic applications using agents were focus on one or intersections or traffic signals. Although these methods improved the road network congestion in some degree, it is difficult to find deep level optimization objectives in the practical application problems and research focus.

In our research, we mainly focused on the road-network congestion problems by using Brownian agent motion model. At the early stage of application of agent models, agents was defined either complex or minimalistic ways. A complex agent can be regarded as an autonomous entity with either knowledge or behavior based rules, performing complex actions such as learning and building its own strategy with multiple attributes [8]. The conceptual design of complex agent is ideal but impractical. The alternative is the minimalistic agent, which has the simplest rule set to guide its decision, without referring the internal attributes. But due to oversimplification, the practical application of such agent is also very limited. To avoid both extremes, Brownian agent approach is proposed [9][10]. A Brownian agent is a minimalistic agent with internal degrees of freedom. Through specific action, Brownian agents are able to generate a self-consistent field which in turn influences their further movement and behavior [9]. The non-linear feedback between the agents and the field generated by themselves results in an interactive structure formation process on the macroscopic level.

The applications with Brownian agent model mostly simulated the agent's own activities and analyzed their macro-emergence. Schweitzer and his colleges began their research on the BA in the early years; they defined a potential attribute which described a two-dimensional plane, the attribute would influent the agent movement decision, and the agents' movements would cause changes of the potential attribute and result in the aggregation phenomenon [11]. Schweitzer also optimized the network topology by using a mix Brownian Agent-based strategy which combined the Boltzmann and Darwin hybrid genetic strategy [12]. Another interesting work was done by Espitia in 2011. He proposed a complex Brownian particle swarm model for solving the routing planning problems [13]. Minazuki focused on the optimization of traffic flow and traffic management, the extent of the traffic congestion can be predicted using a model based on the Brownian motion process [14]. Li and Dan proposed a conflict detection algorithm based on Brownian motion, their algorithm had better results for practical application of automated air traffic control systems [15].

Compared to the previous agent application, the characteristic of Brownian Agent was more macroscopic, their whole behaviors and merging characters are more suitable for global optimization. In our work, the design of intelligent transportation system should at least achieve two objectives. One is the shortest routing length to the destination, and the other is the avoidance of the adjacent high-density congestion area. With a multi-objective optimization perspective, this paper proposed a new method which solved the road-network congestion problem by combining two objectives of shortest routing and congestion avoidance. Especially, we applied the approach of Brownian agent to find the next intersection of road network to avoid congestion. Vehicles spontaneously move to the destination, and the entire network congestion distribution would be optimized at the same time. By means of computer simulation, we proved the efficiency and applicable of our model in solving road-network congestion problem.

The rest of the paper is organized as follows: Section 2 describes the model through ODD protocol. Section 3 gives experimental settings and discusses the results of computer simulations. Section 4 analyzes the simulation results. Finally, Section 5 gives concluding remarks and an outlook of future work.

2   Model Description with ODD Protocol

The model description follows the ODD (Overview, Design concepts, Details) protocol for describing individual- and agent-based models [16].

2.1   Purpose

The Multi-Objective Optimization Algorithm with Brownian Agent Model is designed to solve the road-network congestion problem. We also focus on the methodology: a multi-objective optimization with Brownian agent model. Vehicles are regarded as Brownian agents, they spontaneously move to the destination, and the entire network congestion distribution would be optimized at the same time. We analyze the various network congestions under a mix strategy by changing the weights to represent different focus on two moving strategies: the shortest path strategy and a mix strategy combining two objectives of shortest routing and congestion avoidance. We repeated the optimization processes of model parameters through agent strategies, in order to reduce the degree of congestion of the whole network, and provide a new model for the road-network congestion and traffic control methods.

2.2   Entities, State Variables, and Scales

Table 1. Entities and Descriptions

Entities	Description	Entities name in the model
Vehicle	mobile nodes of the road-network	Id(integers from 1 to 500)
Intersection	immobile nodes of the road-network where vehicle passed or located	Id(integers from 1 to 39)

Table 2. State Variable and Descriptions

State variables	Descriptions	Variables name in the model
Links between Interactions	The connection between intersection nodes	adjMatrix
Density of Intersection	The number of vehicles at each intersection node	locationDensity
Source Node Set	The list of intersection nodes where vehicle departures	start
Destination Node Set	The list of intersection nodes where vehicle moves to	end
Vehicle Path	The list of intersection nodes where vehicles passed by	pathMap
Waiting Vehicles	The vehicles of waiting queue at each intersection node	waitQueue
Vehicle State	The states of vehicles at present intersection, either mobile or immobile	vehicleState

2.3   Process Overview and Scheduling

In the simulation model, each vehicle would choose one of its neighbor intersections with the minimum value as next moving target at each simulation step. The minimum value is addressed as an attribute of intersection nodes, estimated by a fitness value of

```
At each simulation cycle
start
              for i = 0 to 500
                  Initialize the vehicles in the network
              end for
              for i = 0 to 39
                  Initialize the intersection nodes in the network
              end for
              for Simulation Step = 0 to the end of simulation step
                  for i = 0 to 500
                      if (Simulation Step == the time step a vehicel should be added)
                          add vehicle to the network
                      end if
                  end for
                  update the information of intersection nodes in the network;
                  for i = 0 to 500
                      if (vehicle in the network)
                          calculate its next jump and update it
                      end if
                      if (vehicle arrived its destination)
                          remove this vehicle
                      end if
                  end for
              end for
End
```

Fig. 1. Pseudo-Code of the Agent Simulation Model

a multi-objective function. At each simulation step, a vehicle in the first position of the waiting queue at present intersection node would move to the next neighbor intersection with minimum attribute value. When a vehicle arrived at its destination, it would be moved out from the road-network. A simulation cycle is defined as one execution of vehicles movement and nodes update. The following pseudo-code describes the process and scheduling of the simulation.

2.4   Design Concepts

Basic principles. The general concepts underlying the models' design is Brownian Agents and Active Particles, which is addressed systematically by Frank Schweitzer [10]. Brownian particles were observed in 1826 by the British botanist Brown (1773-1858). According to the concept of Brownian Agents that Schweitzer mentioned, Brownian Agents can be described by external variables and internal degrees of freedom. The external variables can be observed from the outside, and internal degrees of freedom can be indirectly concluded only from observable actions. During the motion, the internal degrees of freedom can be described as indirect influence of the environment condition. In our model, vehicle agents will leave those intersection nodes with a high density in order to avoid congestion. With a multi-objectives optimization perspective, we used two objectives of shortest routing and congestion avoidance. The internal degree of freedom can be reflected by dynamics of vehicle agents' decisions on next movement. For the entire network, vehicle agents clustered in one intersection node would lead to a density increasing, causing other vehicle agents to skip this intersection to find another path, through which to alleviate the network congestion.

Emergence. Different moving strategies would lead to a different congestion distribution. Even with the same strategy, the distribution would show some features.

Adaptation. Vehicle agents would make their moving decisions based on the attributes (a combination influence of shortest path and congestion avoidance) of location nodes. Vehicle agents behaviors would lead to the network congestion changed. Such a feedback between vehicle agents and the network state generates agent's adaption.

Objectives. The objective of the model is to alleviate the entire network congestion. The congestion of each intersection node is measured by the density of vehicle agents. And, the congestion of the entire network is estimated by the density distribution of the whole network.

Stochasticity. When vehicle agents moves in the road-network, its source and destination intersection node, and the time step when the vehicle agent put into the network are randomly generated. For the calculation of next jump, a Gaussian random number is employed to simulate the stochastic behaviors during such process.

Observation. The data collected from the agent-based model are the time consumption when a vehicle arrives at the destination intersection and the dynamics of vehicles density at each location node during the entire simulation.

Road-Network description. We define the attributes U_x of a intersection node in the following:

$$U_x = preA(r,t)desiG(r,t) \tag{1}$$

Where *preA(r, t)* represents the constant influence on intersection node *r* with time *t*, *desiG(r, t)* denotes the influence of local vehicle density of the intersection node. At an initial stage, we set the value of *preA(r, t)* as 1 to simplify the experiments.

According to the statistical data from the internet, the numbers of vehicles through an intersection varied in time, average numbers were 28 or 29 cars per one minute. Therefore, we define the vehicle density as follows: if the number of vehicle agents is greater than or equal to 28, the density is set to 1; otherwise the density is computed as the vehicle number plus one divided by 28.

2.5   Initialization

At the initial stage, The road-network topology is show in Fig.2, the nodes distribution were same with the network in [12].

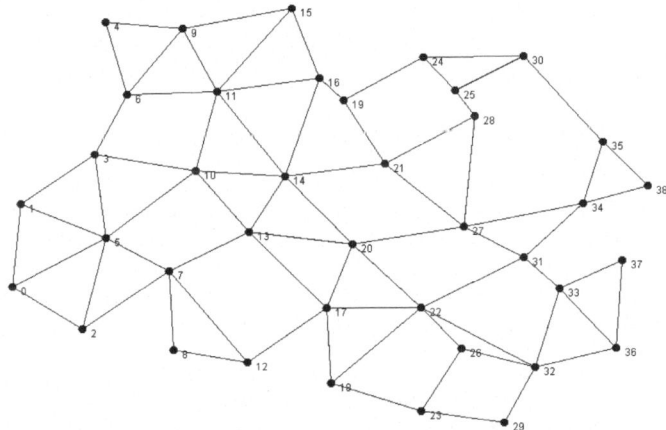

Fig. 2. The Road-Network Topology of the Simulation

2.6   Sub Models

The sub model is agent mobile model, introduced by equation (2):

$$\frac{dx_i}{dt} = v_i \, , \quad m\frac{dv_i}{dt} = -\gamma_0 v_i - \frac{\partial U(x)}{\partial x}\Big|_{x_i} + \sqrt{2k_B T\gamma_0}\xi_i(t) \tag{2}$$

Equation (2) was another type of Langevin equation within external potential. In our model, we did not consider the friction factor γ_0 . $\dfrac{\partial U(x)}{\partial x}$ was regarded as the environment factor at location. $\sqrt{2k_B T\gamma_0}\xi_i(t)$ was the Gaussian random disturbance. We set a fitness function involves two objectives as in Equation (3). Where Λ represents a utility value of adjacent intersection node. Vehicle agents would choose the intersection node with minimum value as next jump. The first term $f(U_x)$ of Equation (3) denotes the attributes of the adjacent node. The second term $g(x)$ represents the restraint of the agent, that is, agents should always move towards destination mode. The parameter λ is used to balance the two objectives (shortest path and congestion avoidance). In order to retain certain randomness of the motion, we add Gaussian random number into the utility function and obtained equation (3).

$$\Lambda(U_x, \lambda) = (1 - \lambda)f(U_x) + \lambda g(x) + Gaussian \qquad (3)$$

3   Experimental Setup and Result Discussion

3.1   Experimental Setup

Given the network topology in Fig.2, the simulation model randomly generated 500 vehicle agents, which were put into the network during the first 50 simulation steps. Each vehicle agent is assigned its source and destination random. For a robust result, each simulation was executed 50 times and the average value was obtained as the final result.

There are two types of vehicle agents defined in our model:

1. In the first type, agents directly used the shortest path of travel in the network. At each simulation step, agents select the intersection node with the shortest path to the destination. We use Floyd Shortest Path algorithm to calculate the shortest path, so we give the name of this type as Floyd Agent.
2. Of the second type, agents move or choose the next movement intersection mode based on the multi-objective utility function (3). We define such type as Mix Agent.

To simplify the experiments, we made the following additional restrictions: each intersection node only allowed one vehicle agent to go through at one simulation step. When vehicles lined up at one intersection node, the simulation model would select the vehicle node at the top of the waiting queue.

3.2   Experimental Result and Discussion

In order to examine the efficiency of our proposed model and algorithms, we summarized the methods of simulation experiments in Table (3).

Table 3. Experimental Descriptions

Group No.	Description	Measurements
Group 1	The effect of λ on network congestion with fixed agent occupation	The average arrival time of agents
		The average vehicle density of 39 intersection nodes
		The density distribution at one simulation step
Group 2	The effect of agent occupation on network congestion with fixed λ	The average time cost and average node density of road-network

The first group of experiments was executed to examine the effect of λ on network congestion with fixed agent occupation. We measured the system performance based on the average arrival time of agents, the average vehicle density of 39 intersections nodes, and the density distribution a one simulation step. In this series of simulations, we set two groups of vehicle agents: the first group has all agents with Shortest Path Strategy, while in the second group the agents with Floyd Strategy or Mix Strategy occupied a 50% rate, respectively.

In the first step of group 1, we tried to find out the effects of different strategies on the agents. Figure 3-5 showed the results of average arrival time under different experimental settings of experiments group 1 in Table (3). Figure 3 gave the average arrival time of Floyd agents with effect of Mix agents, figure 4 showed the average arrival time of Mix agents with the effect of weight(λ), Fig.5 showed the relationship between arrival time cost of Mix agents and the weight.

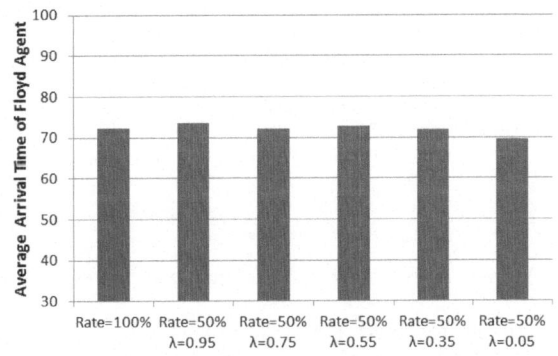

Fig. 3. The Effects of Mix Agents with Different Weight on Floyd Agents

In Fig.3, the x-axis represented a set of situations distinguished by agent proportion (rate) and weights (λ) of the agents with the shortest path strategy; the y-axis denoted the average arrival time of the Floyd agents, described by simulation steps. The first column of the figure showed the average time step when all the agents were Floyd agents and they arrived the destination. The second column gave the average time step when Floyd agents and Mix agents respectively occupied a half rate, the weight (λ) was assigned value 0.95. The rest columns of Figure 3 ranged the weight from 0.75 to 0.05. Based on the results, we found that the average time steps of Floyd agents were in the scale of (60, 80), no matter the various weight of Mix agents. The results indicated that the changes of Mix agents had little effect on the average arrival time of Floyd agent.

In Fig.4, the x-axis represented 50 simluation trials by three different weight of Mix agent, the y-axis denoted the average arrival time of agents, described by simulation steps. Compared the simulation results with the results of Floyd agents in Fig.3, we found that the average arrival time of Mix Agent is longer than Floyd Agent; and the value would be longer when the weight (λ) decreased. Based on the description of equation (3), we found these agents tended to avoid congestion. This tendency became more apparent when the weight was getting smaller.

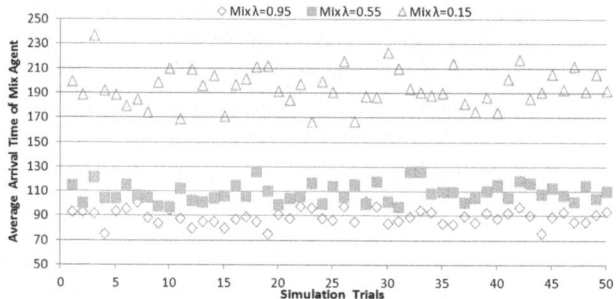

Fig. 4. Average Arrival Time of the 50% Mix Agents in the Network with Different Weight

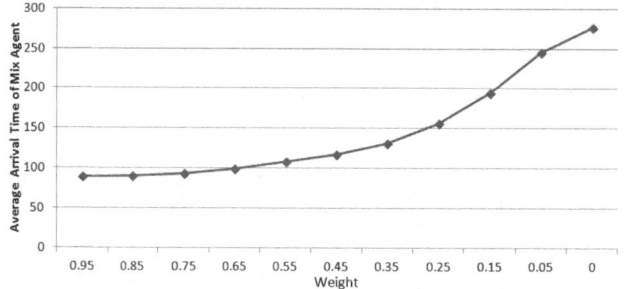

Fig. 5. Average Arrival Time of Mix Agent with Different Weight

In Fig.5, the *x*-axis represented the different weights, the y-axis denoted the average arrival time of the Mix Agents, described by simulation steps. The results indicated that the average arrival time of the Mix Agent would be longer when the weight was smaller. This increasing tendency represented in Fig.5 became greater when the weight was set below 0.35.

In the second step of group 1, we studied the effect of Mix Agent to the network congestion. We analyzed the feasibility of improving the network congestion by multi-objective algorithm with Brownian Agent. Fig.6-7 showed the results of congestion improvements under different experimental settings of experiments group 1 in Table (3).

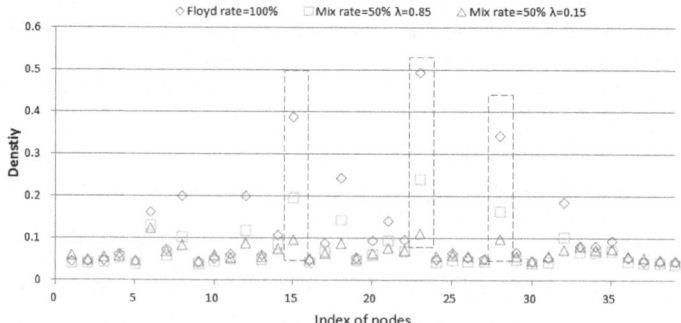

Fig. 6. Density of 39 nodes of the Network

In Fig.6, x-axis represented the index of 39 nodes, and y-axis represented the average density of the 39 nodes. The calculation of density was defined in Section 2. The three kinds of splashes denoted the density of agents in the network with three types of moving strategies as the complete shortest path strategy, the Floyd and Mix agent occupied a 50% rate respectively with different weight values as 0.85, 0.15. From the results, we found that the entire network congestion decreased obviously when the weight of Mix Agent decreased. The results could be observed distinguished among those nodes selected by the rectangles. Because Mix Agent were more inclined to avoid congestion node when the weights decreased according to equation (3), thus the average density of the network nodes was significantly decreased.

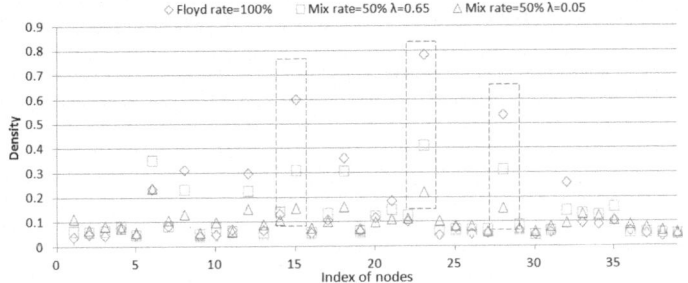

Fig. 7. Density of 39 Intersection Nodes at Time Step 49

Fig.7 gave the density distribution of the network node at one selected simulation step. By sorting the density distribution of 100% Floyd Agents, we found that the time step 49 held the most serious congestion during the whole simulation process. Therefore, we picked up this single time step to verify the feasibility of Mix Agent to improve the congestion of the entire network. Based on the results shown in Fig.7, we found that the congestion of the intersection nodes selected by the rectangles had been notably improved.

According to the results of experiments described in Table (3), we could conclude that the Mix Agents using the multi-objective algorithm would greatly alleviate the congestion of the special intersession nodes and the entire network. Meanwhile because of the shunt in the congestion intersection node, Mix Agents arrival time may be increased.

In the second group of experiments described in Table (3), we tried to found the effects of agents' proportions on the simulation results. The parameters were set as follows: the weight of Mix Agents was 0.35, the occupation rates of two types of agents were set to 25%: 75%, 75%: 25%. Fig.7-8 showed the simulation results changed when modifying the occupation rate.

From the results of Fig.8-9, we found that the greater the occupation rate of Mix Agent was, the smaller the network congestion became. On the other hand, the more the number of Mix Agent was, their average time steps became longer with fixed weights.

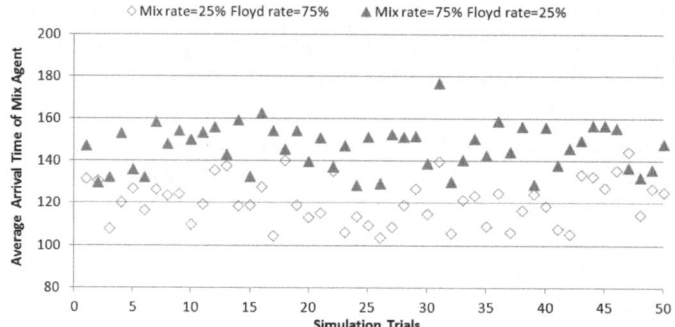

Fig. 8. Average arrival time of Mix Agent with different occupation rate

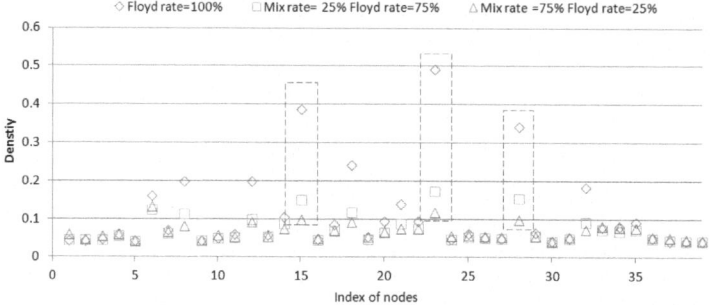

Fig. 9. Density of nodes with different Agent occupation rate

Compared with other congestion control model or algorithm, just like Chiu introduced vehicle navigation systems, which were equipped with Dynamic Route Guidance System, providing shortest distance path of given target location with a multi-objective algorithm [17]. Yoshikawa et al. proposed a hybrid genetic algorithm to solve path optimization [18]. The traditional road-network congestion optimization was focus on the route optimization. Our experiment was based on the entire network, the individual can sense the surrounding environment, from the macro point of view, improved the network congestion, the method herein used is of creativeness.

4   Conclusion

This paper proposed a new method which solved the road-network congestion problem by combining two objectives of shortest routing and congestion avoidance. By means of computer simulation, we implemented our proposed method with a predefined road-network topological structure. We tested the parameters sensitivity by scaling the proportion of agent with different moving strategies and the weights of Mix agent. The simulation results proved the applicability and efficiency of our proposed method for alleviating the network congestion distribution, and the intersections within a higher vehicle density were observed decreased.

The bigger average time consumption with Mix agent, which indicated a mix strategy by considering both effects of shortest path and congestion avoidance might result more time cost than the shortest path strategy. But the actual traffic situation is far more complicated, and the intersection waiting time consumption seems bigger than the cost of detours. Therefore, our model made its sense in its applicability and efficiency of solving road-network congestion problem by a multi-objective optimization algorithm with Brownian agent model.

5   Future Works

In the present version, our model only simulated agent movement via network nodes, while in the real transportation system, the vehicles mobile continuously and could not jump to the next intersection. In the future work, we will change agent motion in line with the actual road condition. Furthermore, other traffic effects, such as some nature impact from the intersection node itself (such as *preA* we mentioned in our equation and model in section 2) should be far more designed and implemented.

References

1. Nagel, K., Schreckenberg, M.: A cellular automaton model for freeway traffic. Journal de Physique I (1992)
2. Gou, C.-X.: Research on highway ram control based on Cellular Automata. In: International Conference on Mechatronics and Automation (ICMA) (2010)
3. Pei, Y.-L., Ci, Y.-S.: Study on Traffic Flow at On-ramp Junctions in Urban Freeway with Cellular Automaton Model. In: International Conference on Management Science and Engineering (ICMSE) (2007)
4. Cui, C.Y., Shin, J.S., Miyazaki, M., Lee, H.H.: Real-time traffic signal control for optimization of traffic jam probability. Electronics and Communications in Japan 96(1), 1–13 (2013)
5. Wang, F.Y.: Agent-based control for networked traffic management systems. IEEE Intelligent Systems 20(5), 92–96 (2005)
6. Du, R.: Urban Traffic Coordination Control System Based on Multi-Agent-Game. In: ICICATA (October 2008)
7. Chin, Y.K.: Q-Learning Traffic Signal Optimization within Multiple Intersections Traffic network. In: 2012 Sixth UKSim/AMSS European Symposium on Computer Modeling and Simulation (EMS) (2012)
8. Müller, J.P., Wooldridge, M.J., Jennings, N.R.: Intelligent agents III: agent theories, architectures, and languages. Springer, Berlin (1997)
9. Schweitzer, F.: Modelling migration and economic aggregation with active brownian particles. Advances in Complex Systems 1(1), 11–37 (1998)
10. Schweitzer, F.: Brownian Agents and Active Particles: Collective Dynamics in the Natural and Social Sciences. Springer, Berlin (2003)
11. Schweitzer, F., Schimansky-Geier, L.: Clustering of active walkers a two-component system. Physica A: Statistical Mechanics and its Applications, 359–379 (1994)
12. Schweitzer, F., Ebeling, W., Rose, H., Weiss, O.: Optimization of Road Networks Using Evolutionary Strategies. Evolutionary Computation 5(4), 419–438 (1998)

13. Espitia, H.E.: Path planning of mobile robots using potential fields and swarms of Brownian particles. In: IEEE Congress on Evolutionary Computation (CEC), New Orleans, LA, June 5-8, pp. 123–129 (2011)
14. Minazuki, A.: Control of vehicle movement on the road traffic. In: 2001 IEEE International Conference on Systems, Man and Cybernetics, vol. 2, pp. 1366–1371 (2001)
15. Li, D., Cui, D.: Air traffic control conflict detection algorithm based on Brownian motion. Journal of Tsinghua University 48(4), 477–481 (2008)
16. Grimm, V., Berger, U., DeAngelis, D.L., Polhill, J.G., Giske, J., Railsback, S.F.: The odd protocol: A review and first update. Ecological Modelling 221, 2760–2768 (2010)
17. Chiu, C.-S.: A Genetic Algorithm for Multi objective Path Optimization Problem. In: ICNC, Yantai, China, August 10-12, pp. 2217–2222 (2010)
18. Yoshikawa, M., Terai, H.: Car navigation system based on hybrid genetic algorithm. In: Proceeding of World Congress on Computer Science and Information Engineering, Log Angeles, USA, October 21, pp. 62–65 (2009)

A Norm-Based Probabilistic Decision-Making Model for Autonomic Traffic Networks

Maksims Fiosins, Jörg P. Müller, and Michaela Huhn

Clausthal University of Technology,
Department of Informatics,
Julius-Albert Str. 4, D-38678, Clausthal-Zellerfeld, Germany
{Maksims.Fiosins,joerg.mueller,michaela.huhn}@tu-clausthal.de

Abstract. We propose a norm-based agent-oriented model of decision-making of semi-autonomous vehicles in urban traffic scenarios. Computational norms are used to represent the driving rules and conventions that influence the distributed decision-making process of the vehicles. As norms restrict the admissible behaviour of the agents, we propose to represent them as constraints, and we express the agents' individual and group decision-making in terms of distributed constraint optimization problems. The uncertain nature of the driving environment is reflected in our model through probabilistic constraints – collective norm compliance is considered as a stochastic distributed constraint optimization problem. In this paper, we introduce the basic conceptual and algorithmic ingredients of our model, including the norms provisioning and enforcement mechanisms (where electronic institutions are used), the norm semantics, as well as methods of the agents' cooperative decision-making. For motivation and illustration of our approach, we study a cooperative multi-lane highway driving scenario; we propose a formal model, and illustrate our approach by a small example.

Keywords: cooperative traffic management, multi-agent decision-making, computational norms and institutions, probabilistic distributed constraint optimization, resampling.

1 Introduction

The growing complexity of traffic management systems (TMS) in conjunction with new technological trends such as the increasing availability and growing amount of real-time traffic data, intelligence and autonomy of vehicular assistance functions (and indeed: of vehicles), and the capability of car-to-X (C2X) communication, create new challenges for future cooperative traffic systems. As an example, the integration of car navigation with intelligent assistance functions and car-to-car communication enables software-based driving assistant not only to support the driver but to make decisions, to take actions, and to communicate with other vehicles and traffic control devices autonomously, i.e., without explicit human command. Current examples of this development are BMWs cross-traffic assistant and traffic light assistant. In the future, we shall see much more advanced services with a higher degree of autonomy. Safety and efficiency of such systems will have crucial impact (positive or negative) on our society [1].

J.M. Corchado et al. (Eds.): PAAMS 2013 Workshops, CCIS 365, pp. 49–60, 2013.

Architectural approaches towards modeling and controlling such future cooperative traffic management systems (CTMS) must (i) support system scalability and reconfigurability, (ii) provide adaptiveness to dynamic and stochastic environments, and (iii) enable a decentralized modeling and coordination approach which allows keeping local structures and decision models simple, and does not require complete models of the environment. We claim that multi-agent systems (MAS) [2] are a promising architectural approach for this purpose, as it provides appropriate paradigms and methods to model autonomy, interaction, and adaptation.

One of the key questions in MAS research and design is how to control the behavior of agents while preserving their autonomy [3]. There are two main answers to this question: The first is to define dedicated services, which coordinate the agents' behavior in terms of action synchronization or resource access planning. An example for this approach is the work on automated intersection control by Dresner and Stone [4]. The second, more decentralized approach employs indirect organizational and social control concepts such as computational norms [5], including permission, obligation or prohibition of states or actions, and provides monitoring, incentives, and penalizing mechanisms to organize and control agent behavior. While both approaches have pros and cons, our research mostly concentrates on the latter aspect, because we argue that direct, centralized control is often unfeasible in large MAS.

In our research we start from concepts and methods from normative multiagent systems [6], which we extend by a distributed constraint semantics and by the ability to deal with uncertainty. Computational norms can be conceived as rules, which define appropriate (or unacceptable) states or actions in a given environment such as maximum speed, minimum distance, or priority at intersections. Compliance to norms is about to effect safe, stable, and efficient functioning of the overall system. Norms lifecycle support mechanisms such as electronic institutions [7] support (i) norm creation, maintenance, and evolution; (ii) provisioning of norms to the agents, and (iii) norm monitoring and enforcement.

Constraints have been proposed as an operational semantics of norms [8], allowing to detect norm violations and optimizing decisions under a given set of norms, based on an established computational framework. We reflect the distributed nature of decision-making situations in traffic scenarios by using distributed constraint satisfaction / optimization (DCSP/DCOP) [9]. In a DCSP/DCOP, each agent controls a subset of the variables and has only local knowledge about constraints of the DCSP or DCOP [10].

Environment uncertainty requires probabilistic decision-making models [11]. Norms are subject to changes, the reasons of which are unknown to the agents. We use a probabilistic distributed constraint satisfaction approach to allow agents analyzing the uncertainty of the environment and making appropriate decisions.

This introductory paper sets out the conceptual and algorithmic pillars of our approach. Starting from a simple application scenario (cooperative multi-lane highway driving), we propose a novel agent-based coordinated decision-making model for autonomic CTMS. We introduce computational norms, describe their semantics in terms of constraints, and formalize deciding norm compliance as a stochastic DCOP. We outline a generic multi-agent architecture for norms provisioning.

The paper is organized as follows. Section 2 presents the motivating scenario. Section 3 describes the overall MAS architecture and models, which support norm provision and interpretation by the agents. In Section 4, we formalize the norm semantics in terms of stochastic constraints. Section 5 presents and discusses an illustrative example. Section 6 contains conclusions and points to future directions.

2 Norms in a Traffic Scenario

In this section we present a simple traffic scenario that is regulated by norms. We consider autonomous vehicles (AV) driving one-way on a multi-lane highway (see Fig. 1). Each AV has its individual goals (destination and preferred arrival time) and each AV respects the physical laws for safe driving; it also knows the traffic rules that apply in a situation. Here we distinguish between two types of rules: (i) basic safety-related rules, which the agent will not willingly break, because doing so would violate the physical integrity of itself or others (e.g., entering a motorway in the wrong direction)[1], and (ii) efficiency-related rules like speed limits that mainly serve to optimizing traffic flows with respect to superordinate targets like maximizing throughput, or minimizing the overall time in traffic congestions or environmental pollution (noise or emissions).

The notion of norms serves us as a conceptual means to express these rules: Norms are behavioral guidelines provided by so-called electronic institutions [7] in order to enforce safety rules and encourage efficiency rules. An institution will offer positive incentives for norm-compliant behavior, and sanctions in case of detected norm violation. For safety norms, we can imagine that an infinitely high penalty will be issued to the violating agent. For efficiency norms, an agent may decide freely whether they fit to its goals, as a norm violation effects neither its physical safety nor results in a capital offense.

Norms refer to the externally observable dynamic state of an AV that consists of a list of parameters like its current location on a certain lane, its speed, and its distance to neighboring vehicles etc. Norms may have a restricted *scope*, e.g. they may only apply for some kind of vehicles in a certain lane section. We assume that norms are published to all traffic participants by the institution.

Examples for norms applying to individual vehicles are:

- *Maximum speed limit:* Such norms recommend an upper speed limit at certain sections of a lane.
- *Minimum speed limit:* These norms are activated, for instance at up-hill sections on certain lanes. They aim at preventing slow vehicles from occupying the lanes that shall be scheduled for the faster ones.
- *Stop at red light:* Such norms prohibit crossing against red light. Compliance of this norm is usually controlled for each traffic light.
- *Prohibition of lane change:* Such norms discourage or prohibit lane changes in heavy-traffic, dangerous road sections, or close to exits.

---

[1] If a safety level is needed to guarantee agents will not coincidentally break rules, even stronger measures like physical precautions need to be taken. This problem is not addressed in this paper.

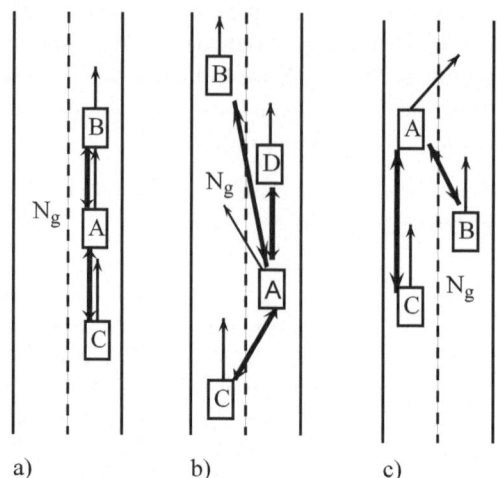

Fig. 1. Examples of group norms for cooperative multi-lane driving in the viewpoint of vehicle A. a) illustrates platooning; b) lane change of a faster vehicle; c) giving way by a slower vehicle.

Group norms require the cooperation of several vehicles:

- *Optimal platooning distance*: This norm specifies an interval for the distance that is recommended between vehicles driving in a convoy on the same lane.
- *Polite lane change by faster vehicles*: Vehicles that aim to drive significantly faster than the vehicle ahead shall change one lane left, if the safety distances to vehicles on the new lane are respected when taking their speed and the possible acceleration of the vehicle itself into account.
- *Polite lane change by slower vehicles*: Vehicles that aim to drive significantly slower than the vehicle behind shall change one lane right. Again, the safety distances to vehicles driving on the right lane have to be considered.

3   Norms-Based Multi-agent Architecture

In this section, we describe an architecture for indirect norm-based control of semi-autonomous vehicles. Our conceptual architecture for norm-based MAS control consists of the controlled MAS and of the electronic institution (system controller). We focus on the agents' viewpoint towards norms rather than on the methods of the norm provision, norm/system monitoring and efficiency analysis from the institution point of view — the system controller is considered a 'black box' for the agents. Thus, we only provide a brief sketch of the institutional side: An institution has three primary tasks: (i) exert indirect control over the system by dynamically providing norms to components (agents); (ii) observe agents and obtain a model by mining their behavior; and (iii) calculate values of system metrics to evaluate efficiency, reliability and controllability of system operation. Based on the metrics and the system model, decisions are made, e.g., about provision of new norms.

Our institutional model is based on the AAOL (Autonomous Agents in Organized Localities) modeling methodology. AAOL provides a metamodel for institution-based multiagent system, which in particular takes the distributedness of institutions and their range of influence into account. In particular, in AAOL, institutions can be associated with a physical or virtual space, a so-called *locality*. The locality of an institution determines the outreach of an institution in terms of the validity of norms as well as the power of norm enforcement. Using localities, we can describe a large range of control regimes, ranging from purely centralized over regional to decentralized. The AAOL model has been described in detail in [12]. In this paper, we extend AAOL by models and methods for constraint-based probabilistic decision-making.

Within a locality, norms act as (hard or soft) constraints to the agents' behavior (while the agent acts within the borders of the locality). We assume that initially each agent acts according to its own interests. Norms restrict this behavior by providing possible sanctions in order to avoid system failures and ineffective system operation due to egoistic behavior of some agents. Within a locality, we assume that norms refer to a system state which will be formalized as a tuple of values each expressing a parameter of a (sub)system as it may be observed by the institution at a certain point in time. A norm consists of (1) a *context* that indicates at which states of the system the norm shall be respected (the locality plus further pre-conditions), (2) a *normative predicate* that specifies the system states preferred by the norm and (3) an *incentive* which is expressed as a function that assigns a positive or negative reward in case the system state complies with or violates the norm. A norm is called *applicable* on an agent, if at least one variable that is addressed in the normative predicate is under the control of that agent. I.e., norms are expressed in terms of (projections of) system states as they are seen from the viewpoint of an institution.

An agent is assumed to be capable to correctly interpret a norm N; i.e., it is able to decide whether the pre-condition applies in the current situation, and it may take the consequences of sanctioning into account for evaluating and choosing its plans. According to its current state and information available, each agent creates a set of alternative plans, each of them containing a sequence of future actions. If egoistic behavior of the agents is supposed, each agent should evaluate the plans according to its preferences and select an optimal plan with respect to the rewards it can obtain by using the plan. A set of norms acts as an additional plan evaluation criterion that forces agents to take possible sanctions (i.e., negative rewards) into account.

We consider the two types of norms identified in Section 2:

- *Single-agent norms*, which restrict plans of single agents in certain situations;
- *Group norms*, which restrict joint plans of multiple agents. Note that group norms are not symmetric in general: they may provide different sanctions to the participating agents.

Each norm is associated with a sanction, i.e. a function that calculates a penalty (negative reward) to be paid by the agent if it violates the norm and has a certain state in the moment of the norm monitoring (e.g. *if* the speed limit is 50 km/h and at the moment of monitoring the speed was 73 km/h *then* the reward is -30). So each plan should be evaluated according to payoff and possible penalties and an optimal plan should be selected. In Section 4 we specify an overall reward function for that purpose.

However, a major complicating factor in this process is uncertainty, which appears in three guises: **uncertainty in plan execution, uncertainty in other agents' plans**, and **uncertainty in norms**. So a model is required that enables probabilistic situation forecasting [13].

Given these different flavors of uncertainty, our goal is to make probabilistic estimation of sanctions from single-agent norms for each individual plan and from group norms for each multi-agent plan. As a method for deciding/detecting cooperative norm compliance, we propose Stochastic Distributed Constraint Optimization (SDCOP) [9]. It enables optimization of certain system-wide characteristics (in our case, the overall reward) under a set of conditions for the entire system. As an optimization approach, resampling can be effective [14].

We propose that each agent is equipped with a 'Probabilistic Constraint Optimizer' (PCO) module, which implements the mentioned SDCOP algorithm and selects an optimal plan for the agent from a predefined plan library under a given set of norms. For each plan in the plan library the PCO module forecasts the situations and estimates sanctions from the available norms. The agent can communicate with other agents in order to make joint plans and estimate sanctions from group norms. Then an optimal plan (with respect to a defined objective function, see Section 4) is selected for execution.

4   Formal Constraint-Based Model of Normative Regulation

In this section we describe a formal model of norm-based decision-making of the vehicle agents. The norms are represented as soft and hard constraints over the system configurations as described in the previous sections.

We define a set of discrete system configurations $Conf = \{\langle c_1(t), c_2(t), \ldots, c_m(t)\rangle \mid t \in \mathbb{N}\}$ where t denotes the discrete time. A global configuration $\mathbf{c}$ represents the system state to which the norms relate. It is composed of local configurations representing the current state of a component, e.g. a vehicle or a traffic light. Each subconfiguration is a vector $c(t) = \langle v_1(t), v_2(t), \ldots, v_k(t)\rangle$, where each parameter describes a characteristics of the component (e.g. $v_1(t)$ may describe the current speed of a vehicle, $v_2(t)$ its distance to the next intersection, v_3 its position etc.). Some of the parameters may be undefined, denoted by "$\perp$", at specific time steps.

The considered MAS consists of a set of n agents $AG = \{ag^1, ag^2, \ldots, ag^n\}$. Each agent ag^j has a set of the internal states $S^j = \{\langle s_1^j(t), s_2^j(t), \ldots, s_{n_j}^j(t)\rangle \mid t \in \mathbb{N}\}$, representing its internal information about itself and its environment. An internal state $s^j(t) \in S^j$ can be translated to a system configuration using a translation function $U^j : S^j \to Conf$. We assume U^j to be a *correct*, but possibly partial view of agent j of the system configuration; i.e., if two agents i and j map their local states $s^i(t)$ and $s^j(t)$ to the system state, and for some parameter $v_k(t)$ within some subconfiguration $c(t)$ both mappings yield a value (i.e. the projections $U^i(s^i(t))|_{c,k} \neq \perp \neq U^j(s^j(t))|_{c,k}$), then $U^i(s^i(t))|_{c,k} = U^j(s^j(t))|_{c,k}$. A correct mapping ensures that any two agents (and the institution) coincide on their common view on the system.

An agent ag^j has a finite set of available actions Act^j. An action execution enforces deterministic state change; the actions from Act^j are used to modify the parameters under the control of the agent. We further assume a set of oracle actions $\omega \in \Omega^j$ that we use to describe what change the agent will observe in its environment as far as it is aware of it like e.g. the traffic light will be red in the next state and the vehicle ahead will be on position x. Formally, there is a deterministic transition function T^j : $S^j \times Act^j \times \Omega^j \to S^j$, which for each state-action pair returns the next state.

Each agent is able to generate a set of alternative plans, whenever needed. In this paper, we assume a planning capability of the agent to be given, so we do not consider details. For simplicity we choose a fixed planning horizon $T \in \mathbb{N}$ that is common to all the agents in the system. A plan $plan^j \in Plans^j$ is an ordered sequence of actions $plan^j = ((a_1, \omega_1), (a_2, \omega_2), \dots, (a_T, \omega_T)), a_k \in Act^j, \omega_k \in \Omega^j$. An execution of the plan $plan^j$ at time t means that the agent selects the pair (a_1, ω_1) at time t, action (a_2, ω_2) at time $t+1$, ..., action (a_T, ω_T) at time $t + T - 1$. If the state $s^j(t) \in S^j$ at the moment t is known and the above mentioned deterministic state transition schema is used, an execution of $plan^j$ generates a defined sequence of the states $s^j(t+1), s^j(t+2), \dots, s^j(t+T)$, where $s^j(t+k) = T^j(s^j(t+k-1), a_k, \omega_k), k = 1, 2 \dots, T$.

The set of norms $Norm$ is finite and fixed. A norm $n \in Norm$ is a tuple $\langle cond, pred, reward \rangle$ where $cond : Conf \to \mathbb{B}$ specifies the *enabling condition* of the norm, $pred : Conf \to \mathbb{B}$ the normative predicate describing the norm compliant states and $reward : Conf \times AG \to (\mathbb{R} \cup \{-\infty\})$ is a reward function, that formalizes the rewards (positive values) and sanctions (negative values) that are imposed on the agents when norm compliance is monitored. Within $Norm$ we distinguish single-agent norms N_a and group norms N_g: A single-agent norm n_a refers only to a single agent, meaning that the set of components on which subconfigurations $cond_a$ and $pred_a$ truly depend, contains exactly one agent[2]. We note that, however, the state of non-agent components may be relevant in a single agent norm, e.g. the norm may state that a vehicle (agent) must stop in case of a red traffic light ahead (component with property $v_{light} = red$). In a group norm n_g, the enabling condition and the normative predicate refer to the status of more than one agent.

In addition we require that at most those agents, on which the norm truly depends, may receive a non-zero reward by the *reward* function. The value $-\infty$ is used in a reward assignment for safety norms that must not be violated.

To reason about norms, an agent must be able to interpret a norm, by mapping its internal state to a system configuration and evaluating the enabling condition, the normative predicate and the reward function. This implies that an agent's perception, its internal state and the translation function U^j need to be sufficiently complete, i.e. the agent must be aware of those parameters of a system configuration that are relevant to a norm. As translation functions are assumed to be correct we can be sure, that all agents that are aware of a certain parameter coincide on its value.

As we described before, a norm aims to restrict an agent's behavior, however an agent can in principle violate it. However, due to its egoistic but rational behavior the agent will take possible sanctions imposed in case of norm violation into account when evaluating its plans.

---

[2] We say a predicate or function p *truly depends on* a component if two system configurations s_1, s_2 exist which differ only by this component, i.e. $s_1 = \langle c_1, c_2, \dots, c_i, \dots, c_k \rangle$ and $s_2 = \langle c_1, c_2, \dots, c_i', \dots, c_k \rangle$, and $p(s_1) \neq p(s_2)$.

Formally, the sanctions for agent j imposed by a norm $n \in Norm$ can be calculated for each state $s^j(t+k)$ in the state sequence produced by the plan $plan^j$, by $reward(plan^j) = \sum_{k=0}^{T} reward(U^j(s^j(t+k)), j)$. We note that via the sequence of oracle actions the effect of future behavior of other components and in particular other agents are taken into account as far as it is represented in the internal state of agent j. However, the prediction is individual for agent j.

A *joint* plan means that a group of agents shares each others plans. Here we will model joint plans as a coincidence of the action sequence of one agent with the oracle sequences on its behavior by the other group members, regarding the effects on those parameters that are under the control of the group of agents: I.e. let $A \subseteq AG$ be a group of agents. Then $plan^A = \{plan^j \mid plan^j \in Plans^j$ for each $j \in A\}$ is called a *joint plan* of A at time t_0 iff for all $i \in A$ the following holds: If $v^{(i)}$ is the mth parameter in the subconfiguration c that represents agent i on the system level and any agent $j \in A$ that is aware of agent i's property $v^{(i)}$, i.e. $U^j(s^j(t))$ yields a value for $v^{(i)}$, then for the two state sequences $s^i(t_0+1), s^i(t_0+2), \ldots, s^i(t_0+T)$ generated from $plan^i$ and $s^j(t_0+1), s^j(t_0+2), \ldots, s^j(t_0+T)$ generated from $plan^j$

$$v^{(i)} = U^i(s^i(t_0+k))|_{c,m} = U^j(s^j(t_0+k))|_{c,m} \text{ for } k = 1, \ldots T,$$

i.e. agent j's prediction on the future of agent i coincides with agent i's plan. Thus the notion of a joint plan formalizes that the agents somehow share their plans. In case of a joint plan, each agent of the group may evaluate the norms individually with respect to its individual rewards. However, it can be sure that the others will behave accordingly. An agent evaluates a $plan^j \in Plans^j$ by summing up the sanctions $reward(plan^j)$ it causes over all applicable norms.

However, in general not every norm violation is monitored and sanctioned. Thus we assume a agent-local likelihood information that may result from its former experience. In order to model it, we introduce an *experience function* $F^j(n) : S^T \rightarrow P(\mathbb{R} \cup \{-\infty\})$, which is associated by agent j with the each norm $n \in Norm$. $F^j(n)$ returns for a sequence of states a probability distribution of the rewards. A sanction or incentive of a plan $plan^j$ of the agent j caused by the norm n is a random variable $X^j_{plan,n}$ with a distribution $F^j(plan^j, n)$;

Then the reward from all norms is also a random variable defined as

$$R^j_{norm}(plan^j) = \sum_{n \in Norm} X^j_{plan^j, n}$$

Each agent $ag^j \in AG$ further has an individual reward function $R^j_{goal}(plan^j)$, which calculates the usability of a plan $plan^j$. The reward function lets us compare the result of different plans relative to the agent goals (for example, the agent wants to reach its destination as quickly as possible; in this case $R^j_{goal}(plan^j)$ may be measured as costs of time).

A total reward $R^j(plan^j)$ of the plan $plan^j$ is calculated as

$$R^j(plan^j) = R^j_{norm}(plan^j) + R^j_{goal}(plan^j).$$

The final reward is a random variable. As a criterion for an optimal plan selection the agent takes into account its expectation $E[R^j(plan^j)]$ and variance $Var[R^j(plan^j)]$

$$Eff^j(plan^j) = \alpha^j E[R^j(plan^j)] + \beta^j \sqrt{Var[R^j(plan^j)]}.$$

Cooperative planning is a process of a maximizing the final reward over a group of agents $A \subseteq AG$ in the system. The goal of the group is to select a joint plan $\{plan^{*1}, plan^{*2}, \ldots, plan^{*n}\} \in Plans^A$ such that the total expected efficiency of the system is maximized:

$$Eff = \max_{Plans^A} \sum_{ag^j \in A} Eff^j(plan^A|^j)$$

The formulated problem is a problem of stochastic DCOP [9].

5   Example

We illustrate our approach by using a simple example. Let us consider a road segment, where three vehicles ag^1, ag^2 and ag^3 are situated. The planning horizon of all the vehicles is $T = 4$.

We use a variant of the Nagel-Schreckenberg traffic model, which means that the road is split to cells and each vehicle occupies exactly one cell. The state of each vehicle j is described by a vector $S^j = \langle s_1^j(t), s_2^j(t), s_3^j(t) \rangle$, where $s_1^j(t)$ denotes the position of the vehicle (number of cells from beginning of the road), $s_2^j(t)$ denotes the lane and $s_3^j(t)$ denotes speed. The movement of a vehicle is possible forward (F) or forward with lane change left (L) or right (R). The relative speeds of the vehicles are expressed by the number of cells which they pass per time unit. We further assume that a vehicle can accelerate (A) or decelerate (D) by one cell per time unit or not change its speed (N). So the set of actions Act^j for each agent j consists of nine actions: $Act^j = \{FA, FD, FN, LA, LD, LN, RA, RD, RN\}$. We finally assume that the subconfigurations $c_i(t)$ of the system configuration $Conf$ are equal to the agent states S^j, i.e. the function U^j is an identity function.

The initial states of the vehicles are $S^1 = \langle 1, 2, 3 \rangle$, $S^2 = \langle 5, 2, 2 \rangle$ and $S^3 = \langle 6, 1, 1 \rangle$. Figure 2 illustrates the initial situation on the road.

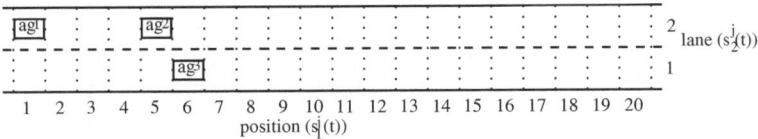

Fig. 2. Example: Initial situation on the road

There are the following norms, which are enabled (*cond* = *true*):

- n_1: Maximum speed limit for all lanes is 4. The norm compliant states are *pred* : $s_3^j(t) \leq 4$ and the reward function of the state $reward(s_3^j(t)) = -(s_3^j(t) - 4) * 10$
- n_2: Minimum following distance for all lanes is 1. The norm compliant states are $pred : \forall k \neq j : (s_2^j(t) = s_2^k(t) \& s_1^k(t) > s_1^j(t)) \rightarrow s_1^k(t) - s_1^j(t) > 1$ and the reward function of the subsequent vehicle $reward(s_1^j(t), s_1^k(t)) = -20$ and of the preceding vehicle $reward(s_1^k(t), s_1^j(t)) = -1$
- n_3: Safety distance for the lane change is 1. The norm compliant states are *pred* : $\forall k \neq j : (s_2^j(t-1) - s_2^k(t-1) = 1) \& (s_2^j(t) = s_2^k(t)) \& (s_1^j > s_1^k) \rightarrow s_1^j(t) - s_1^k(t) > 1$ and the reward function of the subsequent vehicle $reward(s_1^j, s_1^k) = -20$ and of the preceding vehicle $reward(s_1^k, s_1^j) = -1$

The agents consider the following alternative plans: $plan_1^1 = \{FN, FN, FN, FN\}$; $plan_2^1 = \{FA, FN, FD, FN\}$; $plan_1^2 = \{FN, FN, RN, FN\}$; $plan_2^2 = \{FN, RN, FN, FN\}$; $plan_1^3 = \{FN, FN, FN, FN\}$. Tables 1, 2 and 3 list the estimated sanctions from the norms for the vehicles ag^1, ag^2 and ag^3 correspondingly.

Table 1. Sanctions for the plans of the vehicle ag^1

Plan	Norm n_1	Norm n_2		Norm n_3		Reward
		$plan_1^2, plan_1^3$	$plan_2^2, plan_1^3$	$plan_1^2, plan_1^3$	$plan_2^2, plan_1^3$	
$plan_1^1$	0	0	0	0	0	10
$plan_2^1$	-10, $p = 0.1$	-20, $p = 0.2$	0	0	0	20

Table 2. Sanctions for the plans of the vehicle ag^2

Plan	Norm n_1	Norm n_2		Norm n_3		Reward
		$plan_1^1, plan_1^3$	$plan_2^1, plan_1^3$	$plan_1^1, plan_1^3$	$plan_2^1, plan_1^3$	
$plan_1^2$	0	0	-1, $p = 0.2$	0	0	10
$plan_2^2$	0	0	0	-30, $p = 0.3$	-30, $p = 0.3$	10

Table 3. Sanctions for the plan of the vehicle ag^3 (reward = 10)

Norm n_1	0			
	$plan_1^1, plan_1^2$	$plan_1^1, plan_2^2$	$plan_2^1, plan_1^2$	$plan_2^1, plan_2^2$
Norm n_2	0	0	0	0
Norm n_3	0	-1, $p = 0.3$	0	-1, $p = 0.3$

Now any distributed constraint optimization algorithm [9] can be applied to find optimal combinations of the agent plans. In our simple case there are only 4 possible combinations of plans, which are shown in Table 4.

We see that the combination of plans $plan_2^1$, $plan_1^2$, $plan_1^3$ corresponds to maximal system efficiency 34.8 and will be selected in the considered situation.

Table 4. Summarized sanctions for possible combinations of the vehicle plans

Plans	ag^1	ag^2	ag^3	Sum	Eff
$plan_1^1, plan_1^2, plan_1^3$	10	10	10	30	30
$plan_1^1, plan_2^2, plan_1^3$	10	10, $p = 0.7$ -20, $p = 0.3$	10, $p = 0.7$ 9, $p = 0.3$	30, $p = 0.7$ -1, $p = 0.3$	20.7
$plan_2^1, plan_1^2, plan_1^3$	-10, $p = 0.02$ 0, $p = 0.18$ 10, $p = 0.08$ 20, $p = 0.72$	10, $p = 0.8$ 9, $p = 0.2$	10	9, $p = 0.02$ 19, $p = 0.18$ 30, $p = 0.08$ 40, $p = 0.72$	34.8
$plan_2^1, plan_2^2, plan_1^3$	20, $p = 0.9$ 10, $p = 0.1$	10, $p = 0.7$ -20, $p = 0.3$	10, $p = 0.7$ 9, $p = 0.3$	40, $p = 0.63$ 30, $p = 0.07$ 9, $p = 0.27$ -1, $p = 0.03$	29.7

6 Conclusion

In this paper, we proposed a constraint-based decision-making model for vehicles in cooperative traffic management. The model supports indirect regulation of the vehicles by a (centralized or federated) authority while preserving and respecting the autonomy of traffic participants. We illustrated our approach by a simple use case scenario and provided a formalism based on stochastic distributed constraint optimization (SDOP). While this paper has outlined the conceptual and algorithmic cornerstones of our approach, numerous future activities are on our research agenda. The next steps will be to provide a detailed description of corresponding optimization algorithms including their implementation and evaluation both in terms of computational complexity / tractability and with real-world traffic data obtained from the PLANETS research project [1]. Longer term issues relate to the study of more expressive norms semantics (in particular by using temporal logic languages), the consideration of more elaborate methods for norm design, norm emergence, and norm efficiency evaluation.

References

1. Görmer, J., Ehmke, J., Fiosins, M., Schmidt, D., Schumacher, H., Tchouankem, H.: Decision support for dynamic city traffic management using vehicular communication. In: Proc. of 1st Int. Conf. on Simulation and Modeling Methodologies, Technologies and Applications (SIMULTECH), pp. 327–332. SciTePress (2011)
2. Müller, J.P. (ed.): The Design of Intelligent Agents. LNCS (LNAI), vol. 1177. Springer, Heidelberg (1996)
3. Conte, R., Castelfranchi, C., Dignum, F.: Autonomous norm acceptance. In: Papadimitriou, C., Singh, M.P., Müller, J.P. (eds.) ATAL 1998. LNCS (LNAI), vol. 1555, pp. 99–112. Springer, Heidelberg (1999)
4. Dresner, K., Stone, P.: Multiagent traffic management: A reservation-based intersection control mechanism. In: 3rd International Joint Conference on Autonomous Agents and Multiagent Systems, pp. 530–537 (July 2004)

5. Boissier, O., Padget, J., Dignum, V., Lindemann, G., Matson, E., Ossowski, S., Sichman, J.S., Vázquez-Salceda, J. (eds.): ANIREM and OOOP 2005. LNCS (LNAI), vol. 3913. Springer, Heidelberg (2006)
6. Boella, G., Torre, L.V.D.: Introduction to normative multiagent systems. Computational and Mathematical Organization Theory 12, 71–79 (2006)
7. Esteva, M., Rodríguez-Aguilar, J.-A., Sierra, C., Garcia, P., Arcos, J.-L.: On the formal specification of electronic institutions. In: Sierra, C., Dignum, F.P.M. (eds.) Agent Mediated Electronic Commerce. LNCS (LNAI), vol. 1991, pp. 126–147. Springer, Heidelberg (2001)
8. Lacey, N., Hexmoor, H.: A constraint-based approach to multiagent planning. In: Proc. of 13th Midwest AI and Cognitive Science Conference, pp. 1–6 (2002)
9. Yokoo, M.: Distributed Constraint Satisfaction: Foundations of Cooperation in Multi-agent Systems. Springer Series on Agent Technology. Springer (2001)
10. Bowring, E., Tambe, M., Yokoo, M.: Multiply-constrained distributed constraint optimization. In: Proc. of the 5th Int. Joint Conf. on Autonomous Agents and Multiagent Systems (AAMAS 2006), pp. 1413–1420 (2006)
11. Fiosins, M., Fiosina, J., Müller, J.P., Görmer, J.: Reconciling strategic and tactical decision making in agent-oriented simulation of vehicles in urban traffic. In: Proc. of the 4th Int. ICST Conf. Simulation Tools and Techniques, pp. 144–151. ACM Digital Library (2011)
12. Huhn, M., Müller, J.P., Görmer, J., Homoceanu, G., Le, N.T., Märtin, L., Mumme, C., Schulz, C., Pinkwart, N., Müller-Schloer, C.: Autonomous agents in organized localities regulated by institutions. In: Proc. of IEEE DEST 2011, pp. 54–61 (2011)
13. Fiosina, J., Fiosins, M.: Cooperative kernel-based forecasting in decentralized multi-agent systems for urban traffic networks. In: Proc. of Ubiquitous Data Mining (UDM) Workshop at the 20th European Conf. on Artif. Intelligence, pp. 3–7 (2012)
14. Fiosins, M., Fiosina, J., Müller, J.P.: Change point analysis for intelligent agents in city traffic. In: Cao, L., Bazzan, A.L.C., Symeonidis, A.L., Gorodetsky, V.I., Weiss, G., Yu, P.S. (eds.) ADMI 2011. LNCS (LNAI), vol. 7103, pp. 195–210. Springer, Heidelberg (2012)

Reactive Coordination Rules for Traffic Optimization in Road Sharing Problems

Mohamed Tlig[1,2], Olivier Buffet[1,2], and Olivier Simonin[2,1]

[1] INRIA, Nancy, France
[2] Université de Lorraine, Nancy, France
firstname.lastname@loria.fr

Abstract. In the context of transportation of goods, autonomous vehicles are considered today as a solution for large platforms. We are interested in managing unexpected events, like failure of a vehicle or presence of obstacles on the road, as they can generate global phenomena and complex traffic congestions (such as traffic jams). We explore solutions to avoid such undesirable emergent behaviors by studying local rules for coordinating agents (vehicles). We focus on managing space sharing conflicts at the local level, i.e. between the involved vehicles. We consider a generic scenario where two queues of vehicles share a single lane. We propose a model of the network as well as the agents, and simple coordination rules that only involve the two vehicles at the front of each queue. We then conduct experiments that allow the analysis and the comparison of the proposed self-regulation rules. We show that the alternating strategy commonly used by drivers can be easily improved to minimize the delay of the different vehicles.

Keywords: Traffic optimization, Multi-Agent Systems, Reactive Coordination, Space Conflict Resolution, Autonomous Vehicles.

1 Introduction

In the context of transportation of goods, autonomous vehicles are considered today as a solution for seaports or other large platforms[1]. However, in real applications, many unexpected events like failure of a vehicle or presence of obstacles on the road can arise and needs to be managed. Such events can generate local congestions, and then, if they persist, global phenomena and complex traffic congestions (such as traffic jams). We explore solutions to avoid such undesirable emergent behaviors by exploring local rules for coordinating agents (vehicles).

We want to manage conflicts at the local level, when they appear, to allow a quick (real-time) regulation, i.e., without requiring to re-plan the routes of all involved agents. Re-planning [1] is not adapted to large multi-agent systems due to its combinatorial complexity. To avoid such a limitation, we are looking for reactive behaviors allowing to minimize delays and, if possible, to repair the plans.

Our approach relies on cooperative behaviors, based on reactive local coordination in multi-agent systems [2, 3]. Coordination is obtained from simple interactions between

---

[1] http://www.intrade-nwe.eu/

J.M. Corchado et al. (Eds.): PAAMS 2013 Workshops, CCIS 365, pp. 61–72, 2013.

neighboring agents, using perceptions and little or no communication. Such assumptions allow to react to conflicts in real time. As examples of successful uses of local reactive coordination, we can mention [3] for multi-robot/flight avoidance, and [4, 5] for multi-robot navigation conflict solving.

Our work addresses the general problem of space sharing in multi autonomous vehicle/robot systems. In such systems, vehicles receive plans, i.e., routes, to follow. These systems are highly sensitive to local delays/conflicts as these will impact on all the vehicles whose plans go past the local blocking. More precisely, as a case study, a road in which a lane is suddenly blocked, e.g., by a vehicle breakdown, requiring that blocked vehicles use the other lane, initially dedicated to vehicles moving in the opposite direction. This problem specifies the problem of sharing a common space among some agents to two infinite queues of agents.

For this purpose we investigate two approaches relying on simple coordination rules, which require only simple communications between the two vehicles at the front of the queues. We aim at ensuring the simultaneous freeing of both queues, while minimizing the delays of the vehicles.

The paper is organized as follows. Section 2 presents previous work. Section 3 describes a formalization of the problem and the multi-agent model, i.e., the definition of the possible actions and decision rules of the agents. Section 4 proposes two decision rules that produce two different strategies. Then Section 5 details several experiments with deterministic and stochastic scenarios, showing the efficiency and limits of the strategies. Finally, we conclude with a discussion of these results and some promising research directions.

2   Related Work

There are two main approaches for modeling urban traffic:

Macroscopic models consider traffic as a flow through a graph. They use analytical models based for example on fluid dynamics [6, 7]. These macroscopic models offer a high-level model, and thus do not describe individual behaviors.

Microscopic models are individual-based (or entity-oriented) models. They describe the movement of each vehicle, as well as their interactions [8–10]. As these models are very detailed, they process a large quantity of data, which is the main restriction on their use for modeling a real network, e.g., a city. In our case, since we want to propose local individual behaviors to solve problems in a portion of a road, we choose to use a detailed model, i.e., a microscopic model.

We focus on controlling autonomous vehicles which transport goods from a source to a destination. As illustrated in Figure 1, let us assume that we have a two-lane road, the traffic being interrupted by an obstacle at $t = 0$ on one of the lanes (e.g., due to a vehicle breakdown). This results in a space sharing problem between two queues of vehicles, which is equivalent to managing a crossroads intersection, but without traffic lights.

This situation is traditionally studied in operations research and queueing theory. To our knowledge, there is no work proposing vehicle behaviors to deal with such conflicts, but various approaches have been proposed to model and analyze traffic flow

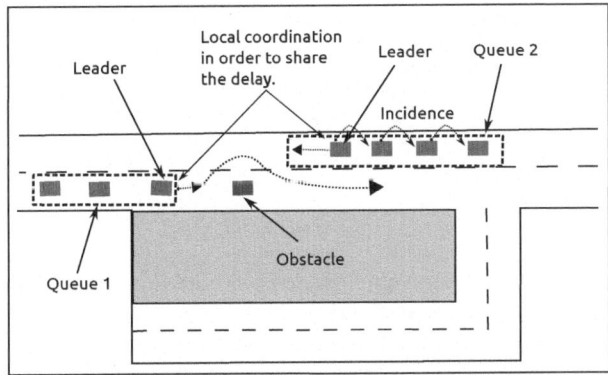

Fig. 1. Two flows of vehicles blocked by an obstacle

interrupted by incidents. In 2002, Hidas proposed a microscopic traffic network simulator with a multi-agent system, and presented lane changing models (unforced, forced, and cooperative) to avoid accidents [11]. His results indicate that only forced and cooperative behaviors reproduce realistic flow-speed relationships in congested situations. Baykal-Gürsoy et al. in 2009 presented a queueing model to describe the traffic flow on a road link that is subject to a roadway incident [12]. For some cases, they present analytical results and compare them to simulation results.

A problem very similar to ours was treated by Tanner [13] in 1953. This is the only paper we know which is interested in the same setting. He defined a mathematical model to estimate delays that occur when two opposing flows (queues) of vehicles try to pass simultaneously through a single lane. All vehicles in this model have the same constant speed and their starting and stopping times are negligible. However, contrary to Tanner, our objective is not to estimate delays that occur in such conflict problems but **to find an efficient approach to reduce delays**.

3   Problem Formalization

In this work, we discretize space and time at an appropriate level to simplify the microscopic model. Behaviors and results remain similar to a continuous model. We use a discrete time step (1 second) and all vehicles have the same constant speed when moving. Space is thus discretized with the unit length l of displacement in $1s$.

3.1   Network Model

The network is modeled here by a set of discrete (directed) arcs of size $n \cdot l$. These arcs are connected together by nodes. Each flow of vehicles in the network follows a particular path, i.e., a sequence of arcs. The traffic is considered as a set of vehicle flows.

Our particular network is modeled by the set of arcs shown on Fig. 2. Here, two flows pass through the network. The first one traverses the arcs A_1, A_2, A_3 and the second one B_1, B_2, B_3. On a particular road –composed by A_2 (for vehicles from source A) and

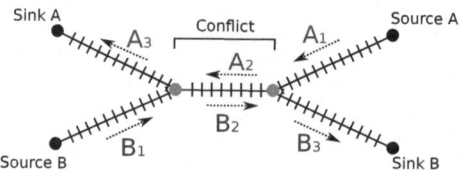

Fig. 2. Representation of the network at hand

B_2 (for vehicles from source B)– vehicles travel in both directions. This is the *conflict* edge, which must be shared by both flows.

Here we consider two flows of vehicles that will fill in the queues of the network in case of obstacle as shown in Fig. 1. The first vehicle in each waiting queue (waiting before the conflict edge) is referred to as its leader. Negotiations about crossing will take place between the two leaders.

3.2   Agent Model

The purpose of this section is to define the agents (the vehicles) and their interactions inside the network.

An agent takes sensory inputs from its environment and performs actions that affect it as outputs. We are interested in autonomous and simple behaviors (i.e, reactive), in order to act locally in real time. Such agents make decisions based only on their local perceptions.

In an agent's model, we distinguish the *action model* and the *decision rules* . The *action model* describes the actions which can be performed by agents. Each action can be executed only under certain preconditions. After executing each action, an effect on the environment is expected. The main problem for an agent is to choose an action in order to best satisfy its objectives. The *decision rules* decide which action to perform. They should, here, allow to (possibly) avoid or solve conflicts by triggering appropriate actions.

Each agent on the network has three internal variables: T_{goal}, the date beyond which the agent is considered to be late; Arc, which indicates in which arc the agent is; and Abs, its position on the current arc in the network, which is incremented as it progresses.

Action Formalism and Model. There is no shared representation formalism in the field of reactive multi-agent systems. In order to describe environment states and transformations, we choose a representation inspired from STRIPS (Stanford Research Institute Problem Solver) as Ferber did in [2]. STRIPS was proposed by Fikes and Nilsson to address planning problems in Artificial Intelligence (AI) [14]. This choice makes a compromise between expressiveness –its ability to describe many problems– and simplicity to ease the development of efficient algorithms.

Each operator is described under the following form (t and $t + 1$ being the current and next time steps):

$\langle name : Action(), \ pre\text{-}condition : A(t), B(t)..., \ post\text{-}condition : C(t + 1), ...\rangle$.

In our case, the action model relies on 3 operators, (which makes use of multi-valued variables): $DoNothing$, $Forward$, and $ChangeArc$.

$DoNothing$ consists in waiting for one time step.

$Forward$ describes the displacement within arcs (not detailed).

$ChangeArc$ describes how an agent moves from one arc to next:

$$\langle name : \quad\quad ChangeArc(),$$
$$pre : \quad\quad Last(Abs, Arc), Free(1, NextArc),$$
$$post : \quad\quad Free_{t+1}(Abs_t, Arc_t), Arc_{t+1} = NextArc_t,$$
$$Abs_{t+1} = 1, \neg Free_{t+1}(1, NextArc_t)\rangle,$$

where $NextArc$ indicates the following arc to the agent. $Free(Abs, Arc)$ is true iff the position Abs of the arc Arc is empty. $Last(Abs, Arc)$ is true iff Abs of the agent is the last position of the arc Arc. Here, if the agent wants to move on an arc, it must verify that it is in the last position of its arc, and that the first position of the next arc is free.

3.3 Optimization Criteria

To estimate a vehicle's delay upon arrival, we must calculate the time remaining for this vehicle to exit the network. Consider a generic scenario where we have two vehicles in the network, $Vehicle$ 1 and $Vehicle$ 2, as shown on Fig. 3. $Vehicle$ 1 wants to enter the conflict edge. However, it must first wait for $Vehicle$ 2 to pass, implying an initial waiting time. When $Vehicle$ 2 leaves the conflict edge, it enters its last arc in the network (B_3), and it is $Vehicle$ 1's turn to pass (on A_2). Finally, to exit the network, $Vehicle$ 1 must go through its last arc (A_3).

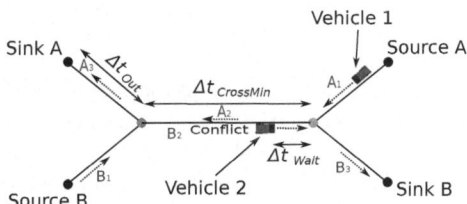

Fig. 3. A particular scenario and the durations that add up to estimate $Vehicle$ 1's traversal time

In this case, the date at which $Vehicle$ 1 reaches its goal is computed as follows:

$$T_{estimated} = T_{real} + \Delta t_{Wait} + \Delta t_{CrossMin} + \Delta t_{Out},$$

where T_{real} is the current date, Δt_{Wait} is the time required to free the conflict edge of vehicles in the other direction, $\Delta t_{CrossMin}$ is the time required to cross the conflict edge, and Δt_{Out} is the time required for the vehicle to cross the last arc in the network.

More generally, we call delay of a vehicle the time lost with respect to the original plan given by the system user.

We define the delay D as $D = \max\left(0, T_{estimated} - T_{goal}\right)$. Now, consider N vehicles $v_1, v_2, v_3, ..., v_N$ in the network and, for each vehicle v_i, its delay D_i. As the arrival of vehicles is stochastic, we have to optimize an expected criterion. We can express our objective to minimize the delay in various ways, in particular with the three following formulas:

$$f_{Sum}(\pi) = \min_{\pi} E\left[\sum_{i=1}^{N}\frac{D_i}{N}\right], \qquad (1)$$

$$f_{Max}(\pi) = \min_{\pi} E\left[\max_{i\in\{1..N\}}(D_i)\right], \qquad (2)$$

$$f_{Sum^2}(\pi) = \min_{\pi} E\left[\sqrt{\sum_{i=1}^{N}\frac{D_i^2}{N}}\right]. \qquad (3)$$

The first formula –a linear criterion– minimizes the average delay over all vehicles, but some vehicles may incur very long delays. The second formula seeks to minimize the worst delay over all vehicles, but may lead to a very bad average delay. That is why we introduce the third formula –a quadratic form–, which is a compromise between equations (1) and (2) using the Root Mean Square of the delay. In all these cases we attempt to have a global behavior that allows sharing delay between agents.

4   Proposed Coordination Behaviors

We propose two strategies relying on coordination rules executed by the vehicles at the front of the waiting queues.

4.1   Alternating

The first behavior is inspired from the civic behavior of drivers when they have to share a one lane road. In case of conflict, vehicles pass alternately, i.e., one at a time, from each side of the *conflict* edge, as in Fig. 4a, with four cars (V_1, V_2, V_3 and V_4) from lane A and two cars (V_5 and V_6) from lane B. The resulting passing order is (from left to right) $V_5\, V_1\, V_6\, V_2\, V_3\, V_4$ or $V_1\, V_5\, V_2\, V_6\, V_3\, V_4$, depending on who goes first between V_1 and V_5.

Alternating is a simple process that does not require high level communications since the order is automatic (regardless of the delays). Only the perception of vehicles on the conflict edge and at its entrance is required. Nevertheless, we must treat the case of the simultaneous arrival on both sides of the conflict edge when it does not contain any vehicle. In this situation, each vehicle transmits a release signal after a (very short) random delay. As soon as a vehicle receives such a signal, and if it does not emit at the same time, it sets out on the road. If both transmit simultaneously, they restart this process.

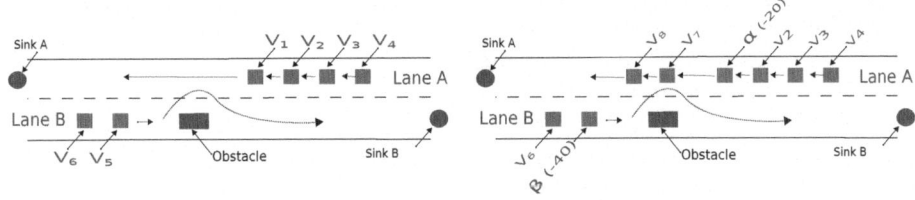

(a) First approach : Alternating vehicles   (b) Second approach : Highest delay first

Fig. 4. Illustration of the two proposed strategies

4.2   Local Greedy Optimization (LGO)

The second behavior tries to optimize the transition by promoting vehicles that are more delayed than others. Delay comparisons are done using the communication between the two agents which want to cross the conflict edge simultaneously. Let us denote α and β the leading vehicles of the queues A and B respectively (assumed nonempty). For decisions to be local, as in the alternating approach, only the two leaders of the waiting queues can communicate together.

For example, consider Fig. 4b, where we noted in parentheses the delay of the two leaders assuming each of them goes first (e.g., vehicle α has 20 seconds of delay). Intuitively, they will go in this order: β then α. But if, as in Fig. 4b, there are vehicles on the conflict edge like V_7 and V_8 (crossing together toward $sink\ A$), choosing the order of passage is not trivial. If α passes first, β will wait an extra time $\epsilon_1 = 40s + \alpha\ crossing\ time$. Else if β passes first, α will wait an extra time $\epsilon_2 = 20s + V_7\ crossing\ time + \beta\ crossing\ time$.

To make this decision, we use the optimization criteria presented in Sec. 3.3. Having chosen to consider only these two vehicles, we restrict the evaluation of the selected criterion to them, and only have to compare two orderings: (1) α before β ($\alpha \rightarrow \beta$), and (2) β before α ($\beta \rightarrow \alpha$).

1. Each vehicle first calculates its two possible delays: $D^v_{\alpha\rightarrow\beta}$ and $D^v_{\beta\rightarrow\alpha}$, where v is α or β, then transmits them to the other vehicle.
2. Each agent compares, based on its own estimates and those received, the two possible passing orders using the optimization criterion at hand. For example, if the criterion used is Formula 2, the passing order will be $\alpha \rightarrow \beta$ if $f^{\alpha\rightarrow\beta}_{Max} = max(D^{\beta}_{\alpha\rightarrow\beta}, D^{\alpha}_{\alpha\rightarrow\beta})$ is less than $f^{\beta\rightarrow\alpha}_{Max} = max(D^{\beta}_{\beta\rightarrow\alpha}, D^{\alpha}_{\beta\rightarrow\alpha})$, else $\beta \rightarrow \alpha$ in the opposite case.

Algorithm 1 gives the decision rule of a leader vehicle (here, β) where $f^{\beta\rightarrow\alpha}_{*}$ (respectively $f^{\alpha\rightarrow\beta}_{*}$) is the value of one of the 3 criteria if β passes before α (resp. if α passes before β).

Algorithm 1. Passage rules for LGO of the vehicle β

---

1 **if** *(agent waiting on the other side)* **then**
2 $\quad$ *Send/receive delays;*
3 $\quad$ **if** $(f_*^{\beta \to \alpha} > f_*^{\alpha \to \beta})$ **then**
4 $\quad\quad$ **if** *(agent on the conflict edge in opposite direction)* **then**
5 $\quad\quad\quad \lfloor$ *wait for release of conflict edge;*
6 $\quad\quad \lfloor$ *ChangeArc();*
7 $\quad \lfloor$ **else** *DoNothing();*
8 **else**
9 $\quad$ **if** *(agent on the conflict edge in opposite direction)* **then**
10 $\quad\quad \lfloor$ *DoNothing();*
11 $\quad \lfloor$ **else** *ChangeArc();*

---

5 Experimental Results

5.1 Simulation

We developed a prototype simulator on the JADE[2] platform (Java Agent Development Framework), which offers a Java middleware to develop agent-based applications.

We reproduce the network as shown in Figures 2 and 3:

- the speed of each vehicle is 10 meters per second (36km/h), thus $l = 10$;
- the length of each arc is 300 meters $(30 \cdot l)$;
- at each entrance of the network, we have installed a source that generates vehicles.

Each source injects vehicles following a Bernoulli process with a parameter $\lambda = \frac{1}{T}$, where T is the average time, in seconds, between two consecutive vehicles.

In all our simulations, we verified that we do not meet the pathological case where a single queue passes, at the expense of the other queue (which is blocked). In the remainder of this paper, we will call Alt the Alternating strategy, and Sum, Max and Sum^2 the three variants of the LGO strategy corresponding to the criteria presented in Formulae 1, 2, and 3.

5.2 Release of the Two Lanes

The particularity of the first presented scenario is that it starts with the Alternating strategy, then, after 50 vehicles have been injected in the network, either we continue with the same strategy $(Alt - Alt)$ or we choose the second strategy (LGO) with one of the 3 criteria $((Alt - *)$. After the injection of 100 vehicles, we stop injections and wait for the network to empty. We used high injection frequencies—thus, dense traffic—with parameter $T = 10$s for the Bernoulli process of each queue.

Fig. 5a shows the simulation results of the Alternating strategy and the 3 variants of the LGO strategy. The curves plotted in Fig. 5a are averages over 100 simulations.

---

[2] http://JADE.tilab.com

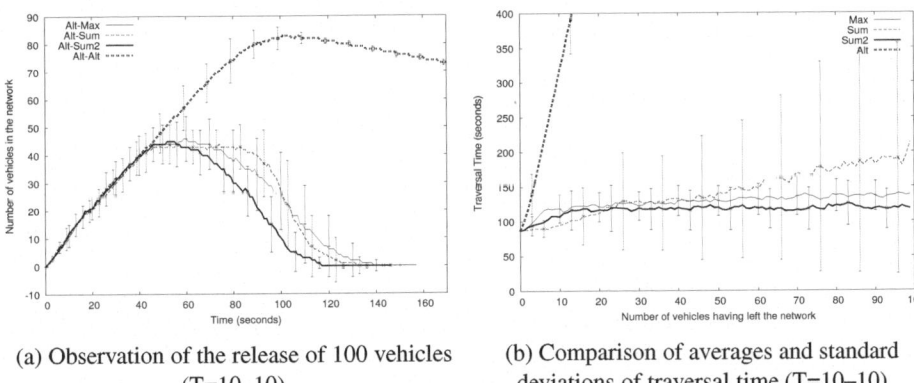

(a) Observation of the release of 100 vehicles (T=10–10)

(b) Comparison of averages and standard deviations of traversal time (T=10–10)

Fig. 5. Observations

The X axis represents the time in seconds, and the Y axis represents the number of vehicles in the network at time t.

The $Alt - Alt$ strategy is not good and takes a lot of time –on average, 600 seconds (not represented)– before releasing the network. Also, when switching to any version of the LGO strategy, the number of vehicles for strategies $Alt - Sum^2$, $Alt - Max$, and $Alt - Sum$ progressively decreases until both paths are finally empty. The fastest evacuation is given by the curve $Alt - Sum^2$. We observe the existence of two stages for the $Alt - Sum$ criterion. Upon the strategy runs, the curve makes a plateau, followed by a steeper slope than on any other curve. This is due to the Sum criterion avoiding to switch queues (as we will see in the next subsection). When there are injections, while one of the queues is running, the other saturates (generations are then forbidden, and therefore the Bernoulli process is not respected). This saturation is a way to limit the increase of the number of vehicles (hence the plateau), and further delays the moment when the total of 100 injected vehicles is reached. Once the injections have stopped, $Alt - Sum$ releases its queues faster by avoiding the wasted time associated to switching queues. We see that $Alt - Max$ and $Alt - Sum^2$ have a slightly higher maximum number of vehicles than $Alt - Sum$, but no such plateau.

5.3   Regulation of a Continuous Traffic

In the second scenario, we do not stop the injections of vehicles as in the previous simulations, but record the traversal time of the first 100 vehicles leaving the network.

Fig. 5b gives the average traversal time of each strategy for injections with $T = 10s$. The X axis gives the number of vehicles having left the network, and the Y axis gives the traversal time in seconds. The plotted curves are averages over 100 simulations.

The Alt strategy is the worst one, again (see Table 1). The Sum criterion is significantly worse than Sum^2 and Max. It does not favor any lane switches (as we will see below) and accumulates vehicles on one of the sides. We observe that the best criteria are Sum^2 and Max with the lowest averages, noting that the minimum traversal time is 87 seconds. Max, besides caring about the worst delay, reduces the standard

Table 1. Summary of Averages and Standard Deviations of traversal time

$Average$	Alt	Sum	Max	Sum^2
$10-10$	1260± 86	142±94	127±22	115±28
$30-30$	782±173	104±28	105±19	102±19

deviation, while Sum^2 works more on reducing the average of the traversal time between vehicles.

Table 1 gives a summary of the measured traversal times with standard deviations
for each strategy and for injections of vehicle flow $T = 10$s and $T = 30$s. With less
frequent injections we find that Sum^2 is the best criterion and that the 3 variants of the
LGO strategy have close averages and standard deviations.

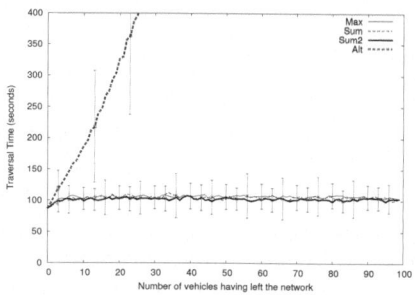

Fig. 6. Comparison of averages and standard deviations of traversal time (T=30–30)

Fig. 6 presents the results of simulations of the control strategies when we increase
the period T to 30s. We can notice that the performance of the strategies Max, Sum
and Sum^2 are almost the same in this fluid traffic condition. However, the Alt strategy
gives the worst results as usual.

To better understand the LGO strategy, Fig. 7 presents the result of a simulation
chosen randomly for each criterion with injections on average every $T = 10$s. Each
curve represents the sequence of 100 vehicles in their output order, with the date of
injections on the X axis, and the traversal time on the Y axis.

The first thing that questions us is that the Sum criterion takes a lot of time before switching queues, unlike Max that switches very often. According to the figures,
the Sum^2 criterion appears as a compromise between the two others. Switching queue
often wastes a lot of time, but not switching queues leads to accumulating delays of
waiting vehicles. Overall, all the measurements show that an approach focused on local coordination rules proves to be efficient to regulate traffic. We demonstrate that an
agent approach, based on the exchange of information between the top vehicles from
each queue, allows to implement an efficient regulation resulting from global delay
optimization criteria.

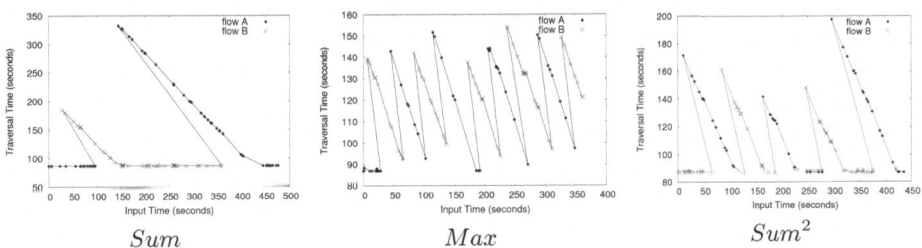

$$Sum \qquad\qquad Max \qquad\qquad Sum^2$$

Fig. 7. Observation of one simulation of each criterion, Input time (x) and Traversal time (y) of vehicles (T=10–10)

6 Discussion

The problem addressed in this paper is to solve space sharing conflicts in a multi-agent system. Only the two vehicles at the front of each waiting queue communicate together in order to know which one goes first. The advantage of our approach is the complete decentralization of the model. Especially, there is no centralized mechanism that manages the intersection (e.g., to receive the delays, to organize an auction...) which is different from the multi-agent approaches to control intersections [15]. Actually, if we consider an exhaustive approach (centralized), and if n and m are the number of vehicles in each queue, the number of vehicle orderings to consider –and thus the algorithm complexity– is the number of ways to interleave the vehicles from both queues (without changing the order within each queue)

$$\binom{n+m}{n} = \frac{(n+m)!}{n!\,m!},$$

which have to be considered at each time step t in order to know the best crossing order. The worst case for a fixed number of vehicles is when $m = n$, whose asymptotic behavior can be derived from Stirling's approximation as:

$$\binom{2n}{n} \sim \frac{4^n}{\sqrt{\pi n}} \text{ as } n \to \infty.$$

The complexity of our approach is significantly lower. It consists in the number of messages sent, i.e., at most two messages in each negotiation.

7 Conclusion

In this article we addressed the resolution of space sharing conflicts between queues of vehicles, or more generally between mobile agents (e.g., robots). For this, we explored agent behaviors based on reactive coordination. We first proposed an approach using only local perceptions (alternating), and then one integrating simple communications between vehicles at the top of the queues. The experimental study has shown the ability to regulate conflicts (congestions) of these behaviors, generated in different traffic scenarios. Congestion phenomena, which are undesirable emergent phenomena, are treated here locally, thus independently of any external planning system, and in real time. The introduction of simple communications of delays significantly improves on the Alternating strategy commonly used by drivers.

We plan to continue this study by generalizing the approaches to any number of queues, but also by proposing to take into account delays of more vehicles present in the queues to further improve traffic management (searching how many vehicles to consider so as to best trade off between complexity and quality). Another perspective is to evaluate the robustness of our strategies, for example in case of communications failures.

Acknowledgement. This work was partially supported by the InTraDE European project (http://www.intrade-nwe.eu).

References

1. Nebel, B., Koehler, J.: Plan reuse versus plan generation: A theoretical and empirical analysis. Artificial Intelligence 76 (1995)
2. Ferber, J.: Multi-Agent Systems. An introduction to Distributed Artificial Intelligence (1999)
3. Zeghal, K.: A comparison of different approaches based on force fields for coordination among multiple mobiles. In: Proc. of IROS (1998)
4. Simonin, O., Ferber, J.: Modeling self satisfaction and altruism to handle action selection and reactive cooperation. In: 6th Int. Conf. on the Simulation of Adaptive Behavior (From Animals to Animats 6), SAB 2000 (2000)
5. Lucidarme, P., Simonin, O., Liegeois, A.: Implementation and evaluation of a satisfaction/altruism based architecture for multi-robot systems. In: Proc. of ICRA (2002)
6. Lighthill, M.J., Whitham, G.B.: On kinematic waves. 2. A theory of traffic flow on long crowded roads. Proc. of the Royal Society of London. Series A, Mathematical and Physical Sciences 229(1178) (1955)
7. Greenshields, B.: A study of traffic capacity. In: Proc. of the Highway Research Board (1935)
8. Simon, P., Nagel, K.: Simplified cellular automaton model for city traffic. Phys. Rev. E 58(2), 1286–1295 (1998)
9. Kosonen, I., Pursula, M.: A simulation tool for traffic signal control planning. In: 3rd Int. Conf. on Road Traffic Control (1990)
10. Meignan, D., Simonin, O., Koukam, A.: Simulation and evaluation of urban bus-networks using a multiagent approach. Simulation Modelling Practice and Theory 15(6), 659–671 (2007)
11. Hidas, P.: Modelling lane changing and merging in microscopic traffic simulation. Transportation Research Part C: Emerging Technologies 10(5-6), 351–371 (2002)
12. Baykal-Gürsoy, M., Xiao, W., Ozbay, K.: Modeling traffic flow interrupted by incidents. European Journal of Operational Research 195(1), 127–138 (2009)
13. Tanner, J.C.: A problem of interference between two queues. Biometrika 40(1/2) (1953)
14. Fikes, R.E., Nilsson, N.J.: STRIPS: A new approach to the application of theorem proving to problem solving. Artificial Intelligence 2(3-4), 189–208 (1971)
15. Dresner, K., Stone, P.: Multiagent traffic management: An improved intersection control mechanism. In: Proc. of AAMAS (2005)

Multimodal Processes Cyclic Steady States Scheduling

G. Bocewicz[1], P. Nielsen[2], Z. Banaszak[3], and Q.V. Dang[2]

[1] Department of Electronics and Computer Science, Koszalin University of Technology,
Koszalin, Poland
`bocewicz@ie.tu.koszalin.pl`
[2] Department of Mechanical and Manufacturing Engineering, Aalborg University,
Aalborg Denmark
`{peter,vinhise}@m-tech.aau.dk`
[3] Department of Business Informatics, Warsaw University of Technology, Warsaw, Poland
`Z.Banaszak@wz.pw.edu.pl`

Abstract. This paper describes a multimodal transportation network (MTN) in which several unimodal networks (AGVs, hoists, lifts, suspended monorail systems, etc.) interact each other via common shared workstations as to provide a variety of demand-responsive workpiece transportation/handling services. The set of transport modes provides connection support for production flows treated as agents trying to realize their origin-destination routes in the MTN. The aim is to provide a declarative model enabling to state a constraint satisfaction problem aimed at multimodal transportation processes (MTP) scheduling, while servicing production flows. In other words, assuming a given topology of MTN, the main objective is to provide the declarative modeling framework enabling to refine conditions guaranteeing the MTP cyclic steady states reachability.

Keywords: multimodal cyclic processes, declarative modeling, constraints programming, cyclic scheduling.

1 Introduction

Multimodal processes scheduling arise in different application domains (such as manufacturing, intercity fright transportation supply chains, multimodal passenger transport network combining several unimodal networks (bus, tram, metro, train, etc.) as well as service domains (including passenger/cargo transportation systems, e.g. ferry, ship, airline, train networks, as well as data and supply media flows, e.g., the cloud computing, the oil pipeline and overhead power line networks) [1], [2], [4], [3], [8]. Multimodal processes executed in multimodal transportation network (MTN), i.e. a set of transport modes which provide connection from origin to destination, can be seen as passengers and/or goods flows transferred between different modes to reach their destination. In that context the MTN can be seen as an environment for multi-agents treated as multimodal process interacting each other via common shared local processes [5].

The throughput of passengers and/or freight (agents) depends on geometrical and operational characteristics of MTN. The problems arising concern of multimodal

J.M. Corchado et al. (Eds.): PAAMS 2013 Workshops, CCIS 365, pp. 73–85, 2013.
© Springer-Verlag Berlin Heidelberg 2013

routing of freight flows and supporting them multimodal transportation processes (MTP) scheduling, and belonging to NP-hard ones. Since the transportation processes executed along unimodal networks are usually cyclic ones, hence the multimodal processes supported by them have also periodic character. That means, the periodicity of MTP depends on periodicity of unimodal (local) processes executed in MTN. Of course, the MTP throughput is maximized by minimization of its cycle time.

It seems to be obvious, that not all the behaviors (including cyclic ones) are reachable under constraints imposed by system's structure. The similar observation concerns the system's behavior that can be achieved in systems possessing specific structural constraints. That means, since system constraints determine its behavior, hence both system structure configuration and desired cyclic schedule have to be considered simultaneously. So, the problem solution requires that the system structure configuration must be determined for the purpose of processes scheduling, yet scheduling must be done to devise the system configuration. In that context, our contribution provides discussion of some solubility issues concerning cyclic processes dispatching problems, especially the conditions guaranteeing solvability of the cyclic processes scheduling. Their examination may replace exhaustive searching for solution satisfying required system functioning.

Many models and methods have been considered so far [7]. Among them, the mathematical programming approach [12], max-plus algebra [9], constraint logic programming [3], [4], [5] Petri nets [10] and multi-agent systems [2] frameworks belong to the more frequently used. Most of them are oriented at finding of a minimal cycle or maximal throughput while assuming deadlock-free processes flow. Note, that processes' operations are blocking if they must stay on a resource (e.g., the station, the machine) after finishing when the next resource is occupied by a job from another process. During this stay the resource is blocked for other processes. The approaches trying to estimate the cycle time from cyclic processes structure and the synchronization mechanism employed (i.e. mutual exclusion instances) while taking into account deadlock phenomena are quite unique.

In that context our main contribution is to propose a new modeling framework enabling to evaluate the cyclic steady state of a given system of concurrent cyclic processes (SCCP) [3] encompassing the behavior typical for material handling and transportation services (see Fig. 1a)) in the flexible manufacturing systems (FMS) [7], [11]. The following questions are of main interest [4]: Does the assumed material handling system, e.g. AGVs, behavior can meet load/unload deadlines imposed by flow of scheduled workpieces processing? Does there exist AGVS enabling to schedule AGVs fleet as to follow lag-free service of scheduled workpieces processing? So, the main question is: Does the MTP treated as multi-agent system [5] can reach their goals subject to constraints assumed on SCCP? In other words, the paper's objective concerns of MTN infrastructure assessment from the perspective of possible FMS oriented requirements imposed on MTP scheduling.

The rest of the paper is organized as follows: Section 2 introduces to the systems of concurrently flowing cyclic processes and a problem formulation. Section 3 provides declarative modeling framework enabling to state and resolve multimodal processes scheduling problems. The cases of multimodal processes cyclic steady states reachability and scheduling are discussed in Section 4. Conclusions are presented in Section 5.

2 Systems of Concurrent Cyclic Processes

Consider the digraph shown in Fig. 1b) representing MTN from Fig. 1a) where three **cyclic local processes** P_1, P_2 and P_3 encompassing hoist operations are distinguished. Processes passing transportation sectors (resources) interact each other via common shared resources. Their routes are specified as follows:

$$p_1 = (R_4, R_3, R_5), p_2 = (R_3, R_1, R_2), \ p_3 = (R_6, R_5, R_1),$$

where: R_1, R_3, R_5 - are shared resources, since each one is used by at least two processes, R_2, R_4, R_6 - are non-shared because each one is used by only one process.

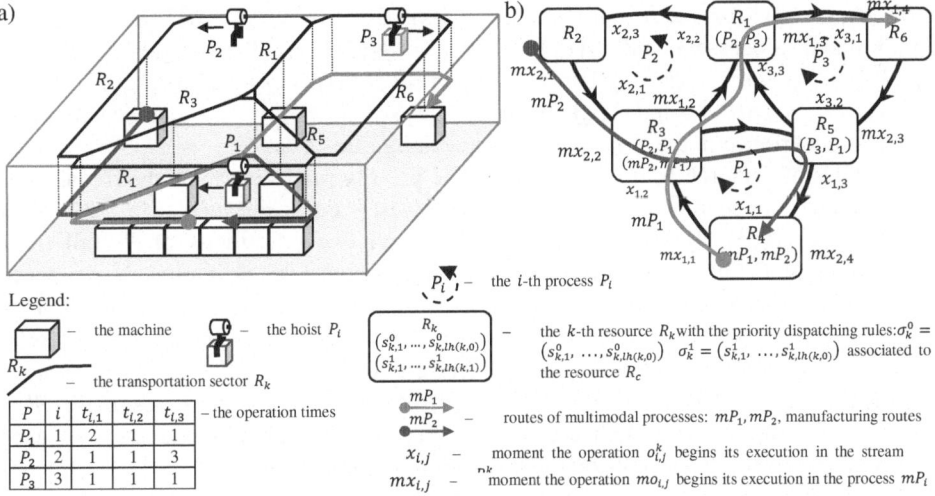

Legend:

P	i	$t_{i,1}$	$t_{i,2}$	$t_{i,3}$
P_1	1	2	1	1
P_2	2	1	1	3
P_3	3	1	1	1

Fig. 1. The example of hoist transportations system a), and its SCCP model representation b)

Apart from local processes, we consider two agents specified by concurrently acting **multimodal processes** (i.e. processes executed along the routes consisting of segments of local processes routes – representing manufacturing routes): mP_1, mP_2. The routes of considered multimodal processes are distinguished by blue mP_1, and red, mP_2 color lines, see Fig 1. The multimodal process route specifying how a multimodal process is executed, can be seen as composed of local cyclic processes route parts. So, the routes mP_1, mP_2 are:

$$mp_1 = (R_2, R_3, R_5, R_4), \ mp_2 = (R_4, R_3, R_1, R_6).$$

where: mp_1, mp_2 - simplified representations of multimodal processes routes:

$$mp_1 = \big((R_2, R_3), (R_3, R_5, R_4)\big), \ mp_2 = \big((R_4, R_3), (R_3, R_1), (R_1, R_6)\big),$$

where: $(R_2, R_3), (R_3, R_5, R_4)$ – parts (subsequences) of routes p_2, p_1, included in mp_1

$(R_4, R_3), (R_3, R_1), (R_1, R_6)$ – parts (subsequences) of routes p_1, p_2, and p_3 included in mp_2.

Both, local and multimodal processes interact each other on the base of mutual exclusion protocol while sharing common resource (transportation sector). The possible resource conflicts are resolved with help of assumed priority dispatching rules determining the order in which processes make their access to common shared resources. For instance, in case of the resource R_3, the priority dispatching rules: $\sigma_3^0 = (P_2, P_1)$, $\sigma_3^1 = (mP_2, mP_1)$ (see Fig. 1b)) determine the orders in which local and multimodal processes (respectively) can access to the shared resource R_3. A sequence σ_1^0 means that the first access is for process P_2, and next to P_1 and once again to P_2, and so on. Similarly, a sequence σ_3^1 means that the process mP_2 can access to R_3 firstly while mP_1 secondly. The process P_i occurs the same number of times in each dispatching rule associated to resources appearing in its route. So, the SCCP shown in Fig. 1b) is specified by the following pair of dispatching rules: $\Theta = (\Theta^0, \Theta^1)$, $\Theta^0 = \{\sigma_1^0, \sigma_2^0, ..., \sigma_6^0\}$ (rules aimed at local processes), $\Theta^1 = \{\sigma_1^1, \sigma_2^1, ..., \sigma_6^1\}$ (rules aimed at multimodal processes) and $f_4(P_1) = f_3(P_1) = f_5(P_1)$; $f_1(P_2) = f_2(P_2) = f_3(P_2)$, $f_6(P_3) = f_5(P_3) = f_1(P_3)$; $f_2(mP_1) = f_3(mP_1) = f_5(mP_1) = f_4(mP_1)$; $f_4(mP_2) = f_3(mP_2) = f_1(mP_2) = f_6(mP_2)$, where: $f_c(P_i)$ / $f_c(mP_i)$ – a number the i-th process occurrence in the c-th priority dispatching rule σ_c^0/σ_c^1.

Besides of resource conflicts resolution the priority rules determine the frequencies of mutual appearance of local processes. For instance, in case of $\sigma_1^1 = (P_1, P_3, P_2, P_1, P_2, P_1)$ it means that for each two executions of P_2 fall three executions of P_1. In general case, the set of dispatching rules Θ implies the sequence of relative frequencies of local processes mutual executions denoted by $\Psi = (\Psi^0, \Psi^1)$, $\Psi^l = (\psi_1^l, \psi_2^l, ..., \psi_n^l)$, where: $\psi_i^l \in \mathbb{N}$ - determines the number of relative, i.e. in relation to other processes, P_i (for $l = 0$) / mP_i (for $l = 1$) occurrence.

In case of SCCP from Fig. 1b) the following sequence is assumed: $\Psi = (\Psi^0, \Psi^1)$ where: $\Psi^0 = (1,1,1)$ and $\Psi^1 = (1,1)$. That means one execution of each local/multimodal process falls on one execution of another one.

In general case, local $P_i \in P = \{P_1, P_2, ..., P_i, ..., P_n \}$, where: n - a number of local processes, and multimodal $mP_i \in mP = \{mP_1, mP_2, ..., mP_i, ..., mP_w \}$,where: w - a number of multimodal processes, processes execute periodically while following the route $p_i = (p_{i,1}, p_{i,2}, ..., p_{i,lr(i)})$ / $mp_i = (mp_{i,1}, mp_{i,2}, ..., mp_{i,lm(i)})$ (where: $lr(i)$ / $lm(i)$ - a length of cyclic process route, $p_{i,j}, mp_{i,j} \in R$, $R = \{R_1, R_2, ..., R_m\}$, m - a number of resources).

Let us assume that: $o_{i,j}$ / $mo_{i,j}$ - denotes the j-th operation executed by the process P_i/mP_i along the route p_i / mp_i, and $t_{i,j}$ / $mt_{i,j}$ $(t_{i,j}, mt_{i,j} \in \mathbb{N})$, denotes the time of the operation $o_{i,j}$ / $mo_{i,j}$ execution. In considered case the operation times of local processes are shown in Fig. 1, and times of all multimodal operations are same. Therefore, the sequence $T_i = (t_{i,1}, t_{i,2}, ..., t_{i,lr(i)})$ / $mT_i = (mt_{i,1}, mt_{i,2}, ..., mt_{i,lm(i)})$ describes the operation times required by P_i / mP_i.

Let us assume, to each shared resource $R_c \in R$ the priority dispatching rules $\sigma_c^0 = (P_{i_1}, P_{i_2}, ..., P_{i_{lp(c)}})$ and $\sigma_c^1 = (mP_{j_1}, mP_{j_2}, ..., mP_{j_{lpm(c)}})$ are associated (where: $i_k \in \{1,2, ..., n\}$, $j_k \in \{1,2, ..., w\}$, $lp(c)$ / $lpm(c)$ - a number of local/multimodal processes dispatched by σ_c^0, P_{i_k} / mP_{j_k} – j_k-th local / multimodal process executed on the resource R_c) determine the local / multimodal processes execution.

Using the above notation, an SCCP can be defined as a tuple [3]:

$$SC = ((R, SL), SM), \quad (1)$$

where: $R = \{R_1, R_2, \ldots, R_c, \ldots, R_m\}$ – the set of resources, $m = |R|$,
$SL = (ST_l, BE_l, SE_l)$ – the structure of local processes, i.e.

> $ST_L = (U, T)$ – the variables describing the layout of local processes,
>> $U = \{p_1, p_2 \ldots, p_n\}$ – the set of routes of local process, n – the number of local processes,
>> $T = \{T_1, T_2, \ldots, T_n,\}$ – the set of sequences of operation times,
> $BE_L = (\Theta^0, \Psi^0)$ – the variables describing the behavior of local processes,
>> $\Theta^0 = \{\sigma_1^0, \sigma_2^0, \ldots, \sigma_c^0, \ldots, \sigma_m^0\}$ – the set of priority dispatching rules,
>> $\Psi^0 = (\psi_1^0, \psi_2^0, \ldots, \psi_n^0)$ – the sequence of relative frequencies of mutual executions of local processes,
> $SE_L = \{eq_{i,j}(ST_L, BE_L)|\ i = 1, \ldots, n;\ j = 1, \ldots, lr(i)\}$ – the set of constraints (equations) linking ST_L and BE_L. $eq_{i,j}(ST_L, BE_L)$ - the time relation between the moments $x_{i,j}$ of operations $o_{i,j}$ beginning for the l-th execution.

$SM = (ST_M, BE_M, SE_M)$ – the structure of multimodal processes, i.e.

> $ST_M = (M, mT)$ – the variables describing the layout of the level of a multimodal process, $M = \{mp_1, \ldots, mp_i, \ldots, mp_w\}$ – the set of routes of a multimodal process, w – the number of multimodal processes mP_i,
> $mT = \{mT_1, mT_2, \ldots, mT_w\}$ – the set of sequences of operation times in multimodal processes,
> $BE_M = (\Theta^1, \Psi^1)$ – the variables describing the behavior of multimodal processes, $\Theta^1 = \{\sigma_1^1, \sigma_2^1, \ldots, \sigma_c^1, \ldots, \sigma_m^1\}$ – the set of priority dispatching rules for multimodal processes,
> $\Psi^1 = (\psi_1^1, \psi_2^1, \ldots, \psi_w^1)$ – the sequence of relative frequencies of mutual executions of multimodal processes,
> $SE_M = \{eq_{i,j}(ST_M, BE_M)|\ i = 1, \ldots, w;\ j = 1, \ldots, lm(i)\}$ – the set of constraints (equations) linking ST_M and BE_M. $eq_{i,j}(ST_M, BE_M)$ - the time relation between the moments $x_{i,j}$ of operations $mo_{i,j}$ beginning.

The constraints $eq_{i,j}(ST_L, BE_L)$ defined for local processes, specify the relation linking the set X and the periodicity α while encompass SCCP cyclic behavior. The set $X = \{X_1, X_2, \ldots, X_i, \ldots, X_n\}$, contains the sequences $X_i = (x_{i,1}, \ldots, x_{i,\psi_i^0 \cdot lr(i)})$ which elements $x_{i,j}$ determine the moments of operation $o_{i,j}$ beginning in the l-th cycle: $x_{i,j}(l) = x_{i,j} + l \cdot \alpha,\ l \in \mathbb{Z},\ (x_{i,j}(l) \in \mathbb{Z}$ – the moment when the operation $o_{i,j}$ starts its execution in the l-th cycle, α – denotes the periodicity of local processes: $\alpha = x_{i,j}(l + 1) - x_{i,j}(l))$. In other words X_i specifies the moments $x_{i,j}$ of operation beginnings in the first cycle ($l = 0$) of the process P_i.

Similarly, the constraints $eq_{i,j}(ST_M, BE_M)$ determine the relation among variables specifying multimodal processes execution (behavior). In case of multimodal processes the moments $mx_{i,j}(l)$ of operations beginning $mo_{i,j}$ are determined by the set of sequence $mX = \{mX_1, \ldots, mX_i, \ldots, mX_w\}$, where: $mX_i = (mx_{i,1},$

$\dots, mx_{i,\psi_i^1 \cdot lm(i)})$, $mx_{i,j}$ – variable specifying the value $mx_{i,j}(l)$: $mx_{i,j}(l) =$ $mx_{i,j} + l \cdot m\alpha$, $l \in \mathbb{Z}$, $m\alpha$ – denotes the periodicity of multimodal processes: $m\alpha = mx_{i,j}(l+1) - mx_{i,j}(l)$. Sequence mX_i specifies the moments $mx_{i,j}$ of operation beginnings in the first cycle ($l = 0$) of multimodal process mP_i.

The constrains SE_L, SE_M determining the behavior of the system specified by (ST_L, BE_L), (ST_M, BE_M) play a key role in course of SCCP performance evaluation. The constraints can be defined in many ways [3], [4], [5] in this paper, however we will define them in terms of the operations precedence digraph concept.

The Constraints SE_L

In order to illustrate an idea standing behind $eq_{i,j}(ST_L, BE_L)$ designing let us consider the following example (see Fig. 2). The operation $o_{1,3}$ (executed by P_1 on the resource R_1) can be started only if the preceding operation $o_{1,2}$ (executed by P_1 on R_6) has been completed $(x_{1,2}(l) + t_{1,2})$ and the resource R_1 has been released, i.e. if the process P_2 (preceding the process P_1 in the rule σ_1^0) occupying the resource R_1 starts its subsequent operation at $x_{2,6}(l) + 1$. So, the relation considered $eq_{1,3}(ST_L, BE_L)$ can be specified by the following formulae:

$$x_{1,3}(l) = max\{(x_{2,6}(l-1) + 1); (x_{1,2}(l) + t_{1,2})\} \tag{2}$$

where: $x_{i,j}(l)$ – the moment of the operation $o_{i,j}$ beginning in l-th cycle

Taking into account $x_{i,j}(l) = x_{i,j} + l \cdot \alpha$ the formulae (2) can be stated as follows:

$$x_{1,3} = max\{(x_{2,6} - \alpha + 1); (x_{1,2} + t_{1,2})\} \tag{3}$$

where: $x_{i,j}$ – the moment of the operation $o_{i,j}$ beginning in first cycle ($l = 0$)

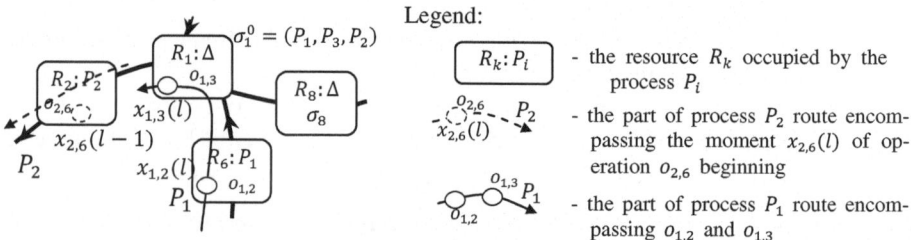

Fig. 2. Illustration of the $x_{1,3}(l) = max\{(x_{2,6}(l-1) + 1); (x_{1,2}(l) + t_{1,2})\}$ calculation

Similarly to the case (3) we can build the constraints SE_L describing the SCCP from Fig. 1b) (see Tab. 1). For all constraints the following principle holds: the moment of the operation $o_{i,j}$ beginning states for a maximum of the completion time of operation $o_{i,j-1}$ preceding $o_{i,j}$ and the release time of the resource $p_{i,j}$ awaiting for $o_{i,j}$:

$eqi,j(STL,BEL)$: *moment of operation* $o_{i,j}$ *begining* =

$$max\{moment\ of\ p_{i,j}\ release, moment\ of\ operation\ o_{i,j-1} completion\},$$
$$i = 1, .., n; \quad j = 1, \dots, \psi_i^0 \cdot lr(i) \tag{4}$$

The considered constraints (4) take into account multiple process executions ψ_i^0 occurring in one cycle.

Table 1. Constraints SE_L describing the SCCP from Fig. 1b)

No	Constraints SE_L	No	Constraints SE_L
1	$x_{1,1} = \max\{x_{1,3} + 1 - \alpha; x_{1,3} + 1 - \alpha\}$	6	$x_{2,3} = \max\{x_{2,2} + 1; x_{2,2} + 1\}$
2	$x_{1,2} = \max\{x_{1,1} + 1; x_{2,2} + 1\}$	7	$x_{3,1} = \max\{x_{3,3} + 1 - \alpha; x_{3,2} + 1 - \alpha\}$
3	$x_{1,3} = \max\{x_{1,2} + 1; x_{3,3} + 1\}$	8	$x_{3,2} = \max\{x_{3,1} + 1; x_{1,1} + 1\}$
4	$x_{2,1} = \max\{x_{2,3} + 1 - \alpha; x_{1,3} + 1 - \alpha\}$	9	$x_{3,3} = \max\{x_{3,2} + 1; x_{2,3} + 1 - \alpha\}$
5	$x_{2,2} = \max\{x_{2,1} + 1; x_{3,1} + 1\}$		

The Constraints SE_M

In a similar way the multimodal processes constraint can be designed, too. It should be noted, however that in case of multimodal processes the operation $mo_{i,j}$ can executes only when the relevant local processes activities occur. So, the moment $mx_{i,j}(l)$ follow $x_{i,j}(l)$. In other words, the parameters mX and $m\alpha$ specifying the behavior of multimodal processes are determined by parameters describing local processes behavior, i.e. moments of operations beginning X and the periodicity α.

For instance, in case the process P_2 executes the operation $o_{2,1}$ at the moment $x_{2,1}(l) = 0 + 5 \cdot l$, $(x_{2,1} = 0, \alpha = 5)$ the operation $mo_{2,2}$ from process mP_2 can be started only at one of the following moments: $0, 5, 10, 15, ...$ (determined by $x_{2,1}(l)$). Values $mx_{2,2}(l)$ are specified by moments of operation $o_{2,1}$ beginning, i.e. the operation executed in the process P_2, and being necessary for execution of $mo_{2,2}$ from the mP_2 (see Fig. 1b).

In that context, the constraints $eq_{i,j}(ST_M, BE_M)$ can be seen as extended version of the principle (4) (taking into account relation between local and multimodal operations):

$$eq_{i,j}(ST_M, BE_M): moment\ of\ operation\ mo_{i,j}\ begining =$$
$$\lceil max\{moment\ of\ mp_{i,j}\ release; moment\ of\ operation\ mo_{i,j-1} completion\}\rceil_{\mathcal{X}_{i,j}} \quad (5)$$

$$i = 1, ..., n; \quad j = 1, ..., \psi_i^1 \cdot lm(i)$$

where: $\mathcal{X}_{i,j}$ – set of values $mx_{i,j}$ following the set of local processes X,
$\lceil a \rceil_B$ – the smallest integer greater than or equal to a in terms of the set B: $\lceil a \rceil_B = \min\{k \in B: k \geq a\}$.

Constraints (5) should be understood in the following way: the moment of the operation $mo_{i,j}$ beginning is equal to the nearest admissible value (determined by set $\mathcal{X}_{i,j}$) being a maximum of both: the completion time of operation $mo_{i,j-1}$ preceding $mo_{i,j}$, and the release time of the resource $mp_{i,j}$ awaiting for $mo_{i,j}$ execution. In other words, the moment of the operation $mo_{i,j}$ beginning belongs to the set $\mathcal{X}_{i,j}$ determined by occurrence of operation of required local process P_i.

The constraints (5) encompassing operations execution order for SCCP from Fig. 1b are shown in Tab. 2.

Problem Formulation: Given the SCCP model (1) specified by sets of routes U and M, the set of resources R, the operation times T and mT, the sets of priority dispatching rules Θ^0 and Θ^1, the sequence of relative frequencies of local processes mutual executions Ψ^0 and Ψ^1, and the sets of constraints linking above mentioned variables SE_L and SE_M. The response to the following question is sought: Does both local and multimodal processes executed in SCCP and modeled by (1) are cyclic? In other words the way of deadlock-free execution of many interdependent agents is sought.

Table 2. Relationship among moments $mx_{i,j}$ of operations (from processes mP_1, mP_2 see SCCP in Fig. 1b) beginning

No	Constraints SE_M	Constraints SE_M
1	$mx_{1,1} = \lceil \max\{mx_{1,4} + 1 - m\alpha; mx_{2,1} + 1 - m\alpha\} \rceil_{x_{1,1}}$	$mx_{1,2} = \lceil \max\{mx_{1,1} + 1; mx_{2,3} + 1\} \rceil_{x_{1,2}}$
2	$mx_{1,3} = \lceil \max\{mx_{1,2} + 1; mx_{1,4} + 1 - m\alpha\} \rceil_{x_{1,3}}$	$mx_{1,4} = \lceil \max\{mx_{1,3} + 1; mx_{1,1} + 1\} \rceil_{x_{1,4}}$
3	$mx_{2,2} = \lceil \max\{mx_{2,1} + 1; mx_{1,2} - 1 - m\alpha\} \rceil_{x_{2,2}}$	$mx_{2,4} = \lceil \max\{mx_{2,3} + 1; mx_{1,2} + 1\} \rceil_{x_{2,4}}$
4	$mx_{2,1} = \lceil \max\{mx_{2,4} + 1 - m\alpha; mx_{2,2} + 1 - m\alpha\} \rceil_{x_{2,1}}$	$mx_{2,3} = \lceil \max\{mx_{2,2} + 1; mx_{2,2} + 1\} \rceil_{x_{2,3}}$

To solve this problem let us consider the property [3] guaranteeing cyclic behavior of local and multimodal processes in case the constraints SE_L and SE_M are consistent. In this context the problem considered boils down to the following question: Does there exist the sets X and mX following constraints SE_L and SE_M? Inconsistency of constraints SE_L and SE_M can be examined using constraint programming techniques.

3   Declarative Approach

Constraints satisfaction problem (SCP) can be used as a formal representation of the above stated problem. Consider CSP (6):

$$CS'_X = (({X, \alpha}, {D_X, D_\alpha}), SE_L) \qquad (6)$$

where: X, α – decision variables, $D_X = \{D_{x_{i,j}} | D_{x_{i,j}} = \mathbb{Z}, i = 1,..,n; \; j = 1, ..., \psi_i^0 \cdot lr(i)\}$, $D_\alpha = \mathbb{N}$ − domains of decision variables X, α, SE_L - the set of constraints linking ST_L and BE_L (e.g. see Tab. 1).

The set X of operations beginning $x_{i,j}$ and the periodicity α follow constraints SE_L consistency, while guaranteeing SCCP cyclic behavior, state for (6) solution.

In order to illustrate an approach proposed let us consider the SCCP from Fig. 1b) while assuming: $X = \{X_1 = (x_{1,1}, x_{1,2}, x_{1,3}), X_2 = (x_{2,1}, x_{2,2}, x_{2,3}),\quad X_3 = (x_{3,1}, x_{3,2}, x_{3,3})\}$, T (see Fig 1), and SE_L (see Tab. 1). The first admissible solution obtained in OzMozart environment consists of X and α presented in Tab. 3.

Table 3. Value of variables X_i and α following local processes from SCCP shown in Fig. 1b)

	$x_{3,1}$	$x_{1,1}, x_{2,1}$	$x_{2,2}, x_{3,2}$	$x_{2,3}, x_{1,2}$	$x_{3,3}$	$x_{1,3}$	α
value $x_{i,j}$:	-1	0	1	2	3	4	5

Similar the multimodal process periodicity can be checked by constraints SE_M consistency examination. The relevant CSP can be stated by the following way (7):

$$mCS'_X = \left((\{mX, m\alpha\}, \{D_{mX}, D_{m\alpha}\}), SE_M \right) \tag{7}$$

where: $mX, m\alpha$ – decision variables, D_{mX}, $D_{m\alpha} = \mathbb{N}$ — domains of decision variables $mX, m\alpha$; SE_M - the set of constraints linking ST_M and BE_M (e.g. see Tab. 2). The constraints SE_M employ the sets $X_{i,j}$ specified by variables X obtained from CS'_X. The sets $X_{i,j}$ consisting moments X operation beginnings necessary for multimodal processes execution are show in the Tab. 4.

Table 4. The sets $X_{i,j}$ following the SCCP shown in Fig. 1b)

	The admissible values of $m^l x_{i,j}^h$ (based on tab. 2)
1	$mx_{1,1} \in X_{1,1} = \{x_{1,1}(l) \mid x_{1,1}(l) = x_{1,1} + l \cdot \alpha, l \in \mathbb{C}\} = \{\dots, 0, 5, 10, 15, \dots\}$
2	$mx_{1,2} \in X_{1,2} = \{x_{1,2}(l) \mid x_{1,2}(l) = x_{1,2} + l \cdot \alpha, l \in \mathbb{C}\} = \{\dots, 2, 7, 12, 17, \dots\}$
3	$mx_{1,3} \in X_{1,3} = \{x_{2,2}(l) \mid x_{2,2}(l) = x_{2,2} + l \cdot \alpha, l \in \mathbb{C}\} = \{\dots, 1, 6, 11, 16, \dots\}$
4	$mx_{1,4} \in X_{1,4} = \{x_{3,1}(l) \mid x_{3,1}(l) = x_{3,1} + l \cdot \alpha, l \in \mathbb{C}\} = \{\dots, 4, 9, 14, 19 \dots\}$
5	$mx_{2,1} \in X_{2,3} = \{x_{2,3}(l) \mid x_{2,3}(l) = x_{2,3} + l \cdot \alpha, l \in \mathbb{C}\} = \{\dots, 2, 7, 12, 17, \dots\}$
6	$mx_{2,2} \in X_{2,2} = \{x_{2,1}(l) \mid x_{2,1}(l) = x_{2,1} + l \cdot \alpha, l \in \mathbb{C}\} = \{\dots, 0, 5, 10, 15, \dots\}$
7	$mx_{2,3} \in X_{2,3} = \{x_{1,3}(l) \mid x_{1,3}(l) = x_{1,3} + l \cdot \alpha, l \in \mathbb{C}\} = \{\dots, 4, 9, 14, 19 \dots\}$

In order to illustrate cyclic behavior of multimodal processes mP_1, mP_2 executed in SCCP from Fig. 1b) let us consider the problem mCS'_X consisting: $mX = \{mX_1 = (mx_{1,1}, mx_{1,2}, mx_{1,3,}, mx_{1,4}), \ mX_2 = (mx_{2,1}, mx_{2,2}, mx_{2,3}, mx_{2,4})\}$, the set SE_M specified in Tab. 3 and Tab. 4. The first admissible solution obtained in Oz-Mozart environment consists of mX and $m\alpha$ shown in Tab. 5.

Table 5. Value of variables mX_i and $m\alpha$ following local processes from SCCP (see Fig. 1b))

	$mx_{2,1}$	$mx_{2,2}$	$mx_{2,3}$	$mx_{1,1}$	$mx_{1,2}$	$mx_{2,4}$	$mx_{1,3}$	$mx_{1,4}$	$m\alpha$
value $mx_{i,j}$:	-3	0	4	5	7	10	11	14	15

Feasible solutions of CS'_X, mCS'_X problems (see Tab. 4 and Tab. 6) follow SE_L and SE_M consistency. The resultant cyclic schedule (see Fig. 3) provides periodicity equal to 5 for local while 15 units of time for multimodal processes.

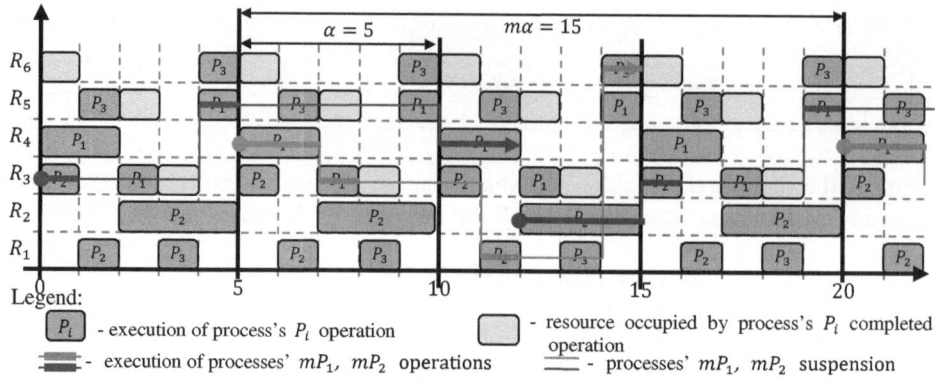

Fig. 3. Local and multimodal processes cyclic schedule for SCCP from Fig.1b)

4   Multimodal Processes Cyclic Steady States Scheduling

The idea of multimodal processes scheduling is shown in Fig. 4. The cyclic steady state of SCCP [3] seen in Fig. 3 follows from subsequent solutions of problems CS_X', mCS_X'. That follows from two levels distinction: SL (local processes structure) and SM (multimodal processes structure). That means each level enables evaluation of particular kind of processes: the SL level provides evaluation of local processes through CS_X', and the SM level provides evaluation of local processes through mCS_X').

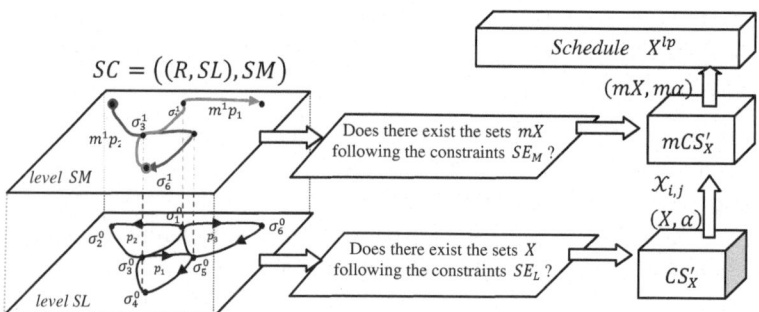

Fig. 4. The idea standing behind of multimodal processes cyclic steady states scheduling

In general case, many different levels of multimodal processes can be recognized as well [4]. The k-th level SM^k of multimodal processes can be seen as a subsystem composed of multimodal process routes M^k network, dispatching priority rules Θ^k, constraints SE_M^k, moments of operation beginnings mX^k, the periodicity $m^k\alpha$, etc., influenced by multimodal processes from the $k-1$-th level. Therefore, in case of multilevel systems evaluation, i.e., consisting of kp levels, the approach shown in Fig. 4, can be generalized by the following algorithm:

function CYCLICSCHEDULEGENERATION $\left(D_X, D_\alpha, D_X^1, D_\alpha^1, ..., D_X^{kp}, D_\alpha^{kp}, SC^{kp}\right)$

$\quad SE_L \leftarrow$ CREATECONSTRAINTS(SL)

$\quad CS_X' \leftarrow \left((\{X, \alpha\}, \{D_X, D_\alpha\}), SE_L\right)$

$\quad (X, \alpha) \leftarrow$ SEARCHONE(CS_X')

$\quad X^{kp} \leftarrow (X, \alpha)$

$\quad$ **if** $X \neq \emptyset$ and $kp > 1$ **then** $SE_M^1 \leftarrow$ CREATECONSTRAINTSM(X, SM^1)

$\quad\quad$ **for** $k \leftarrow 1$ **to** lp

$\quad\quad\quad m^k CS_X' \leftarrow \left((\{m^k X, m^k \alpha\}, \{D_X^k, D_\alpha^l\}), SE_M^k\right)$

$\quad\quad\quad (m^k X, m^k \alpha) \leftarrow$ SEARCHONE$(m^k CS_X')$

$\quad\quad\quad$ **if** $m^k X \neq \emptyset$ **then** $X^{kp} \leftarrow \left(X^{kp}, (m^k X, m^k \alpha)\right)$

$\quad\quad\quad\quad SE_M^{(k+1)} \leftarrow$ CREATECONSTRAINTSM$(m^k X, SM^{(k+1)})$

$\quad\quad\quad$ **else**

$\quad\quad\quad\quad X^{kp} \leftarrow \emptyset$ **break**

$\quad\quad\quad$ **end**

$\quad\quad$ **end**

$\quad$ **end**

$\quad$ **return** X^{kp}

end

where: $D_X, D_\alpha, D_X^k, D_\alpha^k, SC^{kp}$ – input data, D_X, D_α/ D_X^k, D_α^k variable domains of X / $m^k X$ and periodicity α/ $m^k \alpha$; $SC^{kp} = \left(((R, SL), SM^1), ..., SM^{kp}\right)$ – sequence determining the SCCP (1), and taking into account multilevel structure of multimodal processes layers [4],

SEARCHONE(CS) –function providing the first admissible solution to the CS problem and implemented in constraint programming languages environment, e.g. OzMozart, in case CS_X' / $m^k CS_X'$ (equivalent to the problem (7) for SM^k) provided is the sequence (X, α) / $(m^k X, m^k \alpha)$ (in case the solution does not exist, components of pairs are empty sets),

CREATECONSTRAINTSL(SL) – function providing the set of constraints SE_L (see (4)) for a given structure SL (1),

CREATECONSTRAINTSM$(m^k X, SM^{(k+1)})$ –   function   providing   the   set   of straints $SE_M^{(k+1)}$ (see (5)) specifying relations between operations of processes at the $k + 1$ level for a given structures $SM^{(k+1)}$, $m^k X$, $SM^{(k+1)}$.

Due to the algorithm the problem CS_X' following system's structure SC^{kp} is considered as first. The cyclic schedule of local processes X states for its solution. Obtained   schedule   enables   to   consider   the   next   problem $m^1 CS_X'$,   employing straints SE_M^1, while searching for multimodal processes cyclic schedule $m^1 X$. Consequently, subsequent problems $m^k CS_X'$ and constraints SE_M^k determined by (function CreateConstraintsM) and preceding level schedule $m^{(k-1)} X$ can be considered. Its solution provides cyclic schedule X^{kp}, consisting schedules $m^k X$ obtained at previous levels. So, the final cyclic schedule can be defined as folows:

$$X^{kp} = \left(\left(\left((X, \alpha), (m^1 X, m^1 \alpha)\right), ...,\right), ..., (m^k X, m^k \alpha)\right), ..., (m^{kp} X, m^{kp} \alpha)\right) \quad (8)$$

where: X, α – sequence of operations beginning in local processes at the first cycle ($l = 0$), and periodicity of SCCP's cyclic steady state,
$m^k X, m^k \alpha$ – sequence of operations beginning in multimodal processes performed at the k-th level of SM^k, and periodicity of multimodal cyclic steady state.
Computation complexity of the algorithm is polynomial $f(kp) \leq |SE_L| + \sum_{k=1}^{kp}|SE_M^k|$ and mainly constrained by CS_X', $m^k CS_X'$ computational complexities. Solution to those problems concerning consistency verification of max (4), (5) constraints type requires a number of steps equal or less than ($|SE_L|$, $|SE_M^k|$).

5   Concluding Remarks

The main advantages to using a declarative framework are the availability of existing techniques and the expendability of constraint-based representations. In case considered such approach has been employed for modeling of SCCP systems (treated as an environment for concurrently interacting agents) and then for studying of their cyclic steady states space reachability. Searching for a set of possible cyclic steady states encompassing potential cyclic behaviors of the SCCP at hand can be useful in many tasks aimed at cyclic scheduling.

Polynomial time complexity of an algorithm providing cyclic schedules X^{kp} implies the considered problem of multimodal processes cyclic steady state reachability is also of polynomial complexity for assumed routes network, priority dispatching rules and operation times. That is because the constraints (4), (5) have a sufficient character [5]. Therefore, in some cases of SCCP processing multimodal processes imposing constraints (4), (5) inconsistency, the cyclic steady state may occur.

Acknowledgements. This work has partly been supported by the EC under 260026-TAPAS.

References

1. Bielli, M., Boulmakoul, A., Mouncif, H.: Object modeling and path computation for multimodal travel systems. European Journal of Operational Research 175(3), 1705–1730
2. Bernaer, S.: A Multi Agent System to Control Complexity in Multi Modal Transport. In: Proceedings of the IEEE Conf. on Cybernetics and Intelligent Systems, pp. 1–6 (2006)
3. Bocewicz, G., Banaszak, Z.: Declarative approach to cyclic scheduling of multimodal processes. In: Golińska, P. (ed.) EcoProduction and Logistics, vol. 1, pp. 203–238. Springer, Heidelberg (2013)
4. Bocewicz, G., Banaszak, Z.: Declarative approach to cyclic steady states space refinement: periodic processes scheduling. International Journal of Advanced Manufacturing Technology (in print, 2013), doi:10.1007/s00170-013-4760-0
5. Bocewicz, G., Wójcik, R., Banaszak, Z.: Cyclic Scheduling for Supply Chain Network. In: Rodríguez, J.M.C., Pérez, J.B., Golinska, P., Giroux, S., Corchuelo, R. (eds.) Trends in PAAMS. AISC, vol. 157, pp. 39–47. Springer, Heidelberg (2012)

6. Korytkowski, P., Wisniewski, T., Zaikin, O.: Multi-criteria approach to comparison of inspection allocation for multi-product manufacturing systems in make-to-order sector. Control and Cybernetics 39(1), 97–116 (2010)
7. Levner, E., Kats, V., Alcaide, D., Pablo, L., Cheng, T.C.E.: Complexity of cyclic scheduling problems: A state-of-the-art survey. Computers & Industrial Engineering 59(2), 352–361 (2010)
8. Friedrich, M.: A multi-modal transport model for integrated planning. In: Proceedings of 8th World Conference on Transport Research, vol. 2, pp. 1–14. Elsevier (1999)
9. Polak, M., Majdzik, P., Banaszak, Z., Wójcik, R.: The performance evaluation tool for automated prototyping of concurrent cyclic processes. Fundamenta Informatice 60(1-4), 269–289 (2004)
10. Song, J.-S., Lee, T.-E.: Petri net modeling and scheduling for cyclic job shops with blocking. Computers & Industrial Engineering 34(2), 281–295 (1998)
11. Trouillet, B., Korbaa, O., Gentina, J.-C.K.: Formal Approach for FMS Cyclic Scheduling. IEEE SMC Transactions, Part C 37(1), 126–137 (2007)
12. Von Kampmeyer, T.: Cyclic scheduling problems, Ph.D. Dissertation, Fachbereich Mathematik/Informatik, Universität Osnabrück (2006)

Using Multi-agent Systems for Developing an Enterprise Modeling Aided Tool

Paul-Eric Dossou[1], Philip Mitchell[1], and Pawel Pawlewski[2]

[1] ICAM, Site de Vendée, 28 Boulevard d'Angleterre,
85000 La Roche-Sur-Yon, France
[2] Poznan University of Technology, ul.Strzelecka 11
60-965 Poznań
`paul-eric.dossou@icam.fr`, `pawel.pawlewski@put.poznan.pl`,
`philip.mitchell@icam.fr`

Abstract. GRAI Methodology is one of the three main methodologies used for enterprise modeling. GRAIMOD is a software tool being developed for supporting the methodology. A new module is being developed in GRAIMOD for treating specially Carbon management and social, societal and environmental dimensions in the enterprise performance improvement. GRAIMOD is being developed on Java architecture by using Jade a platform of multi-agents system and Jess a platform for defining and elaborating rules base. A focus is made for presenting the orientations taken in this development and difficulties met.

Keywords: Multi-agent systems, Expert system, enterprise modelling, performance, reference models, rules, Knowledge.

1 Introduction

The economic situation in Europe and in USA is unbelievable. Indeed, at the end of 2012, the president of USA had to stop his Christmas holidays for discussing with the congress for finding very quickly solution against the fiscal cliff predicting for the end of the year if republicans and democrats did not find solution. In France, 6 months after the election of the new president, communists were joking with his promises during the election campaign. Capitalists were crying against the high level of taxes and globally against the policy of the new government. These situations were not exceptional but generalized all over the European countries. The only prescription given to the PIIGS (Portugal, Ireland, Italy, Greece and Spain) and other European countries is an increase in taxation and a reduction in government expenditure. Enterprises were looking for solutions to reduce cost and improve their performance. Nobody knows exactly how to solve the situation but in terms of economy but also performance for enterprises.

Enterprise modeling is regularly used for preparing enterprises to the outcome of the crisis. Indeed, the improvement of the enterprise global performance is the main objective of this use. Enterprises need to find the best way to resist the present crisis and then to improve in order to be more efficient. GRAI Methodology is one of the three main methodologies (with PERA, CIMOSA) of enterprise modeling [4].

J.M. Corchado et al. (Eds.): PAAMS 2013 Workshops, CCIS 365, pp. 86–93, 2013.
© Springer-Verlag Berlin Heidelberg 2013

To support this methodology different tools are been developed. GRAIMOD, is the last one being developed by using JAVA technology, JADE and JESS platforms, and an open architecture and structure [8], [10].

In this paper, the basic concepts of GRAIMOD are presented. The changes due to integration of a special module GRAI_SSE for social, societal and environmental dimensions and its sub-module GRAICARB destined for carbon footprint management is presented. Then, the use of JESS, JADE and JAVA for developing GRAIMOD is presented. Finally perspectives for the rest of development phase will be presented.

2   GRAIMOD: Existing Concepts and Architecture

GRAI Methodology is one of the three main methodologies used for analyzing and designing enterprises. The GRAI approach is composed of four phases: An initialization phase to start the study, a modeling phase where the existing system is described, an analysis phase to detect the inconsistencies of the studied system and a design phase during which the inconsistencies detected are corrected and a new system proposed. These concepts could be used to insure the transforming of enterprises which meet the real market needs (globalization, relocation, capacity to be proactive, cost optimization, lead time, quality, flexibility, etc....) and have to be adapted.

An enterprise is completely described according to GRAI Methodology by finding five models: functional (functions of the enterprise and their links), physical (the production system), informational (the net, tools and informational flows), process (suite of sequences or tasks), ant decisional (structure of orders, hierarchic organisation). Then these models could be improved for increasing enterprise performance.

GRAIMOD is a new tool being developed by ICAM Engineer School for proposing concrete solutions to improve enterprises according to new market evolutions. Nowadays, it contains five modules working around three sub modules (figure 1).

GRAIKERN is a graphic editor used for representing the different models associated to GRAI methodology. It is an interface. **GRAIWORKER** is the work base elaborated for managing, modifying and capitalising knowledge about the studied case. **GRAITRANS** is a **Transfer Interface** used for putting the new case in GRAIXPERT in order to improve its Cases Base [1], [2], [3]. The reference model elaborated for each enterprise domain will be improved by the acquisition of this new model in GRAIXPERT between the different modules

GRAIXPERT is a hybrid expert system for managing the analysis of the existing system and proposing a new system [12], [16]. It is composed of two sub-modules in interaction with GRAIKERN: the Knowledge Capitalization (KCM) and the Knowledge Based System (XPERTKBM). **GRAIMANAGER** is a management module used for organising the different interactions between the modules of GRAIMOD. It controls and manages the system's interactions with the users [5], [6].

GRAISUC is a module used for managing the choice of an ERP or SCM tool for an enterprise. It is composed of two sub-modules SpeMM and SpeCM. The Specification Management Module (SpeMM) is used for choosing the appropriate ERP or SCM Tool of an enterprise. The specifications obtained are capitalised in the Specification Capitalisation Module (SpeCM) .

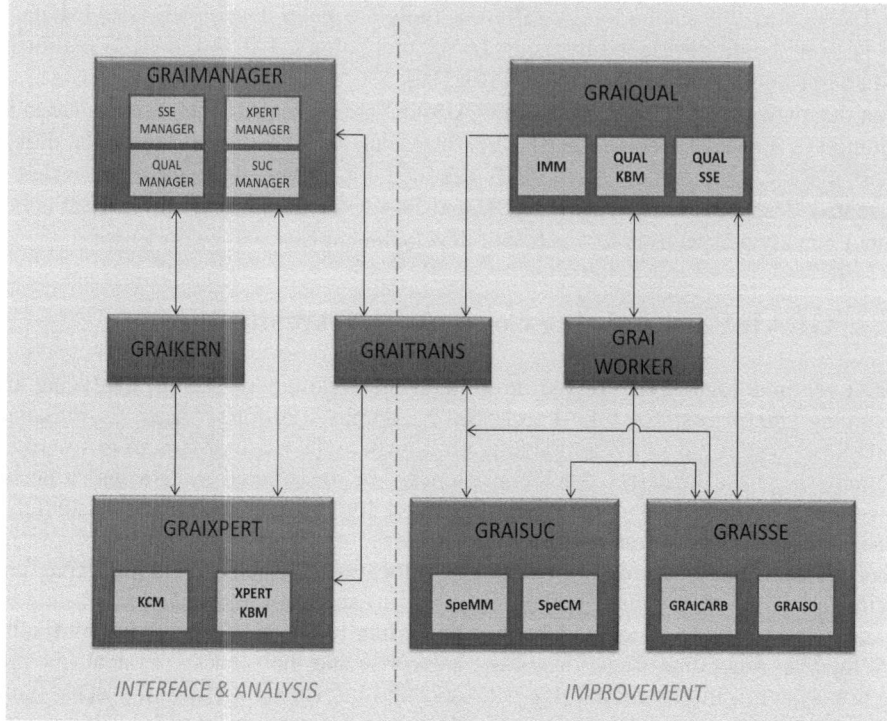

Fig. 1. New Architecture of GRAIMOD

GRAIQUAL is a module used for managing quality approach implementation or quality improvement in an enterprise [7]. It contains two sub-modules IMM and QUALKBM. The Improvements Management Module (IMM) is used for managing the different quality action plans of the enterprise. The Quality Knowledge Base Module (QUALKBM) is being elaborated for containing the rules related to quality certifications in order to use them for improving or elaborating quality in an enterprise. The module GRAIQUAL of GRAIMOD is able and efficient for defining how to improve enterprises basing in criteria like quality, lead time and cost. Indeed, a fourth criterion allowing carbon management is proposed. Then this criterion has to be combined to the others for really improving enterprises according to the actual context of enterprises.

GRAI_SSE is the new module being developed specially for integrating social, societal and environmental dimensions in the improvement of enterprises. It is composed of a sub-module GRAICARB destined to manage carbon footprint and GRAI_SO being elaborated for improving the other aspects of environmental, social and societal dimensions.

It appears that a focus has to be made on the use of this criterion. A new module **GRAI_SSE** is being added to GRAIMOD in order to pinpoint the environmental, societal and social dimensions in enterprises. This module would integrate for example changes associated to carbon management, ISO 26000, ISO 14000 implementations, social and societal evolutions impacts on enterprises but also territorial collectivities (states, associations, districts, etc.) [9]. The objective is not to dissociate this criterion but to obtain a best combination by really studying this aspect of the enterprise in order to propose appropriate solutions. The difficult enterprise context due to the crisis and the research of alternative solutions to the basic QCD (Quality, Cost and Delivery date) optimization, are the cause of this new focus on how social, societal and environmental dimensions are important and how it is benefit for enterprises to find a new optimized solution by focusing on these aspects.

The architecture of this system contains three different bases for managing the study of a new case. A model base is used for managing elaborated reference models. A rule base is used for analyzing the models of the system in question. And a case base is defined for capitalizing different studies for future use. This tool proposes the combination of CBR (Case Based Reasoning) and Multi-agent systems for solving enterprise modeling problem and improving enterprise performance.

A new typology of enterprises is being elaborated by realizing a detailed study on Vendee enterprises. The results would be presented later but this new typology allows to define enterprises making a different management form by integrating alternative considerations. The capitalist model based on market economy, is not totally efficient. Then it appears that elaboration of a typology taken into account this aspect and pinpointing the enterprises with alternative solutions is welcome. A questionnaire has been elaborated and sent to enterprises.

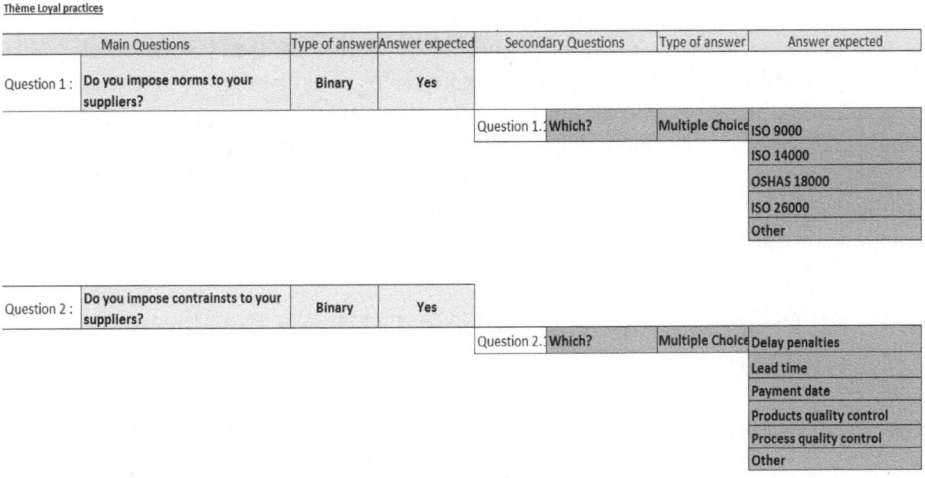

Fig. 2. Example of questionnaire for enterprise typology elaboration

3   GRAICARB a New Sub-module for Managing Carbon Footprint

GRAICARB is composed of different modules. CARBMM is a module for managing carbon reduction policy of enterprises. It used allows to define and manage according to social, societal and environmental dimensions and to elaborate and manage improvements based on these aspects. CARBKBM is destined to contain rules related to ISO 14000 certification and carbon management rules in order to be able to implement or improve enterprises according to this norm. The structure of this sub-module is the same to GRAIQUAL structure (figure. 3).

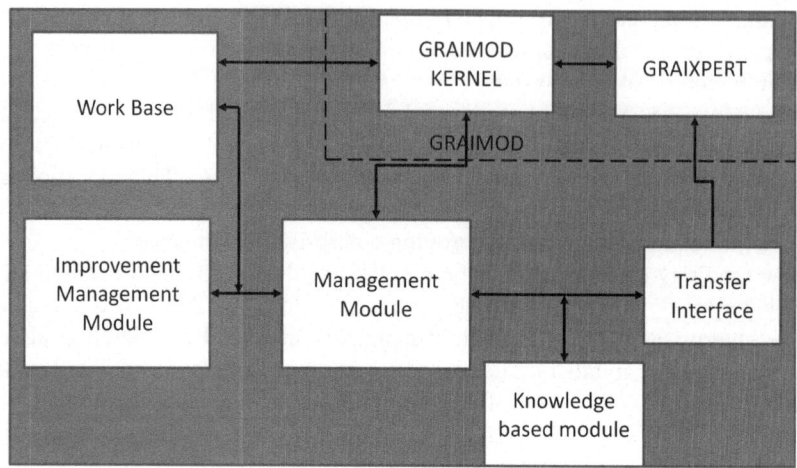

Fig. 3. Architecture of GRAICARB

Carbon footprint management is an approach. It represents the elaboration of evaluation project and gas emission reduction. Six key steps could be defined: growing awareness of carbon management, Definition of the study area, Data acquisition, Results exploiting, Elaboration of reduction action plan, Executing reduction action plan.

The approach chosen is based on the method proposed by ADEME (French environment agency). It is composed of the previous steps, specific calculation rules, calculation software tool (database) and the associated documentation.

4   Multi-agent Systems, JESS and JADE for Developing GRAIMOD

GRAIMOD is being developing by using Java. The platform used for muti-agent systems is JADE. For defining agents for GRAIMOD, and in accordance with enterprise modeling, it is decided to use training agent. This choice is adapted to the problem solving method used for defining concepts of GRAIMOD. This method combines different reasoning like Case Based Reasoning, decomposition reasoning, generalization and particularization reasoning and transformation reasoning. It is clear that the agents defined for the phases related to enterprise performance improvement have to learn quickly in accordance with the possible changes (old cases, reference models associated to typology, etc.) Indeed, the choice was difficult because of the advantages of BDI (Beliefs, Desires, and Intentions) architecture, but we chose the training agents because of their particularity to learn.

This system is used for defining how to improve the enterprise performance and for capitalizing the process followed. The language associated to Jade platform is FIPA ACL (Agent Communication Language) [11], [14]. The reference model of a muli-agent platform is described in the following figure where the roles of some key agents necessary for the platform management and specify the components of agent management language and language ontology [13], [15].

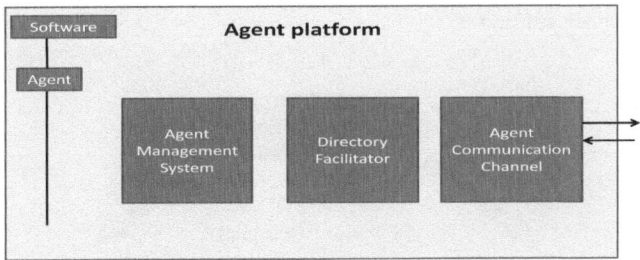

Fig. 4. Reference model for a FIPA Multi-agent platform

The development of GRAIMOD by using these concepts allows to obtain the architecture in figure 5. This architecture is adapted to the previous concepts of GRAIMOD.

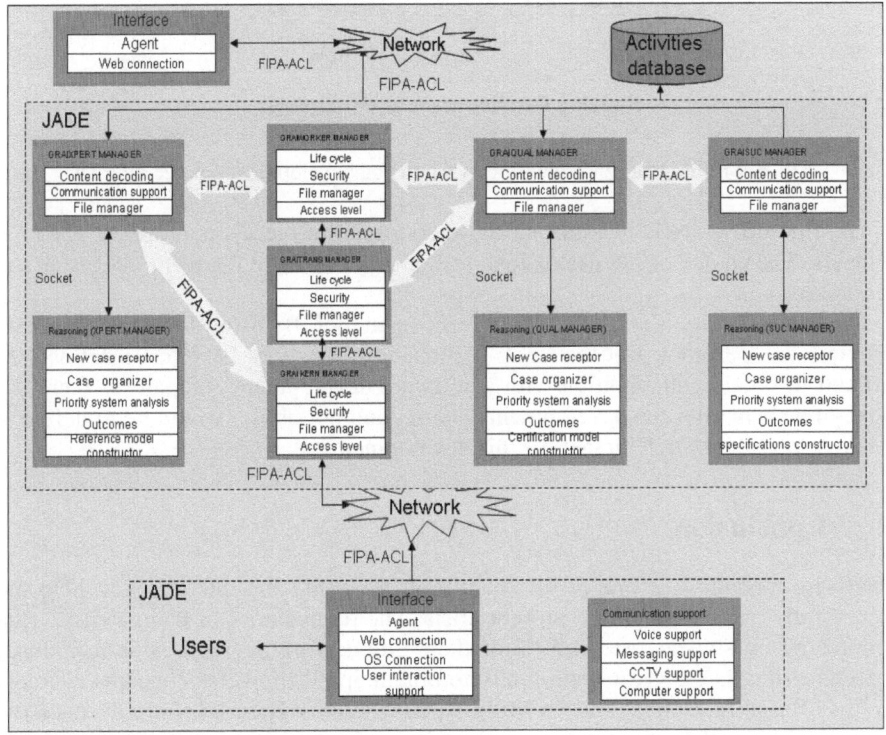

Fig. 5. Architecture of GRAIMOD in a Java environment

For GRAICARB the new sub-module, the concept of housing development model seems to be interesting. The following figure presents the housing development multi-agent representation in which each occupant or household can be modelled as an agent that uses resources in the development environment and can communicate with other occupant agents. Indeed, the human behaviour has been taken into account and six interrelated models could be defined (waste, CO2, water, ecosystem Health, economic and social). The opportunity to use this concept and adapt it for developing GRAICARB is being studied.

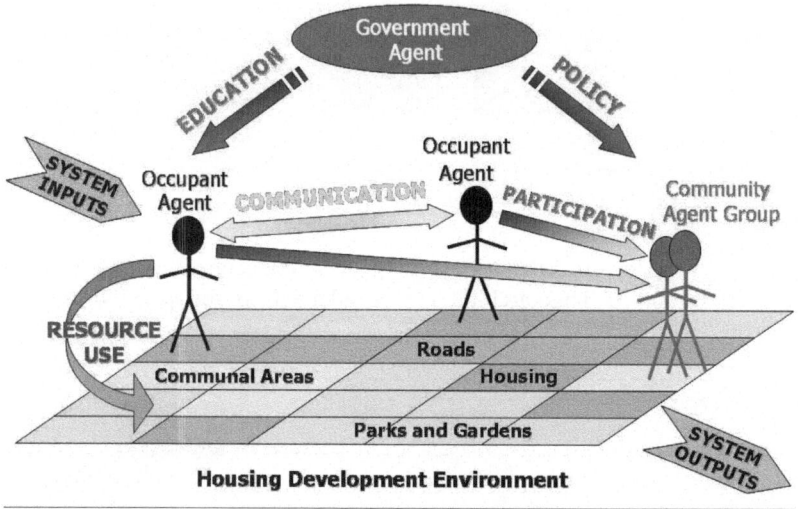

Fig. 6. Multi-agent representation of a housing development (source internet)

The first difficulty is to translate these concepts into terms appropriate for IT developers. The choice of the use of Java technology and Jade Platform integrates some constraints.

The last difficulty is related to the type of open tool. By using Java, the objective is to obtain an open tool. But the rights associated to this tool have to be defined. It is difficult to obtain collaboration with a software development company if there is no money for them after the development. The second possibility would be to define and obtain a special research budget for this development.

5   Conclusion

Enterprise modelling is one of the main tools available for enterprises to help them successfully come through the present crisis. The particularity of Icam Vendee (Icam Group), where students spend 50% of their Engineering degree course in industrial apprenticeship, is the great opportunity to obtain applications for concepts developed on Case Based Reasoning and on Multi Agent Systems Theories. Indeed, this advantage is used for elaborating a new Enterprise typology by using Vendee enterprises and for enriching the bases og GRAIMOD.

A new module GRAI_SSE is being developed in GRAIMOD especially for social, societal and environmental dimensions. A zoom is made on GRAICARB a sub-module of GRAI_SSE. The development of GRAIMOD associated to GRAI Methodology for managing the different phases of this method and improving enterprises will allow to upgrade the expertise given to SMEs for helping them during the crisis and preparing them for the future.

GRAIMOD is being developed in a Java environment, particularly with Jade platform and FIPA-ACL Language. JESS is being used for developing the rule engine of the software tool. The main difficulty is the lack of expertise of developers in the use of multi-agent concepts. Collaboration with specialists is the way being followed at this stage of development.

References

1. Aamodt, A.: Case-Based Reasoning: foundational issues, methodological variations, and system approaches. Artificial Intelligence Communications 7(1), 39–59 (1994)
2. Burke, E.K., et al.: Structured cases in case-based reasoning – reusing and adapting cases for time-tabling problems. The Journal of KBS 13(2-3), 159–165 (2000)
3. Brown, D.C., Chandrasekaran, B.: Expert system for a class of mechanical design activities. In: Knowledge Engineering in CAD. Elsevier, Amsterdam (1985)
4. Chen, D., Doumeingts, G., Vernadat, F.B.: Architectures for enterprise integration and interoperability. Past, present and future. Computers in Industry 59, 647–659 (2008)
5. Dossou, P.E., Mitchell, P.: Using case based reasoning in GRAIXPERT. In: FAIM 2006, Limerick, Ireland (2006)
6. Dossou, P.-E., Mitchell, P.: Implication of Reasoning in GRAIXPERT for Modeling Enterprises. In: Omatu, S., Rocha, M.P., Bravo, J., Fernández, F., Corchado, E., Bustillo, A., Corchado, J.M. (eds.) IWANN 2009, Part II. LNCS, vol. 5518, pp. 374–381. Springer, Heidelberg (2009)
7. Dossou, P.E., Mitchell, P.: How Quality Management could improve the Supply Chain performance of SMES. In: FAIM 2009, Middlesbrough, United Kingdom (2009)
8. Dossou, P.-E., Pawlewski, P.: Using Multi-agent system for improving and implementing a new enterprise modeling tool. In: Demazeau, Y., Dignum, F., Corchado, J.M., Bajo, J., Corchuelo, R., Corchado, E., Fernández-Riverola, F., Julián, V.J., Pawlewski, P., Campbell, A. (eds.) Trends in PAAMS. AISC, vol. 71, pp. 225–232. Springer, Heidelberg (2010)
9. European commission: Responsabilité sociale des entreprises: une nouvelle stratégie de l'UE pour la période 2011-2014, Brussels, Belgium (2011)
10. Ferber, J.: Multi-agent system: An Introduction to distributed Artificial Intelligence. Addison Wesley Longman, Harlow, ISBN 0-201-36048-9
11. Friedman-Hill, E.: JESS, the rule engine for the JAVA platform, version 7.1p2. Sandia National Laboratories (2008)
12. Russell, S.J., Norvig, P.: Artificial Intelligence. A Modern Approach. Prentice-Hall, Englewood Cliffs (1995)
13. Sen, S., Weiss, G.: Learning in Multiagent Systems. In: Weiss, G. (ed.) Multiagent Systems: A Modern Approach to Distributed Artificial Intelligence, ch. 6, pp. 259–298. The MIT Press, Cambridge (1999)
14. Sycara, K.P.: Multi-agent systems. AI Magasine, American Association for Artificial Intelligence, 0738-4602-1998 (1998)
15. Wooldridge, M.: Intelligent Agents. In: Weiss, G. (ed.) Multiagent Systems: A Modern Approach to Distributed Artificial Intelligence, ch. 1, pp. 27–77. The MIT Press, Cambridge (1999)
16. Xia, Q., et al.: Knowledge architecture and system design for intelligent operation support systems. The Journal Expert Systems with Applications 17(2), 115–127 (1999)

A Multi-agent Control Architecture for Supply Chains Using a Predictive Pull-Flow Perspective

J. Lemos Nabais[1], Rudy R. Negenborn[2], R.B. Carmona Benítez[3], Luís F. Mendonça[4],
João Lourenço[5], and M. Ayala Botto[6]

[1] IDMEC, Department of Informatics and Systems Engineering
Setúbal School of Technology, Polytechnical Institute of Setúbal, Setúbal, Portugal
joao.nabais@estsetubal.ips.pt
[2] Delft University of Technology, Marine and Transport Technology
Transport Engineering and Logistics, Delft, The Netherlands
r.r.negenborn@tudelft.nl
[3] School of Business and Economics, Universidad Anáhuac México Norte
Huixquilucan, México
rafael.carmona@anahuac.mx
[4] IDMEC, Escola Superior Naútica Infante D. Henrique
Department of Marine Engineering, Paço d'Arcos, Portugal
luismendonca@enautica.pt
[5] INESC, Department of Informatics and Systems Engineering
Setúbal School of Technology, Polytechnical Institute of Setúbal, Setúbal, Portugal
joao.lourenco@estsetubal.ips.pt
[6] IDMEC, Instituto Superior Técnico, Technical University of Lisbon,
Department of Mechanical Engineering, Lisboa, Portugal
ayalabotto@ist.utl.pt

Abstract. Supply chains are large-scale distribution networks in which multiple types of commodities are present. In this paper, the operations management in supply chains is posed as a tracking control problem. All inventory levels in the network should be kept as close as possible to the desired values over time. The supply chain state is disturbed due to client demand at the end nodes. A multi-agent control architecture to restore all inventory levels over the supply chain is proposed. First the model for the supply chain is broken down into smaller subsystems using a flow decomposition. The operations management for each subsystem will be decided upon by a dedicated control agent. The control agents solve their problems using a pull-flow perspective, starting at the end nodes and then propagating upstream. Adding new components to the supply chain will have as a consequence the inclusion of more control agents. The proposed architecture is easily scalable to large supply chains due to its modular feature. The multi-agent control architecture performance is illustrated using a supply chain composed of four levels (suppliers, consolidation, distribution, end nodes) using different levels of predictions about client demands. With the increase of prediction demand accuracy the proposed control architecture is able to keep the desired inventory level at the end nodes over time, which makes it suitable for use for just in time production strategies.

Keywords: supply chains, multi-agent systems, model predictive control, inventory level.

J.M. Corchado et al. (Eds.): PAAMS 2013 Workshops, CCIS 365, pp. 94–105, 2013.
© Springer-Verlag Berlin Heidelberg 2013

1   Introduction

Supply chain are complex systems in which multiple organizations (suppliers, manufacturers, retailers, and customers) are contributing to move commodities or services from a source node to a destination node [1]. The strong coupling between organizations restricts achieving optimal performance of the whole system. Currently, the increase of production far from the final customer poses a challenge to the existing supply chains. The problem is growing in complexity and new methodologies are required to support decisions leading to a more effective cooperation between organizations. This cooperation depends on the type of supply chain in terms of freedom to exchange information. In a vertical integration all organizations are owned by the same company and therefore the information can be shared freely. In horizontal integration different organizations are owned by different companies with possibly conflicting objectives and competitive issues, making the exchange information more restricted.

In this paper we consider client demand as an exogenous input at the end nodes that disturbs the supply chain state: inventory levels. Operations management is required to assign flows between nodes such that the client demand is satisfied while keeping the inventory at a desired level. This paper proposes a multi-agent control architecture to keep the desired inventory levels over the supply chain. As supply chains may be large-scale systems we propose a flow decomposition [2] to obtain smaller subsystems. A control agent is assigned to each subsystem and is responsible for determining decisions (flows assignment) over time. The control agent will solve an optimization problem at each time step in accordance to the Model Predictive Control (MPC) strategy. MPC has shown successful applications in the process industry [3], and is now gaining increasing attention in fields like supply chains [4], power networks [5], water distribution networks [6] and road traffic networks [7]. In supply chains, costs can be associated to flows and quantities of stored commodities. Using mathematical models to describe the flows inside supply chains it is possible to make predictions about the future behavior of the supply chain. The MPC controller can determine which actions have to be chosen in order to obtain the best performance. At each time step the controller first obtains the current state of the system it controls. Then it formulates an optimization problem, using the desired goals, existing constraints, disturbances and prediction information if available. The possibility to include prediction information in the optimization problem motivates the selection of this control strategy. Through this mechanism the different control agents can exchange information about their current and future decisions increasing their cooperation by avoiding multiple agents to answer to the same client demand. The order by which the control agents solve their problems is a so-called pull-flow perspective, starting from the end nodes, where the exogenous input is applied, and propagated towards the source nodes.

This paper is organized as follows. In Section 2 the model used for describing the multi-commodity flows in supply chains is given. The operations management problem is formulated in Section 3 and addressed using a multi-agent MPC architecture where each control agent solves an optimization problem at each discrete time step. The performance of the proposed architecture is tested through numerical experiments in Section 4 for a hypothetical supply chain taking into account different prediction accuracies. In Section 5 conclusions are drawn and future research topics are indicated.

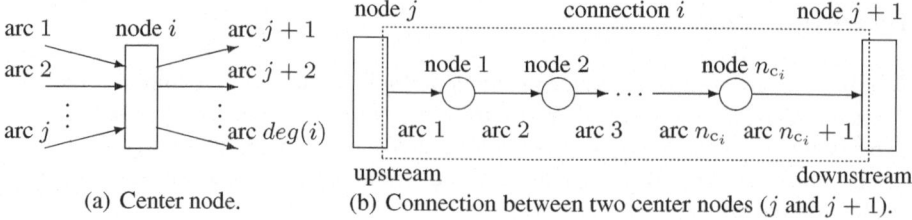

(a) Center node.   (b) Connection between two center nodes (j and $j + 1$).

Fig. 1. Components in a supply chain to model the storage and transport phenomena ($deg(i)$ stands for node i degree)

2   Modeling Supply Chains

A supply chain is a network and can be described as a graph $\mathcal{G} = (\mathcal{V}, \mathcal{E})$ [8], where the nodes $\mathcal{V}$ are related to physical locations and the arcs $\mathcal{E}$ represent the available transport between nodes. At a macroscopic level, i.e., from a management perspective, supply chains exhibits two major phenomena: storage ability in well defined areas where commodities can be produced, manufactured or simply stored, and the transport delay (which is the time necessary to transport commodities between two nodes using the available transport). The storage ability is related to the so-called center nodes that can have multiple arriving and departing connections (see Fig. 1(a)). The transport delay for each connection is modeled as a succession of nodes with limited storage capacity (related to the transport capacity) between two center nodes (see Fig. 1(b)). Each connection has one upstream center node from where it pulls commodities, and it also has one downstream center node to where it pushes commodities. Connections can share the limited transport capacity to guarantee the desired flows between nodes. Supply chains are therefore complex systems with coupled dynamics and coupled constraints.

The complexity of the supply chain model is determined by:

- n_t: number of commodity types considered;
- n_c: number of connections existing in the supply chain;
- n_{c_i}: number of nodes belonging exclusively to connection i;
- n_n: number of center nodes in the supply chain that are further divided into source (upstream) nodes n_n^u, end (downstream) nodes n_n^d and store nodes n_n^s;
- n_l: number of levels present in the supply chain, including the source (upstream) and end node (downstream) levels.

For illustration purposes consider the supply chain represented in Fig. 2. The supply chain is divided into four levels $n_l = 4$ (source, consolidation center, distribution center and end node levels) with a total of $n_n = 11$ center nodes connected through a total of $n_c = 17$ connections. The supply chain transports $n_t = 3$ commodities (products A, B and C) generated at dedicated sources. As particular features the supply chain presents (1) the possibility to transport commodities between the distribution centers, (2) there are some end nodes that can be served by more than one connection and (3) available connections have different transport delays.

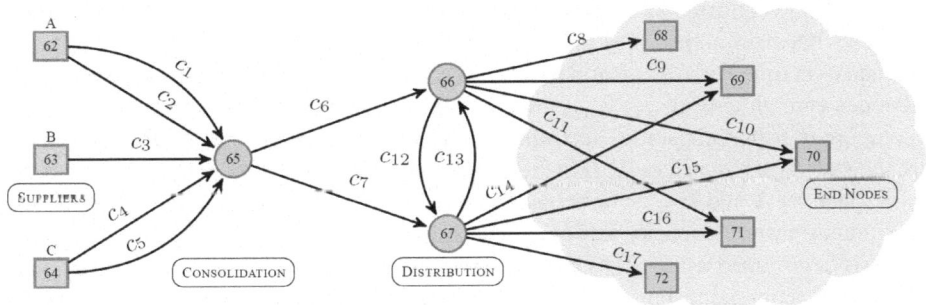

Fig. 2. Example of supply chain with three commodities, products A, B and C. For the sake of readability the 61 connection nodes are omitted.

2.1 Proposed Centralized Dynamical Model

The supply chain is seen as a network of storage areas described as queues that are connected by transport capacity represented by links. The proposed supply chain model for describing the supply chain dynamics is based on a flow perspective. The total number of nodes inside the supply chain n_y is associated with the network topology,

$$n_y = n_n + \sum_{i=1}^{n_c} n_{c_i}. \tag{1}$$

For each node in the supply chain a state-space vector $\bar{\mathbf{x}}_j(k)$ is defined; the individual state-space vectors of the nodes are merged to form the state-space vector $\mathbf{x}(k)$ of the complete supply chain,

$$\bar{\mathbf{x}}_j(k) = \begin{bmatrix} x_j^1(k) \\ x_j^2(k) \\ \vdots \\ x_j^{n_t}(k) \end{bmatrix}, j = 1, \ldots, n_y, \quad \mathbf{x}(k) = \begin{bmatrix} \bar{\mathbf{x}}_1(k) \\ \bar{\mathbf{x}}_2(k) \\ \vdots \\ \bar{\mathbf{x}}_{n_y}(k) \end{bmatrix}, \tag{2}$$

where $x_j^t(k)$ is the quantity per commodity type t at node j at time step k. The dimension of the state-space vector $\mathbf{x}(k)$ is given by $n_t n_y$. The model for the supply chain dynamics can now be represented in a compact form as

$$\mathbf{x}(k+1) = \mathbf{A}\mathbf{x}(k) + \mathbf{B}_u\mathbf{u}(k) + \mathbf{B}_d\mathbf{d}(k), \tag{3}$$

$$\mathbf{y}(k) = \mathbf{C}\mathbf{x}(k), \tag{4}$$

$$\mathbf{x}(k) \geq \mathbf{0}, \tag{5}$$

$$\mathbf{u}(k) \geq \mathbf{0}, \tag{6}$$

$$\mathbf{y}(k) \leq \mathbf{y}_{\max}, \tag{7}$$

$$\mathbf{P}_{uu}\mathbf{u}(k) \leq \mathbf{u}_{\max}, \tag{8}$$

$$\mathbf{x}(k) \geq \mathbf{P}_{xu}\mathbf{u}(k), \tag{9}$$

where $\mathbf{u}$ is the control action vector with length $n_\mathrm{u} = n_\mathrm{t}(n_\mathrm{y} - n_\mathrm{n} + n_\mathrm{c})$ representing the flows between nodes, $\mathbf{d}$ is the exogenous input vector related to the downstream demand over time with dimension $n_\mathrm{t} n_\mathrm{n}^\mathrm{d}$, $\mathbf{y}$ is the current volume per commodity type at all nodes with dimension n_y, $\mathbf{y}_\mathrm{max}$ are the maximum node storage capacities, $\mathbf{u}_\mathrm{max}$ the maximum transport capacities according to the supply chain design, $\mathbf{A}$, $\mathbf{B}_\mathrm{u}$, $\mathbf{B}_\mathrm{d}$ and $\mathbf{C}$ are the state-space matrices, $\mathbf{P}_\mathrm{xu}$ is the projection from the control action set $\mathcal{U}$ into the state-space set $\mathcal{X}$ and $\mathbf{P}_\mathrm{uu}$ is the projection matrix from the control action set $\mathcal{U}$ into the maximum transport capacity set $\mathcal{U}_\mathrm{max}$. The supply chain state, $\mathbf{x}$, at the next time step, $k + 1$, is determined using (3) as a function of the current supply chain state, $\mathbf{x}(k)$, plus the control action contribution, $\mathbf{u}$, decided upon by the supply chain manager, and the corresponding exogenous inputs, $\mathbf{d}$, capturing the client demand. The control action $\mathbf{u}$ is the flow per commodity type between nodes and is imposed through a corresponding transport capacity allocation. Inequalities (5)–(9) are necessary in this framework for imposing the supply chain structural layout and assumptions made:

Nonnegativity of States and Flows: negative storage is not physically possible, imposed by (5), and all flows are assumed to be nonnegative, this is guaranteed by (6);

Storage Capacity: each node has to respect its own storage capacity and this is represented by (7);

Maximum Transport Capacity: the supply chain structural layout in terms of transport capacity is represented by (8);

Feasible Flows: not all flows that satisfy (5) and (6) are allowed. The assigned flow has to respect the quantity per commodity type available in the related node and therefore equation (9) constraints this relation.

2.2   Supply Chain Decomposition

Real supply chains may consist of tens of center nodes and handle hundreds of commodity types. It is critical to alleviate the computational burden introduced when considering the central model (3)–(9) such that a solution is reached in admissible time. Using a node/arc numbering in a push-flow perspective (from the sources towards the end nodes) it is possible to obtain a highly structured state-space model without the need to further mathematical manipulations [9]. Although the network is composed of several center nodes it is important to note that a connection is by definition the path between two center nodes. Therefore the interference of a single connection into the set of center nodes is done solely at two nodes. A subsystem i is defined as the node collection related to a connection i plus the associated source and end nodes [2]. The state-space vector $\mathbf{x}_i$ for subsystem i will be composed of the corresponding $\bar{\mathbf{x}}_j$ state-space vectors,

$$\mathbf{x}_i(k) = \begin{bmatrix} \bar{\mathbf{x}}_{n_{C_i} - n_{c_i} + 1}(k) \\ \bar{\mathbf{x}}_{n_{C_i} - n_{c_i} + 2}(k) \\ \vdots \\ \bar{\mathbf{x}}_{n_{C_i} - 1}(k) \\ \bar{\mathbf{x}}_{n_{C_i}}(k) \\ \bar{\mathbf{x}}_i^{\mathrm{in}}(k) \\ \bar{\mathbf{x}}_i^{\mathrm{out}}(k) \end{bmatrix}, \quad n_{C_i} = \sum_{j=1}^{i} (n_{c_j}), \quad 1 \leq i \leq n_\mathrm{c}, \quad (10)$$

with length n_t $(n_{c_i} + 2)$ belonging to state-space set $\mathcal{X}_i$ where $\bar{\mathbf{x}}_i^{in}$ and $\bar{\mathbf{x}}_i^{out}$ are the state-space vectors related to the source and end nodes for connection i respectively. The state-space model for subsystem i is given by,

$$\mathbf{x}_i(k+1) = \mathbf{A}_i\mathbf{x}_i(k) + \mathbf{B}_{u_i}\mathbf{u}_i(k) + \mathbf{B}_{d_i}\mathbf{d}_i(k) + \sum_{j=1, j \neq i}^{n_c} \mathbf{B}_{u_{i,j}}\mathbf{u}_j(k) \quad (11)$$

$$\mathbf{y}_i(k) = \mathbf{C}_i\mathbf{x}_i(k), \quad (12)$$

where $\mathbf{y}_i$ is the total quantity of commodities at subsystem i nodes, $\mathbf{u}_i$ is the control action for subsystem i with length n_t $(n_{c_i} + 1)$ belonging to set $\mathcal{U}_i$, $\mathbf{d}_i$ is the exogenous input vector associated with subsystem i, $\mathbf{A}_i$, $\mathbf{B}_{u_i}$, $\mathbf{B}_{u_{i,j}}$ $\mathbf{B}_{d_i}$ and $\mathbf{C}_i$ are the state-space matrices for subsystem i. The last term in (11) is responsible for the information exchange between control agents, in particular regarding their future behavior, to avoid that two or more control agents respond to the same demand. The complete subsystem i model is obtained including constraints of nonnegativity of states and flows, storage capacity, maximum transport capacity, and feasible flows to the state space (11)–(12).

3   Supply Chain Operations Management

To limit the problem dimension to be solved at each time step, a control agent is assigned to each subsystem obtained from the supply chain using the flow decomposition of the previous section. This approach leads to a scalable and modular control architecture. Adding new connections and nodes has as consequence the inclusion of more control agents. In order to assure the cooperation between the different control agents it is critical to assure or promote information exchange between control agents regarding their current and predicted future decisions to avoid multiple agents to answer to the same client demand. Control agents solve their problems, one after another, using the information of the previous control agent but no communication iterations are performed between control agents [10].

3.1   MPC Formulation for One Control Agent

Control agent i will solve the operations management for subsystem i following an MPC strategy. MPC is an online optimization-based control approach that minimizes an objective function subject to constraints at each time step.

The solution to the optimization problem is an optimal sequence of control actions over the prediction horizon that give the best predicted performance. The controller implements only the component corresponding to the first time step until the beginning of the next time step, in a receding horizon fashion. At the next time step the MPC controller searches for the solution of a new optimization problem, i.e., by obtaining new information about the current state, available prediction information, and goals.

The cost function of a control agent is defined in accordance to the application field and it is generally a function of the subsystem states and control actions that the agent controls over the prediction horizon N_p,

$$J_i\left(\tilde{\mathbf{x}}_{k,i}, \tilde{\mathbf{u}}_{k,i}, \tilde{\mathbf{x}}_{ref,i}\right) = \sum_{l=0}^{N_p-1} f\left(\mathbf{x}_i(k+1+l), \mathbf{u}_i(k+l), \mathbf{x}_{ref,i}(k)\right), \quad (13)$$

where $\tilde{\mathbf{x}}_{k,i}$ is the vector composed of the state-space vectors for each time step over the prediction horizon $\left[\mathbf{x}_i^T(k+1), \ldots, \mathbf{x}_i^T(k+N_p) \right]^T$, $\tilde{\mathbf{u}}_{k,i}$ is the vector composed of the control action vectors for each time step over the prediction horizon $\left[\mathbf{u}_i^T(k), \ldots, \mathbf{u}_i^T(k+N_p-1) \right]^T$, $\mathbf{x}_{\mathrm{ref},i}$ is the desired inventory level vector, $\tilde{\mathbf{x}}_{\mathrm{ref},i}$ is the vector composed of the desired inventory level vectors for each time step over the prediction horizon $\left[\mathbf{x}_{ref,i}^T(k), \ldots, \mathbf{x}_{ref,i}^T(k+N_p-1) \right]^T$ for control agent i. The MPC formulation for control agent i can be stated as:

$$\min_{\tilde{\mathbf{u}}_{k,i}} \quad J_i\left(\tilde{\mathbf{x}}_{k,i}, \tilde{\mathbf{u}}_{k,i}, \tilde{\mathbf{x}}_{\mathrm{ref},i}\right) \tag{14}$$

$$\text{subject to} \quad \mathbf{x}_i(k+1+l) = \mathbf{A}_i\mathbf{x}_i(k+l) + \mathbf{B}_{\mathrm{u}_i}\mathbf{u}_i(k+l) + \mathbf{B}_{\mathrm{d}_i}\mathbf{d}_i(k+l) + \ldots$$

$$\ldots + \sum_{j=1, j\neq i}^{n_c} \mathbf{B}_{\mathrm{u}_{i,j}}\mathbf{u}_j(k+l), \tag{15}$$

$$\mathbf{y}_i(k) = \mathbf{C}_i\mathbf{x}_i(k), \tag{16}$$

$$\mathbf{x}_i(k+1+l) \geq \mathbf{0}, \tag{17}$$

$$\mathbf{u}_i(k+l) \geq \mathbf{0}, \tag{18}$$

$$\mathbf{y}_i(k+l) \leq \mathbf{y}_{\mathrm{max},i}, \tag{19}$$

$$\mathbf{P}_{\mathrm{uu},i}\mathbf{u}_i(k+l) \leq \mathbf{u}_{\mathrm{max},i}, \tag{20}$$

$$\mathbf{x}_i(k+l) \geq \mathbf{P}_{\mathrm{xu},i}\mathbf{u}_i(k+l), \tag{21}$$

where $\mathbf{y}_{\mathrm{max},i}$ is the maximum capacity for the nodes of control agent i, $\mathbf{u}_{\mathrm{max},i}$ represents the available transport resources according to the network's structural layout for control agent i, $\mathbf{P}_{\mathrm{uu},i}$ is the projection matrix from the control action set $\mathcal{U}_i$ into the transport resource set for control agent i, $\mathbf{P}_{\mathrm{xu},i}$ is the projection from the control action set $\mathcal{U}_i$ into the state-space set $\mathcal{X}_i$.

3.2 Multi-agent Control Architecture

The order in which the control agents solve their problems at each time step can be fixed over time or depend on the current supply chain state and predictions. For the sake of simplicity we consider that the order $\mathbf{o}(k) = \left[o_1 \cdots o_{n_c} \right]$, with $1 \leq o_i \leq n_c$, by which the control agents solve their problems is fixed over time and is a supply chain configuration parameter set before the beginning of operations management. The order of control agents is set following a pull-flow perspective: first the control agents related to the end nodes solve their problems to keep the desired inventory levels. This will pull commodities from the distribution center level. Then the control agents related to the distribution centers solve their problems, pulling commodities from the consolidation level and so on, until the control agents that pull commodities from the source nodes.

The starting control agent is responsible for setting the total amount of transport capacity that is available $\theta^0 = \mathbf{u}_{\mathrm{max}}$ for the current time step and the current prediction for future decisions set $\mathcal{P}^0 = \{\tilde{\mathbf{u}}_{k-1,o_1}, \ldots, \tilde{\mathbf{u}}_{k-1,o_{n_c}}\}$. After the initial configuration iterations are executed. The starting control agent (o_1) has all transport capacity available. Each control agent o_i ($i = 1, \ldots, n_c$), one after another, performs the following steps at an iteration (see Fig. 3):

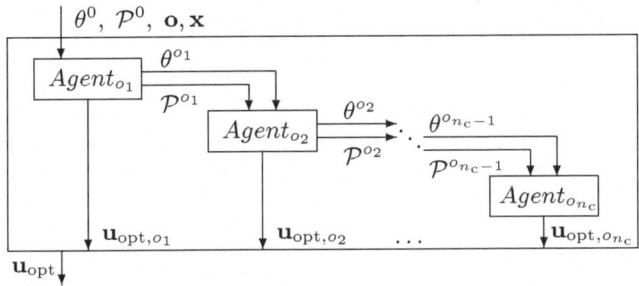

Fig. 3. Multi-agent control architecture schematics at a time step

- the maximum admissible transport capacity for control agent o_i is determined as the minimum between the subsystem maximum transport capacity $\mathbf{u}_{\max,o_i}$ and the transport capacity not yet assigned,

$$\mathbf{u}_{\max,o_i} = \min\left(\mathbf{P}_{\max,o_i}\theta^{o_{i-1}}; \mathbf{u}_{\max,o_i}\right), \tag{22}$$

where $\mathbf{P}_{\max,o_i}$ is the projection matrix from the global transport capacity set $\mathcal{U}_{\max}$ to the maximum transport capacity set $\mathcal{U}_{\max,o_i}$ for subsystem o_i;
- the optimal control action $\mathbf{u}_{\mathrm{opt},o_i}$ is the first time step component of the control agent optimal sequence over the prediction horizon $\tilde{\mathbf{u}}_{\mathrm{opt},o_i}$ found solving the MPC problem (14)–(21) for control agent i;
- the available transport capacity to the next control agent o_{i+1} is updated:

$$\theta^{o_{i+1}} = \theta^{o_i} - \mathbf{P}_{\mathrm{mu},o_i}(k)\mathbf{u}_{\mathrm{opt},o_i}(k), \tag{23}$$

where $\mathbf{P}_{\mathrm{mu},o_i}(k)$ is the projection matrix from control agent o_i handling resource set $\mathcal{U}_{o_i}$ to the control action set $\mathcal{U}_{\max}$;
- the predictions for future decisions are updated and denoted by $\mathcal{P}^{o_{i+1}}$ replacing the control agent initial prediction $\tilde{\mathbf{u}}_{k-1,o_i}$ by the new optimal sequence found $\tilde{\mathbf{u}}_{\mathrm{opt},o_i}$.

4   Simulation Experiments

The proposed architecture is applied to the supply chain presented in Fig. 2. We focus on addressing the supply chain operations management as a flow assignment problem using the multi-agent architecture presented in Section 3. The structural design of the supply chain is out of the scope of this paper. For the sake of clarity we consider constant inventory levels over time. The performance obtained with the multi-agent architecture will be evaluated for three different configurations concerning the prediction accuracy available to the control agents: exact prediction (Test A), constant prediction (Test B) and no prediction (Test C).

Table 1. Connection details for the considered supply chain

Parameters	c_1	c_2	c_3	c_4	c_5	c_6	c_7	c_8	c_9	c_{10}	c_{11}	c_{12}	c_{13}	c_{14}	c_{15}	c_{16}	c_{17}
Transport [hours]	14	8	8	8	14	8	8	6	8	12	10	8	8	10	12	8	6
Source node	62	62	63	64	64	65	65	66	66	66	66	66	67	67	67	67	67
End node	65	65	65	65	65	66	67	68	69	70	71	67	66	69	70	71	72
Nodes (n_{c_i})	6	3	3	3	6	3	3	2	3	5	4	3	3	4	5	3	2
Flows	7	4	4	4	7	4	4	3	4	6	5	4	4	5	6	4	3
Transport cost	1	5	5	5	1	5	5	5	5	5	5	5	5	5	5	5	5
Transport capacity	260	100	100	100	260	80	80	30	30	30	30	10	10	30	30	30	30

Table 2. Supply chain average demand for end nodes (quantity per time step)

Commodity	end node 68	end node 69	end node 70	end node 71	end node 72
A	7.0	9.8	12.6	9.8	7.0
B	8.4	8.4	11.2	1.2	5.6
C	5.6	7.0	9.8	8.4	4.2
Total	15	18	24	21	12

4.1 Setup

The supply chain monitoring and management decision update is done every 2 hours. All supply chain nodes work on a 24 hour daily basis. The end nodes are opened to clients from 8 am to 10 pm. The first disturbance will be available at 10 am translating the consumption per commodity type between 8 am and 10 am. The supply chain can be delivering commodities to supermarkets or raw materials to industries for example.

Using 2 hours as time step size, the transport delay per connection is translated into the required number of nodes to capture this phenomena (see Table 1). The supply chain model has 61 nodes to capture the transport delay for all connections: transport delays are assumed fixed. For end nodes 69, 70, and 71 commodities can be delivered from both distribution centers using a *master* connection (less transport time) or a *slave* connection (higher transport time). The supply chain demand is created as a random demand per time step for all commodities at the five end nodes (center nodes 68 to 72, for average values see Table 2). The inventory levels are set to support the associated average demand during two, three and two complete days for the end nodes, distribution centers, and consolidation center respectively. To increase the demand challenge applied to the supply chain two demand peaks are set: one at the fourth day (a factor of 1.5) and one at the eight day (a factor of 2).

Control agent i is assigned to connection i. All control agents solve the MPC problem using a prediction horizon of 7 steps corresponding to the biggest connection transport delay at the supply chain. As a cost function a linear penalty for deviations from the desired inventory level and transport costs is used. The state weights for the objective function are set in a pull perspective; in that sense the benefit for staying at a *downstream* node has to be bigger than the benefit staying at an *upstream* node. The order by which the control agents solve their problems is the following: $c_{15}, c_{10}, c_{16}, c_{11}$,

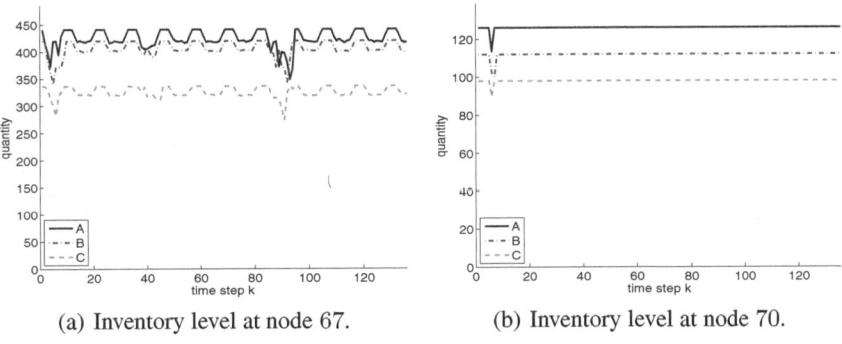

(a) Inventory level at node 67.   (b) Inventory level at node 70.

Fig. 4. Inventory levels for exact demand prediction (test A)

c_9, c_{14}, c_{17}, c_8, c_6, c_{13}, c_7, c_{12}, c_1, c_2, c_3, c_5 and c_4. When multiple connections arrive at the same center node priority was given to the closest or to the cheapest connection. The multi-agent architecture is solved at each time step of the simulation using the MPT v2.6.3 toolbox [11] with the CDD Criss–Cross solver for linear programming problems. The simulations are performed using MatLab R2009b on a personal computer with a processor Intel(R) Core(TM) i7 at 1.60 GHz with 8 GB RAM memory in a 64-bit Operating System.

4.2   Results Analysis

The computational burden can be associated to the control action matrices $\mathbf{B}_u$ and $\mathbf{B}_{u_i}$. Using the proposed decomposition it is possible to reduce the matrix dimension from 50544 elements to 2736, this is a reduction of 94.4%. Naturally the ratio of nonzero elements grows from 0.009 to 0.171. For test A, the average computation time for each time step was 27.04 s, with a maximum time of 40.8 s and a minimum time of 17.1 s.

Increasing the accuracy of the available demand prediction the multi-agent architecture is able to keep the desired inventory levels at the end nodes, see Fig. 4(b). The architecture uses the available prediction to anticipate future events and start to move commodities in advance. Although the inventory level at the end nodes remain constant the other nodes face variation in their inventory levels (see Fig. 4(a)). With an accuracy decrease on the demand prediction the control agents do not have the necessary information to anticipate correctly the future demand. As a consequence the inventory levels at the end nodes start to face bigger oscillations and can run out of stock (see Fig. 5). As is to be expected, the average deviation from the initial inventory level is smaller for control agents that use exact demand prediction and is bigger for the case of no demand prediction (see Table 3). Due to the supply chain structural design all demand predictions show significant deviation at end node 68. The exact demand prediction concentrates all deviation in commodity C. End node 70 has the worst indicators among the exact demand prediction which is justified by the higher demand and transport delay from the distribution centers associated.

Fig. 6 shows the state evolution for connection 10 which is the *slave* connection for node 71. Commodities are only dispatched from the connection source node if they are

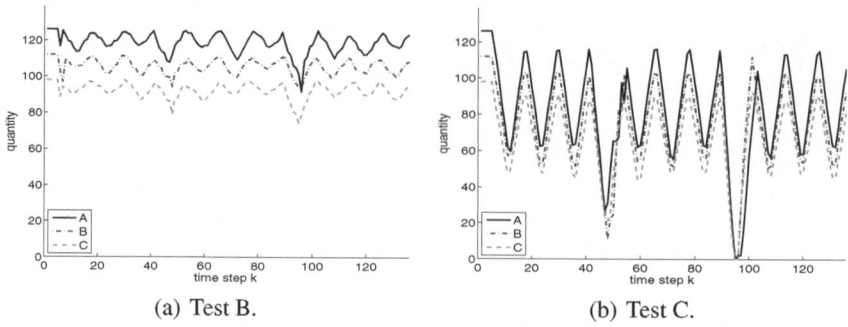

(a) Test B.

(b) Test C.

Fig. 5. Inventory levels at end node 70

Table 3. Inventory analysis for the entire simulation time (exact/close/none demand prediction), bold values stands for out of stock

Deviation	end node 68	end node 69	end node 70	end node 71	end node 72
$\max_A$	0.0/9.5/39.5	0/26.8/68.0	12.5/34.3/**126.0**	0.0/39.0/67.5	0.0/5.3/34.7
$\max_B$	0.0/31.7/73.6	0/12.1/**84.0**	11.8/18.0/**112.0**	0.0/28.6/**112.0**	0.0/6.2/30.2
$\max_C$	46.0/17.1/33.6	0/14.8/62.1	8.3/23.4/**98.0**	0.0/25.0/78.0	2.1/4.3/21.7
mean_A	0.0/2.2/11.8	0.0/3.6/22.4	0.1/7.4/43.5	0.0/4.2/22.4	0.0/1.8/11.5
mean_B	0.0/2.8/15.5	0.0/3.3/21.0	0.2/6.5/37.1	0.0/4.1/27.3	0.0/1.5/9.2
mean_C	1.5/1.9/9.7	0.0/2.8/16.1	0.1/5.8/32.3	0.0/3.6/21.4	0.0/1.2/7.0

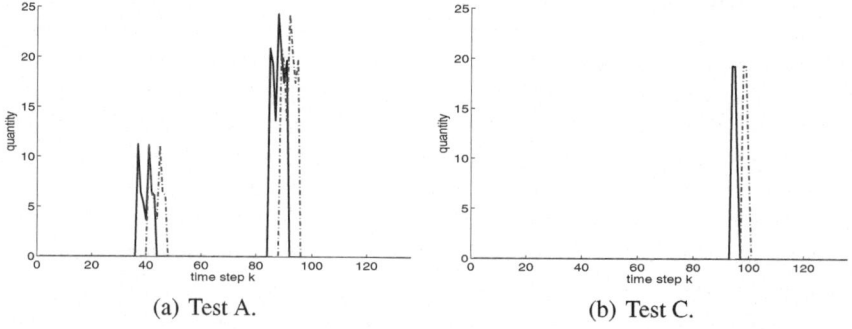

(a) Test A.

(b) Test C.

Fig. 6. Quantity of commodities at first and last nodes for connection 10 (full line: $\overline{x}_{i,1}$, dash-dot line: $\overline{x}_{i,n_{c_i}}$)

guaranteed to be accepted at the connection end node. There is no waiting queue at the connection. Decreasing the accuracy in demand prediction makes the slave connection to transports a lower volume of commodities leading to the decrease of inventory levels at the end node. For exact prediction, commodities are delivered at node 70 using the *master* connection with the ratios 1.00, 0.95, 0.77 for commodities of type A, B, and C respectively. As no distinguish is made in terms of commodities the *slave* connection has a higher impact for the last commodity type.

5   Conclusions and Future Research

The tracking control problem for multi-commodity supply chains has been addressed in this paper through a multi-agent control architecture using a pull-flow perspective. When the demand prediction is accurate the control architecture is able to continuously restore the inventory levels at the end nodes. This is the case in which the supply chain is delivering commodities to clients that know their demands in advance. For situations in which the demand is unknown by nature (as in the case of supermarkets) the control architecture performance will be depending on the prediction accuracy.

In future research the proposed control architecture will be extended to consider the inventory levels as a decision variable in the optimization problem. The question is to set the best level of inventories over the supply chain such that the demand is still fulfilled while minimizing storage costs. The case in which the supply chain is composed by distinct economic actors will also be considered. In this case, the information exchange between control agents is restricted and they may give conflicting objectives. Therefore, negotiation between control agents has to be included into the proposed architecture.

Acknowledgements. This research is supported by the VENI project "Intelligent multi-agent control for flexible coordination of transport hubs" (project 11210) of the Dutch Technology Foundation STW, a subdivision of the Netherlands Organisation for Scientific Research (NWO) and by the Portuguese Government, through Fundação para a Ciência e a Tecnologia, under the project PTDC/EEACRO/102 102/2008 - AQUANET, through IDMEC under LAETA.

References

1. Ballou, R.H.: Business Logistics – Supply Chain Management: Planning, Organizing, and Controlling the Supply Chain. Prentice Hall (2004)
2. Nabais, J.L., Negenborn, R.R., Botto, M.A.: Hierarchical Model Predictive Control for Optimizing Intermodal Container Terminal Operations. Submitted to a Conference (2012)
3. Maciejowski, J.M.: Predictive Control with Constraints. Prentice Hall, Harlow (2002)
4. Maestre, J.M., Muñoz de la Pena, D., Camacho, E.F.: Distributed MPC: A supply chain case. In: 48th IEEE Conference on Decision and Control and 28th Chinese Control Conference, Shanghai, China, pp. 7099–7104 (December 2009)
5. Geyer, T., Larsson, M., Morari, M.: Hybrid emergency voltage control in power systems. In: Proceedings of the European Control Conference, Cambridge, UK, paper 322 (2003)
6. Negenborn, R.R., Van Overloop, P.J., Keviczky, T., De Schutter, B.: Distributed model predictive control of irrigation canals. Networks and Heterogeneous Media 4, 359–380 (2009)
7. Hegyi, A., De Schutter, B., Hellendoorn, J.: Optimal coordination of variable speed limits to supress schock waves. IEEE Trans. Intelligent Transportation Systems 11(1), 102–112 (2005)
8. Ahuja, R.K., Magnanti, T.L., Orlin, J.B.: Network Flows. Prentice Hall, New Jersey (1993)
9. Sezer, M.E., Šiljak, D.D.: Decentralized Control. In: Levine, W.S. (ed.) The Control Handbook, pp. 779–793. CRC Press (1996)
10. Negenborn, R.R., Sahin, A., Lukszo, Z., De Schutter, B., Morari, M.: A non-iterative cascaded predictive control approach for control of irrigation canals. In: Proc. IEEE Int. Conf. on Systems, Man, and Cybernetics, San Antonio, Texas, pp. 3652–3657 (October 2009)
11. Kvasnica, M., Grieder, P., Baotić, M.: Multi-parametric toolbox, MPT (2004), http://control.ee.ethz.ch/~mpt/

Situated MAS Approach for Freight Trains Assembly

Pawel Pawlewski

Poznan University of Technology, ul.Strzelecka 11, 60-965 Poznań
pawel.pawlewski@put.poznan.pl

Abstract. The paper presents the results of conducted researches which concern one of the major cargo operators in Poland. The researches focus mainly on improving functioning cargo operator by developing a system for assisting the process of making decisions relating to setting a draft of trains. In the paper the requirements of the system assisting the dispatcher's decision making in a company providing cargo transport services are defined and data necessary to create a basis for decisions to be made are identified. Author proposes the idea of a "freezable database" as a solution facilitating the system for assisting the decision-making using situated multiagent technology.

Keywords: Situated Multi-agent systems, database, supply chain, transport.

1 Introduction

The Council of Supply Chain Management Professionals [1] defines supply chain management as follows: "Supply Chain Management encompasses the planning and management of all activities involved in sourcing and procurement, conversion, and all logistics management activities. Importantly, it also includes coordination and collaboration with channel partners, which can be suppliers, intermediaries, third-party service providers, and customers. In essence, supply chain management integrates supply and demand management within and across companies. Supply Chain Management is an integrating function with primary responsibility for linking major business functions and business processes within and across companies into a cohesive and high-performing business model. It includes all of the logistics management activities noted above, as well as manufacturing operations, and it drives coordination of processes and activities with and across marketing, sales, product design, finance and information technology."

The cooperation between companies that constitute a supply chain is one of the most significant factors affecting lives of the whole communities.

The comparison of the crisis in the automotive industry and the so-called dot-com bubble burst shows clearly that the impact of the automotive crisis on the world economy is much stronger. It is a clear example of how a supply chain influences the life of a whole region. The complexity of cars nowadays calls for a great number of diverse components used in the process of production. The Motor & Equipment Manufacturers Association (MEMA) estimates this number to be about 3,800 components. Given the fact that some components may have to be used more than once in a single

J.M. Corchado et al. (Eds.): PAAMS 2013 Workshops, CCIS 365, pp. 106–117, 2013.

car, their total number rises up to about 35,000. Such complexity and the general tendency to reduce the time and cost of delivery has encouraged the Original Equipment Manufacturers (OEMs) to seek different procedures in order to improve the designing, preparation and production processes on the global scale. The main goal of OEMs is to provide an offer that would base on the correlation between the product and the consumer's preferences by developing "build to order" products [2] which provide a wide range of options to be selected by customers. OEMs have to develop highly efficient manufacturing processes. Any optimization of material flows in manufacturing requires both identification of supporting processes on the system level, as well as a thorough analysis of operations involved. For contemporary manufacturing enterprises, which offer a rich portfolio of products and rely on vast networks of suppliers and customers, documenting the layout of these networks is both an effort and time-consuming task. On the one hand, such an effort poses a challenge capturing the complete picture of these networks on the process level, and on the other, it also requires identifying the activities having most impact on the supply chain effectiveness.

It is transport that makes it possible to implement the supply chain. In March 2011 the European Commission published the new White Paper on Transport. The new transport policy supports also the development of multimodal transport. These goals can be set into four main directions [3]:

1. reduction of the greenhouse gases emission by 60% by 2050 comparing to the 1990 level;
2. efficient core network for multimodal intercity travel and transport;
3. clear urban transport and commuting;
4. creating global hubs in the European Union for long-distance travel and intercontinental flights.

In order to achieve these goals, the European Commission states the following actions should be taken [3]:

- Halve the use of 'conventionally-fuelled' cars in urban transport by 2030; phase them out in cities by 2050; achieve essentially CO2-free city logistics in major urban centers by 2030;
- Reach 40% level of cow-carbon sustainable fuels in aviation by 2050; also by 2050 reduce EU CO2 emissions from maritime bunker fuels by 40% (if feasible 50%);
- 30% of road freight over 300 km should shift to other modes such as rail or waterborne transport by 2030, and more than 50% by 2050, facilitated by efficient and green freight corridors;
- By 2050, complete a European high-speed rail network. Triple the length of the existing high-speed rail network by 2030 and maintain a dense railway network in all Member States. By 2050 the majority of medium-distance passenger transport should go by rail;
- Establish a fully functional and EU-wide multimodal TEN-T 'core network' by 2030, with a high quality and capacity network by 2050 and a corresponding set of information services;

- By 2050, connect all core network airports to the rail network, preferably high-speed; ensure that all core seaports are sufficiently connected to the rail freight and, where possible, inland waterway system;
- Deploy the modernized air traffic management infrastructure (SESAR) in Europe by 2020 and complete the European Common Aviation Area; Deploy equivalent land and waterborne transport management systems (ERTMS – European Rail Traffic Management System, ITS – Intelligent Transport Systems for road transport, RIS – River Information Services, SSN – the EU's maritime information systems SafeSeaNet and LRIT – Long Range Identification and Tracking of vessels). Deploy the European Global Navigation Satellite System (Galileo);
- By 2020, establish the framework for a European multimodal transport information, management and payment system;
- By 2050, move close to zero fatalities in road transport. In line with this goal, the EU aims at halving road casualties by 2020. EU should be a world leader in safety and security of transport in all modes of transport.

The above mentioned actions support the optimization of the performance of multimodal logistic chains. They should also increase the efficiency of transport services and infrastructure utilization with application of the new schemes for information management.

The conducted investigations concern one of the major cargo operators in Poland and they focus mainly on improving its functioning by developing a system for assisting the process of making decisions relating to setting a draft of trains.

This papers highlights concentrate on:

- the requirements of the system assisting the dispatcher's decision making in a company providing cargo transport services,
- identifying data necessary to create a basis for decisions to be made,
- the idea of a "freezable database" as a solution facilitating the system for assisting the decision-making,
- the proposal of a multi-agent technology, which makes it possible to manage the operations of database freezing, especially on situated multi-agent system (SMAS) where the agents and the environment as treated as the complementary parts of a system, which can mutually affect each other.

The article is divided into six sections. Section 2 refers to the situation of PKP Cargo and challenges the company has to face. Section 3 defines the problem of assisting the dispatcher's decision making and Section 4 focuses on the technology to be applied. Section 5 presents solutions using agent technology for database freezing. Finally, Section 6 provides conclusions and suggestion for the further stages of the project.

2   Multimodal Transport in Supply Chain

The paper discusses issues related to the analysis of supply chains using multimodal approach. A supply chain is actually a complex and dynamic supply and demand network [4]. This network is formed by suppliers and companies which are connected using different kinds of transport. The identification of ineffective processes in both internal and external flow chains requires proper tools for the analysis and decision making.

Both logistic practice and literature on the subject provide various interpretations of intermodal and multimodal networks and transport [5]. These notions are similar in their scope and meaning, yet there are two significant differences between them. According to the Convention on International Multimodal Transport of Goods [6], the multimodal system of transport is defined as an internally integrated system of carrying goods along with accompanying services provided with use of at least two modes of transport on the basis of a multimodal transport contract. The multimodal transport contact is concluded by a multimodal transport operator who assumes responsibility for the performance of the contract. In case of intermodal transport, also at least two modes of transport are involved, however its specific feature is the fact that in the whole freight lane only one unit load is used.

The advantages of limiting the use of intermodal transport are as follows [7]:

- the possibility of offering combined freight services so that benefits can be derived from various modes of transport,
- the possibility of reducing the cost of moving goods without deteriorating the quality of freight services,
- the possibility of reducing damages and losses as well as handling and storage of goods by using pallets and containers,
- increasing the elasticity of deliveries by providing customers with better availability of services over time and space.

In simple words, we can assume that an intermodal chain of deliveries is a specific kind of multimodal logistics, which is characterized by a unified load unit, constant in the whole freight line. In the logistic practice the most commonly used multimodal solutions are sea-air transport and rail-air transport. The multimodality in transport results from the development of containerization: various modes of transport have become more closely related due to fact that the modes of freight, storage and loading of unified load units had to become similar[8].

One of the companies that implement transport between the elements of a supply chain is PKP Cargo Logistics [9] – the operator of a rail cargo system in Poland. It is one of the largest operators in Poland offering an extensive set of services that can be tailored for the needs of individual customers. PKP Cargo Logistics provides all top quality services within the transportation chain: from a given freight sender to receiver. The company specializes in rail, intermodal, motor and railroad-and-ferry transport and offers a wide range of services for external partners, e.g. servicing railway sidings. The potential of the group in the European market is reinforced by certificates allowing PKP Cargo Logistics for independent organization of transports in the Czech Republic, Germany and Slovakia. Owing to fact that the company PKP Cargo International was established, with its seat located in Bratislava, there are plans to develop transport services entirely outside Poland, mainly in the countries of Central and Southern Europe. The group possesses 2.7 thousand locomotives and almost

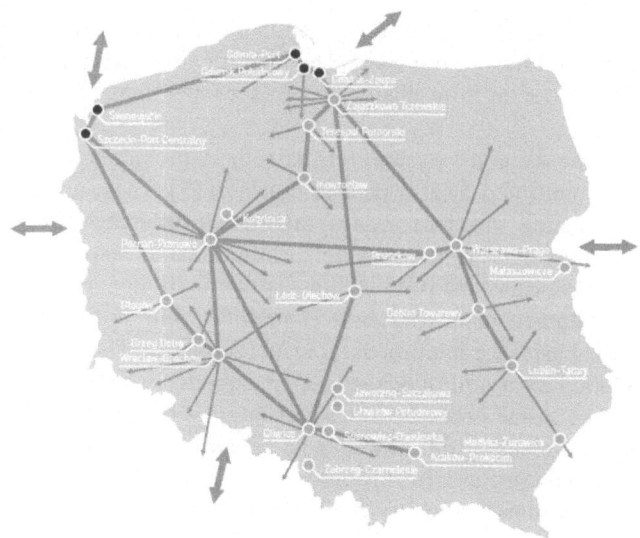

Fig. 1. Logistics centers an terminals in Poland [9]

70,000 freight railway cars. Railway rolling stock is repaired by the company's own technical facilities. Moreover, the group has its own logistics centers and terminals in the most important locations in Poland, e.g. on the land and sea borders (Figure 1)

Throughout the last ten years PKP Cargo provided a wide range of services, such as:

- conventional transportation of consignments, such as full load trains or in the form of distributed transportation, both domestically and internationally,
- intermodal transport, including extensive service of all freight units: containers, semitrailers and swap bodies, full customer service in container terminals as well as reloading and storage of goods in cargo handling areas in border regions,
- railroad-and-ferry transport on the route from Świnoujście to Ystad,
- transport of cars,
- specialized transport services of extraordinary and dangerous loads.

3 Problem Definition

PKP Cargo Logistics has made investments into the monitoring of trains (drafts of cars) in particular regions. Such an investment makes it possible to keep track of the train courses, providing current information and technical data of individual locomotives. The applied GPS technology allows for observing the status of particular railway lines in an Internet browser: pointing to an object with mouse will display information about a train, its timetable, delays, the technical data of a locomotive. On the basis of the obtained information next steps, related with assisting the dispatcher's decisions, can be taken. The dispatcher's decision making is about matching a locomotive, freight railway cars and engine driver so that the requested criteria are met in the best possible way. Current decisions are made by dispatchers whose experience and intuition play a crucial role in the process. However, contemporarily, the amount of available information goes far beyond human perception abilities and, therefore, it is necessary to deploy an assisting system. In this context, the main objective of the project is to develop an IT application assisting the dispatcher's decision making. The idea of the assistance is to generate a list of the best relations:

locomotive <> train <> engine driver

based on information obtained from monitoring train courses, status of locomotives and status of engine drivers. The notion of the best relations refers to the main objective function, which is defined in the following way:

- minimization of the number of locomotives in motion,
- maximization of the number of locomotives awaiting allocation,
- minimization of assignment-awaiting time of a locomotive,
- and an additional objective function:
- minimization of the number of employed engine drivers,
- maximization of the number of engine drivers awaiting assignment,
- minimization of assignment-awaiting time of an engine driver.

It should be emphasized that the objective function here is different than that defined, for instance, for an airline, i.e. maximizing the number of planes in motion.

The developed application ought to be designed in such a way that it can be used as a component assisting and improving the operation of the rail traffic management system in a given area. The applied standards should be compatible with ERTMS – European Rail Traffic Management System, the standard introduced in the European Union.

As already mentioned, the application provides a list of the best relations. Yet, the final decision is made by a dispatcher, who has to accept or reject the list in a given period of time, e.g. within 30 minutes since it was issued. In case the list is rejected, a reason must be given why there is a need to search for another best solution.

The application has to take into account limitations, where the set of limitations can be defined. The possible limitations are, e.g.:

- train stoppage time no shorter than 90 minutes,
- return of a locomotive to the home station due to inspection – time limit no later than 2 days before the inspection,
- time for "awaiting the best solution" between consecutive decisions – a quarter of an hour.

At the same time, certain rules need to be obeyed and they also can be defined, for instance:

- Assign a locomotive to the a train closest in geographical terms.
- Assign a engine driver to a train closest in geographical terms.
- Match the right type of locomotive to the proper train and route parameters.
- Now, the data have been defined that are the basis for searching the best relations:

- Traction vehicle – a locomotive, i.e. one object; yet, there may possibly be two locomotives for one train (this case is now ignored)
- Traction team – an engine driver, i.e. one object

The database of engine drivers includes the knowledge of routes by a driver and the knowledge of a locomotive; therefore the following relationships are important:

Type of engine driver <-> type of route
Type of engine driver <-> type of locomotive

- Trains – the possible status of trains
  AWAITING – number of trains awaiting a locomotive off the track
  ON THE ROUTE – number of trains on the track
  ARRIVAL at the destination
  RUN WITHOUT locomotive change, yet with engine driver change
  RUN WITH locomotive change and river change
  ASSIGNED – number of trains with assigned locomotives
- Locomotives – possible states of locomotives
  ON THE ROUTE – number of locomotives on the routes
  ARRIVAL at the destination
  PASSING – they continue running the same train (ON/OFF THE ROUTE)
  NOT ASSIGNED locomotives – have no job to do
  REPAIR SHOP – number of locomotives in a repair shop – completion time is crucial – it affects decisions on the assignment
- Disturbances
  Objective delays – types of delays
  Breakdowns – types of breakdowns
  Accidents – types of accidents
- Timetable in which routes are defined – the problem of route selection is not the subject of the project, however, the project must be compatible with the current timetable and decision module in the traffic management system.
- Locomotive parameters
- Train parameters
- Route parameters (or decision variables: in case of the project they will define limitations and boundary conditions for the presented optimization problem)

It should be taken into consideration that the presented-above data change dynamically in time, which is obviously related with rail traffic.

4   Situated Multiagent Technologies

For the designed application a situated multi-agent system (SMAS) idea will be used. The main idea of a situated MAS (SMAS) is to define the agents and the environment as complementary parts of a system, which can mutually affect each other [10]. A classical MAS is usually defined as a loosely coupled network of problem solvers (agents) that are autonomous, heterogeneous in nature and interact with each other and with an environment they are situated in [11]. Each agent has incomplete information about the problem, access to local decentralized data and acts in an asynchronous mode, which means that there is no global system control. Agents, thanks to their capability of executing in a proactive way and reacting to the environment changes, can easily adapt to the situated space dynamism, heterogeneity and unpredictability. The agents' sociality allows the scalable decomposition of the decentralized agent organizations and enables autonomous interactions of agents from different classes, as happens in the human real world [12].

Situated computing is viewed as a new activity-centered computational paradigm, in which applications are increasingly embedded into a physical environment and can understand the user's behavior. The analysis of changes in the user context and activities is necessary to get information about the user's situation independently of applications. This information is passed to applications to enhance interaction with them. Dealing with the increasing applications is a big challenge for software engineers. In the last 20 years, multi-agent systems (MAS) have been put forward as a key methodology to develop and to tackle the complexity of self-managing large-scale distributed systems and can be applied in solving the problems with the social components.

As mentioned above, the main idea of a situated MAS (SMAS) is to define the agents and the environment as the complementary parts of a system, which can mutually affect each other [13]. The situated environment determines the situated agents' perception and influences their deliberation and actions. Contrary to knowledge-based agents, situated agents do not use long-term prediction and planning of their actions. They perform situated actions, which are determined by the current agent's position and the state of the environment. The actions of the agents in the situated computing can be executed simultaneously and can interfere with one another. The environment in this system is much more than just an infrastructure for message brokering and transport systems. In SMAS both agents and environment can be extended to the first-ordered application level, where application environment defines an abstract representation of the domain, in which situated agents operate. Thus, the SMAS is usually modeled as a multi-layer heterogeneous system with different types of agents and environment representation at each level.

The general concept of three-level model of situated MAS [14] is depicted in Figure 2.

It is composed of the following three layers:

- MAS application layer, which usually consists of two-sublayers: the application specific logic, where application agents and environment are situated, and a supporting MAS framework. Agents in this layer are the autonomous entities which can interact with the environment and other agents using some logical rules. The application environment provides an application specific representation of the domain to the agents.
- Execution platform layer composed by a middleware and an operating system. Middleware offers a software platform on which distributed applications can be executed. It provides support for remote procedure calls, threading, load balancing, communication, etc.
- Physical infrastructure layer built up of the processors, network, etc., on which the execution platform is run.

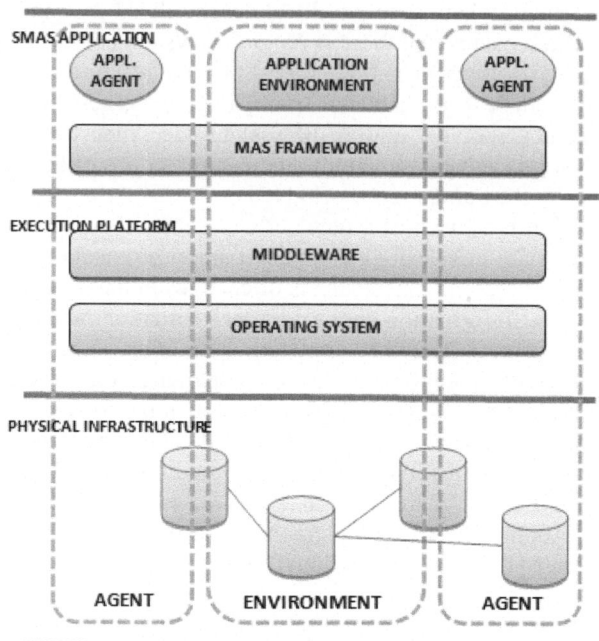

Fig. 2. Three-level model of situated MAS (based on [14])

The physical infrastructure in the model can be centralized or distributed, as a constraint of the application or a result of the well-considered architectural decision. In a centralized setting, agents experience the environment as one shared entity that is locally accessible. In a distributed setting, agents can be aware of distribution or distribution may be transparent to agents. Distribution of an environment is supported by the generic middleware infrastructure. The agents and the environment in fact span all three-layers of the model (depicted by dashed lines in Figure 2). Formally, a situated agent is defined as an application agent, which is 'separated' from the agents' infrastructure. However, the implementation of the application agent is based on the MAS framework model that exploits middleware and the operating system. Finally, the agent's software is executed on physical devices. The analogous characteristics can be defined for the environment.

5   Proposed Solution

In the proposed solution the following process assumption has been made: a process is assigned to an object, therefore as process we understand a specific train in motion or awaiting. It is crucial here to determine the process boundaries: the beginning and the end of a process. It isI assumed that the process boundaries are as follows: for the process beginning – the moment a train enters a region or when it starts its run, for the process end – the moments it leaves a region or when it finishes its run.

The boundaries of a system are marked by the geographical area of a region according to the structure of PKP Cargo.

The designed SMAS can contain two main types of agents, namely (a) sensor agents responsible for managing information, and (b) effector agents performing actions on the ambient where they live. An environment is modeled as a 3D virtual domain. All information data is recorded in a database. The proposed solution is based on the concept of "freezable database", whereas two versions will be considered: operation "on demand" and operation "in the background".

In the version "application operating on demand" (Figure 3), the following scenario of operations was applied:

- A dispatcher generates a signal informing of the intention to make a decision.
- A contemporary database is created, as an effect of collecting data from available sources.
- Database is "frozen" for a specified period of time.
- The algorithm of "resource allocation' operates on the "frozen" database.
- The "list of the best relations " locomotive<->train<->engine driver is generated.
- Data is deleted or copied to the database.

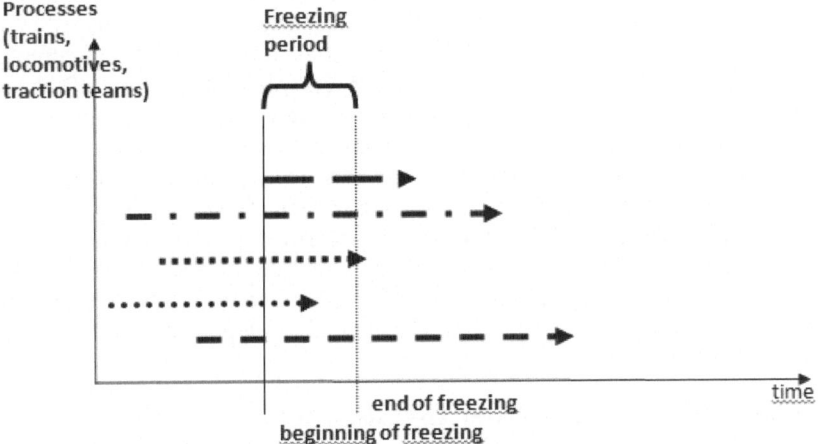

Fig. 3. "Freezing" of database version 1

In the version "application operating in the background" (Figure 4) the following scenario of operations was applied:

- Software agent creates and freezes a database once in a while, for example in cycles.
- In a given point in time there are two databases "frozen" and "freezable". As a result, operations should be faster – unless the time of "freezing", consisting of time of database making and data collecting, is significant.

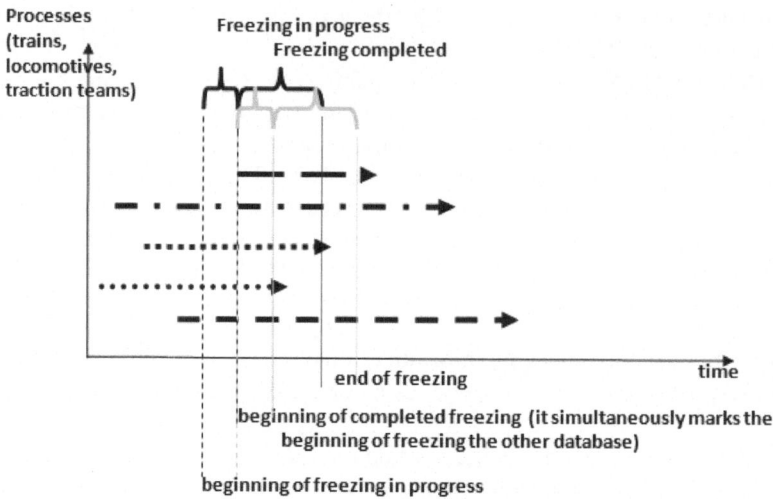

Fig. 4. "Freezing" of database version 2

Additional information about the current state of the environment and the monitoring of the whole system is provided by a web portal. The system is managed in a centralized way by an operating center. The interactions among the system components are managed (and allowed) by the middleware layer, which plays a role of the service provider in the system. The middleware can accept 'raw data' and 'commands' as the input. The raw data come from the sensor agents and they are passed to the 'conversion logic' module, which decides about the data storing and/or translation. Commands are issued by the components to obtain a service. They are passed to the 'core' or to the 'look-up table' modules that contain information about all system components. The whole system can be executed at a mobile ad hoc network (MANET) infrastructure, physical p2p networks. JADE or multichannel adaptive information system (MAIS) reflective architecture can be applied to support this model.

6   Conclusions and Further Investigations

The article presents the results of current investigations on developing an application assisting dispatcher's decision making with use of multi-agent technologies. A special emphasis was put on deploying the idea of situated multi-agent system SMAS. Another proposed solution was database system based on the concept of the so called "freezable database", which makes it possible to assign locomotives and engine drivers (resources) in dynamically changing conditions. Further stages of investigations will include:

- Determining the availability of data, their sources, rules, limitations and objective function. The result will be a project of "freezable database" with data sources, recommendations for obtaining data, determination of rules, detailed objective functions.
- Developing an algorithm.

- Validation of the algorithm – both in a simulation system and a real system.
- Project of implementation. The result will be documentation of the implementation, determination of milestones, definition of implementation parameters, determination of measuring instruments and methods.

References

1. http://cscmp.org/about-us/supply-chain-management-definitions (2012)
2. Holweg, M., Pil, F.K.: The Second Century. Reconnecting Customer and Value Chain through Build-To-Order. MIT Press, Cambridge (2004)
3. Roadmap to a Single European Transport Area – Towards a competitive and resource efficient transport system. COM, Brussels (March 28, 2011)
4. Wieland A., Wallenburg C.M.: Supply-Chain-Management in stürmischen Zeiten, Berlin (2011)
5. Golinska, P., Hajdul, M.: Agent-Based System for Planning and Coordination of Intermodal Transport. In: Corchado, J.M., Pérez, J.B., Hallenborg, K., Golinska, P., Corchuelo, R. (eds.) Trends in PAAMS. AISC, vol. 90, pp. 99–107. Springer, Heidelberg (2011)
6. UNC - United Nations Convention on International Multimodal Transport of Goods, Geneva, May 24 (1980)
7. Seidl, M., Šimák, L.: Integracja transportu w systemach logistycznych, Zeszyty Naukowe. Logistyka i Transport/Międzynarodowa Wyższa Szkoła Logistyki i Transportu we Wrocławiu 1(8), s.159–s.167 (2009)
8. Bocewicz, G., Banaszak, Z.: Declarative modeling of multimodal cyclic processes. In: Golinska, P., Fertsch, M., Marx-Gómez, J. (eds.) Information Technologies in Environmental Engineering. Environmental Science and Engineering – Environmental Engineering, vol. 3, pp. 551–568. Springer, Heidelberg (2011)
9. https://www.pkp-cargo.pl/adx/file/album_10latpkpcargo.pdf (2011)
10. Weyns, D., Holvoet, T.: A Formal Model for Situated Multi-Agent Systems. Fundamenta Informaticae 63, 1–34 (2004)
11. Wooldridge, M.: Intelligent Agents. In: Weiss, G. (ed.) Multiagent Systems: A Modern Approach to Distributed Artificial Intelligence, ch. 1, pp. 27–77. The MIT Press, Cambridge (1999)
12. Siebers, P.O., Macal, C.M., Garnett, J., Buxton, D., Pidd, M.: Discrete-Event Simulation is Dead, Long Live Agent-Based Simulation! Journal of Simulation 4(3), 204–210 (2010)
13. Kolodziej, J., Xhafa, F.: Supporting situated computing with intelligent multi-agent systems. International Journal of 'Space Based and Situated Computing' 1(1), 30–42 (2011)
14. Weyns, D., Vizzari, G., Holvoet, T.: Environments for Situated Multi-agent Systems: Beyond Infrastructure. In: Weyns, D., Van Dyke Parunak, H., Michel, F. (eds.) E4MAS 2005. LNCS (LNAI), vol. 3830, pp. 1–17. Springer, Heidelberg (2006)

Simultaneous Scheduling of Machines and Mobile Robots

Quang-Vinh Dang and Izabela Nielsen

Dept. of Mechanical and Manufacturing Engineering, Aalborg University, Aalborg, Denmark
{vinhise,izabela}@m-tech.aau.dk

Abstract. This paper deals with the problem of simultaneously scheduling machines and a number of autonomous mobile robots in a flexible manufacturing system (FMS). Besides capability of transporting materials between machines, the considered mobile robots are different from other material handling devices in terms of their advanced ability to perform tasks at machines by using their manipulation arms. The mobile robots thus have to be scheduled in relation to scheduling of machines so as to increase the efficiency of the overall system. The performance criterion is to minimize time required to complete all tasks or makespan. A heuristic based on genetic algorithm is developed to find the best solution for the problem. A numerical example is investigated to demonstrate results of the proposed approach. The implementation of the proposed approach in a multi-agent system is also generally described.

Keywords: Scheduling, Mobile Robots, Genetic Algorithm, FMS.

1 Introduction

The automation technology in combination with advances in production management has dramatically changed the equipment used by manufacturing companies as well as the issues in planning and control. With these changes, highly automated and unmanned production systems have become more popular in several industrial areas, e.g., automotive, chemical, robot, and pump manufacturing. An automatic production system consists of intelligent and flexible machines and mobile robots grouped into cells in such a way that entire production of each product can be performed within one of the cells. Mobile robots capable of moving around within their environment and not fixed to one physical location are among various advanced material handling techniques that are finding increasing applications in today manufacturing. However, besides transporting a variety of part types from one point to another without human intervention, mobile robots are more significantly advanced than automated guided vehicles (AGVs) in the capability of performing various value-added tasks on different machines (or workstations) based on their manipulation arms. The tasks include such processes as machine tending, pre-assembly, and quality inspection. Moreover, using mobile robots can lead to production efficiency gains such as less energy usage or lower tool-changing costs than typical industrial robots. The advanced abilities of the mobile robots pay the way for establishing transformable production systems that combine the best features of both fully automated and strictly manual manufacturing

J.M. Corchado et al. (Eds.): PAAMS 2013 Workshops, CCIS 365, pp. 118–128, 2013.
© Springer-Verlag Berlin Heidelberg 2013

environments. In this paper, a particular problem is taken into account. The problem consists of a number of operations of different tasks which are processed on flexible machines. The processes of the operations need the participation of the mobile robots which not only transport parts of tasks from one machine to another where needed but also perform the operations of tasks on the machines. In that context, mobile robots play the role of agents, attempting to reach goals while following rules specific for a given production system. The considered systems are thus treated as multi-agents ones in which each robot can be seen as an autonomous object capable of undertaking decisions about moving, feeding, and completing operations, etc. [6]. However, to utilize the systems in an efficient manner requires the ability to properly schedule operations of tasks on machines and agents. Hence, it is important to plan in which sequence the machines and agents process the operations so that performance criteria can be achieved while satisfying a number of practical constraints.

The problem of simultaneous scheduling of machines and mobile robots has been modeled in several respects comparable to the problems of simultaneous scheduling of machines and AGVs which have attracted interest of researchers in recent decades. Ulusoy and Bilge [13] and Bilge and Ulusoy [2] propose an iterative heuristic based on the decomposition of the master problem into two sub-problems. Ulusoy et al. [14] describe a genetic algorithm (GA) approach for concurrent scheduling machines and AGVs. Abdelmaguid et al. [1] introduce a hybrid method composed of a GA for scheduling of machines and a heuristic for scheduling of vehicles. Jerald et al. [10] deal with the problem of scheduling of parts and AGVs in an FMS environment using adaptive GA. Reddy and Rao [12] present a hybrid multi-objective GA for scheduling of machines and AGVs in FMS. Lin et al. [11] model an AGV system by using network structure and propose an effective evolutionary approach for solving a kind of AGV problems. Deroussi et al. [8] develop a simple metaheuristic approach in which a new solution representation based on vehicles rather than machines to solve the problem of simultaneous scheduling of machines and AGVs. Bocewicz et al. [3-4] deal with the problem of AGV operation synchronization mechanism in FMSs where transport processes can be modeled as a system of cyclic concurrent processes sharing common resources, e.g., machines. Bocewicz and Banaszak [5] present a new modeling framework enabling to prototype and evaluate multimodal cyclic processes, e.g., vehicles, which share common machines while comparing their cyclic steady state.

Although much related research has been completed, the problem of simultaneous scheduling of machines and mobile robots has not yet been studied in the literature. Furthermore, the surveyed genetic algorithms to agent-based solutions are not well suited and cannot be directly used to solve this problem due to the lack of a suitable mechanism to simultaneously assign tasks to machines and mobile robots while taking into account precedence and routing constraints. In this problem, the considered mobile robots have not only the capability of transporting parts of tasks similar to other material-handling devices but also the advanced capability of performing tasks at destination machines by using their manipulation arms. In other words, after transporting parts of the tasks to the destination machines, the mobile robots have to stay at those machines and complete performing the tasks before moving to other places. Moreover, this problem is composed of two interrelated decision problems that are scheduling of machines and scheduling of mobile robots (or vehicles). Both problems are known to be NP-hard [8] resulting in a more complicated NP-hard problem when they are taken into account simultaneously. In that context, our main contribution is to develop a computationally efficient heuristic based on genetic algorithm, a promising algorithm to this class of problems, so as to find the best solutions for the problem of simultaneous scheduling machines and mobile robots. Compared to other optimization methods, the major benefit of GA regards multiple directional search using a set/population of candidate solutions which enables GA to search in several directions simultaneously. In this way, many paths to the optimum are processed in parallel that leads to a clear improvement in performance. Furthermore, since information from many different regions is used, GA is resistant to remain trapped in a suboptimal solution and able to move away from it if the population finds better solutions in other areas. In this paper, the best solutions achieved by the genetic algorithm-based heuristic are useful for decision making at operational levels and the proposed approach enables to model and evaluate scheduling tasks of multi-agent systems.

The remainder of this paper is organized as follows: in the next section, problem description is presented while a heuristic based on genetic algorithm is developed in Section 3. A numerical example is conducted to demonstrate results of the proposed approach in Section 4. Section 5 generally describes how the proposed approach has been implemented and interacted with other components in a multi-agent system. Finally, conclusions and future research directions are drawn in Section 6.

2   Problem Description

The work is developed for an FMS which products parts or components for the pump manufacturing industry at a factory. In the FMS, a set of independent tasks has to be processed without pre-emption on a set of machine tools along with a set of identical mobile robots (agents). Each task consists of a sequence of operations. Each machine and each mobile robot can process only one operation at one time, and each operation can be processed by only one machine and one mobile robot at the same time. Note that in this FMS processing operations at machines has the participation of mobile robots. This results from the mobile robots' advanced abilities which enable them not only to transport parts from one machine to another but also performing operations on the machines to which the parts are transported. The considered FMS can be seen as a multi-agent system.

To enable the construction of a simultaneous schedule for the machines and mobile robots, assumptions are considered as follows:

- Each task is available at the beginning of the scheduling period.
- Each operation sequence of each task (the routing of each part type) is available before making scheduling decisions.
- Each mobile robot can transport only one kind of parts at a time.
- There is sufficient output buffer space at each machine.
- Traveling time is only machine-dependent and deterministic. Processing time is also deterministic.
- Such issues as traffic congestions, mobile robot collisions, machine failures, scraps are not considered in this paper.

Making decisions on scheduling machines and mobile robots simultaneously is a part of the real-time activities of production planners. It means that the best solution must be quickly obtained at the beginning of (re)scheduling periods. Furthermore, concerning the problem belonging to NP-hard class, computation time exponentially grows with the size of the problem, e.g., more number of tasks, machines, or mobile robots. It is therefore necessary to develop a computationally effective algorithm, namely a GA-based heuristic, which determines in which sequence the machines and mobile robots should handle tasks so as to minimize time required to complete all tasks or makespan while satisfying a number of practical constraints.

3   Genetic Algorithm-Based Heuristic

In this section a genetic algorithm, a broadly applicable search approach imitating the evolutionary process in nature, is used to develop a heuristic which is allowed to convert the mentioned problem to the way that best solutions could be found. In GAs, each individual solution is represented in the form of a finite length string called a chromosome. A chromosome is composed of a set of locations known as genes that contain discrete values pertaining to a problem solution. Through the use of genetic operators such as crossover, mutation, and selection to the chromosomes of selected solutions are in a systematic fashion to generate a new generation of solutions moving towards the optimization of certain criteria [9]. The GA-based heuristic shown in Fig. 1 consists of the following main steps: genetic representation; initialization; decoding operator and fitness evaluation; genetic operators including selection, crossover, and mutation; repair operator; termination criteria.

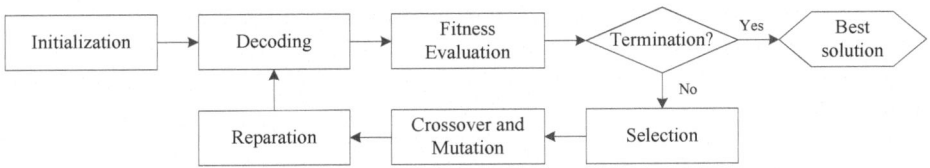

Fig. 1. Flow chart of GA-based heuristic

3.1   Genetic Representation

One of the main concerns when applying GAs to an optimization problem is to find an appropriate coding scheme that transforms feasible solutions into representations amenable to genetic search and reversibly decode these representations [1]. For the problem under consideration, a feasible solution can be encoded by a chromosome representing both operation sequencing and mobile robot assignment. Consequently, each gene in the chromosome is made up of two parts. The first part refers to an operation on a specific machine which is assumed to be scheduled at its earliest starting time. The second part identifies the mobile robot that will transport parts from any machine to that machine and then perform that operation on that machine. The chromosome length is equal to the total number of operations of all tasks. Fig. 2 below illustrates a feasible chromosome of an example problem with 5 operations of 2 tasks, 3 machines, and 2 mobile robots.

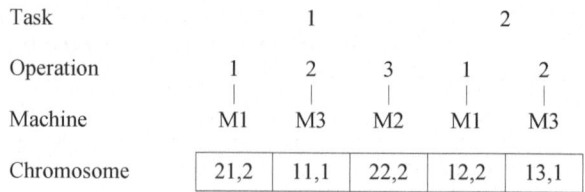

Fig. 2. Illustration of a feasible chromosome

3.2   Initialization

Random chromosomes are generated for providing solutions to the initial population. A chromosome is constructed of gene by gene. Each gene is first assigned an eligible operation (an operation is said to be eligible if all its predecessors are assigned). Then, one of the mobile robots is randomly chosen to complete the gene. If the chromosome is not yet complete, the eligible set of operations is updated and the process continues. The pseudocode of the initialization method is given below.

```
Procedure: Initialization
Begin
    D ← {op_i|op_i: first operations of all tasks};
    R ← {1,...,n_r};//n_r: number of mobile robots;
    Repeat
       Select an operation op_i ∈ D;
       Assign op_i to a mobile robot mr ▢ R;
       D ← D/{op_i};
       If (successor of op_i exists) Then
          D ← D ∪ {successor of op_i};
    Until (D := ∅)
End
```

3.3   Decoding Operator and Fitness Evaluation

The decoding operator and fitness evaluation are described in the pseudocode below.

```
Procedure: Decoding and Fitness Evaluation
Begin
   For i = 1 To chromosome_length
      op ← operation at location i in the chromosome;
      mc ← machine of op;
      pd ← predecessor of op in the task sequence;
      mr ← mobile robot of op;
      If (pd := ∅) Then st ← 0;
      Else st ← pd.completion_time;
      ns ← number of scheduled operations on machine mc;
      If (ns > 0) Then
         ls ← last operation scheduled on machine mc;
         ct ← ls.completion_time;
```

```
    If (st < ct) Then st ← ct;
sr ← mr.last_work_destination;
    If (pd ≠ ∅) Then md ← machine of pd;
    Else md ← or;
    et ← travel time between sr and md;
    lt ← travel time between md and mc;
    ft ← Max(pd.completion_time, mr.last_work_time) + et
                                                    + lt;

    If (st < ft) Then st ← ft;
    op.completion_time ← st + op.processing_time;
    mr.last_work_time ← op.completion_time;
    Schedule op on machine mc and mobile robot mr;
  End
  C_max ← Max(op_j.completion_time|op_j: last operations of
                                        all tasks);
End
```

3.4   Genetic Operators

Selection, crossover, and mutation are three main genetic operators. For selection, various evolutionary methods can be applied to this problem. $(\mu + \lambda)$ selection is used to choose chromosomes for reproduction. Under this method, μ parents and λ offspring compete for survival and the μ best out of the set of offspring and old parents, i.e. the μ lowest in term of the makespan, are selected as the parents of the next generation. This selection method guarantees that the best solutions up to now are always in the parent generation [6-7].

Crossover operator generates offspring by combining the information contained in the parent chromosomes so that the offspring will have desirable features from their parents. The Roulette-wheel selection is first used to select the parent chromosomes based on their fitness values. Then, a uniform crossover operated with probability P_c will be used to generate offspring as follows. Starting from the first operations on the parents, iteratively, one of the parents is randomly selected. The next unconsidered operation of the selected parent becomes the next operation on the first offspring while the next unconsidered operation of the other parent is the next operation of the second offspring. If the mobile robot selected for that operation is the same on both parents, then that selection is also made on the child; if not, one of the mobile robots of the parents is randomly chosen. Fig. 3 below depicts the uniform crossover.

Mutation operator produces spontaneous random changes in various chromosomes. For the current encoding method, there are two mutation operators, one for each part of a gene and with a probability P_m. The first mutation operator selects two random positions on a chromosome and swaps the operations with respect to those positions. Note that the chromosome may be infeasible in terms of precedence constraints after the operation mutation. Hence it has to be adjusted by using the repair operator in Section 3.5. The second mutation operator replaces the mobile robot assignment at a gene with one of the mobile robots which is randomly chosen. This may lead to the same mobile robot assignment for a particular gene, and aim to prevent the loss of any good assignment.

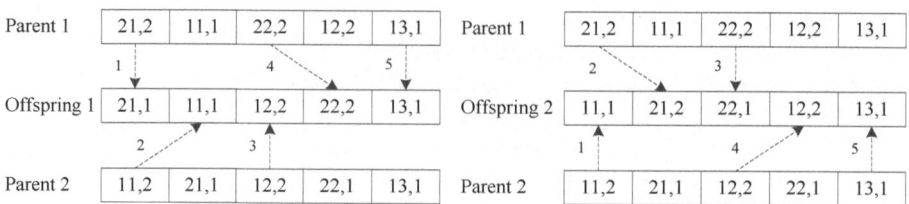

Fig. 3. Uniform crossover

3.5   Repair Operator

A repair operator is developed to validate chromosomes with any precedence violations after the mutation operators. This operator involves the exchange of locations of
operations belonging to the same task such that a valid sequence of operations is
achieved. The following pseudocode describes how the repair operator works.

```
Procedure: Repair Operator
Begin
   For i = 1 To chromosome_length - 1
      opᵢ ← operation at location i in the chromosome;
      pdᵢ ← predecessor of opᵢ in the task sequence;
      ex ← True
      Repeat While (pdᵢ ≠ Ø) And (ex := True)
         For j = i + 1 To chromosome_length
            opⱼ ← operation at location j in the chromosome;
            If (pdᵢ := opⱼ) Then
               ex ← True;
               Exchange locations of opᵢ and opⱼ;
               Update opᵢ at location i and pdᵢ of opᵢ;
               Exit For
            Else ex ← False;
         End
   End
End
```

3.6   Termination Criteria

Termination criteria are used to determine when the GA-based heuristic should be
stopped. Note that making decision on which sequence mobile robots and machines
should handle tasks is a part of real-time activities of production planners. Therefore,
on the one hand, if the best solutions over generations do not converge to a value, the
maximum generation G_m would be used to stop the run. On the other hand, if the best
solution does not improve over G_c consecutive generations, it would not be valuable
to continue searching.

4   Numerical Example

In this section, an example problem is generated to examine performance of the GA-based heuristic. An FMS in the example problem has three machines M1, M2, and M3. There independent tasks with a total of seven operations are to be carried out. Two identical mobile robots are used to process the operations on three machines. The processing times of the operations are given in Table 1. This table also gives the precedence constraints among the operations in each task, e.g., the second operation of task 1 can be carried out only after the first operation of task 1 is complete. The traveling times of mobile robots from one machine to another are given in Table 2.

Table 1. Processing time of operations of tasks

Task	Operation	Machine	Processing time
1	1	M1	30
	2	M3	42
2	1	M2	24
	2	M1	18
	3	M3	36
3	1	M2	30
	2	M3	24

Table 2. Traveling time of robots from one machine to another

From/To	M1	M2	M3
M1	0	12	12
M2	16	0	20
M3	12	12	0

For GA parameters, the population size of 50 is used and probabilities of crossover P_c and mutation P_m are set to be 0.6 and 0.1, respectively. The termination is stop at the generation G_m of 200 or if no improvement is made after G_c of 50 generations. The proposed heuristic has been programmed in VB.NET and run on a PC having an Intel® Core i5 2.67 GHz processor and 4GB RAM. Fig. 4 shows the convergence of the best solution of the proposed heuristic.

The best solution obtained is given as: 21,2 - 11,1 - 12,1 - 31,2 - 22,2 - 23,2 - 32,1. The time required to complete all tasks or makespan is 160 time units and the computation time in this case is less than a second. The best solution of the example problem is depicted graphically by a Gantt chart with a small modification made to represent the schedules of the mobile robots. As shown in Fig. 5, a row is added to each mobile robot in order to show time intervals during which a mobile robot is transporting and performing its assigned operations. These time intervals are illustrated by non-colored bars and colored bars for transporting and performing the assigned operations to/at the destination machines, respectively. Note that the time interval needed to complete transporting may include part for an empty trip depending on the previous location of the mobile robot. This part is represented in the Gantt chart by using a shaded area in the non-colored bar, e.g., operation 32 is transported from machine 2 to machine 3 by mobile robot 1 at machine 3.

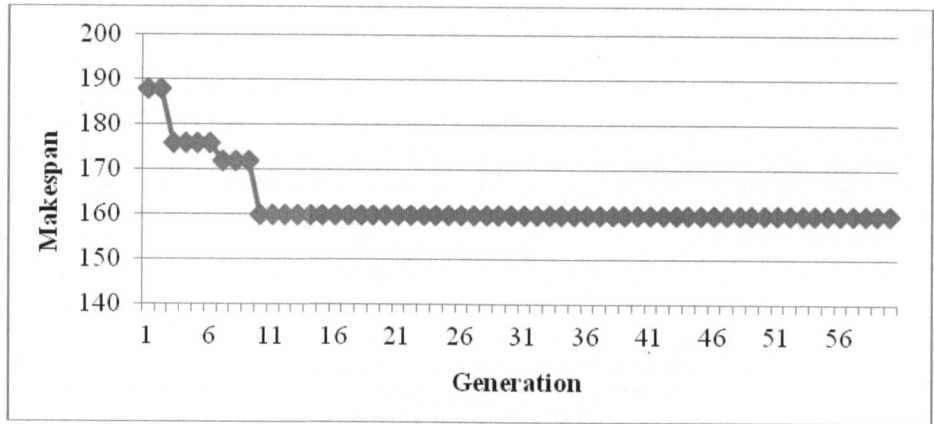

Fig. 4. Convergence of the GA-based heuristic

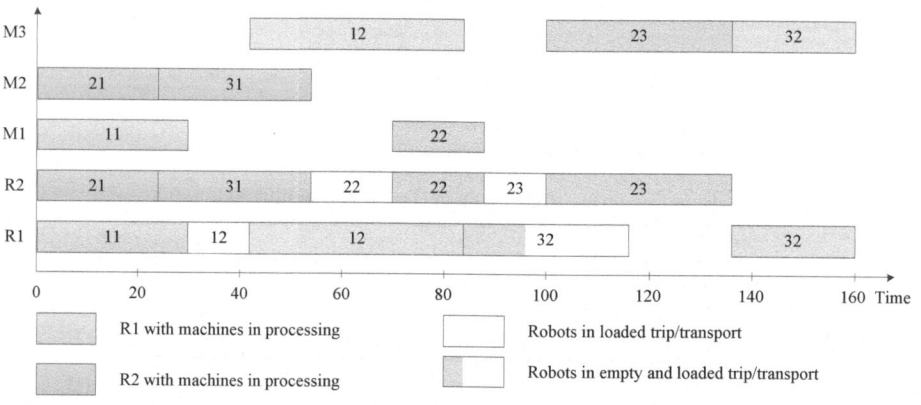

Fig. 5. Gantt chart for the best solution of the example problem

5   Implementation of Proposed Approach in Multi-agent System

This section generally describes how the proposed approach has been implemented in a multi-agent system and highlights the interactions between difference components. The proposed genetic algorithm-based heuristic, the decision-making nucleus, is integrated into the Mission Planning (MP) module of the Mission Planner and Controller (MPC). At first, the input data is derived from an operator through a user interface provided by the MPC or from Manufacturing Execution System (MES). Then, the MP module uses the input data to generate the best schedule/plan which serves as an input to the Mission Control (MC) module of the MPC (this best schedule is also shown to the operator via the user interface). Next, the MC module uses XML-based TCP/IP communication via a wireless network to command mobile robots to execute tasks in succession according to the best schedule and feedback from these mobile robots. In practice, there might be some unexpected events such as breakdown of machines or mobile robots. These events will be reported by MES or the mobile robots so that the MC module is able to update current status of the shop floor and then call the MP module to reschedule the machines and mobile robots if needed. The MP module will in turn use the current status as new input, re-optimize to find an alternative schedule, and send this schedule back to the MC module for execution. Fig. 6 below depicts the aforementioned multi-agent system architecture.

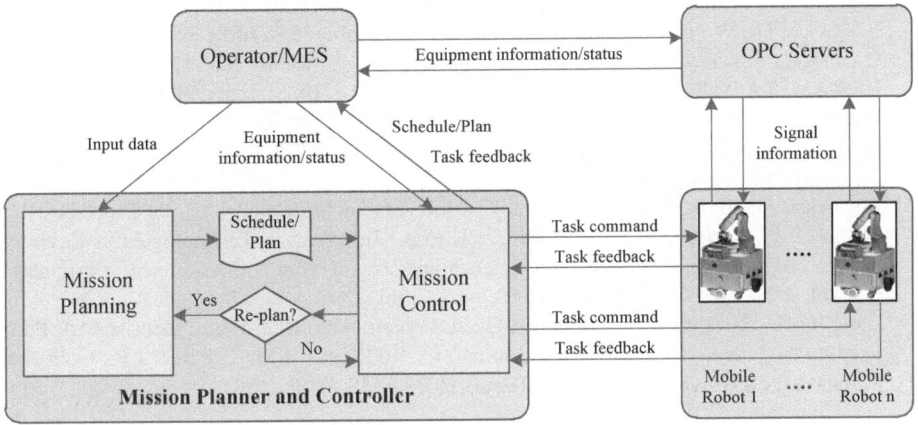

Fig. 6. Multi-agent system architecture

6   Conclusions

In this paper, a problem of simultaneous scheduling of machines and autonomous mobile robots in an FMS environment is studied. To complete all tasks in minimum possible time, it is important for production planners to determine in which sequence the mobile robots and machines should transport and process operations of tasks while satisfying a number of practical constraints. The main novelty of this research lies in the consideration of the participation in performing tasks at machines of the mobile robots. A genetic algorithm-based heuristic was developed to find the best solutions for the problem. An example problem was generated to demonstrate the efficiency of the proposed heuristic. The result showed that the proposed heuristic was significantly fast to obtain the best solution. The solution is useful for decision making at operational levels and the proposed approach provides a solid framework that enables to model and evaluate scheduling tasks of multi-agent systems. The implementation of the proposed approach and its interaction with other components in a multi-agent system was also generally described and highlighted. For further research, lot-sizing procedures for parts with respect to the capacity of the mobile robots should be considered as integral part of the optimization process. Furthermore, rescheduling mechanisms based on obtained schedules and feedback from the mobile robot fleet and machines should be also developed to deal with real-time disturbances.

Acknowledgments. This work has partly been supported by the European Commission under grant agreement number FP7-260026-TAPAS.

References

1. Abdelmaguid, T.F., Nassef, A.O., Kamal, B.A., Hassan, M.F.: A Hybrid GA/Heuristic Approach to the Simultaneous Scheduling of Machines and Automated Guided Vehicles. Int. J. Prod. Res. 42, 267–281 (2004)
2. Bilge, Ü., Ulusoy, G.: A Time Window Approach to Simultaneous Scheduling of Machines and Material Handling System in an FMS. Oper. Res. 43, 1058–1070 (1995)
3. Bocewicz, G., Wójcik, R., Banaszak, Z.: AGVs Distributed Control Subject to Imprecise Operation Times. In: Nguyen, N.T., Jo, G.-S., Howlett, R.J., Jain, L.C. (eds.) KES-AMSTA 2008. LNCS (LNAI), vol. 4953, pp. 421–430. Springer, Heidelberg (2008)
4. Bocewicz, G., Wójcik, R., Banaszak, Z.: On Undecidability of Cyclic Scheduling Problems. In: Karagiannis, D., Jin, Z. (eds.) KSEM 2009. LNCS (LNAI), vol. 5914, pp. 310–321. Springer, Heidelberg (2009)
5. Bocewicz, G., Banaszak, Z.: Declarative Modeling of Multimodal Cyclic Processes. In: Golinska, P., Fertsch, M., Marx-Gómez, J. (eds.) Information Technologies in Environmental Engineering. Environmental Science and Engineering – Environmental Engineering, vol. 3, pp. 551–568. Springer, Heidelberg (2011)
6. Dang, Q.-V., Nielsen, I.E., Bocewicz, G.: A Genetic Algorithm-Based Heuristic for Part-Feeding Mobile Robot Scheduling Problem. In: Rodríguez, J.M.C., Pérez, J.B., Golinska, P., Giroux, S., Corchuelo, R. (eds.) Trends in PAAMS. AISC, vol. 157, pp. 85–92. Springer, Heidelberg (2012)
7. Dang, Q.V., Nielsen, I., Steger-Jensen, K., Madsen, O.: Scheduling a Single Mobile Robot for Part-feeding Tasks of Production Lines. J. Intell. Manuf. (2012), doi:10.1007/s10845-013-0729-y
8. Deroussi, L., Gourgand, M., Tchernev, N.: A Simple Metaheuristic Approach to the Simultaneous Scheduling of Machines and Automated Guided Vehicles. Int. J. Prod. Res. 46, 2143–2164 (2008)
9. Goldberg, D.E.: Genetic Algorithms in Search, Optimization, and Machine Learning. Addison-Wesley, New York (1989)
10. Jerald, J., Asokan, P., Saravanan, R., Delphin Carolina Rani, A.: Simultaneous Scheduling of Parts and Automated Guided Vehicles in an FMS Environment Using Adaptive Genetic Algorithm. Int. J. Adv. Manuf. Technol. 29, 584–589 (2006)
11. Lin, L., Shinn, S.W., Gen, M., Hwang, H.: Network Model and Effective Evolutionary Approach for AGV Dispatching in Manufacturing System. J. Intell. Manuf. 17, 465–477 (2006)
12. Reddy, B.S.P., Rao, C.S.P.: A Hybrid Multi-Objective GA for Simultaneous Scheduling of Machines and AGVs in FMS. Int. J. Adv. Manuf. Technol. 31, 602–613 (2006)
13. Ulusoy, G., Bilge, Ü.: Simultaneous Scheduling of Machines and Automated Guided Vehicles. Int. J. Prod. Res. 31, 2857–2873 (1993)
14. Ulusoy, G., Sivrikaya-Şerifoğlu, F., Bilge, Ü.: A Genetic Algorithm Approach to the Simultaneous Scheduling of Machines and Automated Guided Vehicles. Comput. Oper. Res. 24, 335–351 (1997)

Characterization of the Radio Propagation Channel in a Real Scenario

María Jesús Algar, Iván González, Lorena Lozano, and Felipe Cátedra

Dept. Ciencias de la Computación, Universidad de Alcalá,
University of Alcalá, 28871 Alcalá de Henares (MADRID), Spain
{chus.algaz,iván.gonzalez,lorena.lozano,felipe.catedra}@uah.es

Abstract. The main goal of this paper is to characterize the radio channel propagation model of studying the impulse response. The observation points have been located along two different areas in the city of Madrid, to analyse LOS and NLOS paths. In order to obtain accurate results the geometry has been modelled with NURBS surfaces, since these allow us to obtain very accurate models of real objects. To perform this work, a deterministic electromagnetic (EM) simulation tool, called NEWFASANT, has been used. This tool is able to achieve this goal applying the Geometrical Theory of Diffraction and taken into account multiple reflections and diffractions between the buildings.

Keywords: channel model, impulse response, GTD, radio localization.

1 Introduction

As a result of the increasing interest on the area related to radio localization and radio coverage studies, powerful computer tools and algorithms are required to carry out the characterization of radio propagation in urban areas. In previous researches [1-2], basics approaches were used to perform this task. However, due to the geometrical complexity of the scenarios and accordingly, the large number of ray paths, it was very difficult if not impossible to analyze realistic environments with these procedures. Therefore, new algorithms have been developed to achieve this goal.

Nowadays, thanks to the advances in computer technology, several software tools provide the analysis of the radio propagation channel model in real scenarios. In particular, this work has been developed using NEWFASANT [3], a fast computer tool that lets us obtain a 3-D ray-tracing propagation model of complex environments such as buildings, urban areas, etc. Several features have been included in this tool to perform the analysis of the impulse response.

NEWFASANT is composed of several modules based on rigorous and asymptotic methods, some of them are:

- FASANT module is based on the high frequency techniques Geometrical Theory of Diffraction (GTD) and Uniform Theory of Diffraction (UTD) [4], addressing the analysis of antennas on board complex bodies and the propagation at indoor or outdoor environments.

J.M. Corchado et al. (Eds.): PAAMS 2013 Workshops, CCIS 365, pp. 129–138, 2013.

- MONURBS module is based on the Method of Moments combined with Characteristic Basis Function Method (CBFM) [5] and a Domain Decomposition procedure [6] to speed-up the computation of the electrical field, the radar cross section, the analysis of reflectors and reflectarrays, radio propagation and the design of antennas and radomes.
- POGCROS module is based on Physical Optics (PO) and Geometrical Optics (GO) [7], to compute the monostatic or bistatic Radar Cross Section (RCS) of complex targets, considering any number of interactions between the surfaces of the geometry.

In this paper, results of the EM simulations to characterize the channel propagation in outdoor environment are presented using FASANT module, that is, applying high frequency techniques. Thanks to the capabilities provided by this tool, the time delay regarding a Dirac delta signal has been obtained. This task has been carried out keeping in view the geometrical model of the city of Madrid, shown in figure 1. Several observation points have been located in two different areas in order to analyse the electrical field between the buildings.

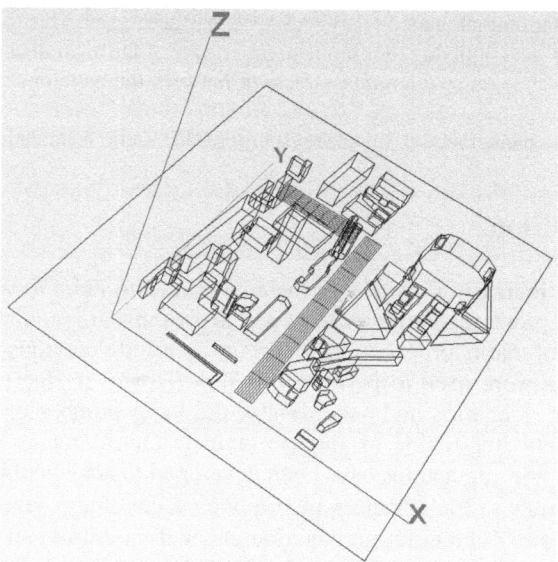

Fig. 1. Geometrical model of the city of Madrid

2   Methodology

Thanks to the efficiency of FASANT as a software tool for the computation of the ray tracing in complex scenarios [8], this module has been used to obtain the electrical field considering multiple interactions between the different parts of the geometry. To achieve this, FASANT applies a ray-tracing algorithm based on the Angular Z-Buffer (AZB) and the Space Volumetric Partitioning (SVP) together with the A* heuristic search methods [9-10]. This fast ray-tracing algorithm speeds up the computation of the electrical field, decreasing the CPU-time and memory resources required for these calculations. The electromagnetic simulations have been accomplished modelling the geometry presented in figure 1 with parametric surfaces. In particular Non-uniform Rational B-Splines (NURBS) [11] surfaces are used. This kind of surfaces efficiently describes the shape of the object using very little information and provides a useful representation of the geometry.

Once the ray-tracing has been obtained, it is easy to perform a post-process in order to analyse the radio channel characteristics. As all the information about the rays have been obtained previously, the time at which each ray (direct ray, reflected ray or diffracted ray) reaches each observation point can be calculated. In this way, a discrete signal composed of Dirac deltas, each one depending on the time of arrival, is built, as depicted in figure 2.

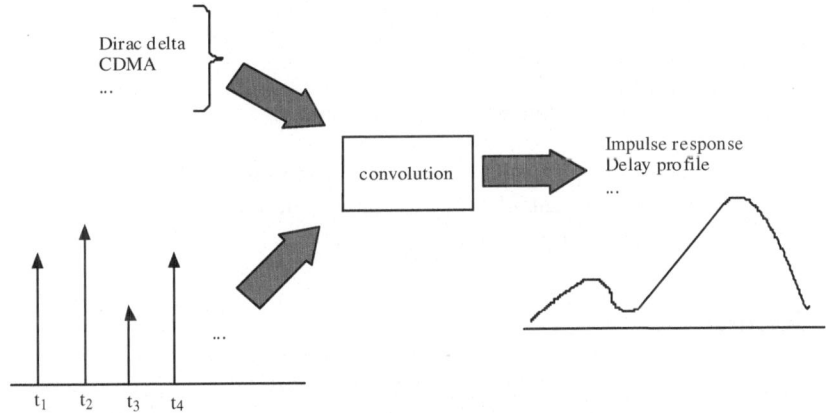

Fig. 2. Convolution process

Before accomplishing the convolution, a specific observation point has to be selected from the whole set of points considered in the previous analysis. Figure 3 illustrates how this information is retrieved.

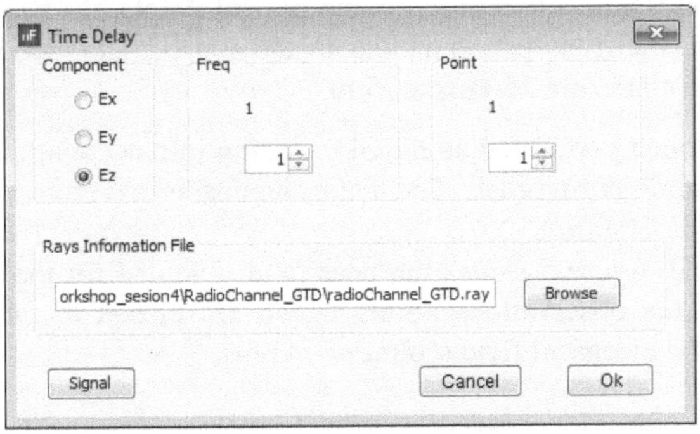

Fig. 3. Time delay definition

Several input signals such as Dirac delta, Sinusoid, Tukey envelope or CDMA, as shown in figure 4, can be convoluted with this signal obtaining the impulse response.

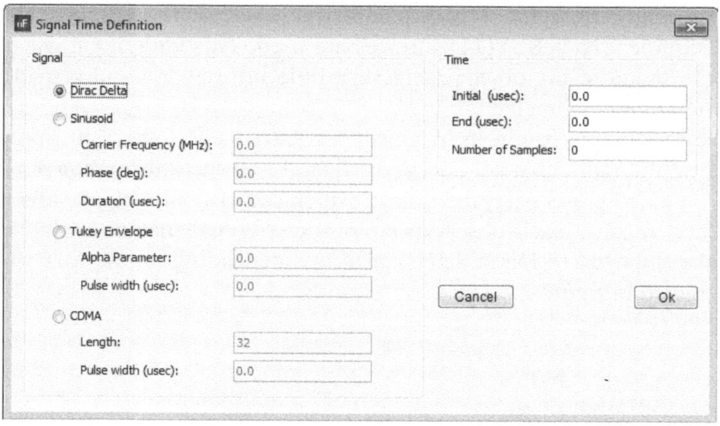

Fig. 4. Signal time definition

Hence, this is a simple process to obtain the different propagation times, due to multi-path propagation, or to calculate the distance from the source to the place where the observation point has been located.

3   Results

After modelling the city of Madrid with NURBS surfaces, the near field on the observation points shown in figure 1 is computed. Two cases have been studied:

- First situation: there is direct visibility between the source and the observation points. An observation plane of 100 points has been placed over the line x = 370 m., in the same lane as the source (see figure 1). The dimensions of this plane are 50 m. x 750 m.
- Second situation: there is no direct visibility between the source and the observation points. A different observation plane of 100 points has been placed over the line y = 750 m. that runs perpendicular to the source lane (see figure 1). The dimensions of this plane are 250 mx x 75 m.

This analysis has been performed at 2.4 GHz, taking into account multiple reflections and diffractions until third order. The feed antenna is a vertical dipole located at (420.0 m., 420.0 m., 30.0 m.).

On the one hand, figure 5 shows the near field obtained for the first situation. As can be observed, the observations points which are closed to the dipole have the greatest value of the electrical field (coloured in red).

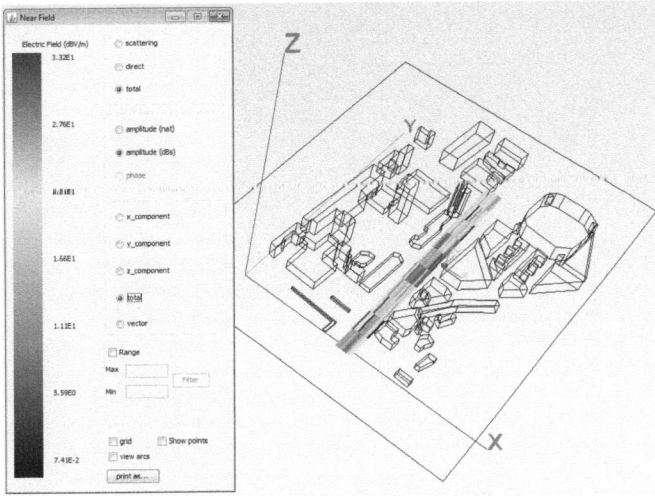

Fig. 5. Near field on the observation points for the first situation

On the other hand, figure 6 shows the near field obtained for the second situation (no direct visibility from the source) with a colour scale.

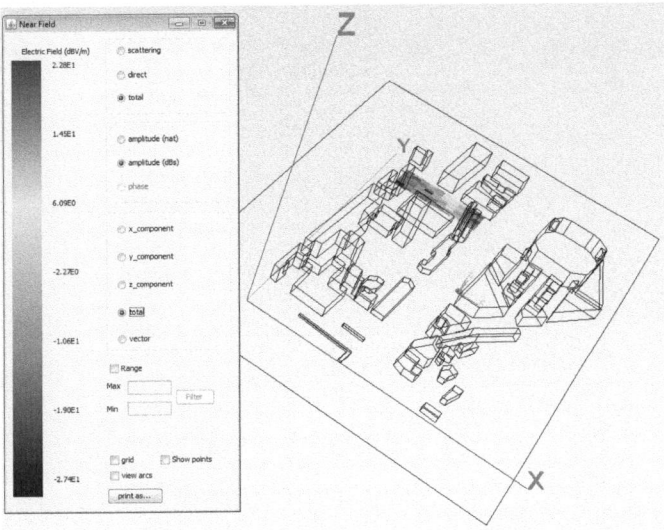

Fig. 6. Near field on the observation points for the second situation

The ray tracing provided by FASANT is shown in figure 7. The simple effects are represented in yellow and the multiple effects are represented in pink. The information about each ray can be visualize: the distance of the path followed by the ray, the propagation time, the effect, the electrical field in the observation point, etc.

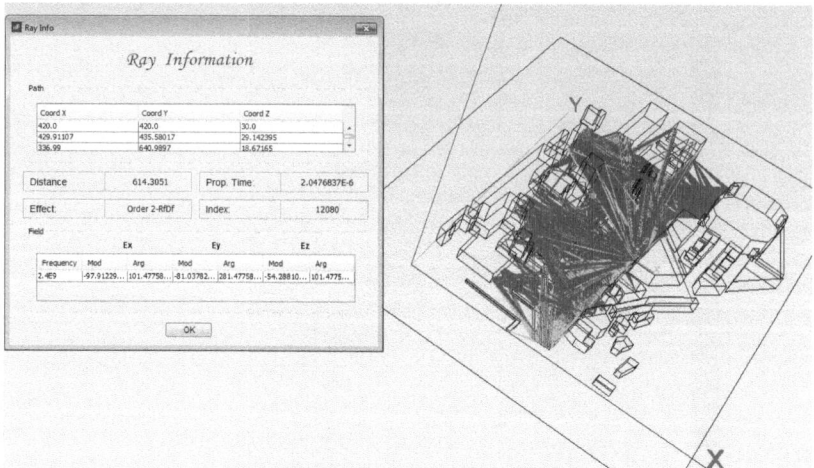

Fig. 7. Ray-tracing representation

To compute the impulse response, Dirac delta and CDMA input signals have been considered. Using the first one, in figure 8 it is shown the impulse response for an observation point within the group with direct visibility, applying the post-processing explained in previous section.

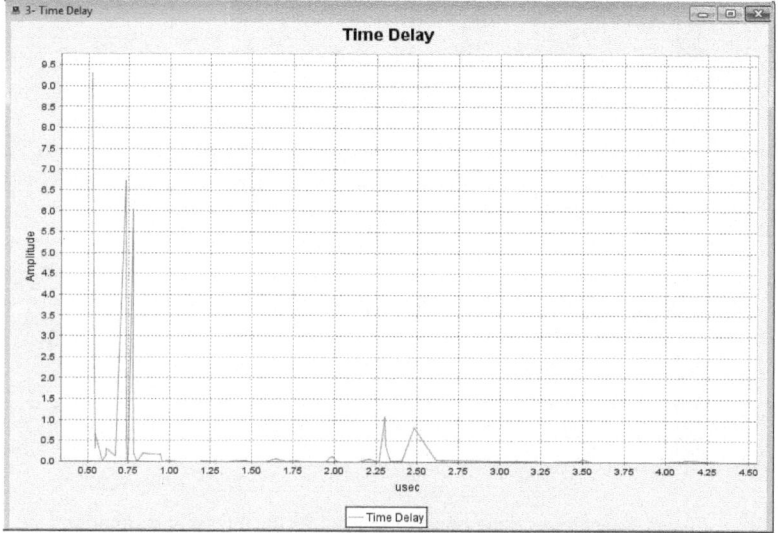

Fig. 8. Time delay considering a Dirac delta for the first situation

Figure 9 shows the impulse response for an observation point without direct visibility. It can be observed the displacement of the maximum amplitude, over the time axis, due to the fact there is not direct ray.

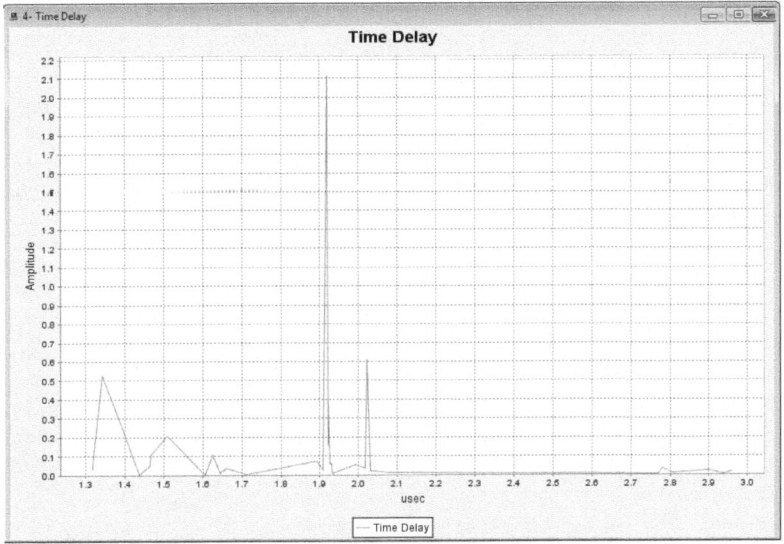

Fig. 9. Time delay considering a Dirac delta for the second situation

From figures 8 and 9 it can be concluded that the first contribution that reach the observation point is the direct ray. Therefore, as in the case plotted figure 9 there is not direct ray, the highest amplitude in this case has been shifted from 0.5 µsec (at this time the direct ray in the case shown in figure 8 reach the observation point) to 1.9 µsec (at this time a multi-path contribution reach the observation point in the case shown in figure 9).

If a CDMA signal is defined as shown in figure 10, the time delay spread presented in figure 11 is obtained for an observation point with direct visibility (367.22, 275.0, 1.5). The highest contribution reaches the point at 0.9 µsec.

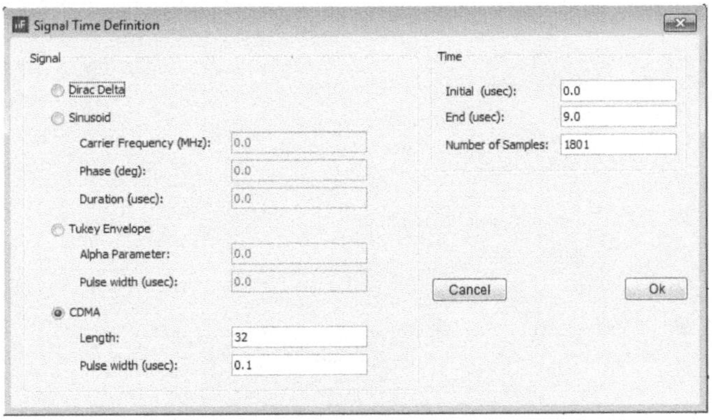

Fig. 10. Definition of the CDMA signal

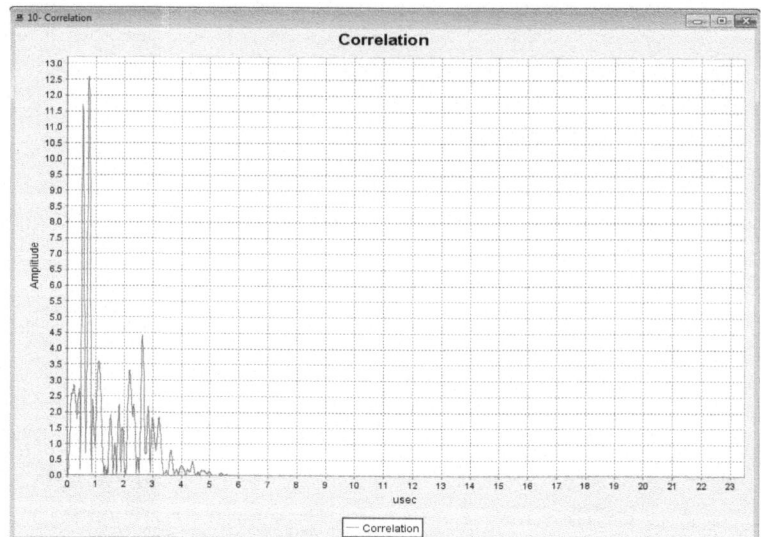

Fig. 11. Time delay spread considering a CDMA for the first case

However, for an observation point without direct visibility the highest contribution experiments a shift from 0.9 μsec to 2 μsec approximately. Figure 12 shows the time delay spread considering a CDMA signal for an observation point located at (241.6, 762.5, 1.5).

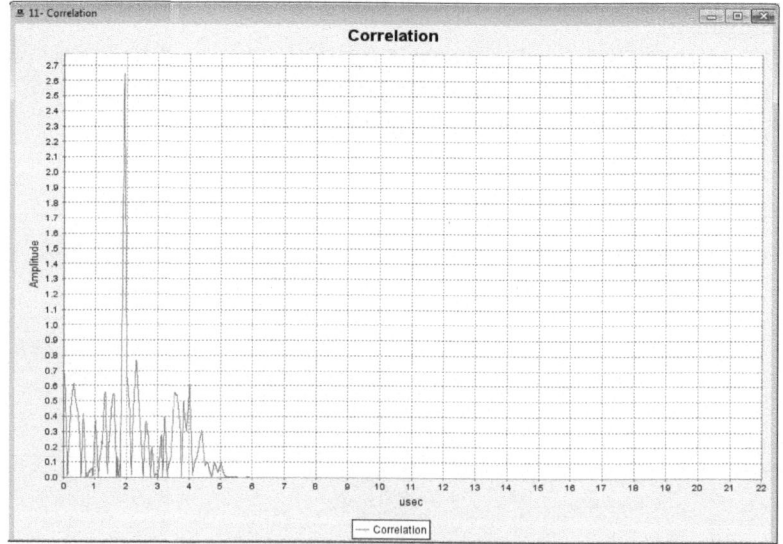

Fig. 12. Time delay spread considering a CDMA for the second situation

4   Conclusions

This paper presents a suitable process to compute the impulse response thanks of the ray-tracing algorithm developed in FASANT tool based on GTD. Convoluting an input signal, such us Dirac delta or CDMA, with a discrete series of contributions, depending on time of arrival, it is easy to characterize the propagation channel model of the city of Madrid. From the analysis of the delay time for the two different groups of observation points, it can be concluded that the first contribution that reaches an observation point is the direct ray. Therefore, when there is NLOS the maximum amplitude suffers a shift over the time axis. FASANT is a suitable software tool for applications like radio localization, pedestrian detection or collision avoidance, thanks to the capability to determine the localization of an object within a complex scenario.

Acknowledgments. This work has been supported, in part by the Comunidad de Madrid Project S-2009/TIC1485 and by the Castilla-La Mancha Project PPII10-0192-0083, by the Spanish Department of Science, Technology Projects TEC 2010-15706 and CONSOLIDER-INGENIO No CSD-2008-0068.

References

1. Hata, M.: Empirical Formula for Propagation Loss in Land Mobile Radio Services. IEEE Transactions on Vehicular Technology VT-29, 317–325 (1980)
2. Cox, D.C.: Multipath Delay Spread and Path Loss Correlation for 910 MHz Urban Mobile Radio Propagation. IEEE Transactions on Vehicular Technology VT-26, 340–344 (1977)
3. NewFasant EM Emulation Software, http://www.fasant.com/
4. Pathak, P.H.: Techniques for high frequency problems. In: Lo, Y.T., Lee, S.W. (eds.) Antenna Handbook, Theory, Application and Design. Van Nostrand Reinhold, New York (1988)
5. Delgado, C., García, E., González, I., Hernández, L., Cátedra, F.: A comparison of the Computational Resources Required by a Domain Decomposition Approach and Other Efficient Numerical Techniques Based on the Moment Method. In: 6th European Conference on Antennas and Propagation, Prague, Czech, pp. 278–282 (2012)
6. García, E., Delgado, C., González, I., Moreno, J., Cátedra, F.: Computational Efficient iterative solution of problems using Characteristic Basis Function Method combines with Multilevel Fast Multipole Algorithm. In: 6th European Conference on Antennas and Propagation, Prague, Czech, pp. 211–214 (2012)
7. Cátedra, F., Lozano, L., González, I., García, E., Algar, M.J.: Efficient Techniques for Accelerating the Ray-Tracing for Computing the Multiple Bounce Scattering of Complex Bodies Modeled by Flat Facet. Applied Computational Electromagnetics Society Journal 25(5), 395–409 (2010)
8. Lozano, L., Algar, M.J., González, I., Cátedra, F.: FASANT: A Versatile Tool to Analyze Radio Localization System at Indoor or Outdoor Environments. In: de Leon F. de Carvalho, A.P., Rodríguez-González, S., De Paz Santana, J.F., Rodríguez, J.M.C. (eds.) Distributed Computing and Artificial Intelligence. AISC, vol. 79, pp. 259–266. Springer, Heidelberg (2010)

9. Delgado, C., Lozano, L., Gutiérrez, O., Cátedra, F.: Iterative PO Method based on Currents Modes and Angular Z-Buffer Technique. In: 2006 IEEE Antennas and Propagation Society International Symposium, Albuquerque, pp. 1853–1856 (2006)
10. Lozano, L., Algar, M.J., González, I., Cátedra, F.: FASANT: A versatile tool to analyse antennas and propagation in complex environments. In: 3rd European Conference on Antennas and Propagation, Berlin, March 23-27, pp. 2088–2092 (2009)
11. Farin, G.: Curves and surfaces for computer aided geometric design. Academic Press (1988)

Dynamic Propagation Analysis in Urban Environments

María Jesús Algar, Iván González, Lorena Lozano, María Fernández,
Gabriel Caballero, and Felipe Cátedra

Dept. Ciencias de la Computación. Universidad de Alcalá,
University of Alcalá, 28871 Alcalá de Henares (MADRID), Spain
{chus.algar,iván.gonzalez,lorena.lozano,felipe.catedra}@uah.es,
{mfernandezv,gabriel.caballero}@edu.uah.es

Abstract. In order to satisfy the demand of the automotive industry about anti-collision systems, related to the protection of pedestrians and drivers, this paper proposes the development of an algorithm that achieves a dynamic analysis of urban scenarios. Typically, some objects of these scenarios can have a translation and/or rotation movement. For each sample of time a new scenario is built according to the information about the movements of the objects. Then, its corresponding simulation is performed using Geometrical Theory of Diffraction to analyse the propagation in outdoor environments and thus, to determine the position of obstacles.

Keywords: GTD, radio localization, anti-collision systems.

1 Introduction

Nowadays, security applications in the field of automotive industry are experiencing significant advances [1]. This field has become of interest since travel safety is an important issue to decrease traffic accidents. At the beginning of the development of security systems, only passive technologies were performed such as airbags and seat belts. Later on, the safety and protection of both pedestrians and drivers has turned to be one of the most important objectives through the adoption of active security mechanisms. In this regard, it is estimated that, within few years, every car will be manufactured with an efficient and accurate anti-collision system. This will be possible thanks to the use of advanced software based on the prediction of the trajectory, analysing a sequence of consecutive images of vehicles, pedestrians and cyclists in urban scenarios.

In this sense, the presence of computers into modern vehicles has become very common. These computers are able to analyse the environment of the vehicle in order to obtain information about the position of possible obstacles, for instance pedestrians, cyclists, etc. Hence, the automotive industry is developing several systems that avoid collisions between the car and any obstacle. Certain factors have to be considered in this process:

- The analysis of the position of pedestrian or obstacles has to be done under any meteorological conditions, such as fog, rain, snow, etc. and with NLOS

J.M. Corchado et al. (Eds.): PAAMS 2013 Workshops, CCIS 365, pp. 139–148, 2013.
© Springer-Verlag Berlin Heidelberg 2013

(non-line-of-sight) between the transmitter and the receiver. Therefore, these systems will work at microwave or millimetre bands because in these frequency bands it is possible to transmit in presence of adverse meteorological conditions or NLOS and to use the information derived from the Doppler shift, due to the movement of the car.

- As the velocity of the car can be very high, all of these analyses have to be done as quickly as possible. For this reason, fast and efficient algorithms are needed.

In order to achieve these goals, the development of the dynamic analysis presented in this paper is based on the use of the high frequency technique Geometrical Theory of Diffraction (GTD) [2]. The application of this technique is very useful in this kind of analysis since it provides the ray path from the source to the observation point in order to analyse the time propagation and the distance [3].

The main goal of this paper is to describe a tool that accomplishes the dynamic propagation analysis in realistic outdoor environments like the geometrical model of the city shown in figure 1.

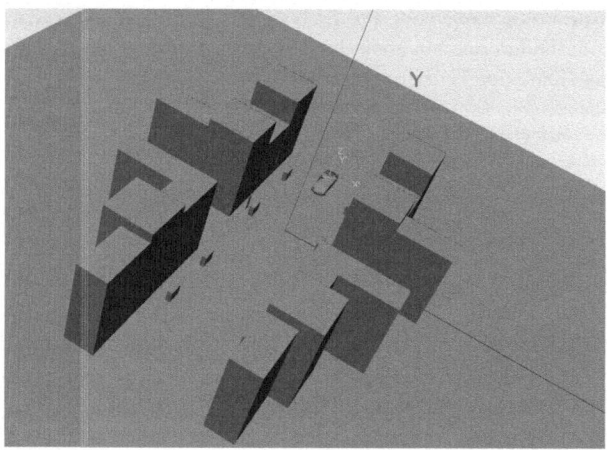

Fig. 1. Geometrical model of the analyzed city

2   Dynamic Procedure

The algorithm to analyze the radio propagation in urban scenarios is based on a batch procedure. This procedure is being implemented within the NEWFASANT tool [4], in the FASANT module [5], which applies the high frequency technique GTD for the analysis of propagation in indoor and/or outdoor environments. A typical scenario in this kind of studies comprises multiple objects: buildings, vehicles, cyclists, containers, urban furniture, etc. Some of them can have a translation and/or rotation movement over time. These movements can be assigned to the object as shown in figure 2.

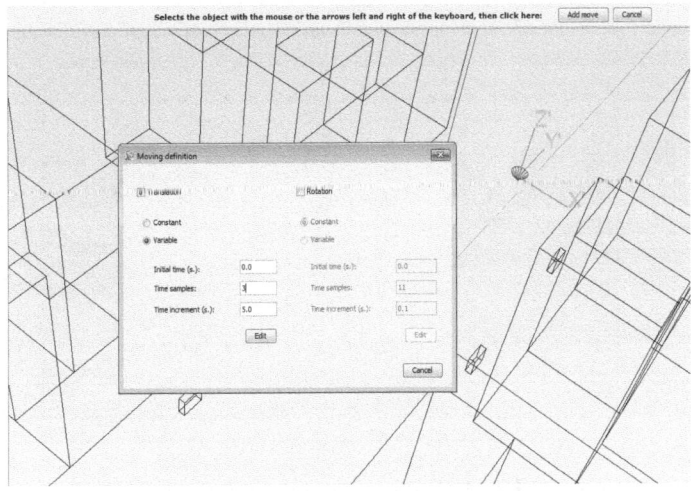

Fig. 2. Assignment of a certain movement to an object

In the case of a variable movement, its characteristics are defined using the tables shown in figures 3 and 4.

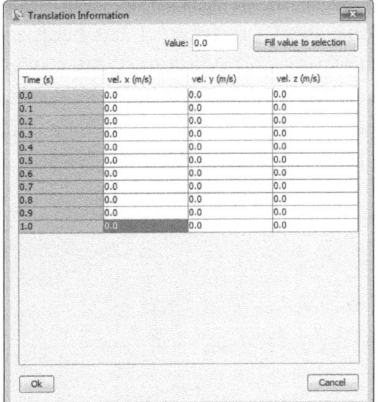

Fig. 3. Translation movement information

On the one hand, to describe the translation movement of an object, only the time and its linear velocity are necessary to be specified, see figure 3. On the other hand, to describe the rotation movement, besides the time and the angular velocity it is necessary to define the rotation axis with two points, see figure 4.

With this information, a distinct scene is associated with each different position of the moving objects. The whole scenes are created automatically once all the movements have been defined. In this way, a dynamic analysis of the propagation over the time can be done in order to study channel parameters. To perform this analysis an efficient ray-tracing technique based on the combination of Angular Z-Buffer (AZB), Space Volumetric Partition (SVP) and A* heuristic search, developed in recent works [6-7], is applied.

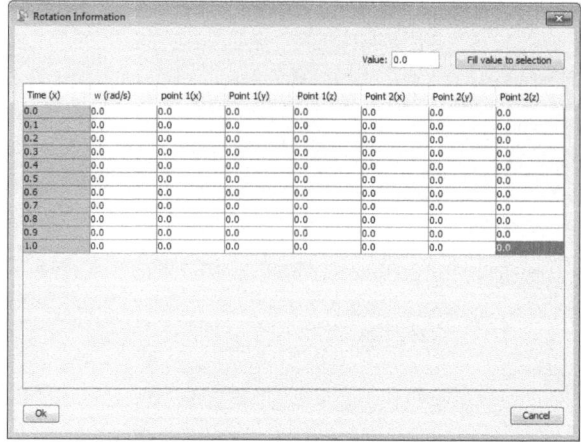

Fig. 4. Rotation movement information

3   Results

The dynamic propagation analysis in a realistic outdoor environment, such as the geometrical model of the city shown in figure 1 has been accomplished. This scenario is composed of several buildings and containers over two perpendicular roads. The car is describing a translation movement on the road over the y axis according to the information shown in figure 5. As the dipole antenna considered in this analysis is always over the car, it has the same translation movement.

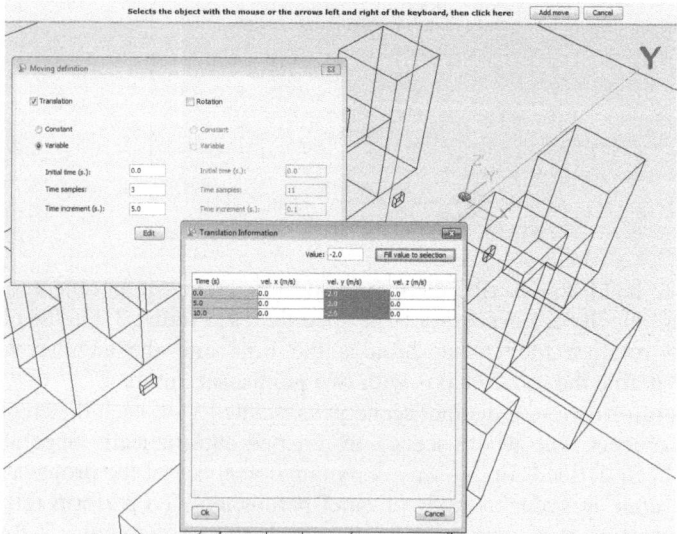

Fig. 5. Translation information movement of the car

A plane of observation points has been located behind one of the containers, see figure1, modelling a human person. This plane has a width of 0.5 m. and a high of 1.75 m.

As mentioned above, the dynamic simulation is achieved according to the translation information. In this particular case study only three time slots have been considered. For the first one, the car is located at (0.0 m., 10.0 m., 0.0 m.) and the dipole is located at (0.0 m., 10.324 m., 1.6 m.). The near field on the pedestrian and the ray-tracing is plotted in figures 6 and 7, respectively.

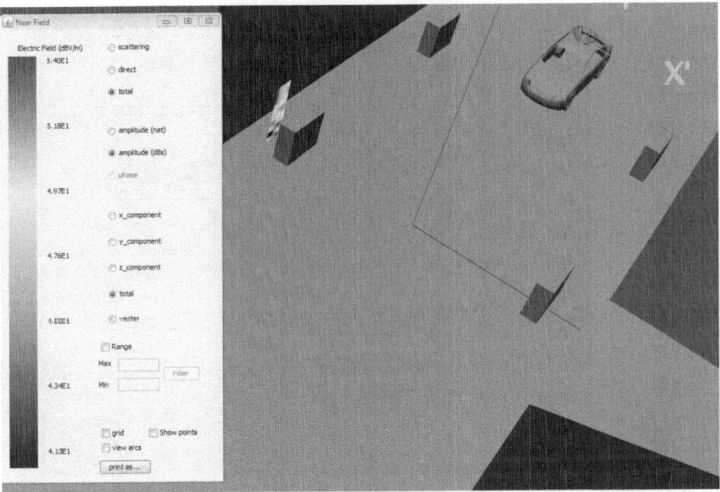

Fig. 6. Image of the near field on the pedestrian for the first time slot

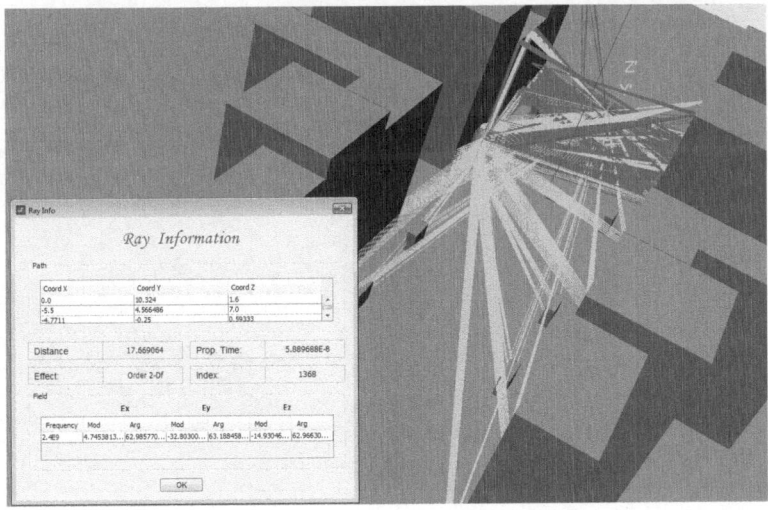

Fig. 7. Image of the ray-tracing for the first time slot

From the ray information it can be obtained its propagation time and the distance of its path between the source and the observation point. Therefore, this information is used to estimate the relative position of the pedestrian from the vehicle for each slot of time.

For the second time slot (t = 5s.), the car has moved from (0.0 m., 10.0 m., 0.0 m.) to (0.0 m., 0.0 m., 0.0 m.). Consequently, the dipole is placed at (0.0 m., 0.324 m., 1.6 m.). Figures 8 and 9 show the near field and the ray-tracing for the second position of the vehicle, respectively.

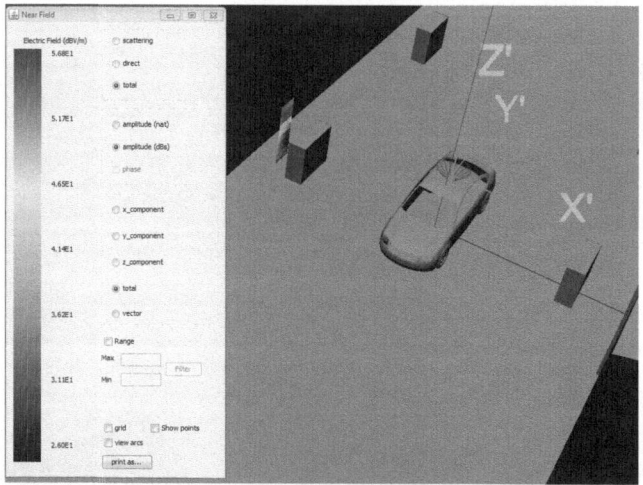

Fig. 8. Image of the near field on the pedestrian for the second time slot

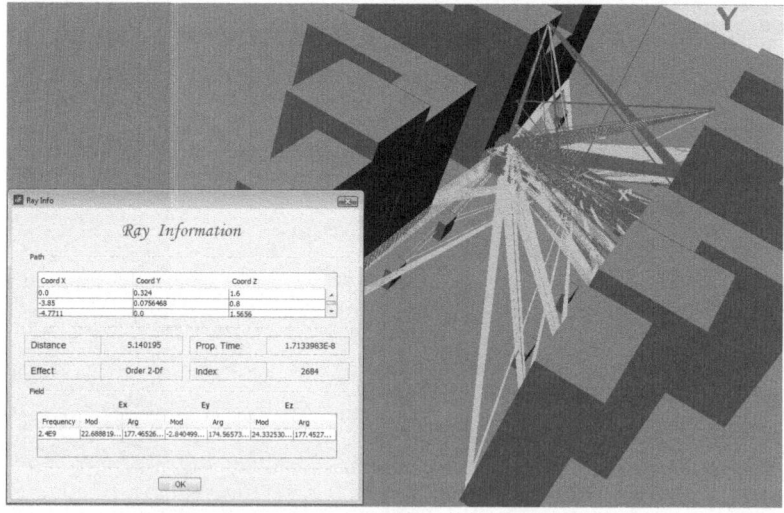

Fig. 9. Image of the ray-tracing for the second time slot

Finally, at the time 10 s., the car is located at (0.0 m., -10.0 m., 0.0 m.) and the dipole is located at (0.0 m., -10.324 m., 1.6 m.). Figures 10 and 11 show the near field and the ray-tracing for the third position of the vehicle, respectively.

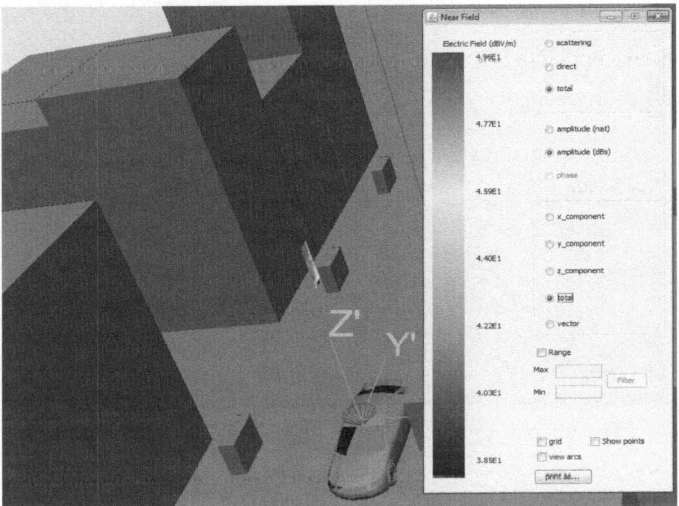

Fig. 10. Image of the near field on the pedestrian for the third time slot

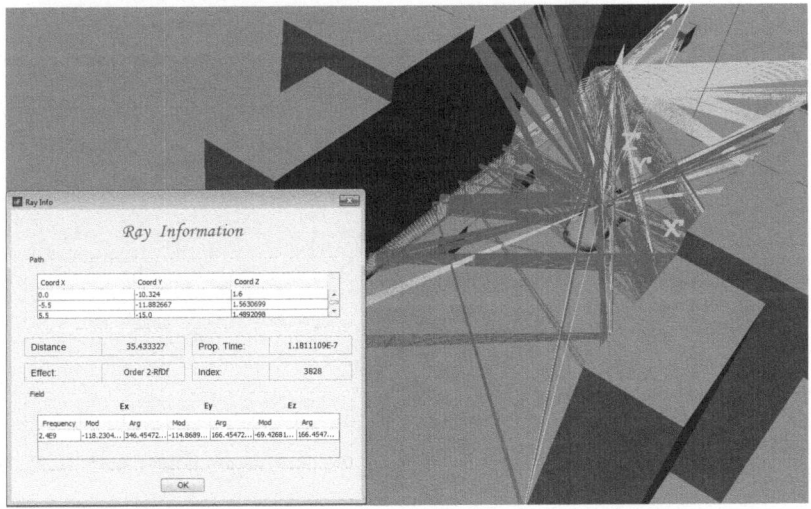

Fig. 11. Image of the ray-tracing for the third time slot

In order to analyze the variation of the near field over the pedestrian (plane of observation points) figures 13, 14 and 15 show the electrical field for three different points. One of these points has been located at the bottom (-4.85, -0.25, 0.01), other has been located in the middle (-4.85, 0.0, 0.78) and the last one has been located at the top (-4.85, 0.25, 1.76) as shown in figure 12.

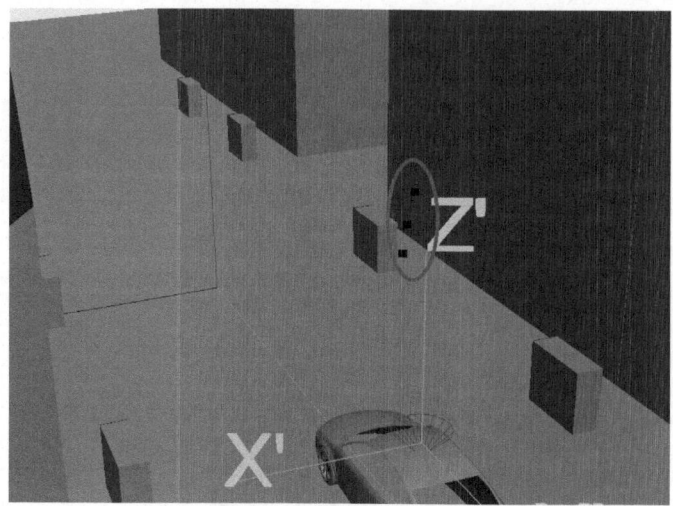

Fig. 12. Observation points representation

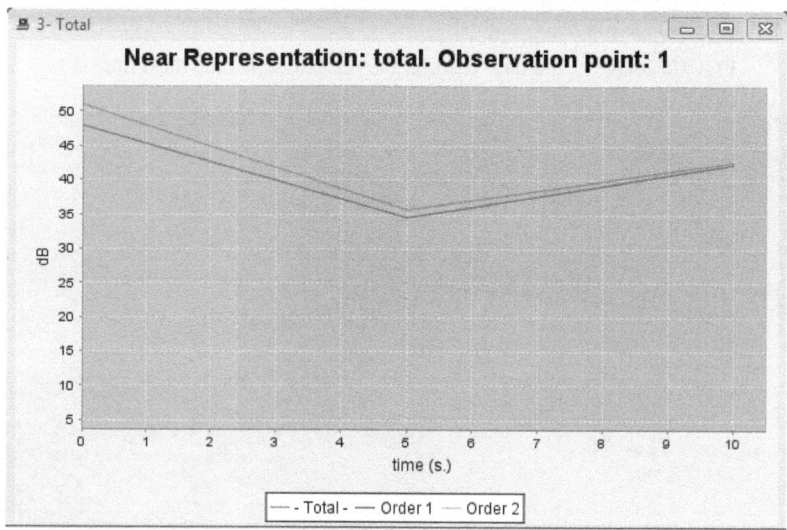

Fig. 13. Near field representation over the time for the observation point (-4.85, -0.25, 0.01)

In the case of point 1, the received value of near field at 0.0 s. is higher than the rest ones since at this time the relative position of this point and the car has direct visibility. When the car moves along the y axis, this point is shadowed by the container.

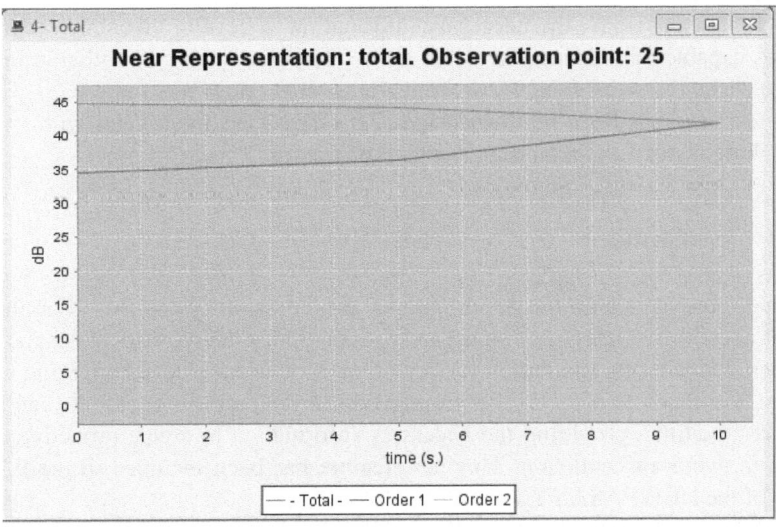

Fig. 14. Near field representation over the time for the observation point (-4.85, 0.0, 0.78)

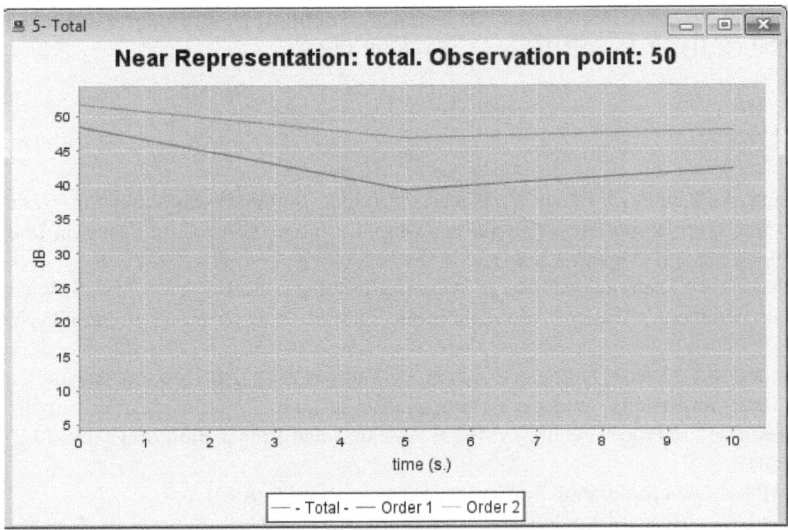

Fig. 15. Near field representation over the time for the observation point (-4.85, 0.25, 1.76)

From these figures it can be concluded that the total electrical field that reaches the observation point located at the top (point 50) is higher than the electrical field that reaches the other two points, because point 50 have direct visibility from the car during the whole movement.   However, point 25 has not this kind of contribution.

As a result, using this dynamic procedure it is possible to track the position of a pedestrian over the itinerary of a car in outdoor urban environments. Similarly, the same technique can be applied to track the position of any other vehicles or obstacles around the car, providing the necessary information to develop dynamic security mechanisms capable of warning the driver about the possible risk of collision in almost real time.

This test case has been performed in a 2.0 GHz Quad Intel Xeon with 24 GB of RAM, taking about 12 min. and 23 s. with 8 processors.

4   Conclusions

This paper presents a help for developing an anti-collision system based on the simulation of consecutive images of an urban scenario. Once the movements of the objects have been defined, one simulation for each time sample is achieved applying GTD. In this way, the characteristics of the propagation in outdoor environments can be analysed over the time, providing the necessary information to create proactive security systems to avoid any collision. This new feature has been included in the FASANT module of the NEWFASANT software tool.

Acknowledgments. This work has been supported, in part by the Comunidad de Madrid Project S-2009/TIC1485 and by the Castilla-La Mancha Project PPII10-0192-0083, by the Spanish Department of Science, Technology Projects TEC 2010-15706 and CONSOLIDER-INGENIO No CSD-2008-0068.

References

1. Huang, A., Xiang, Z., Jiang, W., Chen, Y.: Vehicle Auxiliary Anti-collision Warning System Based on Positioning in Electronic Map. In: International Conference on Information Engineering and Computer Science, ICIECS 2009, pp. 1–4, 19–20 (2009)
2. Pathak, P.H.: Techniques for high frequency problems. In: Lo, Y.T., Lee, S.W. (eds.) Antenna Handbook, Theory, Application and Design. Van Nostrand Reinhold, New York (1988)
3. Cátedra, M.F., Pérez, J., Saez de Adana, F., Gutiérrez, O.: Efficient ray-tracing techniques for three-dimensional analyses of propagation in mobile communications: application to picocell and microcell scenarios. IEEE Antennas and Propagation Magazine 40(2), 15–28 (1988)
4. NewFasant EM Simulation Software, http://www.fasant.com
5. Lozano, L., Algar, M.J., González, I., Cátedra, F.: FASANT: A Versatile Tool to Analyze Radio Localization System at Indoor or Outdoor Environments. In: de Leon F. de Carvalho, A.P., Rodríguez-González, S., De Paz Santana, J.F., Rodríguez, J.M.C. (eds.) Distributed Computing and Artificial Intelligence. AISC, vol. 79, pp. 259–266. Springer, Heidelberg (2010)
6. Delgado, C., Lozano, L., Gutiérrez, O., Cátedra, M.F.: Iterative PO Method based on Currents Modes and Angular Z-Buffer Technique. In: 2006 IEEE Antennas and Propagation Society International Symposium, Albuquerque, pp. 1853–1856 (2006)
7. Lozano, L., Algar, M.J., González, I., Cátedra, F.: FASANT: A versatile tool to analyse antennas and propagation in complex environments. In: 3rd European Conference on Antennas and Propagation, Berlin, March 23-27, pp. 2088–2092 (2009)

Combining Machine Learning Techniques and Natural Language Processing to Infer Emotions Using Spanish Twitter Corpus

Gonzalo Blázquez Gil, Antonio Berlanga de Jesús, and José M. Molina Lopéz

Applied Artificial Intelligence Group, Universidad Carlos III de Madrid,
Avd. de la Universidad Carlos III, 22, 28270, Colmenarejo, Madrid, Spain
{gonzalo.blazquez,antonio.berlanga,josemanuel.molina}@uc3m.es
http://www.giaa.inf.uc3m.es

Abstract. In the recent years, microblogging services, as Twitter, have become a popular tool for expressing feelings, opinions, broadcasting news, and communicating with friends. Twitter users produced more than 340 million tweets per day which may be consider a rich source of user information. We take a supervised approach to the problem, but leverage existing hashtags in Twitter for building our training data. Finally, we tested the Spanish emotional corpus applying two different machine learning algorithms for emotion identification reaching about 65% accuracy.

Keywords: Emotion Context, Emotion Recognition, Microblogging, Twitter, Features extraction, Machine Learning.

1 Introduction

Affective Computing (AC) or Emotion-oriented computing is a branch of Artificial Intelligence (AI) that deals with the design of systems and devices that can recognize, interpret, and process human affective states (moods and emotions).

In [1] Picard described three types of affective computing applications: 1) systems which detect user emotions, 2) systems that express what a human would perceive as an emotion (e.g., an avatar, robot, and animated conversational agent), and 3) systems that can actually "feel" an emotion. This paper we will try to create a system which detect user emotions from text using Social Networks Sites.

The question of how humans perceive emotions has become central for the researchers of affective computing [2]. Emotions are fundamental to human experience, perception, and everyday tasks such as learning, communication, and even rational decision-making. Hence, to create a systems able to recognize emotions gives us new clues to understand people behavior.

Although human emotion sensing may be obtained from a wide range of behavioral cues: gestures, facial expression [3], movements [4], speech or physiological signals (heart rate, salivation, ...). In this case, thanks to the rapid growth

J.M. Corchado et al. (Eds.): PAAMS 2013 Workshops, CCIS 365, pp. 149–157, 2013.

of textual content, such as microblog posts, blog posts, forum discussions, and social networks sites (SNS), we propose to develop an automatic tool for identifying and analyzing people's emotions expressed through Computer Mediated Communication (CMC), in concrete using Natural Language Processing Techniques (NLP).

NLP is the application of computational models to tasks involving human language text. NLP research has been active since the dawn of the modern computational age in the early 1950s, but the field has grown in recent years, thanks to the amazing development of the internet and consequent increase in the availability of online text. Nowadays, following the trend, the research in the field of emotion detection from textual data emerged to determine human emotions from another point of view.

Previous works in emotion recognition using NLP methods used small datasets, about thousands of entries, which makes difficult to well-define which emotion is triggered by an events or situations. To overcome the lack of sufficient labeled data is possible to use Social Networks Sites where daily users share their personal information [5]. SNS manage an uncountable gigabytes of useless user information and it is possible to consider SNS's as an emotional sensor [6].

There are different SNS; Twitter, Facebook, Instagram, etc; however not all the SNS are well-fitted to retrieve Emotions from text content. Twitter contains a very large number of short messages (140 characters) created by users. Twitter's audience varies from normal people to celebrities, company representatives, politicians, etc. Relying on the twitter hashtags which are used to mark keywords or topics in a Tweet, we automatically develop an user emotion-annotated training dataset.

The paper deals with the topic of recognizing people's emotion context by analyzing data from Twitter (Microblogging platform).

2   Natural Language Processing

While express emotion through face-to-face channels is easy to recognize, Computer-Mediated Communication (CMC) may be cause confusion. To understand nuances of the expressions, jokes, detecting subjective opinion documents or expressions, non-verbal cues may be an arduous task for humans and an impossible task for computers.

Identifying the expressed emotions in text is very challenging for at least two reasons. The first one is that emotions can be implicit by specific events or situations. In the next sentence *When I see a cop, no matter where I am or what I'm doing, I always feel like every law I've ever broken is stamped all over my body*, it is possible to infer that the person is scared or fear. Second one, gathering distinction between different emotions purely on the basis of keywords can be very subtle.

Although there is not any standard emotion word hierarchy, focus on the related research about emotion recognition, normally emotion is expressed as joy, sadness, anger, surprise, hate, fear according to the Ekman six basic emotions [7].

In the context of emotion detection NLP is normally based on finding certain predefined keywords as happy, sad, anger, etc. A little overview about NLP features extraction techniques is presented:

- Part-of-Speech (POS): In corpus linguistics, part-of-speech tagging is the process of marking up a word in a text (corpus) as corresponding to a particular part of speech, based on its definition, as well as its context. It is also called word class, a category into which words are placed according to the work they do in a sentence. Commonly, there are 8 parts of speech (or word classes) and they are divided into two groups:

  - Open classes: nouns, verbs, adjectives, and adverbs.
  - Closed classes: pronouns, prepositions, conjunctions, and interjections.

  The most common way to classify using POS features is reduced to calculate the percentage of words belonging to each POS in a tweet.
- LIWC Dictionary[1]: Linguistic Inquiry and Word Count3 (LIWC) is a text analysis software which provides a dictionary covering about 4,500 words and word stems from more than 70 categories. The software is available in 11 languages (Spanish is included).

  In this case, the classification method counted the number of positive/ negative words based on the set of collected emotion words, and used the percentage of words that are positive and that are negative as features.
- Adjectives: In sentiment analysis, adjectives are usually considered as effective features since they can be good indicators of sentiment. Some research [8] shows that using adjectives alone produces competitive results with those obtained by using n-grams in sentiment classification of movie reviews. In order to classify each tweet adjective is included in a feature vector.
- Emoticons: Other way to face NLP is rely on the used emoticons. Some recent work, however, notes that emoticons can provide emotion information and improve CMC [9]. Emoticons are described as graphic representations of facial expressions that are included in electronic messages.
- N-grams: In the fields of computational linguistics and probability, an n-gram is a contiguous sequence of n items from a given sequence of text or speech. An n-gram could be any combination of letters. However, the items in question can be phonemes, syllables and letters, although using words give more information to the developer.

2.1 Emotion Representation

As well as the emotion does not have a commonly agreed theoretical definition, a categorization or representation model there is no consensus. Nowadays, there exist two different ways to depict emotions: Categorical and dimensional.

Categorical model of emotion has its roots in the evolutionary theories which claims that emotions are biologically determined, discrete and belong to one

---

[1] http://www.liwc.net/

of a few groups. These groups are consider fundamental or *basic*. However, the
problem is which emotions are considered basic. In this case, according with [7]
definition of affective state the basic emotions are normally considered: happiness, sadness, surprise, fear, anger and disgust.

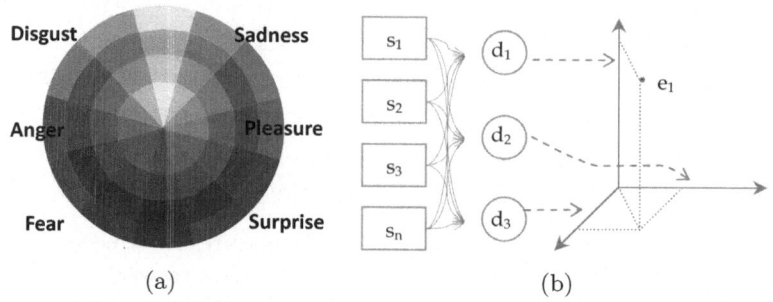

(a)   (b)

Fig. 1. Emotion representation: Categorical (a) and Dimensional model (b)

This model reduce sharply the number of emotions. Some researchers think
that any basic emotion may be decomposed into secondary emotions. This process is very similar to the way that any color is a combination of some basic
colors. Emotions are extracted by mixing and matching the basic emotional
labels as if in a palette of primary colors *Palette theory* as figure 1(a) shows.

In contrast to categorical model, dimensional models do not fix a finite set
of emotions. Alternately, they attempt to find a finite set of underlying features
into which emotions can be decomposed, any combination of features give a
different affective state. Under this model, emotions are described in terms of
three components or dimensions [10]. The first dimension aims to describe the
degree of pleasantness underlying the emotional experience. The second one
describes the level of activation of the emotion and finally the last one defines
the level of attention or rejection.

The three dimension approach is synthesized in figure (b) where a concrete
emotion (e) is the result of the intersection between every different dimensions
(d) whose values are determined by pattern of signals (s).

3   Building a Data Set for Emotion Analysis in Twitter

Due to Twitter restrictions is not possible to use a previous Twitter emotion
dataset [11] to compare machine learning techniques. We had to create our own
dataset to test NLP techniques in Spanish Tweets.

In this section, it is described how we automatically created a labeled emotion
dataset from Twitter SNS. Selected emotions were 6 (fear, anger, sadness, happiness, surprise, and disgust.) according to the Ekman research [7], also called
six universal emotions.

Table 1. Matching between emotion hashtags with six universal emotions

Emotion	Hashtag	Instances
Fear	#Miedo, #terror and #aprension	19.39%
Disgust	#Indignado, #asco and #repulsivo	23.74%
Sadness	#Triste, #sad and #infeliz	18.80%
Happiness	#Feliz, #happy and #contento/a	36.28%
Surprise	#Sorprendido, #sorprendida and #sor-persa	0.90%
Anger	#Furioso/a, #cabreado/a, #mosqueado/a and #enfadado/a	0.85%

We firstly collected at least 3 sets of emotion words for 6 different emotions (e.g., word "feliz" for emotion happiness) from existing psychology literature [12]. Subsequently, we retrieved tweets that have one of these emotion words as a hashtag (e.g, #feliz) using Twitter streaming API. Each collected tweet was automatically labeled with one emotion according to its hashtag (See Table 2).

Full sentiment analysis for a given question or topic requires many stages, including but not limited to:

1. Extraction of tweets using Twitter4J which is an unofficial Java library for Twitter API.
2. Filtering out spam and irrelevant items from those tweets. The main filtering steps the we follow are:
   - Anonymized username: We anonymize the usernames since they do not provide relevant emotional information and also in the way to avoid malicious use of the data.
   - Manual retweets (also known as "RT") are deleted because they do not give us relevant information.
   - Tokenization is difficult in the social media domain, and good tokenization is absolutely crucial for overall system performance. Standard tokenizers, usually designed for newspapers or scientic publications, perform poorly because of the Twitter slang. However, we create a tokenizer which treats hashtags, @-replies, abbreviations, strings of punctuation and emoticons as tokens.
   - Removing stopwords we remove prepositions and conjunctions from the set of words since they do not provide enough meaning to the Tweet.
   - Delete repeated characters: All repeated characters like spaces or repeated vowel are deleted in order to join words with the same meaning and slang differences (e.g. holaaaaaaa -¿ hola).
   - Negation form: "no" word is attached to the word which follows it. For example, th next sentence "No quiero ir" will form two different tokens: "no+quiero", "ir". Such a procedure allows to improve the accuracy of the classication since the negation change completely the meaning of

the sentence since it plays a special role in an opinion and sentiment expression [13] and [14].

3. Identifying subjective tweets. A set of filtering heuristics was developed to select the most valuable tweets:

   - We kept only the tweets with the emotion hashtags at the end. In previous works was proved that the most relevant words are at the end of a Tweet [15].
   - We discarded tweets which have less than five tokens, since they may not provide sufficient context to infer emotions.
   - URL del Tweets which contains URL links since the relevant information is stored in the link (e.g. http://example.com).

After the filtering process was conclude, totally, we collected 21,991 relevant tweets from a period spanning December 28th 2012 until January 8th 2012.

4 Emotion Classification Results

We train classifiers with unigram features for each emotion class using Multinomial Naive Bayes (MNB) for predicting the emotion category of the sentences in our corpus. MNB provides good performance with a large-scale dataset and has previously given good performance in sentiment classification experiments.

Table 2. Machine learning accuracy (ngrams)

Features	Number of ngrams	Accuracy
ngram(n=1)	2264	65.12%
ngram(n=2)	1381	47.64%
ngram(n=3)	164	36.40%
ngram(n=1,2)	3645	49.72%

According to the described features above, one of the best method to analyze emotions in microblogging context is using N-grams. The most common sizes for n are 2 (bigrams), 3 (trigrams) and 4 (four-grams) because unigrams are too narrow a unit of analysis.

In each experiment, we represent every sentence by a features vector indicating if a ngrams appears in the sentence or not. It is made a Boolean feature for each n-gram, which is set to true if and only if the n-gram is present in the tweet.

Our main goal for these experiments is to compare different features in NLP using Spanish Twitter Corpus. Taking into account microblogging text characteristics which maximum text length is 140 characters, we chose small n values. Hence, we decided to compare results between different values of n: Unigrams (n=1), Bigrams (n=2), Trigrams(n=3) and the Unigrams and Bigrams (n=1, 2) combination.

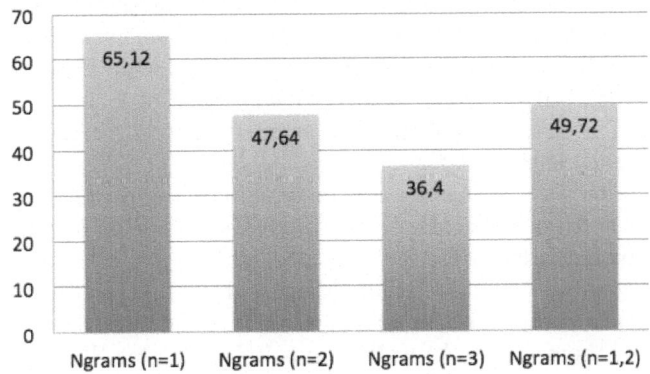

Fig. 2. ngram total accuracy

Fig. 3. Accuracy for each emotion

In the first experiment, we use only corpus based unigram features. We obtain high precision values for all emotion classes (as shown in Table 4). Besides, Table 4 shows the overall performance of MNB classifier (trained with all tweets) on each emotion category.

Our experimental results show that unigrams yields better performance than using unigrams alone. While the number of ngrams are increasing the accuracy decreases (from 65.12% to 36.40%). The number of ngrams and the accuracy show that unigrams provides the best performance to infer twitter user emotion. This validates our previous premise since we consider unigrams can help learn lexical distributions well using short sentences (AS Tweets) in order to accurately predict human emotion categories.

It is important to highlight that for the three most popular emotion (joy), which account for 36.28% of all tweets, the classifier achieves precisions of over 75% (Unigrams). On the contrary, performance declines can be seen on less popular emotions (i.e., Surprise and Anger), which consist of 1.75% of all the tweets in our dataset. The precisions of these two emotion categories are relatively high (with lowest precision of 58.1%).

Interestingly, how is decreasing continuously the performance on the evaluation data comes from using bigger n-grams together with the lexicon features and the microblogging features.

Specifically, combining unigrams and bigrams decrease the accuracy to 49.72%. Hence, further incorporation of trigrams was not implemented due to bad result for using one of them alone. As well as existing works on NLP emotion recognition [8] using unigrams alone is better than applying either bigrams, trigrams or a combination of unigrams and bigrams.

5   Conclusions

In this paper, we investigate the utility of linguistic features for detecting the sentiment of Twitter messages in Spanish. Besides, we evaluate whether our training data with labels derived from hashtags is useful for training emotional classifiers.

Moreover, we culled Spanish emotion tweets covering 6 emotion categories for automatic emotion identification. The experimental results show that the feature of unigrams presents better performance than, bigrams, trigrams and the combination of both of them. We achieved the highest accuracy of 65.12% with is more or less the same accuracy that other researchers have obtained in previous works using English Twitter datasets.

Considering future works are to increase the accuracy of the classication, we should discard common n-grams, measured using Chi-squared. For example taking the top 1,000 n-grams. Besides, it is possible to reduce misspellings and grammatical error in order to unify ngrams.

Acknowledgments. This work was supported in part by Projects MEyC TEC2012-37832-C02-01, MEyC TEC2011-28626-C02-02 and CAM CONTEXTS (S2009/TIC-1485).

References

1. Picard, R.: Affective computing (1997)
2. Cowie, R., Douglas-Cowie, E., Tsapatsoulis, N., Votsis, G., Kollias, S., Fellenz, W., Taylor, J.: Emotion recognition in human-computer interaction. IEEE Signal Processing Magazine 18(1), 32–80 (2001)
3. Soyel, H., Demirel, H.: Facial expression recognition using 3D facial feature distances. In: Kamel, M., Campilho, A. (eds.) ICIAR 2007. LNCS, vol. 4633, pp. 831–838. Springer, Heidelberg (2007)

4. Reilly, J., Ghent, J., McDonald, J.: Modelling, classification and synthesis of facial expressions. In: Affective Computing: Emotion Modelling, Synthesis and Recognition, pp. 107–132
5. Wang, W., Chen, L., Thirunarayan, K., Sheth, A.: Harnessing Twitter 'Big Data' for Automatic Emotion Identification (2012), knoesis.wright.edu
6. Blázquez Gil, G., Berlanga, A., Molina, J.: Incontexto: Multisensor architecture to obtain people context from smartphones. International Journal of Distributed Sensor Networks 2012 (2012)
7. Ekman, P., Friesen, W.: Facial action coding system: A technique for the measurement of facial movement (1978)
8. Pang, B., Lee, L., Vaithyanathan, S.: Thumbs up?: Sentiment classification using machine learning techniques. In: Proceedings of the ACL 2002 Conference on Empirical Methods in Natural Language Processing, vol. 10, pp. 79–86. Association for Computational Linguistics (2002)
9. Derks, D., Bos, A., Von Grumbkow, J.: Emoticons and online message interpretation. Social Science Computer Review 26(3), 379–388 (2008)
10. Schlosberg, H.: Three dimensions of emotion. Psychological Review 61(2), 81 (1954)
11. Petrovic, S., Osborne, M., Lavrenko, V.: The Edinburgh twitter corpus. In: Proceedings of the NAACL HLT 2010 Workshop on Computational Linguistics in a World of Social Media, pp. 25–26 (2010)
12. Shaver, P., Schwartz, J., Kirson, D., O'Connor, C.: Emotion knowledge: further exploration of a prototype approach. Journal of Personality and Social Psychology 52(6), 1061 (1987)
13. Wilson, T., Wiebe, J., Hoffmann, P.: Recognizing contextual polarity: An exploration of features for phrase-level sentiment analysis. Computational Linguistics 35(3), 399–433 (2009)
14. Pak, A., Paroubek, P.: Twitter as a corpus for sentiment analysis and opinion mining. In: Proceedings of LREC, vol. 2010 (2010)
15. De Choudhury, M., Counts, S., Gamon, M.: Not all moods are created equal! exploring human emotional states in social media. In: Sixth International AAAI Conference on Weblogs and Social Media (2012)

Comparing Agent Interactions of Distributed and Centralized Multi-Agent Systems for Context-Aware Domains

Javier Carbo[1], Nayat Sanchez-Pi[2], David Griol[1], and Jose M. Molina[1]

[1] Group of Applied Artificial Intelligence (GIAA), Carlos III University of Madrid,
Avda de la Universidad Carlos III, 22. Colmenarejo. Madrid, Spain
{javier.carbo,david.griol,josemanuel.molina}@uc3m.es

[2] Documentation Active & Intelligent Design Laboratory of Institute of Computing
(ADDLabs), Fluminense Federal University,
156, Passos da Ptria Street. Boa Viagem, Niteri, Rio Janeiro, Brazil
nayat@addlabs.uff.br

Abstract. Comparing the communication overhead of Multi-Agent Systems (MAS) is a complex problem and it does not have a single form. Distributed architectures of MAS are assumed to have greater robustness than centralized approaches. But the corresponding cost in terms of agents interactions is not often quantified in order to fairly evaluate the relative benefits of them. The present work focuses on evaluating interaction relevance (measured through the involved concepts and produced reactions). So, in this paper, we describe the assignment of evaluation values to agents interaction of a distributed and a centralized specific MAS architectures applied to the same context-aware domain. Due to the dependant nature of the relevance of the messages, the evaluation had to be ad-hoc, but here we provide an example of how interesting is this alternative in order to evaluate any MAS architecture theoretically.

Keywords: Multi-Agent Systems, Evaluation, Context-Aware Architectures.

1 Introduction

Context-aware systems combine ubiquitous information, communication, with enhanced personalization, natural interaction and intelligence. Context-aware systems should be able to adapt their operations to the current context without explicit user intervention and taking environmental context into account. Particularly when it comes to using mobile devices, as context data may change so rapidly, it is desirable that programs representing users react specifically to their current location, time and other environment attributes and adapt their behaviour according to the changing circumstances as Agent technology does.

The evaluation of context-aware MAS makes possible to understand the behaviour, and to compare the various systems between them. There are several works addressing evaluation in MAS and are characterized i.e., for its architectural style [1]; for its agent-oriented methodologies based on the software engineering related criteria and characteristics of MAS [2]; [3] or for the complexity of interactions [4]. Evaluation

J.M. Corchado et al. (Eds.): PAAMS 2013 Workshops, CCIS 365, pp. 158–165, 2013.

of the distributed nature of agent systems and the complexity of the interaction inside them make their evaluation a hard task. Interactions are the most important characteristic of any complex software as autonomous agents according to [5], as a problematic of evaluation.

Interaction-based evaluations have been addressed by other researchers. These studies have verified that this kind of evaluation originates different types of problems [4]. Firstly, the effect of an interaction unit (a single message) in an agent system could be equivalent to the definition of n units (messages) in another system. This way, the weight assigned to the same interaction is 1 in the first system and is n in the second. Secondly, the interaction units that are received and cannot be used by an agent could be a bias in the measurement of interaction in MAS.

Our proposal is partially inspired on [4]. The first task is to classify the possible received messages into specific sets sharing the same type. Then, a weight is associated to a message according to its type. If two messages with the same type produce very different effects on the agent, then this assignment does not provide a correct solution. The effects of considering interactions as the main feature of the evaluation, consists of initially processing a message and then deciding a responsive action. The message processing consist of the memorization that deals with the change at the internal state caused by the received message, and the decision concerns the choice of the action that will be handled.

2   Distributed and Centralized MAS for Context-Aware Problems

The proposed agent-based architectures manage context information to provide personalized services by means of users interactions with conversational agents. As it can be observed in Figure 1, the distributed architecture consists of five different types of agents that cooperate to provide an adapted service. *User agents* are configured into mobile devices or PDAs. Providers are implemented by means of *Conversational Agents* that provide the specific services. A conversational agent includes a software that accepts natural language as input and generates natural language as output, engaging in a conversation with the user. A *Facilitator Agent* links the different positions to the providers and services defined in the system. A *Positioning Agent* communicates with the ARUBA positioning system [6] to extract and transmit positioning information to other agents in the system. Finally, a *Log Analyzer Agent* generates user profiles that are used by Conversational Agents to adapt their behaviour taking into account the preferences detected in the users' previous dialogues.

The alternative MAS architecture involves two kinds of agents: User and System Agent. While User agent has no changes, the System agent plays all the roles of Positioning, Facilitator, Conversational and Log Analyzer agents of the distributed alternative.

The free software JADE (Java Agent Development Framework)[1] has been used for the implementation of both architectures. It that complies with the FIPA specifications and the agent platform can be distributed across machines and the configuration can be controlled via a remote GUI.

---

[1] http://jade.tilab.com/

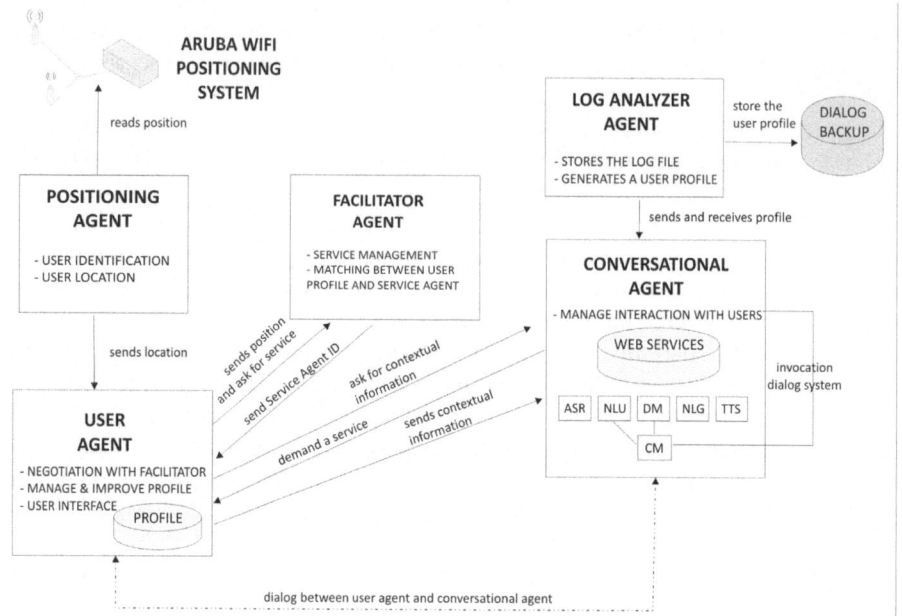

Fig. 1. Schema of the distributed MAS architecture

We also defined an generic ontology for context-aware systems [6]. It contains eight concepts: *Location* (*XCoordinate* int, *YCoordinate* int), *Place* (*Building* int, *Floor* int), *Service* (*Name* String), *Product* (*Name* String, *Characteristics* List of Features), *Feature* (*Name* String, *Value* String), *Context* (*Name* String, *Characteristics* List of Features), *Profile* (*Name* String, *Characteristics* List of Features), *DialogLog* (*Log* List of Features).

Our ontology also includes six predicates with the following arguments: *HasLocation* (*Place*, *Position*, and *AgentID*), *HasServices* (*Place*, *Position*, and *List of Services*), *isProvider* (Place, Position, AgentID, Service), *HasContext* (*What*, *Who*), *HasDialog* (*DialogLog* and *AgentID*), *HasProfile* (*Profile* and *AgentID*), and *Provide* (*Product* and *AgentID*).

The interaction of User agents with the other agents in the distributed MAS follows a protocol which consists of the several phases. Some phases involve an interaction, we consider four possible interaction types: present, request, answer, and inform. Each message of next phases is classified into one of them:

1. The ARUBA positioning system is used to extract information about the positions of the different agents in the system. This way, it is possible to know the positions of the different User Agents and thus extract information about the Conversational Agents that are available in the current location. No message involved.
2. The Positioning Agent reads the information about position (coordinates *x* and *y*) and place (*Building* and *Floor*) provided by the ARUBA Positioning Agent by reading it from a file, or by processing manually introduced data. No message involved.

3. The Positioning Agent communicates the position and place information to the User Agent. Present message.

4. Once a User Agent is aware of its own location, it communicates this information to the Facilitator Agent in order to find out the different services available in that location. Request message

5. The Facilitator Agent informs the User Agent about the services available in this position. Inform message.

6. The User Agent decides the services in which it is interested. No message involved.

7. Once the User Agent has selected a specific service, it communicates its decision to the Facilitator Agent and queries it about the service providers that are available. Request message.

8. The Facilitator Agent informs the User Agent about the identifier of the Conversational Agent that supplies the required service in the current location. Inform message.

9. The User Agent asks the Conversational Agent for the required service. Request message.

10. Given that the different services are provided by context-aware Conversational Agents, they ask the User Agent about the context information that would be useful for the dialogue. The User Agent is never forced to transmit its personal information and preferences. This is only a suggestion to customize the service provided by means of the Conversational Agent. Request message.

11. The User Agent provides the context information that has been required. Inform message

12. The conversational agent manages the dialogue providing an adapted service by means of the context information that it has received. No message involved.

13. Once the interaction with the Conversational Agent has finished, the Conversational Agent reads the contents of the log file for the dialogue and send this information to the Log Analyzer Agent. Inform message.

14. The Log Analyzer Agent stores this log file and generates a user profile to personalize future services. This profile is sent to the Conversational Agent. Inform message.

While centralized MAS architecture does not include phases 4 and 5, since they are implemented internally by the System agent.

3 Evaluation Proposal Based on Agents Interaction

An evaluation that simply quantifies number of interactions brings up different types of problems [4]. First, the effect of an interaction unit (a single message) in an agent system may be equivalent to n units (messages) in another system. The weight of the interactions realizing the same work is 1 and it is n in the second. Later, the interaction units that are received and cannot be used by an agent may be a bias in the measurement of interaction in MAS. Therefore, we take the idea of [4] about how to overcome these problems. The first idea is to classify the possible received messages into different types. Then, a weight is associated to a message according to its type. But we also require to measure the effects of interactions. They consist of the processing of the message and then a responsive action. The processing is realized by: memorization that treats the part of change at the internal state caused by the received message, and the decision that concern the choice of the action that will be handled. According to this model, two kinds of functions are considered:

- A function *Interaction* associates weight to the message according to its type. Function *Interaction* can be computed adopting the primitives proposed by [7] to the type of interaction. This work consists of the already defined four possibilities of message types: present, request, answer, and inform. We note $M^A_{received}$ as the set of messages which may be received by agent A, and the function *Interaction* associates a weight value for each received message by agent A:

$$Interaction = M^A_{received} \rightarrow \text{weight of message type} \qquad (1)$$

- This solution partially solves the problem and it works when two messages of the same type have equivalent effects on the agent. So, we introduce Φ that associates weight to the message according to the change provoked on the internal state and the actions triggered by its reception. This function evaluates the treatment of a message in agent systems. For better understanding Φ is divided into two functions: one that evaluates Decision, DD^A and another that evaluates Memorization, MM^A. The function MM^A associates a value to the variation of the internal state (caused by message received). We note as So^A the set of possible original internal states for the agent A while Sf^A is the set of final internal states for agent A. To quantify, some measurable characteristics of the internal state must be defined. The specification of these characteristics is related to the application domain. Since these characteristics have an associated weight, then the function MM^A is considered as the sum of these weights:

$$MM^A = So^A \times Sf^A \rightarrow \text{sum of weights of state characteristics that changed} \qquad (2)$$

Concerning DD^A, this function associates a value to the triggered actions (results of the message received). To quantify, certain type of actions must be defined. A type of actions having a weight. Then, the value of the function DD^A is considered as the sum of the weights of triggered actions where A^A stands for the set of actions may be done by agent A:

$$DD^A = A^A \rightarrow \text{sum of weights of triggered actions} \qquad (3)$$

Then, the function Φ dependant of the change of internal state and of triggered actions due to the message received, is then defined as the sum of these functions DD^A and MM^A.

The approach then focuses on the evaluation of interactions in MAS based on this function combination: *Interaction* $+ \Phi$. We have now to compute functions and assign weights to each message for each agent interaction.

3.1   Weights vs Type of Message: Function *Interaction*

First we compute function *Interaction* according to the exchanged messages of distributed and centralized architectures previously presented. The message types have to be distinguished because of the different basic behaviors that they model from the sender or the receiver points of view:

- A request includes a change of state of the sender, waiting for the answer.
- An inform includes no change of state for both the sender and the receiver. It might generate other informs, and possibly answers.
- A present includes a possible change in the state of the sender and/or of the receiver. Typically, a present will enable entering a society and introduce itself to other agents

3.2   Weights vs Treatment of a Message: Function Φ

Next we have to evaluate the function Φ that computes the variation of internal state caused by memorization step and decision step. Memorization is evaluated by function MM^A, since we have an ontology described in Section 2 we can measure that changes according to number of involved concepts and attributes. We could also consider the relevance of attributes and concepts giving different weights to any of them. We consider three levels of relevance: low, medium and high.

Then we need to compute DD^A function that associate the variation of internal state caused by decision step. This function associates a value to the triggered actions. To quantify, certain type of actions must be defined. Each type of actions should have a weight. The set of actions involved in our agent system can be classified as external and internal. The external actions corresponds to the communicative responses to the given message, where the weight of this reactive action is equivalent to the weight of the content included in the responsive messages. Then, the value of the function DD^A is considered as the sum of the weights of triggered actions. Again we classify the weight in three categories: low, medium and high.

3.3   Context Aware Domain: An Airport Scenario

In order to define a case of use, we used a scenario inspired in the Airport domain which uses the JADE implementation of centralized and distributed architectures previously mentioned. Our airport scenario has six different rooms that do not overlap with each other. In these rooms one or more services can be provided. Providing each of these services involves filling a given number of concept attributes belonging to the airport Ontology. The number of involved attributes is highly variable (from the simplest services such as register and finger to the most complex ones in the commercial zone). Rooms, services, and range of possible number of involved attributed per service are defined in Table 1.

Each service of these paths involves a cycle of the 14 execution phases of our context aware system as we defined it previously. As we also mentioned in Section 4.1, several types of messages were distinguished. Now we proceed to associate adhoc numerical values to these message types:

Table 1. Initial setup of services in the Airport scenario

Service	Service #	Room	Room #	Max Attributes x Service	Min Attr. x Serv.
Register	1	Airport	1	4	2
Customs	2	Customs	2	3	1
Magazines	3	Commercial	3	4	2
Restaurant	4	Commercial	3	2	
Spa	5	Commercial	3	3	2
Shop	6	Commercial	3	2	2
Office	7	Office	4	3	2
Checkin	8	Checkin	5	7	3
Finger	9	Finger	6	1	0

Table 2. Final weights of agents interactions

Phase	Message type	Internal processing	Attributes Relevance	Attributes involved	Final weight
1	0	0	0	0	0
2	0	0	0	0	0
3	1.5	0	1.5	4	$1.5 + 1.5*4$
4	2	1	1.5	4	$2+1+1.5*4$
5	1	0	1.5	$2*s$	$1+1.5*2*s$
6	0	2	0	0	2
7	2	0	1.5	2	$2+1.5*2$
8	1	1	1.5	Service_Overlapping	$1+1+1.5*Service\_Overlapping$
9	2	0	1.5	2	$2+1.5*2$
10	2	0	2	na_s	$2+2*na_s$
11	1	2	2	na_s	$1+2+2*na_s$
12	0	0	0	0	0
13	1	1	2	na_s	$1+1+2*na_s$
14	1	1.5	2	%overlappingLog	$1+1.5+2*\%overlappingLog*na_s$

- request: 2 (a change of state, a reaction produced)
- inform: 1 (no change of state)
- present: 1.5 (1 or 2 change of state)

Additionally we have to give specific values to the labels: maximum, medium and minimum. We consider weights of 1, 1.5 and 2 respectively. And we can then conclude the final weight of each phase as it is shown in Table 2, where na_s stands for the number of attributes involved in the corresponding agent interaction since it is not a constant value, it is different for each service s (see Table 1).

If we consider that our Airport domain has no overlapping services, and that the number of services per room is one but in commercial zone, where it is 4, then we will have the total weights for every step involved in these 14 phases of the distributed architecture will be $29 + 3*s + 1.5*Service\_Overlapping + 2*\%overlappingLog*na_s + 6*na_s))$, in function of the interest of the particular user in each possible commercial service (s). In our case if we asume that Service_Overlapping=0 and %overlappingLog=1, then total cost will be $29 + 3*s + 8*na_s$.

Since centralized architecture did not include phases 4 and 5, with a corresponding cost of 10+3*s, the relative benefits of using a centralized architecture in interactions terms would be: $(10 + 3*s) / (29 + 3*s + 8*na_s)$. Since this benefits are still depending on values of variables s and na_s, we plan to define a montecarlo simulation to obtain aproximate values of this relative benefit of using a centralized approach.

4   Conclusions

Evaluation for Context-Aware agent systems needs to be conducted to compare architecture alternatives. In this paper, we have described one of these comparisons of Multi-Agent Systems (MAS) based on their agents interactions. This approach based on the weight of the exchanged messages by the agents opens a new way to compare and evaluate the efficiency (in terms of communications overhead) of different MAS architectures. We have assigned evaluation values according to a Context-aware problem to show how a final comparative measure can be obtained. Our approach allowed us to experience the problems of giving values to such weights that are obviously ad hoc. As future work we would aim to include more experimentation on different problem domains and MAS architectures with this evaluation technique.

Acknowledgments. This work was supported in part by Projects MEyC TEC2012-37832-C02-01, MEyC TEC2011-28626-C02-02 and CAM CONTEXTS (S2009/TIC-1485).

References

1. Davidsson, P., Johansson, S., Svahnberg, M.: Characterization and evaluation of multi-agent system architectural styles. In: Garcia, A., Choren, R., Lucena, C., Giorgini, P., Holvoet, T., Romanovsky, A. (eds.) SELMAS 2005. LNCS, vol. 3914, pp. 179–188. Springer, Heidelberg (2006)
2. Mylopoulos, J., Kolp, M., Giorgini, P.: Agent-oriented software development. In: Vlahavas, I.P., Spyropoulos, C.D. (eds.) SETN 2002. LNCS (LNAI), vol. 2308, pp. 3–17. Springer, Heidelberg (2002)
3. Giunchiglia, F., Mylopoulos, J., Perini, A.: The tropos software development methodology: Processes, models and diagrams. In: Proceedings of the First International Joint Conference on Autonomous Agents and Multiagent Systems, pp. 63–74. ACM Press (2002)
4. Joumaa, H., Demazeau, Y., Vincent, J.: Evaluation of multi-agent systems: The case of interaction. In: 3rd International Conference on Information and Communication Technologies: From Theory to Applications, pp. 1–6. IEEE (2008)
5. Wooldridge, M., Ciancarini, P.: Agent-oriented software engineering: The state of the art. In: Ciancarini, P., Wooldridge, M.J. (eds.) AOSE 2000. LNCS, vol. 1957, pp. 1–28. Springer, Heidelberg (2001)
6. Sánchez-Pi, N., Fuentes, V., Carbó, J., Molina, J.M.: Knowledge-based system to define context in commercial applications. In: Proc. of the 8th ACIS Conference SNPD 2007, Tsingtao, China, pp. 694–699 (2007)
7. Gaspar, G.: Communication and belief changes in a society of agents: Towards a formal model of autonomous agent. In: Descentralized A. I. 2, pp. 245–255. Elsevier Science, Amsterdam (1991)

Recommending POIs
Based on the User's Context and Intentions

Hernani Costa, Barbara Furtado, Durval Pires,
Luis Macedo, and Amilcar Cardoso

CISUC, University of Coimbra, Portugal
{hpcosta,macedo,amilcar}@dei.uc.pt, {bfurtado,durval}@student.dei.uc.pt

Abstract. This paper describes a Recommender System that implements a Multiagent System for making personalised context and intention-aware recommendations of Points of Interest (POIs). A two-parted agent architecture was used, with an agent responsible for gathering POIs from a location-based service, and a set of Personal Assistant Agents (PAAs) collecting information about the context and intentions of its respective user. In each PAA were embedded four Machine Learning algorithms, with the purpose of ascertaining how well-suited these classifiers are for filtering irrelevant POIs, in a completely automatic fashion. Supervised, incremental learning occurs when the feedback on the true relevance of each recommendation is given by the user to his PAA. To evaluate the recommendations' accuracy, we performed an experiment considering three types of users, using different contexts and intentions. As a result, all the PAA had high accuracy, revealing in specific situations F_1 scores higher than 87%.

Keywords: information overload, machine learning algorithms, multiagent systems, personal assistant agents, recommender systems, user modelling.

1 Introduction

Nowadays, we are experiencing a huge growth in the quantity of information available. This was mainly caused by the advent of communication technology which humans cannot handle properly, and made critical the need for intelligent assistance when browsing, searching or exploring for interesting information. In order to cope with this superabundance, Recommender Systems (RS) are a promising technique to be used, for instance in location-based domains [1,2]. The majority of RS' approaches focus on either finding a match between an item's description and the user's profile (Content-Based [3,4,5]), or finding users with similar tastes (Collaborative Filtering [6,7,8]). These traditional RS consider only two types of entities, users and items, and do not put them into a context when providing recommendations – context, in ubiquitous and mobile context-aware systems, can be defined as the location of the user, in order to identity people and objects around him, and the changes in these elements [9]. However, the most

J.M. Corchado et al. (Eds.): PAAMS 2013 Workshops, CCIS 365, pp. 166–177, 2013.

relevant information for the user may not only depend on his preferences and context, but also in his current intentions [10]. For example, the very same item can be relevant to a user in a particular context, and completely irrelevant in a different one. This is due to the fact that user's preferences and intentions change over time. For this reason, we believe that it is important to have the user's context and intentions in consideration during the recommendation process [11,12,2,13,14,15].

In this work, our goal is to develop a RS that implements a Multiagent System (MAS). Given the user's context and intentions and the sources at our disposal, it will be imperative to create a system capable of recommending POIs in a selective fashion [16]. Additionally, we intend to ascertain how well-suited different Machine Learning (ML) algorithms are to automatically filter irrelevant POIs. After collecting a small set of POIs from a Web location-based service and updating these manually with extra information, three different users' models via stereotypes are created by using a set of rules. Our assumption is that the system will be able to understand the differences between each user, since each one has unique preferences, intentions and behaviours, resulting in different recommendations for different users, even if their context is the same. In order to accomplish that, a MAS was embedded with the purpose of provide selective information to the users [17]. The recommendations' accuracy will be evaluated by correlating the recommendations outputs given by these algorithms, with nine human judges.

The remaining of the paper starts with a presentation of the system's architecture (section 2). Then, section 3 provides an overview of the experimental set-up, and section 4 describes the results obtained. Finally, section 5 presents the final remarks.

2   System Architecture

In this section, we present the system's architecture and all its components used in this work (see figure 1). This architecture can be seen as a *middleware* between the user's needs and the information available.

More specifically, the `Master Agent` is responsible for starting, not only the Web agents, but also the PAAs, described in figure 1 as $PAA_1 \cdots PAA_n$. The system is capable of retrieving POIs' information from several location-based services. However, for the purpose of this work it is only used the Foursquare service, which explains why we used only one Web agent ($Agent_{fourquare}$).

$Agent_{foursquare}$ implements several methods available through the Foursquare API[1], allowing it to start requesting for POIs in a pre-defined area (see section 3.1). During this process, it filters all the POIs that do not belong to the categories we will use in this experiment, and stores the remaining POIs in our system's database (presented in figure 1 as `POIs Database`). This autonomous agent is constantly searching for new information, and verifying if the data stored in the database is up-to-date.

---

[1] https://developer.foursquare.com

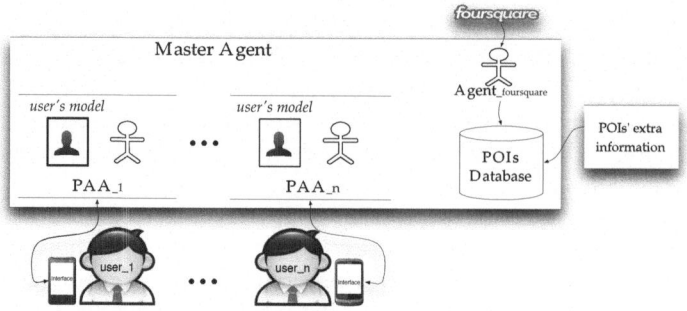

Fig. 1. System's Architecture

Due to the fact that Foursquare service did not have all the information needed for the experiment, we decided to gather more information about the POIs on the field (e.g., POIs' price, timetable, dayOff, as well as some of the attributes missing). This allowed us to have more details about each POI in order to fulfil the set-up requirements of the experiment (see section 3). Thus, this extra information was used to update the POIs' attributes in the database.

As we can see in figure 1, each user has a PAA assigned to him. This agent expects the user to make a request, and, based on his context and intentions (see section 3.2), recommends a list of nearby POIs. In order to improve its recommendations, the PAA continuously learns from the user's experiences. Concretely, each PAA implements a probabilistic classifier to assign a probability value to the relevance of each POI, given the current user's context and intention. Therefore, when the feedback of the true relevance of each recommendation is given by the user to his PAA, the PAA updates its model (described in figure 1 as user's model). As a result, the agent learns every time the user decides to make a request and give his feedback.

3   Experiment Set-Up

Our main objective is to demonstrate how we can face the information overload problem in the location-based service domain by using a MAS architecture. More precisely, it is our intention to take advantage of the multiple independent, autonomous, and goal-oriented units, so called PAAs. In addition, we intend to verify how accurate different ML algorithms perform the task of predicting the user's preferences, while taking his context and intentions into account.

To achieve this goal, an effectiveness evaluation of our system will be performed in section 4. But firstly, we start by explaining the experiment set-up. In detail, the area where we will perform the experimentation is presented in section 3.1. Then, the main attributes used to define the user's context and intentions are presented in section 3.2. Finally, section 3.3 presents the user stereotypes considered in this work, as well as how their models were created.

3.1   Area of Work

The experimentation was performed in Coimbra (Portugal). The number of POIs existent in the city made it impossible to manually update all the POIs retrieved with the extra information needed to this experiment. Thus, a smaller part of the city that had more POIs density and diversity (Coimbra's Downtown) was used. Furthermore, the type of POIs used were restricted to {Food, Shopping, Nightlife} (the categories that contain more POIs in this area). The number of sub-categories for Food are 44, Shopping 8 and Nightlife 11, with 271, 10 and 84 different POIs, respectively. The extra information manually gathered from these 365 places was the POI's price, the day off and the timetable (the possible values for each attribute is explained in the next topic).

3.2   Defining Context and Intentions

Context is the key to personalise the automatic recommendations made by the PAAs for their users. Thus, a set of attributes need to be defined in order to characterise the POI's context, as well as the user's context and intentions. Since these attributes need to be combined, an interface was used to visualise current user location, i.e., his context and intention. The main attributes used to define the user, the POI and the information available in the interface are shown in figure 2.

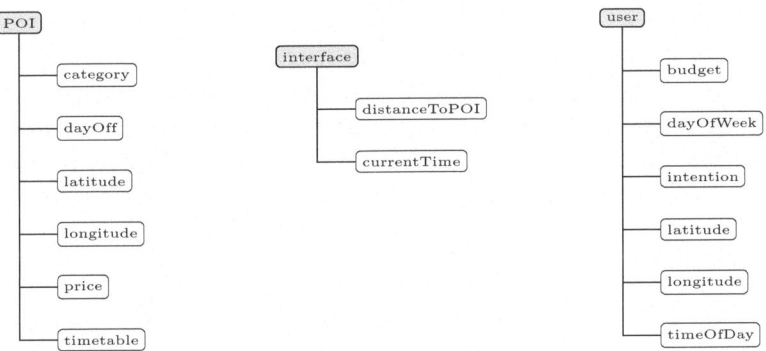

Fig. 2. Main attributes used to define the context of the user, POI and the interface

Possible values for each attribute of the POI's context are:

◇ category = {food, shopping, nightlife},   actually   we   use   the sub-category, e.g., food = ⟨sandwichShop, vegetarian, etc.⟩, shopping = ⟨men'sApparel, women'sApparel, etc.⟩ and nightlife = ⟨wineBar, disco, etc.⟩

◇ dayOff = {a day of the week or combinations}

◇ price = {cheap, average, expensive}, e.g., for lunch {cheap≤5€; 5€>average≤7€; expensive>7€}

⋄ `timetable = {morning, afternoon, night, or combinations}`

Possible values provided by the `interface` are:

⋄ `distanceToPOI = {near≤ 200m; 200m >average≤ 300m; far> 300m}`
⋄ `currentTime = {current day of the week and period of the day (morning, afternoon or night)}`

Possible values for each attribute of the user's context are:

⋄ `budget = {low, medium, high}`, e.g., for lunch `{low≤5€; 5€>medium≤7€; high>7€}`
⋄ `dayOfWeek = {current day of the week}`
⋄ `goal = {coffee, lunch, dinner, party}`, e.g., drink coffee in a `{bakery, coffeeShop, etc.}`, have lunch and dinner in `{burgers, BBQ, etc.}` and party in a `{bar, disco, etc.}`
⋄ `timeOfDay = {morning, afternoon or night)}`

After defining the main attributes considered in this work, we are now able to explain how these were used to create the users' models.

3.3   Datasets and Users Model Description

As one of the goals in this work is the study of different user's profiles, we have created three different types of users, which we believe to be very common in our society:

· u_1 — a user which prefers POIs that are **cheap** and **near**
· u_2 — a user which prefers POIs that are **near**
· u_3 — a user which prefers POIs that are **expensive**

Another objective for this work is the analysis of different probabilistic classifiers suitable for the task of filtering irrelevant POIs, in a completely automatic fashion. For this purpose, two different Bayes classifiers (Naïve Bayes and BayesNet) and two versions of the C4.5 decision tree learner (J48 pruned and unpruned), available through the Weka API[2], were implemented.

However, the cold-start problem [18] needs to be resolved. In order to overcome this problem, a set of rules were used to create three datasets for the three user stereotypes. In detail, the rules used (described in equation 1) consider not only the type of user, but also his goals (i.e., intentions) when given automatic feedback to the POIs in a specific situation. The values given by these rules are binary, 1 if satisfies the user's goal or ∅ if not. To create the datasets we simulated 420 *runs*, for each type of user. For the sake of clarity, a run (r) represents a combination of the user's context and goals with the POIs' context (all the POIs retrieved by the interface in the radius of 400m), i.e., a situation. The resulted datasets, represented as d_1, d_2 and d_3, contain:

· d_1 = 5844 instances, 1371 classified as 1 and 4473 as ∅
· d_2 = 6014 instances, 1774 classified as 1 and 4240 as ∅
· d_3 = 6259 instances, 2590 classified as 1 and 3669 as ∅

---
[2] `http://weka.sourceforge.net/doc`

The dataset number (d_n) correspond to the user type (u_n).

$$R(Goal(u_n)) = \begin{cases} \forall Goal(u_1) \; if \; (distance \leq 200m \;\&\& \\ \qquad\qquad price = cheap), \quad R(u_1) = 1 \\ \forall Goal(u_2) \; if \; (distance \leq 200m), \quad R(u_2) = 1 \\ \forall Goal(u_3) \; \underline{if \; (price = expensive)}, \; R(u_3) = 1 \\ \qquad otherwise, \qquad\qquad\qquad R(u_n) = \emptyset \end{cases} \qquad (1)$$

4 Results

Our experiment can be divided into three different evaluations. Firstly, we made a manual evaluation and calculated the exact agreement between the human judges (section 4.1). Then, using the feedback of the judges about the true correctness of the recommendations, a 10 times tenfold cross-validation was performed with purpose of evaluating the ML algorithms' performance (section 4.2). Finally, well-know metrics were used to compare and analyse the recommendations given by the PAAs with manual evaluation (section 4.3).

4.1 Manual Evaluation

To test our approach, it was used a set of scenarios from real situations. More precisely, in this experiment it were used 3 locations (the ones that had more POI density) in 5 different situations (i.e., considering different user's contexts and intentions). These combinations were named runs (r). Next, it is presented the first 5 runs (location, time of day, day of the week and goal).

$r_1 = $ [40.208934, -8.429067, Morning, Sunday, Coffee]
$r_2 = $ [40.208934, -8.429067, Morning, Monday, Coffee]
$r_3 = $ [40.208934, -8.429067, Afternoon, Wednesday, Lunch]
$r_4 = $ [40.208934, -8.429067, Night, Thursday, Dinner]
$r_5 = $ [40.208934, -8.429067, Night, Saturday, Party]

Then, these runs were manually evaluated by a set of human judges, whose purpose was to analyse the exact agreement (EA) between them, as well as to compare the PAAs' recommendations with their evaluation.

In this experiment it was used 9 human judges (H), divided into three group (G) of 3 people, to evaluate one of the 3 stereotypes (u), i.e., $G_1 = \langle u_1 \rightarrow H_1, H_2, H_3 \rangle$, $G_2 = \langle u_2 \rightarrow H_4, H_5, H_6 \rangle$ and $G_3 = \langle u_3 \rightarrow H_7, H_8, H_9 \rangle$. They were asked to give their personal opinion for a list of scenarios (15 runs), but never contradicting the user's profile they were evaluating.

To perform this evaluation, we have created a user interface using Google Maps[3], see figure 3. The blue icon represents the current user's location, and the other icons represent all the POIs retrieved by the recommender system. Clicking in each POI's icon, the judges could see an information window

---

[3] http://code.google.com/apis/maps/index.html

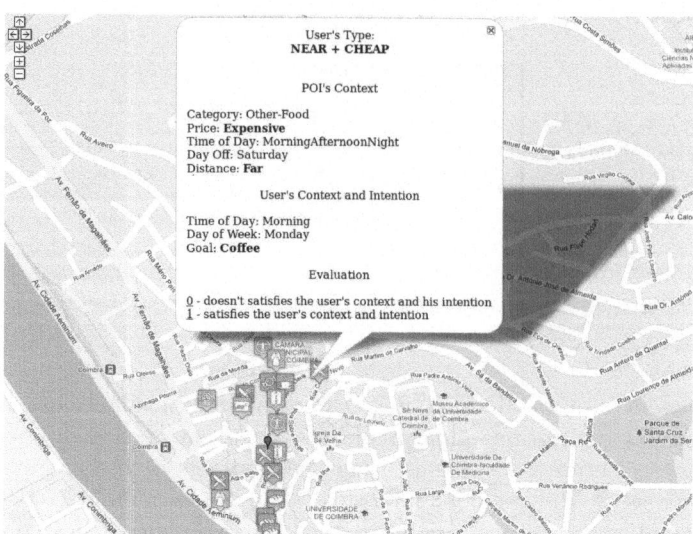

Fig. 3. Manual evaluation example

describing the context of each situation, together with the user's intention. With this information, the judges could perform their evaluation, clicking in the option they prefer. The POIs' names were omitted to avoid that the judges' personal opinion influenced the evaluation. It was important to do this to prevent discrepancy between the judges preferences and the user's profile that they were evaluating. Each human judge was asked to assign one of the following values to each POI, according to the current user's context and POI's context:

∅ - if the POI does not satisfy the user's context and his intention;
1 - if the POI satisfies the user's context and his intention.

The EA among the judges (for the 15 runs) in the G_1 (group one) resulted in 99.4%, 100% for the G_2, and finally 99.4% for the G_3. Despite of the small set of judges, the EA among them, means they have very similar opinions, for all the stereotypes evaluated, validating the data that will be used in the following sections.

4.2   Preliminary Results

To make the evaluation test, it was chosen the 10 times tenfold cross-validation [19]. This test was performed over the instances used in the training with the recommendations given by the algorithms for the 3 types of users, for the 15 runs. Table 1 presents the percentage of correctly and incorrectly classified instances, and also the statistics for the classifiers used (BayesNet, J48 pruned, J48 unpruned and Naïve Bayes, presented as **BN**, **J48**$_p$, **J48**$_u$ and **NB**, respectively).

Table 2 shows in detail the accuracy of the classifiers for the user stereotype u_3. For each prediction class (**Cl**), it is presented the percentage of true positive

Table 1. Classifiers' statistics for the three user stereotypes

	u_1				u_2				u_3			
	BN	J48$_p$	J48$_u$	NB	BN	J48$_p$	J48$_u$	NB	BN	J48$_p$	J48$_u$	NB
Correctly classified instances	99.14	98.57	100	99.43	97.43	100	100	97.71	99.71	99.43	99.43	99.71
Kappa statistic	0.98	0.97	1	0.99	0.95	1	1	0.95	0.99	0.99	0.99	0.99
Mean absolute error	0.05	0.02	0	0.05	0.05	0	0	0.06	0.03	0.006	0.006	0.03
Root mean squared error	0.10	0.11	0	0.11	0.14	0	0	0.15	0.08	0.06	0.06	0.08
Relative absolute error	9.25	3.37	0	10.93	9.45	0	0	11.09	5.92	1.36	1.36	6.90
Root relative squared error	21.18	23.05	0	22.60	28.43	0	0	30.53	15.98	12.60	12.60	16.73
Total number of instances	350				350				350			

Table 2. Cross-validation's statistics for the user stereotype u_3

	TP	FP	P	R	F_1	ROC A.	Cl
BN	99.50	0.49	100	99.50	99.75	99.85	$\emptyset$
	100	0.00	99.33	100	99.67	99.85	1
J48$_p$	98.61	0.13	99.07	98.61	98.84	99.29	$\emptyset$
	98.50	0.14	99.78	98.51	98.14	99.29	1
J48$_u$	98.61	0.14	99.07	98.61	98.84	99.29	$\emptyset$
	98.51	0.15	97.78	98.51	98.14	99.29	1
NB	99.50	0.49	100	99.50	99.75	99.85	$\emptyset$
	100	0.00	99.33	100	99.67	99.85	1

(**TP**), false positive (**FP**), precision (**P**), recall (**R**), F_1 score (**F_1**) and ROC Area (**ROC A.**). The results shows high accuracy for the classes $\emptyset$ and 1, this is due to the fact that the number of instances in the training dataset was balanced.

4.3   Performance Evaluation

In order to observe the relation between the manual evaluation and the output values given by the classifiers, the correlation coefficients between them were computed using the Spearman's coefficient, where $\rho : -100 \leq \rho \leq 100$ (see equation 2).

$$\rho(m_i, x_i) = \frac{\sum_i (m_i - \overline{m})(x_i - \overline{x})}{\sqrt{\sum_i (m_i - \overline{m})(x_i - \overline{x})}} \tag{2}$$

Table 3. Correlation coefficients' results for the three user stereotypes

		BN	J48$_p$	J48$_u$	NB	B
u_1	H$_1$	48.50	49.00	49.00	48.50	100
	H$_2$	48.50	49.00	49.00	48.50	100
	H$_3$	49.25	49.72	49.33	49.25	98.78
	EA$_{G_1}$	48.50	49.00	49.00	48.50	100
	B	48.50	49.00	49.00	48.50	–
u_2	H$_4$	49.01	48.56	48.56	47.34	100
	H$_5$	48.67	48.21	48.21	46.99	99.39
	H$_6$	49.01	48.56	48.56	47.34	100
	EA$_{G_2}$	49.01	48.56	48.56	47.34	100
	B	49.01	48.56	48.56	47.34	–
u_3	H$_7$	49.43	56.50	56.50	49.43	100
	H$_8$	49.43	56.50	56.50	49.43	100
	H$_9$	48.24	55.27	55.27	48.24	97.27
	EA$_{G_3}$	49.43	56.50	56.50	49.43	100
	B	49.43	56.50	56.50	49.43	–

To evaluate the predictions' results, it was created a baseline (**B**) that classifies each instance based on a set of rules (the same rules used to create the training datasets, see equation 1). This baseline acts like a trusted base of comparison with the ML algorithms predictions. Table 3 shows the correlation outputs for the three user stereotypes, as well as the exact agreement for each group of judges (EA$_{G_n}$, where n corresponds to the user stereotype).

The high correlation ($\approx$100) between the judges (H$_n$) and the baseline (**B**) resulted in a perfect monotone increasing relationship, what can be seen as an evidence of the trustiness of their feedback. Although the ML algorithms have lower correlation compared with the baseline, as expected, all of them have positive correlation, revealing in specific situations correlation scores higher than 56% (which can been seen as a good hint to support this approach).

To test the algorithms' accuracy, F_1 scores were calculated for the 3 types of users (u_1, u_2, u_3). Table 4 presents the results with the mean ($\bar{x}$) and the standard deviation (σ) for the 15 runs. In order to avoid some of the ambiguity that could arise when considering only the feedback given by one judge, F_1 was calculated by using the EA of each group (i.e., the EA$_{G_n}$, where n corresponds to user stereotype).

Again, it was used a baseline (**B**, see equation 1) to compare the accuracy between the algorithms. For the sake of clarity, the runs represent different user's intentions, more specifically, runs: $\{r_1, r_2, r_6, r_7, r_{11}, r_{12}\}$= goal coffee; $\{r_3, r_8, r_{13}\}$= goal lunch; $\{r_4, r_9, r_{14}\}$= goal dinner; and $\{r_5, r_{10}, r_{15}\}$= goal party. As we can see, higher values are obtained for the goals lunch, dinner and coffee (see the underline values in the r_3, r_4 and r_{11}, respectively), and lower values are obtained for the goal party (see for instance r_{15}). This happens because the goal party is only valid at night and a lower number of POIs suits that goal,

Table 4. F_1 results (%) for the three user stereotypes

	BN	J48$_p$	J48$_u$	NB	B	BN	J48$_p$	J48$_u$	NB	B	BN	J48$_p$	J48$_u$	NB	B
r_1	26.67	37.50	37.50	26.67	100	31.58	30.00	30.00	31.58	100	26.67	28.57	28.57	26.67	100
r_2	37.50	47.06	47.06	37.50	100	40.00	38.10	38.10	40.00	100	26.67	28.57	28.57	26.67	100
r_3	70.19	76.19	76.19	76.19	100	78.57	78.57	78.57	78.57	100	81.82	85.71	85.71	81.82	100
r_4	76.19	72.73	72.73	76.19	100	78.57	78.57	78.57	78.57	100	81.82	81.82	81.82	81.82	100
r_5	15.38	13.33	13.33	15.38	100	21.05	21.05	21.05	11.11	100	26.67	26.67	26.67	26.67	100
r_6	40.00	40.00	40.00	40.00	100	40.00	33.33	33.33	40.00	100	40.00	57.14	57.14	40.00	100
r_7	40.00	40.00	40.00	40.00	100	33.33	33.33	33.33	33.33	100	40.00	57.14	57.14	40.00	100
r_8	66.67	66.67	66.67	66.67	100	75.00	75.00	75.00	75.00	100	54.55	75.00	75.00	54.55	100
r_9	66.67	57.14	57.14	66.67	100	75.00	75.00	75.00	75.00	100	54.55	54.55	54.55	54.55	100
r_{10}	66.67	57.14	57.14	66.67	100	57.14	57.14	57.14	57.14	100	66.67	66.67	66.67	66.67	100
r_{11}	72.73	69.57	69.57	72.73	100	75.00	75.00	75.00	75.00	100	87.50	87.50	87.50	87.50	100
r_{12}	53.57	60.00	60.00	55.56	100	51.72	63.64	63.64	55.56	100	42.86	72.73	72.73	50.00	100
r_{13}	60.00	60.00	60.00	60.00	100	57.14	57.14	57.14	57.14	100	36.36	44.44	44.44	36.36	100
r_{14}	60.00	57.14	57.14	60.00	100	60.00	57.14	57.14	60.00	100	36.36	36.36	36.36	36.36	100
r_{15}	60.00	57.14	57.14	60.00	100	63.16	57.14	57.14	63.16	100	71.43	71.43	71.43	71.43	100
	u_1					u_2					u_3				
$\overline{x}$	54.55	54.11	54.11	54.68	100	55.82	55.34	55.34	55.41	100	51.59	58.29	58.29	52.07	100
σ	18.56	16.31	16.31	18.56	0.00	18.96	19.65	19.65	20.36	0.00	21.43	21.29	21.29	21.30	0.00

which lead the classifiers to perform worse in these situations. Contrarily, the goal `coffee` is valid in all times of day, resulting in a lot more instances and, consequently, the classifiers' improvement is faster. For example, for the r_{11}, u_3, all the algorithms have 87.50%.

In general, the algorithms performed similarly, however some of them had a higher mean, for a specific user stereotype. For instance, **NB** had better F_1 scores for u_1, for $u_2 \to$ **BN**, and for $u_3 \to$ **J48$_p$** and **J48$_u$**.

To sum-up, ML algorithms can be a powerful technique, in location-based services, to predict which content will be interesting for a determined user. Nevertheless, with more data and more usage the recommendations' accuracy could be improved.

5 Conclusions

In this paper, we discussed the combination of context and intention-awareness with RS, applied in a location-based application. We pointed out what advantages are earned in using, besides the context, the user's intentions, and how to integrate both into a location-based RS. We also presented our system's architecture and described its advantages. ML techniques were used to train the classifiers, more precisely Naïve Bayes, BayesNet and J48 (pruned and unpruned).

Additionally, we created an experimental set-up to evaluate the algorithms' performance, for three types of users. Firstly, a 10 times tenfold cross-validation test was made. Secondly, in order to observe the relation between the manual evaluation and the output values given by the PAAs, the correlation coefficients between them were computed. Finally, we performed an information retrieval task consisting on the identification of correct recommendations, given by the ML algorithms. All of them had high accuracy, revealing in specific situations F_1 scores higher than 87%.

In the future, we are planning numerous improvements to this work, such as: the use of new information sources, as well as their aggregation; take into account new attributes (e.g., POI's quality by considering the number of check-ins and the users' reviews); implement and compare other ML algorithms; analyse other users' profiles; and allow the user to change what values fit in each attributes (e.g., what price is considered cheap, as well as allow the user to select his budget). We think that with more data and more usage the recommendations' accuracy could improve. Furthermore, we plan to analyse the system accuracy when applying selective attention metrics, such as surprise [20], in the recommendation outputs. Finally, we intend to make the application available to the community in order to get more feedback and also to test our system in other situations.

Acknowledgments. Work funded by Fundação para a Ciência e Tecnologia — Project PTDC/EIA-EIA/108675/2008, and by FEDER through Programa Operacional Factores de Competitividade do QREN — COMPETE:FCOMP-01-0124-FEDER-010146.

References

1. van Setten, M., Pokraev, S., Koolwaaij, J.: Context-Aware Recommendations in the Mobile Tourist Application COMPASS. In: De Bra, P.M.E., Nejdl, W. (eds.) AH 2004. LNCS, vol. 3137, pp. 235–244. Springer, Heidelberg (2004)
2. Biancalana, C., Flamini, A., Gasparetti, F., Micarelli, A., Millevolte, S., Sansonetti, G.: Enhancing Traditional Local Search Recommendations with Context-Awareness. In: Konstan, J.A., Conejo, R., Marzo, J.L., Oliver, N. (eds.) UMAP 2011. LNCS, vol. 6787, pp. 335–340. Springer, Heidelberg (2011)
3. Balabanović, M., Shoham, Y.: Fab: Content-Based, Collaborative Recommendation. Commun. ACM 40(3), 66–72 (1997)
4. van Meteren, W., van Someren, M.: Using Content-Based Filtering for Recommendation. In: ECML/MLNET, Workshop on ML and the New Information Age, Barcelona, Spain, pp. 47–56 (2000)
5. Melville, P., Mooney, R.J., Nagarajan, R.: Content-Boosted Collaborative Filtering for Improved Recommendations. In: 18th National Conf. on AI, pp. 187–192. AAAI, CA (2002)
6. Konstan, J.A., Miller, B.N., Maltz, D., Herlocker, J.L., Gordon, L.R., Riedl, J.: GroupLens: applying collaborative filtering to Usenet news. Commun. ACM 40(3), 77–87 (1997)

 7. Billsus, D., Pazzani, M.J.: Learning Collaborative Information Filters. In: 15th Int. Conf. on Machine Learning, pp. 46–54. Morgan Kaufmann, San Francisco (1998)
 8. Das, A.S., Datar, M., Garg, A., Rajaram, S.: Google news personalization: scalable online collaborative filtering. In: 16th Int. Conf. on World Wide Web, pp. 271–280. ACM, NY (2007)
 9. Schilit, B.N., Theimer, M.M.: Disseminating active map information to mobile hosts. IEEE Network 8(5), 22–32 (1994)
10. Costa, H., Furtado, B., Pires, D., Macedo, L., Cardoso, A.: Context and Intention-Awareness in POIs Recommender Systems. In: 6th ACM Conf. on Recommender Systems (RecSys 2012), 4th Workshop on Context-Aware Recommender Systems (CARS 2012). ACM (2012)
11. Woerndl, W., Eigner, R.: Collaborative, Context-Aware Applications for Inter-networked Cars. In: 16th IEEE Int. Workshops on Enabling Technologies: Infrastructure for Collaborative Enterprises, pp. 180–185. IEEE, DC (2007)
12. Adomavicius, G., Mobasher, B., Ricci, F., Tuzhilin, A.: Context-Aware Recommender Systems. AI Magazine 32(3), 67–80 (2011)
13. Baltrunas, L., Ludwig, B., Peer, S., Ricci, F.: Context Relevance Assessment and Exploitation in Mobile Recommender Systems. Personal and Ubiquitous Computing, 1–20 (2011)
14. Huang, H., Gartner, G.: Using Context-Aware Collaborative Filtering for POI Recommendations in Mobile Guides. In: Advances in Location-Based Services. Lecture in Geoinformation and Cartography, pp. 131–147. Springer, Vienna (2012)
15. Costa, H., Macedo, L.: Emotion-Based Recommender System for Overcoming the Problem of Information Overload. In: Corchado, J.M., Bajo, J., Kozlak, J., Pawlewski, P., Molina, J.M., Julian, V., Silveira, R.A., Unland, R., Giroux, S. (eds.) PAAMS 2013 Workshops. CCIS, vol. 365, pp. 178–189. Springer, Heidelberg (2013)
16. Macedo, L.: Selecting Information based on Artificial Forms of Selective Attention. In: 19th European Conference on Artificial Intelligence (ECAI 2010), pp. 1053–1054. IOS Press (2010)
17. Costa, H.: A Multiagent System Approach for Emotion-based Recommender Systems. PhD proposal, University of Coimbra, Coimbra, Portugal (2012)
18. Schein, A., Popescul, A., Ungar, L., Pennock, D.: Methods and Metrics for Cold-Start Recommendations. In: 25th Int. ACM SIGIR Conf. on Research and Development in Information Retrieval, pp. 253–260. ACM, NY (2002)
19. Refaeilzadeh, P., Tang, L., Liu, H.: Cross-Validation. In: Encyclopedia of Database Systems, pp. 532–538. Springer (2009)
20. Macedo, L.: A Surprise-based Selective Attention Agent for Travel Information. In: 9th Int. Conf. on Autonomous Agents and Multiagent Systems (AAMAS 2010), 6th Workshop on Agents in Traffic and Transportation (ATT 2010), pp. 111–120 (2010)

Emotion-Based Recommender System for Overcoming the Problem of Information Overload

Hernani Costa and Luis Macedo

CISUC, University of Coimbra, Portugal
{hpcosta,macedo}@dei.uc.pt

Abstract. Nowadays, we are experiencing a huge growth in the available information, caused by the advent of communication technology, which humans cannot handle by themselves. Personal Assistant Agents can help humans to cope with the task of selecting the relevant information. In order to perform well, these agents should consider not only their preferences, but also their mental states (such as beliefs, intentions and emotions) when recommending information. In this paper, we describe an ongoing Recommender System application, that implements a Multiagent System, with the purpose of gathering heterogeneous information from different sources and selectively deliver it based on: user's preferences; the community's trends; and on the emotions that it elicits in the user.

Keywords: information overload, multiagent systems, personal assistant agents, recommender systems, user modeling.

1 Introduction

The recent explosive growth of information (e.g., in the World Wide Web) has made critical the need for intelligent assistance when users browse, search and explore for interesting information. With new data being created everyday (e.g., in social networks as Facebook, Twitter and online newspapers), humans continuously receive a superabundance of information, which they cannot handle by themselves [1,2]. Moreover, as the number of people and subjects being followed increases, the time required to get through to the social updates they emit also increases, causing a loss of productivity. Additionally, as social updates are broadcast in real-time, humans are frequently interrupted, with can reduce their ability to focus on a demanding task, especially when the social updates are not relevant for their current task (i.e., the interruption could induce a costly cognitive disruption).

In this context, Personal Assistant Agents (PAAs) can be used to retrieve, filter and recommend only relevant information to the user [2,3,4]. Actually, in the last years there has been a remarkable interest in the development of PAAs. These agents have been successfully integrated in available mobile

J.M. Corchado et al. (Eds.): PAAMS 2013 Workshops, CCIS 365, pp. 178–189, 2013.

devices and made their way to the general public. One of the most popular is SIRI[1], a PAA developed by the homonymous company bought by Apple in 2010, and whose technology is now fully integrated into the iPhone 4S. Google released "Google move" after buying CleverSense[2], a company that developed ALFRED/Seymour PAA. More recently, Nuance, the company behind the speech recognition technology in the Siri and dictation features on the iPhone, iPad and OS X, has released a new Siri-like API called Nina[3]. Nina virtual assistant persona, as the company calls it, enables natural conversation, by understanding what users say and mean, and also remembers the context of what is said to refine the results. Even chatbot technology has recently seen a renewed and rising interest with Existor[4] and the chatting software developed by Cleverbot[5] and Tayasui[6].

However, personalised, contextualised and emotional Recommender System (RS), that implements a Multiagent System (MAS) and also integrates heterogeneous sources, are still to come [2]. The user's interests involves a wide range of domains (e.g., politics, sport), which are physically or logically distributed (in terms of their availability and sources). Consequently, it is mandatory to have some kind of retrieval system capable not only of gathering information, but also of filtering it selectively, according to the interests and emotions that this information elicits in the user. For example, nowadays people do not want, or do not have the necessary time, to read all the feeds subscribed, catch up with all the events that will occur or all their friends social notifications [5]. As far as we know, especially concerning the Portuguese language, the literature approaches do not overcome the aforementioned problems. More precisely, they do not take into consideration people's intentions and desires, combined with their social networking habits and also the community trends, into real usable RS application. In order to accomplish that, a MAS will be embedded with the purpose of provide selective information to the users [2].

We believe that it is possible to create an emotion-based RS application, with individual users' agents, capable of filter out irrelevant or emotionless information [2]. Thus, the system needs to handle the people's mental states and also to understand that everyone is different from each other, i.e., everyone has different desires, intentions, interests and motivations to read a specific piece of information [6,7,3]. In order to overcome this information overload problem [1], we identified five tasks that our system needs to be able to perform: *collect* information from different sources; *extract* information from the news, e.g., facebook notifications, tweets or daily news [8]; *represent* the extracted information into a structured representation [9]; *share* information between agents, e.g., users' preferences and emotional features [10]; *deliver* information

---

[1] www.apple.com/iphone/features/siri.html
[2] www.thecleversense.com
[3] www.nuance.com/meet-nina
[4] www.existor.com
[5] www.cleverbot.com
[6] www.tayasui.com

based on the learned or expected human's preferences, intentions and goals, taking advantage of the structured knowledge and the agents community [7].

2 Related Work

Recommender Systems (RS) can be categorised into three main categories [11]: Collaborative Filtering (CF), Content-Based (CB), and Hybrid approach which combines the previous two methods. The first experiments in the RS area adopted pure CF approaches [12], which consist in calculating similarities among users. Knowing the user's neighbours (users with similar opinions or tastes), the system recommends items according to the neighbours' preferences. In fact, with this approach, as more users rate items, more accurate the recommendations become. There are two main paradigms in this approach: *model-based* and *memory-based* techniques, being the latter one the dominant paradigm. In contrast to memory-based CF, where it is used the entire user-item rating dataset to generate a prediction, the model-based CF technique groups different users from the training database into a small number of classes based on their rating patterns.

Another possible approach in RS is CB recommendations, which consists in giving recommendations to a user, based on his past data or personal preferences [13], without involving data from other users. To make that possible, RS must be able to extract content from the items, to verify which content correlates the most with the user's preferences [13]. For example, some works show promising results in different domains, e.g., movies and books [14,15]. Both works used Information Extraction (IE) and text categorisation to create descriptions of products, with the purpose of analysing their similarities with the users' profiles.

Both CB and CF approaches have advantages, but also some shortcomings. Pure CB systems, in some domains, can have problems in the IE process, i.e., some content can be hard to be structured and classified [16]. Another problem that can occur is *overspecialisation* [16]. If the system is programmed to only recommend items with high similarity to the user's previous preferences, the user will never receive recommendations of other types of items. On the other hand, pure CF systems suffer from *cold-start* problems [17]. Whenever a new item is added to the system's database, it does not have any rating, which makes it impossible to be recommended to any user. If a user has unique tastes, and no one has rated the 'same' items he did, he will not receive any recommendations. A similar problem can also occur if the number of items in the database is much larger than the number of users, which makes it difficult to find users that have rated the same items [16].

All these problems led various authors to experiment hybrid RS that merged CF and CB approaches [16,12,17]. These systems have been applied to various domains, such as adaptive hypermedia, content personalisation and user profiling [16,12]. Hybrid recommenders combine users' ratings (CF) with meta-data about the items (CB). Consequently, they overcame some of the problems that each of the previous approaches had.

More recently, several authors have been trying to use context in RS. However, having the user's context in consideration adds an additional dimension of complexity to RS, hence ratings may be valid in only one particular context [18]. Nevertheless, RS can be improved by enrichment with various sorts of contextual information (e.g., relationship among users in social media sites, collaborative tagging, background message of items, timestamp of user actions [19,20]. In the literature, context – for example in ubiquitous and mobile context-aware systems – was initially defined as the location of the user, in order to identity people and objects around him, and the changes in these elements [21]. Therefore, other factors have been added to this definition (e.g., date, season, and temperature) [22]. Some associate the context with the user [23], while others emphasise how context relates to the application [24]. An overview of the notions of context can be found in Adomavicius et al. [25].

Despite of several approaches proposed and new dimensions added to RS, most of the existing RS applications do not take information about human emotions [26] into consideration when recommending information [27]. Consequently, recommender applications are commonly unable to adapt to the constantly changing and evolving users' preferential states. This is partially caused by the difficulty of categorising and representing emotional states [28,29].

Nevertheless, an innovative system, addressed to the restaurant domain, is presented in [27]. In this work, a new approach to model users for RS based on the emotional factor, is described. The model they developed takes into account different attributes related to emotions, which purpose is capturing personality features of a user, e.g., familiarity (confidence) in customer's relationships; degree of patience that a user has on waiting for being served; the efficiency the user needs to feel; and the curiosity to know exotic restaurants. According to the authors, by adding emotional features to the user profile, recommendations are improved regarding the degree of acceptance from the user. It is important to refer that this model is developed taking into account both a CB approach on the information of an isolated user, and a CF approach based on the information provided by the users' community.

More recently, Mostafa et al. [30] presented the Emotion Sensitive News Agent (ESNA), whose purpose is to categorise news stories from different RSS sources into eight emotion categories, according to their emotional content. However, in this approach the affective information conveyed through text is analysed by using a *rule based* approach to assign a numerical valence (i.e., a positive or negative value to assign positive or negative sentiment to the input text). Additionally, the recommendation process considers the cognitive and appraisal structure of emotions [31], and also takes into account the users' preferences.

To sum up, there is a lack of research on applications that use emotion 'in context', and this ability to detect emotions explicitly or even implicitly will add a rich dimension to RS applications.

3   Approach

Figure 1 presents the proposed main components for the emotion-based RS. This system architecture can be seen as a *middleware* between the user's needs (explicit or implicit [32]) and the available information. Its purpose is to deliver information to the user in a selective fashion. As we know, user's intentions and actions are not usually isolated processes, but tend to be influenced by their social environment [5]. However, identifying a user's goals and intentions is not a straightforward task, relying on complex plan recognition [33]. Thus, besides considering the user's model (i.e., preferences, intentions and emotions, represented in the figure 1 as *individual knowledge* and *emotional features*), the agent (PAA) should also contemplate the social networking trends. In the context of this work, trends consist of new data that elicits novelty, surprise or even curiosity in the system community. For this matter, the implementation of collaborative agents to share and discover new trends is imperative.

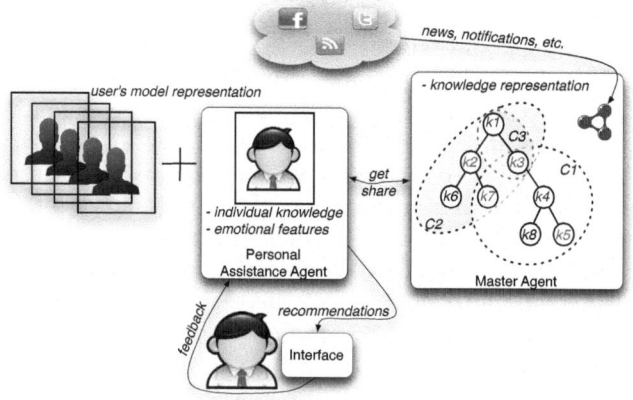

Fig. 1. Emotion-Based RS's Architecture

The user's agent will work as a selective recommender filter. It will compare its user model with the others PAAs and infer new potentially interesting information, even if not suitable for the user's list of implicit preferences [34]. Briefly, these agents will operate in an environment where some of their individual knowledge is shared.

For the system to perform well, it will be necessary to create a structured knowledge representation that these agents can take advantage of when performing tasks. This structure needs to incorporate both the gathered information and the social trends given from the users' *feedback* [35] (e.g., number of views for a specific item and its emotional impact). The emotional impact could be measure by asking the user what was the emotion that a specific information causes in him.

Another system requirement is the use of keyphrases to group sets of similar items (represented in figure 1 as k_n and C_n, respectively). Keyphrases provide a brief summary of a document's contents. More specifically, keyphrases are a concise representation of documents. As large document collections, such as news articles, become widespread and are created every second, the value of such summary information increases. Thus, keyphrases are particularly useful because they can be interpreted individually and independently of each other. Moreover, keyphrases are usually chosen manually [36]. Despite less prone to errors, this task is hardly repeatable, time-consuming and sometimes subjective. Consequently, our system needs to extract keyphrases from heterogeneous Web sources and represent it into a formal representation, in a completely automatic fashion.

The approach we propose for extract information from heterogeneous sources also needs to take into account the news' polarity. A basic task in sentiment analysis is classifying the polarity of a given text at the document, sentence, or word level - whether the expressed opinion in a document, a sentence or word is positive, negative, or neutral (presented in figure 1 as k_n, in different color tones). Commonly, this is done by determining the keyphrases polarity using automated ML algorithms, such as latent semantic analysis or support vector machines. More sophisticated methods can detect the holder of a sentiment (i.e., the person who maintains that affective state) and the target (i.e., the entity about which the affect is felt) [37]. In the future, we intend to relate the user's model with the news' polarity, for example by taking advantage of the SentiLex[7], to recommend only news that satisfies the user's emotional preferences.

The resulting knowledge base will make easy the retrieval by browsing and searching. Furthermore, it will allow clustering information into broader categories. To identify these domains, presented in figure 1 as C_n, it will be necessary to create associations between "close in context" objects. Specifically, clustering algorithms will be used to classify similar objects into different groups – more general topics than simple keyphrases – that will be used to send a list of main topics to the user, in order to start modelling the user's preferences and solve the cold-start problem.

Another method in the knowledge representation process that we intend to take advantage of, is collaborative keyphrasing, when available in the sources. In order to understand the benefits and limitations of using social generated keyphrases for indexing and retrieval purposes, it is important to investigate: to what extent the community influences keyphrasing behaviour; their effects in the represented knowledge; and whether this influence helps or hinders search and retrieval in our knowledge base. Indeed, some Web sources already use social keyphrasing (e.g., Twitter and Delicious) to identify topics of interest. Another important system requirement is its aggregation feature, i.e., we need to develop an aggregator component capable of gathering items from a wide number of Web-sources, such as Facebook, Twitter and RSS feeds.

---

[7] http://dmir.inesc-id.pt/project/SentiLex-PT_02

4 Experimentation and Evaluation

The experimentation phase starts with the definition of the evaluation process that will be applied to the system described in the approach section. The experimentation should be taken using data from real world usage with field tests. The system must be evaluated taking into account the interaction of the user with the system. Firstly, explicitly feedback given by the user will be used to access the system accuracy. Then, the accuracy will be inferred by the system, using an implicit feedback mechanism (like total reading time and past click behaviour [38,39].

4.1 Information Extraction

The utility of the extraction methods and knowledge extracted must be evaluated taking into account the *quality* and the *quantity* of the data extracted. The quality depends on the amount of keyphrases that are correctly identified, and the quantity depends on the number of keyphrases extracted among those that should have been extracted. There exists two main evaluation approaches: manual evaluation and the use of gold standard.

Manual Evaluation is the most classic type of evaluation. Due to its complexity, it is sometimes easier to transmit the principles that should be considered in the evaluation process to human judges, rather than encode a system to automatically evaluate the resource according to these principles. Most of the times, automatic evaluation can not be used, being the evaluation done manually by relying heavily on time consuming work from domain specialists. The disadvantages are: monotonous work, hard to repeat and also subjective to the judge's criteria. Gold Standard is a resource (e.g., could be another knowledge base) that certainly is correct – possibly because it was manually created by specialists. The new resource can be compared to a golden standard according to some criteria in order to assess its accuracy. Usually there are used three common measures in Information Retrieval, precision, recall and F_1.

For the purpose of this work, if possible a golden standard will be used to analyse the results' reliability, Besides that, manual evaluation of a small but representative part of the results need to be performed, in order to analyse the various stages of the development.

4.2 Recommendations

As we already mentioned, the aim of a RS is to predict appreciable items to the user. To do that we strongly believe in our approach to provide selective recommendations according to the user's preferences. However, the expected results from this hypothesis are likely to be subjective, since it cannot be measured accurately because their interpretation may vary under the user's perspectives. Nevertheless, the system must be evaluated taking into account the quality of the data recommended through the PAAs according to several defined evaluation' metrics, as well as in terms of the system's performance and usability.

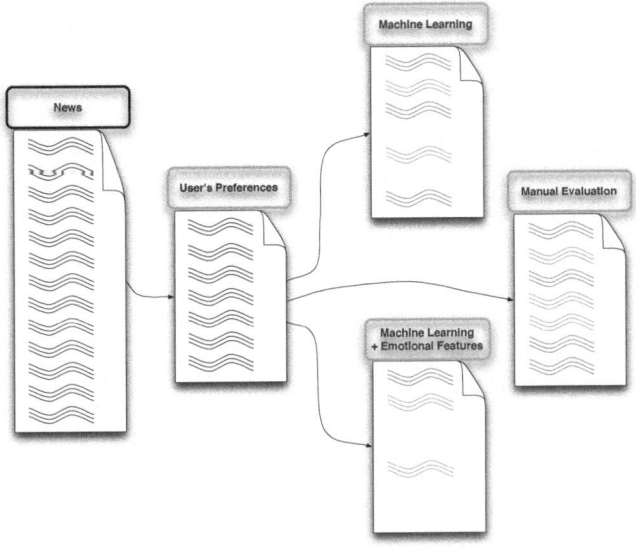

Fig. 2. An example scenario of the evaluation process

The recommendations' quality will depend on the amount of items that are correctly recommended, which can be measured by analysing the users' feedback. To test the system' accuracy, we intend to observe the relationships between the manual evaluation and the output values given by both Machine Learning (ML) and ML with emotional features. In figure 2, we present an example scenario of the evaluation process. On the left, with label *"News"*, we have all the news stored in the system, then, after choosing his preferences (with label *"User's Preferences"*) the user will receive only news from specific thematics. However, this is not enough to prevent the users from receiving irrelevant information, as we show on the right side of the figure, with label *"Manual Evaluation"*, where the green and red items represent interesting and not interesting items to the user, respectively. But, accordingly to the scenario in the figure, our assumption is that using ML and ML with emotional features it will be possible to improve the system' accuracy (labels *"Machine Learning"* and *"Machine Learning + Emotional Features"*, respectively). After analysing the results from the situation presented in figure 2, it is expected higher accuracy when using ML with emotional features techniques, than without using them (see table 1). In short, our assumption can be considered very promising, being a good starting point.

The performance is commonly evaluated through the time the system consumes while executing the expected tasks, but also relates to how the system scales and keeps responding under different circumstances.

To evaluate the usability, questionnaires will be used to assess users' satisfaction. Still concerning usability, before starting the interface implementation process, we intend to make questionnaires to humans in order to

Table 1. Results from the scenario presented in figure 2

	Precision(%)	Recall(%)	F_1(%)
User's Preferences	≈43	100	≈60
Machine Learning	60	≈66	≈63
Machine Learning + Emotional Features	≈66	≈66	≈66

identify their needs. For instance, to understand how they would like to consult the news, what is the better way to provide feedback and to recommend news to others.

5 Expected Contributions

In this work, our goal is to develop a RS that delivers information in a selective fashion. Given the user's expectations and the sources at our disposal, it will be imperative to create a system that performs near real time. To do that, and taking advantage of the belief-desire theory of emotion [40], as well as of the techniques developed in the fields of Artificial Intelligence, RS, Natural Language Processing, MAS and Affective Computing, we will create an emotion-based RS (described in the previews section). The expected outcomes are:

- ◇ Knowledge extraction from assorted sources and contexts into a structured representation.
- ◇ Beyond the standard data available on the Web (e.g., daily news), we intend to study how can RS benefit from social networking integration (such as friends recommendations, i.e., facebook notifications and tweets). Moreover, we intend to answer the question: − Will social networking integration increase the users usage and contributions in our application?
- ◇ A comparative view of the most common algorithms used to identify keyphrases. Study the most suitable metrics to weight keyphrases and how these metrics may be used to identify clusters (crucial to learn main categories in the knowledge base).
- ◇ Not only analyse for how long past information may be considered useful for the system, but also for the users [41].
- ◇ Identify the best structure to represent all the knowledge produced, not only the extracted data but also the information created by the agents (e.g., feedback and emotional features).
- ◇ Create dynamic and automatic user's models and study which are the most suitable for the users' demands.
- ◇ Analyse the impact of sharing information among the agents in order to answer this question: − Does the introduction of collaborative recommendations improve the system's trust?
- ◇ Finally, and most important, analyse if the affect-based PAA avoid their human owners from receiving irrelevant or emotionless information, outperforming

the non-affect-based ones. Analysing the impact of affective features in the recommendations' accuracy.

Information overload has many negative implications, not only in personal life, but also in organisations, business and in the world economy in general [1]. As a result, this work intends to minimise some of these negative implications in human life. Although this work is directed for Portuguese, we intend to perform some experiments in English, in order to contribute and receive feedback from the international community. Furthermore, it is our intention to apply the resulting contributions in other application domains, such as navigation systems.

6   Concluding Remarks

The research proposal presented in this article is an answer to the growing demand on RS. More precisely, it addresses the lack of emotion-based RS, specially concerning real-time textual information. The importance of this kind of systems has been shown and, as far as we know, there is no research in this area for Portuguese or even for English.

This work will be focused in the development of a RS capable of filtering irrelevant and emotionless news to the user, by using a MAS approach and taking advantage of techniques developed in the fields of Artificial Intelligence, RS, Natural Language Processing, MAS and Affective Computing. Firstly, it will be implemented an aggregation module to acquire daily news from heterogeneous sources. Then, information extraction techniques will be used to extract the most relevant items. These items will be stored in a knowledge base that will provide support to the user's agent, when retrieving and storing information. These PAA will take advantage of their model and the community trends when recommending a new piece of information.

References

1. Bawden, D., Holtham, C., Courtney, N.: Perspectives on Information Overload. Aslib Proceedings 51(8), 249–255 (1999)
2. Costa, H.: A Multiagent System Approach for Emotion-based Recommender Systems. PhD proposal, University of Coimbra, Coimbra, Portugal (2012)
3. Costa, H., Furtado, B., Pires, D., Macedo, L., Cardoso, A.: Context and Intention-Awareness in POIs Recommender Systems. In: 6th ACM Conf. on RS, 4th Workshop on Context-Aware Recommender Systems. ACM (2012)
4. Costa, H., Furtado, B., Pires, D., Macedo, L., Cardoso, A.: Recommending POIs Based on the User's Context and Intentions. In: Corchado, J.M., Bajo, J., Kozlak, J., Pawlewski, P., Molina, J.M., Julian, V., Silveira, R.A., Unland, R., Giroux, S. (eds.) PAAMS 2013 Workshops. CCIS, vol. 365, pp. 166–177. Springer, Heidelberg (2013)
5. Joly, A., Maret, P., Daigremont, J.: Enterprise Contextual Notifier, Contextual Tag Clouds towards more Relevant Awareness. In: ACM Conf. on Computer Supported Cooperative Work (CSCW 2010). ACM (2010)

6. Macedo, L.: Selecting Information based on Artificial Forms of Selective Attention. In: 19th European Conference on Artificial Intelligence (ECAI 2010), pp. 1053–1054. IOS Press (2010)
7. Knijnenburg, B.P., Reijmer, N.J., Willemsen, M.C.: Each to His Own: How Different Users Call for Different Interaction Methods in Recommender Systems. In: 5th ACM Conf. on RS, pp. 141–148. ACM, NY (2011)
8. Ritter, A., Clark, S., Mausam, Etzioni, O.: Named Entity Recognition in Tweets: An Experimental Study. In: Conf. on Empirical Methods in Natural Language Processing, EMNLP 2011, pp. 1524–1534. ACL, PA (2011)
9. Sacco, O., Bothorel, C.: Exploiting Semantic Web Techniques for Representing and Utilising Folksonomies. In: Int. Workshop on Modeling Social Media, pp. 9:1–9:8. ACM, NY (2010)
10. Guy, I., Ronen, I., Raviv, A.: Personalized Activity Streams: Sifting through the "River of News". In: 5th ACM Conf. on RS, pp. 181–188. ACM, NY (2011)
11. Adomavicius, G., Tuzhilin, A.: Toward the Next Generation of Recommender Systems: A Survey of the State-of-the-Art and Possible Extensions. IEEE Trans. on Knowledge and Data Engineering 17(6), 734–749 (2005)
12. Billsus, D., Pazzani, M.J.: Learning Collaborative Information Filters. In: 15th Int. Conf. on Machine Learning, pp. 46–54. Morgan Kaufmann Publishers Inc., San Francisco (1998)
13. van Meteren, W., van Someren, M.: Using Content-Based Filtering for Recommendation. In: ECML/MLNET Workshop on Machine Learning and the New Information Age, Barcelona, Spain, pp. 47–56 (2000)
14. Mooney, R.J., Roy, L.: Content-Based Book Recommending Using Learning for Text Categorization. In: 5th ACM Conf. on Digital Libraries, pp. 195–204. ACM, NY (2000)
15. Mukherjee, R., Jonsdottir, G., Sen, S., Sarathi, P.: MOVIES2GO: An online voting based movie recommender system. In: 5th Int. Conf. on Autonomous Agents, pp. 114–115. ACM, NY (2001)
16. Balabanović, M., Shoham, Y.: Fab: Content-Based, Collaborative Recommendation. Commun. ACM 40(3), 66–72 (1997)
17. Schein, A., Popescul, A., Ungar, L., Pennock, D.: Methods and Metrics for Cold-Start Recommendations. In: 25th Int. ACM SIGIR Conf. on Research and Development in Information Retrieval, pp. 253–260. ACM, NY (2002)
18. Woerndl, W., Schlichter, J.: Introducing Context into Recommender Systems. In: AAAI, Workshop on RS in e-Commerce, Vancouver, Canada, pp. 22–23 (2007)
19. Burke, R.: Hybrid Recommender Systems: Survey and Experiments. User Modeling and User-Adapted Interaction 12(4), 331–370 (2002)
20. Adomavicius, G., Sankaranarayanan, R., Sen, S., Tuzhilin, A.: Incorporating Contextual Information in Recommender Systems using a Multidimensional Approach. ACM Trans. Inf. Syst. 23(1), 103–145 (2005)
21. Schilit, B.N., Theimer, M.M.: Disseminating active map information to mobile hosts. IEEE Network 8(5), 22–32 (1994)
22. Brown, P.J., Bovey, J.D., Chen, X.: Context-aware Applications: From the Laboratory to the Marketplace. IEEE Personal Communications 4(5), 58–64 (1997)
23. Dey, A.K., Abowd, G.D., Salber, D.: A Conceptual Framework and a Toolkit for Supporting the Rapid Prototyping of Context-Aware Applications. Human-Computer Interaction 16(2), 97–166 (2001)
24. Rodden, T., Chervest, K., Davies, N., Dix, A.: Exploiting Context in HCI Design for Mobile Systems. In: Workshop on Human Computer Interaction with Mobile Devices, pp. 21–22 (1998)

25. Adomavicius, G., Mobasher, B., Ricci, F., Tuzhilin, A.: Context-Aware Recommender Systems. AI Magazine 32(3), 67–80 (2011)
26. Picard, R.: Affective Computing. MIT Press, MA (1997)
27. González, G., Lopez, B., Rosa, J.L.D.L.: The Emotional Factor: An Innovative Approach to User Modelling for Recommender Systems. In: AH 2002, Workshop on Recommendation and Personalization in e-Commerce, Spain, pp. 90–99 (2002)
28. Parrott, W.: Emotions in Social Psychology: Key Readings. Key Readings in Social Psychology. Taylor & Francis (2000)
29. Stickel, C., Ebner, M., Steinbach-Nordmann, S., Searle, G., Holzinger, A.: Emotion Detection: Application of the Valence Arousal Space for Rapid Biological Usability Testing to Enhance Universal Access. In: Stephanidis, C. (ed.) Universal Access in HCI, Part I, HCII 2009. LNCS, vol. 5614, pp. 615–624. Springer, Heidelberg (2009)
30. Al Masum Shaikh, M., Prendinger, H., Ishizuka, M.: Emotion Sensitive News Agent (ESNA): A system for user centric emotion sensing from the news. Web Intelligence and Agent Systems 8(4), 377–396 (2010)
31. Ortony, A., Clore, G.L., Collins, A.: The Cognitive Structure of Emotions. Cambridge University Press (1990)
32. Lee, C.H.L., Liu, A.: Modeling Explicit and Implicit Service Request for Intelligent Interface Design. In: CISIS, pp. 742–747 (2009)
33. Jonsson, A.: Natural Language Generation without Intentions. In: 12th European Conf. on Artificial Intelligence, Workshop on Planning and Natural Language Generation, pp. 102–104 (1996)
34. Woerndl, W., Huebner, J., Bader, R., Gallego-Vico, D.: A Model for Proactivity in Mobile, Context-Aware Recommender Systems. In: 5th ACM Conf. on RS, pp. 273–276. ACM, NY (2011)
35. Salton, G., Buckley, C.: Improving Retrieval Performance by Relevance Feedback. JASIS 41(4), 288–297 (1990)
36. Abulaish, M., Anwar, T.: A web content mining approach for tag cloud generation. In: 13th Int. Conf. on Inf. Integration and Web-based Applications and Services, pp. 52–59. ACM, NY (2011)
37. Kim, S.M., Hovy, E.: Identifying and Analyzing Judgment Opinions. In: Main Conf. on Human Language Technology Conf. of the North American Chapter of the ACL, HLT-NAACL 2006, pp. 200–207. ACL, PA (2006)
38. Carreira, R., Crato, J.M., Gonçalves, D., Jorge, J.A.: Evaluating adaptive user profiles for news classification. In: 9th Int. Conf. on Intelligent User Interfaces, IUI 2004, pp. 206–212. ACM, NY (2004)
39. Liu, J., Dolan, P., Pedersen, E.R.: Personalized News Recommendation Based on Click Behavior. In: 15th Int. Conf. on Intelligent User Interfaces, IUI 2010, pp. 31–40. ACM, NY (2010)
40. Reisenzein, R.: Emotions as Metarepresentational States of Mind: Naturalizing the Belief-Desire Theory of Emotion. Cognitive Systems Research 10(1), 6–20 (2009)
41. Li, L., Zheng, L., Li, T.: LOGO: A Long-Short User Interest Integration in Personalized News Recommendation. In: 5th ACM Conf. on RS, pp. 317–320. ACM, NY (2011)

A Review on Mobile Applications
for Citizen Emergency Management

David Gómez, Ana M. Bernardos, Javier I. Portillo, Paula Tarrío, and José R. Casar

Data Processing and Simulation Group, Dpt. Signals Systems and Radiocommunications,
School of Telecommunications Engineering, Technical University of Madrid
Av. Complutense 30, Madrid, Spain
{david.gomez,abernardos,javierp,paula,jramon}@grpss.ssr.upm.es

Abstract. Mobile devices may be a powerful tool to help in case of emergency, not only for the person or people in danger but also for those ones giving assistance to them, professionally or not. In order to determine how mobile applications are currently being used in this area and the possibilities for innovation, this paper gathers the result of a review of about more than 250 applications commercially available. These applications have been featured to analyze their value proposition (e.g. main service goal, target user or pricing approach) and their operational features, with respect to their level of context-awareness and the discovery and notification of emergencies. Additionally, the paper proposes the functional design of a mobile application for Citizen Emergency Management, which takes advantage of the gap of the available offer.

Keywords: mobile applications, emergency management, technology analysis.

1   Introduction

The generalization of smartphones and tablets has been key for the implementation of ubiquitous computing concepts [1], in which information and communication technologies merge with daily environments to facilitate interaction with them. These devices are nowadays easily accessible, usable and provide a wide amount of sensing capabilities (e.g. detection of location and proximity, noise, light, activity, resource consumption) that may be used to deliver highly adaptive services. From the developers' point of view, a significant improvement has been the delivery of simple application programming interfaces to facilitate gathering this sensor-based context information. A wide range of applications, from location-based games to augmented travel guides, has quickly flooded the market.

Mobile applications are also supporting people when dealing with emergencies or risky unexpected situations in which anybody can be involved: road accidents, natural disasters such as floods, health problems as heart attacks, personal safety danger or fires. To date, there is a very diversified offer, which goes from providing escape guidelines during a fire in a building [2] or during nuclear accidents [3] to help elderly people when in a medical emergency [4]. Road accident detection through mobile sensing is also available [5-7].

J.M. Corchado et al. (Eds.): PAAMS 2013 Workshops, CCIS 365, pp. 190–201, 2013.
© Springer-Verlag Berlin Heidelberg 2013

This paper focuses on analyzing this offer, in order to find the innovation gap for delivering value through an integrated mobile application that serves to strengthen the link between citizens and public security authorities. In next sections, we include an analysis for emergency applications that are currently available in Google Play. The employed methodology for the analysis is detailed in Section 2. Afterwards, Section 3 contains the value proposition analysis, including information about the applications' main service goals, their target users and their commercial approach. Section 4 contains the operational analysis, taking into consideration what type of technology is needed for the applications to work. Finally, Section 5 makes a proposal to develop a Citizen Emergency Management 112/911-like mobile application, by gathering existing functionalities and adding new ones. Section 6 concludes the paper.

2   Methodology for Data Gathering

Nowadays, the consumer of mobile technology has a wide variety of options regarding devices. In particular, the Operating System (OS) is a discerning feature: Android (from Google), iOS (from Apple), Symbian OS (from Nokia), BlackBerry OS (from RIM) or Windows Phone (from Microsoft) are the most popular options. Whereas Apple with iOS holds the first position with respect to market share, including all its devices (iPhone, iPad, iPod) [8], Android is on the top of smartphone sales [9]. Application developers seem to prefer iOS for its facility to be monetized, because of the commercial/service deadlock in which Apple users are closed after initiating the use of this operative system. With respect to the number of available applications, iOS outdoes Android, however Android provides an extensive set of free applications and it is rapidly increasing the number of available ones, reaching more than 472.000 in January 2013 [10]. When comparing the information that can be retrieved from the application markets, it happens that data in 'App Store' (catalogue from Apple) do not include particularities on technical aspects. On the contrary, Google Play reports about the device's resources that an application will need to work properly (permissions).

All in all, Google Play from Android is thus a reasonable choice to gather information about the available applications, providing equilibrium between quantity of registries and functional variety, and access to relevant information.

Thus, our analysis is based on the set of emergency-related applications available in Google Play. Google Play, the substitute of former Android Market since March 2012, is Google's tool for digital distribution, the channel to provide several services as music, movies or books, apart from applications for their devices. To extract the records for our analysis, we have configured a search that has been executed on the English language website, using the keyword 'emergency' with following filters: 'All prices', 'SafeSearch: off', 'Sort by: Relevance'. After a first screening of the results, we selected the 250 applications at the top of the list as a representative sample of the functional diversity (the resulting list was containing more than 1.000 applications). It is important to note that, on the initial dataset, filtering has been needed, as there are applications where the 'emergency' word appears in their description but then is not focused on providing any kind of emergency-related service. For instance, 'City of Friends' application is a game for children, but its description contains 'emergency' word because it is based on emergency teams.

For each application in our list, we collected data such as description, required Android version, Google Play ategories[1], installs, price, content rating, current Android OS version, number of downloads, application size, developer, rating based on user reviews, date of last update, and required permissions useful to infer information about techniques and technologies on which the applications rely on. The gathered registries were retrieved in April-June 2012.

On this data, together with the applications' description and their websites (when available), we extracted aggregated information about two main aspects: the application value proposition and its technical operational features. Table 1 shows the analysis model, summarizing the info sources, the specific features of interest and the feature description for each main aspect.

Table 1. Model for analysis. The marketplace refers to Google-Play

General aspects to consider	Info source	Specific features to analyze	Features description
Value proposition	Category in marketplace	General application scenario	Classification in user scenarios from Google-Play categories
	Application description	Main service goal	Functional value proposition
		Target user	Victims, rescue teams, voluntaries, witnesses, general public
		User revenue model	Paid vs. free applications
Operational features	Permissions in marketplace	Level of context-awareness	Use of location information
		Emergency detection method	Proactive or automatic
		Emergency notification method	Phone call, SMS, social network, email, sound&light alarm

3   Analysis of the Value Proposition for the Existing Mobile Emergency Application Offer

All the 250 applications that were collected are related to emergency detection, notification or management, but designed to work in different scenarios. To have a general view of the type of general emergency application categories that are available, we have considered Google Play categories as an initial element for classification[1]. Figure 1 shows that most of applications are classified in 'Health & Fitness' or 'Medical'

---

[1] Google Play categories, available in: http://support.google.com/googleplay/android-developer/bin/answer.py?hl=en&answer=113475&topic=2897459&ctx=topic

sections, which gather 61 and 60 applications, respectively. The following more populated category is 'Tools', with 25 applications related to emergency assistance. 'Travel & Local' includes applications dedicated to help people who have been affected by an emergency during a trip (21 applications); for instance, 'Bangkok Emergency' is targeting tourists and residents in Bangkok and contains useful information, e.g. phone number of police, to retrieve if an user is victim of an emergency. It is important to bear in mind that the classification into categories is done under the personal criteria of the application developer. This can led to biases or misclassifications, which may for instance explain the amount of applications in 'Lifestyle' category.

Figure 1 also includes the commercial terms under which applications are offered to the market (free or paid applications). In Google Play, the number of free applications over the total is around 77% [10]. Accordingly, the number of free emergency-related applications exceeds the paid group significantly (63.2 % free, 36.8 % paid). There is an exception, the 'Medical' scenario, which includes different type of applications: from those used to help someone that has suffered a sudden health problem (as a heart attack) to interactive health guidebooks (about anatomy, medicines, drugs or first aid). In this case, the percentage of free applications over the total is just 13.6 %. Moreover, the most expensive application has been classified inside of this group with a cost of 127,47€.

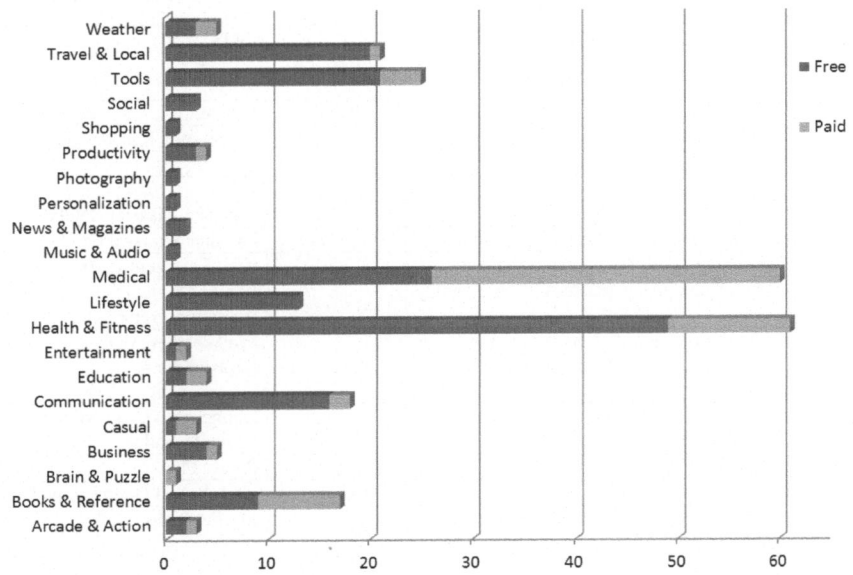

Fig. 1. Category vs. number of applications, sorted by user revenue model

On this initial classification, and after going in depth into the description for each application, we have grouped applications by considering their main functional service goals. Results are gathered in Table 2, together with the percentage of applications in each of them and some sample applications.

In this functional taxonomy, the most numerous group is related to health emergencies (as it was in Google Play categories), containing applications focused on providing help during heart attacks, blood pressure problems, diabetes disease or epilepsy.

The identified groups are not disjoint, being possible for an application to belong to more than one single group. For instance, 'Emergency button' generate an alert requesting help to predefined contact, so it belong to three categories: 'Personal safety', 'Accidents' and 'Health problems'. The majority of applications (41.2% of applications, 103) have been classified as belonging to two different groups. 34% (91) belongs to a single one, and 8% (20) are classified in three different groups. The remaining ones, 14.4% (36), belong to at least 4 groups (with a maximum of 7 groups).

Table 2. List of functional service goals

Main functional service goal	Percentage over total	Examples of applications
Asking for help from the police (safety personal)	58(23.2%)	Emergency Panic Button Guard My Angel SOSbeacon Mayday Emergency Lite
Providing attendance during traffic accidents	45(18%)	Emergency Alert (MarketVer) Car Crash Emergency App
Requesting aid in air accidents	21 (8.4%)	Rega
Asking for help when someone suffers a health problem (e.g. heart attack, epilepsy, blood pressure, diabetes)	127(50.8%)	iSOS
Monitoring security and control of places	1(0.4%)	UAlberta
Activation hard sounds or striking lights for Attracting attention	14(5.6%)	Emergency Rescue Alarm
Receiving information about happened incidents.	16(6.4%)	Fema National Disaster Safety Center
Providing instructions to solve a certain emergency	106(42.4%)	Disaster Survival Guide
Monitoring and tracking of user application position	2(0.8%)	ICE: Emergency Contact
Supplying instructions to evacuate the emergency place.	9(3.6%)	Ready TN Arlington Prepares
To report information about Natural disasters or weather alerts. Furthermore, it is included as to act in these situations	32(12.8%)	Pro Weather Alert Disaster Alert
Teaching right people's behavior when the emergency includes dangerous materials	8(3.2%)	Dangerous Goods Manual Cargo Decoder
Requesting aidduring Fires	27(10.8%)	Ready Plan
Providing help in Sky accidents	1(0.4%)	Notfall App Bergrettung Tirol
Giving suitable instructions for solving an emergency that is suffered by a pet	2(0.8%)	My Pet Record

With respect to the final user (Fig. 2), we have identified the following groups: victim (59%), professionals rescue team (14%), rescue voluntary (14%), witness (7%), and general public (that has not been affected by the emergency) (6%). The majority of them have been developed for victims, in comparison with the next group, professional rescue team, that has a lower percentage, 59% versus 14 %.

4   Operational Features of Current Mobile Emergency Applications

In this Section, we analyze the emergency application set by considering the resources and technologies they rely on, in order to have some aggregated information about how they work. To do so, we consider the application description and the permissions it needs to work in the mobile device (for each application, Google Play records gather data about the permissions that a user must provide to enable the application use). Permissions are listed in y-axis in Figure 3. This figure also shows the amount of applications needed permissions of each type.

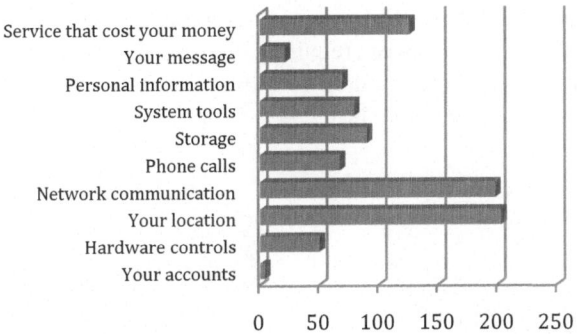

Fig. 2. Permissions requested by analyzed applications

The most requested permissions were: 1) access to location data (fine location, coarse location, mock location); 2) access to communication resources (creation of Bluetooth connection, full Internet access); 3) use of communication tools (SMS sending, directly call phone numbers). Figure 4 shows the number of applications using different kinds of the three previously mentioned resources.

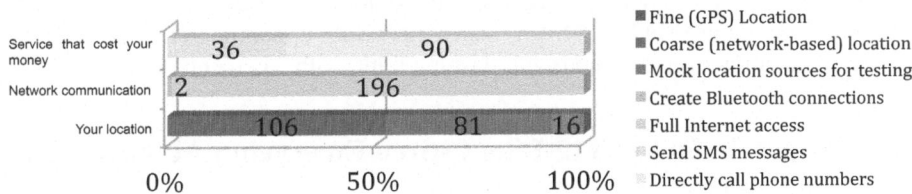

Fig. 3. Applications by used permissions

Depending on the application functionalities, the use of sensors or access to personal data may be needed. For example, most of applications use the GPS sensor when they need to know about the user's location. Location information is necessary for a significant number of applications (81.2% applications over the total): 106 use the GPS sensor, while 81 relies on the network-based location system. Most of them combine both techniques, as GPS do not work indoors, where network-based localization is available. If we assimilate location information use to context-awareness, we could say that most of current emergency applications include context-aware features. Although location provides a lot of information about the user's situation, this approach to context-awareness is obviously reductionist. Some more context-aware features may be supposed for an application from the use of 'personal information' permissions; in the dataset, 27.6 % applications need access calendar events, contact list or system logs in their operation.

Other aspect to consider is how emergency detection is done (Figure 5a). In our application review, two possibilities appear, proactive (manual) or automatic. Automatic detection can be performed by using the inertial sensors embedded in the devices, e.g. through accelerometer or gyroscope measures, as these sensors are enough to discover whether there has been a sudden movement (1.44% of applications). Other automatic detection procedures imply the estimation of user's position relying on GPS or on the network information (2.17%). With respect to proactive methods, user-triggered models are the most common ones: requiring the user to touch any virtual or real element (94.92%) or identifying pre-defined movements (such as shaking the device). This last option is not very common, just 1.44% of applications use it.

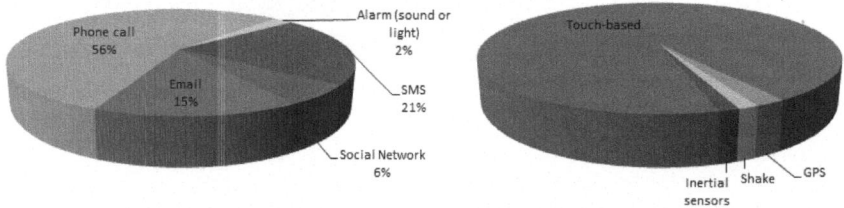

Fig. 4. a) Methods to detect an emergency; b) Techniques to communicate an emergency

'Service that cost your money' permission is oriented to get access to communication channels, for instance voice calls or SMS sending (36 and 90 applications respectively). At the moment of communicating an emergency, the two most popular techniques are the traditional phone calls (more than 56% of applications use this method) and SMS sending (21%). As it can be seen in Figure 5b, the rest of the techniques include email sending (15%), social networks updating (6%) and the least frequent, activation of hard sounds and flashing light, with a percentage of only 2%.

5   Proposal of a 911/112-Like Citizen Emergency Management Application

Our objective with this prior analysis was to detect common features of the existing offer of applications in the emergency field. From it, we derived that no application has been created to serve citizens in emergency situations that are to be managed and solved by a public emergency service. Additionally, few applications focus on handling the great potential of citizens as witnesses and volunteers. Thus we hereby describe a 911-112 mobile application, which relies on mobile sensors and communication capabilities to provide assistance to emergency victims but also to intelligently handle the information and service that can be provided by non-affected citizens.

5.1   Main Service Goal

The leitmotif of the application is to provide its user with direct contact to the Emergency Control Center (ECC), when involved in an emergency scenario. One important change over the existing applications is that the proposed application envisions different type of user roles (Section 5.2), which will get different functionalities adapted to their needs (Section 5.3). In particular, the application should enable: a) emergency detection; b) emergency notification; c) information gathering, both from the victim and from witnesses; d) the management of the victim's smartphone to enable information gathering and resource saving (e.g. battery optimization); e) the management of volunteer groups; and f) the provision of information to the citizen in an emergency situation.

Most of existing applications are focused on the victim role. Their main goal is to request assistance or to notify an emergency. Normally, a voice call is the used method for sending the alert, although others, such as sms, email, social networks (e.g. Twitter) are employed. Applications[2] such as 'Eyewatch', 'Defend call', 'Rave mobile safety', 'Guardly', 'Mobyle Emergency Call', 'FEMA' or 'Fire Department app' illustrate the aspects above. The latter emphasizes the volunteer role, giving the ECC the possibility of searching a volunteer knowledgeable in cardiac resuscitation who can deliver urgent help if nearby, prior to the arrival of the health services, improving response times.

5.2   Target User/Roles

Our application can serve a user under different profiles, i.e. victim, witness, volunteer or citizen:

- The *victim* role is applied when the user is the person that suffers an emergency. Under the victim role, the user has to be capable of easily notifying the emergency, and its mobile device has to optimize its resources to enable maximum lasting performance.
- A *witness* can provide relevant information to help in the emergency solving: e.g. if there is a call alerting from a fire, the people around the fire can give their view on the situation spontaneously and on request from the ECC. This information has to be provided in an interoperable way.
- The *volunteer* role is a profile that the user has to have proactively enabled. When a user volunteers, he can be requested to give help if he is in the vicinity of the emergency area, taking into account his profile and skills. This feature would facilitate the ECC task when organizing citizens' help, which may be chaotic due to lack of resources and information.
- The *citizen* role is the default profile; it enables the user to receive information about active emergencies that may affect him.

The application changes the user role both automatically and manually, depending on the situation.

---

[2]   Example application websites: `www.eye-watch.in`, `www.defencall.com`, `www.ravemobilesafety.com`, `www.guardly.com`, `www.mobileemergency call.com`, `www.fema.gov/app`, `www.firedepartment.mobi`

5.3   Operational Features Description

As previously said, the application may work in different modes (Table 3):

a) Victim Mode. To be used by people in danger, it provides a panic button and gesture-based notification, which will establish a direct communication with the ECC. When the panic state is triggered, a notification including the most accurate location information available will be generated. Data about the mobile device will be also provided (model, battery-time-to-live). At the same time, the ECC will try to establish a confirmation voice call, following normal protocols. Even if it is not successful, the ECC will consider that the emergency has been notified. When the panic state is enabled, the mobile device will enter in a resource optimization mode (shutting down applications, optimizing connectivity and sensing access). In case that the victim is not able to cooperate, the application will enable a management mechanism that will make possible a limited access to the device, enabling information requests (about location, microphone activation, etc.). To enable this mode, it is necessary to have direct access to the device's resources (GPS, inertial sensors, communications, microphone, camera, etc.).

b) Witness Mode. The application offers a structured and easy form for witnesses to provide all the necessary information in an effective way. Only the type of incident is a mandatory field, but the form allows gathering information descriptors such as incident category, place, date, multimedia contents (video/images) and other additional fields that will enable data collection about number of people or victims in the emergency scenario. This mode will also enable requests from the ECC that may request specific information from people in the emergency coverage area. This implies that devices with this application may proactively publish location information, and users may agree with the ECC to provide some personal information under an agreement. Once more, the application must handle resource access (GPS or camera).

c) Volunteer Mode. The difference with the witness mode is that the volunteer does not need to be present in the emergency coverage area, but nearby. If a given user has agreed to volunteer, the ECC will be able to request him to go to an information point to receive instructions to help effectively in the emergency scenario. If the ECC has information about the profile or skills of the volunteer, it would also be possible to make selective resource assignment. The volunteer's location is needed.

d) Information Mode. The application also works as permanent communication channel with the emergency services: it will be able to receive location-filtered information on nearby incidents and guidelines to behave (e.g. those affecting mobility).

When analyzing the application following the structure in Section 2, we can note that:

- The *level of context-awareness*, understood in terms of use of location information is high, as every profile will provide its localization information for different purposes and with different accuracies. For example, victims and witnesses will notify the emergency together with their location; in the former case, the device manager component will optimize the location components to enable maximum duration of the batteries, until the emergency is over. Volunteers will provide their location whenever the ECC triggers a query to gather data about the people in a given area. Citizens will filter alerts taking into account their location.

- *Emergency detection method*: the envisioned detection methods are proactive, giving the user the possibility of notifying the emergency by touch interaction, through a button or a form (when victim or witness) and by gestures (e.g. shaking the device when victim).
- *Emergency notification method*: the notification method will be voice or data-based (form or alert sent).

Table 3. Citizen Emergency Management Application: summary of functionalities

Role	Mobile application	Control Emergency Center
Victim	Detecting emergencies through touch/gesture-based techniques	Confirmation of the received alert
	Generating an alert to ECC with accurate location data	
	Sending the mobile device's information (as model, battery-time-to-live, operating mode)	Establishing communication with the victim through voice call
	Providing critical personal information if the communication with the victim is possible.	
	Allowing access to context data obtained from device (location, images from camera, voice from microphone)	Acquisition of information relevant to victim from his/her device
	Externally controlling device's modules as operating modes (flight, silence, normal or meeting); microphone or vibration module.	Controlling the victim's device.
Volunteer	Providing location information.	Providing protocol commands to aid in the resolution of the emergency.
	Sending useful information to the ECC.	
	Receiving protocol instructions to solve the emergency.	Requesting information about the emergency.
Witness	Contributing with useful information to solve an emergency through structured- predefined reports sending.	
Citizen	Visualization of nearby incidents	Work as dissemination channel in cases of epidemic situations, natural disasters as earthquakes, fire or flooding.

5.4   Some Relevant Technical Aspects for Implementation

The main components implementing the functionalities above in the mobile application are drawn in Figure 6. The mobile application has a structure that consists of three different layers (from up to bottom levels: *Interface*, *Service logic* and Access *to sensor and communications*). When *Alert receiver* detects an emergency, it notifies the warning to the *Service logic* layer. Then, this one creates an alert through *Alert generator* module.

An important aspect for this emergency system is how to exchange data between user and ECC. The messages exchanged between the mobile agent and the ECC have to be structured and organized. A possibility is to design an exchange schema based on the Common Alerting Protocol (CAP[3]), created by the OASIS organization for alert generation. Other options could use the Emergency Data Exchange Language

---

[3] CAP specification: http://docs.oasis-open.org/emergency/cap/v1.2/
CAP-v1.2-os.html

(EDXL) standard, Australian Standard 3745, Standard Emergency Warning Signal (SEWS), NFPA 110 or CSA Z1600.

With respect to the architectural paradigm that could support the application, some of the provided functionalities makes reasonable to think about REST as driving architectural paradigm. REST is the acronym of Representational State Transfer, an architecture style designed for distributed systems. REST is based on resources: a resource is an element of information identified by an URI (Uniform Resource Identifier). Any requested information could be understood as a query to a resource: e.g. camera, battery state, etc. According to REST style, all functionalities of our system (location, modes of device, battery, camera, microphone, vibration module, reports, visualization of news and instructions of coordination) will be interpreted and treated as resources. Resources are exchanged between the network components using XML format and HTTP protocols, and define an operation set with predefined commands (GET, POST, PUT and DELETE). Its interoperability, scalability and easiness to exchange information among components are among the found advantages. REST communications are done lightly and without information overload. The data transfer speeds up due to the small size of the exchanged messages and allows optimizing energy consumption. The centralized architecture is due to the need of having a coordinating institution with a global vision of the available resources.

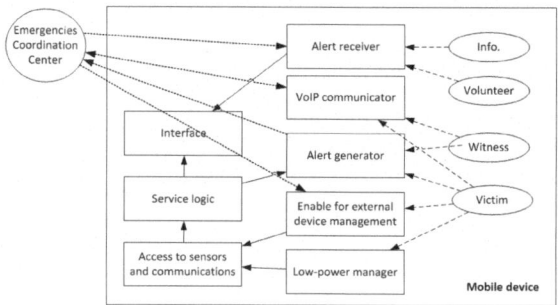

Fig. 5. Application components

6   Conclusions

This research shows the conclusions of an analysis of 250 Android emergency applications from Google Play database. The information in the market (general data and permissions) allows obtaining information about the applications' value proposition and about their operational features. Data show that more than a half of applications target victims affected by the emergency. Rescue teams, witness or citizens attract lower attention as application users. In order to trigger an emergency alert, developers prefer proactive user-initiated approaches, as detection of free false alarms is an advantage when the procedure remains manual. In any case, sensors enable some automation: changes in the user position or specific measurements of inertial sensor may trigger automatic alarms; detection of special movements (e.g. device shaking) may also facilitate manual notifications. With respect to notifications, most of applications communicate the alerts employing phone calls.

The performed research shows that there is gap for innovation to propose a general 911/112 application that could connect citizens and Emergency Control Centers, providing a wide record of functionalities to the users under different profiles. This tool organizes the emergency actor into a set of roles: victim, witness, volunteer and citizen, and could serve to help victims, considering aspects from notification to device management to optimize the acquisition of data and resources during the event. It can also help to organize volunteers in a more effective way and to obtain information from witnesses in a structured way, giving the people coordinated instructions to move around the area of disaster. The application is nowadays under construction using a REST architectural approach.

Acknowledgements. This work has been supported by the Government of Madrid under grant S2009/TIC-1485 (CONTEXTS) and by the Spanish Ministry of Science and Innovation under grant IPT-2011-1052-390000.

References

1. Weiser, M.: The computer for the 21st century. Scientific American 265(3), 94–104 (1991)
2. Sax, C., Lawrence, E.: Point-of-Treatment: Touchable E-nursing User Interface for Medical Emergencies. In: 3rd International Conference on Mobile Ubiquitous Computing, Systems, Services and Technologies, Sliema, Malta, pp. 89–95 (2009)
3. Tsai, M.-K., Lee, Y.-C., Lu, C.-H., Chen, M.-H., Chou, T.-Y., Yau, N.-J.: Integrating geographical information and augmented reality techniques for mobile escape guidelines on nuclear accident sites. Journal of Environmental Radioactivity 109, 36–44 (2012)
4. Chu, L., Wu, S.-J.: An Integrated Building Fire Evacuation System with RFID and Cloud Computing. In: 7th International Conference on Intelligent Information Hiding and Multimedia Signal Processing, Dalian, China, pp. 17–20 (2011)
5. Zaldivar, J., Calafate, C.T., Cano, J.C., Manzoni, P.: Providing accident detection in vehicular networks through OBD-II devices and Android-based smartphones. In: IEEE 36th Conference on Local Computer Networks (LCN), Bonn, Germany, pp. 813–819 (2011)
6. Thompson, C., White, J., Dougherty, B., Albright, A., Schmidt, D.C.: Using Smartphones to Detect Car Accidents and Provide Situational Awareness to Emergency Responders. In: 3rd ICST Conf. Mobile Wireless Middleware, Operative Systems, and Apps., Chicago, USA, pp. 29–42 (2010)
7. White, J., Thompson, C., Turner, H., Dougherty, B., Douglas, C.: WreckWatch: Automatic Traffic Accident Detection and Notification with Smartphones. Mob. Netw. Appl. 16, 285–303 (2011)
8. Asthana, A., Asthana, R.G.S.: IOS 5, Android 4.0 and Windows 8 – A Review. BEACON IEEE 31, 33–43 (2012)
9. Gartner's report: Market Share: Mobile Devices, Worldwide, 2Q12, http://www.gartner.com/resId=2117915
10. Android market stats "Free vs. paid Android apps", http://www.appbrain.com/stats/

Indoor Augmented Reality
Based on Ultrasound Localization Systems

David Gómez, Paula Tarrío, Juan Li, Ana M. Bernardos, and José R. Casar

Data Processing and Simulation Group, Dpt. Signals Systems and Radiocommunications,
School of Telecommunications Engineering, Technical University of Madrid
Av. Complutense, 30, Madrid, Spain
{david.gomez,paula,li.juan,abernardos,jramon}@grpss.ssr.upm.es

Abstract. Augmented reality applications are beginning to reach the general public due to the widespread use of smartphones and tablet devices. Most AR systems require the use of image processing techniques to superimpose the virtual information over the image of the real world. However, this may quickly consume the battery of the user's device. In this paper, we design and implement an AR system for indoor environments that relies on an external ultrasound localization system and on the inertial sensors embedded in the device to estimate the position and orientation of the user. The system was implemented on a tablet device, offers several functionalities, such as visualization of virtual objects and interaction with the virtual view, and aims at providing appropriate accuracy for a satisfactory user experience without the need of using costly vision-based techniques.

Keywords: augmented reality, ultrasound localization, indoor environments, human-computer interaction services.

1 Introduction

Augmented reality (AR) systems consist in overlaying virtual information over an image of the real world in runtime. Although a first AR system definition was not proposed until 1997 by Azuma [1], a prototype using this technology had been designed by Shuterland [2] almost 30 years before. An aspect to be considered in this kind of system is the device that is used to present the virtual information to the user. For instance, Shuterland employed a head-mounted display. However, nowadays the most popular kind of devices employed for AR systems are smartphones and tablet devices, which have a huge presence in the society. Their popularity is due to the advantages offered to both system developers and end users, such as lightness, easy use, the possibility of accessing to the embedded sensors for getting context information, and the availability of displays suitable to present the virtual information to the user.

AR systems rely on knowing the exact relative position and orientation between the user and the surrounding virtual objects. To obtain this information, three different approaches are currently followed [3]. The first approach consists in using image processing techniques to analyze the information that is continuously taken by a

J.M. Corchado et al. (Eds.): PAAMS 2013 Workshops, CCIS 365, pp. 202–212, 2013.

camera in the user's device and estimate the position and orientation of the objects in the scene. The accuracy of this technique is quite high, but its computational cost is also high and problems due to lighting or occlusions may appear. Some examples of this approach can be found in [4], [5] and [6]. The second approach obtains the required information from inertial and positioning data coming from specific sensors outside or inside the user's device (for example, positioning systems such as GPS for outdoor environments and inertial sensors embedded in the device), as in [7]. This approach has a much lower computational cost, which implies a lower battery cost. However, its accuracy may not be enough, especially in indoor environments, where centimeter-level accuracy is necessary to present the virtual objects in the correct position. Finally, the third approach (followed for example in [8]) combines the two previous methods to obtain a high accuracy with not very high computational costs.

In this paper we are interested in developing an AR system for indoor environments using the second approach. Our objective was to analyze to which extent the accuracy in this kind of systems can be enough for a satisfactory user experience. To this end, we propose to use an external ultrasound localization system to estimate the position of the user with centimeter-level accuracy, and to estimate the user orientation from the inertial sensors embedded in the user's device. The proposed system was implemented on a tablet device with Android OS and offers several functionalities, such as visualization of virtual objects and interaction with the virtual view.

The paper is organized as follows. Section 2 reviews previous work on augmented reality services for indoor environments. Section 3 describes the functionalities that were selected for our AR system. Section 4 describes the architecture of the proposed system. Section 5 details how the position and orientation information are obtained. Section 6 presents a discussion of the results. Finally, section 7 concludes the paper and proposes some future research work.

2   Previous Work on Indoor AR

Although the most popular and widespread mobile augmented reality services are targeted at outdoor environments (mainly for tourism applications, e.g. the PRISMA project [9]), there is also a large number of proposals designed for indoor environments.

Indoor guiding and navigation services are among the most popular ones. For instance, [10] proposes a system that allows users to supervise and control a mobile robot that navigates in an indoor environment through an AR interface. Another example of this kind of application can be found in [5], which combines AR and indoor location techniques to provide the user with necessary indications for indoor building navigation.

A popular application of AR-based indoor guiding and navigation are guided tours in museums. Generally, these services augment the information of displayed art objects (paintings, sculptures, etc.). For example, [8] describes an AR museum guidance system that overlaps a 3D model over the real object by combining sensors and vision methods to accurately determine the position of the object with respect to the user. In [11] another museum visiting application is proposed. In this case, the device's screen is divided in two parts, one half showing an AR view and the other half indicating the direction the visitor should follow. Another example appears in [12], which describes an AR multimedia museum guide prototype.

Obtaining contextual information about objects or people is another possible service that can be developed in indoor environments using an AR interface. This kind of service has been used for example in [4], to provide the user with information about objects/people of interest inside a laboratory, and in [6] to provide additional information about identified books inside a library.

Finally, another application of indoor AR falls in the field of interior design and decoration. The possibility of testing a piece of furniture in our house without having to buy it first using an AR application can be very useful. This idea was used by SnapShop[1] to implement *SnapShop Showroom*, an application for mobile devices that allows the user to test how the products from a famous decoration store would fit in their houses.

All reviewed applications for indoor environments use visual recognition methods to display the virtual world in the corresponding position on the real image, either by following a plain vision-based approach ([4-6], [10-12] and SnapShop Showroom), or a hybrid approach, as in [8]. In this paper, we aim at studying the accuracy of plain location-based techniques by designing an AR system that does not use vision-based techniques and analyzing if the provided accuracy is sufficient for a satisfactory user experience.

3   Augmented Reality Functionalities

Our AR system was devised to provide several AR services to the user in a friendly and intuitive way. To this end, we decided to implement the user application over a tablet device, so that the display area was big enough to show the virtual objects with appropriate resolution. Moreover, we designed the system to provide the following functionalities:

- Visualization of virtual objects: The user application shows virtual objects superimposed on the real scene captured by the camera, as shown for example in Fig.1.a.This kind of functionality can be used for several applications, such as entertainment (for instance, by showing animated characters for children) or interior design and decoration (by allowing the user to select virtual objects, and their characteristics, and move them over the scene to the position that best fits her preferences).
- Visualization of icons associated to real objects: Some objects of the real world may have associated virtual information or may be prepared to respond or react to some user's actions. In order to let the user know which objects of the surroundings may be of his interest, the AR application shows an icon in the image superimposed over the corresponding real object, as shown in Fig.1.b.
- Retrieving information about (or associated to) real or virtual objects: By touching on a virtual object or an icon associated to a real object, the user can retrieve

---

[1] www.snapshopinc.com/

information associated to that object, which will be shown in the user's device. For example, a window in a room may have associated weather information, a shelf in a library may provide information about its books, a work of art in a museum may include descriptive information or details about the author, etc.

- Interacting with real or virtual objects: The user may desire to request an object to perform a given action. To this end, a menu showing the possible actions that the object is able to perform will appear when the user touches its icon (or the object itself, in the case of virtual objects). The user may then select an action, which will be executed by the object. Some examples of this functionality include turning the lights on/off by interacting with the light switch, displaying a multimedia content on the TV, or making a virtual animated character dance or sing.

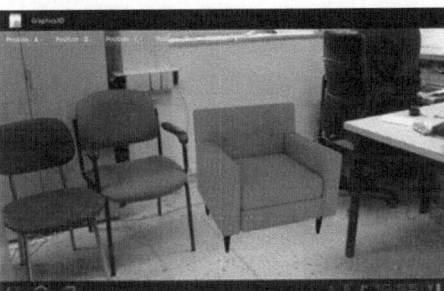

Fig. 1. Snapshots of the AR application. Left: virtual sofa integrated with the environment. Right: icon indicating the position of a real object (a television).

These functionalities enable a wide variety of AR services, including the ones reviewed in section 2 (indoor guiding and navigation, guided tours including augmented information, providing contextual information, etc.).

4   AR System Architecture

Our location-based AR system was developed over a context-aware architecture that consists of three key elements: i) a sensor/acquisition layer, which is responsible for capturing the user context (position, in the case of our AR system); ii) a management platform, which offers services based on the acquired context; and iii) the service consumers.

In our case, the *sensor layer* corresponds to an ultrasound localization system (see details in section 5.1) that estimates the 3D position of the user and sends this information to the management platform through an available REST [13] API. When a new position estimation is received, the *management platform* generates a localization event, which will be sent to the service consumers that are subscribed to this kind of events. In our case, the *service consumer* is the AR application running in a Motorola Xoom tablet with Android 4.0.4 operating system.

The AR application was developed using Java and OpenGL. It provides a traditional AR-based view, where virtual icons associated with real objects or virtual objects associated with real locations are superimposed in real-time on the user's device screen, as shown in Fig. 1.

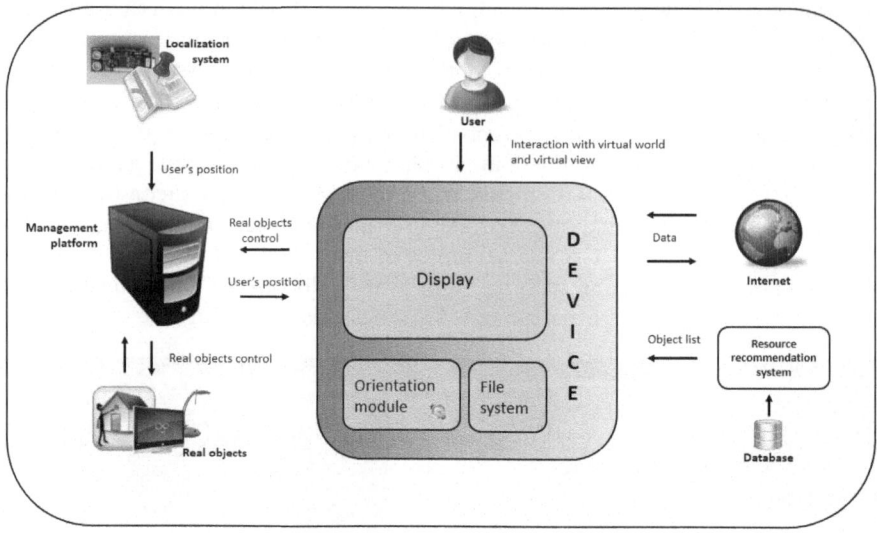

Fig. 2. Flow scheme from AR application

A flow diagram of the AR application and its interactions with external systems is shown in Fig. 2. The main component of the application is the *Display module*, which displays the virtual resources over the camera view using OpenGL ES [2] (OpenGL for Embedded System). In order to show these resources in the correct location from the user's perspective, their relative position and orientation with respect to the user is needed. Therefore, the position and orientation of the user must be calculated (section 5 details how this is done). The orientation is obtained from the *orientation module*, located inside the user's device, and user's position is obtained from an external *localization system*, connected to the device through the *management platform*.

The list of virtual resources is saved in a database that includes the position and orientation of the object in the real environment, the associated image (2D icon or 3D model) and the information or actions associated to the object. As the number of virtual elements in a given environment can be very large, a selection mechanism may be required to filter the complete set of available resources in order not to burden the user with unnecessary information. To this end, a *resource recommendation system* was implemented to give different priorities to the virtual elements depending on spatial information, as described in [7].

Finally, when the user asks for the information associated to an object, the application will retrieve it either from files internally stored in the *file system* or from an external site in the Internet. In the case that the user selects an action to perform over a real object, the command will be sent to the management platform, which actuates on the selected object with the desired action.

The architecture is similar to that presented in [7], but in this paper, we include new functionalities. The two main innovations are the accurate indoor localization

---

[2] http://www.khronos.org/opengles/

system based on ultrasounds, which enables a fully working system in which the user can move through all the deployment area, and a new and wide range of services launched through the virtual resources.

5 Localization and Orientation

As mentioned above, our AR system relies on the position and orientation of the user to establish its relationship with the virtual elements and display the appropriate icons in the user's device screen. We next describe how this information is obtained in our system.

5.1 Ultrasound Localization System

In order to accurately estimate the position of the user, we deployed a localization system based on the Cricket nodes [14], as shown in Fig. 3. Cricket nodes use the combination of radio frequency (RF) and ultrasound technologies to estimate the distance between two nodes. In our system, several nodes (beacons) are mounted in the ceiling at known 3-dimensional coordinates, while the user carries the mobile node to be localized. Beacons transmit concurrent RF and ultrasound signals. Since the propagation speed of RF (speed of light) is much faster than that of the ultrasound (speed of sound), the mobile mote can estimate the distance to a beacon from the Time Difference of Arrival using the following expression:

$$\delta T = \frac{d}{v_{us}} - \frac{d}{v_{rf}} \tag{1}$$

where d is the distance, v_{us} is the speed of sound and v_{rf} is the speed of light. Since $v_{rf} \gg v_{us}$, the following approximation can be used:

$$d \approx \delta T \cdot v_{us} \tag{2}$$

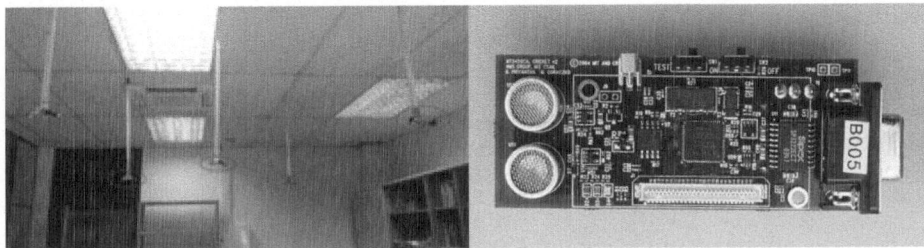

Fig. 3. Final deployment of our Cricket localization system (left) and picture of a Cricket device (right)

The speed of sound varies according to environmental factors such as temperature and humidity, so Cricket uses an on-board temperature sensor to compensate for changes in speed of sound due to temperature variations. Finally, the mobile node sends the distance estimations to each of the beacons inside its coverage to a computer, which calculates the position of the mobile mote using a positioning algorithm. In our case, we used the classical circular algorithm [15], which iteratively minimizes the sum-square error using a gradient search.

In the original Cricket system, the mobile mote is connected to a computer through the serial port, which limits the area where the user can move. In order to get rid of this restriction, a base station was added in our system. In this way, the mobile node sends the estimated distances to the base station through the wireless link and when the base station receives this information, it forwards it to the computer through the serial port.

In order to localize the user, the ultrasound receiver has to be integrated with or attached to her mobile device. To do so, there are several points which should be taken into consideration. First, as the radiation pattern of the Cricket devices is highly directional, the mobile mote should be kept parallel to the ground and pointing to the ceiling where the beacons are deployed. Second, even when the mobile node is pointing to the ceiling, the signals will not pass through the peak of the radiation diagrams, as shown in Fig. 4. If the angle between the main axis of the mobile node and the line joining the mobile node to the beacon is too big, distance estimations are not accurate. We have seen through a set of experiments that to obtain accurate distance estimations, the angle should be lower than 45 degrees. This reduces the amount of beacons that can be used for estimating the distance at a given position. Taking into account that to calculate the 3-dimensional coordinates of the mobile mote, at least three beacons should be heard from each position in the deployment area, the beacon deployment needs to be quite dense. In our case, we finally used 7 beacons to cover a 20 m^2 area (see Fig. 3. left).

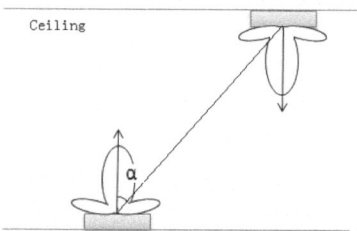

Fig. 4. Illustration of the relative positions and the radiation diagrams of an anchor node (in the ceiling pointing down) and a mobile node (pointing up)

The main advantages of using this kind of localization system are that the accuracy is high enough for indoor AR applications (in the order of few centimeters), that it is easy to use and manage, and that the costs due to computation and communication are much lower than for systems using computer vision. On the downside, the system requires line-of-sight paths between the beacons and the listener, and the deployments need to be dense, as the range of the ultrasound is very low (around 10 meters). According to this, this kind of localization system is appropriate for indoor environments without many obstacles. It could be used, for example, for guided tours in museums or interaction in smart spaces.

5.2   Orientation Estimation

As mentioned above, augmented reality applications need to know the direction to which the user is looking to determine the virtual resources that should be displayed at each moment. In our case, we suppose that this direction coincides with the orientation of the camera axis of the user's device, which is continuously calculated by the AR application by accessing to the data acquired from the accelerometers and magnetometers embedded on the device. The orientation is calculated as a rotation matrix that can be used to transform the sensor measurements from the device coordinate system into the world coordinate systems (see Fig. 5). This rotation matrix is directly obtained with the Android API through the *SensorManager.getRotationMatrix*[3] function.

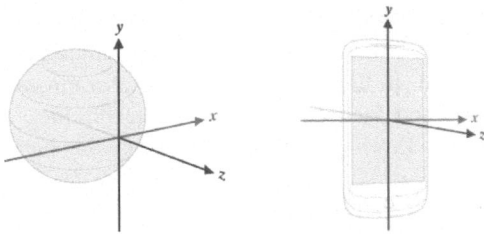

Fig. 5. Definition of the world coordinate system (left) and the device coordinate system (right). The world coordinate system defines Z pointing towards the sky at the position of the user, Y tangential to the ground and pointing towards magnetic north, and X as the vector product Y×Z. The device coordinate system is defined relative to the screen of the device, with Z pointing towards the outside of the front face of the screen.

In practice, as the sensors embedded in the device introduce a small noise in the measurements, the orientation matrix is continuously changing, even when the user's device is completely immobile, causing slight movements on the screen. To overcome this effect, an alpha filter was implemented over the raw accelerometer data and the raw magnetometer data, providing smoother measurements to calculate the rotation matrix. In particular, the filtered data is calculated as:

$$y_n = (1 - \alpha)y_{n-1} + \alpha\, x_n \tag{3}$$

where α is a configurable parameter according to needs; y_{n-1} is the previous estimated filter output; and x_n corresponds to current sample data. The parameter α was set to obtain an acceptable time delay in the filter response (1100 ms), according to the following expression:

---

[3] http://developer.android.com/reference/android/hardware/SensorMa nager.html#getRotationMatrix(float[], float[], float[], float[])

$$\alpha = 1 - 10^{-1/\frac{d}{t_s}} \qquad (4)$$

being d the desired delay in the filter response and t_s the sampling period (in our case, 60 ms for the accelerometer sensor and 120 ms for the magnetometer sensor).

6   Discussion

In order to evaluate the accuracy of the proposed system, we carried out some tests in which the tablet device was situated in different positions of the deployment area and with different orientations. From the user's point of view, we observed that the virtual objects were displayed quite close to their theoretical position over the real image (see for example Fig. 1.b, where the TV icon appears nearly in the center of the real TV). In most of the cases, the displacements were small and totally acceptable for the user to interact with the virtual scene. From these preliminary tests we can conclude that using a plain localization-based approach may be appropriate for a big number of indoor AR applications, in which a completely perfect match between the virtual and real worlds is not required. In these cases, this type of approach should be preferred with respect to vision-based techniques or hybrid techniques, as the computational complexity will be much lower and this will extend the battery life of the user's device.

From a technical point of view, we have identified two main challenges in the proposed system. First, the ultrasound localization system provides an accuracy of few centimeters, which we believe is high enough for most indoor AR applications. However, in order to achieve this, a very dense deployment with line-of-sight paths between the beacons and the listener is required. This will raise the cost of the deployment, especially when there is a wide area to cover. A possible solution could be to use a different indoor localization system with high accuracy, such as those based on UWB technology, which also provide centimeter-level accuracy, but do not require line-of-sight and have a greater coverage. Second, the main source of inaccuracies was found to be the error in the orientation estimation, specially due to the magnetometer sensor. This sensor needs to be calibrated manually by the user for a correct performance, but even so, when the device is situated close to metallic objects, the magnetometer provides inaccurate data. Further research is needed to overcome this problem.

7   Conclusion

In this paper we have designed and implemented an AR system for indoor environments that aims at providing appropriate accuracy from the user's perspective without the need of using costly vision-based techniques. The system was implemented on a tablet device and relies on an external ultrasound localization system and on the embedded inertial sensors to estimate the position and orientation of the user. We could observe from our preliminary tests that, although the matching between the real and the virtual views is not perfect, the errors are not very big, so this approach may be appropriate for numerous indoor AR applications.

As an ongoing work, we are carrying out more extensive tests in order to evaluate the accuracy of the system in a quantitative way. We are also currently working on the optimization of the proposed filter for the orientation measurements and on the implementation of a tracking filter for the position information. As future work, we are planning to evaluate the user experience by carrying out an extensive set of user tests using the proposed system. The energy consumption of the user's device will be a key aspect to analyze in these tests.

Acknowledgements. This work has been supported by the Government of Madrid under grant S2009/TIC-1485 (CONTEXTS) and by the THOFU project (CENIT CDTI).

References

1. Azuma, R.: A Survey of Augmented Reality. Presence 6, 355–385 (1997)
2. Sutherland, I.: A head-mounted three dimensional display. In: Proceedings of the Fall Joint Computer Conference, Part I, New York, USA, pp. 757–764 (1968)
3. Zhou, F., Duh, H., Billinghurst, M.: Trends in augmented reality tracking, interaction and display: A review of ten years of ISMAR. In: 7th IEEE/ACM International Symposium on Mixed and Augmented Reality, Cambridge, UK, pp. 193–202 (2008)
4. Ajanki, A., Billinghurst, M., Gamper, H., Järvenpää, T., Kandemir, M., Kaski, S., Koskela, M., Kurimo, M., Laaksonen, J., Puolamäki, K., Ruokolainen, T., Tossavainen, T.: An augmented reality interface to contextual information. Virtual Real. 15, 161–173 (2011)
5. Mulloni, A., Seichter, H., Schmalstieg, D.: Handheld augmented reality indoor navigation with activity-based instructions. In: Proceedings of the 13th International Conference on Human Computer Interaction with Mobile Devices and Services, New York, USA, pp. 211–220 (2011)
6. Hahn, J.: Mobile augmented reality applications for library services. New Library World 113, 429–438 (2012)
7. Iglesias, J., Gomez, D., Bernardos, A.M., Casar, J.R.: An Attitude-Based Reasoning Strategy to Enhance Interaction with Augmented Objects. In: 6th International Conference on Innovative Mobile and Internet Services in Ubiquitous Computing (IMIS), Palermo, Italy, pp. 829–834 (2012)
8. Oh, J., Lee, M.-H., Park, H., Park, J.-I., Kim, J.-S., Son, W.: Efficient mobile museum guidance system using augmented reality. In: International Symposium on Consumer Electronics, Vilamoura, Portugal, pp. 1–4 (2008)
9. Fritz, F., Susperregui, A., Linaza, M.T.: Enhancing cultural tourism experiences with augmented reality technologies. In: 6th International Symposium on Virtual Reality, Archaeology and Cultural Heritage, VAST, Pisa, Italy (2005)
10. Nunez, R., Bandera, J.R., Perez-Lorenzo, J.M., Sandoval, F.: A human-robot interaction system for navigation supervision based on augmented reality. In: Electrotechnical Conference, Torremolinos, Malaga, Spain, pp. 441–444 (2006)
11. Dong-Hyun, L., Park, J.: Augmented Reality Based Museum Guidance System for Selective Viewings. In: Proceedings of the Second Workshop on Digital Media and its Application in Museum Heritage, pp. 379–382. IEEE Computer Society, Washington (2007)

12. Damala, A., Cubaud, P., Bationo, A., Houlier, P., Marchal, I.: Bridging the gap between the digital and the physical: design and evaluation of a mobile augmented reality guide for the museum visit. In: Proceedings of the 3rd International Conference on Digital Interactive Media in Entertainment and Arts, New York, pp. 120–127 (2008)
13. Fielding, R.T.: Archittectural Styles and the Design of Network-based Software Architectures. Doctoral dissertation, University of California, Irvine, USA (2000)
14. Bodhi, N.: The Cricket Indoor Location System. Doctoral dissertation, Massachusetts Institute of Technology, Massachusetts, USA (2005)
15. Tarrío, P., Bernardos, A.M., Casar, J.R.: Weighted Least Squares Techniques for Improved Received Signal Strength Based Localization. Sensors 11, 8569–8592 (2011)

Dynamic Signature Verification on Smart Phones

Ram P. Krish, Julian Fierrez, Javier Galbally, and Marcos Martinez-Diaz

Biometric Recognition Group - ATVS, EPS - Univ. Autonoma de Madrid
C/ Francisco Tomas y Valiente, 11 - Campus de Cantoblanco - 28049 Madrid, Spain
{ram.krish,julian.fierrez,javier.galbally,marcos.martinez}@uam.es

Abstract. This work is focused on dynamic signature verification for state-of-the-art smart phones, including performance evaluation. The analysis was performed on database consisting of 25 users and 500 signatures in total acquired with Samsung Galaxy Note. The verification algorithm tested combines two approaches: feature based (using Mahalanobis distance) and function based (using DTW), and the results are shown in terms of EER values. A number of experimental findings associated with signature verification in this scenario are obtained, e.g., the dominant challenge associated with the intra-class variability across time. As a result of the algorithm adaptation to the mobile scenario, the use of a state-of-the-art smart phone, and contrarily to what has been evidenced in previous works, we finally demonstrate that signature verification on smart phones can result in a similar verification performance compared to one obtained using more ergonomic stylus-based pen tablets. In particular, the best result achieved is an EER of 0.525%.

Keywords: Biometrics, dynamic signature verification, smart phones, Mahalanobis distance, Dynamic Time Warping (DTW).

1 Introduction

Dynamic (or on-line) handwritten signature is one of the modalities within biometrics that has vital importance in terms of establishing the identity of an individual, mainly because of the social and legal acceptance of handwritten signatures as a means for person identification in the day-to-day life [1]. The latest innovations in touch screen technologies have provided a feasible environment for dynamic signature verification in smart phones and mobile scenarios.

Despite the fact that the technology innovations have made it to a point where dynamic signature acquisitions is easy in smart phones, inherently signature verification faces some challenges which are in general applicable to either smart phones or more ergonomically designed signature pads. The latter scenario (i.e., pen-based digitizing tablets) is commonly studied in the signature verification literature [1]. The purpose here is to adapt established technology previously developed for digitizing tablets for smart phones, and then evaluate its performance and discuss some of its particularities.

J.M. Corchado et al. (Eds.): PAAMS 2013 Workshops, CCIS 365, pp. 213–222, 2013.

More specifically, two of the challenges faced in signature verification are *intra-class* variability where the individual has slight variations in their own signature writing styles over a period of time, and *inter-class* variability where some other person tries to mimic or simulate the signature of an individual to get an illicit access through a signature verification system. Traditionally, it has been thought that these sources of variability, specially the intra-class variability, is much higher in mobile scenarios compared to desktop digitizing tablets for signature verification, which results in degraded verification performance in mobile scenarios [2]. Nevertheless, this comparison has always been evidenced using limited mobile acquisition devices, far from the capabilities of state-of-the-art touch-based and stylus-based smart phones [3].

With regard to the inter-class variability, forgeries can be classified as two types, *random* forgeries and *skilled* forgeries. In *random* forgeries the forger has no information regarding the target signature, whereas in case of *skilled* forgeries the forger has knowledge about the target signature [1]. In the present work, only random signatures are considered.

With respect to the kind of information used in the recognition process, the signature verification can be classified into *feature* based systems and *function* based systems [4]. In feature based systems, a set of global features derived from the signature sample is used, whereas in function based systems, temporal sequences which encapsulate the local properties of the signature samples are used.

As introduced before, in this paper we present the results of the adaptation of an already existing dynamic signature verification algorithm for smart phones. As with any technology, there are some pros and cons associated with smart phones in the context of signature verification, though there is a growing interest in the use of portable devices for personal authentication. For signature verification, one advantage is related to the acquisition hardware, as with touch or stylus based smart phones there is no need for specialized external hardware for signature recognition. Most smart phones come with enough computing power, good quality touch screens and supports pen based input which makes them a feasible platform for dynamic signature verification.

Coming to the challenges, usually smart phones do not provide big display areas which affects user interaction and leads to large intra-class variability, the quality of the signature acquisitions can show high disparity based on the quality of the touch screens and the amount of information that can be captured is limited as pressure, pen-azimuth and other attributes which could lead to improved performance cannot be captured. Finally, in smart phones it is also important to consider the security of the templates [5].

As also introduced before, the public domain evaluations of dynamic signature verifications like BioSecure Multimodal Evaluation Campaign (BMEC-2007) [3], and BioSecure Signature Evaluation Campaign (BSEC'2009) [2] have shown that the performance of dynamic signature verification with databases captured on handheld devices are significantly lower compared with databases captured on ergonomically designed signature pads or tablet PCs. The main reasons for such

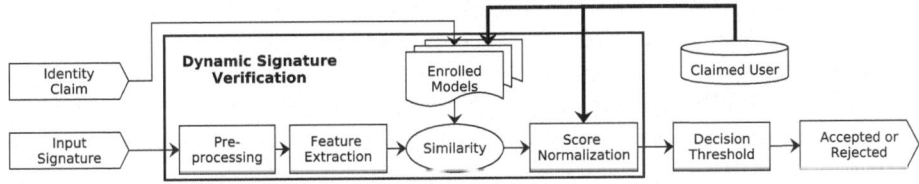

Fig. 1. General architecture of dynamic signature verification system

performance variations are the challenges discussed previously, such as small display area, quality of touch screen sample acquisitions and limited attributes of the samples acquired.

This paper is structured as follows. The general architecture of a dynamic signature verification system is described briefly in Section 2, and the hybrid system combining Mahalanobis distance and DTW used in the experimental work is described in Section 3. Next the database, experiment protocol and results are presented in Section 4, and conclusions drawn in Section 5.

2 Dynamic Signature Verification

The general architecture adopted by most dynamic signature verification systems is depicted in Fig. 1. The various stages and techniques involved are summarized as follows:

1. *Data Acquisition:* The dynamic signature data is in general acquired using devices like digitizing tablets or through the touch screen technologies provided on Tablet PCs, PDA or Smart Phones. The dominant attributes captured are x and y pen positions, and their timestamps. Depending on the functionality provided by the device, other attributes such as pressure, pen-azimuth, pen-up positions, etc can also be captured.
2. *Acquisition Rate:* Most of the devices used for dynamic signature acquisition operate between 100 to 200 samples per second. This sampling frequency is considered to be an accurate discrete time representation of the signature, which is justified by the fact that the bio-mechanical sequence related with such activity operates at a maximum frequency range of 20-30 Hz.
3. *Feature Extraction:* The performance of any biometric system depends largely on how well we can extract various types of discriminant features from the given sample. For dynamic signature data, the methods are traditionally classified into two : *feature-based* which use a set of global features, and *function-based* which use temporal sequences [1].
4. *Enrollment:* Depending on the methodology chosen for matching, and the number of training signatures available, the way signatures are enrolled can be classified into *reference-based* where features extracted from the signature are stored as templates, and *model-based* where a statistical model representing the signatures is generated [1].

5. *Similarity Computation:* In feature-based systems, the similarity score is calculated using Euclidean distance or Mahalanobis distance, whereas in a function-based system, the similarity score is calculated using Dynamic Time Warping (DTW) or Hidden Markov Models (HMM). Traditionally function-based systems have in general shown to perform better than feature-based systems.

6. *Score Normalization:* The similarity scores could be normalized to a given range of values. Score normalization helps when multiple algorithms are used in a system and eventually the scores need to be fused for a final decision.

2.1 Applications and Commercial Systems

A wide variety of applications with commercial importance can be designed over the concept of dynamic signature verification. In general, the main applications cover signature forensics, signature authentications, signature surveillance, digital rights management based on signatures and biometric cryptosystems based on signatures. More specifically, in a smart phone scenario which also serves as a computing platform, the possible applications could be payments in commercial environments, legal transactions, user logins, client validations and cryptobiometrics

There are also many commercial companies selling products designed based on dynamic signature verification. To mention a few of them, Sigma Technologies[1], Communication Intelligence Corporation, SOFTPRO and Cyber-SIGN [1].

3   Verification System Used in This Work

The verification system used in this work combines both feature-based and function-based approaches. The architecture of the hybrid system used in this work is shown in Fig. 2.

In the feature-based system, a set of global features are extracted from the given signature sample as presented in [6]. This feature set comprises 100 global features that include many of the features previously studied in the literature. These features can be divided into four categories based on their inherent properties, namely *time* based, *speed and acceleration* based, *direction* based and *geometry* based. More detailed explanation regarding these features can be found in [3].

To adapt the given feature set into the scenario of smart phones, a feature selection that minimizes the EER is performed using Sequential Forward Feature Selection (SFFS) on this 100 feature global set, which also reduces the dimensionality of the feature vector for the current scenario. This also helps optimizing the run time computational complexity of the system in general.

Normalization is performed on all the global features using *tanh* normalization [7], and the Mahalanobis distance is computed for the similarity score as explained in [8][9].

---
[1] http://www.sigmatechnologies.es

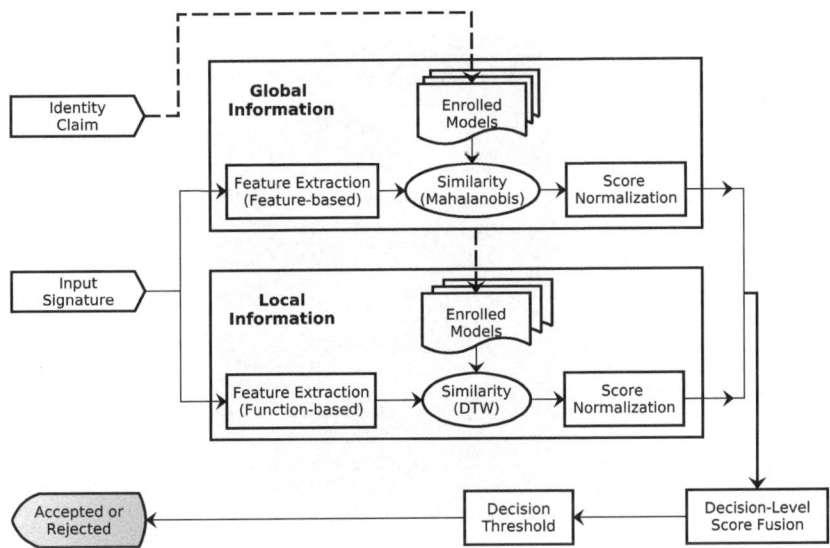

Fig. 2. The hybrid system combining features and functions used in this experiment

Function-based approaches are in general classified into *local* and *regional* based on the kind of matching strategy used. In *local* approach, time functions are directly matched using some elastic matching technique, whereas in *regional* approaches, the time functions of the signature are segmented into regions and their corresponding feature vectors are matched using Hidden Markov Models.

In this work, a *local* approach is employed and the matching is performed using Dynamic Time Warping. From the given signature sample, a set of time functions and their first and second derivatives are used as the feature set which is explained in [10]. It is also shown in this work that the contributions made by second derivatives in general are not so good, so an optimal subset of the second derivatives based on their discriminative power is used.

The score generated using DTW is normalized using *tanh* normalization, and the final match score is obtained as a weighted average of both Mahalanobis distance and DTW elastic distance.

4   Experiments

The signature samples for this experiment are acquired using Samsung Galaxy Note. The database is locally collected within our research lab and comprises 25 users and 20 signatures per user which totals to 500 signatures for the database. The acquisition device and some example signatures are shown in Fig. 3.

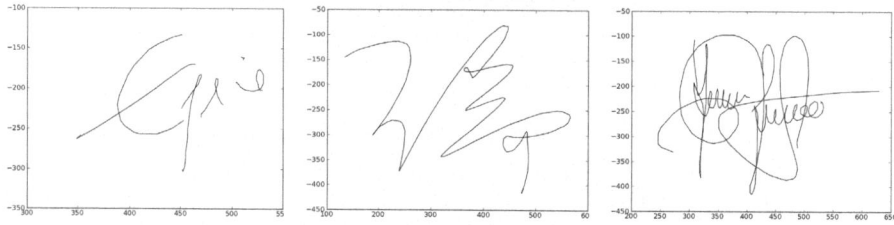

Fig. 3. Acquisition software running on Samsung Galaxy Note and example signatures

4.1   Acquisition Protocol

The signatures are captured in two different sessions with an average gap of 5 days between them, and each session involves two different phases.

In the first acquisition session, 5 signatures are first acquired on Samsung Galaxy Note (first phase) then the user is given a short time break, then again 5 signatures of that particular user are acquired (second phase). So, in the first session, 10 signatures of each user are acquired. The second acquisition session also repeats the same procedure.

The number of signature samples totals to 20 signatures per user. Total number of signatures in the database equals 500 signatures (25×20).

4.2   Evaluation Protocol

The signatures collected from the first acquisition session are used for enrollment in three different ways:

1. First three signatures of the first phase, named as Galaxy3.
2. First five signatures of the first phase, named as Galaxy5.
3. First three signatures of the first phase, and two signatures of second phase, named as Galaxy32.

As test signatures we used the signatures acquired from first session as for Experiment 1, and the signatures from the second session for Experiment 2 (in both cases all the signatures not used for enrollment). In our experiments, we considered only random forgeries, comparing the enrolled model at hand with all test signatures from all the other subjects for generating the impostor scores. Evaluation using skilled forgeries will be conducted in future research.

4.3 Experiment 1 : Intra-session Matching

In this experiment, only the signatures acquired in the first session of the database acquisitions are used. The enrolled models, as well as the signatures against which the system is tested come from the first session. Since all the signature samples come from the first session, the typical intra-class variations across time are not totally captured in this experiment. Fig. 4 shows the system performance of this experiment.

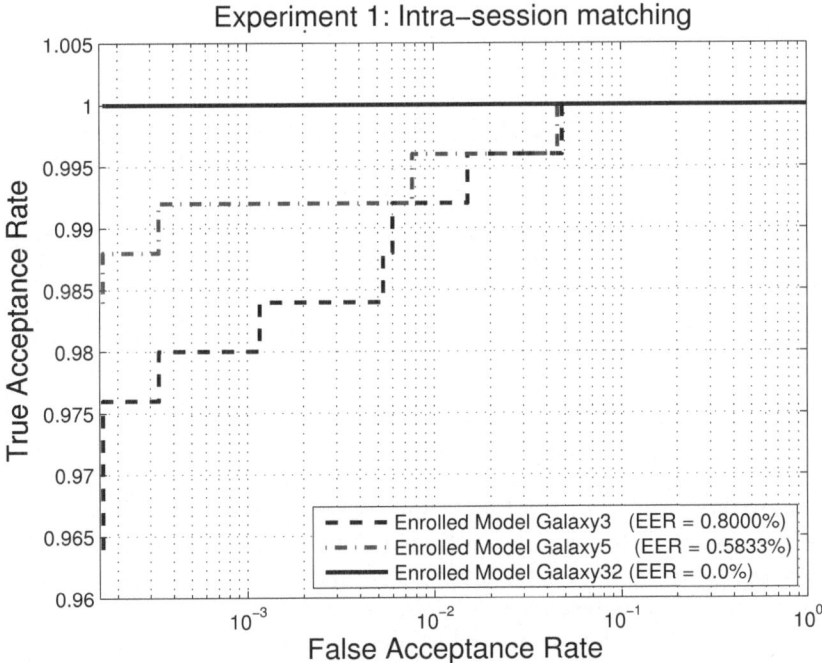

Fig. 4. ROC curve for Experiment 1, which considers enrollment and test signatures from the same session

4.4   Experiment 2 : Inter-session Matching

In this experiment, the enrolled model comes from the first session of database, and the test signatures come from the second session of database acquisition. This experiment helps us to understand better about the problem of intra-class variability of individual users with time variability because the signatures in the second session are collected with an average gap of 5 days with respect to first session. Fig. 5 shows the system performance of this experiment.

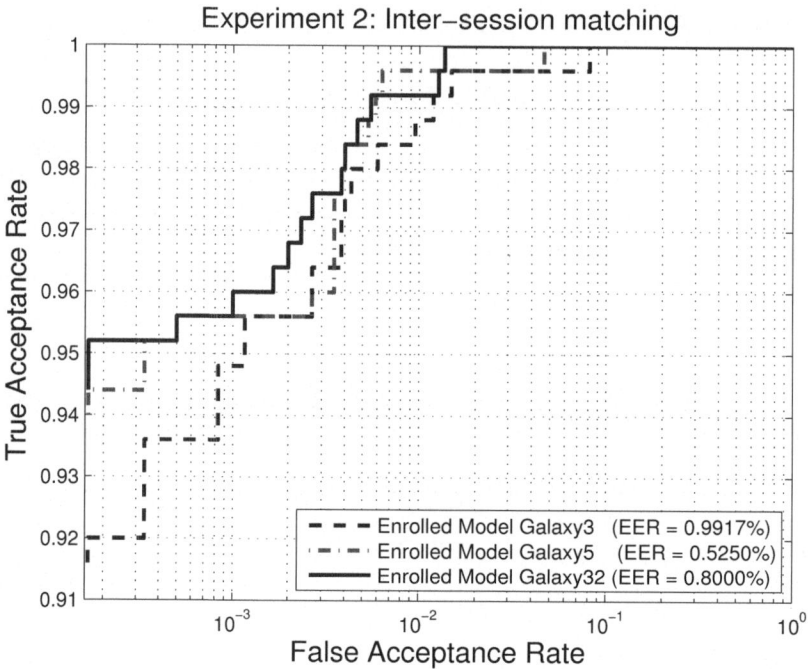

Fig. 5. ROC curve for Experiment 2, which considers enrollment and test signatures from different sessions (5 days gap on average)

4.5   Results and Discussion

An EER of 0% is obtained in the Experiment 1 (see Table 1), where the model signature is enrolled with information from the first session, 3 signatures from the first phase and 2 signatures from the second phase. This clearly shows that there was not much intra-class variability within the first session of acquisitions, but for the same set of models compared against the signatures acquired from the second session which was collected over a break of 5 days, the EER is found to be 0.8%, where we notice a higher intra-class variability. The best EER obtained in this scenario is 0.525%.

Table 1. Results in terms of EER values for both experiments

Enrolled Model	EER values in %	
	Experiment 1	Experiment 2
Galaxy3	0.8000	0.9917
Galaxy5	0.5833	0.5250
Galaxy32	0.0000	0.8000

In the BioSecure Signature Evaluation Campaign (BSEC'2009) [2], the *UAM-DTWr* system was ranked the first in the evaluation with an EER value of 0.51% which was a system specially tuned for random forgeries. The evaluation was performed on the BioSecure database. The protocol and various evaluation results are detailed in [2].

5   Conclusion

In this work, we adapted a hybrid version of an existing signature verification system for smart phones. The experiments were conducted on a dynamic signature database that was collected within our research lab on a state-of-the-art stylus-based smart phone (Samsung Galaxy Note). Different experiments were conducted to understand better the effect of intra-class variability with respect to time. The adapted hybrid system has shown promising results, and we obtained a best result with an EER of 0.525%, comparable to the one obtained by the top ranked systems in international evaluations using digitizing tablets [2]. We also discussed about the pros and cons associated with smart phones in the context of personal authentication and other applications built over signature verification concepts.

Acknowledgment. This work has been supported by Sigma Technologies, S.L., Madrid, Spain, and the following projects: Contexts (S2009/TIC-1485) from CAM, Bio-Challenge (TEC2009-11186) and Bio-Shield (TEC2012-34881) from Spanish MICINN, and Catedra UAM-Telefonica.

References

1. Fierrez, J., Ortega-Garcia, J.: On-line signature verification. In: Jain, A.K., Ross, A., Flynn, P. (eds.) Handbook of Biometrics, pp. 189–209. Springer (2008)
2. Houmani, N., Mayoue, A., Garcia-Salicetti, S., Dorizzi, B., Khalil, M., Moustafa, M., Abbas, H., Muramatsu, D., Yanikoglu, B., Kholmatov, A., Martinez-Diaz, M., Fierrez, J., Ortega-Garcia, J., Alcob, J.R., Fabregas, J., Faundez-Zanuy, M., Pascual-Gaspar, J., Cardeoso-Payo, V., Vivaracho-Pascual, C.: Biosecure signature evaluation campaign (bsec2009): Evaluating online signature algorithms depending on the quality of signatures. Pattern Recognition 45(3), 993–1003 (2012)

3. Martinez-Diaz, M., Fierrez, J., Galbally, J., Ortega-Garcia, J.: Towards mobile authentication using dynamic signature verification: useful features and performance evaluation. In: Proc. Intl. Conf. on Pattern Recognition, ICPR (December 2008)
4. Fierrez-Aguilar, J., Krawczyk, S., Ortega-Garcia, J., Jain, A.K.: Fusion of local and regional approaches for on-line signature verification. In: Li, S.Z., Sun, Z., Tan, T., Pankanti, S., Chollet, G., Zhang, D. (eds.) IWBRS 2005. LNCS, vol. 3781, pp. 188–196. Springer, Heidelberg (2005)
5. Freire, M.R., Fierrez, J., Galbally, J., Ortega-Garcia, J.: Biometric hashing based on genetic selection and its application to on-line signatures. In: Lee, S.-W., Li, S.Z. (eds.) ICB 2007. LNCS, vol. 4642, pp. 1134–1143. Springer, Heidelberg (2007)
6. Fierrez-Aguilar, J., Nanni, L., Lopez-Peñalba, J., Ortega-Garcia, J., Maltoni, D.: An on-line signature verification system based on fusion of local and global information. In: Kanade, T., Jain, A., Ratha, N.K. (eds.) AVBPA 2005. LNCS, vol. 3546, pp. 523–532. Springer, Heidelberg (2005)
7. Jain, A.K., Nandakumar, K., Ross, A.: Score normalization in multimodal biometric systems. Pattern Recognition 38(12), 2270–2285 (2005)
8. Galbally, J., Fierrez, J., Freire, M.R., Ortega-Garcia, J.: Feature selection based on genetic algorithms for on-line signature verification. In: Proc. IEEE Workshop on Automatic Identification Advanced Technologies, AutoID, pp. 198–203 (June 2007)
9. Galbally, J., Fierrez, J., Ortega-Garcia, J.: Performance and robustness: a trade-off in dynamic signature verification. In: Proc. IEEE Intl. Conf. on Acoustics, Speech and Signal Processing, ICASSP, pp. 1697–1700 (March-April 2008)
10. Martinez-Diaz, M.: Dynamic signature verification for portable devices. Master's thesis, Universidad Autonoma de Madrid (November 2008)

Analysing Facial Regions
for Face Recognition Using Forensic Protocols

Pedro Tome, Ruben Vera-Rodriguez, and Julian Fierrez

Biometric Recognition Group - ATVS, Escuela Politecnica Superior
Universidad Autonoma de Madrid
Avda. Francisco Tomas y Valiente, 11 - Cantoblanco - 28049 Madrid, Spain
{pedro.tome,ruben.vera,julian.fierrez}@uam.es

Abstract. This paper focuses on the analysis of automatic facial regions extraction for face recognition applications. Traditional face recognition systems compare just full face images in order to estimate the identity, here different facial areas of face images obtained from both uncontrolled and controlled environments are extracted from a person image. In this work, we study and compare the discriminative capabilities of 15 facial regions considered in forensic practice such as full face, nose, eye, eye brow, mouth, etc. This study is of interest to biometrics because a more robust general-purpose face recognition system can be built by fusing the similarity scores obtained from the comparison of different individual parts of the face. To analyse the discriminative power of each facial region, we have randomly defined three population subsets of 200 European subjects (male, female and mixed) from MORPH database. First facial landmarks are automatically located, checked and corrected and then 15 forensic facial regions are extracted and considered for the study. In all cases, the performance of the full face (faceISOV region) is higher than the one achieved for the rest of facial regions. It is very interesting to note that the nose region has a very significant discrimination efficiency by itself and similar to the full face performance.

Keywords: Forensic, biometrics, face recognition, facial regions, forensic casework.

1 Introduction

Automatic face recognition has been extensively researched over the past two decades. This growth is due to its easy acquisition and its important role in a growing number of application domains, including access control, video surveillance, and its wide use in government issued identity documents (e.g., passport and driving's license) [9].

An area where these kinds of systems have obtained an increased emphasis is the forensic field [7,13]. Forensic science analyses data collected by law enforcement agencies in order to prove or disapprove the guilt of a suspect with high confidence under the legal system.

J.M. Corchado et al. (Eds.): PAAMS 2013 Workshops, CCIS 365, pp. 223–230, 2013.

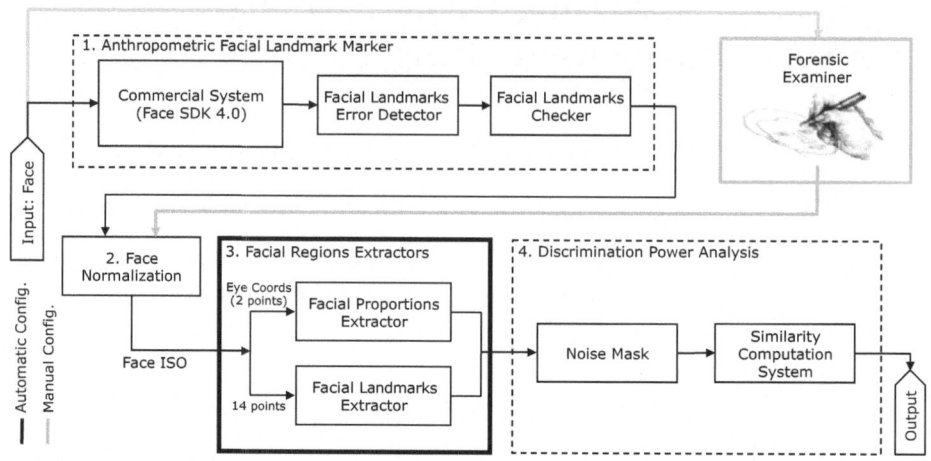

Fig. 1. Experimental framework

While DNA and fingerprint forensic identification are two of the most reliable and available identification methods in forensic science, automatic face recognition technology needs to improve the set of available tools to determine a person's identity, particularly from video surveillance imagery. Such progress for forensic face recognition is one of the goals of the FBI's Next Generation Identification program [15].

Automatic face recognition systems are generally designed to match images of full faces. However, in practise, forensic examiners focuses carry out a manual inspection of the face images, focussing their attention not only on full face but also on individual traits. They carry out an exhaustive morphological comparison, analysing the intra-variability of a face, trait by trait on nose, mouth, eyebrows, etc., even examining soft traits such as marks, moles, wrinkles, etc. On the other hand, there are several studies [22,20,12,21] based on realistic scenarios trying to understand the effect of the different variability factors in this field.

As Jain et al. decribe as future work in [8,7,2], facial regions-based system for matching and retrieval would be of great value to forensic investigators.

There are some previous works where region-based face recognition is studied [19,5,11,4,1,16] but these papers do not focus their attention in the regions usualy considered by forensic experts. In this work, we have extracted facial components (called from now facial regions) following forensic protocols from law enforcement agencies, allowing us to study the discriminative power of different facial regions individually. In particular we address in this paper the problem of finding the most discriminative areas of the face for recognition.

Understanding the discrimination power of different facial regions on a wide population has some remarkable benefits, for example: *i*) allowing investigators to work only with particular regions of the face, *ii*) preventing that incomplete, noisy, and missing regions degrade the recognition accuracy. Further, a better

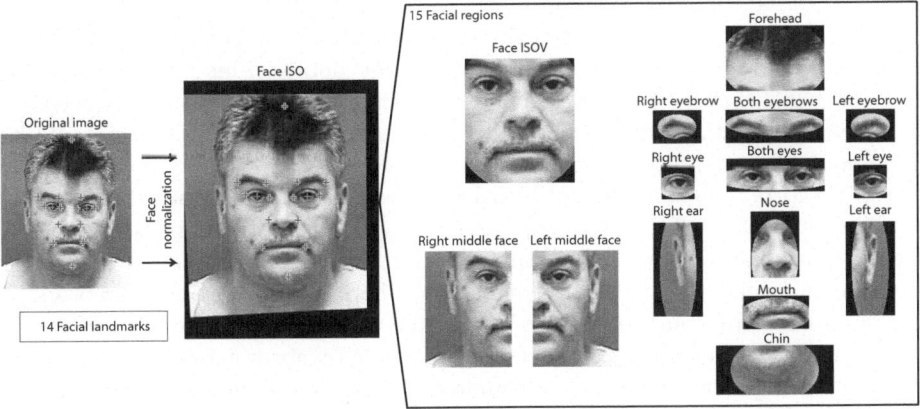

Fig. 2. Facial regions extraction

understanding of facial regions-based face recognition should facilitate the study of individuality models.

In summary, the main contribution of the paper is an experimental study of the discriminative power of different forensic facial regions on a wide population using forensic protocols. Additionally, we propose a novel framework for facial regions extraction useful for controlled and uncontrolled scenarios.

The rest of the paper is organized as follows. In Section 2, we provide an overview of the automatic facial region extraction procedure. Section 3 presents the analysis of the extracted facial regions defining the database used, the experimental protocol followed, the feature extraction and classification used and the experimental results achieved. We conclude in Section 4 with a discussion and summary of our work.

2   Facial Regions Extraction

This section describes the experimental framework developed to extract the different forensic facial regions analysed in this work.

The traditional inspection procedure of the law enforcement agencies carried out by forensic examiners is mainly based on manual and individual skills of the human examiners using some general image processing tools. Automatic approaches of image processing could help the examiners to reduce the human subjective decisions, reaching higher precisions. In this sense, we have developed a useful tool able to extract different facial regions as summarized in Fig. 1.

The presented experimental framework has two different configurations in order to find the facial landmarks for extraction of the facial regions: automatic and manual . Automatic configuration uses a commercial system [1] that provides 65 facial points of which only 13 are used. These 13 facial landmarks plus a

---

[1] Luxand, Inc. http://www.luxand.com.

new point that indicate the top of the head (defined by us) (see Fig. 2) are used as inputs to a facial landmarks error detector developed by us based on distances, angles and symmetries between these points. This system allows us to know which facial landmark is correctly located and which of them needs to be corrected. On the other hand, the location of these facial landmarks could be done manually by a forensic examiner.

After a correct facial landmark location, faces are normalized based on the ISO standard [6] with an *Interpupillary Pixel Distance* (IPD) of 75 pixels. Therefore, facial regions can be extracted with a standard size for all faces.

In our approach we have implement two different facial region extractors: *i*) based on human facial proportions, and *ii*) based on facial landmarks. The first one extracts the facial area of interest of the face (eyebrows, eyes, nose, mouth, etc.) using just the two eyes coordinates, following simple facial proportions rule [10,3]. The mentioned extractor would be of interest in challenging uncontrolled scenarios where landmarks are very difficul to be extracted automatically. On the other hand, the second extractor, based on facial landmarks correctly located, allows to extract the facial regions with high precision.

The experimental framework implemented extracts of 15 different facial regions as can be seen in Fig. 2. The election of these 15 regions is based on protocols from Spanish Guardia Civil [18] and NFI [14], two of the most important national forensic science laboratories in Spain and Netherlands, respectively.

3   Facial Regions Analysis

This section decribes how facial regions extracted from a face are analysed in order to evaluate their discriminative power. Firstly, the database and the experimental protocol adopted for this work are presented. Then, the feature extraction and classification will be described and finally, the experimental results will be detailed.

3.1   Database

The experiments are carried out on a subset of the MORPH Non-Commercial Release database [17]. MORPH contains 55.000 frontal face images from more than 13.000 subjects, acquired from 2003 to late 2007. The distribution of ages ranges from 16 to 77 with an average age of 33. The average number of images per individual is 4 and the average time between pictures is 164 days, with the minimum being 1 day and the maximum being 1.681 days. The MORPH database is divided in 5 subsets named: *i*) African, *ii*) European, *iii*) Asian, *iv*) Hispanic and *v*) Other.

The subset "European" comprises 2.704 subjects (2.070 males plus 634 females) and has been selected for these experiments. Fig. 2 shows an example in our dataset together with their extracted regions.

3.2 Experimental Protocol

For the experimental work of this paper we discarded those subjects with less than three images and chose three images per subject with the smallest gap between acquisitions in order to reduce the time lapse effect.

Then using this selection, three population sets were randomly chosen in order to analyse the discrimination power of each facial region on different populations: *i*) 200*female*, *ii*) 200*male*, and *iii*) 200*mix* (100 male+100 female).

Each population subset of 200 subjects with 3 face images each is then divided into: *i*) a training set comprising the first sample (enrolment template); and *ii*) an evaluation set comprised of the other two images available for each subject.

3.3 Feature Extraction and Classification

Regarding feature extraction and classification, a system based on PCA-SVM was adopted to compute the discrimination power between different facial regions. Different noise masks were applied to each facial region (Fig 2) (e.g. 75×101 (width $\times$ height) for nose region). PCA was applied to each facial region over the training set retaining 96% of variance. This leads to a system where the original image space (e.g. of 7.575 dimensions for nose region) is reduced to 200 dimensions. Similarity scores are computed in this PCA vector space using a SVM classifier with linear kernel.

3.4 Experimental Results

This section describes the experimental analysis of individual features of each facial region and their discrimination power (represented by EER) over the different 3 population datasets. Results are shown using ROC curves with EERs (in %).

The discrimination power of each defined forensic facial region for the three studied population datasets is presented in Fig. 3. As can be seen, doing a global analysis, faceISOV region reaches the highest performance compared to the other facial regions, followed by the nose and middle faces regions. It is worth highlighting that the faceISOV and middle faces include other facial regions considered. However, the nose region does not, hence it is important to remark that the nose region has a very high and important discrimination power with respect to the other regions of the face. Ranking the remaining facial parts regarding their discrimination power, the eye regions come next, followed by eyebrows, mouth and chin. The worst results were obtained for the chin, which could be explained due to difficulty to locate the corresponding landmark. As it was expected, ears achieved worse results due to the common occlusion by hair and the pose. It is important to note that mouth region achieves poor performance, it could be due to variability having a not neutral expression: open, closed, smiling, etc.

As can be seen in Fig. 3 (middle and bottom), faceISOV for male and female populations has more or less the same performance, but in general discriminative results for the male population were better than female, due to less variability.

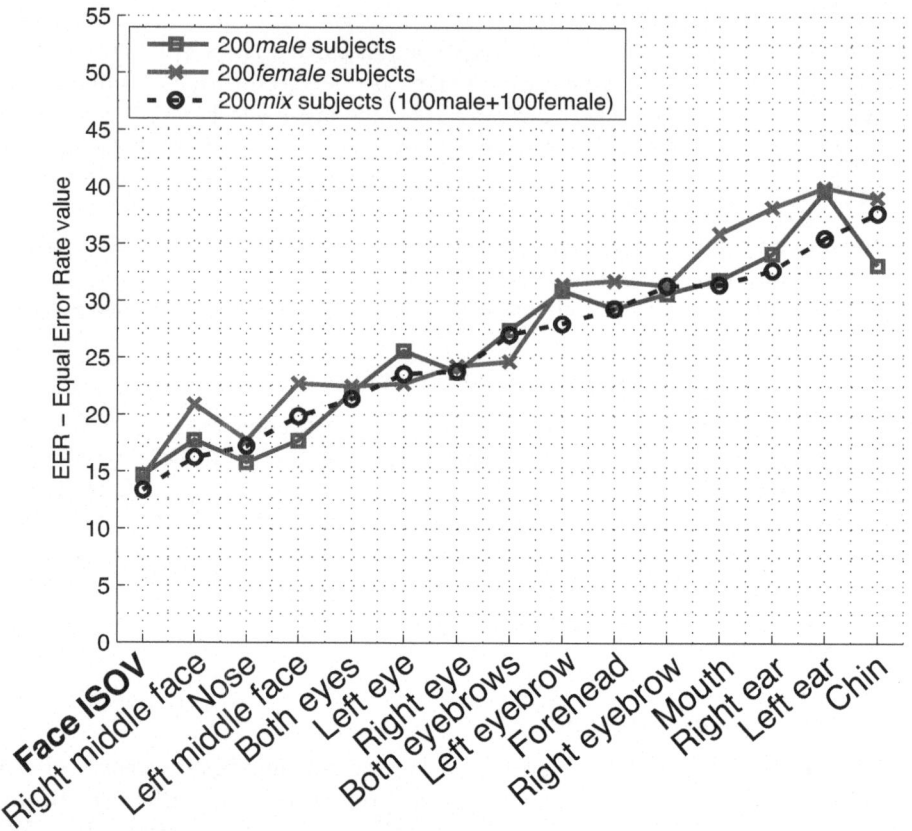

Fig. 3. EER values for verification performance of different facial regions obtained for the three popilation sets: 200*mix* (dashed black line), 200*female* (solid red line), and 200*male* (solid blue line). See one example of the different regions in Fig. 2.

4   Conclusions

In the present work, an experimental framework for the extraction of different facial regions of a face has been presented and used to understand their discrimination power. The discrimination efficiency of each facial region has been studied considering three different populations obtained from the MORPH database. In all cases, the performance of the full face named faceISOV region is higher than the one achieved by the rest of facial regions. In a real forensic scenario, partial faces are considered very often for recognition due to occlusions or other factors, hence this individualized study is very useful in order to give some insight into the expected degradation when working with partial faces. Furthermore, the nose region has a very significant discrimination efficiency by itself and similar to full face performance. There are notable differences between male and female performances on different facial regions and in general men achieve better discriminative reults for their facial regions compared to women, most likely due to less variability of appearance. This work highlights the benefits of adequate analysis of facial regions from a face in order to better understand the facial intra-variability.

Acknowledgement. P. Tome is supported by a FPU Fellowship from Univ. Autonoma de Madrid. This work has been partially supported by contract with Spanish Guardia Civil and projects BBfor2 (FP7-ITN-238803), Bio-Challenge (TEC2009-11186), Bio-Shield (TEC2012-34881), Contexts (S2009/TIC-1485), TeraSense (CSD2008-00068) and "Cátedra UAM-Telefónica".

References

1. Ali, T., Tome, P., Fierrez, J., Vera-Rodriguez, R., Spreeuwers, L., Veldhuis, R.: A study of identification performance of facial regions from cctv images. In: 5th International Workshop on Computational Forensics, IWCF 2012 (2012)
2. Bonnen, K., Klare, B., Jain, A.K.: Component-based representation in automated face recognition. IEEE Transactions on Information Forensics and Security 8(1), 239–253 (2013)
3. Gunes, H., Piccardi, M.: Assessing facial beauty through proportion analysis by image processing and supervised learning. International Journal of Man-Machine Studies 64(12), 1184–1199 (2006), http://dblp.uni-trier.de/db/journals/ijmms/ijmms64.html#GunesP06
4. Gupta, S., Markey, M.K., Bovik, A.C.: Anthropometric 3d face recognition. Int. J. Comput. Vision 90(3), 331–349 (2010)
5. Heisele, B., Serre, T., Poggio, T.: A component-based framework for face detection and identification. Int. J. Computer Vision 74(2), 167–181 (2007), http://dx.doi.org/10.1007/s11263-006-0006-z, doi:10.1007/s11263-006-0006-z
6. ISO/IEC JTC 1/SC 37 N 504: Biometric data interchange formats part 5: Face image. International Organization for Standardization (2004)
7. Jain, A.K., Klare, B., Park, U.: Face recognition: Some challenges in forensics. In: FG, pp. 726–733. IEEE (2011)
8. Jain, A.K., Klare, B., Park, U.: Face matching and retrieval in forensics applications. IEEE MultiMedia 19(1), 20 (2012)
9. Jain, A.K., Ross, A.A., Nandakumar, K.: Introduction to Biometrics. Springer Science+Business Media, LLC (2011), http://ebooks.ub.uni-muenchen.de/27631/
10. Jefferson, Y.: Facial beauty-establishing a universal standard. IJO 15(1), 9 (2004)
11. Li, F., Wechsler, H., Tistarelli, M.: Robust fusion using boosting and transduction for component-based face recognition. In: Proceedings of the 10th International Conference on Control, Automation, Robotics and Vision, ICARCV 2008, Hanoi, Vietnam, December 17-20, pp. 434–439. IEEE (2008), http://dx.doi.org/10.1109/ICARCV.2008.4795558
12. Li, S.Z., Jain, A.K. (eds.): Handbook of Face Recognition, 2nd edn. Springer (2011)
13. Meuwly, D., Veldhuis, R.: Forensic biometrics: From two communities to one discipline. In: 2012 BIOSIG - Proceedings of the International Conference of the Biometrics Special Interest Group (BIOSIG), pp. 1–12 (2012)
14. Netherlands Forensic Institute (NFI): http://www.forensicinstitute.nl

15. Next Generation Identification:
    http://www.fbi.gov/about-us/cjis/fingerprints_biometrics/ngi/ngi2
16. Ocegueda, O., Shah, S.K., Kakadiaris, I.A.: Which parts of the face give out your
    identity? In: CVPR, pp. 641–648. IEEE (2011),
    http://dblp.uni-trier.de/db/conf/cvpr/cvpr2011.html#OceguedaSK11
17. Ricanek, K., Tesafaye, T.: Morph: a longitudinal image database of normal adult
    age-progression. In: 7th International Conference on Automatic Face and Gesture
    Recognition, FGR 2006, pp. 341–345 (2006), doi:10.1109/FGR.2006.78
18. Spanish Guardia Civil (DGGC): http://www.guardiacivil.es/
19. Tistarelli, M.: Active/space-variant object recognition. Image and Vision Comput-
    ing 13(3), 215–226 (1995),
    doi:http://dx.doi.org/10.1016/0262-8856(95)90841-U
20. Tome, P., Fierrez, J., Fairhurst, M.C., Ortega-Garcia, J.: Acquisition scenario anal-
    ysis for face recognition at a distance. In: Bebis, G., Boyle, R., Parvin, B., Koracin,
    D., Chung, R., Hammoud, R., Hussain, M., Kar-Han, T., Crawfis, R., Thalmann,
    D., Kao, D., Avila, L. (eds.) ISVC 2010, Part I. LNCS, vol. 6453, pp. 461–468.
    Springer, Heidelberg (2010)
21. Tome, P., Vera-Rodriguez, R., Fierrez, J., Ortega-García, J.: Variability compen-
    sation using NAP for unconstrained face recognition. In: Omatu, S., Paz Santana,
    J.F., González, S.R., Molina, J.M., Bernardos, A.M., Rodríguez, J.M.C. (eds.)
    Distributed Computing and Artificial Intelligence. AISC, vol. 151, pp. 129–139.
    Springer, Heidelberg (2012),
    doi:http://dx.doi.org/10.1007/978-3-642-28765-7_17
22. Zhang, X., Gao, Y.: Face recognition across pose: A review. Pattern Recognition,
    2876–2896 (2009)

Analysis of Gait Recognition on Constrained Scenarios with Limited Data Information

Ruben Vera-Rodriguez, S. Gabriel-Sanz, Julian Fierrez, Pedro Tome, and J. Ortega-Garcia

ATVS, Escuela Politecnica Superior - Universidad Autonoma de Madrid, Avda. Francisco Tomas y Valiente, 11 - 28049 Madrid, Spain
{ruben.vera,silvia.gabriel,julian.fierrez, pedro.tome,javier.ortega}@uam.es

Abstract. This paper is focused on the assessment of gait recognition on a constrained scenario, where limited information can be extracted from the gait image sequences. In particular we are interested in assessing the performance of gait images when only the lower part of the body is acquired by the camera and just half of a gait cycle is available (SFootBD database). Thus, various state-of-the-art feature approaches have been followed and applied to the data. Results show that good recognition performance can be achieved using such limited data information for gait biometric. A comparative analysis of the influence of the quantity of data used in the training models has been carried out obtaining results of 8.6% EER for the case of using 10 data samples to train the models, and 5.7% of EER for the case of using 40 data for training. Also, a comparison with a standard and ideal gait database (USF database) is also carried out using similar experimental protocols. In this case 10 data samples are used for training achieving results of 3.6% EER. The comparison with a standard database shows that different feature approaches perform differently for each database, achieving best individual results with MPCA and EGEI methods for the SFootBD and the USF databases respectively.

Keywords: Biometrics, gait recognition, video surveillance.

1 Introduction

Surveillance of public spaces is growing at an unprecedented pace in response to crime and global terrorism. For example, currently, in the UK there are reportedly more cameras per person than in any other country in the world [1]. Due to the computational improvement of the current technologies and the increase of this type of devices during these last few years in certain open areas or even closed places, the deployment of non-invasive biometric technologies becomes important for the development of automated visual surveillance systems as well as for forensic investigations. The biometric technologies more suitable for these scenarios are face and gait recognition. Others such as iris or even ear would work under more controlled conditions [2].

J.M. Corchado et al. (Eds.): PAAMS 2013 Workshops, CCIS 365, pp. 231–239, 2013.

This paper is focused on gait recognition under limited data conditions. Gait is a relatively new biometric which utilizes the manner of walking to recognize an individual [3]. Compared to biometrics such as the iris or fingerprint recognition, this technique presents two main advantages: the recognition is performed at a distance and there is no need to cooperation from the users [4]. Both of these characteristics are also present in the case of face recognition, but gait has also the advantage of being able to work with low image resolution. On the other hand, the case of gait recognition is a very difficult task due to the huge amount of variability factors that can affect the gait recordings in real scenarios, such as persons walking to different directions, occlusions due to other people or clothing, different lighting conditions, etc.

In this paper six state-of-the-art feature extraction approaches for gait recognition have been followed to compare their recognition performances using a limited gait database which contains only the lower part of the body, SFootBD database (Swansea University, UK). Two configurations of this database were followed using 10 and 40 data samples for model training respectively. Then, these results were compared with a second and more ideal database used by many researchers, the USF database (University of South Florida, USA), where the gait images represent the whole body of the person. Finally, the best three individual feature approaches, GEI, EGEI and MPCA, were fused to increase the discrimination power of the systems obtaining results of 8.6% and 5.7% EER respectively for SFootBD 10 and 40 data samples in the training stage, and 3.6% EER for USF database which uses 10 data samples for model training. This shows that even with limited gait information the results are very promising.

The remainder of the paper is organized as follows. Section 2 describes the two databases used to evaluate the performance. Section 3 describes the different feature approaches followed. Section 4 reports the experimental work and Section 5 draws the final conclusions.

2   Gait Databases

Due to the importance of databases which are essential tools to evaluate the biometric recognition systems, in this paper we have carried out experimental work on two gait databases whose properties differ from one another allowing to obtain a comparative analysis of the results.

The first database used is the SFootBD [5]. This database is comprised of four biometric modes: footstep, gait, face and speech, using only the gait mode in this case. This database was captured without supervision obtaining therefore more realistic biometric samples (example shown in Figure 1(top)). This gait dataset is comprised of 130 users and 9893 gait image sequences but only having information for half of a gait cycle (left-right) and the lower half of the human body. The SFootBD is a much more limited database compared to the next database in terms of the amount of available information. Therefore, this database can be seen as a more realistic scenario for a gait application, e.g. a forensic case.

On the other hand, the second gait database used in this paper is the USF database [6]. This database contains sequences of gait images from 122 users,

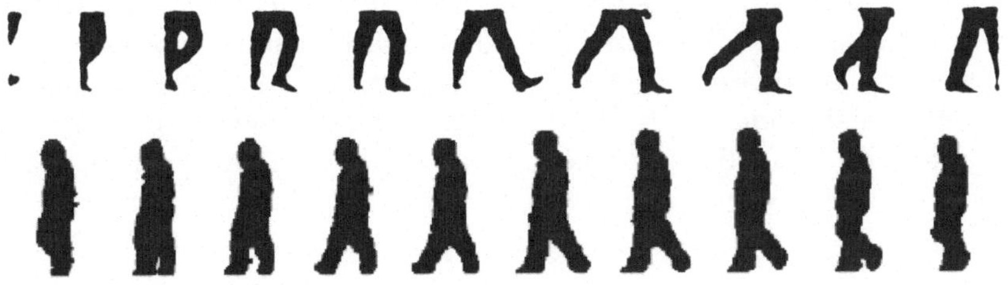

Fig. 1. Examples of gait sequences of the two databases considered in this paper. SFootBD database on the top row and USF database on the bottom row.

1870 with a half gait cycle (right-left) and the whole body shape. This database is comprised of 12 probes and 1 gallery with the persons walking under different conditions. In this paper only a subset of probe A was evaluated which is comprised of 71 users and 1458 gait sequences. This dataset contains sequences with a certain type of shoe, walking over grass. Figure 1(bottom) shows an example gait sequence from this database.

Regarding image alignment for the different feature approaches, the USF database was aligned using the position of the head. For the case of the SFootBD, the images were aligned to a central position using the position of the waist.

3   Feature Extraction

During the last few years, many algorithms have been developed to extract the discriminative information for gait recognition. In general, there are two main feature approaches: appearance-based and model-based [7]. Appearance-based approaches are focused on identifying persons using their silhouette, shape, geometrical measures, etc. On the other hand, model-based approaches are focused on identifying persons using the kinematic characteristics of the walking manner. The majority of the state-of-the-art approaches are appearance-based.

In this paper, an analysis of the state-of-the-art was conducted selecting six feature approaches, which were implemented and tested with different conditions. These algorithms are: Active Energy Image (AEI) [8], Multilinear Principal Component Analysis (MPCA) [9], Gait Flow Image (GFI) [3], Gait Energy Image (GEI) [10], Motion Silhouette Contour Template (MSCT) [3] and Enhance Gait Energy Image (EGEI) [11].

Results achieved for these six feature approaches are shown in Section 4. The three approaches obtaining best individual performance were: GEI, EGEI and MPA and are described in more detail next.

The first feature approach considered, one of the most popular to date, is called Gait Energy Image (GEI) [10]. In this case, a single image is obtained by averaging the binary silhouettes of a pedestrian over one gait cycle. Therefore, this method is an appearance-based approach. As Figure 2 shows, the image obtained represents by means of the intensity of each pixel, the frequency (energy) of body occurrence at the position of each pixel for a complete walking cycle. This algorithm was developed in 2006 [10] and although it is not as new as the other ones, the good results reflect the effectiveness of it. This method allows an easy implementation and reduces the time, storage and computational costs but it is heavily affected by factors such as the clothing and persons carrying objects.

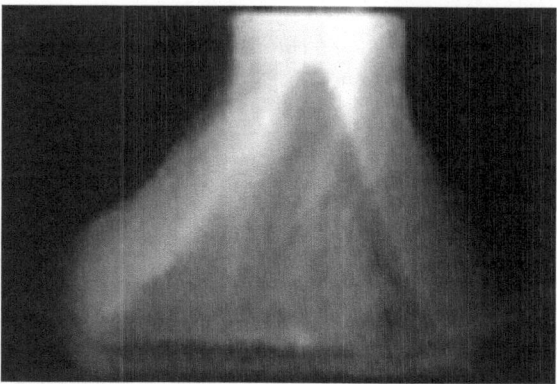

Fig. 2. Example of Gait Energy Image (GEI) for SFootBD database

The second feature approach considered, called Enhanced Gait Energy Image (EGEI) [11], is based on enhancing the previous GEI method. For this, an averaged GEI image representing each user class is used to construct a dynamic weight mask (DWM) by variance analysis. This mask is applied to the original GEI images to obtain the EGEI images. Finally, this method uses a Gabor filter bank in order to emphasize the most discriminative parts of the body image as shown in Figure 3. This technique is computationally more expensive than the GEI method, but allows to improve the results in cases of having much noisier environments.

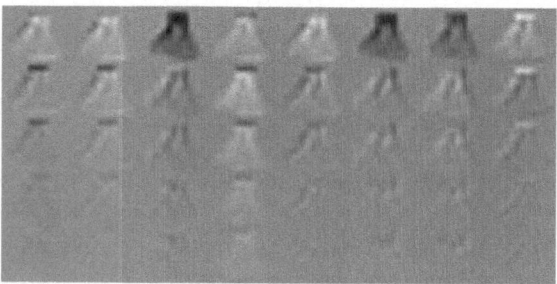

Fig. 3. Example of Enhanced Gait Energy Image (EGEI) for SFootBD database

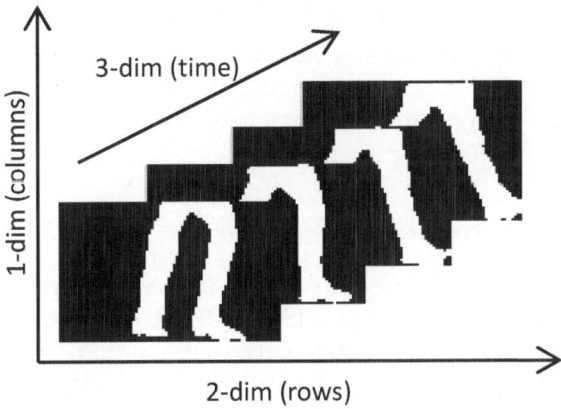

Fig. 4. Example of Multilinear Principal Component Analysis (MPCA)

The third approach considered in this paper, called Multilinear Principal Component Analysis (MPCA) [9], is an extension of the popular algorithm PCA. As can be seen in Figure 4, the data is arranged in several dimensions to form a tensor. In our case, four dimension tensors are used: two spatial dimensions of the images, a time dimension and another dimension for the different data examples. Once the tensor is ready, MPCA can drastically reduce the high dimensionality of the original data into low dimension feature vectors which are used in the classification stage.

4 Experimental Work

4.1 Experimental Protocol

To carry out the experimental work to study the discriminative power of different gait recognition systems using limited data, both databases considered were divided into training and test sets. Two configurations were considered for SFootBD database, using 10 and 40 data samples for model training, being 59 and 40 the number of users present in the training set respectively. The case of USF database was only set to 10 data samples for model training, having 71 users. It is worth mentioning that SFootBD is comprised of 130 users which are all present in the test set, so in this configuration there is a impostor dataset comprising data for the remaining users, which makes this an open-set scenario, more challenging than the case of the USF database.

Reduction of feature dimensionality was performed over the six feature approaches considered. Firstly, principal component analysis (PCA) was applied, analysing different number of principal components (PC). The case of MPCA did not require to use PCA. Later, linear discriminant analysis (LDA) was used to further extract the most relevant information. Finally, support vector machine (SVM) with a RBF kernel was employed as the classifier to obtain the recognition results.

Experiments are carried out for both identification (1 vs. all) and verification (1 vs. 1) working modes. In the first case, top rank identification performance is obtained using cumulative match characteristic (CMC) curves, and for the case of verification DET curves are obtaining giving the equal error rate (EER) as a measure of the performance.

4.2   Evaluation of Results

The first experiment was set to compare the individual performance of the six feature approaches considered (AEI, MSCT, GFI, GEI, EGEI and MPCA) over the two gait databases using the same data configuration, i.e., 10 data samples for training. Results are shown in Table 1. It is interesting to note that the number of PCA components was smaller in all cases but one (MPCA) for the SFootBD compared to the USF database, most likely for the lower amount of information contained (approximately a quarter of the information as only half of the gait cycle is visible for the lower part of the body).

Table 1. Results achieved for both SFootBD database with 10 and 40 signals to train the models and USF database, with rank 5 identification rate and EER both in %

	SFOOTBD 10		SFOOTBD 40		USF 10	
	Rank 5 ID	EER	Rank 5 ID	EER	Rank 5 ID	EER
AEI	69.1	16.4	82.5	11.4	85.6	9.2
MSCT	75.1	13.5	85.8	9.4	88.3	7.9
GFI	72.6	14.4	85.2	9.8	86.0	9.6
GEI	77.8	12.7	86.5	8.6	96.4	4.0
EGEI	79.8	11.9	88.0	7.6	96.4	4.1
MPCA	83.2	9.8	89.9	6.4	95.5	5.4
FUSION	**85.6**	**8.6**	**90.5**	**5.7**	**97.1**	**3.6**

As can be seen in Table 1, the GEI, EGEI and MPCA approaches obtained much better individual performance compared to AEI, MSCT, GFI, for both identification (rank 5) and verification (EER) experiments. Much better results were achieved for the case of USF database as was expected. But results in the order of 10% EER were achieved for the SFootBD which is good. It is interesting to note that the different feature approaches perform differently from one database to another. GEI and EGEI approaches perform better than MPCA for the USF database, while MPCA is the best approach for the SFootBD. This is due to the missing information of the SFootBD, as GEI and EGEI approaches are proven to work very well when the whole silhouette is visible.

The second experiment was the analysis of the influence of the amount of training data in the performance. For this only SFootBD was used with the two configurations of 10 and 40 data samples for model training. Table 1 shows

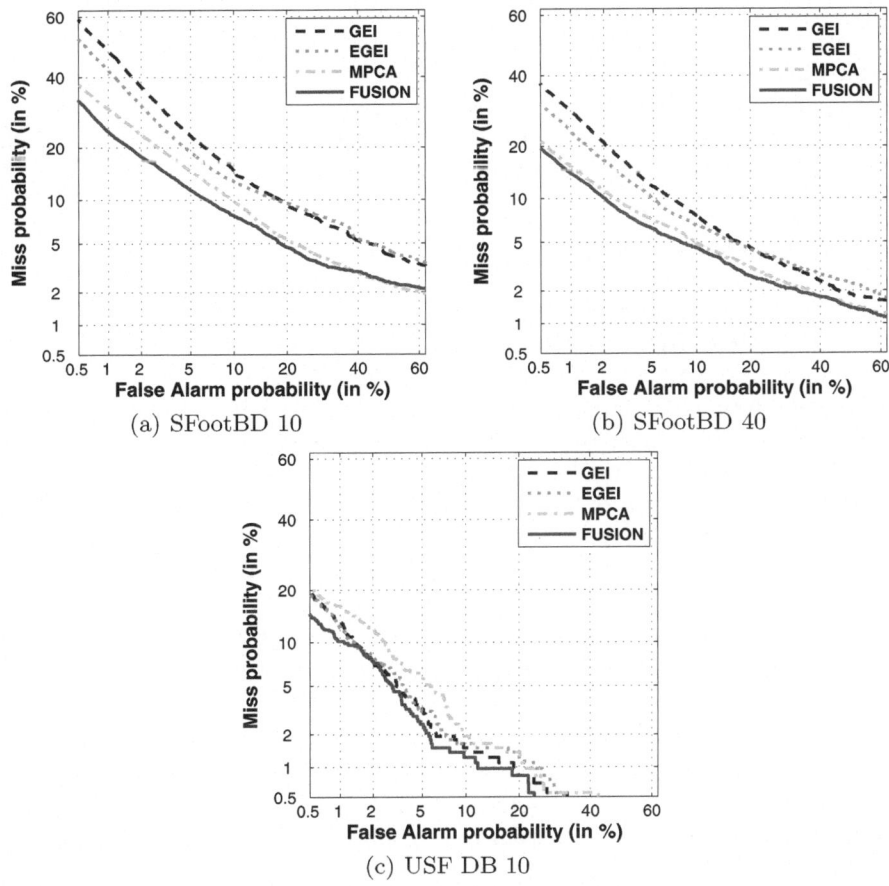

Fig. 5. DET Curves for both SFootBD database with 10 and 40 signals to train the models and USF database comparing the three best feature approaches and their fusion at the score-level.

how the results improve significantly when more data is included in the training models, getting close to the results achieved for the USF database. The same trends in the approaches are observed.

The third experiment was the fusion of the best three feature approaches in order to further improve the recognition performance of the system for a limited gait database. The fusion was carried out at the score-level using a simple product rule.

Figure 5 shows four DET curves for the three selected feature approaches and the fusion for the SFootBD (configurations 10 and 40) and USF databases respectively. As can see in Figures 5(a) and 5(b), the approach which provides better results for the case of the SFootBD is MPCA (9.8% and 6.4% EER respectively). The fusion of the three approaches achieved also a small improvement in terms of identification rate (85.6% and 90.5% for rank 5 respectively) and

EER (8.6% and 5.7% respectively). Table 1 shows an overview of the main results achieved. In contrast to these results Figure 5(c) shows results for the case of the USF database where the three feature approaches provide very similar identification rates, achieving a slightly better performance for EGEI (96.4% of rank 5 identification rate). The fusion of the three approaches achieves a small improvement obtaining 97.1% rank 5 identification rate and 3.6% EER.

5 Conclusions

In this paper, an evaluation of gait recognition systems over data with limited information (SFootBD) has been carried out. For this, six state-of-the-art feature approaches (AEI, MSCT, GFI, GEI, EGEI and MPCA) have been applied to the gait data. Similar experimental work has been followed over an ideal gait database (USF database) in order to compare results. In both cases best individual performance has been achieved for GEI, EGEI and MPCA feature approaches and a fusion of the three has been carried out at the score-level. As expected, there are significant differences in the performance of these approaches over the two databases, but more than acceptable results (85.6% of rank 5 identification rate and 8.6% of EER) have been achieved over the limited gait database, showing that using only the lower part of the body provides significant discriminative information for person recognition.

Acknowledgements. This work has been supported by projects Contexts (S2009/TIC-1485), Bio-Challenge (TEC2009-11186), Bio-Shield (TEC2012-34881) and "Catedra UAM-Telefonica". Ruben Vera-Rodriguez is supported by a Juan de la Cierva Fellowship from the Spanish MINECO.

References

1. http://www.guardian.co.uk/uk/2009/mar/02/westminster-cctv-system-privacy (2009)
2. Nixon, M., Bouchrika, I., Arbab-Zavar, B., Carter, J.: On the use of biometrics in forensics: gait and ear. In: Proc. of European Signal Processing Conference, EUSIPCO (2010)
3. Trivino, G., Alvarez-Alvarez, A., Bailador, G.: Application of the computational theory of perceptions to human gait pattern recognition. Pattern Recognition 43(7), 2572–2581 (2010)
4. Han, S., Zhi-Wu, L., Guo-Yue, C.: A gait recognition method using L1-PCA and LDA. In: Proc. International Conference on Machine Learning and Cybernetics, vol. 6, pp. 3198–3203 (2009)
5. Vera-Rodriguez, R., Mason, J., Fierrez, J., Ortega-Garcia, J.: Comparative analysis and fusion of spatio-temporal information for footstep recognition. IEEE Transactions on Pattern Analysis and Machine Intelligence 99 (2012)
6. Sarkar, S., Phillips, P.J., Liu, Z., Vega, I.R., Grother, P., Bowyer, K.W.: The humanID gait challenge problem: data sets, performance, and analysis. IEEE Transactions on Pattern Analysis and Machine Intelligence 27(2), 162–177 (2005)

7. Nixon, M.S., Carter, J.N.: Automatic recognition by gait. Proceedings of the IEEE 94(11), 2013–2024 (2006)
8. Zhang, E., Zhao, Y., Xiong, W.: Active energy image plus 2DLPP for gait recognition. Signal Processing 90(7), 2295–2302 (2010)
9. Lu, H., Plataniotis, K.N., Venetsanopoulos, A.N.: Multilinear principal component analysis of tensor objects for recognition. In: Proc. of the 18th International Conference on Pattern Recognition, vol. 2, pp. 776–779 (2006)
10. Han, J., Bhanu, B.: Individual recognition using gait energy image. IEEE Trans. Pattern Anal. Mach. Intell. 28(2), 316–322 (2006)
11. Yang, X., Zhou, Y., Zhang, T., Shu, G., Yang, J.: Gait recognition based on dynamic region analysis. Signal Processing 88(9), 2350–2356 (2008)

A Self-configurable Agent-Based System for Intelligent Storage in Smart Grid

Juan M. Alberola, Vicente Julián, and Ana García-Fornes

Departament de Sistemes Informàtics i Computació,
Universitat Politècnica de València,
Camí de Vera s/n. 46022, València. Spain
{jalberola,vinglada,agarcia}@dsic.upv.es

Abstract. Next generation of smart grid technologies demand intelligent capabilities for communication, interaction, monitoring, storage, and energy transmission. Multiagent systems are envisioned to provide autonomic and adaptability features to these systems in order to gain advantage in their current environments. In this paper we present a mechanism for providing distributed energy storage systems (DESSs) with intelligent capabilities. In more detail, we propose a self-configurable mechanism which allows a DESS to adapt itself according to the future environmental requirements. This mechanism is aimed at reducing the costs at which electricity is purchased from the market.

Keywords: smart grid, multiagent systems, storage.

1 Introduction

Smart grid technologies are positioned as one of the leading frameworks to build the next generation of systems and applications. Intelligent functions are expected to provide the smart grid with self-corrective and reconfiguration features, by creating a more complex interaction behavior among intelligent devices [1]. To address these issues, the multiagent system paradigm is widely agreed to be one challenging approach to build these systems [2, 3, 4, 5, 6].

In the last few years, agent-based technologies have been used to model smart grid systems, mostly focused on optimizing the system performance. In [7], agents represent customers which are faced with a multi-scale decision-making problem along temporal and contextual dimensions. The objective of these agents is to maximize the utility focused on these dimensions by learning the information of time-series. In [8], authors propose a model for dynamic coalition formation to approximate optimal micro-grid configurations.

The multiagent paradigm is envisioned as a strong solution to different approaches based on the smart grid, however, little work has been done focused on the use of agent-based techniques for storage management in these domains. Related to this issue, in [3] authors present an agent-based model for micro-storage management in the micro-grid. They propose a strategy based on game theory which reduces costs and carbon emission and converges to an efficient storage

J.M. Corchado et al. (Eds.): PAAMS 2013 Workshops, CCIS 365, pp. 240–250, 2013.

behavior. Their storage strategy proposed is focused on a learning mechanism that decides on when to store energy and when to use the stored energy in home devices. However, agents are self-interested with the aim of maximize their individual monetary profit. Therefore, conflicts that may arise depending on the distributed decision-making (e.g. a limited number of devices allowed to charge simultaneously at the same moment) are not considered.

The use of widely distributed energy storage systems (DESSs) with intelligent monitoring, communications, and control will enable the power grid of the future [9]. According to [10], the storage opportunity involves multiple interests with value propositions: (1) electric energy time-shift for purchasing electricity during periods when price is low to use the stored energy or to sell it when the price is high; (2) electric supply capacity for reducing the need to buy new central station generation capacity; (3) sub-station on-site power for managing equipments when the grid is not energized; (4) energy storage to provide highly reliable electric service; and so on. A DESS optimally located on the grid allows to maintain control over the grid and to the service reliability [9]. Storage can be applied at the energy production, at the transmission system, at the distribution system, and on the customer's side [11].

One of the benefits from storage that has been discussed in the literature long ago is referred to the use of storage systems for energy arbitrage. This involves purchasing electric energy during periods when the price is low, to charge the storage devices, so that the stored energy can be used or sold at a later time when the price is high [10]. This approach have been also studied in other works [12, 13, 14]. These decisions depend on different factors such as the market prices, the storage costs, the transmission costs, etc. In addition, depending on the storage device system, different parameters are associated to each one such as the efficiency, the charge rate, the storage response, the energy retention time.

To this respect, we focus on how intelligent storage systems can be build to achieve optimal configurations in the smart grid. We propose a self-configuration mechanism in order to provide a DESS with intelligent storage for improving the efficiency level. This mechanism uses an organizational representation of the DESS and focus on an adaptation of the roles played by agents. The objective of this process is aimed at scheduling the supplying and charging periods in order to reduce the electricity purchasing cost for supplying the system.

The rest of the paper is organized as follows. Section 2 presents the DESS model. Section 3 explains in detail the self-configuration mechanism. Section 4 shows the evaluation of the mechanism proposed. Finally, Section 5 presents some concluding remarks.

2   DESS Model

The DESS modeled in this work represents a group of storage devices which are geographically distributed (Figure 1). Each one of these devices is able to supply its stored electricity for a given area (e.g. a neighborhood, a town, etc.). The self-configuration mechanism is aimed at deciding for any storage device, when to store electricity by purchasing it from the market and when to use the stored electricity. Therefore, the optimal configuration is aimed at minimizing the cost of purchasing the electricity demanded by the areas during several periods of time (e.g. hourly, daily, etc.). The optimal configuration is dependent on the current and future electricity purchasing prices, and the current and future electricity demand. For reasons of clarity, in this work we assume an homogeneous system of storage devices in order to omit some of the parameters which could influence the optimal configuration, such as the standby losses or the transportation losses.

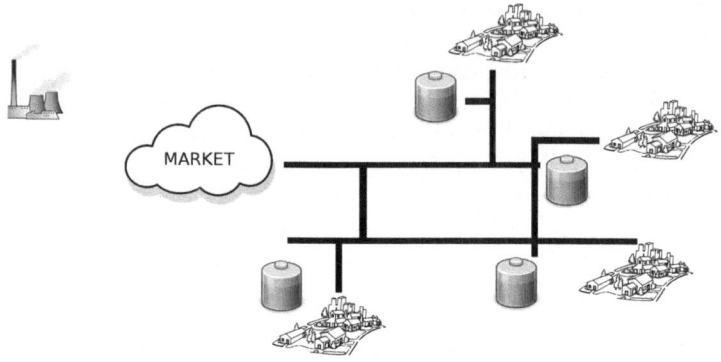

Fig. 1. Representation of the DESS

The optimal configuration that is obtained, represents a decision-making problem that determines the state of each storage device. Similar to other real-life problems, a conflict may emerge in this problem when different and autonomous decisions are taken distributively. As an example, if all storage devices decide to charge simultaneously, this could cause to exceed the generation or the transportation capacity. In order to solve this conflict, our approach selects the most optimal configuration according to the domain restrictions and not only by considering the individual preferences of the storage devices.

Since this problem determines a distributed scenario, we represent the group of storage devices as autonomous agents with organizational capabilities, in order to configure them according to the organizational constraints that must be fulfilled. These constraints are referred to the limited capacity of the transportation system, which determines the maximum number of storage devices that can be charged simultaneously. Based on our previous definition of dynamic organization [15], we model the DESS as a multiagent system $G^t = \langle \mathcal{A}^t, \mathcal{R}, \mathcal{P}^t, \Lambda^t, \Delta_i^t, \Phi \rangle$, where:

- $\mathcal{A}^t = \{a_1 \ldots a_n\}$ denotes the set of agents that are associated to the storage devices. Each agent a_x is able to supply electricity to its specific area x and has associated different parameters for a given moment t: $L(a_x)^t$ represents the electricity load; $Q(a_x)^t$ represents the electricity supplied to the area; and $P(a_x)^t$ represents the electricity purchased from the market.

- $\mathcal{R} = \{supplier, charge, idle\}$ denotes the set of roles which agents can play. We define three possible roles that agents can play (but not simultaneously) depending on the state of the storage device. An agent a_x playing the *supplier* role refers that the electricity demanded by the area x is supplied from the storage device; an agent playing the *charge* role refers that the storage device is being charged by purchasing electricity from the market, and the electricity demanded by the area is also directly supplied from the market; finally, an agent playing the *idle* role is neither charging its storage device nor supplying electricity to its corresponding area.
- $\mathcal{P}^t = \{\mathcal{S}^t, \mathcal{C}^t, \mathcal{I}^t\}$ denotes the three subsets of agents depending on the roles that they are playing at the moment t. We define $\mathcal{S}^t \subseteq \mathcal{A}^t$ as the subset of agents that are playing the *supplier* role at the moment t. We define $\mathcal{C}^t \subseteq \mathcal{A}^t$ as the subset of agents that are playing the *charge* role at the moment t. Finally, we define $\mathcal{I}^t \subseteq \mathcal{A}^t$ as the subset of agents that are playing the *idle* role at the moment t.
- $\Lambda^t = \lambda^{t+1} \ldots \lambda^m$ denotes the sequence of electricity purchasing price estimations for the following moments. A given electricity purchasing price λ^y represents the estimated price at which the electricity can be purchased from the market at the moment y. For reasons of simplicity, this estimation is the same for every storage device.
- $\Delta_i^t = \delta_i^{t+1} \ldots \delta_i^m$ denotes the sequence of forecast demand of electricity associated to each area for the following moments. A given demand δ_i^y represents the forecast demand of electricity for the area i at the moment y.
- Φ denotes the set of constraints that must be fulfilled at each moment. As we stated above, we enforce that the number of storage devices that can be simultaneously charged at the same time does not exceed a predefined value $Nmax$, which corresponds to the limit capacity of the transportation system: $\phi_1 :\mid \mathcal{S}^t \mid \leq Nmax$.

3 Self-configuration Mechanism

The self-configuration mechanism is intended at providing the decision-making process which determines the state of each storage device at any moment. This mechanism provides a general vision of the whole system and allows to determine the specific consequences of each change of state in the rest of the system.

This mechanism is based on our previous work about role reallocation for organizational adaptation in agent societies [16]. This work obtains the adaptation with the highest potential for improvement in utility based on the costs of adaptation. Similarly, the self-configuration mechanism presented in this paper, obtains the roles configuration of the storage devices which minimizes the electricity purchasing costs, depending on the electricity purchasing price and the electricity demand for the forthcoming moments. The problem of predicting future electricity purchasing prices is widely studied in other works such as [17, 18, 19], and is out of the scope of this work.

In order to determine the state of the storage device for the following moment, we define the concept of impact associated to each possible role that can be played by each agent. This impact represents the measurement of the effects of playing a role in terms of system utility based on the costs for carrying out each this action. This impact measures the different alternatives that can be chosen from the current storage devices configuration in order to adapt it, based on the benefits and costs of each alternative. Computing the impact becomes essential in order to empirically specify the value of each possible configuration before changing the state of the storage devices. Given the DESS model presented in Section 2, following we define the notation for obtaining the impact measurements for playing each possible role allocation.

First, each area can be supplied by its corresponding storage device, or directly by the market at the current electricity purchasing price. In this last case, considering δ_x^{t+1} as the forecast demand of electricity for the next moment $t+1$ associated with the area x, if this demand is supplied from the market, this will be purchased at the price λ^{t+1}, which defines the following cost for supplying the area x from the market:

$$S(x,m)^{t+1} = \delta_x^{t+1} \times \lambda^{t+1}$$

Otherwise, if this demand is supplied from the storage device, this will be supplied at the following supplying cost:

$$S(x,a_x)^{t+1} = \delta_x^{t+1} \times \bar{p}^{\,t+1}$$

being $\bar{p}^{\,t+1}$ the average price of the stored electricity in a_x, according to the prices at which this stored electricity was previously purchased from the market:

$$\bar{p}^{\,t+1} = \begin{cases} \lambda^{t+1} & \text{for } t=0 \\ \frac{(L(a_x)^t \times \bar{p}^{\,t}) + (P(a_x)^t \times \lambda^t) - (Q(a_x)^t \times \bar{p}^{\,t})}{L(a_x)^t + P(a_x)^t - Q(a_x)^t} & \text{for } t>0 \end{cases}$$

In the above equation, the variables $L(a_x)^t$, $Q(a_x)^t$ and $P(a_x)^t$ represent the electricity load, the electricity supplied, and the electricity purchased as denoted in Section 2. In this case, the electricity supplied to the area by the agent a_x for the next moment $t+1$ corresponds to $Q(a_x)^{t+1} = \lambda^{t+1}$. Otherwise, if the electricity is supplied from the market, this value is null: $Q(a_x)^{t+1} = 0$. Hence, the cost for supplying a given area x can be calculated depending on which source supplies the electricity.

When the electricity is supplied from the storage device, the load of this device will be reduced to: $L(a_x)^{t+1} = L(a_x)^t - \delta_x^{t+1}$. This causes that each storage device needs to be charged eventually from the market. In case that the storage device is charged at the moment $t+1$, the cost associated to this charge is calculated as the amount of electricity purchased according to the electricity purchasing price at this moment:

$$C(a_x)^{t+1} = N(a_x) \times \lambda^{t+1}$$

being $N(a_x)$ the predefined amount of electricity that this storage device can charge (it could be related to the charge rate of each device). In this case, the electricity purchased from the market will be: $P(a_x)^{t+1} = N(a_x)$. Otherwise, $P(a_x)^{t+1} = 0$.

If the storage device is not charged in the next moment $t + 1$, it will be able to supply electricity until its reserves are running out (denoted as the moment $t + n$). Being $L(a_x)^{t+1} = L(a_x)^t$, the charge could be postponed to a future moment t', which is comprised in the period of time up to $t + n$, at which the electricity purchasing price is the cheapest one, formally:

$$(t+2 \leq t' \leq t+n) \wedge \left(\delta_x^{t'} = \operatorname*{argmin}_{i \in [t+2, t+n]} (\delta_x^i) \right) \wedge \left(\sum_{i=t+2}^{i=t+n} \delta_x^i \leq L(a_x)^t \right) \wedge \left(\sum_{i=t+2}^{i=t+n+1} \delta_x^i > L(a_x)^t \right)$$

According to the above notation, the impact for an agent a_x for playing the *supplier* role at the moment $t + 1$ is measured as: (1) the cost required for supplying the electricity demanded from the storage device; (2) the benefits for not supplying this electricity from the market at the next moment; (3) the cost for charging the storage device in the future moment t' (the best case); and (4) the benefits for not charging the storage device at the next moment:

$$I(a_x, supplier)^{t+1} = S(x, u_x)^{t+1} - S(x, m)^{t+1} + C(a_x)^{t'} - C(a_x)^{t+1}$$

We must note that in order to an agent a_x being able to play the *supplier* role, it must maintain the supply availability, i.e. the current load of the storage device must be higher than the expected demand for the next moment, otherwise, this storage device cannot be a supplier:

$$\phi_2 : L(a_x)^t < \delta_x^{t+1} \rightarrow I(a_x, supplier)^{t+1} = \infty$$

The impact for an agent a_x for playing the *charge* role at the moment $t + 1$ is measured as: (1) the cost required for supplying the electricity demanded from the market at the next moment; (2) the benefits for not supplying this electricity from the storage device; (3) the cost for charging the storage device at the next moment; and (4) the benefits for not charging the storage device in the future moment t' (the best case):

$$I(a_x, charge)^{t+1} = S(x, m)^{t+1} - S(x, a_x)^{t+1} + C(a_x)^{t+1} - C(a_x)^{t'}$$

The impact for an agent a_x for playing the *idle* role at the moment $t + 1$ is measured as: (1) the cost required for supplying the electricity demanded from the market at the next moment; (2) the benefits for not supplying this electricity from the storage device; (3) the cost for charging the storage device in the future moment t' (the best case); and (4) the benefits for not charging the storage device at the next moment:

$$I(a_x, idle)^{t+1} = S(x, g)^{t+1} - S(x, a_x)^{t+1} + C(a_x)^{t'} - C(a_x)^{t+1}$$

Finally, we measure the impact of a whole self-configuration of the system as the aggregation of the impact of each role allocation:

$$I(\mathcal{P}^{t+1}) = \sum_{a \in \mathcal{S}^{t+1}} I(a, supplier)^{t+1} + \sum_{a \in \mathcal{C}^{t+1}} I(a, charge)^{t+1} + \sum_{a \in \mathcal{I}^t} I(a, idle)^{t+1}$$

Given the state of the system defined as $G^t = \langle \mathcal{A}^t, \mathcal{R}, \mathcal{P}^t, \Lambda^t, \Delta_i^t, \Phi \rangle$, some agents could be reallocated to play other roles in the future moment $t + 1$. A role reallocation process entails transforming the current set of role allocations $\mathcal{P}^t$ into $\mathcal{P}^{t+1}$. Each one of the possible role allocations determines a different G^{t+1} with an associated impact $I(\mathcal{P}^{t+1})$.

Let Θ denote the set of all the possible different role allocation that can be obtained from the current configuration. The challenge of the self-configuration mechanism is to find the specific role allocation $\widehat{\mathcal{P}}^{t+1}$ that minimizes the role allocation impact:

$$I(\widehat{\mathcal{P}}^{t+1}) = \operatorname*{argmin}_{\mathcal{P}^{t+1} \in \Theta} I(\mathcal{P}^{t+1})$$

4   Evaluation

In this section we present some experiments for testing the performance of the self-configuration mechanism applied to the DESS model. For these experiments, the system is composed at any moment by a set of five agents $\mathcal{A}^t = \{a_1, a_2, a_3, a_4, a_5\}$ and the electricity demand and purchasing price is changing during 50 time-steps. Being t the current time-step, the demand for a given area $x = [1..5]$ for the next time-step is calculated according to the following formula: $\delta_x^{t+1} = \delta_x^t \times random[0.95, 1.05]$. Due to the objective of the self-configuration mechanism is not focused on the price prediction but is focused on improving the performance of the system, we assume that the electricity purchasing price changes progressively by following a sequence from a lowest price of 3c/kWh up to a highest price 6c/kWh. In this experiment, the maximum number of devices that are allowed to charge simultaneously is defined as $Nmax = 3$.

In the first experiment (Figure 2) we test the performance of the DESS when the self-configuration mechanism is applied. Therefore, the configuration of the system at any moment reflects the role allocation which minimizes the impact.

In Figure 2(a) we show the aggregated cost for satisfying the demand of all the areas during the 50 time-steps. We compare the performance of the self-configuration mechanism with the performance of a static mechanism, in which the charge is carried out when it is needed, i.e. when the storage device has not enough electricity stored for supplying the following time-step. In Figures 2(c) and 2(d) we show the electricity purchasing price at any moment in order to compare it with the cost.

We can observe that the performance of the self-configuration mechanism is always better (the cost is lower) than the mechanism which charges the devices when it is needed. This is because the self-configuration mechanism changes the configuration of the storage devices by taking into consideration the forthcoming electricity demand and the purchasing price. Therefore, this mechanism configures the system for supplying the electricity in the following time-steps according to these parameters. It can also be observed that the average cost is decreasing on time when the self-configuration mechanism is used, while it is oscillating (as the electricity purchasing price oscillates) when the charges are carried out when they are needed. The average cost during the 50 time-steps is $492.54e \pm 50.68$ with

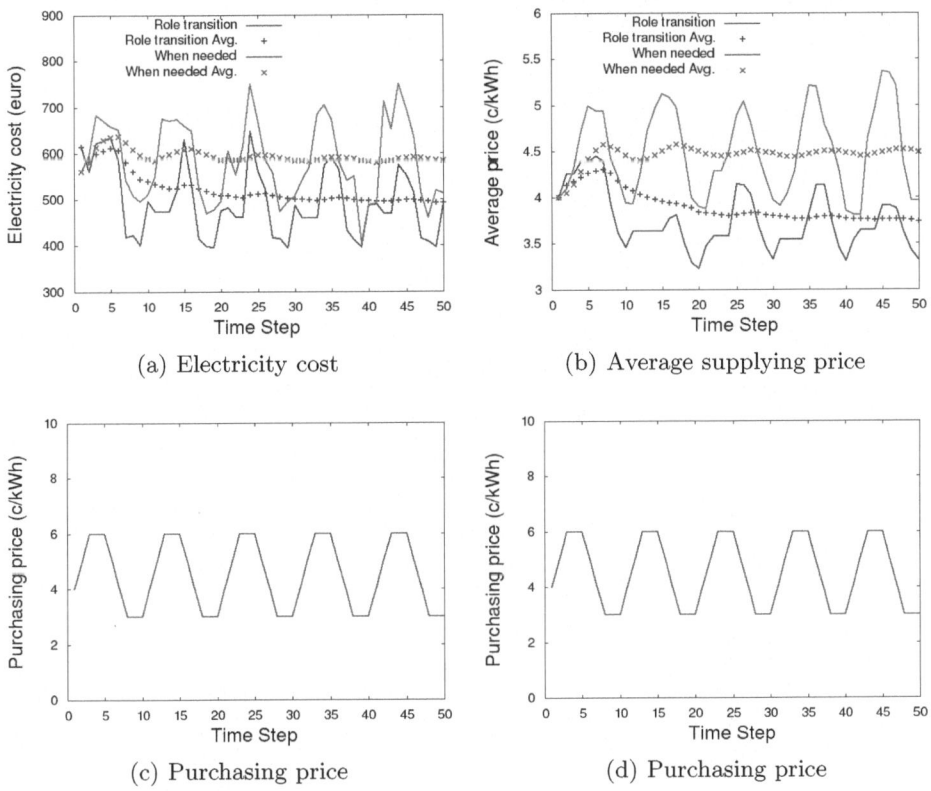

(a) Electricity cost

(b) Average supplying price

(c) Purchasing price

(d) Purchasing price

Fig. 2. Smart grid performance in a progressive electricity purchasing price scenario

a 95% confidence interval when using the self-configuration mechanism. In contrast, this cost is 584.33e±66.27 if the storage devices are charged when it is needed. This causes a whole economic difference between both approaches of 4579.63e during the 50 executions.

In Figure 2(b) we show the average price of all the storage devices at any time. Similar to the above figure, the average price is lower for the self-configuration mechanism. The average price for all the iterations is 3.74e when using the self-configuration mechanism and 4.49e when not, which represents an average price reduction of almost 17%.

In the second experiment we want to test the number of agents which are playing each role depending on the purchasing price changes. In order to observe more clearly the behavior of both strategies, we present an scenario in which the purchasing price changes from the lowest value to the highest one (Figure 3(b)). Thus, the differences between purchasing and supplying electricity may be quite different from one time-step to the following one. The objective of this experiment is to demonstrate how the self-configuration mechanism is able to adapt the role configuration according to the price is expected to abruptly

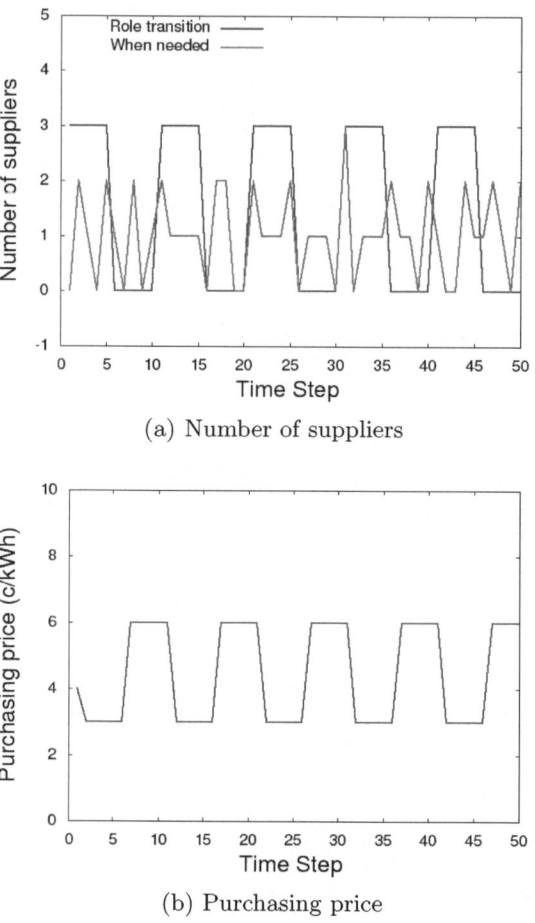

(a) Number of suppliers

(b) Purchasing price

Fig. 3. Smart grid performance in a progressive electricity purchasing price scenario

increase or decrease in the next few moments. In Figure 3(a) we show the number of storage devices which are simultaneously purchasing electricity (i.e. playing the *charge* role) at each time-step. We can observe that the self-configuration mechanism is able to configure the system in order to charge simultaneously the highest number of allowed devices (3) when the price is low and it is expected to increase in the next few moments. Similarly, the number of devices that are simultaneously charged is reduced to 0 when the price is the highest one and it is expected to decrease in the next few moments. We can observe that the storage devices are charging and the areas are supplied directly from the market when the price is low. This stored electricity is then supplied to the areas when the purchasing price remains high. In contrast, when the devices are charged when needed, the number of devices that are charged simultaneously do not follow any pattern. In this experiment, differences between both approaches are even higher than in the first experiment. The average cost during the 50 time-steps is 413.58$e\pm$1.03 with a 95% confidence interval for the self-configuration mechanism and 574.05e pm86.77 if the storage devices are charged when it is needed. This causes a whole economic difference between both approaches of 8023.39e during the 50 executions. The average price for all the iterations is 3.14e when using the self-configuration mechanism and 4.07e when not, which represents an average price reduction of almost 23%. Therefore, the self-configuration mechanism is able to reduce the cost for purchasing the energy demanded by the areas during a long-time period. This is caused because the role allocation adaptation allows to obtain the configuration with the highest potential for cost reduction, according to the future purchasing prices and demand.

5 Conclusions

We proposed a self-configuration mechanism which provide distributed storage in smart grids with intelligence. This mechanism is based on organizational adaptation by role reallocation. The representation of the DESS by means of a multiagent organization provides different future challenges such as including other organizational dimensions to be adapted (such as the agent population) and to improve the organizational interaction and cooperation among agents.

The decision-making process associated to the self-configuration mechanism, obtains the solution which minimizes the electricity supplying costs for satisfying the demand of the areas. As we observed in the experiments, these costs can be significantly reduced when taking into account the future prices and demand. In addition, since the objective is to maximize the utility of the whole system, conflicts that can emerge from individual utilities are solved due to the global view of the system. What is more, the configuration of the storage devices fits the current and future parameters of the environment by adjusting the number of devices that are charging and supplying energy at any moment.

Acknowledgments. This work has been partially supported by projects TIN2012-36586-C03-01 and TIN2011-27652-C03-01.

References

[1] Momoh, J.A.: Smart grid design for efficient and flexible power networks operation and control. In: IEEE PES Power Systems Conference and Exposition, pp. 15–18 (2009)
[2] Pipattanasomporn, M., Feroze, H., Rahman, S.: Multi-agent systems in a distributed smart grid: Design and implementation. In: IEEE/PES Power Systems Conference and Exposition, pp. 1–8 (2009)
[3] Vytelingum, P., Voice, T.D., Ramchurn, S., Rogers, A., Jennings, N.R.: Agent-based micro-storage management for the Smart Grid. In: Proceedings of the 9th International Conference on Autonomous Agents and Multiagent Systems, pp. 39–46 (2010)

[4] Vytelingum, P., Voice, T.D., Ramchurn, S., Rogers, A., Jennings, N.R.: Intelligent agents for the smart grid. In: Proceedings of the 9th International Conference on Autonomous Agents and Multiagent Systems, pp. 1649–1650 (2010)

[5] Van Dam, K.H., Houwing, M., Bouwmans, I.: Agent-based control of distributed electricity generation with microcombined heat and power-cross-sectoral learning for process and infrastructure engineers. Computers & Chemical Engineering 32, 205–217 (2008)

[6] Oyarzabal, J., Jimeno, J., Ruela, J., Engler, A., Hardt, C.: Agent based Micro Grid Management System. In: International Conference on Future Power Systems, vol. 18(8) (2005)

[7] Reddy, P.P., Veloso, M.M.: Factored Models for Multiscale Decision Making in Smart Grid Customers. In: Proceedings of AAAI 2012, the Twenty-Sixth AAAI Conference on Artificial Intelligence (2012)

[8] Mihailescu, R.C., Vasirani, M., Ossowski, S.: Dynamic coalition formation and adaptation for virtual power stations in smart grids. In: Proc. of the 2nd Int. Workshop on Agent Technologies for Energy Systems, pp. 85–88 (2011)

[9] Nourai, A.: Installation of the First Distributed Energy Storage System (DESS) at American Electric Power (AEP). Technical report, Sandia National Laboratories (2007)

[10] Eyer, J., Corey, G.: Energy Storage for the Electricity Grid: Benefits and Market Potential Assessment Guide. Technical report, Sandia National Laboratories (2010)

[11] Mohd, A., Ortjohann, E., Schmelter, A., Hamsic, N., Morton, D.: Challenges in integrating distributed Energy storage systems into future smart grid. In: IEEE International Symposium on Industrial Electronics, pp. 1627–1632 (2008)

[12] Costa, L., Bourry, F., Juban, J., Kariniotakis, G.: Management of energy storage coordinated with wind power under electricity market conditions. In: 10th International Conference on Probabilistic Methods Applied to Power Systems, pp. 259–266 (2008)

[13] Pinson, P., Chevallier, C., Kariniotakis, G.N.: Trading Wind Generation From Short-Term Probabilistic Forecasts of Wind Power. IEEE Transactions on Power Systems 22(3), 1148–1156 (2007)

[14] Maly, D.K., Kwan, K.S.: Optimal battery energy storage system (BESS) charge scheduling with dynamic programming. IEE Proceedings-Science, Measurement and Technology 142(6), 453–458 (1995)

[15] Alberola, J.M., Julian, V., Garcia-Fornes, A.: Multi-Dimensional Adaptation in MAS Organizations. IEEE Transactions on Systems, Man, and Cybernetics, Part B: Cybernetics (in press, 2013)

[16] Alberola, J.M., Julian, V., Garcia-Fornes, A.: Multi-dimensional Transition Deliberation for Organization Adaptation in Multiagent Systems. In: Proc. 11th Int. Conf. on Aut. Agents and MAS, AAMAS 2012, pp. 1379–1380 (2012)

[17] Conejo, A.J., Plazas, M.A., Espinola, R., Molina, A.B.: Day-Ahead Electricity Price Forecasting Using the Wavelet Transform and ARIMA Models. IEEE Transactions on Power Systems 20(2), 1035–1042 (2005)

[18] Mohsenian, A.H., Leon-Garcia, A.: Optimal Residential Load Control With Price Prediction in Real-Time Electricity Pricing Environments. IEEE Trans. Smart Grid 1(2), 120–133 (2010)

[19] Szkuta, B., Sanabria, L., Dillon, T.: Electricity price short-term forecasting using artificial neural networks. IEEE Transactions on Power Systems 14(3), 851–857 (1999)

Strategies for Cooperation Emergence
in Distributed Service Discovery

E. del Val, M. Rebollo, and V. Botti

Departament de Sistemes Informàtics i Computació,
Universitat Politècnica de València,
Camí de Vera s/n. 46022, València. Spain
{edelval,mrebollo,vbotti}@dsic.upv.es

Abstract. In distributed environments where entities only have a partial view of
the system, cooperation plays a key issue. In the case of decentralized service discovery in open agent societies, agents only know about the services they provide
and who are their direct neighbors. Therefore, they need the cooperation of their
neighbors in order to locate the required services. However, cooperation is not
always present in open and distributed systems. Non-cooperative agents pursuing
their own goals could refuse to forward queries from other agents to avoid the
cost of this action; therefore, the efficiency of the decentralized service discovery
could be seriously damaged. In this paper, we propose the combination of local
structural changes and incentives in order to promote cooperation in the service
discovery process. The results show that, even in scenarios where the predomi-
nant behavior is not collaborative the cooperation emerges.

Keywords: Cooperation, Complex Networks, Service Discovery.

1 Introduction

There are distributed systems where the cooperation of all the entities that participate
in them is required to obtain a good performance that provides benefits for all the participants. Some of the scenarios where cooperation is required are: wireless ad-hoc
networks where nodes rely on other nodes to forward their packets in order to reach the
destination node; file sharing in P2P systems [1]; streaming applications [2], discussion
boards [3], on-line auctions [4], or overlay routing [5]. If participants that decide not
to contribute in order to maximize their own benefits and exploit the contributions of
the others appear in these scenarios, they will obtain a high rate of benefits in the short
term. However, these benefits decrease as the number of selfish participants increases,
thereby damaging the performance of the whole system. There are models of genetic
and cultural evolution that confirm that the opportunity to take advantage of others un-
dermines and often eliminates cooperation [6]. These cooperation problems are also
known as social dilemmas (i.e., the tragedy of the commons, the free-rider problem, the
social trap). The promotion and stabilization of cooperation in scenarios of this type has
been considered to be an area of interest [7].

Several mechanisms have been proposed to promote and maintain cooperation in different scenarios. In scenarios where individuals interact repeatedly, selfish or altruistic

J.M. Corchado et al. (Eds.): PAAMS 2013 Workshops, CCIS 365, pp. 251–262, 2013.
© Springer-Verlag Berlin Heidelberg 2013

actions would be returned in future. Therefore, a common mechanism to facilitate the emergence of cooperation is *direct reciprocity* [8]. When agents do not always interact with the same individuals, *indirect reciprocity* [9] or *tags* [10] are used. *Punishment* has also been considered to promote cooperation and to overcome the "tragedy of the commons" [6]. Punishment is present in human societies where sanctioning institutions apply a punishment to those that do not obey the law. In systems where such centralized institutions do not exist, individuals are willing to punish defectors even though this implies a cost for them [11]. In general, punishment has been proven to be an efficient way to maintain cooperation [12, 13].

Many approaches that are used to promote cooperation assume well-mixed populations where everybody interacts with equal frequency with everybody else. However, real populations are not well-mixed. In real populations, some individuals interact more often than others; therefore, to understand the social behavior of the systems it is important to consider the social structure. The social structure is represented by a network where links are established by the individuals following certain preferences. There are several works that analyze the influence of the network structure in the emergence of cooperation. These works study how structural parameters such as clustering or degree distribution affect the emergence and maintenance of cooperation [14–17].

Another issue that it is important to consider is how local changes can influence the collective social behavior. Eguíluz et al. [18] present a model that uses the Prisoner's Dilemma game [19] and *social plasticity* in random undirected networks of agents. Agents update their behavior in discrete time steps using an imitation strategy that considers the payoff of neighbors. The social plasticity (i.e., changes in structural links) is considered when an agent imitates a defector in order to facilitate the replacement of an unprofitable relationship with a new one that is randomly chosen. Griffiths et al. [20] propose a mechanism that considers context awareness and tags of agents to promote cooperation. Moreover, agents can remove part of their connections with agents that are not cooperative and add connections with others that can improve cooperation. There are other approaches that also make use of rewiring techniques and partial observation to facilitate the emergence of cooperation [21].

In this paper, we present a proposal that promotes cooperation in the service discovery process among agents that are located in a network structure. In this context, cooperation plays an important role since agents only have a partial view of the network and need the cooperation of their neighbors in order to forward queries to locate the required resources or services. This becomes even more difficult when there are self-interested agents that do not cooperate with other agents in order to avoid the cost of forwarding queries. We combine two mechanisms in order to promote cooperation: incentives and social plasticity. The main differences between our approach and other proposals are: (i) we consider the social structure where agents are located instead of a well mixed population; (ii) we have considered different criteria for the assignment of incentives for the agents participate in the search process; (iii) structural local changes are also taken into account in combination with incentives; the structural changes are not random, agents break links with those neighbors that have non-cooperative behavior, and instead of replacing them randomly, the agents look for another agent based on their preferences; (iv) taking into account local information about the degree of cooperation of their neighborhood, agents are able to detect when it is more appropriate to include social plasticity. The proposed combination of mechanisms has been tested and the results show that even in adverse situations where there is a large number of non- cooperative (non-cooperator) agents our proposal obtains good results and the performance of the system is not seriously affected.

The paper is structured as follows. In section 2, we describe the model where we integrate the cooperation mechanisms. This section contains the description of the service discovery process, presents the incentives mechanism and the social plasticity, and finally we describe how agents selects each action during the service discovery process. Section 3 presents a set of experiments where we evaluate the performance of our proposal. Finally, section 4 presents conclusions and final remarks.

2   Model for Cooperation in Service Discovery

Consider a network of agents $A = \{1, ..., n\}$ connected by undirected links in a fixed network represented by the adjacency matrix g. A link between two agents i and j, such that i and $j \in A$, is represented by $g_{ij} = g_{ji} = 1$, where $g_{ij} = 0$ means that i and j are not connected. The set of neighbors of player i is $N_i = j|g_{ij} = 1$. We assume that $g_{ii} = 0$. The number of neighbors of i is denoted by k_i, which is the cardinality of the set $N_i(g)$. Each agent in the network plays a role r_i and offers at least one service associated with that role s_i. An agent has an initial behavior that can be cooperative (c) or not cooperative (nc). Moreover, each agent has an initial budget b that it is equal for all the agents in the system.

A link between two agents i and j is established considering a probability. This probability is based on the similarity between the roles played by the agents i and j and the services provided by them as well as their degree of connectivity. Therefore, agents have a greater probability of establishing links with agents that have similar attributes than with dissimilar ones. The result of using this criterion to establish links between agents is a network structure based on similarity and degree that has an exponential distribution of its degree of connection. This structure facilitates the task of decentralized service discovery only considering local information [22].

2.1   Service Discovery

The service discovery starts when agent $i \in A$ needs to locate an agent that plays certain role and offers certain service in order to deal with one of its goals. The agent i, in order to start the process estimates if it has enough budget b to reach the target. In the case that the budget is enough, agent i creates a query at time t $q_i^t = \{s_{tg}, r_{tg}, TTL, \varepsilon, \{\}\}$, which consists of: the required semantic service description (s_{tg}), the organizational role that the target agent should play (r_{tg}), the Time To Live that represents the maximum number of times that the query can be forwarded (TTL), the ε established by i that represents how similar should be the target agent that i is looking for, and the list of identifiers of the agents that participate in the search process (initially this list is empty).

In the discovery process, when an agent that is similar enough to the target is found, the agent i is informed and the process ends. Otherwise, agent i should choose one of its neighbors to forward the query q_i^t. The selection of the the most promising neighbor is based on the similarity between the neighbor and the target (similarity-based factor that considers the semantic similarity between the services and the roles of two agents) and the number of neighbors of the neighbor (degree-based factor)[22].

$$\mathcal{F}_{Ni}(tg) = \operatorname{argmax}_{j \in N_i} P(\langle j, tg \rangle) \tag{1}$$

For each neighbor j, $P(\langle j, tg \rangle)$ determines the probability that the neighbor j redirects the search to the nearest network community where there are more probabilities of finding the agent tg.

$$P(\langle j, tg \rangle) = 1 - \left(1 - \left(\frac{H(j, tg)}{\sum\limits_{k \in N_i} H(k, tg)} \right) \right)^{k_j} \tag{2}$$

where $H(j, tg)$ is the semantic similarity between the roles and services of agents j and tg. For a detailed mathematical definition of this measure we refer the reader to [22]. The discovery process ends when the number of forwards exceeds the TTL or when the target agent that provides the required service is found.

Actions and Incentives. When a neighbor j receives a query q_i^t, it has a set of possible actions $Acc = \{\rho, \infty, 1, 2, ..., k_i, \emptyset, \lambda\}$, where:

- ρ is asking for a service
- ∞ is providing the service
- $\{1, ..., k_i\}$ is forwarding the query to one of its neighbors $\in N_i$
- $\emptyset$ is doing nothing
- λ rewiring a link

The actions of an agent in the network have associated a cost, a benefit, or a reward. If an agent asks for a service to a provider, it has to pay the provider β. If an agent provides a service, it earns a payoff p. Forwarding a query is costly c, but an agent earns a payoff α if the query ends successfully. Otherwise, the payoff is 0. If an agent chooses the action $\emptyset$, its payoff is 0. The agent can also decide rewiring a current structural relation with a neighbor and looking for a new one. The rewiring action has a cost γ. Formally:

$$u_i^t(a_i^t) = \begin{cases} -\beta & \text{if } a_i^t = \rho \\ p & \text{if } a_i^t = \infty \\ -c & \text{if } a_i^t \in \{1, 2, ..., k_i\} \\ 0 & \text{if } a_i^t = \emptyset \wedge \nexists t' \leq t : a_i^{t'} \in \{1, 2, ...k_i\} \\ \alpha & \text{if } a_i^t = \emptyset \wedge \exists t' \leq t : a_i^{t'} \in \{1, 2, ..., k_i\} \wedge \exists j \in A : a_j^t = \infty \\ -\gamma & \text{if } a_i^t = \lambda \end{cases} \tag{3}$$

The agent that initiates the service discovery process distributes incentives α among the agents that participate forwarding a query. The use of incentives tries to provide a reward to those agents that cooperate during the discovery process. We have considered different types of mechanisms to distribute incentives:

– mechanisms that uniformly distribute the incentives among all the agents that participated in the forwarding process of a query that ended successfully. We consider two different mechanisms that differ from who is the entity that provides the incentives to the other agents. In one mechanism the system is the entity responsible of providing the incentives to the agents. We call this mechanism *System*, and the other one where the agent that initiates the discovery process provides the incentives. We called this mechanism *Fixed*.

– mechanisms that use a criterion to distribute the incentives in a non-uniform way among all the agents that participated in the forwarding process of a query that ended successfully.

   • *Path*: the reward depends on the length of the path. The shorter path to locate the provider agent is, the higher reward the agents will received.
   • *SimDg*: the reward for an agent that participates in the forwarding process depends on its similarity with the target agent and its degree of connection. The participants that are closer to the target agent and have a high degree of connection will receive a higher reward than the other participants.
   • *InvSimDg*: the reward for an agent that participates on the forwarding process depends on its similarity with the target agent and its degree of connection. The participants that are distant to the target agent and have a low degree of connection will receive a higher reward that the other participants.

Social Plasticity. The structure of the network influences interactions of agents, therefore it is important to provide agents mechanisms to be able of changing their local structure in the network. For that reason, we consider the rewiring action λ in our model. Through interactions during the service discovery process, agents are able to change their structural relations taking into account which neighbors provide profitable relationships and which do not. This feature is called social plasticity [18]. Social plasticity is the capacity of individuals to change their relationships as time passes. Specifically, in our system, each agent maintains information related to its neighbors. This information consists of the number of times a neighbor has refused to forward one of its queries (r_{ij}).

In order to evaluate the utility of a link, an agent i uses a decay function that calculates the probability of maintaining a link with j taking into account the number of queries that it would have sent through neighbor j but j refused to forward. This function is a sigmoid that ranges between [0,1].

$$P_{decay}(rq_{ij}) = \frac{1}{1 + e^{\frac{-(rq_{ij}-d)}{y}}} \tag{4}$$

where the constant y is the slope and d is the displacement. These constants are established by the agent. The most influential constant is d. The displacement d indicates how benevolent an agent is with respect the non-cooperative behavior of its neighbors. A high value of d means that the agent is going to consider a higher number of refuses in order to make a decision about looking for another neighbor. A low value means that it is not permissive with the number of refuses. The function $P_{decay}(rq_{ij})$ returns a value in the range [0,1], where 0 indicates that the agent does not consider that the number of rejects from its neighbor is enough to make a decision about rewiring, and 1 indicates that it is necessary to change the link. There criterion that we have considered for establishing a new link with another agent in the network consists on looking for a neighbor that offers similar services to the previous one.

In order to find a trade-off between the number of structural changes and the emergence of cooperation, the use of the rewiring action λ mechanism is affected by the number of cooperator agents that an agent has in its neighborhood. If the number of cooperator neighbors is under a certain threshold σ, the mechanism used to facilitate the emergence of cooperation is the social plasticity mechanism combined with the mechanism based on incentives. Otherwise, the mechanism used is based on incentives only.

2.2 Action Selection

Agents choose which will be the next action taking into account: (i) the similarity between itself and the target agent; and (ii) previous actions of their neighbors and an imitation strategy. An agent i has an information structure $H_i^t = \{\pi_i^t(c), \pi_i^t(nc)\}$ that stores information about the budget that the agent has when its behavior was cooperative $\pi_i^t(c) = \sum_{t' \leq t} u_i^{t'}(a_i^{t'}), a_i^{t'} \in Acc - \{\emptyset\}$ and when it was non-cooperative $\pi_i^t(nc) = \sum_{t' \leq t} u_i^{t'}(a_i^{t'}), a_i^{t'} \in Acc - \{1, ..., k_i\}$. Moreover, an agent i stores the number of times it sends a query to one of its neighbor j and it rejected forwarding it (rq_{ij}).

When an agent i receives a query q_i^t at time t, it chooses one of these actions using the following criterion:

- do the task itself when its service and role are enough similar to the service and role of the target agent tg.

$$a_i^t = \infty \text{ if } |H(i, tg)| \geq \varepsilon \tag{5}$$

- do nothing when its service and role are not enough similar to the target agent and, considering information from previous stages, agent i finds that the neighbor with highest benefit did not cooperate in the stage $t - 1$.

$$a_i^t = \emptyset \text{ if } |H(i, tg)| < \varepsilon \wedge a_j^{t-1} = \emptyset, j \in \text{argmax}(H_1^{t-1}, ..., H_{k_i}^{t-1}) \tag{6}$$

- forwarding the query to one of its neighbors $j \in N_i(g)$ when its service and role are not enough similar to the target agent and the neighbor with highest benefit cooperated in the stage $t - 1$.

$$a_i^t = j \text{ if } |H(i, tg)| < \varepsilon \wedge a_j^{t-1} \neq 0, j \in \text{argmax}(H_1^{t-1}, ..., H_{k_i}^{t-1}) \tag{7}$$

where

$$j \in \text{argmax}_{j \in \{1, ..., k_i\}} P(\langle j, tg \rangle) \tag{8}$$

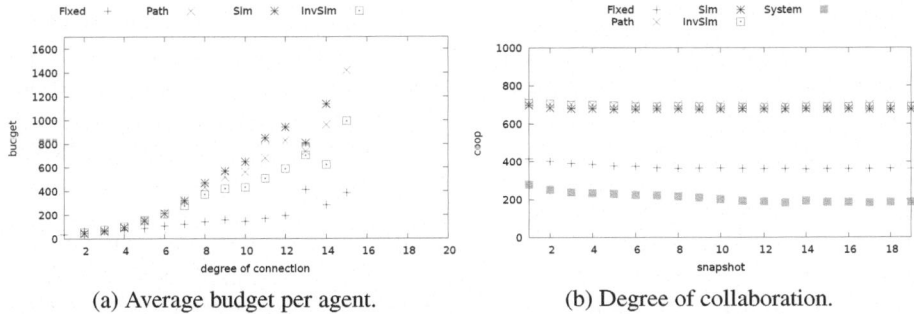

(a) Average budget per agent.   (b) Degree of collaboration.

Fig. 1. 1a Average budget per agent with an specific degree of connection when agents use incentives. 1b Evolution of the degree of cooperation in the system when agents use incentives.

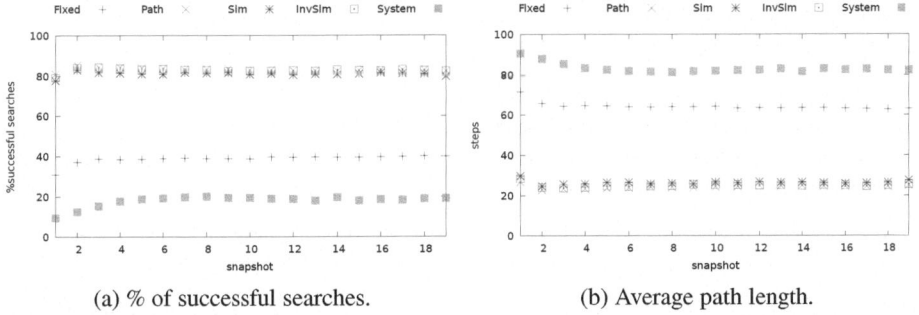

(a) % of successful searches.   (b) Average path length.

Fig. 2. 2a Evolution of the percentage of discovery processes that end before TTL when agents use incentives. 2b Evolution of the average number of steps in successful discovery processes when agents use incentives.

- rewiring a link with probability P_{decay} when agent i forwarded a query to a neighbor j in the stage $t - 1$, it rejects forwarding the query at stage t, and the number of cooperative agents in the neighbor is under a threshold σ.

$$a_i^t = \lambda \text{ if } a_i^{t-1} = j \wedge a_j^t = \emptyset \wedge |coop| < \sigma, coop \subseteq N_i(g) | j \text{ is a cooperator} \quad (9)$$

3 Experiments

In this section we evaluate the effects of different criteria for the distribution of incentives and the social plasticity in the emergence of cooperation in a decentralized service discovery system.

The tests were performed on a set of 10 undirected networks based on preferences where the degree of connection followed and exponential distribution. The networks were populated by 1,000 agents and the average degree of connection was 2.5. Each agent had a initial budget $b = 100$. The agents played one role and offered one semantic web service associated to this role. Initially, the agents were uniformly distributed over 16 roles, which were defined in an organizational ontology. The set of semantic service descriptions used for the experiments was taken from the OWL-S TC4 test collection[1].

All the agents in the system had the same probability of generating service queries. A query was successfully solved when an agent that offered a similar service (i.e., the degree of semantic match between the semantic service descriptions and roles was over a threshold $\varepsilon = 0.75$) was found before the TTL ($TTL = 100$). The query distribution in the system was modeled as a uniform distribution. In the experiments, we made a snapshot of all of the metrics every time 5,000 queries were solved in the system in order to see the evolution of the metrics. In all the experiments we did 19 snapshots. The costs, benefits, and incentives of the actions were the following: $\beta = 0.5, p = 0.5, c = 0.01, \alpha = 0.02$ (when the mechanism distributes uniformly the incentives), and $\gamma = 0.1$. For the mechanisms that distribute the incentives in a non-uniform way, agents distribute the quantity of 0.5 among the agents that participate in the discovery process considering the different criteria.

The metrics that we considered in the experiments were:

- the success of the service discovery processes
- the average path length of the discovery process
- the degree of cooperation in the system
- the average budget that an agent has.

For the experiments we considered two scenarios to see the effects of cooperation mechanisms:

- an scenario where, initially, 40% of the network cooperated and the 60% did not cooperate and only incentives were used
- an scenario where, intially, 40% of the network cooperated and the 60% did not cooperate and incentives and social plasticity were used.

3.1 Incentives

In these tests we evaluated the different ways that the agent that started the search process and found the provider agent distributed the incentives among the agents that participated in the process. Figure 1a shows the final budget of agents with certain degree. The x-axis shows the degree of connection of the agents and y-axis shows the average budget that agents with certain degree of connection had available in the last snapshot. In general, agents with a high degree of connection were the agents that obtained higher benefits due to they participated in more service discovery process, and usually, these processes were shorter and had more probability of success. The strategies that better distributed the incentives were the *Fixed* and the *InvSimDg* since it gave more incentive to those agents that were far from the target and had a low degree of connection.

Regarding the results related to the degree of cooperation in the system, the strategies that gave a fixed incentive to the participants in the discovery process obtained

---

[1] http://www.semwebcentral.org/projects/owls-tc/

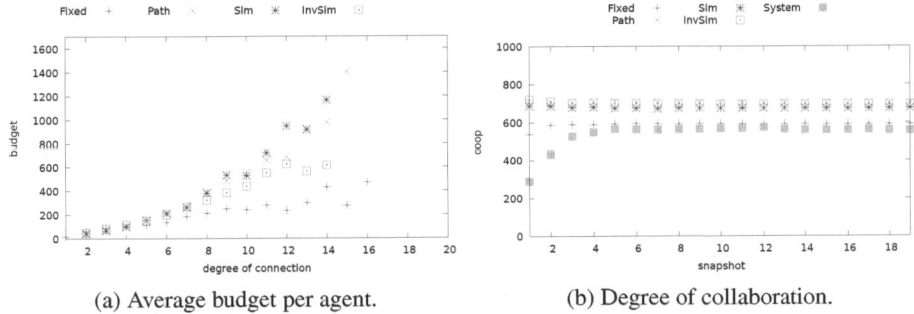

(a) Average budget per agent.   (b) Degree of collaboration.

Fig. 3. 3a Average budget per agent with an specific degree of connection when agents use incentives and have social plasticity. 3b Evolution of the degree of cooperation in the system when agents use incentives and have social plasticity.

a lower degree of cooperation than the strategies that did not distribute the incentives uniformly. In Figure 1b these results are shown. The x-axis shows the snapshots and the y-axis the number of agents that cooperate. Although the strategies that do not distribute uniformly the incentives benefit the hubs of the network, this fact provides a higher degree of cooperation. As consequence, the average number of steps required in the search process to reach the target agent decreases (see Figure 2a) and the percentage of queries successfully solved increases (see Figure 2b).

3.2   Incentives and Social Plasticity

In these tests we incorporated social plasticity. Agents used incentives to promote cooperation but also they rewired links that they considered that were not being useful. The value for the threshold σ to decide if it was appropriate using social plasticity was 0.25. The values of the parameters of the slope y and the displacement d were 1 and 7 respectively. In general, it can be observed that the use of social plasticity improves the results obtained only considering incentives. Regarding the final budget of the agents, the use of social plasticity implies a small decrease in the budget of the agents. However, the use of social plasticity increases degree of cooperation achieved in the system (see Figure 3b). This fact is more significant in the case of strategies that use a uniform distribution of the reward. The increase of the degree of cooperation in the system facilitates the service discovery decreasing the average path length of the discovery processes (see Figure 4b) and increasing the success (see Figure 4a). This improvement is more significant than the improvement obtained only with the use of incentives. Finally, we analyzed the number of structural relations that were modified using different mechanisms for distributing the incentives (see Figure 5). The results show that the incentive mechanisms that distribute the benefit in a non uniform way require less structural changes to increase the cooperation in the system.

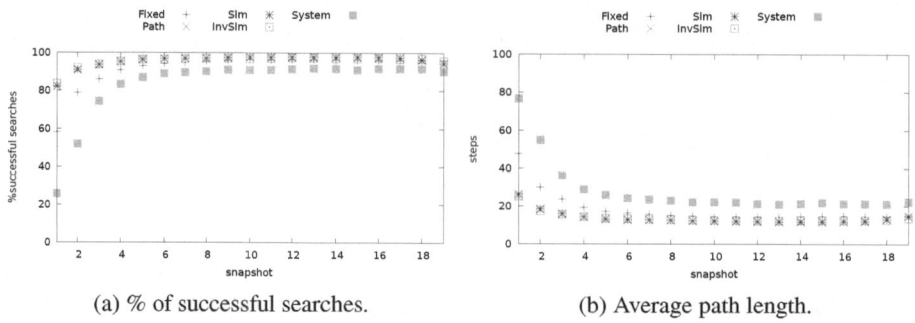

(a) % of successful searches.   (b) Average path length.

Fig. 4. 4a Evolution of the percentage of discovery processes that end before TTL when agents use incentives and have social plasticity. 4b Evolution of the average number of steps in successful discovery processes when agents use incentives and have social plasticity.

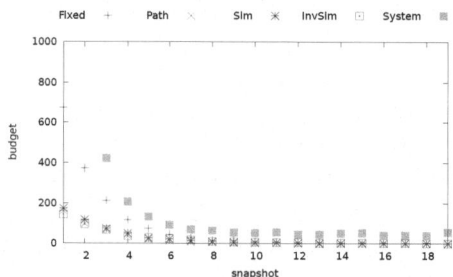

Fig. 5. Number of rewired structural relations when social plasticity is considered when agents use incentives and have social plasticity

4   Conclusions

This article addresses the problem of emergence of cooperation in scenarios where cooperation is required to achieve a good performance that benefits all of the participants. Specifically, our proposal focuses on the emergence of cooperation in decentralized service discovery scenarios where agents need the cooperation of their neighbors in order to locate other agents that offer services that they require. Therefore, if selfish agents appear in the system, in the long term, as the number of non-cooperator agents increases, the service discovery process could be seriously compromised. For this reason, it is important to provide mechanisms that facilitate the emergence and maintenance of cooperation. In this paper, we present the combination of two mechanisms to facilitate the emergence of cooperation in open societies of agents where not all the agents have cooperative behavior.

In the model that we presented, agents can use incentives in order to promote cooperative actions such as the forwarding action in the discovery process. We have considered different mechanisms to distribute these incentives. Some of them take into account the same quantity of reward for all the participants in a successful search process. Others distribute the reward among all the participant non-uniformly considering an specific criterion. In general, the non-uniform distribution benefits the agents with a high degree of connection due to participate in a higher number of successful discovery processes, and therefore, this fact increases their budgets cooperating. Consequently, other agents imitate their behavior and, therefore cooperation increases.

Moreover, we also considered the inclusion of structural changes (social plasticity) based on the degree of cooperation of their neighbors. As the number of times a neighbor refuses to forward a query increases, the probability of changing this relation increases. If an agent decides to change a neighbor, it chooses a neighbor with similar functional features to the previous one. The inclusion of social plasticity in the system increases the degree of cooperation achieved in the system, mainly when the incentive mechanism used is based on a fixed reward distribution.

The experiments confirm that this combination of mechanisms promote cooperation in service discovery scenarios where the number of non-cooperator agents is higher than the number of cooperators. The increase of the degree of cooperation in the system improves the performance of the system reducing the average number of steps required to reach the target and increasing the number of service discovery processes.

Acknowledgements. Work partially supported by the Spanish Ministry of Science and Innovation through grants TIN2009-13839-C03-01, TIN2012-36586-C03-01, CSD2007-0022 (CONSOLIDER-INGENIO 2010), FPU grant AP-2008-00601 awarded to E. del Val.

References

1. Sun, Q., Garcia-Molina, H.: Slic: A selfish link-based incentive mechanism for unstructured peer-to-peer networks. In: Proceedings of the 24th International Conference on Distributed Computing Systems (ICDCS 2004), pp. 506–515. IEEE Computer Society, Washington, DC (2004)
2. Lin, W., Zhao, H., Liu, K.: Incentive cooperation strategies for peer-to-peer live multimedia streaming social networks. IEEE Transactions on Multimedia 11(3), 396–412 (2009)
3. Gu, B., Jarvenpaa, S.: Are contributions to p2p technical forums private or public goods? - an empirical investigation. In: Proceedings of the 1st Workshop on Economics of Peer-to-Peer Systems (2003)
4. Shneidman, J., Parkes, D.C.: Rationality and self-interest in peer to peer networks. In: Kaashoek, M.F., Stoica, I. (eds.) IPTPS 2003. LNCS, vol. 2735, pp. 139–148. Springer, Heidelberg (2003)
5. Blanc, A., Liu, Y.K., Vahdat, A.: Designing incentives for peer-to-peer routing. In: Proceedings of the 24th Annual Joint Conference of the IEEE Computer and Communications Societies, vol. 1, pp. 374–385 (March 2005)
6. Hardin, G.: The tragedy of the commons. Science (162), 1243–1248 (1968)
7. Doran, J.E., Franklin, S., Jennings, N.R., Norman, T.J.: On cooperation in multi-agent systems. The Knowledge Engineering Review 12, 309–314 (1997)
8. Nowak, M.A.: Five Rules for the Evolution of Cooperation. Science 314(5805), 1560–1563 (2006)

 9. Nowak, M.A., Sigmund, K.: Evolution of indirect reciprocity by image scoring. Nature 393(6685), 573–577 (1998)
10. Sigmund, K.: Sympathy and similarity: The evolutionary dynamics of cooperation. Proceedings of the National Academy of Sciences 106(21), 8405–8406 (2009)
11. Hauert, C., Traulsen, A., Brandt, H., Nowak, M.A., Sigmund, K.: Via Freedom to Coercion: The Emergence of Costly Punishment. Science 316(5833), 1905–1907 (2007)
12. Sigmund, K., Hauert, C., Nowak, M.: Reward and punishment. P. Natl. Acad. Sci. USA (19), 10757–10762 (2001)
13. Sigmund, K.: Punish or perish? retaliation and collaboration among humans. Trends in Ecology and Evolution 22(11), 593–600 (2007)
14. Pujol, J.M., Delgado, J., Sangüesa, R., Flache, A.: The role of clustering on the emergence of efficient social conventions. In: IJCAI, pp. 965–970 (2005)
15. Ohtsuki, H., Hauert, C., Lieberman, E., Nowak, M.A.: A simple rule for the evolution of cooperation on graphs and social networks. Nature 441(7092), 502–505 (2006)
16. Santos, F.C., Santos, M.D., Pacheco, J.M.: Social diversity promotes the emergence of cooperation in public goods games. Nature 454(7201), 213–216 (2008)
17. Hofmann, L.M., Chakraborty, N., Sycara, K.: The evolution of cooperation in self-interested agent societies: a critical study. In: Proceedings of the 10th International Conference on Autonomous Agents and Multiagent Systems, vol. 2, pp. 685–692 (2011)
18. Eguiluz, V.M., Zimmermann, M.G., Cela-Conde, C.J., Miguel, M.S.: Cooperation and emergence of role differentiation in the dynamics of social networks. American Journal of Sociology 110, 977 (2005)
19. Axelrod, R.M.: The evolution of cooperation. Basic Books, New York (1984)
20. Griffiths, N., Luck, M.: Changing neighbours: improving tag-based cooperation. In: Proceedings of the 9th International Conference on Autonomous Agents and Multiagent Systems, vol. 1, pp. 249–256 (2010)
21. Villatoro, D., Sabater-Mir, J., Sen, S.: Social instruments for robust convention emergence. In: Walsh, T. (ed.) Proceedings of the International Joint Conference on Artificial Intelligence, pp. 420–425 (2011)
22. Val, E.D., Rebollo, M., Botti, V.: Enhancing Decentralized Service Discovery in Open Service-Oriented Multi-Agent Systems. Journal of Autonomous Agents and Multi-Agent Systems (2012)

Probabilistic Argumentation Frameworks: Basic Properties and Computation

Pierpaolo Dondio

School of Computing, Dublin Institute of Technology,
Kevin Street 2, Dublin, Ireland
pierpaolo.dondio@dit.ie

Abstract. In this paper we analyze probabilistic argumentation frameworks PAF, defined as an extension of Dung abstract framework in which each argument n is asserted with a probability p_n and where an argumentation semantics is used to compute arguments' status. We start by extending recent definitions of *PAF* removing the hypothesis of arguments independence, extending the computation to preferred semantics and defining the distribution of various probabilities induced over arguments acceptability status. We then prove some basic properties linking grounded and preferred *PAF* and we describe the first algorithm to compute the probability of acceptance of each argument. We end our work with an application of *PAF* to legal reasoning.

Keywords: Argumentation Theory, Semantics, Probabilistic Reasoning.

1 Introduction

Abstract argumentation frameworks were introduced by Dung [2] to analyze properties of defeasible arguments, i.e. arguments whose validity can be disputed by other conflicting arguments. An abstract argumentation framework is a directed graph where nodes represent arguments and arrows represent the attack relation.

Various semantics have been defined to identify the set of acceptable arguments. We follow the labeling approach proposed by Caminada [6], where a semantics assigns to each argument a label *in*, *out* or *undec*, meaning that the argument is considered consistently acceptable, non-acceptable or undecided (i.e. one abstains from an opinion). We deal with grounded and preferred semantics. The grounded semantics is a skeptical semantics that maximizes the set of arguments with label *undec*, and it does not allow an argument to reinstate itself by counter-attacking the attacking argument. Preferred semantics is a credulous semantics that maximizes the in set.

In Dung's original work, arguments are treated as abstract entities that are fully asserted or not asserted at all, and there are no degrees related to either arguments or attacks' relations. Abstract argumentation is often too strict and coarse to support a decision making process. The situation is described by Dunne [10], who underlines how an abstract argumentation' solution is often an empty set or several sets with nothing to distinguish between them. In quest for gradualism in argumentation, few

J.M. Corchado et al. (Eds.): PAAMS 2013 Workshops, CCIS 365, pp. 263–279, 2013.
© Springer-Verlag Berlin Heidelberg 2013

approaches tried to marry probability calculus and argumentation semantics, defining probabilistic argumentation frameworks PAF. In a PAF an argumentation semantics is used to identify under which conditions a set of arguments is acceptable, while probability calculus quantifies how likely those conditions are. The main motivation of this paper remains the need for a usable gradualism in argumentation.

This paper contributes to the study of PAF from different angles. We extend recent definitions of PAF by removing the hypothesis of arguments independence, by extending the computation to preferred semantics and defining various probabilities distribution induced over argument's acceptability status. This theoretical extension mainly relies on previous works by Li [4] and Hunter [11]. We then prove some basic properties linking grounded and preferred PAF and we describe the first algorithm to compute the probability of acceptance of each argument, representing the core of our contribution. We end our work with an application of PAF to legal reasoning.

The paper is organized as follows: in section 2 we recall the pre-requisites of abstract argumentation; section 3 introduces our proposal for $PAFs$. In section 4 we prove some basic properties, in section 5 we describe our algorithm to compute arguments' acceptance probabilities while section 6 describes related works to date.

2   Background Definitions

Definition 1 (Abstract Argumentation Framework) Let U be the universe of all possible arguments. An argumentation framework is a pair (Ar, R) where Ar is a finite subset of U and $R \subseteq Ar \times Ar$ is called attack relation.

Let's consider AF $= (\text{Ar}, \text{R})$ and Args $\subseteq$ Ar.

Definition 2 (conflict-free). Args is conflict-free iff $\nexists a, b \in$ Args $|$ a R b

Definition 3 (defense) Args defends an argument $a \subseteq Ar$ iff $\forall b \in Ar$ such that b R a, $\exists c \in$ Args such that c R b. The set of arguments defended by Args is denoted F(Args).

Definition 4 (indirect attack/defense) Let a, b $\in$ Ar and the graph G defined by (Ar, R). Then (1) a indirectly attacks b if there is an odd-length path from a to b in the attack graph G and (2) a indirectly defends b if there is an even-length path (with non-zero length) from a to b in G.

Labeling. A semantics identifies a set of arguments that can survive the conflicts encoded by the attack relation R. In the labeling approach a semantics assigns a label to each argument. Following [6], the choice for the set of labels is: *in, out* or *undec*.

Definition 5 (labeling/conflict free). Let AF $= (\text{Ar}, \text{R})$ be an argumentation framework. A labeling is a total function L : Ar $\rightarrow$ {in, out, undec}. We write in(L) for $\{a \in \text{Ar} | L(a) = in\}$, out(L) for $\{a \in \text{Ar} | L(a) = out\}$, and undec(L) for $\{a \in \text{Ar} | L(a) = undec\}$. We say that a labeling is conflict-free if no IN-labeled argument attacks an (other or the same) IN-labeled argument.

Definition 6 (complete labeling). Let (Ar, R) be an argumentation framework. A complete labeling is a labeling that for every $a \in$ Ar holds that:

1. if a is labeled *in* then all attackers of a are labeled *out*
2. if all attackers of a are labeled *out* then a is labeled *in*
3. if a is labeled *out* then a has an attacker labeled in,
4. if a has an attacker labeled *in* then a is labeled out
5. if a is labeled *undec* then it has at least one attacker labeled *undec* and it does not have an attacker labeled *in*.

Theorem 1. (proved in [6]) Let AF = (Ar , R) be an argumentation framework. L is the grounded labeling iff L is a complete labeling undec(L) is maximal (w.r.t. set inclusion) among all complete labelings of AF. L is the preferred labeling iff $in(L)$ or $out(L)$ are maximal.

In figure 1 two argumentation graphs are depicted. The grounded semantics assigns the status of *undec* to all the arguments of (A) (always the case if there are no initial arguments), while in (B) it assigns the label *in* to a and c, and *out* to b. Note how a reinstates c. The preferred semantics agrees with the grounded for (B) (always the case when the *undec* set of the grounded is empty), but it produces two different labelings for the AF A, one with $in(L_1) = \{b\}$, $out(L_1) = \{a, c\}$, $undec(L_1) = \emptyset$ and the other with $in(L_2) = \{a, c\}$ and $out(L_2) = \{b\}$ and $undec(L_2) = \emptyset$.

Fig. 1. Two Argumentation Graphs (A) and (B)

3   Probabilistic Argumentation Frameworks

Our discussion of probabilistic argumentation frameworks starts from what Hunter [11] defines the *constellations approach,* which we aim to extend.

A probabilistic argumentation framework *PAF* associates a joint probability distribution to the set of arguments. The probabilistic nature of arguments implies that an argument premises are not always satisfied and therefore, given an argumentation framework of n arguments, 2^n different scenarios are possible, each of them obtained by assigning the status of satisfied or not satisfied to each argument. Each scenario – corresponding to a spanning sub-graph - can be labeled according to a chosen semantics by assigning an *in, out* or *undec* label to each argument. As a result, for each argument we know the subsets of scenarios where they are labeled *in, out* or *undec,* and for each subset we can compute the corresponding probability using the joint distribution P. Let's refer to these probability distributions over arguments as P_{IN}, P_{OUT}, P_U.

Definition 7 (PAF). A probabilistic argumentation framework PAF is a couple (A, P) where $A = (Ar, R)$ is an abstract argumentation framework with a finite set of arguments Ar and an attack relation R on $Ar \times Ar$; and P is a joint probability distribution over elements of Ar.

P is the probability that an argument holds *on its own,* in isolation, before the dialectical process starts. It is the likelihood that the probabilistic premises of the argument are satisfied, and therefore the argument claim can be used in the argumentation process. Our aim is to compute P_{IN}, P_{OUT}, P_U for each argument, the probabilities that the argument will be labeled *in, out* or *undec* under the chosen semantics, and therefore argument claim is accepted, rejected or undecided. We note how P ranges from a full joint probability table of 2^n entries to the situation of complete independence of arguments, where a single scalar number attached to each argument suffices. Indeed the joint probability is a first form of argumentation, a way to defeat arguments on the ground that an argument does not co-exist with another. For instance, two arguments a and b might have $P(a \wedge b) = 0$, meaning that they actually exclude each other and they cannot be present in the same scenario. The joint probability excludes some scenarios that are impossible and quantifies the not null probability of the others. However, it is not the only form of defeasibility, since obviously even two totally independent arguments might rebut each other or one undercut the other. This second form of defeasibility is encoded in the attack relation R, that might identify cycles among arguments and that is used by the chosen semantics to label arguments. While the joint probability P deals with the existence of arguments and it does not contain all the effect of the argumentation process, P_{IN}, P_{OUT}, P_U deal with the validity of the arguments in the argumentation process. Algorithm 1 proposes a brute force approach to compute P_{IN} (P_{OUT}, P_U are analogous).

Algorithm 1 - Brute force approach for computing P_{IN}

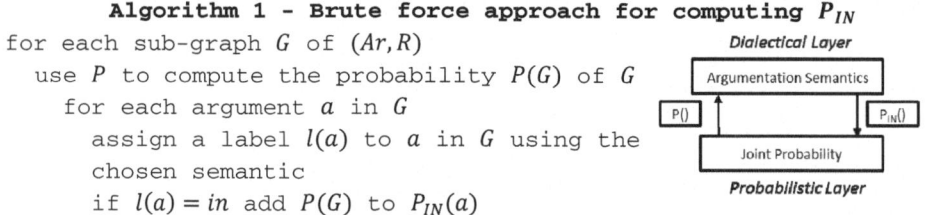

```
for each sub-graph G of (Ar,R)
  use P to compute the probability P(G) of G
    for each argument a in G
      assign a label l(a) to a in G using the
      chosen semantic
      if l(a) = in add P(G) to P_IN(a)
```

The difference between $P(a)$ and $P_{IN}(a)$ is crucial. $P(a)$ is the probability of argument a in isolation, before the argumentation process combines arguments, while $P_{IN}(a)$ is the probability of a being labeled *in* by the chosen semantics. $P_{IN}(a)$ entails the effect of the argumentation process on a: the fact that a's conclusion might be rebutted or one of the premises of a invalidated by other arguments. There might be a case where a has high probability to hold in isolation, but it is completely invalidated in the argumentation process. It can be completely true that a: *Joe got full marks in his math test, so he is good at math*, but it might be also known with certainty that b: *Joe copied the test*. Therefore $P(a) = P(b) = 1$, but since b attacks (undercuts) a, then $P_{IN}(a) = 0$ (the conclusion does not hold anymore) and $P_{IN}(b) = 1$.

If we consider the 3 previous definitions of *PAF*s by Li [4], Hunter [11] and Thimm [12], Li's approach is the one we evolve, while Hunter's work goes in a complementary direction described later. In Li's definition P is not a joint probability but a scalar function $Ar \rightarrow [0,1]$ and a similar scenario-like approach (extension-based rather than argument-based) is used. It is only fully probabilistic approach, while later approaches are going in a different direction discussed later. Li's work is limited to fully independent arguments with grounded semantic, and no exact computation behind the brute force algorithm is analyzed. We therefore intend to (1) extend the definition introducing new concepts and analyze the consequences of allowing arguments to be dependent – which appears a key issue, (2) consider preferred semantic, (3) prove some key properties and (4) provide algorithms to compute P_{IN}.

In [11] Hunter tackles the hypothesis of independence, not treated by Li. He introduces a *justification* perspective on the probability of an argument, that makes it possible for two arguments, one based on *p* and the other on *not(p)*, to be present at the same time in the same sub-graph (see pag. 21 in [11]). If an argument premises contain *p* and another argument contains *not(p)*, as far as $P()$ is a probability measure over arguments (as we assume in this work) those two arguments will never be on the same scenario (sub-graph), since they are based on mutually exclusive premises. The *justification* measure described by Hunter is a generic non probabilistic uncertainty measure over arguments. For instance, *p* and *not(p)* can be fully asserted at the same time if a possibility function is defined over *p* – defining a situation of total ignorance. Our assumption that *P* is a probability distribution does not preclude rebuttals on the same sub-graph. We clarify with an example. The two statements **r**: *x is red* and ¬**r**: *x is not red* rebut each other and, if they are given as initial facts, (i.e. ⊢ **r**) they are necessarily mutually exclusive, since *P* satisfies the Kolmogorov axioms and therefore $P(r \wedge \neg r) = 0$. On the contrary, the two arguments **t**: *Tom says that x is red, so x is red* and **j**: *John says that x is not red, so x is not red* are again rebutting arguments, but in general $P(t \wedge j) \geq 0$. The relation between $P(t)$ and $P(j)$ is encoded in the joint probability *P*. It could be the case that Tom never speaks when John speaks (so that **t** and **j** result totally dependent: $P(t|i) = 0$) or they can be independent, or something in between. It can indeed be $P(t) + P(j) > 1$ but $P(t) + P(\neg t) = 1$ and, using the constellations approach, always $P_{IN}(t) + P_{IN}(j) \leq 1$ (proven in [11]).

Thrimm in [12] (and Hunter [11] in his epistemic approach) starts from a complementary angle. Both authors assume that there is already an uncertainty measure – potentially not probabilistic - defined on the admissibility set of each argument (i.e. P_{IN} is given as a function $P_{IN}: Ar \rightarrow [0,1]$). Starting from P_{IN} rather than *P* poses the question: which P_{IN} assignments are acceptable? The authors both argue that only a subset of these measurements can be sensibly associated to an argumentation framework. They define a series of rules to identify a rationally acceptable probability distribution of P_{IN}, such as the rationality and *p-justificability* properties. The good news is that, if *P* is a probability distribution over arguments, as we assume, then P_{IN} satisfies Hunter's rationality property

We follow a complementary approach, since our aim is to start from *P* (assumed a probability measure) and then compute P_{IN}. We also believe it is a more justified process to start from what is known about an argument (*P*) and study how the argument is modified in the dialectical process (P_{IN}) and how P_{IN} is computed.

3.1   Formalizing Scenarios and Their Probabilities

Given a framework $PAF = ((Ar, R), P)$ with $|Ar| = n$, a scenario is a subgraph of *Ar*, i.e. an element of $S = 2^{Ar}$. We focus on particular sets of scenarios, i.e. elements of 2^S. Given an argument $a \in Ar$, we define:

$$A = \{s \in S \,|\, a \in s\} \quad ; \quad \bar{A} = \{s \in S \,|\, a \notin s\}$$

that are the sets of scenarios where argument *a* exits (when probabilistic premises are assumed to be satisfied) and does not exist. We can propagate the probability $P(a)$ of argument *a* to its related sets of scenarios *A* and $\bar{A}$. First we notice that if a scenario *s* is composed by *j* arguments of *Ar* required to exist and $n - j$ arguments required to not exist, the probability of *s* is:

$$P_s(s) = P(e_1 \wedge e_2 \wedge ... \wedge e_j \wedge \overline{e_{j+1}} \wedge ... \wedge \overline{e_n})$$

The probability of a set of scenarios A is the sum of the probabilities of each scenario in A. Using the theorem of the total probability (or by marginalization):

$$P_{ss}(A) = \sum_{s \in A} P_s(s) = P(a) \text{ and } 1 - P(a) = P_{ss}(\bar{A})$$

i.e. the probability $P(a)$ that the argument exists in one of the sub-graphs (scenarios) of Ar is the probability of the set of all the sub-graphs containing a. Since P is a joint probability over Ar, P can be used instead of P_{SS} and P_s to quantify the probabilities of both scenarios and set of scenarios as well, since a set of scenarios can be seen as a logical proposition containing arguments joint by the connectives $\{\wedge, \vee, \neg\}$.

We write AB for the intersection of set of scenarios, $A + B$ for the union of scenarios. Therefore AB means all the scenarios where a and b exist, while $A + B$ means all the sets of scenarios where a or b does not exists. The associate probabilities are $P(AB) = P(a \wedge b)$, $P(A + \bar{B}) = P(a \vee \neg b)$.

3.2   Labeling Scenarios and Acceptance

Given a scenario $s \in S = 2^{Ar}$, the labeling of s simply follows the rules of the chosen semantics. We therefore define a scenario labeling $\mathcal{L}$ as a total function over the cartesian product of arguments in Ar and scenarios in S, therefore $\mathcal{L}: Ar \times S \rightarrow \{in, out, undec\}$. When labeling a scenario, we follow this choice: an argument a is labeled out in all the scenarios where a does not exist (i.e. it is out because it is not satisfied on its own) or when it exists but it is labeled out by the semantic, representing the effect on a of the other arguments.

In the case of grounded semantics there is only one labeling per scenario s, that we call $\mathcal{L}^g(s)$. In the case of preferred labeling there could be more than one valid labeling per scenario. Each preferred labeling for scenario s is referred as $\mathcal{L}_i^{pr}(s)$ and the set of the preferred labeling of a scenario as $\ell^{pr}(s) = \{\mathcal{L}_1^{pr}(s), .., \mathcal{L}_n^{pr}(s)\}$. We call $in(\mathcal{L}^x(s))$, $out(\mathcal{L}^x(s))$, $undec(\mathcal{L}^x(s))$ the sets of argument labeled in, out, $undec$ in the labeling $\mathcal{L}^x(s)$, x in $\{g, pr\}$. In order to study how an argument behaves across scenarios in S, we define the following set of scenarios. For grounded semantics:

$$A_{IN}^g = \{s \in S : a \in in(\mathcal{L}^g, s)\}; \ A_{OUT}^g = \{s \in S : a \in out(\mathcal{L}^g, s)\}$$

$$A_U^g = \{s \in S : a \in undec(\mathcal{L}^g, s)\}$$

which represent all the scenarios where argument a is labeled in, out or $undec$. When it comes to preferred semantic, since there could be more than one labeling for each scenario s, we define two extreme sets, corresponding to a skeptical and credulous attitude. The credulous set is identified by requiring argument a to be labeled in at least in one of the valid preferred labeling for s. Therefore we define:

$$A_{IN}^{pr+} = \{s \in S : (\exists \ \mathcal{L}^{pr}(s) \in \ell^{pr}(s) : a \in in(\mathcal{L}^{pr}, s))\}$$

$$A_{OUT}^{pr+} = \{s \in S : (\exists \ \mathcal{L}^{pr}(s) \in \ell^{pr}(s) : a \in out(\mathcal{L}^{pr}, s))\}$$

$$A_U^{pr+} = \{s \in S : (\exists \ \mathcal{L}^{pr}(s) \in \ell^{pr}(s) : a \in undec(\mathcal{L}^{pr}, s))\}$$

While the skeptical sets are:

$$A_{IN}^{pr-} = A_{IN}^{pr} \setminus (A_{OUT}^{pr} \cup A_U^{pr}) \quad ; \quad A_{OUT}^{pr-} = A_{OUT}^{pr} \setminus (A_{IN}^{pr} \cup A_U^{pr})$$

$$A_U^{pr-} = A_U^{pr} \setminus (A_{OUT}^{pr} \cup A_{IN}^{pr})$$

representing scenarios where argument a has the same label in all the preferred labeling of a scenario. It is $A_{IN}^{pr-} \subseteq A_{IN}^{pr+}, A_{OUT}^{pr-} \subseteq A_{OUT}^{pr+}, A_U^{pr-} \subseteq A_U^{pr+}$ and the two sets of scenarios identify an upper and lower probability level. We add a last useful notation. We write A_{out} for all the scenarios where a is labeled *out* when it exists. Note that $A_{OUT} = \bar{A} + A_{out}$.

Definition 8. We define the following probabilities of acceptance of argument a:

$$P_A^g = P(A_{IN}^g), P_A^+ = P(A_{IN}^{pr+}), P_A^- = P(A_{IN}^{pr-})$$

The following are called probability of rejection:

$$\overline{P_A^g} = P(A_{OUT}^g), \overline{P_A^+} = P(A_{OUT}^{pr+}), \overline{P_A^-} = P(A_{OUT}^{pr-})$$

And finally these are the undecided probability:

$$U_A^g = P(A_U^g), U_A^- = P(A_U^{pr-}), U_A^+ = P(A_U^{pr+})$$

Example 1. Let's consider the graph of figure 1, assumed independent, and let's study the properties of argument a There are 3 independent arguments, therefore $2^3 = 8$ scenarios, $S = \{\emptyset, \{a\}, \{b\}, \{c\}, \{a, b\}, \{a, c\}, \{b, c\}, \{a, b, c\}\}$. Let's presume $P(A) = P(B) = P(C) = 0.8$. Let's start computing A_{IN}^g. Argument a is labeled *in* in all the scenarios where it is asserted and b is not asserted (and c becomes irrelevant). Using our notation $A = A\bar{B}$ (i.e. the set of scenarios $\{\{a\}, \{a, c\}\}$. It is *undec* when all the arguments are present, i.e. the single scenario $A_U^g = ABC$ (i.e. $\{\{a, b, c\}\}$) and it is labeled *out* when it is not asserted or when b is *in* and c is *out*, i.e. $A_{OUT}^g = \bar{A} + AB\bar{C}$ (set $\{\emptyset, \{b\}, \{c\}, \{a, b\}, \{b, c\}\}$). By inserting numerical values we have:

$$P_A^g = 0.16, \ U_A^g = 0.512, \ \overline{P_A^g} = 0.328.$$

Regarding preferred semantic, we can verify that:

$$A_{IN}^{pr+} = A(\bar{B} + BC), P(A_{IN}^{pr+}) \equiv P_A^+ = 0.672$$
$$A_{IN}^{pr-} = A\bar{B}, P(A_{IN}^{pr-}) \equiv P_A^- = 0.16$$
$$A_U^{pr+} = A_U^{pr-} = \emptyset$$
$$A_{OUT}^{pr+} = \bar{A} + AB, P(A_{OUT}^{pr+}) \equiv \overline{P_A^+} = 0.84$$
$$A_{OUT}^{pr-} = \bar{A} + AB\bar{C}, P(A_{OUT}^{pr-}) \equiv \overline{P_A^-} = 0.328.$$

We note how $P_A^g = P_A^-$ and $\overline{P_A^g} = \overline{P_A^-}$. In 4 we show that this is not always the case.

4 Basic Properties

Proposition 1 (Basic relations)

$$a) \ P_A^g + \overline{P_A^g} + U_A^g = 1 \quad b) \ P_A^+ + \overline{P_A^+} + U_A^+ \geq 1 \quad c) \ P_A^- + \overline{P_A^-} + U_A^- \leq 1$$

a) follows from the fact that grounded labeling always exists and it is unique for each scenario. b) follows from the fact that preferred labeling might assign different labels to the same argument in a scenario, and c) from the fact that under preferred labeling the skeptical set might be empty in some scenarios.

Note from b) and c) how the skeptical and credulous sets define a possibility and necessity measure on the corresponding preferred sets. This is a consequence of the multiple preferred labeling of a scenario and the credulous acceptance of arguments. Since we do not have any reason to prefer one label to another in the scenarios where an argument is accepted credulously, a probability measure can be defined invoking the *principle of indifference* and by equally splitting the probability of those scenarios.

Definition 9. We define the *indifferent preferred probabilities* as follows:

$$P_A^i = P(A_{IN}^{pr-}) + \frac{1}{3} P(A_{IN}^{pr+} \cap A_{OUT}^{pr+} \cap A_U^{pr+}) + \frac{1}{2} P(A_{IN}^{pr+} \cap A_{OUT}^{pr+}) + \frac{1}{2} P(A_{IN}^{pr+} \cap A_U^{pr+})$$

The probability of rejection and the undecided probability are defined in the same way. It can be proved that $P_A^i + \bar{P}_A^i + U_A^i = 1$.

Proposition 2 (Conditions for $A_U^g \neq \emptyset$)

$$\forall\, a \in Ar, (A_U^g \neq \emptyset \Leftrightarrow \exists\, cycle\ C\ in\ Ar \wedge \exists\, path\ from\ an\ element\ of\ C\ to\ a)$$

$\Rightarrow$ Ad absurdum, if there are no cycles, then none of the subgraps of (Ar, R) has one, and therefore in all the scenarios any argument can be labeled *in* or *out* starting from some initial arguments. Therefore $A_U^g = \emptyset$ contradicting the hypothesis.

If there are cycles, but none of them is connected to argument a, then a is either initial or it is connected only to initial arguments, and therefore is labeled *in* or *out*.

$\Leftarrow$ Let's consider a scenario s containing argument a plus all the arguments in the cycle C and, if a does not belong to C, all the arguments connecting C to a. In this scenario s then a is surely labeled *undec* and therefore $s \in A_U^g$ that implies $A_U^g \neq \emptyset$.

Proposition 2b (version for preferred semantic)

$$\forall\, a \in Ar, (A_U^{pr} \neq \emptyset \Leftrightarrow \exists\, odd - length\ cycle\ C\ in\ A \wedge \exists\, path\ from\ an\ element\ of\ C\ to\ a)$$

Under preferred semantic, even-length cycle can be consistently labeled with two dual assignments, while odd-length cycles leads to an inconsistent situation where all the arguments result labeled *undec*. Therefore using the same argument above, the presence of odd-length cycles are a necessary and sufficient condition for $A_U^{pr} \neq \emptyset$

Proposition 3. Conditions for $A = A_{IN}$ (the dialectical process has no effect on a).

a) $A = A_{IN}^{pr+} \Leftrightarrow \forall\, b \in Ar, R(b, a) \rightarrow R(a, b)$

b) $A = A_{IN}^g \Leftrightarrow \nexists\, b \in Ar : R(b, a)$

Proof of a). We need to prove that argument a is labeled *in* under preferred semantics every time it exists *iff* argument a attacks all its attackers.

$\Rightarrow$ If, ad absurdum, $R(b, a)$ but not viceversa, then in the scenario s containing only a and its attacker b, a results labeled *out*, and $A \supset A_{IN}^{pr+}$

$\Leftarrow$ If a attacks all its attackers in all scenarios s containing a then, under preferred semantic, we can always consistently assign a label *in* to a and a label *out* to all its attackers, therefore there is at least one labeling assigning *in* to a and $A = A_{IN}^{pr+}$.

Proof of b).

$\Rightarrow$ If, ad absurdum, there is an argument b so that $R(b,a)$, then in the scenario s containing <u>only</u> a and its attacker b, a results labeled *out* or *undec* (if a counter attacks b), and $A \supset A_{IN}^g$

$\Leftarrow$ if $\nexists\, b \in Ar : R(b,a)$, then a is an initial argument and is labeled IN in all the scenarios where it exists, therefore $A = A_{IN}^g$

Proposition 4. Relationships between grounded and preferred acceptability sets.
Given a PAF $((Ar, R), P)$ and an argument a it follows that:

(1) $A_{IN}^{pr+} \supseteq A_{IN}^{pr-} \supseteq A_{IN}^g$ *therefore* $P_A^+ \geq P_A^- \geq P_A^g$ *and* $P_A^i \geq P_A^g$

(2) $A_U^g \supseteq A_U^{pr+} \supseteq A_U^{pr-}$ *therefore* $U_A^g \geq U_A^+ \geq U_A^-$ *and* $U_A^i \leq U_A^g$

(3) $A_{OUT}^{pr+} \supseteq A_{OUT}^{pr-} \supseteq A_{OUT}^g$ *therefore* $\overline{P_A^+} \geq \overline{P_A^-} \geq \overline{P_A^g}$ *and* $\overline{P_A^i} \geq \overline{P_A^g}$

We now prove (1), 2 and 3 follow the same approach.

Step 1. Possibility of the equality $A_{IN}^{pr+} = A_{IN}^{pr-} = A_{IN}^g$.

If Ar is acyclic, grounded and preferred semantics agree: $A_{IN}^{pr+} = A_{IN}^{pr-} = A_{IN}^g$.

Step 2, $A_{IN}^{pr+} \supseteq A_{IN}^{pr-}$

If a is present in all the labelings of a scenario, it is also present in at least one. Therefore $A_{IN}^{pr+} \supseteq A_{IN}^{pr-}$. On the contrary, let's consider a scenario composed by an even-length cycle. Argument a can be labeled *out* or *in*, therefore belonging to A_{IN}^{pr+} but not to A_{IN}^{pr-}

Step 3. $A_{IN}^{pr-} \supseteq A_{IN}^g$

If a scenario belongs to A_{IN}^g, that means that argument a can be labeled unambiguously starting from some initial arguments and, if there are some *undec* arguments in the scenario, they do not affect a status. Therefore, even under preferred semantics argument a is labeled *in* in all the labelings.

Step 4. Possibility of $A_{IN}^{pr-} \supset A_{IN}^g$

Let's consider the argumentation graph where a is attacked by b, and b is attacked by c and d, and c and d rebut each other (known as an example of floating assignment). Here it is $P_A^+ = P_A^- > P_A^g = 0$. In fact, there are two preferred extensions and a is labeled *in* in both.

5   Computing A_{IN}

The aim of this section is to provide an algorithm to compute A_{IN}, A_{OUT} under grounded and preferred semantics. The baseline brute force approaches forces to compute the chosen semantics in all the 2^n scenarios. The complexity of computing A_{IN} is clearly above polynomial, but the proposed algorithms are a first optimization that drastically reduces the computation in many situations, since it allows computing several set of scenarios in a single step and it also has an approximate version useful to answer threshold queries, described in section 3.3.

5.1   Grounded Semantics

We present an algorithm to find A_{IN}^g, A_{OUT}^g in the case of grounded labeling. Given a starting argument a and a label $l \in \{in, out\}$, we need to find the set of scenarios where argument a is legally labeled l.

The idea is to traverse the transpose graph (a graph with reversed arrows) from a down to its attackers, propagating the constraints of the grounded labeling. While traversing the graph, the various paths correspond to set of scenarios. The constraints needed are listed in definition 6 and theorem 1. If argument a - attacked by n arguments x_n - is required to be labeled in, we impose the set A_{IN} to be:

$$A_{IN} = A \cap \left(X_{1_{OUT}} \cap X_{2_{OUT}} \cap ... \cap X_{n_{OUT}} \right) \tag{1}$$

i.e. argument a can be labeled in in the scenarios where:

1. a exists - set A and
2. all the attacking arguments x_i are labeled out (sets $X_{i_{OUT}}$).

If a is required to be labeled out, the set of scenarios is:

$$A_{OUT} = \bar{A} \cup \left(X_{1_{IN}} \cup X_{2_{IN}} \cup ... \cup X_{n_{IN}} \right) \tag{2}$$

i.e. a is labeled out when it does not exist or when at least one of the attackers is labeled in. Therefore we recursively traverse the graph finding the scenarios that are compatible with the starting labeling of a. The sets $X_{N_{OUT}}$ and $X_{N_{IN}}$ are found when we reach terminal nodes. When we reach a terminal node – that corresponds to an initial node in the original graph - we enforce the following conditions on the terminal node a:

3. if a is required to be in then $A_{IN} = A$
4. if node a is required to be out then $A_{OUT} = \bar{A}$

The way we treat cycles guarantees that we identify only grounded complete labelings. If a cycle is detected, this means that the path visited corresponds to a scenario containing a cycle connected to the initial node a - or a belongs to the cycle. According to proposition 2, we stop visiting that specific path and the path - and the corresponding set of scenarios - is discarded along with all the paths/scenarios linked by a logical AND to the cyclic path, since under grounded labeling they do not contribute to A_{IN} or A_{OUT}.

Algorithm 2 FindSet(A,L,P) Algorithm

```
A is a node ; L is the label - either IN or OUT
FindSet(A,L,P):
Cset initialized to empty

if A in P:
    FindSet(A,L,P)= empty_set //Cycle found
```

```
if L = IN:
    if A terminal:
        return FindSet(A,L,P) = a
    else:
        add A to P
        for each child C of A
            Cset = Cset AND FindSet(C,OUT,P)
            FindSet = a AND Cset
if L = OUT:
    if A terminal:
        return FindSet(A,L,P) = NOT (a)
    else
        add A to P
        for each child C of A
            Cset = Cset  OR FindSet(C,IN,P)
            FindSet = NOT(a) OR (a AND Cset)
```

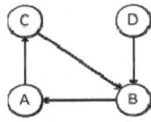

Fig. 2.

Example 3.1. Table 1 describes the steps for computing A_{IN} in the graph of figure 2.

Table 1. Recursively applying Algorithm 2

	Node, label	Constraint	Parent List	Comment
1↓	A_{IN}	$A_{IN} = A \cap B_{OUT}$	[]	*a must exist and b=OUT*
2↓	B_{OUT}	$B_{OUT} = \bar{B} \cup (B \cap (C_{IN} \cup D_{IN}))$	[a]	*b is out when b does not exist or b exists and c = in or d = in*
3=	C_{IN}	$C_{IN} = C \cap A_{OUT}$	[a,b]	*c=IN when c exists and a=OUT. Cycle with a, $C_{IN} = \emptyset$*
4=	D_{IN}	$D_{IN} = D$	[a,b]	*d is initial*
5↑	B_{OUT}	$B_{OUT} = \bar{B} \cup (B \cap D)$		
6↑	A_{IN}	$A_{IN} = A \cap (\bar{B} \cup (B \cap D)) = A\bar{B} + ABD$		

Exploting Rebuttals. We note that, if a and b are rebuttals, it is:

$$A_{IN}^g = A\bar{B}, \; A_{OUT}^g = \bar{A}, \; A_U^g = AB$$

$A_{OUT}^g = \bar{A}$ suggests an optimization to algorithm 2. The computation of A_{OUT}^g results independent from its rebuttals and all the arguments connected to a exclusively via b. This implies a new terminal condition for A_{OUT}. While we are visiting node a, if a has only rebutting attackers   the constrain for A_{OUT} is: $A_{OUT} = \bar{A}$ instead of $A_{OUT} = \bar{A} \cup \left(X_{1_{IN}} \cup X_{2_{IN}} \cup ... \cup X_{n_{IN}} \right)$.

5.2   Extension to Preferred Labeling

The constraints used in algorithm 2 – argument a is *in* when all the attackers are *out* and a is *out* if one attacker is *in* – are proper of any complete labeling. The way algorithm 2 treats cycles – it always assigns to their arguments the *undec* label – guarantees that we collect only grounded complete labeling. Since a preferred labeling is complete, the extension of algorithm 2 to the case of preferred semantics requires changing only the way cycles are treated. First we prove the following lemma.

Lemma 5.1. If a is labeled *in* (or *out*) in a complete labeling of a scenario, then the scenario can be assigned to A_{IN}^{pr+} or (A_{OUT}^{pr+}).

Proof. If a is labeled *in* in a complete labeling C of a scenario s, either C is the preferred one maximizing $in(C,s)$ w.r.t. to set inclusion, or there is another C' with $in(C,s) \subset in(C',s)$. Since $a \in in(C,s)$, then $a \in in(C',s)$ and s contributes to A_{IN}^{pr+}.

We go back to the treatment of cycles. When a cycle is detected, the labeling of an even-length cycle is consistent, since the argument that is visited twice and identifies the cycle is required to have the same label. On the contrary, an odd-length cycle create an inconsistent *undec* labeling not contributing to A_{IN}^{pr+} or A_{OUT}^{pr+}. Therefore we assign a path (=set of scenarios) to A_{IN}^{pr+} when a consistent cycle is found, while we reject the scenario otherwise. Note how the skeptical sets A_{IN}^{pr-} and A_{OUT}^{pr-} can be derived once the credulous sets are computed. While traversing the graph, we therefore need to remember the label required for an argument to check if the cycle can be consistently labeled. We remind that A_{out} (small letter for the label) identifies the set of scenario where argument a exists and it is labeled *out* (note that $A_{OUT} = \bar{A} + A_{out}$). Let's consider the graph depicted in figure 3. The graph contains both odd and even length cycles. Table 2 shows the steps required to compute A_{IN}^{+} .

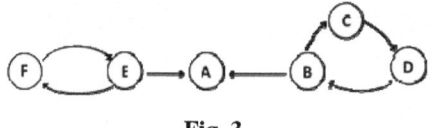

Fig. 3.

Table 2. Computing A_{IN}^{pr+} of figure 3

1	$A_{IN} = AB_{OUT}E_{OUT}$		
2a	$B_{OUT} = \bar{B} + B_{out}D_{IN}$	2b	$E_{OUT} = \bar{E} + E_{out}F_{IN}$
3a	$B_{out}D_{IN} = B_{out}DC_{OUT}$	3b	$E_{out}F_{IN} = E_{out}FE_{OUT}$
4a	$B_{out}DC_{OUT} = B_{out}D\bar{C} + B_{out}DCB_{IN}$ $= BD\bar{C} + \emptyset$ *(inconsistent cycle)*	4b	$E_{out}FE_{OUT} = EF$ $\left(\begin{array}{c} \textit{consistent cycle:} \\ e \textit{ and } f \textit{ exist}, e = in, f = out \end{array}\right)$
5a	$B_{OUT} = \bar{B} + BD\bar{C}$	5b	$E_{OUT} = \bar{E} + EF$
6	$A_{IN}^{pr+} = A(\bar{B} + BD\bar{C})(\bar{E} + EF) = A(\bar{B}\bar{E} + \bar{B}EF + BD\bar{C}\bar{E} + BD\bar{C}EF)$		

Note how the 3-length cycle creates an inconsistent situation $B_{out}DCB_{IN}$ (argument b has to exist and be labeled *in* and *out* at the same time) while $E_{out}FE_{OUT}$ can be labeled consistently (the cycle is consistent when argument e is required to exist and labeled *out*. We can verify that A_{IN}^{pr-} differs from A_{IN}^{pr+} since it discards the even-length cycle EF, therefore the path AEF is not in A_{IN}^- .

5.3   Answering Threshold Queries

We now describe a way of incrementally approximating A_{IN}. Algorithm 2 finds and combines paths terminating in node a of odd length (if we are computing A_{IN}) or even length (for A_{OUT}). We note how shorter paths identify a larger set of scenarios, meaning that arguments closer to a have a higher impact on A_{IN} or A_{OUT}. This suggests that A_{IN} and A_{OUT} could be approximated incrementally, by collecting paths of increasing length and combining them according to the constraints of the semantics.

The idea is that a path can be ended at any step of the computation by imposing the last argument on the path to be non-existent. The result obtained is an approximation since we neglect the scenarios in which the last argument exists but results labeled *out*. We can anyway estimate the range of error in terms of number of scenarios neglected, producing at each step an interval for A_{IN} and A_{OUT}, A_U. The computation can be stopped when the error is below a certain level, resulting in an effective method to answer threshold queries of the kind *"is P_{IN} more than a value x"? "Is A_{IN} composed by more than x number of scenarios"?*

The computation starts locally and it expands the frontier of the sub-graph. At each step n, we impose that arguments at distance n from root node a are forced to not exist. By doing so, when n is odd, the scenarios found will contribute to A_{IN} since we collect path of even-length (plus the nth argument that is set to not existent), while when n is even we contribute to A_{OUT}.

Let's consider example of figure 3. In order to keep the discussion independent form the probability assigned to each argument, we reason in terms of number of scenarios assigned to A_{IN}, A_{OUT} or A_U. In the example there are 6 arguments (a and other 5) and therefore 64 scenarios to be assigned. Trivially, half of them – when a does not exist – contribute to A_{OUT}. The other 32 has to be assigned, so we start from the following intervals: $A_{IN} = [0,32], A_{OUT} = [32,64], A_U = [0,32]$, where the intervals show the minimum and maximum number of scenarios for each set.

At step 1, the approximation impose that the direct attackers b and e do not exist, defining the set of scenarios $A\overline{BE}$ incrementing A_{IN}. Since there are 6 arguments, $A\overline{BE}$ identifies 8 scenarios assigned to A_{IN} and the intervals are updated as follows: $A_{IN} = [8,32], A_{OUT} = [32,56], A_U = [0,24]$.

At step 2 we expand the frontier and we collect path of length 1 + 1 argument set to non-existent to terminate the path. The sub-graph now goes as far as arguments f and d, i.e. the arguments at distance 2, that we impose to be not existing. We found the two paths $AB\overline{D}$ and $AE\overline{F}$, contributing to A_{OUT} . We rewrite them as $AB\overline{D} + A\overline{B}E\overline{F}$ to keep them disjoint (note how d and f are forced to be non-exisitent). Therefore the new scenarios $AB\overline{D} + A\overline{B}E\overline{F}$ contribute to A_{OUT}. They are $8 + 4 = 12$ scenarios, and therefore we have $A_{IN} = [8,20], A_{OUT} = [44,56]$ and $A_U = [0,12]$ and so on.

6   An Application to Legal Reasoning

In this section we present an application of PAF to legal reasoning. In order to under-stand PAF 's application, we need to reveal something on the underlying nature of the arguments, so far treated as abstract entities with a probability attached.

An argument a is a couple $\langle P, C \rangle$ where P (called support of a) is a set of proposi-tions of a language L, and C is a conclusion (called claim of a) inferred from the set P ($P \vdash C$), and P is the minimal set in L from which C can be inferred. An argument a rebuts b if the negation of $claim(b)$ can be deducted from (a) ; argument a undercuts argument b if it is possible to deduct from $claim(a)$ the negation of part of the sup-port of b (see [11] for a detailed formalization of arguments).

Paul and John are under trial for the assassination of Samuel. The following evi-dence is available. First it is known with certainty that John enter the murder's room at 1pm and left at 3, while Paul entered at 3pm and he was found by the policemen at 5pm. The police report suggests that there is evidence to believe that the probability that Sam died between 1 and 3 is 60% and between 3 and 5 is 40%. With so little evidence, the judge builds the following arguments:

R_J: John was in the room btw 1 to 3, Sam died btw 1 and 3 $\rightarrow$ John is the killer

R_P: Paul was in the room btw. 3 and 5, Sam died btw 3 and 5 $\rightarrow$ Paul is the killer

From the description above, the probability of each argument is: $R_J = 0.6, R_P = 0.4$ and they are based on mutually exclusive premises, since $P(R_J \wedge R_P) = 0$. Therefore, the scenarios with not null probability are only 2 rather than 4.

On an argumentation graph the two arguments rebuts each other, but since $P(R_J \wedge R_P) = 0$, each of them generate a scenario with only itself asserted, where they are obviously labeled in. In depicting the graph in figure 4, we show with a grey line rebuttals between arguments derived from mutually exclusive premises, that are never together in a scenario. We marked with P the arguments whose conclusion is against Paul and with J the arguments against John. Other arguments are marked with a = signal, they do not directly add to the conclusion but they interact with P and J.

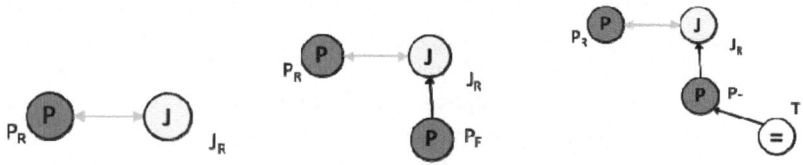

Fig. 4. Argumentation Graphs for the legal case

If we call G_p and G_J the set of scenarios where Paul or John are guilty (i.e. at least one argument supporting the conclusion is labeled in), we have $G_p = R_P, G_J = R_J$ and the grounded probabilities are 0.5 for each of them.

Let's add new evidence. During the trial, John's lawyer asks for a fingerprint anal-ysis of the murder weapon. The results are the follows: with probability 0.7 the fin-gerprints are Paul's. The lawyer therefore proposes a new argument:

F_P: The fingerprints are Paul's $\rightarrow$ Paul shot Sam btw 3 and 5

This argument undercuts J_R (it leads to conclude that the assumption that Sam was shot by John and died btw 1 and 3 is wrong). Therefore, as represented in figure 5 center, as long as the fingerprints are Paul's, Paul is guilty (prob. 0.7). When fingerprints are considered not valid (the remaining set of scenarios with probability 0.3), Paul is guilty when R_P holds, and John is guilty when R_J holds. The set of scenario for Paul's is $G_P = F_P + \overline{F_P}R_P$ while John's set is $G_J = \overline{F_P}R_J$. Inserting numerical values the grounded probabilities are 0.82 for Paul and 0.18 for John.

Anyway, a further analysis by the police labs states that the weapon was tempered, and the test is only 50% reliable. The new argument (with probability 0.5):

T: the test is void $\rightarrow$ fingerprints are not a valid evidence

enters the graph (figure 5 right), undercuts the validity of F_P (that obviously assumed the test validity). Now F_P is valid when T is not. The resulting set of scenarios is: $G'_P = F_P\overline{T} + (\overline{F_P} + F_PT)R_P$ and $G_J = (\overline{F_P} + F_PT)R_J$ as can be verified with algorithm 2. The grounded probabilities are now 0.61 (Paul) and 0.39 (John).

Paul's lawyer counter-attacks using the testimony of a credible witness, that heard a shot at 2pm, when only John was in the room. The witness is reputable credible with a probability of 0.8. A new argument is put forward:

W: A shot was heard at 2pm, John was in the room at 2 $\rightarrow$ John shot Sam

The new argument J_W is therefore undercutting P_R and rebutting F_P. Note how it only rebuts F_p since only the conclusions are conflicting. Therefore the final graph is depicted in figure 5. By applying algorithm 2 the sets are $G_P = \overline{W}G'_P$ (since, when W is out, the situation is as before while, when W is in, none of the two argument R_p or F_P is in (one is *out*, the other is *undec*). Paul's probability goes down to 0.122. Now $G_J = W(\overline{F_P} + F_PT) + \overline{W}(\overline{F_P} + F_PT)R_J$, that has a probability of 0.598.

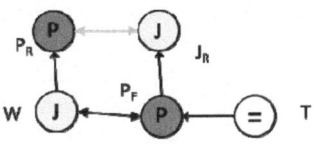

Fig. 5.

Our illustrative example has some interesting points. First, the use of the joint probability that reduces the number of scenarios to consider; second, the way arguments are modeled on the graph and third the way computation can be improved. We do not test 2^5 scenarios, since algorithm 2 simplified the computation.

7   Related Works

The idea of merging probabilities and abstract argumentation is present in Dung's work [3], even if a more detailed formalization is due to Li et al. [4] already discussed, along with the works by Hunter [11] and the analysis of Thimm [12]. Regarding other works investigating gradualism in argumentation, we first mention Pollok's work on degrees of justification [8]. Pollock rejects the use of probabilities to propagate numerical values on an argumentation framework, but he considers probabilities the only valid proxy for argument strength, and he uses the statistical syllogism as the standard comparison to measure strengths. Pollock considers arguments' strengths as cardinal quantities that can be subtracted. The accrual of arguments is denied – except the case of a rebutting and an undercutting argument – and it is the argument with the maximum strength that defines the attack. In a chain of arguments, it is the argument with minimum strength that defines the strength of the conclusions. In [1], the authors propose an argumentation framework with various degrees of attacks. The authors extend a work by Martinez [10] that first extended Dung's argumentation framework introducing different levels of attacks. [7] has first suggested the use of weights both on arguments and on attacks and Dunne et al. [9] have proposed weighted argument systems, in which attacks has a numeric weight, indicating how reluctant one would be to disregard the attack. Authors accept that attacks can have different weights, and such weight might have different interpretation: an agent-based priority voting, or a measure of how many premises of the attacked argument are compromised. Note how in the second case the weight is defined by the attacked and attacking argument structure, i.e. it is derived by the logical structure of the attacked argument. Finally, an approach that tries to combine Bayesian networks to argumentation theory can be found in [5], where authors use argumentation constructs – usually argumentation schemes and their critical questions – over a classical Bayesian network.

8   Conclusions and Future Works

In this paper we analyzed probabilistic argumentation frameworks. We provided an extension of Li's constellation approach; we explored the case where arguments are no more treated ad independent. We provided an algorithm to compute the probability of acceptance of each argument under grounded and preferred semantics. We also proved some properties of PAF that links grounded and preferred probabilistic frameworks. We believe to have provided enough applicative example and analysis to further justify research in the field. Future developments are the extension to other forms of uncertainty management such as possibility and fuzzy/multi-value logic. Much work has to be done over the computational aspects. Computing A_{IN} is clearly above polynomial complexity and the presented algorithm reduces considerably the steps to define the set of scenario A_{IN} (or A_{OUT}), but it is still subject to combinatorial explosion in some cases. This opens the door for various future optimizations such as keeping a memory of the nodes already visited, or by optimizing the simplification of boolean expressions.

References

1. Claudette, C., Caroline, D., Lagasquie-Schiex, M.C.: Acceptability semantics accounting for strength of attacks in argumentation. In: 19th ECAI, Lisbon, Portugal, pp. 995–996 (2010)
2. Dung, P.: On the acceptability of arguments and its fundamental role in nonmonotonic reasoning, logic programming and n-person games. Artificial Intelligence 77, 321–357 (1995)

3. Dung, P., Thang, P.: Towards (Probabilistic) Argumentation for Jury-based Dispute Resolution. In: COMMA 2010, pp. 171–182. IOS Press, Amsterdam (2010)
4. Li, H., Oren, N., Norman, T.J.: Probabilistic Argumentation Frameworks. In: Modgil, S., Oren, N., Toni, F. (eds.) TAFA 2011. LNCS (LNAI), vol. 7132, pp. 1–16. Springer, Heidelberg (2012)
5. Grabmair, M., Gordon, T., Walton, D.: Probabilistic Semantics for the Carneades Argument Model Using Bayesian Networks. In: Baroni, P., et al. (eds.) Proc. of COMMA 2010, pp. 255–266. IOS Press, Amsterdam (2010)
6. Baroni, P., Caminada, M., Giacomin, M.: An introduction to argumentation semantics. Knowledge Eng. Review 26(4), 365–410 (2011)
7. Barringer, H., Gabbay, D., Woods, J.: Temporal dynamics of support and attack networks: From argumentation to zoology. In: Hutter, D., Stephan, W. (eds.) Mechanizing Mathematical Reasoning. LNCS (LNAI), vol. 2605, pp. 59–98. Springer, Heidelberg (2005)
8. Pollock, J.L.: Defeasible reasoning with variable degrees of justification. Artificial Intelligence 133(1-2), 233–282 (2001)
9. Dunne, P., et al.: Inconsistency Tolerance in Weighted Argument Systems. In: Proceedings of the Eighth Joint Conference on Autonomous Agents and Multi-Agent Systems, AAMAS 2009, pp. 851–858. ACM Press (2009)
10. Martinez, D.C., Garcia, A.J.: An abstract argumentation framework with varied-strength attacks. In: Proc. of KR, pp. 135–143 (2008)
11. Hunter, A.: A probabilistic approach to modeling uncertain logical arguments. International Journal of Approximate Reasoning 54(1), 47–81 (2013)
12. Thimm, M.: Probabilistic Semantics for Abstract Argumentation. In: Proceedings of 20th European Conference of Artificial Intelligence, pp. 750–755. IOS Press (2012)

A Negotiation Approach
for Energy-Aware Room Allocation Systems

Sergio Esparcia[1], Victor Sánchez-Anguix[1], and Reyhan Aydoğan[2]

[1] Departamento de Sistemas Informáticos y Computación
Universitat Politècnica de València
Camino de Vera s/n, 46022 - Valencia, Spain
{sesparcia,sanguix}@dsic.upv.es
[2] Interactive Intelligence Group
Delft University of Technology
Delft, The Netherlands
R.Aydogan@tudelft.nl

Abstract. This paper addresses energy-aware room allocation management where the system aims to satisfy individuals' needs as much as possible while concerning total energy consumption in a building. In the problem, there are a several rooms having varied settings resulting in different energy consumption. The main objective of the system is not only finding the right allocations for user's need, but also minimizing energy consumption. However, the users of the system may have conflicting preferences over the rooms to be allocated for them. This paper pursues how the system can increase user satisfaction while achieving its goals. For that purpose, an adaptation of the mediated single text negotiation model is introduced. The proposal seeks to guarantee an upper bound on energy consumption by pruning the negotiation space via a genetic algorithm, and to take advantage of the negotiation for increasing user satisfaction. Experiments suggest that the adaptations improve the performance.

Keywords: automated negotiation, room allocation, energy consumption.

1 Introduction

The primary energy consumption in the world in 2004 has been reported as 11059 MToe (Million of Tonnes of Oil Equivalent), while it was 6034 MToe in 1973 [1]. That shows that we are consuming more and more energy over time. Due to the decreasing of the amount of the energy resources and the environmental effects of excessive energy consumption, reducing energy consumption has become a critical issue.

Buildings are one of the main sources of energy consumption, and its consumption is increasing rapidly. For example, in 2004, in the European Union, buildings consumed 37% of the final energy, more than transport, whose consumption was a 32%, and the industry, which consumed a 28% of the total energy consumption. In this territory, the energy consumption increases 1.5% each year [1]. Therefore, it seems clear that keeping the energy consumption of a building under control is important for the environment of our planet. This leads to the need for the emergence of energy-aware systems aiming to minimize the energy consumption inside buildings. For example, the Government of

J.M. Corchado et al. (Eds.): PAAMS 2013 Workshops, CCIS 365, pp. 280–291, 2013.

the Region of Valencia (Spain) established the minimum air conditioning temperature to 26 centigrade degrees at workplaces during summer in order to reduce the electricity consumption [2]. Although this rule is aimed to reduce the energy consumption and consequently to save the environment and reduce energy expenses, it may not satisfy everyone at the same degree in the society. For example, this temperature may be too hot for some workers who have difficult working conditions under very warm summer days. Therefore, it is desired to meet the individuals' preferences at the same time while reducing the energy consumption.

In this paper, we address the problem of energy-aware scheduling and resource allocation. Our primary aim is to minimize the energy consumption, but we also desire to satisfy the individuals' preferences as much as possible. The proposed system is based on the assignment of activities around different rooms of a building. This case-study is a revision of the scenario presented in [3]. The building belongs to a university, and its rooms are dedicated to a certain purpose (teaching, meeting, etc.). Thus, they have different equipments that allow them to carry out different purposes. The activities are managed by the building manager, who is responsible for distributing the different activities. The activities are sent to the building manager by staff members that require a room with specific features with a start and end time. The goal of the building is finding a proper room allocation for the requested activities. However, the number of available spots for an activity are limited. Therefore, it is necessary to solve this problem by taking into account the constraints imposed by the petitions and the characteristics of the different rooms. Due to differences between rooms, users have different preferences. For example, a user may be interested on a specific room because of different reasons, like the location of the room (the closer to his office, the better), its capacity (not too big, not too small), the acoustics and luminosity inside this room, the quality of the equipment (a user may look for new computers or other new equipments), etc.

A classic solution to this problem is applying some optimization algorithm, such as a genetic algorithm. However, the preferences of the participants may not be known and they may be patients. In such a case, the applied optimization technique will produce a solution by only considering the system's preferences, minimizing energy consumption. Therefore, it is necessary to take into account the agents' preferences when allocating the activities. In order to deal with this problem, we present a multiparty negotiation approach in which the system generates possible room allocations, and asks to each participant whether or not it is acceptable for them, and refines its offer based on their feedback. It is worth noting that the preferences of the participants are kept as private. The proposed approach is a variant of the mediated single text negotiation protocol [4] adapted to the present domain. Using negotiation presents the following advantages: (i) each user participates as a software agent that keeps its preferences private; (ii) negotiation is a "human" process (i.e. it is understandable by people) where humans can directly participate at some point; and (iii) allocations can be renegotiated, which allows systems to adapt themselves to changes.

The rest of this paper is structured as follows: Section 2 describes the case-study and the problem that is intended to be solved. Section 3 explains the negotiation model that is followed to solve the previously presented scenario. Section 4 presents the results of the experiments carried out using this negotiation model. Finally, Section 5 depicts the related work on this topic, as well as the conclusions and future work on this topic.

2   Problem Description

This case study focuses on how to manage the petitions of activities to be carried out in the different rooms of a building in a university. The type of activities that can be carried out inside a room are limited by two factors: (i) the capacity of the room, and (ii) the equipment of the room. The building is open during weekdays (from Monday to Friday) and closes on weekends. The working hours of the building are from 8:00 to 20:00. The activities take place in slots of 60 minutes, starting at the minute :00 each hour and finishing at the :59 of the same hour. The activities can last from one to n slots.

The scheduling of activities in the rooms is controlled by the building manager. The users of the building (the agents that are responsible for each activity) send their petitions to the building manager, who is responsible for managing petitions and finally making public an adequate schedule. A petition includes the number of people that will participate in the activity, the type and quantity of equipment they require, the start time of the activity, and the number of slots of an hour that they need.

Additionally, there is another requirement imposed by the building manager that has to be taken into account. Its objective is keeping energy consumption at a reasonable limit (i.e. minimize energy consumption). The energy consumption is calculated as the sum of the consumption of the whole set of rooms. Then, the consumption of each room is the sum of the individual consumption for each unit of equipment used. The system is a multiagent system described as $MAS = \langle R, A, E, s \rangle$, where R is the set of rooms of the building, A is the set of agents representing the users that make petitions, E is the set of the different equipment that a room may have, and s is the building manager.

2.1   Rooms

A room $r_1 \in R$ is defined by means of three features: its capacity (ca), the number of units per equipment type it has (h), and the average consumption per hour of each type of equipment (co). These features are represented as follows:

$$\begin{aligned} ca &: R \to \mathbb{N} \\ h &: R \times E \to \mathbb{N} \\ co &: R \times E \to \mathbb{R} \end{aligned} \tag{1}$$

where the function ca defines, given a room $r_i \in R$, the number of people that fit inside that room. Given a room $r_i \in R$ and a type of equipment $eq_j \in E$, the function h returns the number of units that the room is equipped with. In the case the room is not equipped with a specific type of equipment, the function returns 0. Finally, the function co returns the consumption (in kW/hour) that a unit of equipment of the type $eq_j \in E$ makes during an hour in the room $r_i \in R$.

2.2   Agent

An agent $a_i \in A$ is represented by means of the petition he makes. This petition includes the number of participants in the activity the agent is requesting (pa), the number of units of each type of equipment that are required (req), the date and time when the activity has to start $(date)$, and the length of the activity (len):

$$pa : A \to \mathbb{N}$$
$$req : A \times E \to \mathbb{N}$$
$$date : A \to T \tag{2}$$
$$len : A \to \mathbb{N}$$

where *pa* returns, given an agent $a_i \in A$, the number of participants on the activity requested by the agent. The function *req* will return the number of units of this type of equipment that the agent requests, given an agent $a_i \in A$ and a type of equipment $eq_j \in E$. In the case of *date*, the moment in time $t \in T$ is represented as:

$$t = \langle day, time \rangle \tag{3}$$

where $day \in \{mon, tue, wed, thu, fri\}$ is the day of the week to carry the activity out, and $time \in [8, 19]$ represents the hour when the activity in the petition is intended to start. Finally, *len* returns the number of hours required by the activity.

2.3 Room Allocation

A room allocation is an assignment of one room per petition $X = (x_1, x_2, x_3, ..., x_A)$ being $x_i \in R$ is the room assigned to agent a_i. It represents a possible solution for the problem presented in this paper. During this work, we will talk indistinctly of room allocation, solution, or offer, since we consider them to be the same object. In order to be valid, the solution has to satisfy the following constraints:

- $\forall x_i \in X, eq_j \in E : h(x_i, eq_j) \geq req(a_i, eq_j)$
  - The room has the required units of equipment requested in the assigned petition.
- $\forall x_i \in X, a_i \in A : ca(x_i) \geq pa(a_i)$
  - The number of participants is lower than the capability of the assigned room.
- $\forall x_i, x_j \in X : \neg overlap(x_i, x_j)$
  - There is no overlap between activities. The function $overlap(x_i, x_j)$ returns *true* if there is an overlap between the activities requested by agents a_i and a_j.

3 Negotiation Model

Our proposal takes inspiration from the mediated single text negotiation protocol presented in [4]. In Klein *et al.*, the mediator initially generates a random bid and asks the negotiating agents to vote for this bid. Each agent can vote to either "accept" or "reject" according to its negotiation strategy. If all negotiating agents vote to accept, the bid is selected as the most recent mutually accepted bid. In further rounds, the mediator modifies the most recent mutually accepted bid by randomly exchanging one value with another one in the bid and queries negotiating agents to vote for the current bid. The negotiation process continues iteratively until a predefined number of rounds is reached. The next section describes the process followed to reach an agreed room allocation, depicting how we adapted the model proposed by Klein *et al.* to our domain.

3.1 Modeling Preferences

Agents' Preferences. Agents have different preferences over room assignments (e.g., walking distance, acoustics, equipment quality, etc.). Thus, as users of the reservation system, agents not only want to have their petitions fulfilled, but also being assigned their most preferred rooms if possible. Given a room allocation X, an agent's satisfaction is only affected by the room which has been assigned to its activity. Thus, the utility function for agent a_i can be defined as $U_{a_i}(X) = sat_i(x_i)$, where $sat_i(x_i)$ defines the satisfaction generated by being assigned a certain room. The function is scaled to $[0, 1]$ so that 1 represents the highest satisfaction and 0 designates the lowest satisfaction obtainable with a room assignment. Each agent aims to maximize its own utility.

Building Manager Preferences. The building manager has the goal of managing agents' petitions and providing an adequate room allocation for the activities that have been requested. However, given the increasing importance of energy consumption in our society, not every room allocation is considered as adequate. Instead, the building manager scores the different room allocations based on the energy consumption stemming from the room assignment. As a manager, his prime goal is minimizing energy consumption. The energy consumption associated to the room allocation X can be defined as:

$$EC_s(X) = \sum_{i=1}^{|A|} \sum_{eq_j \in E} req(a_i, eq_j) * co(x_i, eq_j) * len(a_i) \tag{4}$$

Basically, it is defined as the sum of each petitions' consumption, where a petition's consumption can be defined as the sum of the consumption generated by the required equipment units during the assigned time.

3.2 Proposed Negotiation Approach

As stated, the negotiation protocol is a variant of the mediated single text negotiation protocol proposed by Klein *et al.* [4] adapted to our domain. The original protocol is based on the existence of a mediator that helps agents reach an agreement by mutating the most recent mutually accepted offer. In our case, the building manager samples a set of low energy consumption allocations by means of a genetic algorithm (GA) before the negotiation. The reasons to this genetic sampling are: (i) the building manager needs to look for good solutions that satisfy the main goal of the system, energy consumption; (ii) the domain is extremely huge (e.g., even for a *small* problem like $|R| = 10$ and $|A| = 10$ the search space is 10^{10}); (iii) employing a metaheuristic like a GA provides an anytime optimization. During the negotiation, the building manager plays the role of mediator and it proposes offers with low energy consumption from the sample obtained from the GA. Hence, a bound on the energy consumption (i.e., a threshold) can be assured, fulfilling the main goal of the system. Then, the negotiation aims to satisfy agents' preferences as much as possible with proposals that are below the aforementioned threshold.

The negotiation protocol goes as follows. In the first negotiation round, the building manager informs of the initial agreement for the group, which is automatically accepted.

From that point on, the manager proposes one offer per round to the group. This offer is then sent to the agents, who cast their votes (either 'better', 'worse', or 'same'). Depending on the specific mechanism employed by the manager, which will be explained later, the offer is accepted or rejected. If the offer is accepted, the manager informs the rest of agents and the offer becomes the most recently accepted solution. The negotiation continues following this iterative process until a number of negotiation rounds N is reached. In the end, the final agreement is the most recently accepted solution.

Agent's Voting Mechanism. During the negotiation agents receive offers from the building manager and they are asked to vote. By default, the first offer proposed by the building manager becomes the initial agreement. In following negotiation rounds, agents can give feedback. Considering that X is the last offer accepted by the group, an agent a_i emits a 'better' vote if $U_{a_i}(X) < U_{a_i}(X')$, it emits a 'worse' vote (i.e., reject) if $U_{a_i}(X) > U_{a_i}(X')$, and it emits a 'same' vote if $U_{a_i}(X) = U_{a_i}(X')$.

Pre-negotiation: Sampling and Defining the Negotiation Space. When the building manager engages agents to agree on a room allocation, it does not suffice with just calculating the optimal solution from the point of view of energy consumption. In fact, it may be likely that the best solution in terms of energy consumption does not generate a high user satisfaction for petitioners. Instead, a set of high quality and significantly different room allocations is needed to look for possible win-win situations. Additionally, constraints imposed over the search space by rooms' limitations and petitions' requirements preclude the building manager from employing simple optimization methods like the ones used to generate new solutions in monotonic search spaces. For that matter a niching genetic algorithm [5,6] is employed to sample solutions before the negotiation starts. Niching genetic algorithms are a special type of genetic algorithm that avoids converging towards a single high quality solution. Instead, the population converges towards different, yet high quality solutions. This effect is accomplished by introducing local competition among similar solutions. Niching genetic algorithms have been used to tackle other complex search spaces in negotiation [7].

Before the negotiation starts, the building manager calculates a set of high quality room allocations in terms of energy consumption. The niching genetic algorithm has the following characteristics:

- Chromosome representation and fitness function: Solutions are represented as a vector of integers, where each vector index represents a petition and its content represents the room where the petition is assigned. For the fitness function, the energy consumption function introduced in Equation 4 is employed. The goal of the genetic algorithm is minimizing the fitness function.
- Initial population: Initially, a population of room allocations is randomly generated. The population has a maximum size of MAX_POP.
- Genetic operators: Crossover and mutation operators are applied over pairs of the genetic pool. More specifically, $\frac{MAX\_POP}{2}$ disjoint pairs of solutions are randomly formed. Genetic operators are applied over such pairs.
    - Crossover operator: It is applied over two parents X_i and X_j, and it generates two different children X_i' and X_i'. It operates on a chromosome per chromosome basis (i.e., attribute per attribute). With an equal probability and given

a certain chromosome index k, the chromosome k from X_i is inherited by X_i' and the chromosome k from X_j is inherited by X_j'. Otherwise the chromosome k from X_i is inherited by X_j' and the chromosome k from X_j is inherited by X_i'. The probability of applying a crossover operator over a pair of solutions is controlled by the p_{cross} parameter.

- Mutation operator: It is applied over one parent and it produces one child. The mutation operator goes chromosome per chromosome and with a probability p_{matt}, it changes the value of the current chromosome to other valid value.

- Selection Operator: It decides the solutions that are to be part of the next generation. It introduces the niching effect by inducing competition between similar solutions. The selection operator is used after each crossover and mutation operation. In the case of the mutation operation, it takes the parent and the child and it decides which one takes part in the next generation. In the case of a crossover operation, the selection operation takes both parents and both children. Each parent is paired up with its most similar child, and then, the selection operator is applied two decide whether the parent or the child go to the next generation. The selection operator is composed of a portfolio containing a deterministic crowding rule $DC(X_1, X_2)$ and a probabilistic crowding rule $PC(X_1, X_2)$. The deterministic crowding rule selects always the solution with the best fitness, whereas the probabilistic crowding rule allows for worse fitness solution to pass to the next generation with a small probability for escaping local minima/maxima. The use of of deterministic crowding and probabilistic crowding is controlled by p_{pc}, which refers to the probability of applying probabilistic crowding rules. The probabilistic crowding rule can be defined as:

$$PC(X_1, X_2) = \begin{cases} X_1 \text{ if random}() \geq p_1 \\ X_2 \text{ otherwise} \end{cases} \tag{5}$$

with $p_1 = \frac{EC_s(X_1)}{EC_s(X_1) + EC_s(X_2)}$.

- Stop criteria: The genetic algorithm stops its execution when the fitness of the best solution has not improved in *MAX_IT* iterations.

Since energy consumption is a prime goal for the system, the building manager may prune from the negotiation space all those solutions that are not the best from an energy perspective. From the sample obtained by the genetic algorithm, the building manager discards all of those solutions whose energy consumption is over a certain threshold. More specifically, if X_{best} is the best solution obtained by the GA, the building manager will discard those solutions X that $EC_s(X) > EC_s(X_{best}) \times tol_s$, where $tol_s > 1$ and it represents the tolerance of the building manager with respect to energy consumption. Therefore, the building manager dictates that any agreement found in the negotiation can be no worse than tol_s times the best solution found by the GA. The set of solutions *NS* from the GA population that are below the threshold become the negotiation space.

Once the negotiation space has been defined by the manager, the manager scales his own utility function as follows:

$$U_s(X) = 1 - \frac{EC_s(X) - EC_s(X_{best})}{EC_s(X_{best}) \times tols_s - EC_s(X_{best})} \tag{6}$$

Negotiation: Proposing and Accepting Solutions. In this paper we introduce special features in the offer proposal and the offer acceptance mechanism to adapt it to our domain. Regarding the offer proposal mechanism, the first offer proposed to the group, which is accepted by default, is the one with the highest utility (i.e., lowest energy consumption) for the building manager. In the next rounds, the offer proposal takes into account the agents' feedback during the negotiation. Since the most recently accepted solution implicitly represents the feedback given by the agents, the building manager proposes an offer from NS (i.e., the filtered sample from the GA), which is the most similar[1] to the most recently accepted solution. Given the fact that an agent is only affected by the attribute corresponding to its room allocation, the manager can keep track of those room assignments that are worse for each agent than the allocation in the most recently accepted solution. For instance, if x_i is the current allocation for the petition made by agent a_i in the most recently accepted offer and the manager proposes x'_i, which receives a 'worse' vote by a_i, then any other solution with x'_i assigned for the petition from a_i will be rejected by the agent. Therefore, when selecting the most similar offer from NS, it skips those solutions that contain values that are known to be worse for each agent's current allocations. If all the solutions from NS are skipped, then the similarity mechanism takes into account every solution in NS.

As for the acceptance mechanism employed by the building manager, we contemplate two options in our initial study similarly to Klein *et al.* [4]:

- Hill Climber Manager: It updates the most recently accepted solution to X when no petitioner emits a 'worse' vote over X (it can emit 'same' votes and be accepted).
- Annealer Manager: It may accept an offer even if some negative votes are received. More specifically, it assigns a probability of acceptance $p_{ac}(X) = e^{\frac{-dE}{T}}$, where T is the virtual temperature which will be declined over time. In this study, we take the remaining number of rounds scaled to $(0,1]$. $dE = \frac{nw}{|A|}$, with nw being the number of 'worse' votes received for the offer X. According to this formula, the building manager is likely to accept an offer X as "most recently accepted offer" if the proportion of 'worse' votes over all votes is low in the beginning. Over time, this probability for the same proportion of 'worse' votes will decrease and the offer becomes unacceptable. In other words, the higher remaining time to complete the negotiation, and the smaller proportion of negative votes, the greater the probability that the the offer X will be accepted even though there are some negative votes for that offer. While approaching the deadline, annealer gradually declines so eventually he will act as a hill-climber and only accepts the offers as most recently accepted offer if all agents use positive vote for them. We restrict the annealing probability only to those offers which received more positive votes than negatives to assure that at least a higher number of petitioners benefit from the new offer. Otherwise the offer is automatically rejected.

4 Experimental Evaluation

In this section, we evaluate the performance of the proposed model in 90 different scenarios. We randomly generated test cases considering a number of rooms $|R|$ equal to

---

[1] Manhattan distance is used.

10, 20, or 30. The number of petitioners $|A|$ was set to be 10, 20, and 30. For every possible combination of $|R|$ and $|A|$, 10 different scenarios were generated. Hence, the total number of generated test cases was $3 \times 3 \times 10 = 90$ (possible number of rooms × possible number of petitions × number of different scenarios). The size of the smallest test cases ($|R| = 10$, $|A| = 10$) is 10^{10} with 10 agents, while the size of the largest test cases ($|R| = 30$, $|A| = 30$) is 30^{30} with 30 agents.

In order to assess the quality of the final agreement, we use a social welfare measure that sums up the utility of the building manager and the agents. We consider that the highest the social welfare, the better performance the model achieves.

$$SW(X) = U_s(X) + \sum_{a_i \in A} U_{a_i}(X) \qquad (7)$$

In our experiments, we compared the performance of our hill climber manager (HC), the performance of our annealer manager (AN), the performance of the best solution found by the genetic algorithm (i.e., no negotiation carried out after the optimization), and the performance of a basic annealer manager (BA). The basic annealer does not keep track of which room values are worse than the current room allocation for each agent. The proposal mechanism just selects the offer which is the most similar to the most recently accepted solution. Additionally, the basic annealer may accept an offer (attending to $p_{ac}(X) = e^{\frac{-dE}{T}}$) even if the number of 'worse' votes received is greater than or equal to the number of 'better' votes. Hence, differently to our annealer manager, it does not assure that the new solution benefits at least more members than it detriments. The inclusion of the basic annealer manager aims to assess the benefits of the adaptations proposed to tackle the present domain. Next, we describe the experiments that we carried out.

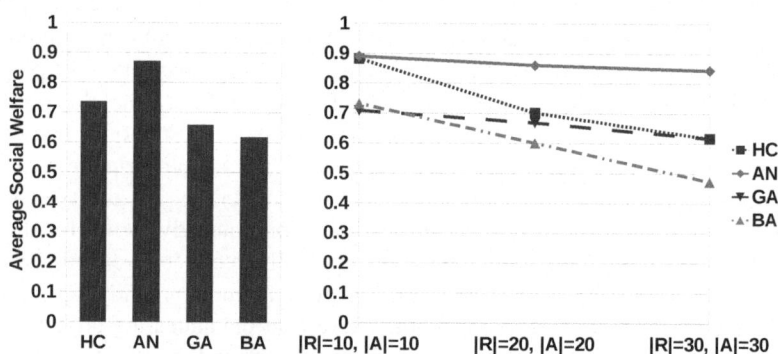

Fig. 1. Average social welfare when the number of negotiation rounds is $N = 100$ for all the test scenarios (left), and average social welfare for increasing problem sizes and agents (right)

First, we measured the social welfare in all of the test cases when the number of negotiation rounds is $N = 100$. The execution of each scenario was repeated four times to capture stochastic differences. The parameters[2] for the genetic algorithm were set to

---

[2] An initial grid search was performed to find good parameters for the GA.

$MAX\_POP = 8192$, $p_{cross} = 70\%$, $p_{matt} = 10\%$, $p_{pc} = 90\%$, and $MAX\_IT = 100$. Additionally, the tolerance of the building manager was set to $tol_s = 1.10$. Therefore, the building manager assures that the final agreement is at most 10% worse than the best solution in terms of energy consumption found by the GA. The same pool generated by the GA was provided to the hill climber, the annealer, and the basic annealer managers. Fig. 1 shows the average social welfare scaled to $[0, 1]$ [3] in all of the scenarios (left side). In order to study the effect of the problem size and the number of agents on the negotiation, we also plotted the average social welfare for test cases with $|R| = 10$ and $|A| = 10$, $|R| = 20$ and $|A| = 20$, and $|A| = 30$ and $|R| = 30$ (right side). It can be observed in the left part of Fig. 1 that our annealer manager is the one that achieves the highest average social welfare (0.87), followed by our hill climber manager (0.73), the genetic algorithm (0.65), and the basic annealer (0.62). The performance obtained by the proposed annealer manager is close to the optimal social welfare obtainable from the genetic pool. An ANOVA test with Bonferroni post-hoc analysis suggested that the differences between the methods are statistically significant. Surprisingly, the basic annealer mediator is slightly worse than using the GA, which suggests that using our heuristic approaches in the proposed annealer manager is more adequate for the case study. When observing the right side of Fig. 1, it can be observed that, as the size of the problem increases and more agents are involved, the performance of the genetic algorithm, the basic annealer, and the hill climber manager decreases. Contrarily, the performance of the annealer manager is only slightly affected. This graphic suggests that the performance of the annealer manager is more robust to the number of negotiating agents and the problem size than the other methods, which is also highly desirable.

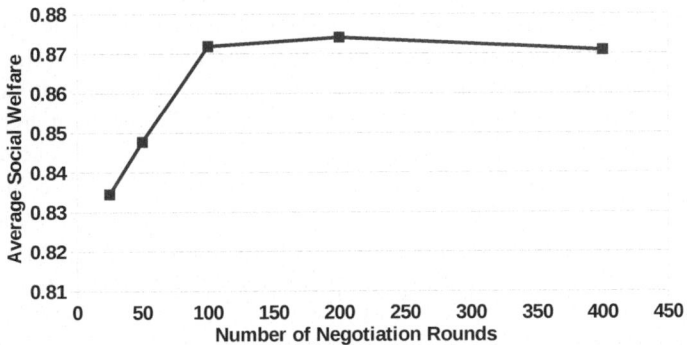

Fig. 2. Social welfare of the annealer manager at the end of the negotiation for different rounds

Finally, in the second experiment we measured the performance of the annealer manager for different maximum number of negotiation rounds. More specifically, N was set to 25, 50, 100, 200, and 400. The rest of parameters was set to the same value as the previous experiment. The results of the experiment are shown in Fig. 2. As it is can be seen, the average social welfare obtained by the annealer manager increases as the number

---

[3] 0 being the lowest, and 1 being the highest social welfare obtainable from the pool.

of negotiation rounds increases. It approximately converges to a maximum value when $N = 100$. From that point, even quadrupling the number of negotiation rounds does not have any effect on the average social welfare. This convergence suggests that additional changes in the core of the annealer manager (e.g., proposal method, acceptance method, etc.) may be necessary to improve its performance. If compared with the average social welfare obtained by other methods in the first experiment, the annealer manager outperforms the rest even when the number of rounds is four times lower (i.e., 0.83 when $N = 25$ versus 0.73 obtained by hill climber manager, 0.65 obtained by the GA, and 0.62 obtained by the basic annealer when $N = 100$). Therefore, it is possible to reduce communication costs and still obtain a higher performance, which is quite desirable in case that a quicker solution is needed.

5   Discussion and Future Work

In this paper, we address the problem of energy-aware room allocation in a building. The system's goal is obtaining an adequate allocation that minimizes consumption while satisfying users' preferences as much as possible. For this matter, we introduce a variant of the mediated single text negotiation protocol [4]. The main differences reside in the fact that (i) the manager desires to minimize energy consumption and it prunes the negotiation space accordingly by means of a genetic algorithm and a threshold; (ii) agents' votes are expressed in three categories that describe their preference with respect to the new allocation ('worse', 'better', 'same'); (iii) since some solutions are not valid, the manager proposes new offers based on a similarity mechanism that takes into account those rooms that do not improve the current agreement for each agent; and (iv) the annealer mechanism ensures that offers are only accepted only if more agents benefit than agents detriment with the new offer. The experiments show that the adaptations carried out in our annealer manager are more adequate for the domain at hand.

Kuo *et al.* [8] propose the use of linear programming for planning and scheduling the time of an operation room. In order to do so, there are taken into account features such as the type of surgery (vascular, trauma, etc.), the time for each specific operation, the economic costs, etc. However, they only focus on maximizing operational issues.

Similarly to our approach, Schumann *et al.* [9] take into account the preferences of the users to maximize their termal comfort while reducing energy consumption. They adjust the thermal control by means of the predicted preferences of agents. In addition to minimizing the energy consumption, we also deal with room allocation.

One of the studies presenting a multiagent system (MAS) approach for energy consumption is that Multi-Agent Home Automation System (MAHAS) [10], a MAS that is used to manage the energy consumption of a house. MAHAS' agents are capable of calculating the consumed energy as well as predicting energy consumption. In this case, MAHAS presents two mechanisms: reactive and anticipative. The reactive mechanism protects the house from violations of energy constraints and it guarantees a good level of inhabitant satisfaction. The anticipative mechanism computes plans for production and consumption of services in a house, anticipating the energy consumption for the devices inside the house. In addition to energy consumption, in our problem we consider room allocation where constraints exist on which activities can be hosted in each room.

Some future lines of work include considering the robustness of solutions with respect to unexpected changes. Additionally, we plan to introduce renegotiation mechanisms for tackling such unexpected events that require the agreement to be adapted. Finally, we also consider studying different proposal based on learning agents' preferences and annealer mechanisms that further improve the performance.

Acknowledgements. This work is supported by TIN2012-36586-C03-01, TIN2011-27652-C03-01, and TIN2009-13839-C03-01 projects of the Spanish government, the FPU grant AP2008-00600 awarded to Víctor Sánchez-Anguix, and the New Governance Models for Next Generation Infrastructures project with NGI grant number 04.17. We would also like to thank anonymous reviewers for their valuable feedback.

References

1. Perez-Lombard, L., Ortiz, J., Pout, C.: A review on buildings energy consumption information. Energy and Buildings 40(3), 394–398 (2008)
2. Plan de ahorro de eficiencia energética de los edificios públicos de la generalitat. Diari oficial de la Comunitat Valenciana (6800), 18038–18044 (June 2012)
3. Sorici, A., Boissier, O., Picard, G., Santi, A.: Exploiting the jacamo framework for realising an adaptive room governance application. In: Proc. DSM 2011, TMC 2011, AGERE! 2011, AOOPES 2011, NEAT 2011, & VMIL 2011, pp. 239–242. ACM (2011)
4. Klein, M., Faratin, P., Sayama, H., Bar-Yam, Y.: Negotiating complex contracts. Group Decision and Negotiation 12, 111–125 (2003)
5. Sareni, B., Krahenbuhl, L.: Fitness sharing and niching methods revisited. IEEE Transactions on Evolutionary Computation 2(3), 97–106 (1998)
6. Mengshoel, O.J., Goldberg, D.E.: The crowding approach to niching in genetic algorithms. Evolutionary Computation 16(3), 315–354 (2008)
7. Sanchez-Anguix, V., Valero, S., Julian, V., Botti, V., Garcia-Fornes, A.: Evolutionary-aided negotiation model for bilateral bargaining in ambient intelligence domains with complex utility functions. Information Sciences 222, 25–46 (2013)
8. Kuo, P., Schroeder, R., Mahaffey, S., Bollinger, R.: Optimization of operating room allocation using linear programming techniques. J. Am. Coll. Surg. 197(6), 889–895 (2003)
9. Schumann, A., Wilson, N., Burillo, M.: Learning user preferences to maximise occupant comfort in office buildings. In: García-Pedrajas, N., Herrera, F., Fyfe, C., Benítez, J.M., Ali, M. (eds.) IEA/AIE 2010, Part I. LNCS (LNAI), vol. 6096, pp. 681–690. Springer, Heidelberg (2010)
10. Abras, S., Pesty, S., Ploix, S., Jacomino, M.: An anticipation mechanism for power management in a smart home using multi-agent systems. In: Information and Communication Technologies: From Theory to Applications, pp. 1–6. IEEE (2008)

Designing Autonomous Social Agents under the Adversarial Risk Analysis Framework

Pablo G. Esteban[1] and David Ríos Insua[2]

[1] Rey Juan Carlos University of Madrid
pablo.gomez.esteban@urjc.es
[2] Royal Academy of Sciences, Spain
david.rios@urjc.es

Abstract. We describe how the Adversarial Risk Analysis framework may be used to support the decision making of an autonomous agent which needs to interact with other agents and persons. We propose several contextualizations of the problem and suggest which is the conceptual solution in some of the proposed scenarios.

Keywords: Game Theory, Adversarial Risk Analysis, Multi-agent systems, Intelligent Agents.

1 Introduction

In [1], we have described a behavioural model for an autonomous decision agent which processes information from its sensors, facing an intelligent adversary using multi-attribute decision analysis at its core, complemented by models forecasting the decision making of the adversary. We call Adversarial Risk Analysis (ARA) to this framework, see [2]. Generally speaking, ARA views a two-person game through two coupled influence diagrams, one for the supported agent and one for the adversary. The supported agent would build an explicit model for the decision-making of the adversary. Given such model, the supported agent may simulate outcomes under it, which will draw on subjective probabilities about the adversary's beliefs, preferences, capabilities and resources. Following such approach, we avoid the standard and unrealistic game theoretic assumptions of common knowledge, through a nested hierarchy of decision analysis models. From the point of view of supporting our agent, the problem is understood as a decision analytic one, see [3], but we consider principled procedures which employ the adversarial structure to forecast the adversary's actions and the evolution of the environment surrounding both of them, therefore, embracing also adaptability: the agent performs as best as it can, given the circumstances. On doing this, the agent would forecast what the other participant thinks about him, thus starting the above mentioned hierarchy. Depending on the level the agent climbs up in such hierarchy, we would talk about a 0-level analysis, 1-level analysis and so on, borrowing the k-level thinking terminology, see [4], [5] and [6]. Our approach has a Bayesian game theoretic flavor, as in [7] and [8].

J.M. Corchado et al. (Eds.): PAAMS 2013 Workshops, CCIS 365, pp. 292–303, 2013.

This model has been implemented within an AISoy1 robot, see [9]. In this paper, we shall refer to multi-agent systems, exploring the social needs of our robotic agent, and how it handles interactions with other agents, both human and robotic ones. We have in mind four possible scenarios, shown in Fig. 1. On the top left, Fig. 1(a), we consider a single agent facing multiple adversaries (agents and users). On its right, Fig. 1(b), several agents compete in their interaction with several users. At the bottom left, several agents, each of them related with only one user, compete in a global scenario, see Fig. 1(c). Finally, bottom right, there are multiple agents cooperating to satisfy themselves and the users, see Fig. 1(d).

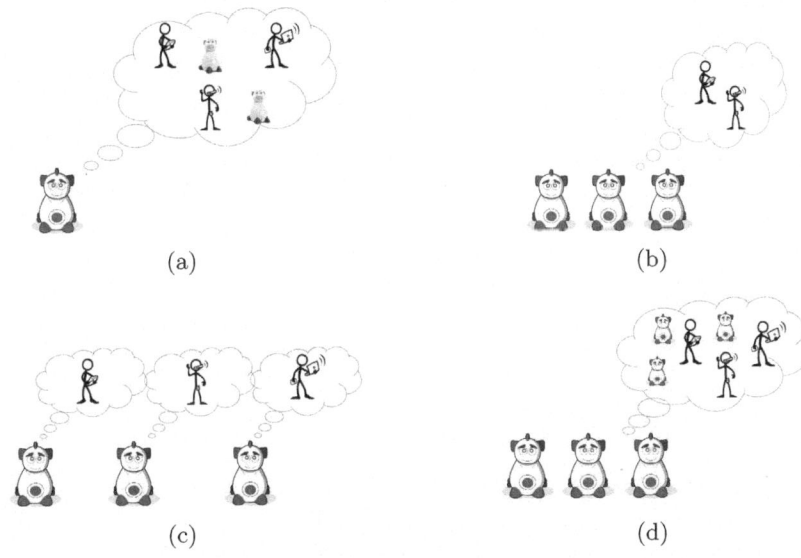

(a)   (b)

(c)   (d)

Fig. 1. Different scenarios take into account

Throughout this paper, we shall explore the interaction among different agents and users, within the scenarios outlined above. Due to space limitations we shall only describe in detail the two first scenarios (Figs. 1(a) and 1(b)), briefly introducing the third one (Fig. 1(c)). Our motivation is the design of societies of robotic agents that interact among them and with one or more users. Those agents may be used as interactive robotic pets, robotic babysitters and teaching assistants or cooperative caregivers for the elderly.

The paper is structured as follows. In Section 2, we provide the basic model for a single agent facing a single adversary. In Section 3, we consider a case in which a decision agent is identifying several users and robotic agents, and makes decisions depending on the adversary is facing, scenario (1(a)). Next, in Section 4, we define two cases of a society of competitive robots which interact with humans, scenarios (1(b)) and (1(c)). For comparative purposes, we deal with them through the standard game theoretic and the novel ARA frameworks. We remain at a conceptual level, describing the solution concepts, although we outline the required modeling. Finally, in Section 5, we end up with some discussion.

2   The Basic Model

We briefly describe, as a starting point, the model in [1] which supports the decision making of an agent A facing a user B. This model will serve as a basis for later elaborations. A and B make decisions, respectively a and b, within finite sets $\mathcal{A}$ and $\mathcal{B}$, which possibly include a *do nothing* action. They are placed within an environment E which changes with the user's actions, adopting a state e within a set $\mathcal{E}$. Essentially, we plan our agent's activities over time within the decision analytic framework, see [3], including models to forecast the adversary behaviour (Adversarial Risk Analysis) and the evolution of the environment. Note that we could view the problem within the game-theoretic framework, see [10], but with our alternative approach we avoid the much debated common knowledge assumptions, see [8] or [11].

Assume that, for computational reasons, we just forecast one period ahead based on a two period memory. We are interested in computing, at each time t,

$$p(e_t, b_t \mid a_t, (e_{t-1}, a_{t-1}, b_{t-1}), (e_{t-2}, a_{t-2}, b_{t-2})) = \qquad (1)$$
$$= p(e_t \mid a_t, b_t, (e_{t-1}, a_{t-1}, b_{t-1}), (e_{t-2}, a_{t-2}, b_{t-2})) \times$$
$$\times\ p(b_t \mid a_t, (e_{t-1}, a_{t-1}, b_{t-1}), (e_{t-2}, a_{t-2}, b_{t-2}))\ ,$$

which forecast the reaction of the user and the evolution of the environment, given the agent action, and the recent history. This constitutes the adversarial part of the model. The first term in (1) will be simplified to

$$p(e_t \mid b_t, e_{t-1}, e_{t-2})\ ,$$

which we call the *environment model*, thus assuming that the environment is fully under control by the user. The second term in (1) will be simplified to

$$p(b_t \mid a_t, b_{t-1}, b_{t-2})\ . \qquad (2)$$

The agent will maintain two models, M_i with $i \in \{1, 2\}$, in relation with (2). The first one, M_1, describes the evolution of the user by himself, assuming that he is not affected by the agent's actions. We call it the *user's model* and describe it through

$$p(b_t \mid b_{t-1}, b_{t-2})\ .$$

The second one, M_2, refers to the user's reactions to the agent's actions, which we describe through

$$p(b_t \mid a_t)\ .$$

We call it the *classical conditioning model*, with the agent possibly conditioning the user. We combine both models to recover (2), through model averaging, see [12]:

$$p(b_t \mid a_t, b_{t-1}, b_{t-2}) =$$

$$= p(M_1)\, p(b_t \mid b_{t-1}, b_{t-2}) + p(M_2)\, p(b_t \mid a_t) \ ,$$

where $p(M_i)$ denotes the probability that the agent gives to model M_i, with $p(M_1) + p(M_2) = 1$, $p(M_i) \geq 0$.

Assume that the agent faces multiple consequences $c = (c_1, c_2, \ldots, c_l)$, that will be of the form $c_i(a_t, b_t, e_t)$, $i = 1, \ldots, l$. We shall assume that they are evaluated through a multi-attribute utility function, see [3]. Specifically, we adopt an additive form

$$u(c_1, c_2, \ldots, c_l) = \sum_{i=1}^{l} w_i u_i(c_i) \ ,$$

with $w_i \geq 0$, $\sum_{i=1}^{l} w_i = 1$, where u_i represents the robot's i-th component utility function and w_i represent the corresponding utility weight.

Our agent aims at maximizing the predictive expected utility, i.e. implements the alternative solving

$$\max_{a_t \in \mathcal{A}} \psi(a_t) = \int \int u(c(a_t, b_t, e_t)) \times [p(e_t|b_t, e_{t-1}, e_{t-2})\, p(b_t|a_t, b_{t-1}, b_{t-2})]\, db_t de_t \ .$$

Planning $(r + 1)$ instants ahead follows a similar parth, but may turn out to be very expensive computationally.

For details on the implementation of this model, including learning, forecasting and decision making, see [1].

3   Supporting an Agent Facing Several Agents and Users

In this Section, we extend our basic model to a case in which the agent faces several adversaries, which may be agents or users, see Fig. 1(a). As an example, assume that our agent (A) is supporting two children (B_1 and B_2) in their daily school assignments, so that, A should be able to identify who is who, to evaluate how correctly each of them is working, and deliver the corresponding score and support.

For that purpose, the agent must be able to identify the adversary he is facing and will have different forecasting models in relation with each of the known opponents. We assume that the agent will face just one adversary at each of the time steps of the scheme described in Fig. 2.

Using some identification method, the agent will guess who is the user/agent it is dealing with and adapt its behaviour accordingly. The difference between facing another agent or a user would essentially be the set of actions available for the corresponding adversary forecasting model. Adversary identification is not a core element of our work. For that purpose we could base the identification of the opponent B_x on eigenface recognition algorithms, see [13] for a face recognition survey, and implement it with the OpenCv libraries, see [14], as we have done.

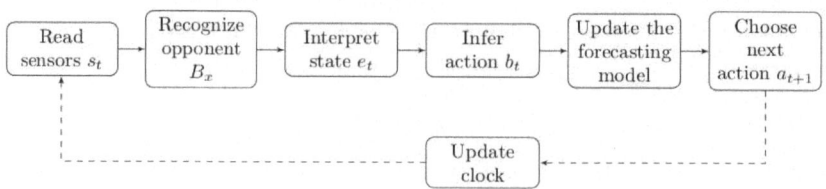

Fig. 2. Agent loop with advesary recognition

We assume that the user is that which maximizes $p(B_x|D_t)$, after obtaining an image of the face of the participant. Our agent will not make any difference among robotic agents as there is no physical difference among them, because we assume they are all robots of the same type.

3.1   Model

As in Section 2, our agent A makes decisions within a finite set $\mathcal{A}$. In this case, there are r adversaries $B_1, \ldots, B_r$ which interact with A. An index x will be used to identify the corresponding adversary. As B_x may be an agent or a user, he makes decisions within the set $\mathcal{A}$, in case it is an agent, or a set $\mathcal{B}$ that will designate the set of available actions to the users, which we assume are the same for all of them.

The agent decision model is similar to that in Section 2. However in this case, the forecasting model is conditional on the guessed adversary, so that (1) becomes

$$p(e_t, b_t \mid a_t, (e_{t-1}, a_{t-1}, b_{t-1}), (e_{t-2}, a_{t-2}, b_{t-2}), B_x) =$$
$$= p(e_t \mid b_t, a_t, (e_{t-1}, a_{t-1}, b_{t-1}), (e_{t-2}, a_{t-2}, b_{t-2}), B_x) \times$$
$$\times p(b_t \mid a_t, (e_{t-1}, a_{t-1}, b_{t-1}), (e_{t-2}, a_{t-2}, b_{t-2}), B_x) \ . \tag{3}$$

Using a similar decomposition, now

$$p(e_t \mid b_t, a_t, (e_{t-1}, a_{t-1}, b_{t-1}), (e_{t-2}, a_{t-2}, b_{t-2}), B_x) = p(e_t \mid b_t, e_{t-1}, e_{t-2}, B_x) \ , \tag{4}$$

and

$$p(b_t \mid a_t, (e_{t-1}, a_{t-1}, b_{t-1}), (e_{t-2}, a_{t-2}, b_{t-2}), B_x) = p(b_t \mid a_t, b_{t-1}, b_{t-2}, B_x) \ .$$

We should note that, when B_x is a robotic agent, the environment model (4) would become $p(e_t \mid e_{t-1}, e_{t-2}, B_x)$, because the agent's action does not affect the environment.

Again, we view this as a problem of model averaging, for each agent B_x:

$$p(b_t \mid a_t, b_{t-1}, b_{t-2}, B_x) =$$

$$= p(M_1|B_x)\, p(b_t \mid b_{t-1}, b_{t-2}, B_x) + p(M_2|B_x)\, p(b_t \mid a_t, B_x) \ ,$$

where $p(M_i|B_x)$ denotes the probability that the agent gives to model M_i, assuming that the adversary is B_x, with $p(M_1|B_x)+p(M_2|B_x) = 1$, $p(M_i|B_x) \geq 0$. Finally, we shall use model averaging over users, defined through

$$p(e_t, b_t \mid a_t, (e_{t-1}, a_{t-1}, b_{t-1}), (e_{t-2}, a_{t-2}, b_{t-2})) =$$

$$= \sum_{B_x} \left[p(e_t \mid b_t, e_{t-1}, e_{t-2}, B_x) \times p(b_t \mid a_t, b_{t-1}, b_{t-2}, B_x) \times p(B_x) \right] \; .$$

The core of the *classical conditioning model* and the *adversary's model* remains as before. In our implementation, we use two matrix-beta models, see [15], to store the corresponding data, a $n \times m$ matrix for the classical conditioning model and a $n \times n \times n$ matrix for the adversary's model, as the set $\mathcal{A}$ had m elements and set $\mathcal{B}$ had n. As the robot faces users and agents, the size of the data structures would be different depending on the type of adversary it is dealing with. This corresponds to a 0-level implementation in that we only appeal to past behaviour of the adversary, possibly as a response to our previous behaviour.

We include also some details about the preference model. As described in [1], each agent aims at satisfying five objectives which are: *being charged, being secure, being taken into account, being accepted* and *being updated*. The first and the last objectives would remain unvaried within the multiagent model, but the other three should be extended to face several users and agents. Generally speaking, those objectives and subobjectives which refer to inference of user's actions, should take into account the actions of each user within the scenario, specifically,

$$u_{21}(attack) = \begin{cases} 1, & \text{if none of the users attacked} \\ 0, & \text{otherwise} \; , \end{cases}$$

and

$$u_{41}(play) = \begin{cases} 1, & \text{if the robot inferred a user or another agent} \\ & \quad \text{playing around} \\ 0, & \text{otherwise} \; . \end{cases}$$

Some subobjectives ought to be extended to include agents' actions as well as users' actions, as it is the case of:

$$u_{313}(asked\ to\ play) = \begin{cases} 1, & \text{if the robot is asked to play by the user} \\ & \quad \text{or by another agent} \\ 0, & \text{otherwise} \; , \end{cases}$$

where *asked to play* refers to detecting an order to play from the user, including the game's title, or a request for playing by another agent (action a_8: *ask for playing*). For additional details, see [1]. The expected utility model would remain the same as in Section 2.

4   Supporting an Agent Competing with Other Agents

We deal now with two competing scenarios in which agents interact with one or more users. In the first case, several agents compete among them to be selected by the users, so that the competition is among the agents. In the second case, each agent interacts with its own user forming a team. Each tandem agent-user will compete against the other participating teams. For comparison, both cases are solved computing the corresponding Nash Equilibria (NE) and under the ARA framework. We assume that there is communication among the agents. Moreover, under the NE framework, we shall assume that there is a computerised trusted third party (CTTP) that would handle the conflict, computing the NE when needed. This may be an external computer or one of the robotic agents that could adopt the role of trusted party. Working under the ARA framework we shall not make such assumptions, but, for convenience, we shall allow agents to communicate.

There will be two different types of communication: among the participating robotic agents and each of them with the CTTP. The agents would be periodically transferring information to interact with each other. Whenever a conflict arises, participating agents would send their beliefs, matrices and parameters, as well as their utilities to the CTTP, who would compute the required solution and send back the corresponding strategies to each participating agent.

For both models, the preference model and the expected utility model would be the same as in Section 3.

4.1   Supporting an Agent within a Society of Competing Agents

In this case, several agents compete among them to accomplish an identical goal, involving users in the scene, see Fig. 1(b). As an example, consider a case in which there are three robots (A, B, C) and two kids (X, Y) in a scene. The kids want to play "Simon says". They would like to have at least one more player to do so. All agents want to play with the kids, but just one of them will play. The robotic agents would compete to be chosen as the third player, being nicer, funnier or whatever, in order to be selected.

Model. We have several agents, under a competing attitude, facing simultaneously one or several users within an environment. To fix the discussion, assume that, as in the example, we have three agents (A, B, C) and two users (X, Y). Agents will perform actions a_{A_t}, a_{B_t} and a_{C_t}, respectively, whereas users will perform b_{X_t} and b_{Y_t} actions, respectively.

We use again a multi-attribute utility function. However, in this case the consequences will depend on the actions of all agents and users:

$$c_i(a_{A_t}, a_{B_t}, a_{C_t}, b_{X_t}, b_{Y_t}, e_t) \ ,$$

for $i = 1, \ldots, l$, where e_t is the environmental state as in Section 2. The utility that the agents will obtain will be, respectively:

$$u_A(a_{A_t}, a_{B_t}, a_{C_t}, b_{X_t}, b_{Y_t}, e_t), \quad u_B(a_{A_t}, a_{B_t}, a_{C_t}, b_{X_t}, b_{Y_t}, e_t),$$

$$u_C(a_{A_t}, a_{B_t}, a_{C_t}, b_{X_t}, b_{Y_t}, e_t) \ .$$

We next describe the forescasting model for agent A,

$$p_A(a_{B_t}, a_{C_t}, b_{X_t}, b_{Y_t}, e_t \mid \tag{5}$$

$$\mid a_{A_t}, (a_{A_{t-1}}, a_{B_{t-1}}, a_{C_{t-1}}, b_{X_{t-1}}, b_{Y_{t-1}}, e_{t-1}), (a_{A_{t-2}}, a_{B_{t-2}}, a_{C_{t-2}}, b_{X_{t-2}}, b_{Y_{t-2}}, e_{t-2})) \ .$$

Assuming that e_t remains exclusively under the users' control, (5) will be decomposed as:

$$p_A(e_t \mid b_{X_t}, b_{Y_t}, e_{t-1}, e_{t-2}) \times p_A(a_{B_t}, a_{C_t}, b_{X_t}, b_{Y_t} \mid$$

$$\mid a_{A_t}, (a_{A_{t-1}}, a_{B_{t-1}}, a_{C_{t-1}}, b_{X_{t-1}}, b_{Y_{t-1}}, e_{t-1}), (a_{A_{t-2}}, a_{B_{t-2}}, a_{C_{t-2}}, b_{X_{t-2}}, b_{Y_{t-2}}, e_{t-2})) \ .$$

Note that in the scheme described in Fig. 2, we assumed that each agent chooses its action depending on the action performed by the user, so that when several agents face the same user, the actions performed by them would be considered simultaneous. For that reason, when our agent A is facing another agent, we assume that the forecasted action of the robotic agent will depend only on the actions previously perfomed by itself and the action of the agent A. Users' actions will depend on all agent's actions. Equation (5) then becomes:

$$p_A(e_t \mid b_{X_t}, b_{Y_t}, e_{t-1}, e_{t-2}) \times p_A(a_{B_t} \mid a_{B_{t-1}}, a_{B_{t-2}}, a_{A_{t-1}}) \times \tag{6}$$

$$\times \, p_A(a_{C_t} \mid a_{C_{t-1}}, a_{C_{t-2}}, a_{A_{t-1}}) \times p_A(b_{X_t} \mid a_{A_t}, a_{B_t}, a_{C_t}, b_{X_{t-1}} b_{X_{t-2}}) \times$$

$$\times \, p_A(b_{Y_t} \mid a_{A_t}, a_{B_t}, a_{C_t}, b_{Y_{t-1}}, b_{Y_{t-2}}) \ .$$

Finally, we find out that our forecasting models for agent A are: the first term of (6) (the *environmental model*), and the rest of (6) which is the model to forecast the adversaries' actions. This second term in (6) will be decomposed in the *adversary models* and the *classical conditioning model*, similarly to what we did in Section 2. The adversary models would be those in which the forecasted action depends on the evolution of their own behaviour as, e.g.:

$$p_A(a_{B_t} \mid a_{B_{t-1}}, a_{B_{t-2}}) \text{ and } p_A(b_{X_t} \mid b_{X_{t-1}}, b_{X_{t-2}}) \ .$$

The classical conditioning models would be those reflecting the reaction to our agent's behaviour as, e.g.:

$$p_A(a_{B_t} \mid a_{A_{t-1}}) \text{ and } p_A(b_{X_t} \mid a_{A_t}) \ .$$

They are combined through model averaging techniques. Forecasting other agents' actions shall be defined as forecasting the user's actions in Section 2, evaluating the evolution of its own behaviour and how reactive is to agent A's actions:

$$p_A(a_{B_t} \mid a_{B_{t-1}}, a_{B_{t-2}}, a_{A_{t-1}}) = \tag{7}$$

$$= p(M_1^B) p_A(a_{B_t} \mid a_{B_{t-1}}, a_{B_{t-2}}) + p(M_2^B) p_A(a_{B_t} \mid a_{A_{t-1}}) \ ,$$

with $\sum_i p(M_i^B) = 1$, $p(M_i^B) \geq 0$, and, similarly, for $p_A(a_{C_t} \mid a_{C_{t-1}}, a_{C_{t-2}}, a_{A_{t-1}})$. In this case, forecasting the users' actions would be extended to include the reaction of the user to the actions of every agent:

$$p_A(b_{X_t} \mid a_{A_t}, a_{B_t}, a_{C_t}, b_{X_{t-1}} b_{X_{t-2}}) = p(M_1^X) p_A(b_{X_t} \mid b_{X_{t-1}}, b_{X_{t-2}}) +$$
$$+ p(M_2^X) p_A(b_{X_t} \mid a_{A_t}) + p(M_3^X) p_A(b_{X_t} \mid a_{B_t}) + p(M_4^X) p_A(b_{X_t} \mid a_{C_t}) \ ,$$

with $\sum_i p(M_i^X) = 1$, $p(M_i^X) \geq 0$, and, similarly, for $p_A(b_{Y_t} \mid a_{A_t}, a_{B_t}, a_{C_t}, b_{Y_{t-1}}, b_{Y_{t-2}})$. Note that

$$p(M_i^X \mid D_t) = \frac{p(D_t \mid M_i^X) p(M_i^X)}{\sum_{i=1}^4 p(D_t \mid M_i^X) p(M_i^X)}, \quad i = 1, \ldots, 4 \ .$$

Computing Nash Equilibria. As we are in a competitive scenario, we are dealing with selfish agents so that each agent will aim at maximizing its expected utility. For example, when A implements a_{A_t}, and the other agents implement a_{B_t} and a_{C_t}, agent A's expected utility would be:

$$\psi_A(a_{A_t}, a_{B_t}, a_{C_t}) = \int \int \int u_A(a_{A_t}, a_{B_t}, a_{C_t}, b_{X_t}, b_{Y_t}, e_t) \times$$
$$\times \left[p_A(b_{X_t} \mid a_{A_t}, a_{B_t}, a_{C_t}, b_{X_{t-1}} b_{X_{t-2}}) \times p_A(b_{Y_t} \mid a_{A_t}, a_{B_t}, a_{C_t}, b_{Y_{t-1}} b_{Y_{t-2}}) \times \right.$$
$$\left. \times p_A(e_t \mid b_{X_t}, b_{Y_t}, e_{t-1}, e_{t-2}) \right] \ db_{X_t} db_{Y_t} de_t \ ,$$

and, analogously, for the other agents. As we pointed out above, we assume that a CTTP would play the role of a trusted party solving the existing conflicts, and there will be communication among the agents. Each agent would send its beliefs, matrices, parameters and utilities, so that, in our example, the CTTP will have available ψ_A, ψ_B and ψ_C which would be common knowledge. Then, the CTTP would compute the Nash Equilibria with methods described, e.g. in [16] or [17].

ARA Solving agents Let us write the problem from the ARA framework point of view. In this case, communication is not required. Under this framework, we are supporting one of the agents (say, agent A), to make a decision facing several users (X and Y) and other agents (B and C). The agent will aim at maximizing its expected utility based on forecasts of the other agents defined through

$$\max_{a_{A_t}} \ \psi_A(a_{A_t}) = \int \int \psi_A(a_{A_t}, a_{B_t}, a_{C_t}) \times \left[p_A(a_{B_t} \mid a_{B_{t-1}}, a_{B_{t-2}}, a_{A_{t-1}}) \times \right.$$
$$\left. \times p_A(a_{C_t} \mid a_{C_{t-1}}, a_{C_{t-2}}, a_{A_{t-1}}) \right] \ da_{B_t} da_{C_t} \ ,$$

where the relevant probability models were described in (7). In a 0-level approach, we may use matrix-beta models to implement these.

4.2   Agent Supporting a User within a Competitive Society of Users

In this case, each agent is interacting with its own user, supporting her within a competition against other user-agent teams, see Fig. 1(c). As an example, consider a case in which three teams are involved, couples robot A - child X, robot B - child Y and robot C - child Z. Each of the teams work on school assignments willing to be chosen as the favourite by the teacher and get the highest grade. Each agent shall support its own user in making decisions, forecasting what the other agents would do. Assumptions similar to those in the previous Section will be made here.

Model. We will have several agents, under a competing attitude, supporting simultaneously their corresponding user within an environment. To fix the discussion, assume that we have three agents (A, B, C) and three users (X, Y, Z) forming agent-user teams. Agents will perform actions a_{A_t}, a_{B_t} and a_{C_t}, whereas users will perform b_{X_t}, b_{Y_t} and b_{Z_t} actions.

We use again a multi-attribute utility function. In this case, the consequences will depend on the actions of all agents and the supported user. The consequences that agent A would face when it is supporting user X are:

$$c_A(a_{A_t}, a_{B_t}, a_{C_t}, b_{X_t}, e_t) \ ,$$

where e_t is the environmental state, as described in Section 2. The utilities that the agents will obtain in our example will be, respectively:

$$u_A(a_{A_t}, a_{B_t}, a_{C_t}, b_{X_t}, e_t), \quad u_B(a_{A_t}, a_{B_t}, a_{C_t}, b_{Y_t}, e_t),$$

$$u_C(a_{A_t}, a_{B_t}, a_{C_t}, b_{Z_t}, e_t) \ .$$

The forescasting model for agent A would be

$$p_A(a_{D_t}, a_{C_t}, b_{X_t}, c_t \ | \tag{8}$$
$$| \ a_{A_t}, (a_{A_{t-1}}, a_{B_{t-1}}, a_{C_{t-1}}, b_{X_{t-1}}, e_{t-1}), (a_{A_{t-2}}, a_{B_{t-2}}, a_{C_{t-2}}, b_{X_{t-2}}, e_{t-2})) \ .$$

Simplifications and assumptions related to the forecasting models would be analogous to those of the previous case. Equation (8) ends up decomposed in:

$$p_A(e_t \ | \ b_{X_t}, e_{t-1}, e_{t-2}) \ ,$$

the *environmental model*, and

$$p_A(a_{B_t} \ | \ a_{B_{t-1}}, a_{B_{t-2}}, a_{A_t}) \times p_A(a_{C_t} \ | \ a_{C_{t-1}}, a_{C_{t-2}}, a_{A_t}) \times \tag{9}$$
$$\times \ p_A(b_{X_t} \ | \ a_{A_t}, b_{X_{t-1}} b_{X_{t-2}}) \ ,$$

the model to forecast the adversary's action, which will be decomposed in the *adversary model* and the *classical conditioning model*, as we did in the previous scenario, then combined, through model averaging techniques.

Computing Nash Equilibria. Again, we are dealing with selfish agents so that each agent will aim at maximizing expected utility. Agent A's expected utility will be

$$\psi_A(a_{A_t}, a_{B_t}, a_{C_t}) = \int \int u_A(a_{A_t}, a_{B_t}, a_{C_t}, b_{X_t}, e_t) \times$$
$$\times \left[p_A(b_{X_t} \ | \ a_{A_t}, b_{X_{t-1}} b_{X_{t-2}}) \times p_A(e_t \ | \ b_{X_t}, e_{t-1}, e_{t-2}) \right] \ db_{X_t} de_t \ ,$$

and, similarly, for the other agents. As in the previous scenario, we assume that a CTTP would solve the existing conflicts, and there will be communication among the agents, so that ψ_A, ψ_B and ψ_C would have common knowledge. The Nash Equilibria may be computed as described in the previous scenario.

ARA Solving agents From the ARA perspective, we are supporting one of the agents (agent A) facing his own user (X) and other agents (B and C), so that, it shall be willing to maximize its expected utility, defined through

$$\max_{a_{A_t}} \psi_A(a_{A_t}) = \int \int \psi_A(a_{A_t}, a_{B_t}, a_{C_t}) \times \left[p_A(a_{B_t} \mid a_{B_{t-1}}, a_{B_{t-2}}, a_{A_t}) \times \right.$$
$$\left. \times\, p_A(a_{C_t} \mid a_{C_{t-1}}, a_{C_{t-2}}, a_{A_t}) \right]\, da_{B_t} da_{C_t}\;.$$

The relevant probability models are described in (9). As before, we use matrix-beta models for their 0-level implementation.

5   Discussion

We have described different scenarios in which a decision agent is facing several adversaries (human and robotic ones).

As future work, we have two more scenarios to develop. Within the first one, we aim at supporting a society of agents, where n agents would like to behave cooperatively towards one or several users, see Fig. 1(d). As an example, suppose three robotic agents that want to support their children with their corresponding weekly school assignments, trying to emulate a cooperative environment in the school. They are under a cooperative attitude, so that they would look for helping the child together to find the best solution that satisfy their common goal. Within the other scenario, moving from the competing towards cooperating attitude shall be studied: agents will then modify their behaviour depending on their experience. To do such a thing, we should define two types of behaviour: selfish and cooperative. Based on certain parameters, the agent would move from a cooperative attitude to a competitive one, or viceversa. Note also, that the ARA models proposed here correspond to 0-level thinking and we could explore 1-level and 2-level thinking ideas.

The field of cognitive processes has recently shown that emotions may have a direct impact on decision-making processes, see e.g. [18]. Advances in areas such as affective decision making [19], neuroeconomics [20] and affective computing [21] are based on this principle. Following this, a potential future work, concerning these models will be addressed towards providing a model for an autonomous agent that makes decisions influenced by emotional factors when interacting with humans and other agents. Our aim with this would be to make interactions between humans and agents more fluent and natural.

Acknowledgments. Research supported by grants from the MICINN project RIESGOS, the RIESGOS-CM project and the INNPACTO project HAUS. We are grateful to discussion with Diego García, from AiSoy Robotics S.L., Jesus Ríos and David Banks.

References

1. Rázuri, J.G., Esteban, P.G., Insua, D.R.: An adversarial risk analysis model for an autonomous imperfect decision agent. In: Guy, T.V., Kárný, M., Wolpert, D.H. (eds.) Decision Making and Imperfection. SCI, vol. 474, pp. 165–190. Springer, Heidelberg (2013)
2. Ríos Insua, D., Ríos, J., Banks, D.: Adversarial risk analysis. Journal of the American Statistical Association 104(486), 841–854 (2009)
3. Clemen, R.T., Reilly, T.: Making Hard Decisions with Decision Tools. Duxbury, Pacific Grove (2004)
4. Stahl, D.O., Wilson, P.W.: On players models of other players: Theory and experimental evidence. Games and Economic Behavior 10(1), 218–254 (1995)
5. Banks, D., Petralia, F., Wang, S.: Adversarial risk analysis: Borel games. Applied Stochastic Models in Business and Industry 27, 72–86 (2011)
6. Kadane, J.B.: Adversarial risk analysis: What's new, what isn't?: Discussion of adversarial risk analysis: Borel games. Journal Applied Stochastic Models in Business and Industry 27(2), 87–88 (2011)
7. Kadane, J.B., Larkey, P.D.: Subjective probability and the theory of games. Management Science 28(2), 113–120 (1982)
8. Raiffa, H.: Negotiation Analysis: The Science and Art of Collaborative Decision Making. Press of Harvard University Press, Cambridge (2007)
9. AISoyRobotics (2010), http://www.aisoy.es
10. Aliprantis, C., Chakrabarti, S.: Games and Decision Making. Oxford University Press (2010)
11. Lippman, S., McCardle, K.: Embedded nash bargaining: Risk aversion and impatience. Decision Analysis 9, 31–41 (2012)
12. Hoeting, J., Madigan, D., Raftery, A., Volinsky, C.: Bayesian model averaging: A tutorial. Statistical Science 4, 382–417 (1999)
13. Zhao, W., Chellappa, R., Phillips, P.J., Rosenfeld, A.: Face recognition: A literature survey. ACM Comput. Surv. 35(4), 399–458 (2003)
14. Hewitt, R.: Seeing With OpenCV, Part 4: Face Recognition With Eigenface (2007)
15. Ríos Insua, D., Ruggeri, F., Wiper, M.: Bayesian Analysis of Stochastic Process Models. Wiley (2012)
16. Nisan, N., Roughgarden, T., Tardos, E., Vazirani, V.V.: Algorithmic Game Theory. Cambridge University Press (2007)
17. Menache, I., Ozdaglar, A.: Network Games: Theory, Models, and Dynamics. Morgan and Claypool Publishers (2011)
18. Busemeyer, J.R., Dimperio, E., Jessup, R.K.: Integrating emotional processes into decision-making models, pp. 213–229. Oxford University Press, New York (2006)
19. Loewenstein, G., Lerner, J.S.: The role of affect in decision making. In: Davidson, R., Scherer, K., Goldsmith, H. (eds.) Handbook of Affective Science, pp. 619–642. Oxford University Press, Oxford (2003)
20. Glimcher, P.W., Camerer, C., Poldrack, R.A., Fehr, E.: Neuroeconomics: Decision Making and the Brain. Academic Press (2008)
21. Picard, R.W.: Affective Computing. MIT Press, Cambridge (1997)

Extracting Behavioural Patterns
from a Negotiation Game

Marco Gomes, Tiago Oliveira, Davide Carneiro, Paulo Novais, and José Neves

Department of Informatics, University of Minho
pg18373@alunos.uminho.pt,
{dcarneiro,toliveira,pjon,jneves}@di.uminho.pt

Abstract. The work presented focuses not only on the behavioural patterns that influence the outcome of a negotiation, but also on the discovery of ways to predict the type of conflict used in the process and the stress levels of the actors. After setting up an experimental intelligent environment provided with sensors to capture behavioural and contextual information, a set of relevant data was collected and analysed, with the underlying objective of using the behavioural patterns (obtained by statistical/probabilistic methods) as a basis to design and present plans and suggestions to the associated participants. In sooth, these proposals may influence in a positive way the course and outcome of a negotiation task in many aspects. This work highlights the importance of knowledge in negotiation, as in other social forms of interaction, providing also some new insights for informed decision support in situations in which uncertainty and conflict may be present.

Keywords: Intelligent Environments, Online Dispute Resolution, Negotiation, Context-Aware.

1 Introduction

Negotiation [1] is a collaborative and informal process by means of which parties communicate and, without external influence, try to reach an outcome that may satisfy both. This process is widely used in the most different fields, including legal proceedings, divorces, parental disputes or even hostage affairs. It may be also used as a mechanism to solve disputes without recurring to the traditional judicial process, i.e., litigation in courts. Undoubtedly, it stands for a highly interdependent process in which each party continuously incorporates information from the other party(ies) to devise answers that might lead to the resolution of the conflict at hand, in the quest for understanding the process through which conflicts are settled. In this particular case, negotiation is incorporated in Online Dispute Resolution (ODR) software and used in a technological context, either supported by technology or under a virtual computational environment. Indeed, being able to capture behaviour patterns performed within a negotiation is very relevant to drive the process. Therefore, modelling this human activity must take into consideration the dynamic, adaptive, and interactive setting of the virtual computational environment in which the negotiation (related to ODR) occurs.

To acquire this kind of contextual and behavioural information, a set of models was developed. Indeed, the information from physical sensors, named low-level context, may

J.M. Corchado et al. (Eds.): PAAMS 2013 Workshops, CCIS 365, pp. 304–315, 2013.

be meaningless, trivial, vulnerable to small changes, or uncertain [2]. A way to mitigate this problem is the extraction of high level context information from raw sensor values [3] in order to attain descriptions of human behaviour that may be relevant to a negotiation. Such specifications include the negotiation style or strategy and the stress state of the parties (when facing a negotiation process). To assess this kind of information the models introduced in [4] were used to classify the negotiation/conflict resolution styles along with a multimodal approach to identify and classify a party's stress progress during a negotiation in a contextually rich and dynamic environment [5].

This work illustrates the process used to extract behavioural patterns from data gathered in a negotiation, performed within an intelligent environment, using game theory. In particular, it focuses on the analysis of behavioural data related to the estimation of stress levels and negotiation/conflict approaches of the actors. The intention is to enrich the knowledge about user states in negotiation processes for the further development of a reasoning system that will generate proposals that may show the way to successful negotiation outcomes.

2   Systematic Behavioral Analysis

The behaviour of a living system includes all the activities that the system would not fulfil if it were not living, with *living* being interpreted either in the classical sense or referring, for example, to a virtual computational machine.

These activities are always the response of the system to some stimuli, or lack of them. Stimuli are said to be internal, when they are originated inside the *body* of the system (e.g. thought, pain, change of state). They are said to be external when originated outside of the *body* of the system and perceived by some receptor cell (e.g. change in the temperature, visual change in the environment, reception of a given message).

The system may be conscious or unconscious of the perceived stimuli. Despite this, the system may respond. This response is said to be voluntary when the system undergoes some reasoning process before acting or involuntary when the system reacts in pre-determined ways, without reasoning about it.

Nothing characterizes an individual better than his/her behaviour. Knowing how an individual reacts to stimuli allows one to foresee their future states. On the other hand, controlling stimuli may allow one to control any individual. This is the way to behaviourism. Therefore, in psychology, the behaviour is influenced an studied in order to address behavioural issues of an individual, ranging from psychological disorders to other matters, such as smoking habits or eating disorders, just to name a few.

In this work, the interest is on knowing how a given party acts in response to specific scenarios (e.g. how does a party behave when under stress or during a negotiation). Introducing the figure of a mediator with access to this information, he/she will be able to make better decisions. As an example, if a mediator knows that a given party generally assumes a highly competitive style during a negotiation, he may try to show that party that such a style might be an obstacle for a successful outcome.

The approach followed focuses on acquiring context information that allows to characterize the behaviour of the human users of the negotiation tool. Moreover, it does it in an absolutely transparent and non-invasive way, i.e., rather than relying on traditional self-reporting mechanisms such as questionnaires in order to infer behaviours, it analyses the actions of the parties, in real-time.

In order to implement such processes, procedures used in social science were analysed. In particular, an algorithm defined by [6] was followed. It provides a complete description of the procedures and principles required to identify the behaviour sources and to perceive not only the relationship between sources and behaviours but how to adjust them in order to influence the doings as preferred.

According to [6], all behavioral research should include:

1. At least one participant;
2. At least one behaviour (which stands for the dependent variable);
3. At least one setting or environment;
4. A system for measuring the behaviour and ongoing visual analysis of data;
5. At least one treatment or intervention condition;
6. Manipulations of the independent variable so that its effects on the dependent one may be quantitatively or qualitatively analysed; and
7. An intervention that will benefit the participant in some way.

The conditions for performing the experiment included the following: ten individuals participated in the study; the behaviour under consideration was the individual's conflict handling style; the environment of the experiment was the Intelligent Systems Lab, at the University of Minho; a system for measuring the behaviour in real-time was developed (it allows one to grasp the evolution of the conflict handling in real-time); the intervention condition denotes that one or more parties evidence negative conflict handling styles (e.g. competitive, avoiding) and should be guided in a proper way, i.e., by letting them know the potential consequences of particular decisions in conflict styles. It is expected that the participants will benefit from this kind of intervention, in the sense that, by improving their negotiation behaviour, the process is more likely to succeed.

3   An Intelligent Environment to Extract Behavioral Information

The variety of user types that can be involved in each Intelligent Environment (IE), and the multitude of potential objectives of each particular environment demands an exhaustive analysis of all components to be included. Therefore, an intelligent environment with diverse devices and functionalities was built, aiming to provide the user's context and state of information to the applications being used. In this case, the developed prototype was in the area of Online Dispute Resolution (ODR).

3.1   Assessing the Level of Stress

In order to assess the level of stress of the parties, a group of devices is considered in the user-area network (Fig. 1). The main requirement when selecting the devices is that they have to provide as much information about the user environment as possible. Moreover, the user has to feel comfortable with them. In that sense, the selected devices are more or less common nowadays; so they do not represent a drawback for the user. Table 1 briefly describes each device and the main characteristics of interest.

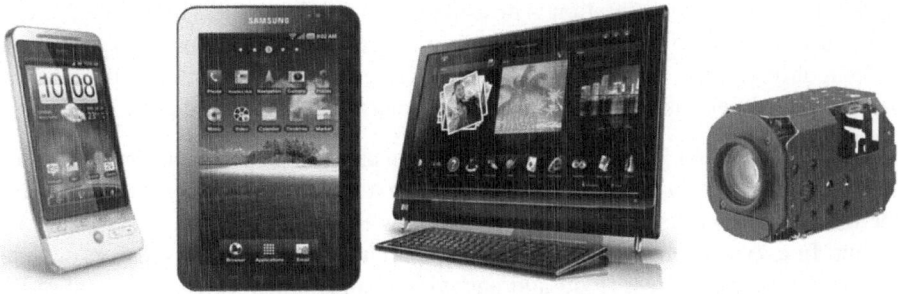

Fig. 1. Devices used to implement the described functionalities

Table 1. Brief description of the functionalities of the devices that constitute the environment

Device	Brief description	Main features
HP Touchsmart	All-in-one PC	touchscreen, web cam, large screen
Samsung Galaxy Tab	Tablet PC	touchscreen, web cam, accelerometer, relatively large screen, mobile, Android OS
HTC PDAs	Smartphones	touchscreen, camera, accelerometer, mobile, Android OS
Sony FCB-EX780BP	25x Super HAD PAL Color Block Camera with External Sync	25x Optical Zoom, Image stabilizer, Day/Night Mode, Privacy Zone Masking

The focus is on devices capable of acquiring data about the behaviour of the users that can be related to stress. The following sources of information (from now on designated sensors), acquired from the respective devices, are considered:

- Touch pattern - the touch pattern represents the way in which a user touches the device and represents a variation of intensity over a period of time. This information is acquired from touchscreens with support for touch intensity.
- Touch accuracy - a comparison between touches in active controls versus touches in passive areas (e.g. without controls, empty areas) in which there is no sense in touching. This information is acquired from touchscreens.
- Touch intensity - the intensity of the touch represents the amount of force that the user is putting into the touch. It is analyzed in terms of the maximum, minimum and mean intensity of each touch. This information is acquired from touchscreens.
- Touch duration - this represents the time span between the beginning and the end of the touch event. This data is acquired from devices with touchscreens.
- Amount of movement - the amount of movement represents how and how much the user is moving inside the environment. An estimation of the amount of movement from the video camera is built. The image processing stack uses the principles established by [7] and uses image difference techniques to calculate the amount of movement between two consecutive frames [8].

- Acceleration - the acceleration is measured from accelerometers in mobile devices. It is useful for building an estimation of how much the user is moving and how he is doing it (e.g. is the user having sudden movements?). Moreover, information from the accelerometer is used to support the estimation of the intensity of touch.

The stress models used in this work were built in a previous experiment. The collection of the data was organized in two phases. In a first phase, participants were required to perform specific tasks through the interaction with the devices in a stress-free environment. In a second phase, they performed similar tasks subject to stressors such as the vibration of the devices, loud and annoying sounds, unexpected behaviors of the devices, among others.

The empirical data gathered in both phases about the participant's interaction patterns and physical response was synchronized and transformed/normalized to allow its joint analysis. The participants of the proposed experiment were volunteer students and professors from our institution. 19 male and female individuals participated in the experiment aged between 20 and 57. All these individuals are familiar with the technological devices used thus the interaction with them was not an obstacle.

The data gathered was analyzed in order to determine statistically significant differences between phase 1 and phase 2 of the data collection. Measures of central tendency and variability were calculated for all variables of interest. The Mann-Whitney-Wilcoxon Statistical test was used to test whether there are actual differences in the distributions of the data. A 0.05 level of significance was considered. The data analysis was performed using Wolfram Mathematica®, Version 8.0.

Based on this analysis of the data we were able to determine which parameters, for each individual, were effectively affected by stress. Using this knowledge, we developed personalized models for stress estimation in real time. Moreover, a more generic model was also developed taking into consideration the data of all the participants. This generic model can be applied in the cases in which a personalized one is not available. The whole process, including the dataset and the results, is further described in [9].

3.2 Assessing the Conflict Handling Style from the Utility of the Proposals

The style of dealing with a conflict that each one has must be seen as having a preponderant role in the outcome of a conflict resolution process, especially on those in which parties interact directly (e.g. negotiation, mediation). Ultimately, it is acceptable to state that the outcome will largely depend on the conflict resolution style of each party and on the interaction of the styles of the parties.

Different approaches can be followed to formalize the way that we respond to conflicts. A well-known definition was presented by Kenneth Thomas and Ralph Kilmann, which encoded the way that we react under a conflict into five different modes. To define these modes, they take into consideration the individual's assertiveness, which denotes how much a party tries to satisfy his own interests, and the cooperativeness, which denotes to which extent the party is willing to satisfy the other's interests. The five different conflict resolution styles defined are as follows:

- Competing - A party that shows this uncooperative style aims at maximizing his own gain, with a consequent minimization of the others. Usually, a competing individual will use his ability to argue, his rank, his social status or whatever advantageous position that he can have to show dominance over the other party. This is thus a power-oriented style;

- Accommodating - An accommodating party will show a behaviour that can be classified as the opposite of a competing one in the sense that he will be cooperative. It may happen that an accommodating party will even neglect his own gain, thus maximizing the one of the others, in order to achieve a solution. Thus, it may be said that there is an element of self-sacrifice. Generally, such a party will tend to show generosity or charity, will be understanding and will easily obey other's orders or desires even if they represent a drawback;

- Avoiding - An individual that shows an avoiding behaviour is most likely not dealing with the conflict as he usually satisfies neither his own interests nor those of the other party. Common behaviours in this conflict style include diplomatically sidestepping or postponing some issue or even withdrawing from threatening or unpleasant situations;

- Collaborating - On the opposite side of avoiding is the collaborative behaviour. This is a cooperative style in which the party shows the willingness to work with the other party in order to find solutions that can be interesting for both. This implies that the party is interested in finding what the fears and desires of the other are and might even try to explore a disagreement in order to learn from other's insights;

- Compromising - A compromising party will generally try to find a fast and satisfactory solution that can be interesting for both parties. This conflict style can be seen as an intermediary one between the competing and the accommodating. A compromising party is generally willing to split the differences between two positions, to exchange some concessions or to seek middle-ground solutions.

The potential relation between the personal conflict style and the utility of the proposals for the resolution of the conflict has been explored in previous work [10]. The utility quantifies how good a given outcome is for a party. In that sense, it is acceptable to argue that a competing party will generally propose solutions that maximize its own utility in expense of that of the other party, while for example a compromising party will most likely search for solutions in an intermediary region. Essentially, we were able to classify the personal conflict style of a party by constantly analysing the utility of the proposals created. The relation between the utility of the proposals and the conflict style is depicted in Figure 2 and further detailed in [10].

3.3 Experiments and Datasets

The negotiation game simulates a business situation involving a manufacturer and a reseller, in which each party has to achieve a desired result in the negotiation or go bankrupt. The desired result was a win/win situation for both parties. The game starts with a random draw of roles (i.e. manufacturer or reseller) for each party. The instructions to win the game were to negotiate a successful deal and make sure that any party did not go bankrupt.

To capture behavioural and contextual information, a test environment was set up in our lab. In this environment, the users were isolated from external stimuli and had

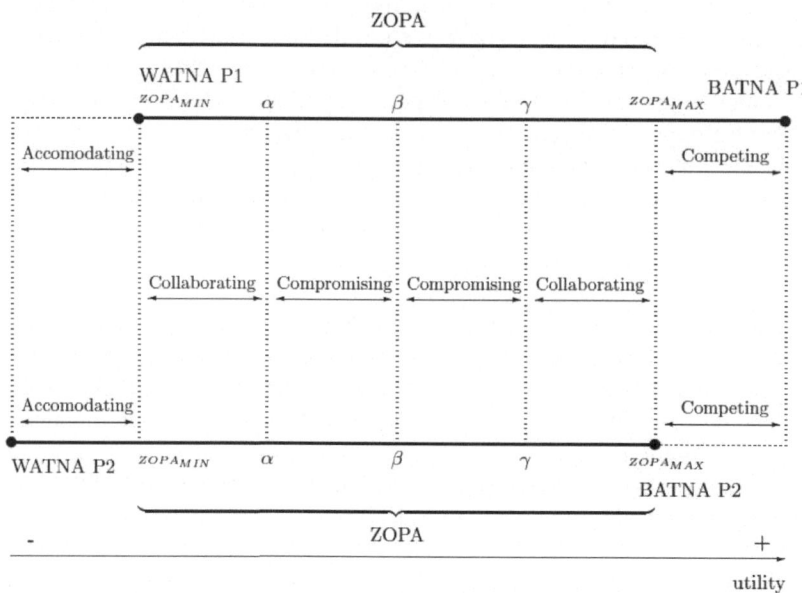

Fig. 2. The relationship between the utility of a proposal and the personal conflict handling style

to play a negotiation game that implied interaction with portable devices. It was developed a sensor-based application for the Android Operating System (Figure 3). The choice of a mobile platform relied on the use of computer based systems that had the capability of sense, interaction, store and manage sensor-based data with portability and platform-independence requirements, like smartphones and tablet computers. The developed application covers the functional needs to perform within an IE. Thus, at each round, the application collects the sensor information (using the classes provided by the Android API) and negotiation information (e.g., the proposal, the text messages) in terms of a temporal window. During the experiments, the information about the user's context was provided by a monitoring infrastructure, which is customized to perform movement detection from a camera located in front of the user and collect and treat the information that comes from the portable devices. The group of sensors used and their associated features included touch intensity (higher levels of touch intensity are associated with increased levels of stress); and touch accuracy (this is a measure of the amount of touches in active controls versus touches in active areas). The resulting datasets are summarized in Table 2.

3.4   The Resulting Behavioural Patterns

Looking over the data it may be concluded that most of the time the parties are using a competitive style, either in stress or calm phases. The evaluation of the progress of the conflict styles during the negotiation process was centred on the average slope of its numeric values. It was concluded that in a stressful state the parties tend to vary

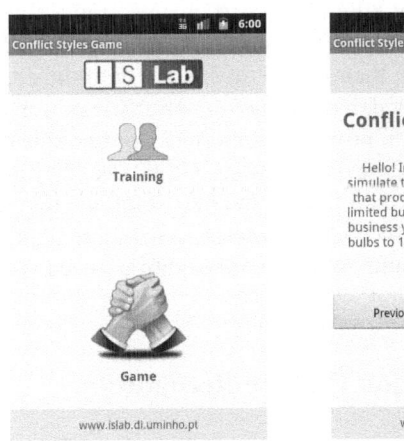  

Fig. 3. Some Android-based application's graphic interfaces

Table 2. Summary of the data generated during the tests. The size of the datasets comprises all the data generated.

data	brief description	size of dataset
Acceleration	Data concerning the acceleration felt on the handheld device while playing the game	33366
Movement	A dataset containing information about the amount of movement during the tests	9137
Touches	This dataset contains information about the touches	590
Proposals	Data concerning the proposals made by the parties in all rounds	59

slowly their way of dealing with the conflict than when they are calmer. Regarding at proposal values made by the parties during the negotiation, similar conclusions may be made. At the training phase both parties change more quickly their conflict styles than during the stressful phase. In the same way, *manufacturers* present a more dynamic proposal evolution than the *resellers*. It may be concluded that in a stressful situation it is more likely that the parties propose more *uncooperative* offers than others in a different situation. This may be explained as a consequence of acting too quickly or relying too much on coercion. When parties are under pressure they may make strategic mistakes or unwanted concessions. It may also lead to bad agreements. These are the natural assumptions that one may draw from these results. Acting too quickly may be a response to external and internal stressors. Indeed, considering the duration of the rounds, one may state that a high percentage of the negotiation rounds performed were shorter under a stressful environment than a stress-free one. However, only a small amount of these cases were statistically significant.

Looking at the statistical data one notices that 80% of the participants used a competitive conflict style in the early moves, 55% improve their styles (shifting towards more cooperative solutions), 35% do not change their competitive style until the end, and 10% become even more competitive. It is stated that *competitors* often use power as the primary tool for handling conflict, and work to prove the importance of one side of the argument in order to win. This may be one of the explanations. Otherwise, they are usually more concerned with winning the game than finding the best solution. Taking into consideration the game pre-conditions, the second hypothesis seems more appropriate, but one may not extrapolate the given results. Additional insights are needed in order to have a better and a more broad explanation.

4   A Probabilistic Model for Negotiation Posture Recognition

Probabilistic models are considered to be one of the best ways to deal with uncertainty in a given domain [11]. When there is a need to predict something based upon relationships that are not yet transparent among variables, probabilistic models offer a comprehensive way to work out the problem. As such, the application of these models to the data collected from the experiment was considered.

4.1   The Probabilistic Network Formalism

To discover possible hidden relationships among the data, we look at Bayesian Networks (BNs) using machine learning techniques. BNs are graphical representations of statistical dependences and independences among variables [12]. The reasons for choosing this representation are related with the fact that a BN provides a network structure and a probability distribution that are easily interpreted by humans and machines, as well as a comprehensive way of dealing with uncertainty. In fact, there are a number of programs that enable a user to manipulate BN parameters and selectively analyse the impact of these changes.

A BN is an acyclic directed graph $G = (V(G), A(G))$ with a set of vertices $V(G) = \{V_1, ..., Vn\}$, where each vertex $V_i \in V(G)$ represents a discrete stochastic variable, and a set of arcs $A(G) \subseteq V(G) \times V(G)$, where each arc $(V_i, V_j) \in A(G)$ represents statistical dependence. A BN defines a joint probability distribution Pr that may be factorized in the following way:

$$Pr(V_i, ..., V_n) = \prod_{i=1}^{n} Pr(V_i \mid \pi(V_i)) \qquad (1)$$

where $\pi(V_i)$ is associated with the set of variables that denote the parents of V_i.

4.2   The Model for Negotiation Style Recognition

Before feeding the data to the learning algorithms, some pre-processing was needed, namely the conversion of the variables round number, proposal value and round duration to nominal variables. The dataset included 103 instances and the set of variables used to acquire knowledge about the model were:

- *ExperienceType:* if the experience occurred under stress conditions or under training conditions;
- *Round:* the round interval to which the instance belongs;
- *Part:* if the role played in the instance was a manufacturer or a reseller;
- *ProposalValue:* the value in euros of the proposal;
- *ConflictStyle:* : the conflict style detected in the negotiation; and
- *RoundDuration:* the estimated duration of the round in terms of time intervals.

There are essentially two ways of learning the structure of BNs: *score-based* search and *constraint-based* search [12]. *Score-based* algorithms search for a BN structure that better fits the data by starting with an initial network and then traversing the search space of structures, removing, adding or reversing arcs in each step. On the other hand, *constraint-based* algorithms carry out a conditional (in)dependence analysis on the data. Based on this analysis, an undirected graph is generated to be interpreted as a Markov network. Given the reduced number of available instances, the method used was *score-based* search since it appears to work better in these cases. The algorithms used to learn the topology of the network were the *hill-climbing* and the *tabu* algorithms which are available in the *bnlearn* package for R. When retrieving the score (measure of fitness of the network to the data) for each network, the one learned by *hill-climbing* was the one with the highest, and so it was the one used to learn the probability distribution of the parameters. The retrieved network is represented in Figure 4. When one observes the BN of Figure 4 it is visible that it is rather sparse, probably due to the small amount of data used to construct it. None of the algorithms used managed to establish a dependence relationship between the *ConflictStyle* and the other variables under study, which does not fit the desired outcome of the process. However, it is noticeable that the *competing style* is the most frequent. Some other relationships were detected, namely

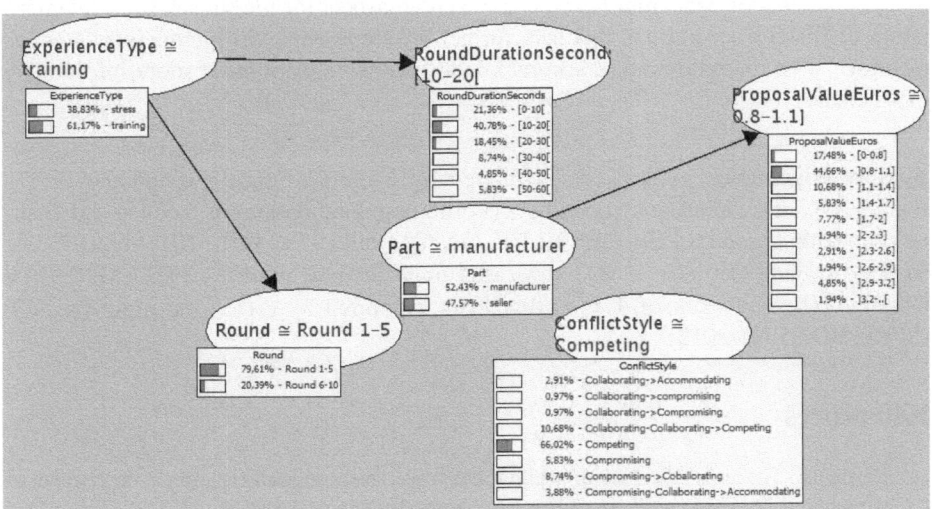

Fig. 4. Representation of the learned network visualized in the SamIam software tool

between *Part* and *ProposalValue*. When the *manufacturer* part is taken, the value of the proposals tends to be at lower intervals than when the *reseller* part is the one chosen. Again, the algorithms did not establish a connection between these two vertices and the other variables. By observing the remaining network, one detects some diverging arcs between *Round*, *ExperienceType* and *RoundDuration* which means that instantiating *ExperienceType* blocks the flow of probabilistic information, i.e., the influence from the *Round* interval to the *RoundDuration* (and vice versa). This means that if the *ExperienceType* is not instantiated, instantiating the *Round* may change the marginal probability distribution of the *RoundDuration*, but if *ExperienceType* is instantiated, instantiating *Round* will not change the probability distribution of *RoundDuration*. This was within the expected outcome.

These results point to the necessity of continuing to develop the experiment in order to gather more data that may uncover the interactions between the variables under analysis.

5 Conclusions and Future Work

After performing the experiments and the data analysis described so far, we are able to conclude that it is effectively difficult to extract consistent and reliable behavioural patterns from the collected data. Indeed, when applying machine learning algorithms to the results of the experiments it was noticed that the gathered data was insufficient for a conclusive answer, despite the fact that the raw statistical data was truly interesting.

In order to provide personalized and adapted services to help the conflict resolution field, the need for knowing the most frequent behaviour patterns is very clear. The patterns expressed by users, namely in negotiation processes, may provide vital information for mediation purposes and thus may help to achieve better outcomes. The ability to learn patterns of behaviour became an essential aspect for the successful implementation of IEs. To accomplish this task further developments will include new sources of information that allow more accurate data and the conception of more informative experiments.

Acknowledgements. This work is funded by National Funds through the FCT - Fundação para a Ciência e a Tecnologia (Portuguese Foundation for Science and Technology) within projects PEst-OE/EEI/UI0752/2011 and PTDC/EEI-SII/1386/2012. The work of Davide Carneiro is also supported by a doctoral grant by FCT (SFRH/BD/64890/2009). The work of Tiago Oliveira is supported by a doctoral grant by FCT (SFRH/BD/85291/2012).

References

1. Raiffa, H.: The art and science of negotiation: how to resolve conflicts and get the best out of bargaining. The Belknap Press of Harvard University Press (1982)
2. Ye, J., Coyle, L., Dobson, S., Nixon, P.: Using situation lattices to model and reason about context. In: Proceedings of MRC 2007: The Workshop of Modeling and Reasoning Context (coexist with CONTEXT 2007), Roskilde, Denmark, pp. 1–12 (August 2007)

3. Bettini, C., Brdiczka, O., Henricksen, K., Indulska, J., Nicklas, D., Ranganathan, A., Riboni, D.: A survey of context modelling and reasoning techniques. Pervasive and Mobile Computing 6(2), 161–180 (2010)
4. Carneiro, D., Gomes, M., Novais, P., Neves, J.: Developing dynamic conflict resolution models based on the interpretation of personal conflict styles. In: Antunes, L., Pinto, H.S. (eds.) EPIA 2011. LNCS, vol. 7026, pp. 44–58. Springer, Heidelberg (2011)
5. Gomes, M., Carneiro, D., Novais, P., Neves, J.: Modelling stress recognition in conflict resolution scenarios. In: Corchado, E., Snášel, V., Abraham, A., Woźniak, M., Graña, M., Cho, S.-B. (eds.) HAIS 2012, Part I. LNCS, vol. 7208, pp. 533–544. Springer, Heidelberg (2012)
6. Cooper, J.O., Heron, T.E., Heward, W.L.: Applied Behavior Analysis. Prentice Hall (1987)
7. Castillo, J.C., Rivas-Casado, A., Fernández-Caballero, A., López, M.T., Martínez-Tomás, R.: A multisensory monitoring and interpretation framework based on the model–view–controller paradigm. In: Ferrández, J.M., Álvarez Sánchez, J.R., de la Paz, F., Toledo, F.J. (eds.) IWINAC 2011, Part I. LNCS, vol. 6686, pp. 441–450. Springer, Heidelberg (2011)
8. Fernández-Caballero, A., Castillo, J.C., Martínez-Cantos, J., Martínez-Tomás, R.: Optical flow or image subtraction in human detection from infrared camera on mobile robot. Robotics and Autonomous Systems 58(12), 1273–1281 (2010); Intelligent Robotics and Neuroscience
9. Carneiro, D., Castillo, J.C., Novais, P., Fernández-Caballero, A., Neves, J.: Multimodal behavioral analysis for non-invasive stress detection. Expert Systems with Applications 39(18), 13376–13389 (2012)
10. Carneiro, D., Gomes, M., Novais, P., Andrade, F., Neves, J.: Automatic classification of personal conflict styles in conflict resolution. In: Atkinson, K.M. (ed.) Legal Knowledge and Information Systems - JURIX 2011: The Twenty-Fourth Annual Conference, pp. 43–52. IOS Press (2011)
11. Sheridan, F.: A survey of techniques for inference under uncertainty. Artificial Intelligence Review 5(1), 89–119 (1991)
12. Jensen, F.V.: Bayesian networks. Wiley Interdisciplinary Reviews: Computational Statistics 1(3), 307–315 (2009)

An Intelligent Tutoring Systems Integrated with Learning Management Systems

Cecilia E. Giuffra P., Ricardo Azambuja Silveira[1], and Marina Keiko Nakayama[2]

[1] Departamento de Informática e Estatística, Universidade Federal de Santa Catarina (UFSC), Florianópolis, SC, Brasil
{giuffra,silveira}@inf.ufsc.br
[2] Departamento de Engenharia e Gestão do Conhecimento, Universidade Federal de Santa Catarina (UFSC), Florianópolis, SC, Brasil
marina@egc.ufsc.br

Abstract. The computer-assisted education is increasingly exploited, as well as the use of Learning Management Systems (LMS). LMS are used in distance learning and classroom teaching as teachers and students support tools in the teaching–learning process. Teachers can provide material, do activities and create assessments for students. Nevertheless, this procedure is done in the same way for all the students, regardless of their performance and behavior differences. This work proposes an intelligent tutoring system (ITS) integrated with LMS to provide adaptability to it, using Moodle as a case study, taking into account student performance on tasks and activities proposed by the teacher and student access on resources.

Keywords: Learning management systems, intelligent tutoring system, multi-agent.

1 Introduction

LMS are defined as learning interactive tools where the content is available online. They allow the teacher to provide feedback to students in learning activities and are considered important resources for education. [1]

LMS are used satisfactorily in e-learning, however, as a rule, they do not operate in an interactive and personalized way with students in providing study materials and tasks. They provide the same pedagogical mediation resources and the same content for all of them, without considering their specific needs. Currently, many researches are made to incorporate features that take into account the individual characteristics of students. [12]

In order to provide adaptability to learning environments, according to student characteristics, and to allow a greater interactivity degree between the learning environment and the users, the research points to the use of resources provided by artificial intelligence (AI) and in particular the use of multi-agent system-based architectures [17].

In agreement with this emerges the motivation of this research: to enhance the teaching–learning process in LMS using artificial intelligence techniques to make the

J.M. Corchado et al. (Eds.): PAAMS 2013 Workshops, CCIS 365, pp. 316–327, 2013.
© Springer-Verlag Berlin Heidelberg 2013

LMS more adaptive and more interactive. This paper proposes the use of agent-based ITS architectures to get personalized teaching strategies, taking into account the student performance, exploring their skills, in order to have better and more effective learning in an intelligent learning environment.

This paper is structured as follows: the second section presents the theoretical reference, the third section presents the definition of the model, the fourth section presents an explanation about the model implementation and the last section presents the conclusions.

2   Background

LMS are technological tools and resources using cyberspace to lead content and enable pedagogical mediation through the interaction between the educational process actors [15]. With the advance of technology the use of these environments has increased because of the ease of providing interaction between student and teacher and the ease of access the content from anywhere and at any time.

For Dillenbourg [8], LMS are not only restricted to distance learning. Web-based education is often associated with distance learning; however, in practice it is also widely used to support classroom learning as a teacher's tool to provide materials, to review tasks, to keep track of the students on course (activity logs) and also to evaluate them. For students, the environment facilitates the delivery of tasks, the obtaining of materials for the course and the monitoring of their evaluation.

LMS can be enhanced with artificial intelligence techniques using cooperative intelligent agents (working in background) or animated pedagogical (interacting with the user). In the cooperative case, a multi-agent modeling is done, where each agent has a specific role and communicates with other agents. These agents are not visible to the user. In the case of pedagogical agents multimedia resources to create an animated character who interacts with the student are used [13]. Resulting in intelligent learning environments.

An agent is a cognitive entity or an abstraction of a device that can perceive its environment through sensors and can act upon that environment through actuators. A human agent has eyes, ears and other parts as sensors, and hands, legs, mouth, and other body parts such as actuators. An agent robot has infrared cameras and locators as sensors and various motors as actuators. A software agent has encoded bit strings as perceptions and actions. [18]

To Wooldridge (2009), an agent is a computer system situated in some environment, capable of perform autonomous actions in order to meet the goals that are delegated to it. In this context, autonomy is to have the ability to decide how to act in order to achieve the goals.

According to [5], an agent always requires a certain amount of intelligence to accomplish their tasks. An agent without intelligence can be any program of traditional software because it also performs specific tasks. Only intelligence allows an agent to perform tasks largely independently, requiring the user participation only to important decisions.

A rational agent is one who chooses perform actions according to their own interests, given the beliefs he/she has about the world. For example, if someone wants to keep itself dry and has the belief that it is raining, then it is rational to take an umbrella when going home. The B.D.I. (Belief, Desire, Intention) model recognizes the importance of beliefs, desires and intentions in rational actions. [20]

An important aspect of B.D.I. architecture is the notion of commitment to previous decisions. A commitment incorporates the balance between reactivity and direction to a goal of an agents oriented system. In an environment that changes constantly, the commitments give a sense of stability to the agent reasoning process. [16].

B.D.I. agents are rational agents who use the own beliefs that they have about the world to realize their desires, having the intention to perform them. The B.D.I. architecture is usually employed for the construction of so-called pedagogical agents.

Pedagogical agents are those whose goal is to help students in the teaching-learning process. According to Giraffa (1999), incorporate agents in an educational program is to intensify the pedagogical aspects desirable in the environment. Pedagogical agents can be divided into agents directed to goals and agents directed to utilities and have as main properties the autonomy, social ability, proactivity and persistence.

In practice, systems with only one agent are not common. The most common are the cases of agents that inhabit an environment containing other agents. The main focus of multiagent systems is to provide mechanisms to create computer systems from autonomous software entities, called agents, that interact through an environment shared for all the agents of a society. (BORDINI, 2001).

According to Bordini et al. [3], there are two major types of multi-agent systems: reactive and cognitive. The reactive acts under a stimulus-response scheme; the cognitive has, in general, few agents because each agent is a complex and computationally heavy system.

The BDI model represents a cognitive architecture based on mental states, and has its origin in the human practical reasoning model. An architecture based on the BDI model represents its internal processes through the mental states: belief, desire and intention, and defines a control mechanism that selects in a rational way the course of actions [9].

In the context of this work, an agent is considered as an autonomous entity, able to make decisions, respond in a timely manner, pursue goals, interact with other agents, and has reasoning and character. This agent is a of type BDI, with beliefs, desires and intentions, and operates in a LMS as an intelligent tutor.

ITS are complex systems involving several different types of expertise: subject knowledge, knowledge of the student's knowledge, and pedagogical knowledge, among others. According to Santos et al. [19], an ITS is characterized for incorporating AI techniques into a development project and acts as a helper in the teaching–learning process.

According to Conati [7], ITS are an interdisciplinary field that investigates how elaborate educational systems provide adapted instructions to the needs of students, as many teachers do.

ITS research has been investigating how to make computer-based tutors more flexible, autonomous and adaptive to the needs of each student by giving them explicit knowledge of the relevant components of the teaching process and reasoning skills to convert this knowledge into intelligent behavior.

To Giraffa and Viccari [11], ITS developments consider a cooperative approach between student and system. Research in ITS is concerned about the construction of environments that enable more efficient learning. [10].

ITS offer flexibility in the presentation of material and have the major ability to respond to students' needs. They seek, in addition to teaching, learning relevant information about the student, providing an individualized learning. ITS have been shown to be highly effective in improving performance and motivation of students [14].

ITS in LMS potentiate the teaching–learning process, making the virtual environment into an intelligent learning environment. Intelligent learning environments use AI techniques to respond to students' needs, making that learning personalized [14].

An intelligent learning environment is a kind of intelligent educational system that combines features of the intelligent tutor traditional system with learning environments [6].

According [17], the intelligent learning environment must build and update the student model in terms of what he/she already knows, which can vary significantly from one student to another.

3   Definition of the Model

The aim of this work is to create an agent architecture and an agent knowledge base that compose an ITS with information obtained from database of a teaching–learning virtual environment. For this, a case study is done based on the Moodle platform architecture, chosen because it is a platform widely used today, in addition to being consolidated from the standpoint of operation, and also to be formally used in the institution where the research is performed.

The classical model of ITS contains the pedagogical model, the student model, the domain base and the control. In the proposed model, two types of agents, called "Bedel" and "tutor" are used. The Bedel Agent and all their knowledge and interaction structure corresponds in the classical model of intelligent tutoring to the Pedagogical Model. The Tutor Agent and all their structure corresponds in the model of intelligent tutors to the Student Model. The content of the discipline, in turn, may be associated with the abstraction of the Domain Base. These correlations are shown in Figure 1.

In the proposed model the teacher chooses the Pedagogical Model to be used in the course, resources (readings, articles, videos) and activities (papers and exams) that he/she considers necessary to exploit optimally all course features during the semester, and configures the Bedel Agent according to this model, through the LMS interface. This agent helps the teacher. It is the tutor of the course.

The Tutor Agent is the agent that has contact with the student. It guides the student, indicating changes in performance, each time an activity is evaluated, encouraging him/her to improve when he/she has had a drop in performance or congratulating him/her when he/she has had a better performance. These guidelines are sent to students through the LMS messages.

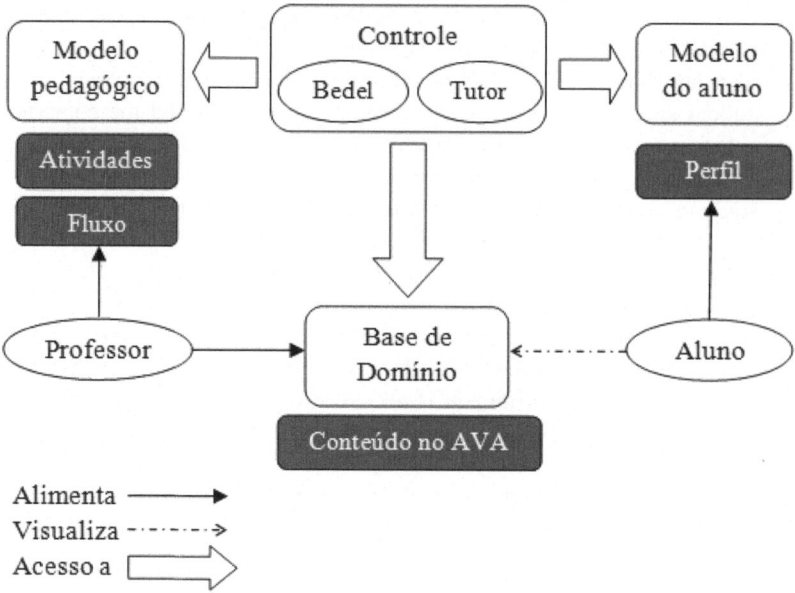

Fig. 1. Classic model with proposed model

The proposed model considers an LMS with a large amount of students, teachers and disciplines, predicting therefore the existence of an Bedel agent for each discipline and an Tutor agent for each student, being that this Tutor agent checks the student's performance in all disciplines in which it is enrolled.

Thus, the model proposes a multi-agent system, with several Tutor agents that communicates with the Bedel agent of each discipline, and Bedel agents providing activities and resources for all discipline students in a personalized way.

This scenario, dynamic and complex, demands the need of independent and autonomous agents that collaborate with each other to achieve the defined purposes, globally, given the directives proposed by each teacher in each discipline, in developing the pedagogical model and the model domain of each one of them.

The system model contains the LMS, the actors (student and teacher, users of the LMS), Bedel and Tutor Agents and the different interactions between them. The teacher adds the resources and activities on the LMS and configure them for the Bedel Agent. After that, the Bedel updates the LMS database to show the resources and activities to the students in a personalized way.

Each time the student accesses the LMS, the Tutor Agent checks the information existing on database about that student and updates the belief it has about him/her. Thereafter, the Tutor agent sends messages to the student using the LMS messaging feature.

The Bedel is the course agent. It constantly checks if any task was evaluated by the teacher, it calculates the students performance and inserts on database the information about their grades and the information required for the LMS to show new activities and resources to the students, taking into account their activity grades and their interaction in different resources of the course.

The database has information concerning the student, such as personal data, performance data and data from student interaction on the system. Every student interaction in the environment is saved in a log on database. Similarly, the student performance in each activity and task is stored on database and is updated every time the student access and interact in the environment, providing rich material for the agent's performance.

In the proposed model, the student model is represented by the student id, his/her grades in the different activities proposed by the teacher and the log information of these activities.

The agents (Bedel and Tutor) access the database as often as necessary to update the course and students information. They share the database information. The Tutor Agent updates the belief that it has about the student and if required, shows a message for him/her about his/her performance. The Bedel Agent gets from database, the configuration of the resources and activities of the course, made by the teacher, moreover, configures their display for each student profile and checks if new tasks were evaluated to send a message to the Tutor Agent with the information of the student to update the belief it has about the student profile data.

In the proposed model, formed by the actors teacher and student and the intelligent tutors Tutor and Bedel, students are grouped into three different profiles, according to their performance (grades) in the tasks and their access on different resources (study materials). These profiles are basic, intermediate and advanced.

This separation into groups takes into account the "grade profile" of each student, which is calculated as follows: The student grade of the last activity assessed by the teacher and the grade of the student access on reading that is a prerequisite for activity are summed. If the student accesses the reading, two points in the activity grade are added. If he/she does not access, four points are added. This difference is given for increasing the possibility to the student who does not access the reading, to have a higher profile grade and then go to a higher level task than the profile that he/she would belong to if he/she had a lower grade, stimulating him/her to read before accomplishing future activities.

After this, the average value of the profile grade field is computed for all students. The lowest value considered for the profile average is 6. The maximum value considered for the profile average is 8.

The student belongs to the average profile if his/her profile grade is 0.5 less or more than the average profile grade in his/her class; for example, if the average profile grade is 7.5, he/she will be in the intermediate profile if he/she has a profile grade between 7 and 8. The student who has a higher grade with more than 0.5 of difference with the average will be in the advanced profile and the student who has a lower grade with more than 0.5 of difference will be in the basic profile.

The Bedel is the course agent. It receives the information entered by the teacher when configuring the tutoring system. With this information, the Bedel knows what behavior it must follow to display the course in a personalized way according to each student profile by inserting the required information on database. Also, the Bedel checks for teacher updates on worksheet, calculates the profile grade of students, calculates the average profile grade, updates the database with these grades and communicates with Tutor Agent to inform the performance of the student with who the Tutor Agent is in contact.

The Tutor Agent is the agent that communicates with the student, it gets information sent by Bedel Agent about the student performance, each time the worksheet is updated and communicates with the student to encourage him/her and congratulate him/her according to what he/she needs at the moment.

The proposed model has the next steps:

Step 1:

- The teacher adds the resources and activities normally in the LMS, using the LMS tools as usual.
- The teacher sets the Bedel Agent using the environment interface including:
  - Level of difficulty (basic, intermediate, advanced and general) for each resource and activity that the teacher added previously in the LMS. The "general" difficulty level is selected when the teacher wants to show some resource or activity to all students equally.
  - The resources and activities where the students should start the process. The first reading (resource) and the first activity are shown for all students and the teacher have to indicate which ones they are.
  - The dependencies between the activities and resources.
- With this information the Bedel Agent knows the resources and activities of the course and knows how the course should be developed for each type of student, according with his/her profile.
- The teacher see the dependency graph generated by the system after the completion of the previous step.

Step 2:

- The teacher assigns grades in the proposed activities, after being performed by the students, and updating the worksheet for all students in the course.
- The Bedel Agent checks that were given grades for all students in a particular activity and calculates the student profile grade using the grade given by the teacher and the access log in the resources flagged as prerequisites of the activity, at the initial configuration of the teacher.
- The Bedel Agent calculates the average of the profile grade of all students and the students are separated by the profile into groups (basic, intermediate or advanced) according to their profile grade. Who has the average grade is in the intermediate profile, who is below the average is in the basic profile and who is above the average is in the advanced profile.

Step 3:

- The Bedel Agent checks the profile to which the students belong and shows the following activities according to that profile.
- Students access the activities in a personalized way, according to the grade obtained in previous activities and their access on the resources (readings).

- Each time the Bedel Agent calculates the profile grade it updates the database with the current student profile, which can go from basic to intermediate or advanced and vice versa, during the time the course is offered.
- The process is repeated from step 2.

4   Implementation of the Model

The model integrates concepts of ITS architectures with LMS that have their use consolidated as Moodle, which are not adaptive for itself only, and can be potentiated with artificial intelligence techniques, resulting in intelligent learning environments which are shown to be adaptive and more suitable to the implementation of teaching defiant methodologies for the student.

The use of agents in the implementation of this model is important because of the agent's ability to adapt to environment changes, showing resources and activities to students in a personalized way, according to their performance in the course, and taking into account the teacher's initial settings.

For the agent implementation the Jason tool was used, which is an interpreter for an extended version of AgentSpeak, oriented agent programming language, implemented in Java. The basic idea of AgentSpeak is to define the know-how (knowledge about how to do things) of a program in the form of plans [4].

The teaching–learning virtual environments are designed to enable the knowledge-building process. Different to conventional software, which seeks to facilitate the tasks achievement by user, learning environments incorporate the complexity to more flexible different forms of users (students), relations, to learn content, and to collaborate. These environments are used by students of various cognitive profiles [2].

According to the research of [1], Moodle has a good architecture, implementation, interoperability and internationalization, besides having a very strong community, is free and its accessibility is average. It has almost the highest score in expected functionality of an e-learning platform, and has the best rating in the adaptation category. In addition, Moodle has personalization features and adaptability.

The version of Moodle LMS used for this work is 2.2, where the task condition resource is available. This condition allows the availability of content and activities with a restriction. This feature must be activated by the Moodle administrator in the environment advanced settings, enabling the option "Enable tracking of completion" and "Enable conditional access." Moreover, in course settings, in "student progress" topic, the teacher must enable the completion tracking option.

With this feature enabled, tasks can be made available only to students who perform the defined prerequisites, which can be: a grade on a specific activity; the viewing of a resource; or his/her grade.

In this work, the availability of resources and activities is done taking into account the student performance and his/her access on the system. The resources and activities are made available to the student depending on his/her profile grade, computed according to his/her performance and participation in the course. The information between the agent system and the LMS is exchanged through the database of the learning environment which contains information about the prerequisites of tasks and resources, defined by the teacher at time of configure the tutor (Fig. 2).

The agents are connected with the LMS through the database. The interface in which the teacher sets the levels and priorities of the resources and tasks in the environment is developed. The database is adapted with the creation of the tables for the profile types, students profile grades, average grades of profiles, availability according to the profile, according to the level of tasks, evaluated tasks, and dependencies of resources and activities set by the teacher, and the integration of the agents actions with the Moodle LMS is done.

The development, in Moodle and using Jason, has 4 steps.

4.1   Tutor Block Development

It was developed a moodle block for the teacher to configure the agent. This block was developed following the Moodle standard programming for creating blocks, using PHP language and accessing the Moodle database using SQL language.

The name of the block was defined as "Tutor Block". Here the teacher sets the level of the different resources and activities, whether they are basic, intermediate or advanced, moreover, choose the first resource and activity, which are available equally to all students, and are the basis for the initial calculation of the student profile grade, and finally chooses the prerequisites for each activity and resource of the course.

After the teacher configures the agent through the block, he/she can see the dependency graph (Fig. 2) generated after setting all prerequisites.

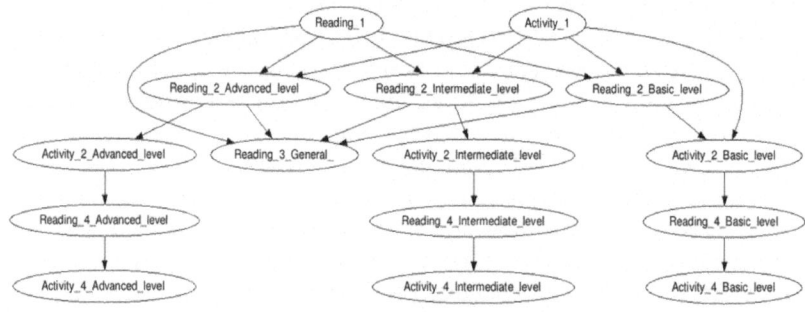

Fig. 2. Dependence graph

4.2   Development of the Calculation of the Student's Profile (Bedel Agent)

The agent programming was performed using the Eclipse IDE, with Jason plugin. The agents were developed with artifacts implemented in Cartago, in the Java language.

The agents' implementation is basically divided into the following files:

- jasonTutor.mas2j: Definition file of the multi-agent system. Here is specified the centralized infrastructure, the Cartago environment and the Tutor and Bedel Agents.
- BD_Artifact.java: File with the artifact code, which makes the connection between the agents and the LMS database.
- tutor.asl: File with the implementation of the Tutor Agent, who is the agent that has contact with the student.
- bedel.asl: File with the implementation of the Bedel Agent, teacher agent who follows the settings defined by the teacher in the LMS block, to show to the students the resources and activities depending on their performance.

4.3   Development of the Availability of Resources and Activities Code (Moodle)

For the availability of resources and activities according to the student profile was created the tutor_profile_availability table in the database, to store the information of the minimum and maximum grades of the intermediate profile. Verifying this information the resources and activities can be provided, according to the students profile.

In addition to this table, the Moodle source code is modified in conditionlib.php method "is_available" by entering the code needed so that resources and activities are shown on the LMS for each student according to their profile, taking the information added by the Bedel Agent into the database, after making the calculation of the grade profile.

At this stage, also, the bedel.asl file is updated, inserting methods that enable communication between it and the Tutor Agent. Sending the student information to him.

4.4   Development of the Tutor Agent - Feedback to the Student

In this step the Tutor Agent code is developed, this implementation is done in the tutor.asl file. This agent is responsible for sending messages of encouragement to the student, depending on his/her performance.

The Tutor Agent has the belief of the student profile grade, which is updated each time the Bedel Agent sends the message with a new profile grade. And according to the student situation the Tutor Agent sends a message to him/her, congratulating him/her or encouraging him/her to improve.

The Tutor Agent must have a LMS user account for sending the messages to the student.

5   Conclusions

In this study is proposed a solution for LMS to assist teachers to provide activities and resources to the students in a personalized way depending on their performance and his/her behavior in the course using an ITS architecture.

Students are assessed by their interaction in the course and the grades obtained in tasks, creating different profiles for groups of students with the same behavior. More advanced tasks are available for students who have improved performance, enabling more efficient learning, exploring student skills, and maintaining a basic level for learning the course content.

Works related to LMS and adaptivity in general differentiate students by learning style – for example, a student who learns better with pictures than with reading lots of text. In this work students are distinguished by their performance, taking into account the grades obtained, and their participation (access) in the various resources available in the course, creating an adaptive environment that constantly updates the profile of students, and therefore, a student with a basic profile, at the end of the course may have an average profile. These profile changes can be studied and displayed to the teacher, in an extension of this model.

The main contribution of this work is to add the advantages of the LMS to intelligent tutors and vice versa, creating an intelligent learning environment.

References

1. Ajlan, A.-A., Husein, Z.: Why Moodle. In: International Workshop on Future Trends of Distributed Computgin System. IEEE (2008)
2. Boff, E.: Collaboration in Learning Intelligent Environments mediated by a Social Agent Probabilistic. Thesis (Ph.D.) Computer Science Course. Federal University of Rio Grande do Sul, Porto Alegre (2008) (in Portuguese)
3. Rafael, B., Renata, V., Moreira Alvaro, F.: Multiagent Systems Fundamentals. In: Ferreira, C.E. (ed.) Informatic Update Day, JAI 2001, vol. 2, ch. 1, pp. 3–44. SBC, Fortaleza (2001) (in Portuguese)
4. Bordini, R.H., Hubner, J.F., Wooldridge, M.: Programming Multi-Agent Systems in AgentSpeak using Jason. Editora Wiley, England (2007)
5. Walter, B., Rüdiger, Z., Hartmut, W.: Intelligent Software Agents – Foundations and Applications. Springer, Heidelberg (1998)
6. Peter, B.: Student model centered architecture for intelligent learning environment. Proceedings of Fourth International Conference on User Modeling (1994), Diponível em: http://www2.sis.pitt.edu/~peterb/papers/UM94.html (Acesso em Dez. 04, 2011)
7. Conati, C.: Intelligent Tutoring Systems: New Challenges and Directions. Paper Presented at the Proceedings of the 21st International Joint Conference on Artificial Intelligence (2009)
8. Dillenbourg, P.: Virtual Learning Environment. In: EUN Conference 2000. Workshop on Virtual Learning Environment (2000), http://tecfa.unige.ch/tecfa/publicat/dil-papers-2/Dil.7.5.18.pdf
9. Fagundes, M.: An environment for development of BDI agents. Course Completion Work. Federal University of Pelotas (2004) (in Portuguese), http://www.inf.ufsc.br/~silveira/INE602200/Artigos/TCC_Moser.pdf
10. Frigo, L.B., Pozzebon, E., Bittencourt, G.: The Role of Intelligent Agents in Intelligent Tutoring Systems. In: Proceedings of the WCETE - World Congress on Engineering and Technology Education, São Paulo, Brasil, pp. 667–671 (2004) (in Portuguese)

11. Giraffa, L.M.M., Viccari, R.M.: The Use of Agents Techniques on Intelligent Tutoring Systems. In: Computer Science SCCC 1998. XVIII International Conference of the Chilean Society, pp. 76–83. IEEE Computer Society, Washington, DC (1998)
12. Graf, S., Kinshuk: Analysing the Behaviour of Students in Learning Management Systems with Respect to Learning Styles. In: Wallace, M., Angelides, M.C., Mylonas, P. (eds.) Advances in Semantic Media Adaptation and Personalization. SCI, vol. 93, pp. 53–73. Springer, Heidelberg (2008)
13. Jaques, P.A., Vicari, R.M.: State of the Art in Intelligent Learning Environments that consider the student affection. Computers in Education 8(1), 15–38 (2005) (in Portuguese)
14. Lima, R.D., Rosatelli, M.C.: An intelligent tutoring system to a virtual environment for teaching and learning. In: IX Workshop de Informática na Escola, Campinas. Anais do XXIII Congresso da Sociedade Brasileira de Computação (2003) (in Portuguese)
15. Pereira, A.T.C., Schmitt, V., Álvares, M.R.C.: Virtual Learing Environments. Culture Bookstore (2007) (in Portuguese), http://www.livrariacultura.com.br/imagem/capitulo/2259532.pdf
16. Rao Anand, S., Georgeff Michael, P.: Bdi Agents: From Theory to Practice. In: Proceedings of the First International Conference of Multiagents Systems. AAAI (1995), Disponível em: https://www.aaai.org/Papers/ICMAS/1995/ICMAS95-042.pdf (Acesso em: Dez. 04, 2011)
17. Silveira, R.A.: Intelligent Distributed Learning Environments. CPGCC da UFRGS, Porto Alegre (1998) (in Portuguese)
18. Russell, S., Norvig, P.: Artificial Intelligence: A Modern Approach. Prentice-Hall, Inc., New Jersey (2002)
19. dos Santos, C.T., Frozza, R., Dhamer, A., Gaspary, L.P.: DÓRIS - Pedagogical Agent in Intelligent Tutoring Systems. In: Cerri, S.A., Gouardéres, G., Paraguaçu, F. (eds.) ITS 2002. LNCS, vol. 2363, pp. 91–104. Springer, Heidelberg (2002)
20. Wooldridge, M.: Reasoning about Rational Agents. The MIT Press, Cambridge (2000)
21. Wooldridge, M.: An Introduction to Multiagent Systems, 2nd edn. John Wiley & Sons Ltd., Hoboken (2009)

Multiagent Based Recommendation System Model for Indexing and Retrieving Learning Objects

Ronaldo Lima Rocha Campos, Rafaela Lunardi Comarella,
and Ricardo Azambuja Silveira

Federal University of Santa Catarina (UFSC) Florianópolis, SC, Brazil
{rcampos,silveira}@inf.ufsc.br, rafaela@egc.ufsc.br

Abstract. This paper proposes a multiagent system application model for indexing, retrieving and recommending learning objects stored in different and heterogeneous repositories. The objects within these repositories are described by filled fields using different metadata (data about data) standards. The searching mechanism covers several different learning object repositories and the same object can be described in these repositories by the use of different types of fields. Aiming to improve accuracy and coverage in terms of recovering a learning object and improve the relevance of the results we propose an information retrieval model based on a multiagent system approach and an ontological model to describe the covered knowledge domain.

Keywords: multiagent system, recommender system, ontology, learn object, information retrieval.

1   Introduction

The efforts and investments needed by educators and educational institutions to produce qualified learning content are considerable. This is especially important in the production of content for distance education because almost all the information and knowledge must be completely and explicitly covered by the learning objects [1]. A learning object is any digital resource reused to support learning. Thus learning objects may be small parts such as images, sounds, videos or more complex parts such as courses or software [1].

Owing to the large cost of producing learning content, there is a strong advantage in improving the possibility of reusing it. Therefore, the development of mechanisms to facilitate the reuse of learning content has attracted the interest of several research groups, organizations and educational institutions around the world.

This scenario explains the heterogeneity of the available technologies used to produce and store learning objects. This heterogeneity makes painful and laborious the interoperability among the different tools used to produce, store and retrieve learning objects. Moreover, it is clear that the lack of effective and specialized LO search tools does not allow wide reuse of the learning objects produced.

The existing tools used to retrieve information about learning objects are usually solely based on a syntax search. This type of search is not an efficient way to recover

J.M. Corchado et al. (Eds.): PAAMS 2013 Workshops, CCIS 365, pp. 328–339, 2013.

learning objects as they used to be in retrieving ordinary documents from the web. The information on regular web pages is not cataloged as it is in LO repositories. This characteristic hinders the use of semantic functions for recovering LOs.

This paper proposes an LO intelligent search model capable of indexing and retrieving learning objects, regardless of the metadata (data about data) standard used, located in different and heterogeneous repositories and provides the user with a ranking of the learning objects based on their profile. This model aims to increase the recovery and re-usability of learning objects by searching the learning content from several different LORs by the teachers, students or learning objects designers. It does so by using multiagent system technologies as well as domain ontologies to support the work of the designed agents in promoting a better recovery and re-usability of learning objects.

To validate the model, a prototype was developed and tested in two learning object repositories, developed under different storage and dissemination technologies, and each with a distinct metadata set. The results show that the proposed model brings improvements in the coverage and recovery of learning objects and recommends LOs that best fit the context of the user who is seeking it.

2   Background

The theoretical model of this research covers the basic concepts related to learning objects as well as formal specification of metadata for the LOs. Furthermore, the use of multiagent systems technology combined with retrieval techniques, usually used for Semantic Web to solve the problem of retrieving objects in distributed and heterogeneous environments using semantic aspects of learning object. The obtained results pointed to use representation of domain ontology to contextualize the domain specific concepts search problems and indexing and weighting information techniques to improve the accuracy, coverage and the performance of search tools.

Learning objects are educational resources that can be used in the learning process supported by technology [3]. Learning objects can be based on text, animations, presentations, images, software, and have to be described by a set of metadata, according to some formal specifications [1]. The learning object is the learning content formally described by its metadata, stored in repositories, which can be combined with other learning objects to create larger objects such as lessons and courses [4].

Digital content repositories are software developed with the objective of storing and organizing digital resources, thus providing search and content retrieving mechanisms [1], [4]. The repositories have interfaces for submission or cataloging content, using one or more data standards, dissemination and harvesting interfaces, communication protocols, and search and retrieval interfaces. Digital repositories should deal with a series of requirements such as storage, cataloging, dissemination, harvesting and search and retrieval. It is not currently possible to distinguish at the current state of the art, just one particular accepted and adopted model, which could be used to guide all of those policies. There is thus, a heterogeneous scenario. The problem of heterogeneity has been addressed in several ways and according to [5], by creating repositories that are highly sustainable, they also become highly heterogeneous because they must deal with various types of storages, access to objects and consulting methods. As for [6], heterogeneity is more technically related, highlighting differences in both the implementation of the repositories (softwares) as well as differences in hardwares that supports them. Thus the concept of heterogeneity for search engines can be set upon two major pillars: access to the resources, and metadata standards used to describe objects. In this article we address these two areas in the model of agents, while mainly focusing on techniques that deal with different metadata standards. Such approach is justified by the difficulty in representing the object semantic in its recovery and integration with other systems, [7] expose that the adoption of only one metadata standard for the integration of various systems is complicated, the demands are different from one system to another and for that reason a mapping technique called Crosswalks is used.

To ensure interoperability, the repositories are adopting one or more disseminating protocols. These protocols came out of the efforts to find efficient forms to replicate not only the structure, but the object of the repositories and end up defining a standard form to obtain access to these objects. In the same way these repositories are different according to the technology and the protocols used: Lightweight Directory Access Protocol (LDAP), Open Archives Initiative protocol for Metadata Harvesting (OAI-PMH; Open Archives Initiative Object Reuse and Exchange (OAI-ORE).

What can be noticed is that even though the access mechanisms to the resources (objects and metadata) deal with a range of technologies, the emergence and adoption of standards to make the systems inter-operable has helped to standardize such accesses. Regarding the description of objects in the current scenario, there is also a range of patterns that have emerged about demands and different ideas and to attend several purposes. Thus the concept of metadata is related to information structures that describe on various aspects, its own resources and, such concept is commonly referred as being the data of the data, or the information about the information [8].

One of the main reasons to use metadata is to simplify information recovery in a relevant way. Moreover, it helps organizing, facilitates interoperation and resource integration, digital identification, filing and preserving. Among the main existing Standards, the most relevant ones and, therefore most adopted are: Dublin Core, LOM and OBAA.

Dublin Core metadata set emerged in 1995 in a workshop sponsored by OCLC and NCSA. Its continuing development and specifications are managed by Dublin Core Metadata Initiative (DCMI) [9]. The initial objective was the creation of some fields to describe web resources by their original authors. With the growth of electronic resources and the lack of describers to catalog them, the standard defined some elements and simple rules to enable such cataloging.

Created by IEEE Learning Technology Standards Committee (LTSC), the Learning Objects Metadata (LOM) is an IEEE standard meant for the reuse and description of educational resources [10]. LOM defines a minimum set of attributes to manage, locate (language) and validate educational objects.

OBAA is a Brazilian technical and functional requirement specification standard for the production, edition and distribution of interactive digital content, allowing them to be used in Web platforms, mobile devices and digital television. This standard was developed by the Federal University of Rio Grande do Sul (UFRGS) in partnership with Vale dos Sinos University (UNISINOS) in response to a call from the Education, Communication, Science and Technology Ministries and used based on the LOM standard. OBAA is an extension of LOM. There were included some elements in the Technical and Educational categories and added another two, Accessibility and Segment Information Table to meet the Brazilian needs with relation to these segments [6].

Regarding theoretical background of software agents we consider a multiagent system with a network of problem solvers who work in conjunction to solve problems which go beyond their individual capability [11]. These problem solvers are essentially autonomous, distributed and heterogeneous in nature. We also adopt the FIPA reference model of agents [12] and use JADE (Java Agent Development Framework) [13] to construct it.

Besides the theoretical background related to multiagent systems and learning objects we consider retrieval techniques used for finding documents. These techniques aim to find the location of information that satisfies specific needs, from digital media [14] and techniques for knowledge representation to ontologies consisting of entities that can be classes, concepts, instances, individuals, relationships, properties, data types and values.

3   The Proposed Model

The objective of this model is to promote better recovery of learning objects, through support of software agents in different repositories with heterogeneous access and metadata. The proposed multi-agent system model was developed to be able to index, classify and retrieve learning objects in different repositories besides ensuring good coverage and recovery for areas of knowledge and prioritize relevant results.

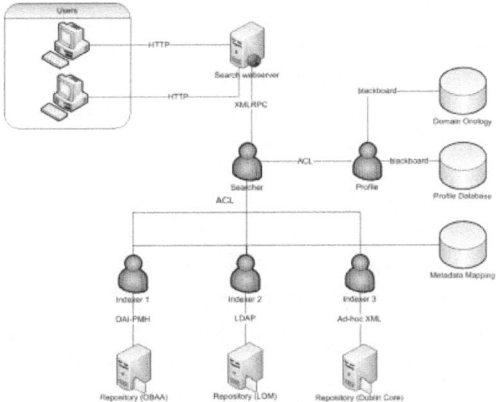

Fig. 1. Multiagent System Architecture

According to Figure 1, the main components are: the multi-agent system, the system of web search, the set of repositories of learning objects, and the foundations of knowledge and profiles. The web search system is responsible for the interface of the multiagent system with the user, receiving user's profile information, and the search terms. Repositories can be completely different, both in content and in technology that was developed and for each type of repository there is an Agent Indexer adapted to handle a heterogeneous environment. Knowledge bases are accessed by the Agent Profile and are responsible for expanding the terms to search and filter the objects returned, since the base profile is responsible for storing user information and is consulted by the Agent Profile. Figure 2 indicates the information flow system.

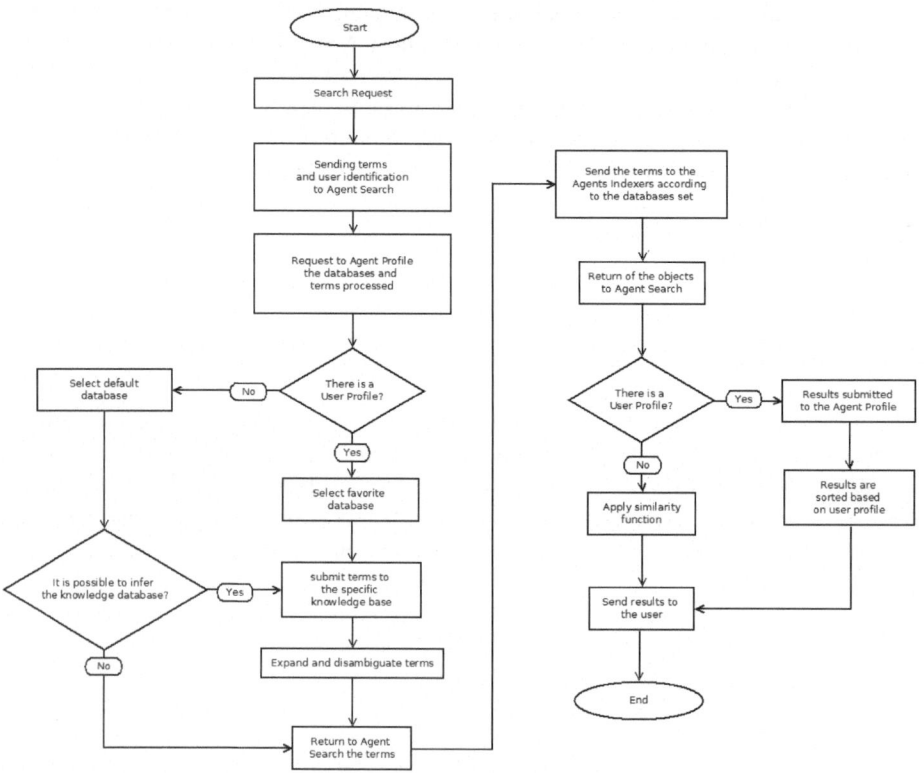

Fig. 2. Information flow chart

Figure 2 indicates the information flow as follows: When the system user accesses the web search system, he is identified and thereafter he may send a search request, through terms (keywords). The web search system receives this request and passes the data request to the multiagent system using a remote procedure call, in a vector containing the search terms and the user ID (if existent). The Search Agent receives the request and sends a message containing the terms and user ID to the Profile Agent, prompting which databases to search and the search terms treated semantically.

With this information, the Profile Agent sends a message to the Profile Database requesting if the user profile exists and user's information. Thereafter, he asks the user about the preferred databases and chooses the specific knowledge base, subjecting it to the search terms to be expanded and detailed. Otherwise, a set of default database is selected and he tries to infer the knowledge area of the terms, if possible, the terms are subjected to a knowledge base for expanding and detailing and following the flow pattern, if not, the terms do not suffer modifications.

After, to define the databases and search terms, the Agent Profile informs the selected Searcher Agent about the databases which triggers the Indexers Agents by sending messages containing the search terms. Such agents will carry out the search in the repositories indexed by them, based on the fields abstract, title and keywords. Once the search is performed, the agents send messages to Searcher Agent, containing the identification of the objects recovered by them.

The Search Agent receives the list of objects and sends it to the Profile Agent. The Profile Agent checks the user information to sort the list of objects. Then the objects are sorted based on the user profile and the sorted list is sent for viewing. If the user profile is not found, the objects are subjected to a similarity function, to avoid possible objects out of context and duplicates.

3.1   Description of Agents

The conceptual model was designed to index any type of repository, using a specialized index agent. The implementation of the model was performed using the JADE framework. The communication between agents is established by exchanging messages in ACL (Agent Communication Language). Specifically, the communication between the agent Profile and profile database is performed by blackboard and similarly the communication of agent Profile with the knowledge base is also established by blackboard. We have implemented an agent who is specialized in communication protocol and an OAI-PMH in the LDAP protocol. Both are capable of indexing any repositories that disseminate their data according to these protocols and adopt the metadata standards: LOM, Dublin Core or OBAA.

The prototype is used to perform indexing in two repositories, UNA-SUS (UFSC) and CESTA 2 (UFRGS). This choice was made because both implement the OAI-PHM protocol and use the LOM metadata standard. The CESTA 2 repository was chosen because it is a multidisciplinary repository with a large set of objects. The UNA-SUS UFSC repository was chosen as well because of its specificity in public health, so you can use all the features of the knowledge bases to expand the search terms since the repository was indexed using the terms of DECS (Brazilian version of MESH).

Searcher Agent

The Searcher Agent acts as a coordinator for the entire process. It interacts with the web system, receiving search requests, and returning the results; ordering the databases to be searched and the terms extended to Agent Profile; requesting objects that meet the search parameters to the Indexer Agents; returning the selected objects to Profile Agent and sorts them by relevance.

The Searcher Agent receives requests from the users, who enter keywords to search and request information about the user agent profile. This information, when available, is stored and used to classify objects. After receiving the search terms the agent uses a system of domain ontologies to expand the terms and build a network of knowledge and then the Searcher Agent requests the Indexer Agents for objects and their description (metadata). With the information from the Indexer Agents, along with the terms and expanded user information, the Searcher Agent ranks the results and sends them to the web search system.

For this purpose the agent communicates with the web search system using a remote procedure call protocol in XML (XMLRPC). The prototype interface was developed in PHP language, with the possibility of user identification. The system is requested using protocol by calling the Search method with a vector containing text information to identify the user and the terms to be searched. As an answer to the call, the web system also receives a text vector, with information of the objects returned by the multiagent system.

Profile Agent

The Profile Agent, in the multiagent system, is responsible for enriching the search, producing specialized and customized search terms according to the user. To perform this task, the agent interacts with two bases: the user profile and a dictionary of terms and knowledge. The Profile Agent is able to retrieve the user's profile, select the appropriate databases according to the user, expand and detail the terms to search, sort and filter the returned objects by relevance and assist in the construction and refinement of profile user.

The Agent Profile begins operating when it receives a request from the Searcher Agent, containing user ID information and the search terms. With the user's identification, the Profile Agent requests for database profiles, if the user's profile exists. Thus the technique that defines user ID must be known by both the agent and the database, and both must be able to communicate in a standard way, using ad-hoc language or blackboard.

Being able to identify and obtain information from the user's profile, the agent sends a message to the profile database requesting which databases the user tends to use in the search and which knowledge base that it uses to treat the terms to search.

To choose the knowledge base, the Agent Profile first checks if there is a user profile and if so, it indicates a base, otherwise it tries to infer which base. This inference is carried out by subjecting the terms of a similarity function with the terms contained in the database; the selected base is the one that has the highest degree of similarity. After choosing the knowledge base, the agent communicates with it by ad-hoc language or blackboard. To this base, the agent will submit the terms and receive the expanded terms for the search.

As an example, the agent provides a communication with the base specializing in medical terms, submits the terms CVA (Cerebrovascular Accident) and Blood Circulation, the base receives the terms, synonyms and expands the communicating agent, in this case the term is synonymous CVA, Cerebral Vascular Accident, Cerebral Stroke, Brain Vascular Accident, etc. and that Blood Circulation is related to Cardiovascular System.

In the second phase, the Agent Profile is tasked with sorting out objects, resulting in the repositories search for relevance. If there is no user's profile selected, the agent will use a similarity function of terms with objects and thus ordains them. If the user's profile exists the agent will also apply a similarity function, albeit using metadata values most used and stored in the user's profile as a filter, giving those objects that fit those values with greater relevance.

As an example, chosen the year 2005, the user's profile contains the date field set to dates greater than 2005, when sorting objects, with objects whose metadata Date meet this definition they receive a higher weight and therefore are ordered as having greater relevance.

Once the results are classified the agent prepares the objects to be sent as an indexed list with relevant information about each object, it's metadata fields content and it's location. The list is submitted to the Searcher Agent, which passes on to the web search system responding to its request. According to this information the system assembles a web visualization of the learning objects information to the user, highlights the most relevant objects and builds a profile update function according to each object shown. This function retrieves the user profile information as it accesses some items shown in the web interface, analyzes the profile fields that refer to metadata, and establishes standards for the calculation of the frequency of the field values, thus updating the profile.

Ontology

The expansion of the search terms, responsible for ensuring greater coverage, is performed by the Profile Agent using the available knowledge bases expressed by specific domain ontology. This ontology is a dictionary of terms that expands beyond the terms, through their synonyms, defines and categorizes them in order to qualify by avoiding ambiguities and terms outside their area of expertise. As an example, in the medical field CVA can mean Cerebral Vascular Accident (more common term) or a reference to a chemotherapy protocol. Viruses can be computer virus or biological virus or the medical field, or even the social area. This ontology follows a standard model, to be consulted by the Agent Profile, as shown in Figure 3.

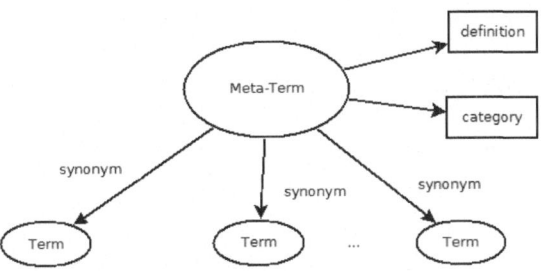

Fig. 3. Model domain ontology

According to Figure 3, the terms are related to a meta-term relationship for a synonym. This meta-term defines a concept or idea at a high level, containing its definition, organizational category and for terms that represent that concept. Since the relationship of meta-term with terms is determined by synonyms, locating a term, you can get your meta-term and following all its synonyms. Thus accomplishing the expansion of the terms. Making use of the same knowledge base, the agent uses the profile definition and synonyms of the terms to calculate the relevance of the objects.

Profile Database

The database profile is used by the agent profile for user information. It can be implemented with different techniques, since the technique accepts messages from the Profile Agent. Each profile contains a series of specific information that define the characteristics of the objects to be recommended, they are: the most used database (preferred) default values for metadata fields, relations with other profiles and knowledge databases.

Initially the system has a set of specialized profiles, focusing on the specifics of each knowledge area addressed by the system. This profile contains information about the most frequently used specialized search databases referring to the area in question and information about which knowledge base is used to treat the terms. Every user who signs up for the system indicates the area that the users belongs to and thereby inherits the specific information in this profile, given the characteristics form relationships with other profiles. As an example, a new user accesses and fits the system, selects the medical field and thus his/her profile is related to the specific profile of the medical field, previously registered in the system. This new profile will inherit the information about which databases are from the medical field and knowledge base to expand the search terms.

As the system indexes different databases, the user can choose to search on a subset, removing those search databases that are less relevant, or adding those databases that can bring additional results, those building a list of more useful and complete databases. This interaction is done directly by the web search system, using advanced search fields. The web system is then responsible for updating the base profile.

One of the important information fields contained in the user profile is the identification of the knowledge base. This knowledge base was previously built through the model specified in the search. This database is referenced by a specialized profile and is inherited by the user when he/she creates his/her profile. Technically, it is a reference, and may be implemented in several ways accessible by the Profile Agent via messaging.

In the prototype the following fields are stored and refined: Date (range), Educational Background, Knowledge Area, Type, Target, Interaction and didactic strategy. These fields were defined based on interviews with two experts, who considered them the most relevant for identifying and filtering of learning objects.

Indexer Agent

The Indexer Agent was modeled to index different object repositories with heterogeneous access mode and several types of objects description. Thus, for each repository indexed in the system, there is a specific Indexer Agent. To perform this task the agent should be able to access the object repositories; obtain the information about the objects it contains, a description of these objects (metadata) and if available, collaborative information such as the number of hits and qualifications and build an index of the collected information.

Access to the repository, objects and their descriptions is performed by a dissemination protocol. The tendency of the repository is to use patterns of dissemination and collection protocols such as the OAI-PMH. However there are cases such as repositories of BVS (Biblioteca Virtual em Saúde, medical repository), in which the mechanism is designed in a specific way (ad-hoc). There are repositories where access is via a data structure in LDAP, or search protocols such as SPARQL. Each Indexer Agent should then be specialized in a repository and its dissemination protocol mechanism, ensuring access to the objects it contains.

Related to the harvesting protocol's capabilities are accessing the repository and obtaining the objects and their descriptions, because each protocol type has a different kind of technical metadata description, for example, the metadata collected by the OAI-PMH are represented in a XML structure. By defining the protocol used by the agent, the object descriptions structures and their metadata, should be also be defined, allowing the agent to understand and retrieve them.

After obtaining the information about the objects and their known structure, the agent builds an index with the information collected. It is through this index that the Indexer Agent returns the objects that where requested by the Searcher Agent. This index must be standardized so that the various objects, from the various repositories, are described and available in a standard way. Using a mapping base, a list of relevant metadata is created to search and map the known standards for this list, creating a standard group of metadata. Thus, not all metadata contained in the objects are mapped, only the relevant ones, making the content simpler and robust.

By adopting a standard, such as LOM, and map the objects to this standard, the entire system operates on a single standard, simplifying the implementation stage of the model and its dissemination. However, if there are some objects that are rarely described or which are represented in a simpler pattern (such as Dublin Core) some fields are not being described. Beyond this, if some objects contain fields that are not in default to be mapped, or its description is incomplete, the search results are impacted.

Using the original description format of the object, instead mapping it, simplifies the agent's work, and ensures complete representation of the object. However brings additional complexity to the other agents in the system, they should be able to understand all metadata standards known to the system.

In the prototype the constructed agents are specialized in the OAI-PMH protocol and are able to recognize Dublin Core, LOM and OBAA patterns, adopting the mapping 1-1 to the OBAA, namely the Dublin Core and LOM patterns are transformed into OBAA. This transformation is simple, because the standard OBAA is an extension of LOM, in other words, all fields present in LOM, are within OBAA. Concerning the Dublin Core standard, this mapping is made by the semantic agreement between fields, for example, the title metadata in the Dublin Core is represented by dc.title and OBAA is represented by obaa.general.title.

Performance

Repositories can contain a large number of objects. Analyzing all of them to select the most relevant to a job search can be very costly. In systems where the response time is not a factor limiting the problem can become irrelevant, but in systems with time related response while large indexes can hinder the response time. To deal if this issue, we have two alternatives; using search algorithms on large indexes or using an auction system for Indexer Agents.

To reduce the search time of the agent in the index objects can adopt any specific algorithm to search large indexes, such as a graph inverted indexes. Divide the index into sub-index ordered by areas or subareas of knowledge, or store the results of searches conducted more for a faster query.

By using an auction system ensures the response time because the Searcher Agent opens an auction of a number of selected objects to the terms and finish in a certain time. Thus, each Agent Indexer query table as auction and is consulting its index, responds with the objects with greater relevance. At the end of the Auction Agent Searcher collects the results.

4   Final Remarks

The proposed model allows searching heterogeneous repositories using semantic features and user's information, increasing coverage and relevance of their results. The option of using an open protocol based on XML for communication between the multiagent and the web search application incorporated features distributed throughout the system, making it more accessible since any application using the protocol is able to communicate with the system. This feature allows the use of the tool in a more transparent way in other systems, like the LMS (Learning Management System). Thus a module for LMS Moodle is being developed, which will allow search and content implementation through its own platform.

At the current stage of development the system is already functional, having implemented the following agents: Searcher; Index (LDAP and OAI-PMH protocol) for CESTA 2 and UNASUS/UFSC; and agent Profile is also integrated with the JENA framework being able to expand and establish relationships between the terms and synonyms referred to it.

The Human-machine interface is through a web application that communicates with the Agent Searcher via XML protocol (XMLPRC library). It is already possible to search the repositories CESTA 2 and UNASUS/UFSC. For now there are two domain ontologies created, information security and medical subjects.

To validate the model we submitted a list of terms to search engine repositories CESTA 2, UNASUS/UFSC and the multiagent system. Of the 22 collected and analyzed results of the first 10, in 5 cases the SMA results are relevant, 4 are the same as the other systems and 1 is irrelevant. Of the remaining results 9 are considered good (they meet the search terms) but not as good as the first 10.

The model for classifying objects based on user's information, statistics and collaborative evaluations of objects, despite being in the initial phase, has already showing a good potential. And because of this potential, is being improved the ontology for the domain of medicine, with the aim of preparing a survey with specialists.

The CESTA 2 repository recently changed your harvest protocol to OAI-PMH they was LDAP at the moment of our tests.

References

1. Downes, S.: Learning Objects: Resources for distance education worldwide. The International Review of Research in Open and Distance Learning 2(1) (2001) (accessed: April 10, 2012)
2. Wiley, D.: Connecting learning objects to instructional design theory: A definition, a metaphor, and a taxonomy. In: Wiley, D.A. (ed.) The Instructional Use of Learning Objects (2000), http://reusability.org/read/chapters/wiley.doc (accessed: July 10, 2012)
3. McGreal, R.: Online Education Using Learning Objects. Routledge, London (2004)
4. Nash, S.S.: Learning Objects, Learning Object Repositories, and Learning Theory: Preliminary Best Practices for Online Courses. Interdisciplinary Journal of Knowledge and Learning Objects (2005)
5. Gil, A.B., De la Prieta, F., Rodríguez, S.: Automatic Learning Object Extraction and Classification in Heterogeneous Environments. In: Pérez, J.B., Corchado, J.M., Moreno, M.N., Julián, V., Mathieu, P., Canada-Bago, J., Ortega, A., Caballero, A.F. (eds.) Highlights in PAAMS. AISC, vol. 89, pp. 109–116. Springer, Heidelberg (2011)
6. Fabre, M.C.J.M., Tarouco, L.M.R., Tamusiunas, F.R.: Reusabilidade de objetos educacionais. RENOTE - Revista Novas Tecnologias na Educação 1(1) (2003)
7. Li, S., Yang, Z., Liu, Q., Huang, T.: Research of web information retrieval based on metadata and OAI. In: IEEE International Conference on Granular Computing, GrC 2008, August 26-28, pp. 383–386 (2008), doi:10.1109/GRC.2008.4664693
8. Bargmeyer, B.E., Gillman, D.W.: Metadata Standards and Metadata Registries: An Overview (2011), http://www.bls.gov/ore/pdf/st000010.pdf (accessed: July 10, 2011)
9. Dublin Core, The Dublin Core Metadata Initiative (2012), http://dublincore.org/ (accessed: June 2, 2012)
10. IEEE-LTSC, Draft Standard for Learning Object Metadata. IEEE Learning Technology Standards Committee (2002), http://ltsc.ieee.org/wg12/files/LOM_1484_12_1_v1_Final_Draft.pdf (accessed: Mai 10, 2011)
11. Wooldridge, M.: An Introduction to Multiagent Systems. John Wiley, England (2002)
12. FIPA. Foundation for Intelligent Physical Agents (2012), http://www.fipa.org/ (accessed: December 10, 2012)
13. JADE, Java Agent Development Framework (2012), http://jade.tilab.com/ (accessed: December 3, 2012)
14. Manning, C.D., Raghavan, P., Schutz, H.: Introduction to Information Retrieval. Cambridge University Press, England (2008)

A Semantic Web Approach
to Recommend Learning Objects

Tiago Thompsen Primo*, André Behr, and Rosa Maria Vicari

Federal University of Rio Grande do Sul,
Informatics Institute, Porto Alegre, RS, Brazil
{ttprimo,arbehr,rosa}@inf.ufrgs.br

Abstract. This work explores the use of Semantic Web techniques as an alternative to traditional educational recommender systems. The proposed model explores the use of Learning Object metadata information and Student academic profile described by knowledge ontologies in order to provide a knowledge structure. This knowlege is stored in an OWL ontology providing domain knowledge and knowledge interoperability. Such ontologies can be used by Recommender Systems to provide educational material recommendations. For a common vocabulary, the core of the ontologies were described with the use of OBAA, a metadata standard that extends IEEE LOM and provides interoperability among hardware platforms to cope with the Brazilian educational context.

Keywords: Semantic Web, Recommender Systems, Ontology.

1 Introduction

Shadbolt et al. define the Semantic Web as a Web of actionable information. Information derived from data through a semantic theory for interpreting the symbols. The semantic theory provides an account of "meaning" in which the logical connection of terms establishes interoperability between systems [1]. A large quantity of interconnected data is relevant for the Semantic Web takes form. This data have to be in a standard, be reachable, and manageable by tools and/or Agents.

The adoption of common conceptualizations, referred as ontologies, achieves the data integration. The ontologies that will furnish the semantics for the Semantic Web must be developed, managed, and endorsed by communities. The idealized Semantic Web makes substantial reuse of existing ontologies and data. It is a linked information space in which data is being enriched and added [1].

Studer et al. presented the ontology term as being "a formal, explicit specification of a shared conceptualization", merging Gruber and Burst definitions [2]. Thus, the education domain can use ontology representation and its search mechanisms for learning objects.

---

* We thank CNPq and UFRGS for the grant and fisical structure to support this research.

J.M. Corchado et al. (Eds.): PAAMS 2013 Workshops, CCIS 365, pp. 340–350, 2013.

The Institute of Electrical and Electronic Engineers (IEEE) characterizes a learning object as an entity, digital or non-digital, that may be used for learning, education, or training [3]. Then, in the Semantic Web context, learning objects must be well-defined. Laleuf and Spalter mentioned that the learning resource representations must support the finest-grained level of granularity required by the core technologies [4].

Learning objects are a useful type of data representation. Standards describe its contents, but those standards do not have well-defined ontologies that can promote information reasoning to derive new knowledge that could be used to provide more accurate educational material suggestions or recommendations.

According to [5] a Recommender System (RS) has the purpose of helping in the process of suggesting or receiving a suggestion. This suggestion may be any object that will help a user or a group of users.

This work intends to gather and unite such definitions on a multidisciplinary research to provide a common ontology engineering approach that encompass a knowledge infrastructure that can provide information reasoning to aid RS. Such approach can be seen as some sort of "cloud education" initiative.

For the ontology representation and engineering process the Web Ontology Language 2 (OWL 2)[1] was chosen, a recommended pattern by the World Wide Web Consortium (W3C). Beyond its wide utilization in the scientific community, it is an ontology specification compatible with the Semantic Web. This representation was made through Protégé[2] tool, a knowledge-based framework, ontology editor, free, and open source. The Hermit reasoner performed the reasoning process, in its version 1.3.6.

The semantic of the learning objects will furnish interoperability between systems. Its also possible to verify the learning object consistency and access its semantic via Universal Resource Identifier (URI). Therefore, an OBAA ontology may be used in recommendation systems, repositories, intelligent agents, or in a learning object authorship application.

Abstractly, each proposed component in this work can be considered an Autonomous Agent. This abstraction is also contemplated by the techniques of the SW, for example, the FOAF standard allows the description of any resource as an agent.

We consider this concept tangent to this work and will not be explicitly used. The choice of this approach was due to the fact that the technologies that enable the WEB act as a kind of "multi-agent system" make use of its concepts, but do not use the technological framework currently available for this purpose.

This paper follows in the Section 2 describes related works and the differences with this proposal. In the Section 3 with the characterization of the OBAA metadata standard, what it provides and its extension from others metadata standards. The steps for the ontology creation are described in Section 4, showing how the metadata information was transposed into ontology concepts. Section 5 illustrates its application, describing learning objects and realizing inferences

---

[1] http://www.w3.org/TR/owl2-new-features/
[2] http://protege.stanford.edu/

about technical and metadata profiles as also the link with the recommender systems.

2   Related Work

Santos and others [6] propose a recommendation model with the goal to support teachers on a specific educational activity, for instance, to prepare a lecture. Their proposed model is built over a service oriented architecture to allow interoperability over educational platforms.

Lee and others [7] proposed a modification to a traditional CF algorithm. They describe the use of semantics for user similarity. This similarity is obtained when the users provide their preferences, those preferences were mapped to knowledge areas extracted from Wikipedia. To determine how similar the users are, they develop a Bayesian Belief Network [3]. The major difference from our research, is that they do not provide ways to share they domain knowledge with other applications.

Klasnja-Milícevíc and others [8] proposed a recommendation module for algorithms tutoring. Their proposal explores, as similarity variables, the use of the students cognitive learning stile to support a Collaborative Filtering RS method. Their student, domain and activities as modeled with the use of ontologies. Their proposed work, are different from the one here proposed because the authors are not considering the reuse of those knowledge by other educational applications.

Considering the related works, [6] its the most similar. Our major difference is that we think that the educational domain can be described with ontologies and the Axioms will provide the intersections between contexts, educational material and users.

3   The OBAA Metadata Standard

There are some metadata standards that define learning objects, such as LOM [3] and OBAA [9]. Metadata is data used to describe other data or loosely defined as data about data, as mentioned by Bargmeyer et al. [10]. This paper proposes an approach to transpose this conceptualizations to an ontology model.

Barcelos et al. cited that the OBAA metadata proposal [11] is one of the OBAA project main results and it defines an extension of the IEEE-LOM standard. This proposal provides several new metadata which allows object interoperability among multiple digital platforms beyond the Web platform, supporting new platforms such as Digital TV and mobile devices. It also provides specific metadata for accessibility and pedagogical issues [12].

The IMS AccessForAll standard provides the metadata accessibility resources [13]. The proposal above also mentions that the proposed metadata intends to ensure freedom to the developer of pedagogical content. Therefore, the professional encounters no technological restrictions. The proposed set of metadata

---

[3] A model to reason about uncertainty.

establishes a wide structure for cataloging, enabling different forms of application according to the needs of each learning object designer.

In the next section we present our ontology creation process, involving the description of classes, properties and individuals. Also we present our reasoning method for such ontology.

4 Ontology Creation Process

The ontology creation process was made from technical reports of metadata standards: LOM [3], OBAA [9], and IMS AccessForAll [13]. The OBAA metadata standard furnishes the data in an organized way (with hierarchy, domain, ranges, etc. defined).

Since the metadata were organized respecting an hierarchy, the ontology began to be created in a top-down approach. Noy and Mcguinnes describe a top-down development as a process that starts with the definition of the most general domain concepts and subsequent specialization of concepts [14].

The remaining section presents how it was described the Class Hierarchy, Properties, Cardinalities, Annotations and Documentation.

4.1 Class Hierarchy

The process started transforming each metadata item in one ontology class, respecting the predetermined hierarchy, resulting in classes and subclasses. Qin and Finneran performed similar methodology, where learning object has each one of its components normalized in a group of classes into a more generic class [15].

The class nomination was made respecting the metadata name proposed in the respective technical reports of LOM, IMS AccessForAll, and OBAA. However, the Protégé tool does not allows entities to have the same name in the same ontology, because of the ontology Unique Name Assumption (UNA). In LOM, for example, the metadata identifiers 1.4, 5.10, 6.3, 8.3, and 9.3 all have the same name: Description.

Thus, to obtain classes with different names, it was concatenated to the metadata name the father metadata name followed to the point character, until it results in a unique name. For example, General and Rights contain the Description metadata. So, the result classes will be General.Description and Rights.Description.

The metadata Rights group contains the metadata Cost, Copyright and Other Restrictions, and Description. This resultant class hierarchy group is illustrated in Figure 1.

In the end, LOM.Technical and LOM.Educational classes were made equivalent respectively to OBAA.Technical and OBAA.Educational. Figure 1 shows these equivalences. Moreover, the Accessibility class from IMS had its superclass set to OBAA.

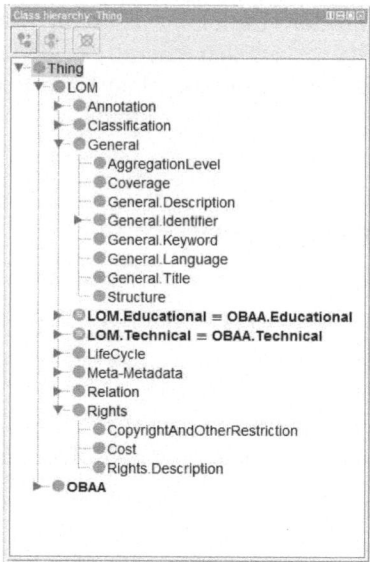

Fig. 1. LOM general hierarchy and detailed hierarchy class of the metadata group Rights

The class hierarchy is used to determinate the domain of a property. This domain is relevant to identify the types of the learning object and classify it posteriorly. Moreover, it is possible to define the cardinality of the property in a class level.

4.2   Properties

The properties were defined according to its the metadata characteristic. Whether the metadata is a leaf node, a correspondent data property will be made; if the metadata is a container type with a maximum cardinality greater than one, an object property will be related to it. So, if a container metadata has cardinality one there will not be an object property for it.

For the nomenclature, the data properties have the same name of the classes. The only difference is that the first letter is in lower case. On the other hand, the object properties are nominated with the prefix "has" followed by the class name.

Last, the properties domains and ranges were defined. The reasoner defines the types of the individual from domains, so it is important for further inference. Whether a metadata has a conditional value space, as in Name (number 4.4.1.2), this restriction is done in the superclass level and the property range is a set with all possible values.

It was chosen to define one property for each class instead of sharing properties in different classes, even if the property would have the same range. This was decided because the reasoner defines the type of the individual always from the property domain. Therefore, if a domain is a union of classes, the profile inference will be prejudiced. Mostly when it is necessary to know which specific property was filled, because a common super class type is assumed. Moreover, the cardinality verification was done in an incorrect way, not been possible to have different cardinalities in different classes for the same property.

The Figure 2 exemplifies a property creation part of Outras Infâncias learning object related to the LifeCycle metadata group. The individuals OutrasInfancias-CORE and OutrasInfanciasLifeCycleContribute1 are linked by the hasLifeCycle.Contribute object property.

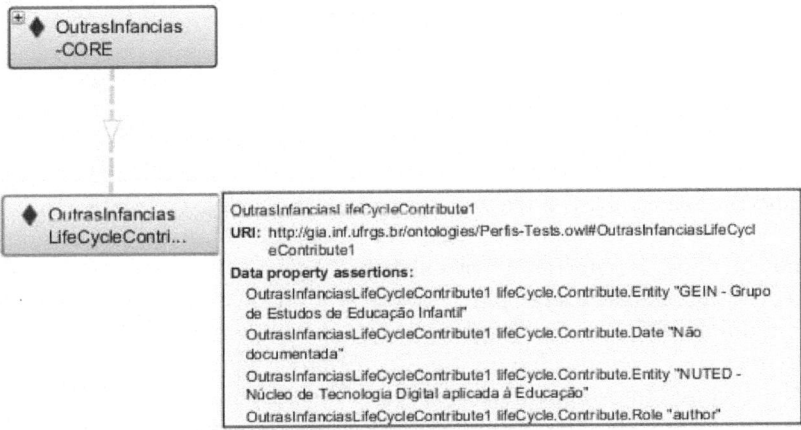

Fig. 2. Properties related to the OutrasInfanciasLifeCycleContribute1 individual

The properties will represent the learning object characteristics. The determined property range consists if the property was filled correctly. It is also possible to relate learning objects by object properties.

4.3 Cardinalities

The property cardinalities were defined according to the technical reports. Each cardinality is associated with the correspondent metadata, restricted by its property.

All the data and object property cardinalities were defined in superclass, aiming a code standard. For example, if a property has cardinality one, it is possible to restrict this cardinality both in superclass and in defining the property as functional. The Figure 3 shows the lifeCycle.Contribute.Role cardinality property and the inherited object property hasLifeCycleContribute.

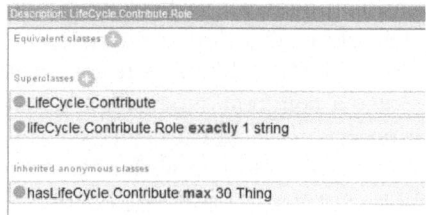

Fig. 3. Cardinalities inherited to the LifeCycle.Contribute.Role class.

The cardinalities limit the number of properties that a learning object must have. So, if a learning object must have just one title, it will be restricted by cardinality.

4.4 Annotations and Documentation

It was used the enhanced annotation capabilities of OWL 2. Then, with OBAA, LOM, and IMS AccessForAll technical reports was possible to create annotations with the same tags of the reports. Also were created comments to the facts that could not be done, as cardinality problems.

Moreover, there is a Protégé plugin called OWL Doc[4] that generates a HMTL page containing all the documentation above mentioned. This allows to have an ontology overview even not having the Protégé tool working.

All the documentation was imported to a website. Thus, it is possible to access all the ontology semantic by its URI. Shadbolt et al. mention that associating a URI with a resource means that anyone can link to it, refer to it, or retrieve a representation of it [1].

4.5 Individuals

Aiming the lowest ontology granularity, a minimum quantity of individuals should be created. Then, only the container metadata with cardinality greater than one will have an individual representation.

With an individual, it is possible maintain the relationship between the data properties of the container metadata and its maximum cardinality. But, it is necessary create an individual for the utilization of this object property always when the container appear in the metadata.

A whole learning object will be represented by one or more individuals. There will be a central individual representing the learning object that links the container representations above. This central individual will also handle the metadata elements that are in containers with cardinality equal to one by data properties.

Then, it will be possible consist this representation, verifying if a property is well-filled. It is also possible get inferences by the reasoning process.

---

[4] http://www.co-ode.org/downloads/owldoc/

5   Ontology Application

The following subsections presents some applications of the OBAA ontology. This ontology would be integrated into recommendation systems, repositories, or a learning object authorship application.

5.1   Learning Object Representation

The learning object representation was made through the learning objects available at the OBAA portal[5]. Following the process above, the learning object Outras Infâncias is exemplified in Figure 4.

There is a main individual, named OutrasInfancias-CORE that is linked with other individuals by object properties. These individuals represent the metadata containers. There are also data properties that are hidden in this figure.

This approach is similar to performed by Gluz and Vicari [16]. The difference is that metadata containers, with cardinality one, are not included in the learning object representation. For example, the Metadata individuals (md001, md002, ...) are not included in this work.

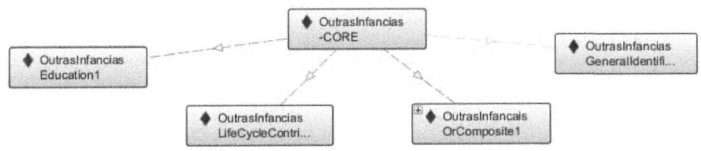

Fig. 4. Individuals related to main individual OutrasInfancias-CORE

In the end, all the individuals are declared as different. Because the reasoner do not assume same individuals when the cardinality is greater than the suggested.

5.2   Development of Application Profiles

Posteriorly, profile ontology was created to classify learning object individuals according some profiles. Technical and metadata profiles were defined. These profiles were defined as equivalent classes to be possible infer individuals as its members. The equivalent class is needed to specify the necessary and sufficient conditions to the reasoner inference.

In this ontology, property chains were created according to the profile. It is necessary to propagate the all the linked individual types to the main individual (the learning object). So, at the end of the inference process, the main individual will be associated with the profile and not the other individuals that compose

---

[5] http://www.portalobaa.org/

the learning object. This chain is also important as an access to the properties of the individuals that composes the whole learning object.

For example, to the PlatformSpecificFeatures node (illustrated in Figure 5), the chain would be compose of PlatformSpecificFeatures, SpecificRequirement, and SpecificOrComposite. Therefore, a chain property will be formed for each node way and level. In this case, an object property named as hasPlatformSpecificFeaturesChain with its chains was created, showed in Figure 6.

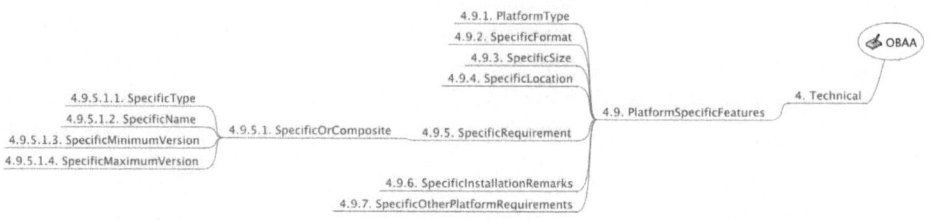

Fig. 5. PlatformSpecificFeatures descendent nodes

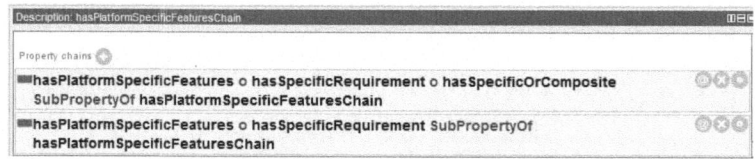

Fig. 6. Object property chains to hasPlatformSpecificFeaturesChain

With technical profiles, it is possible to classify determined learning object according its supported technology. Figure 7 exemplifies a learning object profile that supports the Ginga digital television technology. This example would have the Specific Name metadata (number 4.9.5.1.2) filled with the value "ginga" and the Language (1.3), for example, filled with "Português do Brasil".

Fig. 7. Learning object technical profile example for Ginga technology

The metadata profiles aim verify if the learning object has or not a metadata filled, independent of which values were filled. The Figure 8 shows the OBAA-Lite profile, defined by Julia da Silva [17], as an ontology equivalent class.

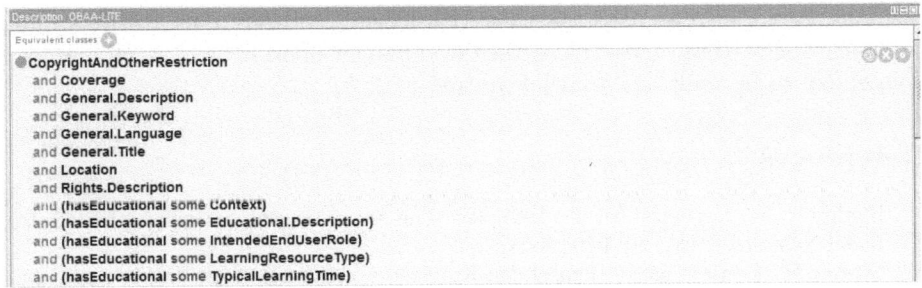

Fig. 8. Equivalent class to OBAA-LITE profile

5.3   The Use of RS

There are two steps for the RS workflow. The first step incorporates the reuse of basic RS methods (Collaborative Filtering, Content Based or Hybrid), with their basic requirements. Their use produce the first list of recommendations which is the result of this step.

The second step is also considered as the post-processing of the first step recommendation list. For its function the set of the $o' \in O$ recommendation is necessary for any user u and at least two sets of metadata and one set of axioms. The first set describes the profile of the user u with information i'_u. The second set describes the object o' with the information i'_o associated. The third set describes a set of application profiles p in the form of axioms with the information i_p associated. Applying reasoning over i'_u, i'_o and the set of axioms i_p originates an final set of recommendations.

Considering the Description Logic, the application profiles are more likely to form the TBOX and the users and learning objects will form the ABOX. To cope with this infrastructure a few definitions on the Educational Content, User Model and Post-Processing had to be made and will be described in the next sections.

6   Conclusion

This work presented how to transpose a standard metadata into an ontology. Further, a learning object was described as an individual member of this ontology and it is also possible to classify individuals from technical and metadata profiles.

Ontologies allow a discourse domain to be verified about its data consistency. It can be done through its axioms. It is also possible classify ontological representations of learning objects according predetermined profiles.

After this experiment, it was noted that the task of create an ontology with a metadata standard for the ontology development is facilitated. The hierarchy classes, the properties, etc. just have to be transposed to the ontology. So, this task would be automatically done by an application. It was also presented that a RS can get benefits with the use of such ontology engineering process.

As a future work, a tool that uses the OBAA ontology will be developed. With this tool, it will be possible that others applications uses it according with its domains. It can also be used together with learning objects repositories aiming to consist such data properly. Also the development of an RS with such ontology is intended to be built as an initial prototype.

References

1. Shadbolt, N., Berners-Lee, T., Hall, W.: The semantic web revisited. IEEE Intelligent Systems 21(3), 96–101 (2006)
2. Studer, R., Benjamins, R., Fensel, D.: Knowledge engineering: principles and methods. Data and Knowledge Engineering 25, 161–197 (1998)
3. Learning Technology Standards Committee of the IEEE: IEEE standard for learning object metadata (draft). IEEE standard 1484.12.1 (2002)
4. Laleuf, J.R., Spalter, A.M.: A component repository for learning objects: A progress report. In: Proceedings of the 1st ACM/IEEE-CS Joint Conference on Digital Libraries, JCDL 2001, pp. 33–40. ACM, New York (2001)
5. Resnick, P., Varian, H.R.: Recommender systems. Commun. ACM 40(3), 56–58 (1997)
6. Santos, O.C., Boticario, J.G.: Modeling recommendations for the educational domain. Procedia Computer Science 1(2), 2793–2800 (2010)
7. Lee, J.W., Lee, S.G., Kim, H.J.: A probabilistic approach to semantic collaborative filtering using world knowledge. Journal of Information Science 37(1) (February 2011)
8. Klašnja-Milićević, A., Vesin, B., Ivanovic, M., Budimac, Z.: E-learning personalization based on hybrid recommendation strategy and learning style identification. Computers & Education 56(3) (April 2011)
9. Vicari, R.M., Gluz, J.C., Santos, E.R., Primo, T.T., Rossi, L.H.L., Bordignon, A., Behar, P., Passerino, L.M., Filho, R.C.M.F., Roesler, V.: Proposta de padrão para metadados de objetos de aprendizagem multiplataforma. Technical Report 01.08.0215.00, Universidade Federal do Rio Grande do Sul (UFRGS) (July 2009)
10. Bargmeyer, B.E., Gillman, D.W.: Metadata standards and metadata registries: An overview (2000)
11. Viccari, R., Gluz, J.C., Passerino, L.M., Santos, E., Primo, T., Rossi, L., Bordignon, A., Behar, P., Filho, R., Roesler, V.: The OBAA proposal for learning objects supported by agents. In: Proceedings of MASEIE Workshop – AAMAS 2010 (2010)
12. Barcelos, C.F., Gluz, J.C., Vicari, R.M.: An agent-based federated learning object search service. In: LACLO 2010 (2010)
13. IMS Global Learning Consortium, Inc.: IMS accessforall meta-data information model. Technical Report Version 1.0 Final Specification (July 2004)
14. Noy, N.F., Mcguinness, D.L.: Ontology development 101: A guide to creating your first ontology. Technical report (2001)
15. Qin, J., Finneran, C.: Ontological representation of learning objects. In: Proceedings of the Workshop on Document Search Interface Design and Intelligent Access in Large-Scale Collections, pp. 52–57. Springer (2002)
16. Gluz, J.C., Vicari, R.M.: Uma ontologia OWL para metadados IEEE-LOM, dublin-core e OBAA. In: Anais do XXII SBIE - XVII WIE, Aracaju, pp. 204–213 (November 2011) ISSN: 2176-4301
17. da Silva, J.M.C.: Análise Técnica e Pedagógica de Metadados Para Objetos de Aprendizagem. PhD in informatics in education, Universidade Federal do Rio Grande do Sul (UFRGS), CDU - 371.694:681.3 (2011)

Learning Objects Repository Management
Using an Adaptive Quality Evaluation Multi-Agent System

Valentina Tabares[1], Néstor Duque[2], Demetrio Ovalle[1], Paula Rodrígucz[1],
and Julián Moreno[1]

[1] Universidad Nacional de Colombia Sede Medellín
{vtabaresm,dovalle,parodriguezma,jmoreno1}@unal.edu.co
[2] Universidad Nacional de Colombia Sede Manizales
ndduqueme@unal.edu.co

Abstract. Availability and correspondence with expectations are desired characteristics in order to guarantee the quality of Learning Objects (LOs) retrieved
from LO repositories during the search process. The administrators of these repositories have the responsibility of ensuring the quality of LOs after applying
their corresponding evaluation. The implementation of metrics applied on relevant characteristics of LOs is a crucial tool for LO evaluation. This paper proposes an approach that uses a Multi-Agent System (MAS) for assessing main
LO characteristics, applying different methods and metrics being adjustable to
different kinds of repositories by employing adaptive parser agents. By using
metadata as main source of information, the metrics allow users to rate the quality of LOs and generates alarms concerning inputs that do not meet the expected
values. The system developed automatically evaluates a large number of resources to facilitate the work of the repository administrators before improving
or publishing the LOs into a repository federation.

Keywords: Learning objects repository management, quality evaluation, metrics,
multi-agent systems.

1 Introduction

The consolidation of digital resources warehouses leads to problems associated with
the exponential growth of data and information stored in repositories. One of these
problems concerns the adequate resource management, ensuring their use and access
and guarantying their specification through metadata that define their context, content, and structure. In addition, such metadata should accurately reflect the communication, action, or decision for which these digital resources were created [1] .

Among the trends of digital resources we can find the following: The learning objects (LOs) available to users; the consolidation of repositories that store these LOs
categorized from specific interests and the implementation of federations of LO repositories that enable centralized searches of distributed digital resources. In general
these trends aim to focus on users' needs and concerns, thus facilitating –in agile and
timely way– the retrieving of relevant, accurate, and relevant information [2].

J.M. Corchado et al. (Eds.): PAAMS 2013 Workshops, CCIS 365, pp. 351–362, 2013.
© Springer-Verlag Berlin Heidelberg 2013

Considering that characteristics such as availability, accessibility, property, versioning, and reusability define the quality of stored LOs and that all of those depend on the quality of the metadata representing them, one of the main challenges is to determine the quality of such metadata being responsible of facilitating the search and retrieval of accurate resources from these LO repositories [3].

To a large extent the usefulness of a learning object repository (LOR) depends on the quality of the metadata that describe their objects. It is common that users perform a search and as a result they obtain big lists of possible LOs that should be reviewed one by one, in order to identify those which are really relevant according to their interests and needs. This process is lengthy and wasteful, and also it must be consider that many of these resources may be are not available. Thus, it runs the risk of generating mistrust and can result in lack of interest for users in this kind of educational materials [4]. Furthermore, this situation is even more serious in the case of the automatic selection of LOs for construction of virtual courses or educational modules.

Different studies show that it is common to find inaccurate, incomplete, and inconsistent metadata in digital repositories. Although formal rules and standards are established in digital repositories, the majority of metadata involved do not comply with these requirements, thus the recovery system delivers to the user data that do not correspond to the resource's content searched or also offers outdated LOs [5][6][7].

Several approaches are possible to deal with this problem. Some research works define the quality of metadata in terms of fundamental concepts such as relevance and accuracy, and for doing so, define automatics metric for their evaluation [8][9]. Other authors present tools that allow to evaluate certain aspects associated with the metadata, as in [10] in which authors propose a web application that measures to what extent LOs are complete considering the Dublin Core standard as a reference and using the OAI - Open Archives Initiative - protocol for metadata harvesting. A infrastructure that takes into consideration both syntactic and semantic aspects of metadata from a qualitative perspective is presented in [11].

This research work proposes a system to support the LORs management by evaluating the quality of the metadata involved within their LOs. The system qualifies the fixation degree according to the policies and standards concerning the adopted metadata, thus generating alarms to those metadata that do not meet the expected values. Although this process is basically guided in the system by the LO metadata however some similarity-based techniques are introduced to perform semantic analysis and thus proceed to refine the results that going far beyond a simple string comparison.

The paper is organized as follows: Section 1 outlines main problems involved in this research and some related works to face those problems. Section 2 presents the system proposed, based on a multi-agent approach that leverages the features of modularity, scalability, and adaptability at the same time allows to act from a distributed perspective that characterizes this kind of problems. Section 3 shows and analyzes the tests carried out at the level of LO repositories management. Finally, conclusions and future work are presented in Section 4.

2   Proposal of Multi-agent Architecture for LO Repositories Management

To support the process of the LORs management and taking advantage of the MAS characteristics, we propose a system that retrieves stored LO metadata from distributed LO repositories and analyzes them by applying metrics in order to verify their quality.

The system applies with versatility evaluations according to the metadata standard under which resources were labeled. The system receives as input the repository or the metadata location, retrieves these metadata, cleans and analyzes them and also makes transformations in order to apply measurement algorithms and hence qualify their quality.

Figure 1 shows the MAS architecture deploying the agents that interact within the system and the communication established among them.

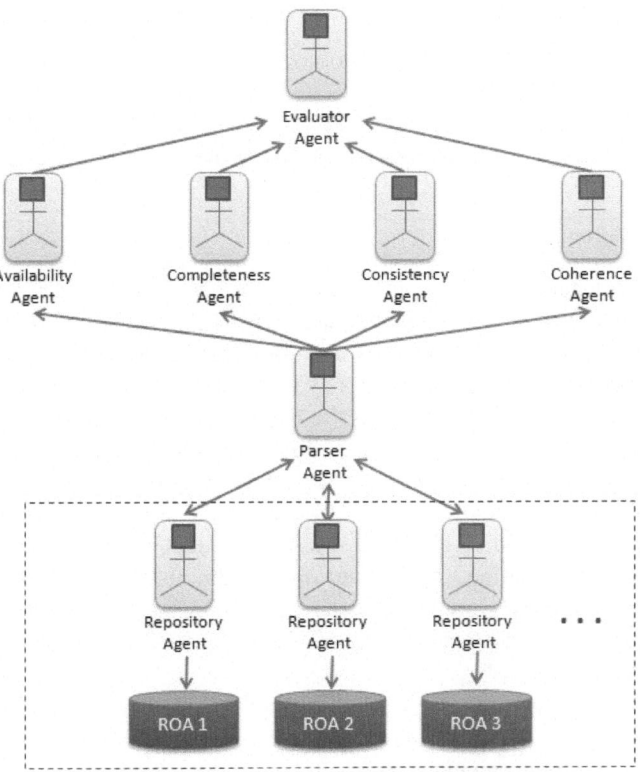

Fig. 1. Multi-agent System Architecture Diagram

2.1   Repository Agent

This agent knows all the information associated with the LOR to be evaluated, and represents this within the system. This agent requires general and specific information about how metadata are delivered. The user can decide to use the standard metadata or define its own structure. Each Repository Agent must send this information to the Parser Agent.

Figure 2 shows the System Interface that allows the registration of the repository to be evaluated and its respective structure.

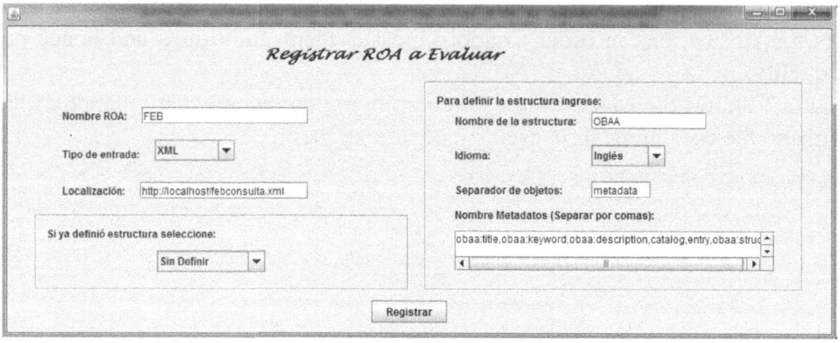

Fig. 2. Registration System Interface

2.2   Parser Agent

The Parser Agent, that simulates the behavior of a parser program, is the component of the system that interprets text as input and builds a data structure, transforming it to the desired format, and then sends this data structure to the evaluation process. The parsers may be programmed by hand or may be (semi-) automatically generated [12].

This agent receives information from the Repository Agent about the LOR on how they deliver their LOs metadata and their structure. The LORs can deliver the LO's metadata in different ways such as plain text, XML, OAI-PMH but also can directly allow the users to access databases of LO's contents. The metadata structure also varies depending on the standard chosen by the ROA or its own rules.

Using the structure defined by the repository administrator, the Parser Agent initiates a process of reading and processing of LO's metadata. This agent recognizes the different labels and extracts the values of the corresponding metadata, creating tag-value pairs.

After being structured the information, this agent is in charge of delivering the data to other agents such as Availability, Completeness, Consistency, and Coherence, in order to proceed with the calculations.

The first column of Table 1 shows the metadata structure that has been defined by the repository administrator. While the second column shows the initial reading of the metadata provided by the LOR the third column shows the metadata in a structured way.

Table 1. Process of recognition of Metadata

Structure defined by the administrator	Initial reading of metadata	Structured metadata	
		Tag	Value
• Título • Idioma(s) • Descripción • Autor(es) • Entidad(es) • Palabras Clave • Versión • Fecha • Ubicación • Formato • Instalación • Requerimientos • Uso Educativo • Costo • Derechos de Autor • Ruta Taxonómica • Fuente Clasificación	O B J E T O I N F O R M A T I V O **Título**: Salud en el computador. **Descripción**: Guía de cuidado. **Palabras Clave**: Ergonomía; salud. Ciclo de Vida. **Autor(es)**: Botero Orduz, Diego. **Entidad(es)**: Dirección Innovación. **Versión**: V.1.0. **Fecha**: 2005. Técnico. **Formato**: zip. **Ubicación**: **Costo**: Libre. **Derechos de Autor**: Copyright 2005 ©. Anotación. **Uso Educativo**: Sugerencias. **Fuente Clasificación**: Áreas de Conocimiento - NBC.	Título	Salud en el computador.
		Descripción	Guía de cuidado.
		Autor(es)	Botero Orduz, Diego.
		Entidad(es)	Dirección Innovación.
		Palabras Clave	Ergonomía; salud.
		Versión	V.1.0.
		Fecha	2005.
		Ubicación	
		Formato	zip.
		Uso Educativo	Sugerencias.
		Costo	Libre.
		Derechos de Autor	Copyright 2005 ©.
		Fuente Clasificación	Áreas Conocimiento - NBC.

2.3   Availability Agent

The characteristic of availability is defined as the possibility that the LO has to be found and used at any time. The avalability agent focuses on the location metadata to determine the level of availability of the evaluated LO, i.e., if it is possible to directly download the LO or if the link that indicates the LO location is active.

In order to calculate the metric the availability agent maps 1 to those cases that the LO is available and 0 otherwise. Since this field can be multi-valued hence the value is divided by the number of found instances. Equation 1 expresses how this metric can be determined. In case that LO does not have metadata location (L = 0), the metric value is 0.

$$AvailabMetric = \frac{\sum_1^n (Mi)}{L} \tag{1}$$

Where L is the number of locations instances, $Mi=1$ if location is available and $Mi=0$ if location is not available

2.4   Completeness Agent

This agent is responsible for assessing whether the metadata associated to the LO describe it as much as possible. In order to determine this value the completeness agent reviews in detail all the metadata instances verifying if it contains values filled with resource information, measuring to what extent the information is available according to the amount of metadata being established by the standard.

Since not all of the LO metadata have the same relevance, a weight is assigned to some of them that are the "most frequently used". Based on the weights defined in [13], the scanning process was performed allowing to tune the weights according to the those LOs metadata that are commonly used in different LO repositories. Figure 3 shows the metadata used for calculating the LOs completeness and their respective weights. However, these weighting factors can be parameterized according to the specific conditions of each LO repository or according to the policies handled by them.

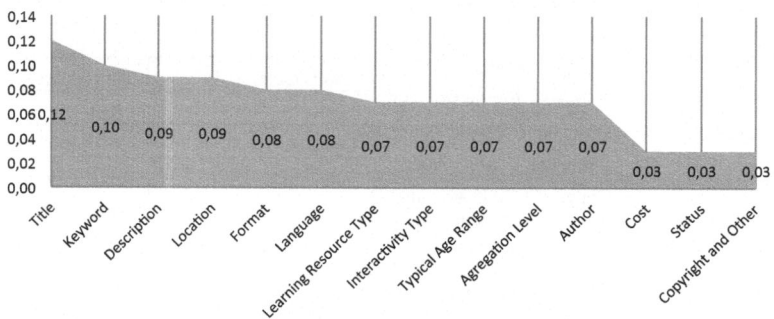

Fig. 3. Weighing Factor

For calculating the metric, a value of 1 is assigned if the metadata have value (not null) and 0 for other case, then such a value is multiplied for the corresponding factor. The accumulate result is the metric value and its range is [0,1]. A value of 1 means that LO is fully complete, whereas a value of 0 means that LO is completely metadata empty. The corresponding formula is shown in Equation 2:

$$ComplMetric = \sum_1^n (ki * Mi) \qquad (2)$$

Where ki is the Weighing Factor, $Mi=1$ if value of metadata is not null and $Mi=0$ if value of metadata is null.

2.5   Consistency Agent

This agent is in charge of estimating the conformity level of LOs according to the metadata standard or structure established by the specific LO repositories to which they belong to. Specifically, the Consistency Agent evaluates a series of defined rules to determine whether LOs are complying with the values defined by the standard. For doing so, the agent must first of all identify which LO standard is associated with the resource in order to proceed with the evaluation. It is important to highlight that this information is supplied by the Parser Agent.

The rules that are defined are mostly of the type If - Then, and their goal is to analyze each of the fields that are not free text. In [13] four rules are presented, which were enlarged and tuned for this research and thus obtaining a total of 15 rules based on standard LOM. It is important to highlight that it is not always possible to apply all rules, since some of metadata are not covered by some LO standards, which means that the rule will not fire. In this case, the agent must first assess the existence of the metadata that is directly involved in the rule before execute it.

An example of these rules is shown as follows:

Rule X: If Difficulty.exist *is* true *and* Dificult.value *in* (very easy, easy, medium, difficult, very difficult) *Then* Mi = 1

If the metadata that is used by the evaluation rule does not exist, this rule must be discarded and hence not affect the metric calculation, since the absence of the field was already taken into consideration in the analysis of the completeness metric.

Equation 3 expresses how was calculated this metric, a value of 1 is assigned if the metadata complies with rule and 0 is assigned otherwise. The accumulate result is the metric value and its range is [0,1]. A value of 1 means that LO is completely consistent, whereas a value of 0 means that LO is completely inconsistent. It could be the case that no rule is fired, so the value of the consistency metric will be equal to 0.

$$ConsisMetric = \frac{\sum_1^n (Mi)}{R} \tag{3}$$

Where R is the number of analyzed rules, $Mi=1$ if metadata complies with the rule and $Mi=0$ if metadata do not complies with the rule

2.6   Coherence Agent

The Coherence Agent is responsible for evaluating the degree in which a set of metadata describe the same resource. In other words, this agent determines the semantic distance between different free text fields.

To implement its behavior this agent must apply an initial filter in order to remove the excess of irrelevant words, then transforms uppercase to lowercase and removes accents by applying text mining operations. This process considers the language of the metadata, which is specified by the repository administrator at the moment that defines the structure of the metadata.

In [13] the Coherence Agent has worked with the following fields: title, keywords and description. Although these fields have great relevance with respect to other metadata and in order to obtain a better implementation of this metric, this agent will scan all the LO metadata reviewing which of them correspond to free text fields and perform the respective calculation by using them.

To calculate the semantic distance the cosine measure is proposed, which measures the similarity between arrays. In this case such arrays are the words contained in the description of the metadata. To obtain K_i the consistency agent applies the knowledge that it possess about the LO repository and fits the metric to these conditions. Equation 4 expresses how this metric can be determined.

$$CohereMetric = \left. \sum_1^k \sum_1^n \frac{Pi * Qi}{\sqrt{(\sum_1^n Pi^2 * \sum_1^n Qi^2)}} \middle/ Ki \right. \tag{4}$$

Where Ki is the number of metadata analyzed, Pi is term frequency i in field 1 and Qi is term frequency i in field 2

2.7   Evaluator Agent

The Evaluator Agent is in charge of analyzing the values obtained by the other agents such as Availability, Completeness, Consistency, and Coherence. Its behavior is based on a production rules system that executes on the facts obtained by the application of the previously defined metrics. Some general examples of the alarm rules triggered by this agent are the following:

- If $AvailabMetric$ = 0 then alarm1;
- If $AvailabMetric$ > 0 and $ComplMetric$ < umbralCompl then run alarm2;
- If not alarm2 and $ConsisMetric$ < umbralConsis then run alarm3;
- If not alarm3 and $CohereMetric$ < umbralCohere then run alarm4;
- If alarm1 and alarm2 and alarm3 then run alarmGral;

These alarms allow the repository administrator identify objects with greater problems in specific metrics and the combination of some of them. In addition, an overall value named "Total metric" is calculated for each LO, which allows to order and classify all the LOs based on their quality measurement.

In order to display the results in a useful and visual way for the repository administrator, the Evaluator Agent employs the semaphore coding, according to the defined threshold values, and highlighting the biggest problems that have been found in the LO's metadata.

The red color identifies the LOs with higher quality problems. That is, if the value of "Total metric" is less than or equal to 0.3 the LO is located in this category. The yellow color is used to present LOs that have low levels of assessment, with a value greater than 0.3 and less than or equal to 0.6, and finally, the green color presents those LOs obtaining the best reviews, greater than 0.6. Figure 4 shows the results obtained after applying metrics as well as by using three colors (red, yellow and green) it is possible to easily categorize LOs according to their metadata quality.

3   Experimental Work

We conducted a case study in which the proposed model was used in three different LO repository scenarios. The MAS was implemented using JADE platform (Java Agent Development Framework) [14].

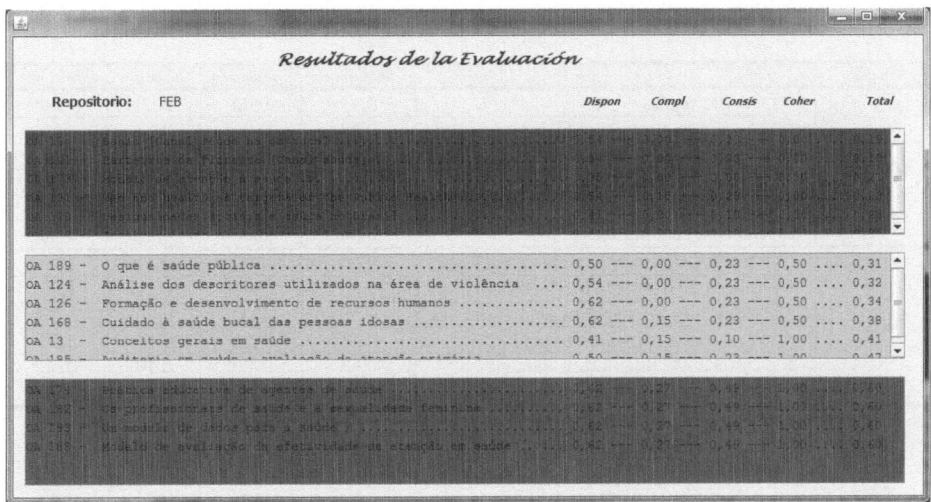

Fig. 4. Deployment of LO Quality Evaluation Results

The selected repositories were Federation Educa Brazil (FEB), Federación de Re positorios de Objetos de Aprendizaje Colombia (FROAC) and Banco de Objetos de Aprendizaje de la Universidad Nacional de Colombia (BOAUNC). For each repository 100 LOs were evaluated in different knowledge areas.

FEB repository is a service provided by the RNP (Rede Nacional de Ensino e Pesquisa) of Brazil in order to have an available infrastructure for the confederation of LO repositories starting from a single search point, hawking as a guiding principle the reuse of these resources [15]. Metadata were directly obtained in XML format. The metadata standard used by FEB is OBAA, a Brazilian initiative aimed at interoperability of LOs on platforms such as Web, digital TV and mobile devices [16].

FROAC is a project of the National University of Colombia (Manizales and Medellín). Its main objective is to build a federation of LORs with a focus on centralized metadata harvesting, storing LOs in a central server, where the users can execute general or advanced searches. This federation provides additional services that support users in the process of searching and selecting of such digital resources [17]. LOM is the metadata standard used to specify LOs, which was initially proposed by the IEEE, grouped into nine categories containing around 50 fields [18]. Metadata were obtained through OAI-PMH interface.

BOAUNC is an initiative of the Dirección Nacional de Innovación Académica of Colombia that provides educational materials developed by teachers from different university faculties. This repository is part of the project entitled "Catalogación de Objetos de Aprendizaje en Instituciones de Educación Superior", promoted by the Ministerio de Educación Nacional [19]. For the experiment, the metadata were obtained through the web search and converted as plain text files.

Table 2 shows the three best and three worst scores for each LOR, generated by the system, ordered from low to high in the ratings. Hence, these values can help repository managers to take action in order to cope with this issue.

In the case of obtaining the LO availability value equal to 0, although other values of the metrics are favorable, the final rating will be poor since the resource is non-available.

Table 2. Top five LOs with worst quality assessment

LOR		Title	Completeness	Consistency	Coherence	Availability
BOAUNC	best	Condicionales	0,63	0,00	0,23	1,00
		Manejo de vectores, TDUs y archivos	0,63	0,00	0,23	1,00
		Diseño de Algoritmos	0,63	0,00	0,23	1,00
	worst	Extracción conocimiento	0,63	0,00	0,23	0,00
		Sistemas multiagentes	0,63	0,00	0,23	0,00
		Sistema de cómputo	0,54	0,00	0,23	0,50
FROAC	best	Test TAAC Comparación de Codigos	0,60	1,00	0,23	1,00
		Ontological Agents Model based ...	0,60	1,00	0,23	1,00
		Multiobjective heuristic search in road	0,60	1,00	0,23	1,00
	worst	Agentes de software desde la ...	0,43	1,00	0,10	0,50
		Test TAAC Simulacion Paralela	0,43	1,00	0,10	0,50
		Agentes con arquitectura CBR-BDI	0,43	1,00	0,10	0,50
FEB	best	Os profissionais de saúde e ...	0,62	0,27	0,49	1,00
		Um modelo de dados para a saúde /	0,62	0,27	0,49	1,00
		Modelo de avaliação da efetividade ...	0,62	0,27	0,49	1,00
	worst	Bahia [Canal saúde na estrada]	0,54	0,00	0,23	0,00
		Ligado em saúde [Ligado em saúde]	0,54	0,00	0,23	0,00
		Ceará [Canal saúde na estrada]	0,54	0,00	0,23	0,00

Other metrics are evaluated even though you can not access the resource, because knowing the quality of other metadata help to repository administrator to take corrective action.

Is worth mentioning that the metric consistency in BOAUNC and FEB repositories are very low due to that the repositories were evaluated according to well known LO metadata standards. To avoid such bad results these repositories should had defined their own consistency rules according to the LO metadata structure that has been adopted.

The fact of identifying the educational resources that present problems allows the repository administrators to take measures for avoiding to offer low quality or unsuitable resources to users. They could exclude these resources from the search results, remove those LOs from the repository, report LO failures to authors, or update them.

Figure 5 shows the general behavior of the evaluations applied to each repository. The evaluations for the three LORs are located in an unfavorable range, below 0.6. It also shows that the LOs that had high assessments belong to the repository FROAC, since it is more in compliance with the standard metadata selected.

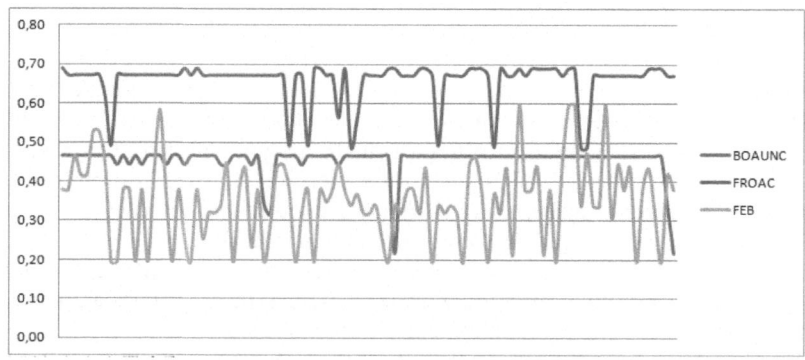

Fig. 5. General evaluations by repository

4   Conclusions and Future Work

The MAS presented adapts its behavior to different types of LO repositories, evaluating LO metadata from different sources and stored in different structures. This evaluation is necessary in order to ensure the quality of the LO repositories and is a management tool very useful for LOR administrators in different processes.

One of the main advantages of our approach is the robustness for the system to automatically evaluate large volumes of metadata which corresponds to a difficult task if it is made manually.

Modeling the problem using a MAS technique was an excellent option that allowed the disintegration of the solution into functional blocks, without losing the systemic point of view. This fact leads to distribute the solution in diverse entities that require specific knowledge, processing and communication between each other.

The implementation of production rules that support the quality metric evaluation process performed by agents take advantage of all the knowledge required by this task enabling the MAS adaptation capabilities, which was one of absolutely essential objectives proposed.

Specifically for the Colombian Federation of Learning Object Repositories FROAC this proposal represents an important factor in order to improve the quality of LOs stored in federated repositories, enabling their assessment before they be accessed and used, always attempting to improve the characteristics of these educational materials. These same benefits are available to other world LOR federations.

As future work, we will add more quality metrics to the system applied on LOs and will work in the validation stage of the results obtained. Finally, as one of the applications and services offered by FROAC, this management tool will be available soon online.

Acknowledgements. The research reported in this paper was funded in part by the COLCIENCIAS project entitled "ROAC Creación de un modelo para la Federación de OA en Colombia que permita su integración a confederaciones internacionales" Universidad Nacional de Colombia, with code 1119-521-29361.

We are grateful with the group of the Federação de Repositórios Educa Brasil – FEB, in Porto Alegre, for their collaboration.

References

1. ISO 15489-1: Information and Documentation - Records Management - Part 1: General (2001)
2. Lugo Hubp, M.: El impacto de los recursos digitales en la bibliotecas. In: UNAM (ed.) Administración de Servicios de Información, p. 173 (2004)
3. Motelet, O., Baloian, N., Pino, J.A.: Learning Object Metadata and Automatic Processes: Issues and Perspectives. In: Learning Objects: Standards, Metadata, Repositories & LCMS, pp. 185–218 (2007)
4. Ochoa, X.: Learnometrics: Metrics for Learning Objects (2008)
5. Bui, Y., Park, J.: An Assessment of Metadata Quality: A Case Study of the National Science Digital Library Metadata Repository (2006)

6. Tabares, V., Duque, N., Moreno, J.: Análisis experimental de la utilidad en la recuperación de objetos de aprendizaje desde repositorios remotos, pp. 1–12 (2011)
7. Bruce, T.R., Hillmann, D.I.: The Continuum of Metadata Quality: Defining, Expressing, Exploiting. Metadata in Practice (2004)
8. Ochoa, X., Duval, E.: Automatic evaluation of metadata quality in digital repositories. International Journal on Digital Libraries 10, 67–91 (2009)
9. Margaritopoulos, T., Mavridis, I., Margaritopoulos, M., Manitsaris, A.: A Conceptual Framework for Metadata Quality Assessment. In: Proc. Int'l Conf. on Dublin Core and Metadata Applications, pp. 104–113 (2008)
10. Nichols, D., Chan, C., Bainbridge, D.: A Tool for Metadata Analysis (2008)
11. Hughes, B.: Metadata Quality Evaluation: Experience from the Open Language Archives Community. In: Chen, Z., Chen, H., Miao, Q., Fu, Y., Fox, E., Lim, E.-P. (eds.) ICADL 2004. LNCS, vol. 3334, pp. 320–329. Springer, Heidelberg (2004)
12. Duque, N.D., Chavarro, J.C., Moreno, R.: Integrando Información de Fuentes Heterogeneas Enfoques y Tendencias. Scientia et Technica XIII, 397–401 (2007)
13. Tabares, V., Rodríguez, P., Duque, N., Vicari, R., Moreno, J.: Multi-agent Model for Evaluation of Learning Objects from Repository Federations - ELO-index. Revista Respuestas, 48–54 (2012)
14. Bellifemine, F., Poggi, A., Rimassa, G.: JADE: A FIPA2000 compliant agent development environment. In: Proceedings of the Fifth International Conference on Autonomous Agents. ACM (2001)
15. UFRGS: FEB – Federação de Repositórios Educa Brasil, http://feb.ufrgs.br/
16. Vicari, R., Gluz, J.C., Santos, E.R., Thompsen Primo, T., Longhi, L.H., Bordignon, A., Behar, P., Passerino, L.M., Machado, R.C., Roesler, V.: Proposta de Padrão para Metadados de Objetos de Aprendizagem Multiplataforma. In: Projeto OBAA (2009)
17. Tabares, V., Rodríguez, P.A., Duque, N.: Modelo Integral de Federación de Objetos de Aprendizaje en Colombia - más que búsquedas centralizadas. In: LACLO 2012 - Séptima Conferencia Latinoamericana de Objetos y Tecnologías de Aprendizaje (2012)
18. Learning Technology Standards Committee: IEEE Standard for Learning Object Metadata. Institute of Electrical and Electronics Engineers, New York (2002)
19. Dirección Nacional de Innovación Académica: Banco de Objetos de Aprendizaje de la Universidad Nacional de Colombia, http://aplicaciones.virtual.unal.edu.co/drupal/

Improving the Entrepreneur's Market Research Strategies Learning Process Using the MaREMAS Environment

Alejandro Valencia, Oscar Salazar, and Demetrio Ovalle

Universidad Nacional de Colombia - Sede Medellín - Facultad de Minas
{javalenca,omsalazaro,dovalle}@unal.edu.co

Abstract. The development of e-learning systems serving as instructors in the marketing research field for new entrepreneurs is an alternative that allows a better use of resources, a broader knowledge of the market, and a creative activity support in the discovery of new potential niche markets. Thus, the purpose of this paper is to improve the entrepreneur's learning process of market research strategies by using the MAS learning environment so-called MaREMAS. The methodologies MAS-CommonKADS and GAIA are integrated with AUML diagrams for system designing. The paper further describes the tasks, architecture and communication model of MaREMAS. In addition, main steps that support entrepreneur's market research learning process are detailed. To validate these aspects a case study in the motorcycle industry is shown. The paper finally concludes with a comparison performed between the learning processes achieved through MaREMAS environment and the traditional learning approach.

Keywords: Agent-based learning environments, market research strategies, entrepreneurship, intelligent learning systems, learning helpers modeling.

1   Introduction

The entrepreneurship impact on the economy of nations has increased in recent years; because of that, this subject has become relevant for the academic literature [1]. In this sense, many researchers have found that entrepreneurship can contribute to economic growth acting as a method to discover and generate knowledge based on the market opportunities recognition and trading [2]. It is thought that an efficient management of the business creation process becomes a filter to guide towards the selection of successful enterprises within a given market [3]. Thus, alternative mechanisms to generate intelligence should be searched in terms of competition and potential markets [4], using generative learning strategies [5], moreover, specific tools to integrate the breadth of knowledge spread on the market are required.

Consequently, the development of systems serving as instructors in marketing research for new entrepreneurs is an alternative that allows a better use of resources, a broader knowledge of the market and stimulates creative activity in the discovery of new potential expansion niche markets. Our agent-based learning environment proposed for Market Research (MR) Learning purposes aims to be an instructor in the

J.M. Corchado et al. (Eds.): PAAMS 2013 Workshops, CCIS 365, pp. 363–374, 2013.
© Springer-Verlag Berlin Heidelberg 2013

marketing research process established by McDaniel and Gates [6], which specifies standard phases of academic literature [5], [7].

The ultimate goal is that the user understands and learns about the stages and components of the MR process, thus, it is proposed a sequential process that allows it to feedback in each of the learning process steps, i.e., a process that serves as guideline to make a proper MR and promote creativity and pro-activity regarding the opportunities offered by the business environment. A Multi-Agent System (MAS) learning environment can provide support in the strategies of market orientation that are compatible with the generation of business intelligence, improving standards of reliability to create the company, and also, filling some gaps that new businessmen have in the marketing orientation due to their limited resources [4].

The rest of the paper is organized as follows: Section 2 outlines main research works related to this research. Section 3 presents a general description of MaREMAS learning environment. Section 4 further describes the MaREMAS's decision making process which involves five stages. While a case study is presented in Section 5, the main advantages and learning assistance generated by MaREMAS is provided in Section 6. Finally, conclusions and future work are presented in Section 7.

2   Related Works

In order to establish a support to entrepreneurs for learning of MR decision-making strategies and for understanding the way the enterprises operate it is necessary to adapt new tools to comply with the challenges and demands that the business sector must face [8]. In the literature, there are some learning mechanisms regarding the selection of research strategies in specific markets and the importance of these processes when making decisions successfully. It is important to note that the set of knowledge required to understand a particular market dynamics is complex and extensive, hence one of the strategies to face this complexity is to encode or categorize the whole knowledge to provide its better systematization, interpretation, and learning [9]. Concerning this subject, it is important to recognize the crucial role of MR learning models that allow the organization to respond to the users, customers or consumers' specific needs. This is particularly important especially for new entrepreneurs who have few knowledge of the markets dynamics and exhibit poor management skills coming from their little experience in the business world [10]. Experiential learning platforms by simulating market environments are considered as an appropriate mechanism to face the uncertainty and current restructuring that occurs in the market [11]. However, concerning the MR in the entrepreneurship field there are few studies about teaching-learning methods for developing, combining, and leveraging of resources to create and maintain competitive advantage in the marketplace, besides allowing to identify and exploit specific market opportunities for new entrepreneurs [9].

Some methods which focus on identifying opportunities have been developed such as the fuzzy multi-attribute decision making that correspond to an index system for generating more reasonable and objective evaluations with respect to the opportunities identified, besides taking into consideration subjective preferences of entrepreneurs, making in this way the results more comprehensive and closer to reality [9].

On the other hand, neural networks is an artificial intelligence promising approach that have already been used being a tool for knowledge discovery that use data previously collected through quantitative methodological designs. An auto-associative neural network is proposed in [12] which aims to find similarities and differences between perceptions of sample populations in a specific MR in order to identify relevant factors of the environment.

Other significant method to reduce uncertainty is the fuzzy comprehensive evaluation that allows the entrepreneur to analyze key market circumstances and hence enable the creation of successful businesses. In addition, other models have been developed for learning and assessment of entrepreneurial environments by using Fuzzy Theory and Analytic Hierarchy Process (AHP) as a support tool for generating accurate, effective, and systematic decisions making [13].

Similarly, the e-learning MR modules are proposed as a very significant option, since they allow to incorporate large amounts of knowledge that can be available for users at any time [14]. Thus, the virtual learning mechanisms are useful for entrepreneurs in order to develop their skills and to strength their business as needed, and also when the market requires them [14]. In addition, learning methods that emulate real-world processes ensure high success rates when applied to real environments. In that sense, MAS are a viable possibility in the entrepreneurship's MR learning process, since these intelligent systems allow to incorporate and manage large amounts of knowledge giving greater value added to the teaching-learning process [11].

When MAS environments are planned to be used in MR, it is important to focus on communication mechanisms associated with the learning support functions that the system could offer. Also, it should be included the situational analysis of a respective market as well as the experience from the human user in order to obtain more accurate results that responds to the requirements of the environment. On the other hand, It is important to incorporate the use of MAS in MR teaching-learning process since it allows the entrepreneurs to modify such strategies concerning the identification of market opportunities but according to the different situations that occur in the environment [8].

Finally, the MAS learning environments are particularly useful because they give clarity to entrepreneurs on strategies for MR decision making, providing them, at the same time, with security and a more objective assessment when analyzing market opportunities, being this approach considered as a reliable mechanism for improving MR teaching-learning process.

3 MaREMAS: General Description

3.1 Methodology

It is important to highlight that a single methodology is not sufficiently complete to reflect the flexibility, interaction among agents and the complexity of the organizational

MAS structures. MAS-CommonKADS and GAIA methodologies were complementary each other in different ways: the GAIA methodology uses an iterative process at each stage of the system development while MAS-CommonKADS approach uses a cyclical process that allows that the analysis and design phases can perform in an evolutionary manner, complementing the lack of tracing and tracking errors and risks attending in GAIA [15]. MAS-CommonKADS and GAIA methodologies were used along with AUML diagrams [6], [16], which is not a methodology but instead focuses on trying to adapt existing development tools in order to enrich agent-based system modeling[17]. The MAS environment raised in this paper is called MaREMAS (Market Research for Entrepreneurs based on a MAS Approach).

3.2   Task Model

This model describes the tasks that agents can perform: objectives of each task, its components and problem solving methods. The decomposition of tasks into sub-tasks are shown in Figure 1.

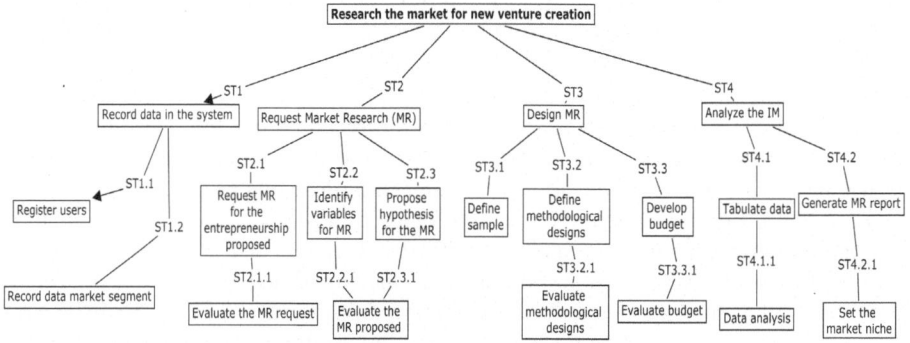

Fig. 1. Task diagram

3.3   MaREMAS's Architecture

The system architecture was conceived using the model of the MAS-CommonKADS design phase. This phase refines the models of the previous phases and decides which architecture is the best suited for each agent and the infrastructure requirements of the agent network [16]. Figure 2 shows the distribution of system components like the own telematic needs of the proposed architecture. It can be seen each of the agents involved in the system and the way they are distributed in different nodes or containers that make up the system.

The lower node represents the MaREMAS's central platform; the other nodes are secondary containers which represent each of the support institutions associated with the system.

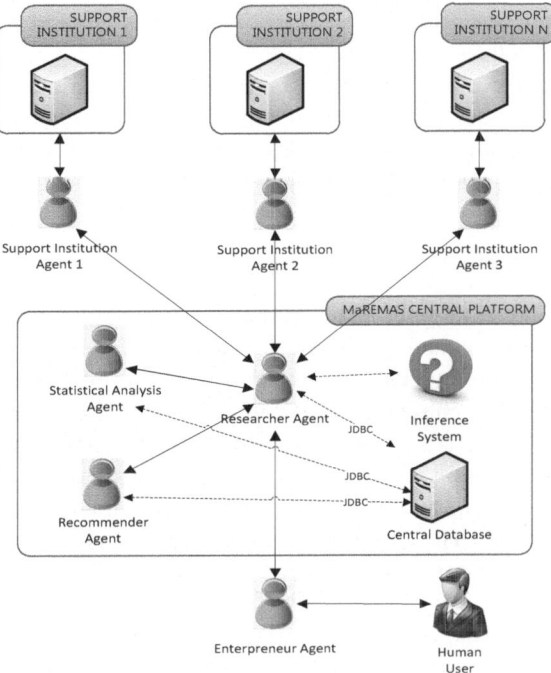

Fig. 2. MaREMAS's architecture

4   MaREMAS: Decision Making Process

The MaREMAS learning environment provides five main stages that support the decision-making process and new entrepreneurs training to acquire MR strategies. Below, these main stages are described along with their sequence diagram set.

4.1   Stage 1: Evaluating and Suggesting MR Variables

This stage attempts to guide the entrepreneur on the variables that must select to perform the MR. The entrepreneur registers analysis variables that considers relevant
after having detailed not only the problem but the characteristics of the MR desired.
MaREMAS analyzes the selected variables by the entrepreneur, watching for previous
research with the same variables and suggests other analysis variables that could be of
interest for the entrepreneur. It is important to highlight that those variables have already been learnt by the system through the research previously conducted. This analysis is requested by the researcher agent, which sends the request to the recommender
agent who is in charge of searching MR both in the central database and in supporting
institutions database which have variables in common with those selected by the user.
The resulting MR when performing this first match are subsequently analyzed by the
recommender agent to suggest or discard variables considered within these MR, this

process is accomplished using the feedback of previous entrepreneurs who have assessed such variables through ratings.

User entrepreneur decides whether to approve the suggestions and qualifies them to generate learning in the system. Through this functionality we are looking to incorporate a collaborative filtering system in MaREMAS, in order to restrict the results of previous MR based on the users' experiences.

4.2   Stage 2: Evaluating and Suggesting MR Hypothesis

The aim of this stage is to guide the entrepreneur in formulating hypotheses to validate using MR, the formulation of these hypotheses is based on the variables previously made. This stage involves the interaction of several agents, the entrepreneur agent initially requested entrepreneur assumptions. Researcher agent then asks the recommender agent suggesting hypotheses from previous MR found in the previous step. This initial formulation of hypotheses is sent to the statistical analysis agent who examine these assumptions and from this analysis to generate information that can be useful for entrepreneurs. The entrepreneur agent receives and displays the initial hypothesis raised by the system as information generated by the statistical analysis agent.

The formulation of these hypotheses oriented the purposes, methodological designs and questions that will have the research. The suggested hypothesis can be rejected by the entrepreneur, qualifying the suggestions made by MaREMAS.

4.3   Stage 3: Evaluating and Suggesting Methodological Designs

The aim of this stage is to guide the entrepreneur on the selection of the methodological designs to be used to collect information based on the definition of the population that will apply the methodological designs defined the variables of interest and the assumptions. With this information, the system makes suggestions about methodological designs that could be useful, giving the advantages and disadvantages of each of the designs.

The system gives the user the possibility of re-evaluating decisions of the system for the purpose of enhancing its elections for new entrepreneurs who use the system and then selecting other methodological designs. The methodological designs proposed by MaREMAS are divided into quantitative and qualitative suggestions depend on the variables considered in the previous stages.

4.4   Stage 4: Evaluating the Budget

The aim of this stage is to assist the entrepreneur about how to evaluate and assign the MR budget. This suggestion is based on the methodological designs selected by the entrepreneur and evaluated by the researcher agent and the agents of the institutions supporting entrepreneurship.

This assessment can be adjusted to the available budgets for each institution so that the system can provide relevant suggestions based on economic factors defined by each institution concerned. That is, each support institution agent knows the budget that has the support institution that represents and from this analyzes the methodological designs selected by the entrepreneur with the purpose of accepting or rejecting. From this, the system provides options for reducing the cost of the proposed budget based on their learning.

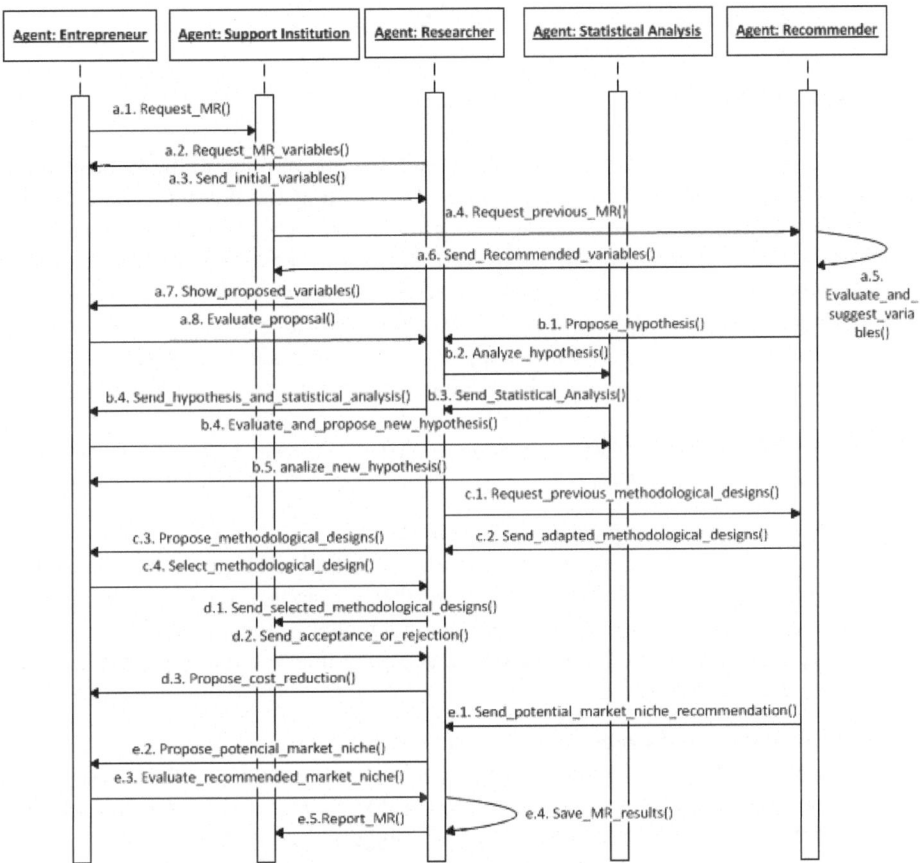

Fig. 3. MaREMAS's sequence diagram

4.5 Stage 5: Suggesting Potential Market Niches Based on the MR Results

This stage aims at guiding the entrepreneur in the identification of market niche it belongs the business idea according to results released by the MR conducted by analyzing data of methodological designs. This is the most important stage of the learning process as it provides a guide to entrepreneur sector about the market sector where it should focus its efforts when creating the company and make marketing processes. In this decision interfere: the researcher, support institution and the entrepreneur, who also evaluated the option provided by MaREMAS to generate learning in the system.

Finally, the researcher agent is in charge of storing the results of MR and reports them to support institutions. In the sequence diagram agents are placed in a horizontal row in the upper diagram, featuring a graphical representation for displaying processes. This scheme facilitates the design and communication of the MAS, representing the simultaneous processing that occurs in MaREMAS.

Figure 3 shows all the interactions performed by agents during decision making process for different stages previously described.

5   Case Study: Motorcycle Industry

Focusing on this case study two MR were considered and applied to the same analysis unit (motorcycle industry) with the purpose of evaluating the recommendations provided by the MaREMAS environment during the learning process. The purpose of the first MR is to offer advice on the motorcycle buying process and the second MR is aimed at advising on purchasing of motorcycle spare parts.

It is important to highlight that both MR were performed previously and already gave results, this in order to perform a supervised learning analysis where it can confront MaREMAS results obtained with those reached without the use of MaREMAS.

Below, each of the stages of the MaREMAS decision making as defined previously will be detailed for the first MR considering that the second MR was stored in the system's knowledge base (KB).

Stage 1: Evaluating and suggesting MR variables
The following variables were initially considered: bike brand, price and years from purchase, based on this MaREMAS evaluated these variables, approved the relevant and suggested considering the age, the budget and gender of the buyer.

The suggestions made by MaREMAS are accepted into the learning process, since they will be used in later stages.

Stage 2: Evaluating and suggesting MR hypothesis
Considering a first hypothesis that linking the motorcycle brand with the budget of the buyer, based on this, the system evaluated this hypothesis and found that age and gender were significant to the budget, since it suggested considering this new hypothesis. Is important to highlight that this hypothesis was considered in the second MR.

Stage 3: Evaluating and suggesting methodological designs
This stage shows the methodological designs proposed by MaREMAS, which are suggested from the ratings given by the entrepreneur who performed the previous MR and from the recommendations made by supporting institutions agents. This suggestion is important for the new entrepreneur, since this means saves in resources such as cost and time.

For this case two types of designs will be selected: the personal and virtual surveys, which were two of the designs considered when making such a research without MaREMAS orientation. Is important to note that the three designs proposed by MaREMAS, were considered in the previous MR.

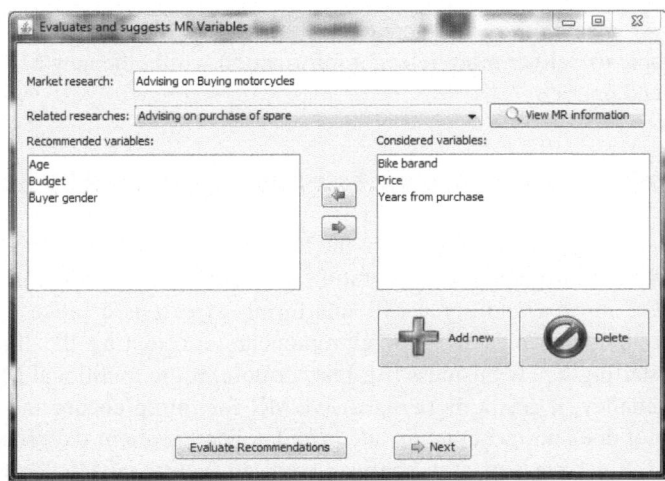

Fig. 4. MaREMAS'interface showing how the system evaluates and suggests MR variables

Stage 4: Evaluating the budget
In the evaluation stage of the budget, the budget ranges suggested system based on the recommendations of the researcher and each of the agents of the supporting institutions. Were entered values within the ranges suggested by some entities support, for others it exceeded the maximum suggested.

MaREMAS gave the responses generated by the supporting institutions and methodological designs in which when the recommendations were followed are accepted, while those which did not follow the suggestions are rejected.

Stage 5: Suggesting potential market niches based on the MR results
The MaREMAS environment, at this stage, recommends some of the niche markets that have in its KB. The niche markets suggested are the following: selling motorcycles, motorcycle business advice, spare parts for motorcycles, among others.

Figure 5 shows the way like MaREMAS increases its knowledge base and so improves its recommendations provided to the user. Also, the system offers better support during the new entrepreneur's learning process.

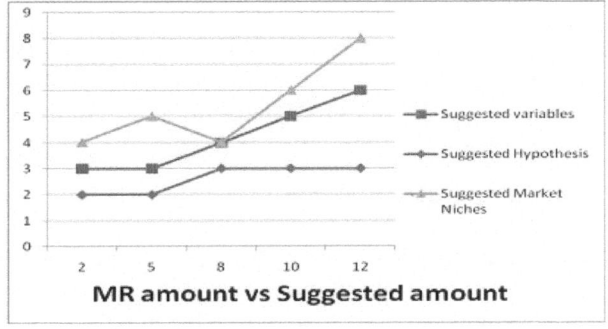

Fig. 5. Results from MaREMAS's case study learning process

Similarly as registered MR are increased in the MaREMAS knowledge base, statistical agent is able to deliver more relevant information within the new MR coming on, saving effort and budget.

6 Advantages and Learning Assistance Generated by MaREMAS

Among the mechanisms used to integrate the MR knowledge it should be included the use of experts and consultants for integrating environmental assessments [18]. However, the execution of a traditional MR and hiring experts is a process that can be costly in time and resources for new entrepreneurs considering the limitations involved when starting a new business [3]. Furthermore, if the traditional MR is carried out by a consultancy, it gets a more expensive MR for entrepreneurs and has the disadvantage that it does not generate an adequate knowledge about the process for subsequent MR. Table 1 presents a comparison between traditional MR learning process and assisted learning software using MaREMAS that highlights main differences.

Table 1. Comparison between MR traditional learning and learning through MaREMAS

MR traditional learning	Learning by MaREMAS environment
Possible difficulty on generating feed-back processes since the information is not systematized	Possible quick feedback due to the systematization of previous MR
Difficulty to monitor entrepreneurs by supporting institutions	Better monitoring structures of entrepreneurs by supporting institutions
Decision making often obvious results of past research	It improves the decision-making processes due to increased availability of information
Learning processes are often theoretical	Promotes the acquisition of MR strategies by learning of theoretical–practical processes
Difficulty in accessing past MR	Allows consult past MR related to a specific topic
Suggestions commonly asynchronous for learning process of MR	Synchronous suggestions delivered by the learning system for a MR
High costs of counseling and consulting for learning a MR	Lower costs associated with counseling and acquisition of knowledge about the MR processes
Generic learning to be adapted subsequently for the support institution that endorses the entrepreneur	Learning processes is oriented to the needs and requirements of a specific support institution
Difficulty in assessing the knowledge acquired by entrepreneurs	It allows the evaluation of knowledge and skills through practical monitoring process conducted by the entrepreneur

7 Conclusions and Future Work

MaREMAS is projected as an e-learning environment tool that serves to potentiate learning in new entrepreneurs in terms of decision-making processes, cost efficiencies to conduct MR and integration of dispersed knowledge in the market, which enables with acquired skills to respond proactively to market opportunities and enabling support institutions to learning about how to identify new opportunities and potential market niches.

It is important to note that initially MaREMAS does not record high indicators of reliability because the system is in a sequential learning process, which becomes more robust as much as entrepreneurs and supporting institutions use the system and enrich their knowledge base.

MaREMAS provides five main stages for learning proper MR processes. These stages are the following: evaluates and suggests MR variables, evaluates and suggests MR hypotheses, evaluates and suggests methodological designs, evaluate the budget and suggests potential market niches based on the MR results. These stages offer the possibility of quick feedback, online information increased availability, and finally allowing new entrepreneurs to evaluate their knowledge and skills through an e-learning process monitoring.

Additional advantages of MaREMAS learning environment concerns the fact that the system promotes in users the acquisition of MR strategies by learning of theoretical–practical processes, allows them to consult past MR related to a specific topic, and offers to new entrepreneurs with synchronous suggestions for a specific MR.

The MaREMAS's learning process case study shows that MaREMAS increases its knowledge base and hence improves further accurate recommendations provided to the user. In addition, it offers lower costs associated with counseling and acquisition of knowledge about the MR processes as well as promotes in users the acquisition of metacognitive skills through the interaction with e-learning environments.

As future work we plan to integrate the system with current MR repositories in order to add more knowledge to the system.

References

1. Chernow, R.A.: Entrepreneurship in American Higher Education. Innovation and Entre-preneurialism in the University 143 (2006)
2. Acs, Z., Szerb, L.: Entrepreneurship, economic growth and public policy. Small Business Economics 28, 109–122 (2007)
3. Cobo Quesada, F.B., Hervé, A., Aparicio Sánchez, M.S.: Emprender en clave de market-ing: propuestas conceptuales y prácticas. Anuario Jurídico y Económico Escurialense 43, 373–392 (2010)
4. González-Benito, Ó., González-Benito, J., Munoz-Gallego, P.A.: Role of entrepreneurship and market orientation in firms success. European Journal of Marketing 43, 500–522 (2009)
5. Liu, S.S., Luo, X., Shi, Y.Z.: Market-oriented organizations in an emerging economy: A study of missing links. Journal of Business Research 56, 481–491 (2003)
6. Wood, M.F., DeLoach, S.A.: An overview of the multiagent systems engineering metho-dology. In: Ciancarini, P., Wooldridge, M.J. (eds.) AOSE 2000. LNCS, vol. 1957, pp. 207–221. Springer, Heidelberg (2001)
7. Bolger, F., Pulford, B.D., Colman, A.M.: Market entry decisions: Effects of absolute and relative confidence. Exp. Psychol. 55, 113–120 (2008)
8. Jia-hai, Y., Shun-kun, Y., Zhao-guang, H.: A multi-agent trading platform for electricity contract market. In: The 7th International Power Engineering Conference, IPEC 2005, pp. 1024–1029 (2005)

9. Li, C., Qian, W.: Entrepreneurial orientation, learning capability and resource leveraging. In: International Conference on Management Science and Engineering, ICMSE 2009, pp. 1594–1601 (2009)

10. Steiner, F., Tarman, R.T., Ihl, J.C., Piller, F.T.: Learning from the customer: Identifying changing user needs during product usage through embedded toolkits for user innovation. In: Portland International Conference on Management of Engineering & Technology, PICMET 2009, pp. 706–716 (2009)

11. Tsay, R.-S.: An Entrepreneurship Emulation Platform. In: IEEE International Conference on Microelectronic Systems Education, MSE 2007, pp. 63–64 (2007)

12. Azcarraga, A.P., Hsieh, M.H., Setiono, R.: Market research applications of artificial neural networks. In: Evolutionary Computation, CEC 2008, IEEE World Congress on Computational Intelligence, pp. 357–363 (2008)

13. Han, J.-Y., Yang, Y.-B., Zhao, Y.-H.: Evaluation of entrepreneurial environment based on fuzzy comprehensive evaluation method. In: 2012 International Conference on Machine Learning and Cybernetics, ICMLC, vol. 1, pp. 305–309 (2012)

14. Welzer, T., Druzovec, M., Venuti, M., Ward, A.E., Yahoui, H.: Implementation of an E-learning Module in Virtual Centre for Entrepreneurship: The development of cultural awareness in students. In: Developments in E-systems Engineering (DESE), pp. 119–122 (2010)

15. Wooldridge, M., Jennings, N.R., Kinny, D.: The GAIA methodology for agent-oriented analysis and design. Autonomous Agents and Multi-Agent Systems 3, 285–312 (2000)

16. Iglesias Fernández, C.A.: Definición de una metodología para el desarrollo de sistemas multiagente. Universidad Politécnica de Madrid (1998)

17. Bayer, P., Svantesson, M.: Comparison of Agent-Oriented Methodologies. In: First Blekinge Institute of Technology Student Workshop on Agent Programming, 21 (2001)

18. Luca, L.M.D., Atuahene-Gima, K.: Market knowledge dimensions and cross-functional collaboration: Examining the different routes to product innovation performance. Journal of Marketing 71, 95–112 (2007)

An Agent-Based Approach for Efficient Energy Management in the Context of Smart Houses

Dima El Nabouch[1], Natalie Matta[1,2], Rana Rahim-Amoud[1],
and Leila Merghem-Boulahia[2]

[1] EDST, Centre-Azm, Laboratoire des Systèmes électroniques, Télécommunications
et Réseaux (LaSTRe), Lebanese University, Lebanon
dima.elnabouch@hotmail.com, rana.rahim@ul.edu.lb
[2] ICD/ERA (UMR CNRS 6279), Troyes University of Technology, France
{natalie.matta,leila.merghem_boulahia}@utt.fr

Abstract. Traditional power systems are centralized systems that supply electricity to end users through unidirectional transmission and distribution networks. The heterogeneity of renewable energy sources has introduced complexity in the transmission and distribution of electricity. Thus, intelligent distributed coordination and real-time information is needed to ensure that the electricity infrastructure will run efficiently in the future. This information enables the grid to meet the challenge of balancing supply and demand by actively sensing and responding to fluctuations in power demand, supply, and costs. In the near future, smart homes will be able to exchange energy, to sell to or buy from different actors available in the market. These new changes will introduce a soft competition in the market where each user will try to get lower contract prices according to his needs. In order to respond to the user's needs while integrating new sources of energy, we propose an agent-based approach for optimizing energy consumption. We present the agents' interactions that aim to procure energy for household activities at a suitable price to satisfy the user's needs. The results showed that these strategies can lead to a more environmental friendly, responsible, and efficient way to consume and distribute energy.

Keywords: smart grid, smart house, multi-agent systems, markets, renewable energy.

1 Introduction

Traditional electrical grids are generally used to carry power from a few central generators to a large number of customers. In contrast, the new emerging smart grid uses two-way flow of electricity and information to create an automated and distributed advanced energy delivery network. The integration of renewable energy sources (e.g. wind, solar, hydroelectric) has introduced complexity in the transmission and distribution of electricity. Therefore, the smart grid is equipped with advanced communication and automated network infrastructure that gathers, distributes, and handles information about the behavior of all participants

J.M. Corchado et al. (Eds.): PAAMS 2013 Workshops, CCIS 365, pp. 375–386, 2013.
© Springer-Verlag Berlin Heidelberg 2013

(suppliers and consumers). Smart grids will improve the efficiency, reliability, economics, and sustainability of electricity services.

A main business process of the energy sector in smart grids has been concerned with the production and distribution of energy. Due to two main forces, deregulation of the energy market and advances in information technology, the energy market is now undergoing significant changes [1]. The contribution of different sellers and producers will introduce a soft competition in the market. Different actors will be involved, and the winner is the one that obtains energy for lower contract prices.

Multi-agent technology has been successfully applied to power system management and operations. The field of multi-agent systems (MASs) offers a rich set of techniques, algorithms, and methodologies for building distributed systems in which desirable system-wide properties can be assured, despite the autonomous and self-interested actions of its components [2]. We propose a new agent-based approach for efficient energy management in the context of smart houses in order to respond to the challenges of electricity supply. We describe the main interactions between the agents that try to purchase the needed energy with minimum prices, in priority from renewable sources of production.

This article is organized as follows. Section 2 introduces some examples of MASs' use in smart grids. The major changes of the energy distribution sector in smart grids are explored in section 3, along with their consequences and benefits. In section 4, a new approach to manage the consumption of energy in smart houses using a multi-agent system is proposed. Furthermore, our proposal is implemented in Jade and the simulation results are illustrated in section 5. Finally, the last section summarizes our contribution and outlines our future research.

2 Related Work

Agent based methods can be used to create specific technical solutions as well as understand the interactions of various elements. Various smart grid researchers and organizations are using agents to create solutions for specific smart grid applications. Researchers are currently developing agent methods to address demand response using dynamic pricing. Game theory will be used as the basis to achieve desired response patterns. For example, a group of households collaborating to reduce their collective peak to average ratio and hence gain an encouraging tariff [3].

Much research attempted to simulate the electricity price elasticity and consequences of implementing demand response programs in a real-time pricing market [4]. In these studies, electricity consumers (i.e. buildings) are usually modeled as predefined, aggregated, and fixed-load profiles on the basis of historic regional electricity consumption data. For example, the PowerMatcher is a field-proven technology for the integration of distributed generation, demand response and electricity storage into the electricity markets and into distribution network management. The results of the field experiments and simulation studies presented in [5] show that the PowerMatcher improves the wholesale market position of energy trade and supply businesses, contributes to active management of electricity distribution networks, raises the electricity system's accommodation ceiling for renewable power generation, and is scalable to mass-application levels [5]. Energy management is not a new application for home and building automation systems. Indeed, the authors of [6] introduced a home automation system for managing and controlling energy in a building, mainly heating, cooling, water heating and lighting. Although this solution of energy management is efficient, it did not deal with the integration of renewable resources of energy that may offer different prices in a competitive market. In addition, it did not manage the scheduling of tasks and it did not consider the condition of each activity in term of priority and the price suitable to achieve it, neither the possibility of delaying some activities in order to obtain better offers. Also, it did not take into consideration the interaction between houses to get a cleaner energy and lower prices.

3 Competition in the Energy Market

As electricity grids are slowly getting smarter, the use of distributed generation (DG) is increasing. DG integration into smart grids offers important advantages such as a clean and sustainable source of electric power, enhanced system reliability, minimized transmission and distribution line losses and costs, as well as congestion avoidance in the transmission system [7].

However, as more renewable DG resources are installed, the interaction and combination of the individual generation sources may confront different challenges. A large scale deployment of distributed generation may affect grid-wide functions such as frequency control and allocation of reserves [6]. This new situation can create several technical problems related to power quality, and voltage stability, reliability, protection, and control. In addition, the current electricity distribution system considers home and working environments as isolated and passive individual energy-consuming units. This consideration severely limits the achieved energy efficiency and sustainability. In fact, it ignores the potential delivered by homes and buildings seen as intelligent networked collaborations where energy can be intelligently managed [6]. Tomorrow's houses and buildings should be considered as proactive customers that negotiate and collaborate as an intelligent network in close interaction with their external environment [8]. The energy grids of the future will be a combination of centralized and decentralized renewable electricity production. Cities, towns and industrial parks will be able to produce their own renewable electricity. However, they will still be connected to the big electricity production centers for backup energy needs.

Meanwhile, buffering and storing solutions are expensive and difficult. In electricity, there is no storage or buffering commodity in the network itself, so the supply/demand balance should be maintained all times to prevent instabilities [7]. The issue is how to keep the balance between demand side and supply in these future systems. As the supply side becomes more inflexible, the flexibility of the demand side should be taken advantage of [6]. Thus, demand response is necessary for the stability of the electricity network's operations. Utilities have to offer tariffs that motivate consumers to save energy and/or shift loads to off-peak periods. This will result in a slightly more open market that is still heavily regulated by the government. Furthermore, sellers are introduced in a free market. The winner is the consumer that could choose the lowest offer for the same service. Ordinary consumers will be able to retrieve their needed energy from the prosumer [1](a neighbor that can supply them) [7].

A smart grid is viewed as an open market trying to achieve a balance between the demand and the supply of energy. The decentralized nature and expected autonomous and intelligent behavior of the smart grid increases the turning to novel information and communication approaches to understand how to build and control this new grid [9]. Recently, multi-agent systems among other ICT approaches, have been proposed to provide intelligent energy control and management systems. The field of MAS offers a rich set of techniques, algorithms and methodologies for building distributed systems in which desirable system-wide properties can be assured. Thus, our approach for the efficient energy management in smart houses will be based on an MAS. The next section defines our MAS-based model and describes its main features.

4   Strategies for Efficient Energy Management

Our agent-based approach models the main actors that participate in a smart grid's electricity market. Consumers are in competition to acquire the needed energy to execute their household tasks. In priority, they refer to prosumers to buy that energy. If they cannot get to an agreement with a prosumer, then they refer to a generator company. The roles and characteristics of the agents representing these actors are (Fig. 1):

1. Generator Company agents (GC): they represent the big generator companies that are the main sources of energy. They can be also big renewable sources that deliver energy over long distances.
2. Prosumer agents: they represent small sources of energy distributed near the consumers. They can produce and consume energy; they produce a smaller quantity of electricity (compared to GC) by using renewable sources of energy [7].
3. Consumer agents: the regular consumer agent is an agent that cannot produce energy but is only a purchaser of energy.

In our proposal, Prosumers prefer to sell the unused quantity of energy of each period because their storage capacities are limited. Furthermore, it is better to refer to Prosumer agents when buying electricity, because they are closer and are electrically connected to regular consumers, thus the cost of transmission is reduced comparing to GC. In addition, renewable energy sources are more environmental-friendly.

---

[1] A prosumer is a smart house or building that produces renewable energy.

The consumers act by determining how much electricity to purchase in each time period. The goal of each agent is to maximize its profit in terms of unit price paid per day. In other words, each user aims to fulfill all its energy requirements for the day with the minimum price paid. The suppliers generate electricity from both renewable as well as non-renewable sources of energy. In our proposal, the demands of consumers are first met with supply from renewable sources. If the renewables cannot meet the total energy requirements of all consumers, then the traditional sources (fossil fuels) are used to meet the shortage in supply.

After defining the agents and their roles, the main variables and rules should be elaborated in order to better explain the different cases. A day is divided into 24 periods (each period is equal to 1 hour). At each period T, a list of activities has to be realized. The agent tries to purchase energy for all the activities of the next period. Each activity will be assigned a priority P according to the user's preferences, and a required quantity of energy. The matrix $activity\,(i,j)$ designates the needed energy for activity j at time i ($T = i$) of the day. An activity's priority can be High, Medium, or Low, and prices are considered to be fixed at each period. The agent begins to respond to the needs of the activity of highest priority first, then the medium and finally the lowest. We denote PR as the price offered by the provider (price/KWh). The user agent's goal is to not exceed the maximum price $PRmax$ that it defines for all types of activities. If the activity is of Medium or Low priority, the offered price P should not exceed the critical price PRc. In addition, an activity can be delayed for a given number of periods DT. If $DT = 0$, this means the activity could not be delayed and therefore the device could not be switched off and there is an urgent need to procure the needed energy. This case covers the condition of most of appliances that are very costly to turn off in the middle of an operation. If $DT = x$ (where $x > 0$), it means that the activity could be delayed of x periods of time.

4.1   Agents Interactions and Sequence of Events

Figure 2 shows the sequence of events taken by the consumer agent when it is trying to procure the required energy at each period of the day [2]. The main objective of our consumer agent is to procure the energy according to his needs. The provider of energy for these activities can be either a prosumer or a generator company, which may offer the needed quantity of energy for a defined price. At each period ($i - 1$), the agent schedules its consumption for the next period (i). First, it refers to prosumers and checks if there are any which can procure the quantity of energy $Q\,(i)$ needed to perform all the activities at the next period (i). The needed energy is (Fig. 2, 1):

$$Q\,(i) = \sum_{0}^{N-1} activity\,(i,j)\,. \tag{1}$$

---

[2] The events are numbered in the diagram of Fig. 2 and refer to the same numbers used in our description of the agent's behavior below.

The consumer agent sends a message to the prosumers containing the needed energy $Q(i)$ (Fig. 2, (2)). It waits for different offers from different providers (Fig. 2, (3)). Its decision will be based on the priority of the activity (Fig. 2, (4)). If there are no prosumers that can provide the needed quantity of energy, then the consumer agent waits another period of time for the activities that can be delayed. For the activities that cannot be postponed, it will refer to GC. As the price offered by a provider at each interval (T) is fixed, the consumer must wait another round in case he was not satisfied with the offered price. In fact, a consumer agent can refer to prosumers when the activity can be delayed, if not it refers to the generator company because there is no time to negotiate.

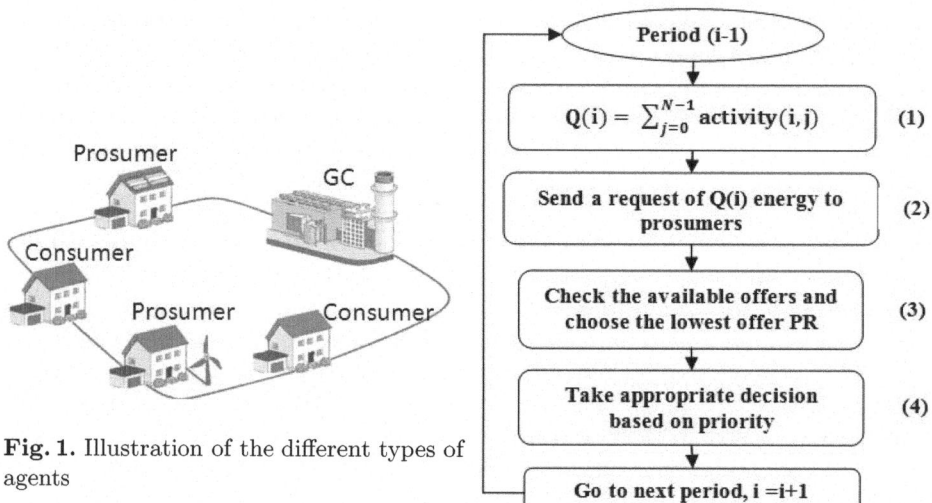

Fig. 1. Illustration of the different types of agents

Fig. 2. Sequence of events of the consumer agent for a given period of the day

4.2   Agent Decision Based on Activity Priority and Offered Price

We distinguish the three following cases:

Case 1: Decision for Low or Medium priority activity. The activity that has a low or medium priority should be executed for a price that does not exceed the critical price PRc. For a given offer PR, the agent checks if the price is lower than the critical price PRc (Fig. 3, (1)). If the offer is adequate, he accepts it and tries to establish a contract for each period (Fig. 3, (2)). If the agent did not find any adequate offer, he tries to delay his activities to another period so he can obtain new offers that may satisfy his requirements (Fig. 3, (3)). If the activity could not be delayed, it is dropped (Fig. 3, (4)).

Case 2: Decision for High Priority activity. When the activity has a High priority, the agent checks if the price offered PR does not exceed the $PRmax$ value (Fig. 4, (1)). If it is the case, he accepts the offer and tries to establish a contract (Fig. 4, (2)). Otherwise, he checks if he can delay the activity to the next period (Fig. 4, (4)). If not, the agent is called for a personal decision (Fig. 4, (3)). According to his preferences, he can decide to refuse the offer or accept the offered price knowing that the price exceeds his price limitation (Fig. 4, (2)).

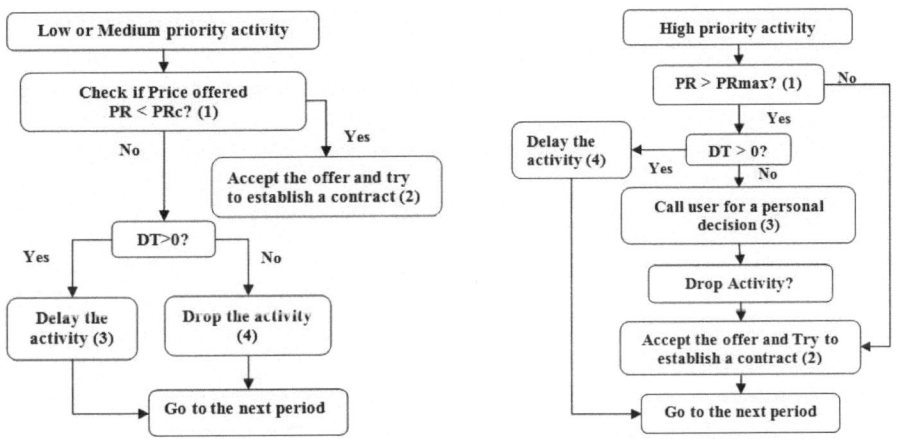

Fig. 3. Flowchart of the consumer agent for activities of Low or Medium priority

Fig. 4. Flowchart of the consumer agent for activities of High priority

Case 3: Decision for an Offered Price PR Lower than PRmin. In this case, the agents who have a storage capacity will take advantage of the situation when the prices offered are very low. In fact, the agent checks if the price offered PR is lower than the minimum price $PRmin$. If it is, then he buys a surplus of energy Qs and stores it, in order to use it later when the prices are very high.

4.3 Contract Establishment between a Consumer and a Prosumer

Once the consumer agent accepts the offer of a particular prosumer, he sends this prosumer an accept message (Fig. 4, (2)). He then waits for ΔT seconds for an agree message from the prosumer in order to establish the contract. If he could not establish the contract within ΔT, he concludes that he is being rejected. While the number of times being rejected is below a defined threshold MaxReject, the agent tries again to get another deal by choosing the next lowest offer. When he has been rejected more than MaxReject times, the consumer agent considers that there is too much competition in the market and he refers to a GC in order not to waste any additional time.

5 Performance Evaluation

In order to validate the performance of the proposed model, we chose JADE to simulate the agents behaviors based on the strategies described in the previous section.

5.1 Simulation Parameters and Considered Scenarios

We have created three simplified scenarios involving four consumer agents (C1, C2, C3, C4), three prosumer agents (P1, P2, and P3), and one GC agent. The day is divided into 24 periods. The tasks of each consumer are generated randomly and their priorities are being assigned randomly too. The simulation parameters are given in Table 1. In addition, in our proposed agent-based approach, the coordination of distributed renewable energy sources relies on the contract net protocol [4]. This coordination technique has been developed and demonstrated by software simulation.

Table 1. Simulation Parameters

Simulation Parameters	Values
Number of periods	24
Number of prosumers	3
Number of consumers	4
Number of GCs	1
Number of activities for each period	Random[0;5]
Priority of each activity	Random[0,1,2]
Number of possible delayed period for the activity	Random[0;24]
Time out delay for receiving offers	120 s
Time out delay for receiving Agree/Refuse messages	120 s
Maximum number of accepted rejections before referring to GCs (MaxReject)	3
Minimum price (PRMin)	30
Maximum price (PRMax)	85
Critical price (PRc)	70

We have considered the following scenarios:

Scenario 1: Consumer does not receive any offer. In this case, the agent C1 does not receive any offer from the prosumers' side and thus he has to refer to GC to obtain the needed energy. This case can happen either because no prosumer can offer energy at this period or because the offer messages did not arrive before the time out delay (120 s).

Scenario 2: Consumer receives different offers from different prosumers. This is the normal case, where the consumer agent sends a request message to the prosumers and receives 3 offers during the waiting period (as we considered 3 prosumers). He chooses the lowest offer and sends an Accept_Proposal message. The prosumer agent sends back an agreement message and thus the contract is established successfully.

Scenario 3: Consumer is rejected by one prosumer (P2) and tries to establish a new offer with another prosumer (P3). In this case, the consumer agent chooses the best offer from P2. But since this offer is already taken by another consumer, P2 sends back a Refuse message, and thus the contract could not be established. Consumer agent needs to choose the next lowest offer of P3 with whom he succeeds to establish a new contract.

In Fig. 5 we show how many periods each scenario could occur for the four consumers in our simulation. We can see that for an average of 34%, a prosumer does not receive any offer. For an average of 74%, the consumer establishes a contract successfully and is being rejected because the offer is already taken by another agent for an average of 23%. Therefore he has to try again to establish a new contract of the second lowest offer with another prosumer.

5.2   Evaluation of Different Study Cases

After showing the different scenarios that can take place in a negotiation for energy purchase, the efficiency of our algorithm will be shown by comparing it to a typical billing scheme used in most electric power systems where some or all consumers pay a fixed price per unit of electricity independently of the cost of production at the time of consumption. The results are shown in Fig. 6 based on the percentage of high priority activities that should take place during the day and the number N of competing consumers:

Case A: 70% of the total activities are High Priority and Number of consumers N=2. In this case, we assign a high priority to 70% of the activities, in order to evaluate the efficiency of the algorithm in an extreme case of a high percentage of urgent activities. As most activities are of high priority, our algorthim tries to respond to the consumer needs. Thus we can see that only 2.5% of the activities are being dropped and those are activities of low or meduim priority, while 6% are being delayed without any discomfort for the consumer. As 2.5% of activtities are dropped, the rest of the activities are completed and the two consumers will accomplish an average monetary profit of 31%.

Case B: 70% of the total activities are High Priority and N=4. In this case, we assign a high priority to 70% of the activities and we have 4 consumers. The results show an average profit of 16.5%, with an average of 10% of activities being dropped and 14% of activities being delayed. In fact, when the number of consumers increases, the competition will increase too and thus the average profit will be lower than the previous case (A).

Case C: 40% of the total activities are High Priority and N=3. As the percentage of activities of high priority decreases, we notice that the average profit increases in comparison to case B where the percentage of activities of high priority was equal to 70%. Even though activities of low and meduim priority constitute 60% of all activities, the agents reach a good profit of average 34.5%, with an average of 6.5% of activities being dropped and 11.5% of activities being delayed.

Case D: 40% of the total activities are High Priority and N=4. In this case, the average profit is 29%, with an average of 14% of activities being dropped and 20% of activities being delayed. The average profit is lower than the average in case C because there is more competition. The percentage of delayed activities increases in order to get lower contract prices. In addition, the number of dropped activities also increases because the percentage of activities of low priority represents a higher percentage, and thus the agent can have more flexibility to drop these activities if no suitable price is found.

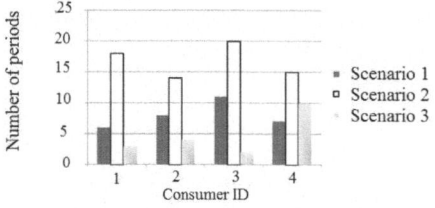 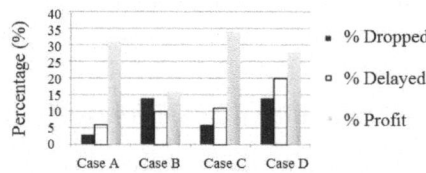

Fig. 5. Number of periods for each scenario

Fig. 6. Average percentage of dropped activities, delayed activities, and monetary profit for the considered cases

5.3 Electricity Cost Comparison

Next, we investigate the differences between conventional billing and the billing scheme we proposed in this paper. The price to pay for the activities of each period of the day is presented showing the profit that can be achieved by a consumer when adopting our approach.

Case of a Regular Consumer. We first consider a regular consumer that has random daily tasks with different priorities. Figure 7 presents a comparison between an example conventional bill and the one that the consumer may pay when the new strategies of our algorithm are adopted. Figure 7(b) shows that activities at $T = 14$ and $T = 15$ are being shifted to off-peak hours and being executed at lower prices. In addition, we can see clearly that the activities at periods $T = 3$, $T = 7$, $T = 10$ and $T = 11$ are accomplished at lower prices due to the contribution of the prosumers in the energy market (Fig. 7(b)).

Case of a Consumer with Constant Consumption. In this case, we present the bill for an agent that has a constant consumption during the day. It needs to procure the same quantity of energy for each period. All its activities are of high priority and cannot be delayed. Figure 8 shows that an agent with constant consumption can also achieve a benefit by establishing inferior contract prices for some periods. In this example, the agent realizes a profit of 11.3% by procuring energy at periods $T = 0$, $T = 2$ and $T = 6$ from prosumers at lower prices.

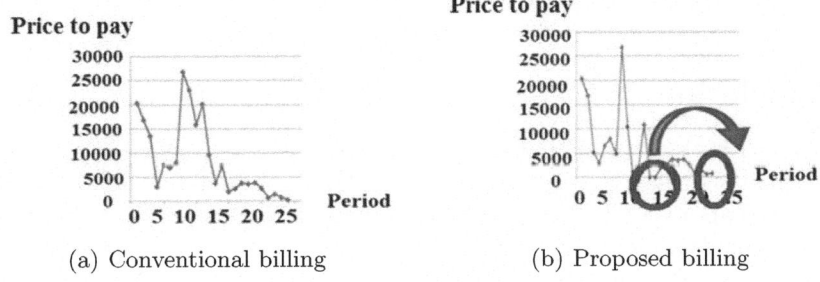

(a) Conventional billing   (b) Proposed billing

Fig. 7. Electricity cost comparison for a consumer with variable consumption

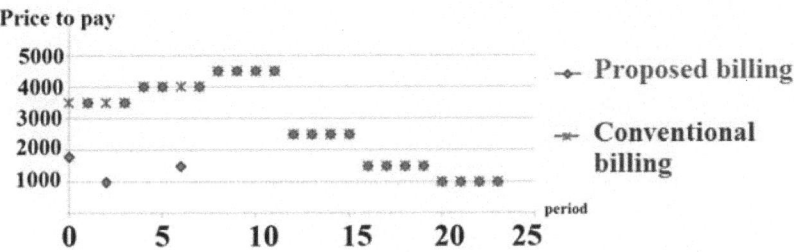

Fig. 8. Electricity cost comparison for a consumer with constant consumption

5.4 Discussion

The previous results show that the percentage of activities of high priority affects the profit of the consumer since he cannot drop those tasks even when the price is critical. In addition, when the percentage of activities being delayed increases, then the probability of achieving a higher profit increases because the activities are being shifted to off-peak hours where the price of electricity is lower. Furthermore, the activities that are being dropped are tasks with low or medium priority. These tasks were scheduled at peak hours, times at which it is not profitable to execute them. They may also be activities of high priority, but in that case it was the agent's personal decision not to complete them due to the high price offered. These results are quite interesting for the consumer since they show that once the activities are prioritize and defined with a delay property, he can choose to shift the activities during peak hours to off-peak hours. In this way, the consumer will succeed to minimize his bill while doing most of his activities and delaying just those activities that can be delayed without causing any inconvenience. In addition, when the number of consumers entering the competition increases, the percentage of delayed activities will increase and the profit may decrease because there will be a higher demand. The benefits of this kind of MAS-based approach are that it leads to a more responsible energy consumption while establishing lower contract prices and reducing harmful emissions which damage the environment.

6 Conclusion

In this paper we have presented an agent-based approach to allow passive houses to participate in the open electricity market. We have simulated different scenarios and evaluated the performance of our proposal. We showed that our scheme can help achieve a more responsible consumption by shifting some activities to off-peak hours, as well as referring to renewable energy sources when it is possible and thus minimizing the pollutant emissions in the environment. Future works include the development of a more detailed description of the GC and prosumers agents' decisions. In addition, the fluctuations in the provision of electric power from renewable energy sources should also be taken into consideration to assure the stability of future power grids. Furthermore, the problem can be extended by adding storage capacity to the prosumer agent and studying its benefits for the agent and its effects on the market. Moreover, electrical vehicles can be added to the scenario to study their interaction with the house (vehicle-to-home).

Acknowledgments. This work was supported in part through grants from the Troyes University of Technology and the Lebanese Association for Scientific Research (LASeR).

References

1. Boman, M., et al.: Energy saving and added customer value in intelligent buildings. In: Third International Conference on the Practical Application of Intelligent Agents and Multi-Agent Technology, pp. 505–517 (1998)
2. Rogers, A., et al.: Intelligent agents for the smart grid. PerAda Magazine (2010)
3. Fadlullah, Z., et al.: A survey of game theoretic approaches in smart grid. In: 2011 International Conference on Wireless Communications and Signal Processing, pp. 1–4 (November 2011)
4. Roozbehani, M., et al.: Dynamic pricing and stabilization of supply and demand in modern electric power grids. In: 2010 First IEEE International Conference on Smart Grid Communications, pp. 543–548 (October 2010)
5. Kok, K., et al.: Dynamic pricing by scalable energy management systems - field experiences and simulation results using powermatcher. In: 2012 IEEE Power and Energy Society General Meeting, pp. 1–8 (July 2012)
6. Bollen, M.H., et al.: Integration of Distributed Generation in the Power System. Wiley (2011)
7. Capodieci, N.: P2p energy exchange agent pltaform featuring a game theory related learning negotiation algorithm. Master Degree Thesis (2010/2011)
8. Dave, S., et al.: A systems approach to the smart grid. In: ENERGY 2011: The First International Conference on Smart Grids, Green Communications and IT Energy-aware Technologies, pp. 130–134 (2011)
9. Logenthiran, T., et al.: Multi-agent coordination for der in microgrid. In: IEEE International Conference on Sustainable Energy Technologies, pp. 77–82 (November 2008)

An Agent-Based Middleware
for Cooperating Smart Objects

Giancarlo Fortino, Antonio Guerrieri, Michelangelo Lacopo,
Matteo Lucia, and Wilma Russo

DEIS, University of Calabria

Abstract. This paper proposes an agent-oriented and event-based
framework for the development of cooperating smart objects. Smart objects are objects of the real life augmented with computing, communication, sensing/actuation and storing functionalities. They are the building
blocks of the future Internet of Things (IoT) towards the construction of
complex smart environments. In the proposed framework, smart objects
are modelled as agents that can cooperate as a multi-agent system to
fulfill specific goals. The framework implementation relies on the JADE
middleware that provides an effective agent management and communication infrastructure. In particular, cooperating smart objects can be
implemented as JADE or Jadex agents and can cooperate through direct
coordination based on ACL message passing and spatio-temporal decou-
pled coordination based on a topic-based publish/subscribe. A simple yet
effective case study referring to a smart office environment constituted
by two cooperating smart objects, is presented to elucidate the proposed
approach.

Keywords: Internet of Things, Smart Objects, Multi-Agent Systems,
Wireless Sensor and Actuator Networks, JADE.

1   Introduction

Recent progresses in electronics, telecommunications and computing are driving
the vision of the Internet of Things (IoT), a world-wide network of interconnected
heterogeneous physical objects (sensors, actuators, smart devices, smart objects,
RFID, embedded computers, etc) uniquely addressable and based on standard
communication protocols [1].

Among several approaches available for building the IoT [2], in this paper
we focus on an IoT defined as a loosely coupled, decentralized system of cooperating smart objects (SOs). An SO is an autonomous, physical digital object
augmented with sensing/actuating, processing, storing, and networking capabilities. It is able to sense/actuate, store, and interpret information created within
itself and around the neighboring external world where it is situated, acts on its
own, cooperates with other SOs, and exchanges information with other kinds of
electronic devices and human users.

To date, research efforts have mainly focused on prototyping middleware infrastructures for the implementation of SO-based smart systems. Apart from

J.M. Corchado et al. (Eds.): PAAMS 2013 Workshops, CCIS 365, pp. 387–398, 2013.

many projects focused on smart environments but not specifically on smart objects, UbiComp [3], FeDNet [4] and Smart Products [5] promote SOs as central entities in developing the IoT infrastructure, even though they differ in many aspects (e.g. programming model, metadata, system architecture, SO architecture, communication model, proactivity, programming language, knowledge management).

To define an IoT infrastructure based on a well-defined distributed computing paradigm which effectively supports the definition of distributed computing entities, their architecture and their coordination, this paper proposes an agent-oriented and event-based framework for the development of cooperating smart objects. The framework relies on the agent paradigm, which is centered on the concept of agent, as it is a well-defined distributed computing paradigm for developing methods and middleware for SOs. Agents are defined as autonomus, proactive, social, and situated entities that can fulfill specific objectives [6]. Therefore, the characteristics of agents perfectly fit those of the SOs. The proposed framework is implemented in JADE [7] and allows to program cooperating smart objects as JADE or Jadex [8] agents that comply with a well-defined event-driven reference architecture. The exploitation of JADE will enable interoperability between SO applications and agent applications based on JADE. Moreover, the proposed smart objects are based on the BMF [9] and SPINE [10] frameworks, which manage their sensor and actuator networks that are based on IoT standards (e.g. IEEE 802.15.4, ZigBee, 6LowPan). The JADE-based framework is finally exemplified through a simple yet effective case study.

The remainder of the paper is organized as follows. Section 2 discusses related work. In Section 3 the event-driven reference architecture for cooperating smart objects is described. Section 4 presents the proposed agent-based framework whereas the case study is detailed in Section 5. Finally conclusions are drawn and future work is briefly discussed.

2   Related Work

Nowadays, the development of architectures and middlewares for SOs is still an emergent research activity. Available works can be roughly classified in three kinds: (i) ad-hoc middlewares fo smart environments that could be reused, after a proper enhancement, for smart objects (e.g. Smart-Its, 2WEAR, Ambient Agoras, Aura, Gaia, iRoom) [11]; (ii) infrastructures focused on an all-inclusive IoT vision, where each object, even a sensor or an RFID, belongs to the IoT [12], [13]; (iii) smart object middleware focused on the development of an SO-based IoT (e.g. FedNet [4], SmartProducts [5], and UbiComp/Gadgetware Architectural Style [3]). In particular, we discuss the latter works as they are specifically focused on SO middleware.

FedNet [4] uses XML metadata to describe the requirements of SO applications, but it does not consider the SO management. FedNet does not provide a SO architecture because it is a high level middleware providing an interface to different SO architectures. For this reason, the proactivity in FedNet is "out of the SO" and applications are able to provide proactivity by orchestrating the SOs. The matching between FedNet application requirements and services provided by SOs together with the proactivity is managed by a (centralized) coordinator. FedNet supports 802.11x (TCP/IP) and bluetooth (RF-COMM) communication protocols.

SmartProducts [5] provides a metadata representation based on OWL and RDF languages. SmartProducts offers an SO architecture which allows the SOs to cooperate with each other in a P2P fashion through the communication middleware named MundoCore that supports several low-level communication protocols. SmartProducts supports proactivity in SOs, which can store knowledge in a proactive knowledge base (through specific APIs) which is associated with a reasoner to gather new knowledge.

UbiComp/GAS [3] uses XML data for the representation and communication of the SOs and their communication. It is based on a middleware named GAS-OS, which is installed on each SO and defines the SO architecture. In Ubi-Comp/GAS, SOs are components of distributed applications collaborating in a P2P fashion. It is based on the plug/synapse model for interconnecting SOs and the proactivity is limited to the substitution of lost synapses. The knowledge management is based on Knowledge Bases (KBs) and on a Prolog inference engine that supports the gathering of new knowledge. The communication protocols provided are TCP/IP and eRDP.

The aim of our proposal is the design and implementation of an event-driven SO architecture suitable for every SO and a distributed high-level P2P framework for SOs based on the agent paradigm. Our framework supports several communication types (message passing and publish/subscribe) and provides proactivity based on inference rules and on local and remote KBs.

3   Event-Driven Architecture for Cooperating Smart Objects

A Smart Object (SO) is a common physical object augmented with sensing, actuation, processing, storing, and communication capabilities. To implement these capabilities, hardware and software components have to be added to its physical structure. In particular, the hardware components provide the objects with augmented capabilities and the software components implement the SO functionalities.

The hardware structure of a SO is typically composed by a computing device (such as a PC/notebook/tablet/smartphone or even an embedded computing node) and a set of wireless/wired sensors and/or actuators nodes. The device computing power is purposely defined depending on the functionalities the SO will provide and on the dimension and complexity of the SO.

The software infrastructure can be logically organized according to a master/slave model, in which the master (or coordinator) is the most powerful device of the SO and can control a set of software entities running on sensor/actuator nodes. The coordinator is the only component having the capability of communicating with other SOs and other external, personal and environmental devices.

The communication capability with other SOs provides the basis for cooperation among SOs to achieve common goals, e.g. data sharing, complex service provisioning, ambient intelligence management, etc.

This simple yet effective SO model is quite general as it can accommodate any size of SOs: small (e.g. pencil, desk, sofa, coffeemaker, door), medium (e.g. motorbike, tram, bus shelter) and large (e.g. building, tunnel, highway). Moreover, in case of large SOs, the coordinator can be hierarchically organized to optimize the SO management functionalities.

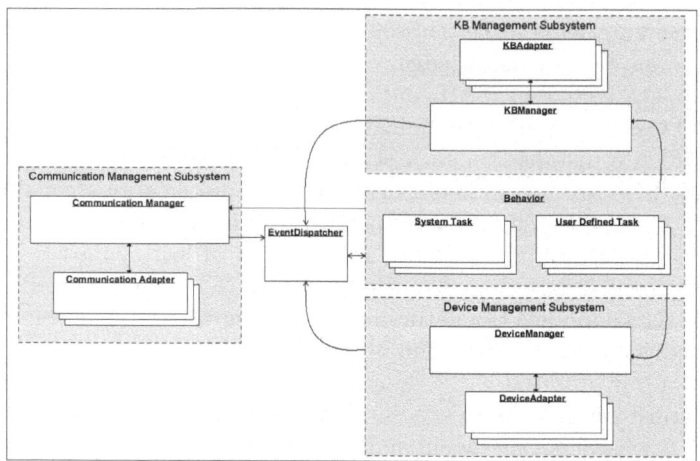

Fig. 1. SO Architecture

The defined cooperating smart objects (CSO) comply with the event-driven architecture (see Fig. 1) which is an instance of the high level architecture reported in [11]. The proposed architecture is composed of a *Behavior* that formalizes the object behavior, an *EventDispatcher* that manages all the internal events of the object, a *Communication Management Subsystem* that manages communications with other CSOs and external entities, a *Device Management Subsystem* that manages the sensor/actuator nodes of the object, and a *KB Management Subsystem* that manages the object knowledge base.

The Behavior component is composed by a set of Tasks. Tasks are software subcomponents programmed to reach specific objectives through a set of operations, involving computation, communication, sensing/actuation, and storage management. They can be either proactive or reactive. Proactive tasks are able to self-trigger to fulfill specific objectives whereas reactive tasks are only triggered by events sent by other internal or external entities. Tasks have also an internal state and can interact with the CSO subsystems and with other tasks.

According to the proposed architecture, as tasks are driven by events, external CSO communication, signals to/from the CSO devices, data to/from the KB are always formalized as events and handled by the EventDispatcher that sends them to the interested tasks. In particular, when the EventDispatcher starts its execution, waits for events. When an event arrives, it is inserted into the event queue of the EventDispatcher, which fetches, filters and, if not discarded, forwards the event only to the interested tasks. More than a task can be target of the same event instance.

Depending on the realization of the architecture, tasks can be implemented following either run-to-completion or multi-threading paradigms.

Tasks can be divided in:

- **System Tasks**: they provide basic services common to all the CSOs. In particular, the system tasks are:
  - *Shutdown/Reboot/Standby* tasks, which respectively implement the shutdown/reboot/standby operations of the CSO.
  - *Discovery* task, which enables the CSOs discovery.
  - *Information Access* task, which provides the information related to the basic CSO functionalities.
  - *Parameter Setting* task, which allows setting the basic parameters of the CSO.
- **User Defined Tasks**: they are application-level tasks designed to define specific CSO behaviors. Examples of User Defined tasks are provided in Section 5.

Events are characterized by two properties: event type and event source type. The types of event can be:

- **Inform**: events containing information;
- **Request**: events formalizing a request;
- **Log**: events for logging purposes;
- **Error**: events representing occurring errors.

The event source types can be:

- **Internal**: the event source is an internal software component.
- **External**: the event source is an external entities or components.
- **Device**: the event source is a CSO device.

A priority among events is defined as follows. Error events have the highest priority whereas the Log events have the lowest one. Inform and Request events have the same priority, which can also be specifically customized.

Device Management Subsystem, Communication Management Subsystem, and KB Management Subsystem are designed to be generic and are respectively based on extensible DeviceAdapters, CommunicationAdapters, and KBAdapters to allow for interaction with different entities through different protocols.

The Device Management Subsystem manages interactions with sensing/actuation devices and is composed by:

- *DeviceManager*, which manages and coordinates different DeviceAdapters.
- *DeviceAdapter*, which allows to interact with sensors/actuators hiding low level-details. In particular, it interprets high-level requests from tasks which translates into the specific sensor/actuator protocol, and receives data from sensors/actuators which makes available to tasks.

The Communication Management Subsystem provides a common interface for different kinds of communication (local or remote) with other CSOs or different devices so as to allow the CSO to manage all the communication in the same way. This subsystem is composed by:

- *CommunicationManager*, which manages and coordinates different CommunicationAdapters.
- *CommunicationAdapter*, which manages all the active connections and monitors the channel to set new connections by hiding low-level mechanisms;

The KB Subsystem provides the CSO with a knowledge base and consists of:

- *KBManager*, which manages and coordinates different KBAdapters.
- *KBAdapter*, which manages a KB containing the knowledge of the CSO. The KB can be local or remote and store information that can be shared among tasks.

4   Agent-Based Implementation

The event-driven architecture for CSOs has been fully implemented and integrated in the JADE middleware (see Fig. 2). CSOs are thus JADE-based agents so exploiting all features of JADE middleware at the agent management and communication levels. In the following subsections we first provide some basic information about the JADE middleware and then describe the JADE-based implementation of CSOs.

4.1   The JADE Middleware

JADE [7] is a FIPA-compliant middleware for the development of distributed multi-agent systems. A JADE agent is defined as a set of behaviors, each of which represents one or more tasks to fulfill. JADE doesn't provide any high-level abstraction for the definition of intelligent behaviors. To this purpose, the Jadex framework [8] has been introduced. It allows to program agents according to the BDI (Belief Desire Intention) paradigm. Specifically, a Jadex agent is defined as a triple: *Goal* (the agent objectives), *Belief* (the agent beliefs), and *Plan* (the agent plan). Jadex provides an execution model based on events that trigger the execution of plans. It is possible to execute Jadex agents on the JADE platform by using the specific adapter.

The agent communication is managed by the JADE platform through ACL message passing according to the FIPA specifications. The agent interaction can

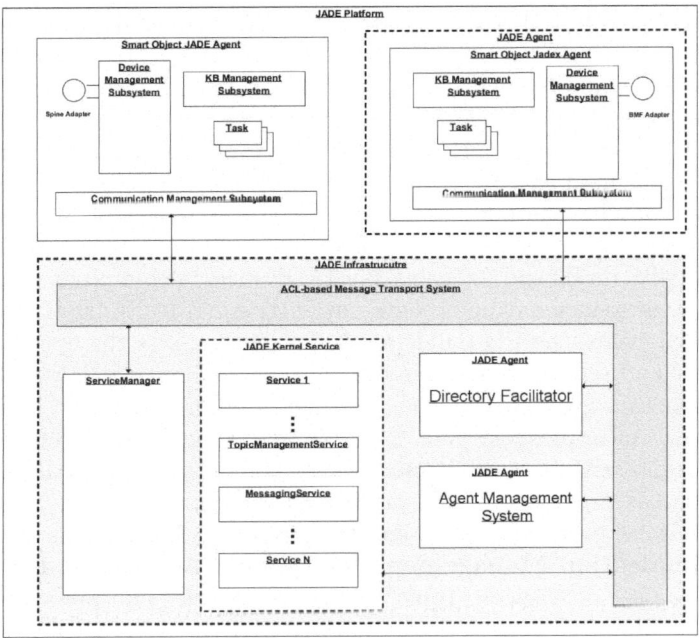

Fig. 2. Realization of the event-driven architecture for CSOs using the JADE middleware

also occur by means of the publish/subscribe pattern based on the topic mechanism. Such mechanism allows to send a given message to many agents without knowing the identity of the target agents. The topic-based communication is implemented in the JADE kernel service, named *TopicManagementService*, which manages the creation and the subscription to topics.

The exploitation of ACL messages and the topic-based coordination allows for interoperability among CSOs that will be able to request services and exchange information with each other and with other FIPA agents.

4.2   Agent-Oriented CSOs

The JADE-based CSO architecture is reported in Fig. 2. CSOs are agents of the JADE platform so they are managed by the AMS (Agent Management System) and can use the DF (Directory Facilitator) to look up other agents. The communication layer is based both on ACL messages and topic-based Publish/Subscribe. In the following we provide the most relevant JADE-based implementation details of the CSO architecture components (see Fig. 1).

– **Task**. Due to the affinity between the Task concept and the concepts of Behaviour (in JADE) and Plan (in Jadex), tasks are defined as JADE Behaviours or Jadex Plans. Thus, the task execution is based on the mechanisms provided by the specific framework.

- **EventDispatcher**. The EventDispatcher (ED) is modelled as an active component (Behaviour or Plan) and operates according to the execution mechanisms of the exploited platforms. For each event submitted to the ED, it adds such an event to its queue and self triggers the event dispatching through an ACL message in JADE or through an event in Jadex. In JADE, each task implemented as a Behaviour will wait for a specific ACL message that, in turn, contains the high-level event to be dispatched to the task. A task will use the *register* method provided by the ED to register to the events of interest with its ID and, by using the JADE message template, will intercept the ACL messages having a conversationID equal to its ID. Thus, for each registered event, the ED builds an ACL message, sets the apposite conversationID and sends the message into the internal system. Jadex is based on events so allowing to distinguish between internal events and input/output messages. As in Jadex a plan can be executed upon the occurrence of an event of interest, an event is uniquely associated to a task (the association could be based either on XML or Java classes). In particular, tasks register the high-level event of interest and the triggering Jadex event to the ED.
- **Communication Management Subsystem**. As shown in Fig. 2, JADE provides a set of services (TopicManagementService and MessagingService) and an ACL-based communication channel for the agent iteraction. To provide communication among CSOs, an active component, named CommunicationManagerMessageHandler has been introduced (as Behaviour in JADE and as Plan in Jadex), which captures the ACL messages targeting CSOs and translates them into external events (see Section 3). Moreover, two other handlers (TCPAdapter and UDPAdapter) have been defined to manage communication with external networked entities based on TCP and UDP.
- **Device Management Subsystem**. The management of wireless sensors/ actuators is carried out through the DeviceManager that handles several DeviceAdapters. In particular, two DeviceAdapters have been realized: the BMFAdapter, which allows to manage wireless sensor and actuator networks (WSANs) based on the BMF framework [9], and the SPINEAdapter, which allows to manage Body Sensor Networks (BSNs) based on the SPINE framework [10]. BMF and SPINE are based on IoT standards protocols such as IEEE 802.15.4, ZigBee, and 6LowPan.
- **Knowledge Management Subsystem**. Currently, the KB is constituted by just one object containing the global state variables of the CSO; ocal variables can also be kept inside the CSO tasks.

5   Designing a Smart Environment through Cooperating Smart Objects

In this section we exploit the agent-oriented framework described in the previous section to develop a case study. In particular, the case study refers to a smart environment composed of two CSOs: a Smart Office (or SmartO) and a Smart Body (or SmartB). The two CSOs will gather information and cooperate to support the working activity of the office user. As shown in Fig. 3: (i) the SmartO is physically composed of an office room with two desks, two PCs with screen, a whiteboard, a projector, and a chair, and is augmented with a set of wireless sensors, organized as a BMF-based WSAN; (ii) the SmartB corresponds to the office user that wears a BSN, which consists of two accelerometer-equipped sensor nodes and a mobile basestation, which is able to recognize the following user activities: standing still, sitting, walking, and laying down.

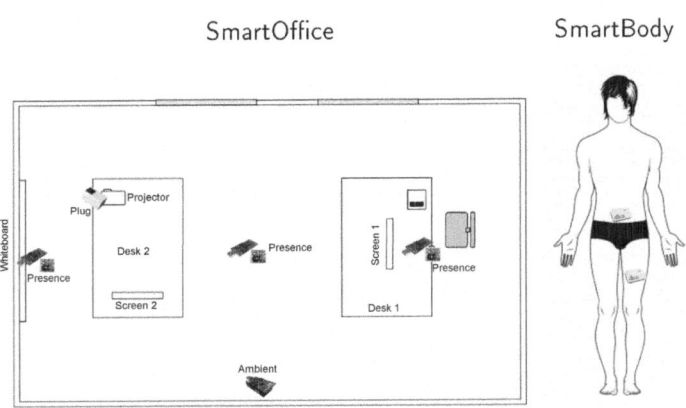

Fig. 3. Physical and hardware structure of the CSOs: Smart Office and Smart Body

5.1 Operating Scenarios

The operating scenarios of the case study refer to a usual working day: entry in the office, work at desk, work at whiteboard, meeting, etc. On the basis of the information gathered, the two CSOs will support the user during the working activity by suggesting to turn the lights and/or the projector off while not used, to take a break, and showing such information on the screen closest to the user. In Table 1 the defined scenarios are described in detail by reporting the correlated inference rules and actions performed by the smart environment.

5.2 Interaction between SmartO and SmartB

Each CSO publishes a set of topics and services that can be exploited by each other or by other entities to implement more complex services. In particular, in Table 2 the topics that the two CSOs publish and subscribe to are reported. Moreover, the provided services can be requested one-shot or according to specific state transitions of the CSO. In particular, the services offered by SmartB allow to query SmartB about the activity the user is currently performing, whereas SmartO, apart from the services for querying the room state (e.g. user presence, temperature, light, etc), provides actuation services that allow the exploitation of the screens.

Table 1. Operating scenarios of the case study

Scenario	Description	Inference	Action
1	User enters in the office	Uncertain position	Information shown on both the screens
2	User at desk 1	Work at desk	Information shown only on Screen 1
3	User is sitting for too long time	User should stand up	Alerting message displayed on Screen 1
4	User moves around the room	Uncertain position, walking	Information shown on both the screens
5	User uses the whiteboard	Work at whiteboard, standing	Information shown only on Screen 2
6	User starts a presentation	Presentation running	Switch screens off (do not disturb), notify information through Twitter
7	Presentation over, user forgets the projector on and sits to Desk 1	Energy wastage	Alerting message sent to the user on Screen 1
8	User leaves forgetting lights on	Energy wastage	Alerting message sent to the user through Twitter

Table 2. Published and subscribed topics

Topic	Publisher	Subscriber
Sitting	SmartB	SmartO
PresentationIsRunning	SmartO	SmartB
Work_at_Desk	SmartO	SmartB
Work_at_Whiteboard	SmartO	SmartB
MorePeopleInTheRoom	SmartO	SmartB

5.3 An Overview of SmartB and SmartO

SmartB has been developed by using the JADE version of the proposed agent framework that can work atop J2SE and J2ME (or Android). The management of the BSN (constituted by two Shimmer nodes, see Fig. 3) is based on SPINE which is integrated through the SPINEAdapter. To display feedback messages to the user, SmartB uses the screen service of SmartO. The KB of SmartB is distributed among its tasks. Some inference rules embedded in SmartB are as follows:

1. $TooLongSitting \Leftarrow SittingTime > 2h \wedge WorkAtDesk$
2. $DoingPresentation \Leftarrow Walking \wedge PresentationIsRunning$
3. $UseScreen1 \Leftarrow DeskUsed \wedge Sitting \wedge \neg MorePeopleInTheOffice$
4. $UseScreen2 \Leftarrow WhiteboardUsed \wedge \neg MorePeopleInTheOffice$

SmartO has been developed by using the Jadex version of the proposed agent framework that can work atop J2SE. The management of the WSAN (constituted by five sensor nodes: three TelosB equipped with presence sensors, one TelosB for ambient sensing, and an Epic smart plug node to measure the power consumption of the projector, see Fig. 3) is based on BMF which is integrated through the BMFAdapter. Moreover, SmartO directly controls the two screens for providing feedback to the user through a specific GUI. The KB consists of a Java class which maintains all the state variables and generates events when the values of such variables change. Some inference rules embedded in SmartO are as follows:

1. $isSomebodyInTheRoom \Leftarrow AmbientPresence \lor isDeskUsed \lor isWhiteboardUsed$
2. $isPresentationRunning \Leftarrow lowAmbientLight \land isSomebodyInTheRoom \land isProjectorOn$
3. $notDisturb \Leftarrow isPresentationRunning$
4. $morePeopleInTheOffice \Leftarrow isPresentationRunning \lor (isDeskUsed \land isWhiteBoardUsed)$
5. $uncertainPosition \Leftarrow morePeopleInTheOffice \lor (isSomebodyInTheRoom \land \neg isWhiteboardUsed \land \neg isDeskUsed)$
6. $waste \Leftarrow isAmbientLightHigh \land (isProjectorOn \lor \neg isSomebodyInTheRoom)$
7. $useScreenOne \Leftarrow isDeskUsed \land \neg notDisturb$
8. $useScreenTwo \Leftarrow isWhiteboardUsed \land \neg notDisturb$

6 Conclusion

This paper has proposed an agent-oriented framework for the development of cooperating smart objects as building blocks for the constitution of even complex smart environments towards the future IoT. An ecosystem of cooperating smart objects is modelled and implemented as a distributed MAS based on the widely used JADE middleware. Finally, a case study has shown the effectiveness of using the proposed approach in developing smart environments based on smart objects. Moreover, apart from the well-recognized benefits to exploit an agent-oriented approach, the exploitation of JADE can facilitate integration with other FIPA-compliant agent systems.

On-going work is being devoted to define tiny cooperating smart objects based on the MAPS (Mobile Agent Platform for SunSPOTs) framework [14], integrate them on the basis of the JADE-MAPS gateway [15], and extend the JADE DF with effective CSO discovery mechanisms. Future work will focus on the customization of the agent-oriented methodology ELDAMeth [16],[17] for the development of smart environments based on the proposed agent-oriented framework.

Acknowledgments. This work has been partially supported by TETRis - TETRA Innovative Open Source Services, funded by the Italian Government (PON 01-00451).

References

1. Vasseur, J.P., Dunkels, A.: Interconnecting Smart Objects with IP - The Next Internet. Morgan Kaufmann (2010)
2. Kortuem, G., Kawsar, F., Sundramoorthy, V., Fitton, D.: Smart Objects as Building Blocks for the Internet of Things. IEEE Internet Computing 14(1), 44–51 (2010)
3. Goumopoulos, C., Kameas, A.: Smart Objects as Components of UbiComp Applications. International Journal of Multimedia and Ubiquitous Engineering 4 (2009)
4. Kawsar, F., Nakajima, T.: A Document Centric Framework for Building Distributed Smart Object Systems. In: Proc. of the 2009 IEEE International Symposium on Object/Component/Service-Oriented Real-Time Distributed Computing, ISORC 2009, pp. 71–79. IEEE Computer Society (2009)
5. Miche, M., Schreiber, D., Hartmann, M.: Core Services for Smart Products. In: Smart Products: Building Blocks of Ambient Intelligence (AmI-Blocks 2009), collocated with AmI 2009 (2009)

6. Luck, M., McBurney, P., Preist, C.: A Manifesto for Agent Technology: Towards Next Generation Computing. Autonomous Agents and Multi-Agent Systems 9(3), 203–252 (2004)
7. Bellifemine, F., Poggi, A., Rimassa, G.: Developing multi-agent systems with a FIPA-compliant agent framework. Softw. Pract. Exper. 31, 103–128 (2001)
8. Pokahr, A., Braubach, L., Lamersdorf, W.: Jadex: A BDI Reasoning Engine. In: Multi-Agent Programming, pp. 149–174 (2005)
9. Fortino, G., Guerrieri, A., O'Hare, G., Ruzzelli, A.: A flexible building management framework based on wireless sensor and actuator networks. Journal of Network and Computer Applications 35(6), 1934–1952 (2012)
10. Bellifemine, F., Fortino, G., Giannantonio, R., Gravina, R., Guerrieri, A., Sgroi, M.: SPINE: A domain-specific framework for rapid prototyping of WBSN applications. Software - Practice and Experience 41(3), 237–265 (2011)
11. Fortino, G., Guerrieri, A., Russo, W.: Agent-oriented smart objects development. In: Proc. of the 2012 IEEE 16th International Conference on Computer Supported Cooperative Work in Design, CSCWD 2012, pp. 907–912 (2012)
12. de Souza, L.M.S., Spiess, P., Guinard, D., Köhler, M., Karnouskos, S., Savio, D.: SOCRADES: A web service based shop floor integration infrastructure. In: Floerkemeier, C., Langheinrich, M., Fleisch, E., Mattern, F., Sarma, S.E. (eds.) IOT 2008. LNCS, vol. 4952, pp. 50–67. Springer, Heidelberg (2008)
13. Floerkemeier, C., Lampe, M., Roduner, C.: Facilitating RFID Development with the Accada Prototyping Platform. In: Proceedings of the Fifth IEEE International Conference on Pervasive Computing and Communications Workshops, PERCOMW 2007, pp. 495–500. IEEE Computer Society, Washington, DC (2007)
14. Aiello, F., Fortino, G., Gravina, R., Guerrieri, A.: A java-based agent platform for programming wireless sensor networks. Computer Journal 54(3), 439–454 (2011)
15. Mesjasz, M., Cimadoro, D., Galzarano, S., Ganzha, M., Fortino, G., Paprzycki, M.: Integrating JADE and MAPS for the development of agent-based WSN applications. In: Fortino, G., Badica, C., Malgeri, M., Unland, R. (eds.) Intelligent Distributed Computing VI. SCI, vol. 446, pp. 211–220. Springer, Heidelberg (2012)
16. Fortino, G., Garro, A., Russo, W.: A discrete-event simulation framework for the validation of agent-based and multi-agent systems. In: Proceedings of WOA 2005 - 6th AI*IA/TABOO Joint Workshop "From Objects to Agents": Simulation and Formal Analysis of Complex Systems, pp. 75–84 (2005)
17. Fortino, G., Russo, W.: ELDAMeth: An agent-oriented methodology for simulation-based prototyping of distributed agent systems. Information and Software Technology 54(6), 608–624 (2012)

Simulating the Impacts of the Energy Consumption Using Multi-agent Systems

Fernanda P. Mota[2], Graçaliz Pereira Dimuro[1,2], Vagner Rosa[2],
and Silvia S. da C. Botelho[1,2]

[1] Programa de Pós-Graduação em Modelagem Computacional
[2] Programa de Pós-Graduação em Engenharia de Computação
Universidade Federal do Rio Grande (FURG)
Av. Itália km 8 – Campus Carreiros
96.201-900– Rio Grande – RS – Brazil
{nandapm2010,gracaliz,vsrosa,silviacb.botelho}@gmail.com

Abstract. Simulation of home use of electric energy is a very powerful tool for the purpose of studying, planning and managing at electric energy distribution companies. This paper presents the initial results obtained considering the paradigm of multiagent systems (namely, the NetLogo tool) for the of energy consumption simulation as a common resource. Distinct profiles of possible behaviors of consumers and household appliances with different powers are modeled and simulated using computational agents.

Keywords: Multiagent Systems, NetLogo, Electricity Consumption.

1 Introduction

Energy consumption is one of the main indicators of economic development and the level of quality of life of any society. It reflects both the pace of activity in the industrial, commercial and services, and also the population's ability to purchase goods and services more advanced technologically, such as cars, appliances and electronics. In late May, the energy consumption in Brazil increased 3.8% over the same period last year, reaching 36.9 milgigawatts-hours (GWh) [1]. The energy consumption of the residential sector presented an average growth of 4.3%. The highlight of this segment was the Northeast, which concentrated 36% of the increasing energy consumption.

According to Brazilian Agency of Electric Energy (ANEEL), the expansion in consumption of energy, although it may reflect the economic boom and the improving quality of life, has negative aspects such as: the possibility of exhaustion of resources used for energy production, the impact on the environment produced by this activity, the high investments required in the search for new energy sources and building new plants [2].

In this sense, the present work represents efforts to provide tools for the analysis of the impacts of energy consumption, using the technique of agent-based simulation,

J.M. Corchado et al. (Eds.): PAAMS 2013 Workshops, CCIS 365, pp. 399–404, 2013.

more specifically, the NetLogo tool. We consider very simple user profiles, just to test the simulation tool and demonstrate its utility. So, these profiles will be used to analyze the behavior of users with different financial income, demonstrating the peculiarities of each of them, by observing the monthly energy consumption

This paper is organized as follows: Section 2 briefly describes the conceptual aspects of multi-agent systems and NetLogo tool. Section 3 shows the initial simulation model developed in this work. Section 4 reports the results that were generated by the implementation of this model, and finally, Section 5 has the conclusions of the article, with final remarks and comments on future work.

2   Multiagent Systems and Netlogo

In the context of Artificial Intelligence, agents are defined as computational entities, embedded in an environment, which are able to perceive it and act on it. A computational agent has specific properties, such as: it operates under autonomous control, perceiving its environment, persists for a period of time, adapts to changes and it is able to accept goals [3]. There are several programming environments that are designed to work with agent-based modeling, however with different advantages, as shown in Table 1.

Table 1. Comparing some agent-based modeling environments [4]

Plataform of MBA	Ascap	Mason	Repast	NetLogo	SWARM
Quantity of users	Low	Growing	High	High	Low
Languages	Java	Java	Java Python	NetLogo	Java Objective C
Speed and Programing	Moderate	Faster	Fast	Moderate	Moderate
Learning Facility	Moderate	Moderate	Moderate	Moderate	Moderate
Documentation	Good	Little	Little	Large	God

We decided to use NetLogo [5], especially because the programming language is very friendly, but also for its portability, abundant documentation, easy access and free use. With this tool, it is possible to build hundreds or thousands of agents, which work in parallel [5]. Using NetLogo, we can explore the behavior of an agent (at the micro level) and this behavior emerges in the behavior of the entire system (at the macro level).

3   Simulation Model

The simulation model of energy consumption based on the agent paradigm that was implemented in Netlogo presents the following elements, as shown in Fig. 1. Observe

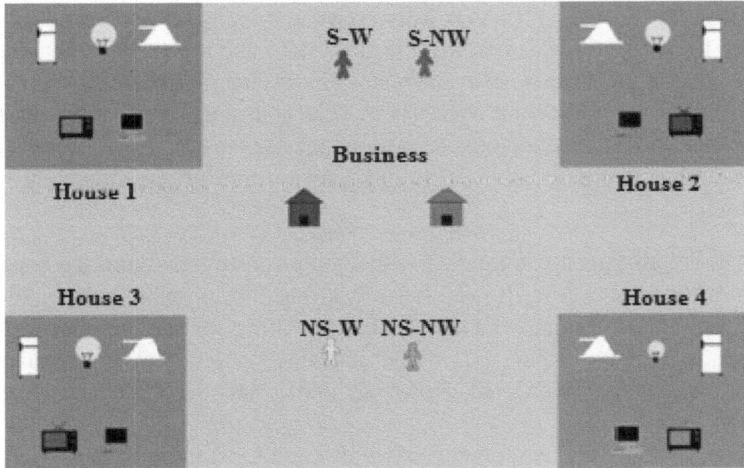

Fig. 1. Interface simulation model at the interface of Netlogo

that the simulation model was developed to be used in Brazil, so see the correspondent translation in the figure caption.

We modeled four houses, each with five types of appliances, with their characteristics and consumption [9], [10], as described below:

- **Analyzed Equipments.** We modeled four houses, each one with five types of equipments: refrigerator, lamp, shower, television and computer, with characteristics and consumption level [6], [7] shown in Table 2.

Table 2. Features and consumption of the equipments

Equipament	Character	Consuption (w/min)
Refrigerator	Refrigerator +Freezer with capacity of 350 Liters	29,5
Lamp	Incandescent bulb of 60watts	1
Shower	Shower in winter mode	91,7
Television	14 inch TV	5
Computer	CPU + monitor	2,5

- ConsumerUsers: We created four different types of consumer users, as described below:
    - **Saver Worker (S-W):** This consumer spends a certain period of time away from home (work period) and has a conscious behavior in the sense that he/she always seeks to shut down any equipment when not using it.
    - **Saver Non-Worker (S-NW):** This consumer is at home all the time (he/she does not have job outside home) and has a conscious behavior in the sense that he/she always seeks to shut down any equipment when not using it.

- **Non-Saver Worker (NS-W):** This consumer spends a certain period of time away from home (work period), but does not have a conscious behavior in the sense that in most cases he/she does not turn off an equipment when not using it.
- **Non-Saver Non-Worker (NS-NW):** This consumer is at home all the time (he/she does not have job outside home), but does not have a conscious behavior in the sense that in most cases he/she does not turn off an equipment when not using it.

The devices are also agents to interact with agents consumers return the consumption of each profile (S-W, S-NW, NS-W, NS-NW), this consumption is dependent on the time that each device remains attached. The probability of staying connected equipment depends on each profile, i.e., if the consumer is economical equipment has a 30% chance of staying connected. However, if it is spender the chance increases to 70%.

Consumers choose the equipment that will connect randomly, that is, except the fridge which is all the time on other equipment have the same probability of being selected and the same chance to stay connected. The equipment is only switched off when the agent returns to it, otherwise it is consuming.

The companies that are represented in the model do not have energy, because this work were concerned only about the residential consumption, not taking into account the consumption of companies and industries, because we want to analyze how the social profile influences in residential consumption.

4   Preliminary Results of the Initial Model

We evaluated the four user profiles considering ten simulation runs, as can be seen in the profiles below, as show in Fig. 2:

- **Consumer 1 (S-W):** This profile had an average consumption of 1778 kw / min per month.
- **Consumer 2 (S-NW):** This profile had an average consumption of 1929 kw / min per month.
- **Consumer 3 (NS-W):** This profile had an average consumption of 3542 kw / min per month.
- **Consumer 4 (NS-NW):** The profile had an average consumption of 3581 kw / min per month.

From the graph, it can be observed that consumers profiles of S-W and S-NW have similar consumption, for although the consumer 2 does not work, he has a economic behavior which causes it to use consume consciously.

Another interesting observation is the behavior of agents NS-W and NS-NW that have a similar performance as the agent who saves forget a machine on he can only turn it off when you return from work, so does the agent not saves. Finally, these two agents consumed more who do economic consumers, because they do not care about the use of the equipment, not considering the conscious consumption and economic.

Electric Power Consumption

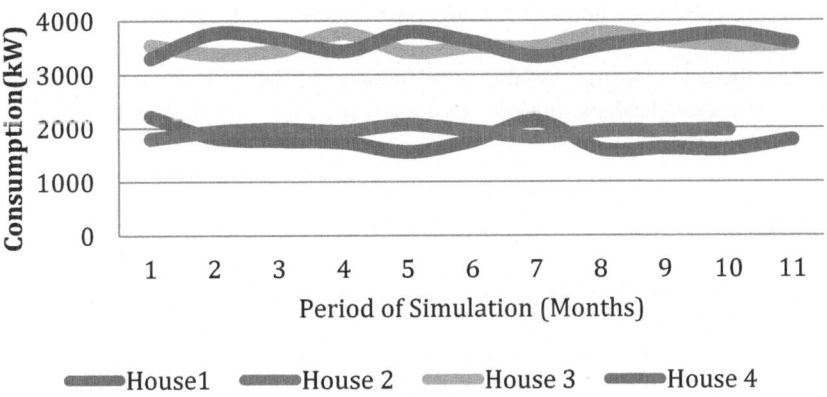

Fig. 2. House 1 is a electric consumption of S-W. House 2 is a electric consumption of S-NW. House 3 is a electric consumption of NS-W. And House 4 is a electric consumption of S-W.

Thus, as expected, the consumer of type NS-NW presents an average of the four higher energy consumption, since he/she passes a longer time period at home, without caring in saving energy. The consumer of type S-W had a lower average consumption because he/she spends a shorter period of time at home and also for being a conscious consumer. However, this simulation presents some consumption peaks due to the fact that he/she can forget about any connected device during the work time (8 hours).

5   Conclusions

As demonstrated in the results we can say that the use of the agent paradigm and NetLogo tool is an interesting alternative for simulating scenarios of electricity user profiles. For the considered user behaviors we have implemented different types of agents, which were inserted in a virtual environment.

We emphasize that these results are of reduced scope, consisting our initial test. We are now seeking referrals to build real world simulations. However, this initial assessment indicates positively to future work with more elements and more profiles to be studied.

For example, as future work, we will create houses with different profiles: many equipments, few equipments, old equipments, modern equipments. We will also extend the model for considering industries. Another perspective is to apply learning techniques (e.g., punishments that affect the behavior of agents), in order to observe, for example, the impact of re-education campaigns for power consumption or government politics of taxes for exceeding energy consumption.

Another interesting future work is to develop a model that has the consumer directly related to consumer income, so you can get more real results. Moreover, one can add more agents to each home, showing consumption of a larger family and not just a single agent.

Finally, there is also the possibility of integrating the data generated by NetLogo interface with GoogleMaps, in order to demonstrate the use of georeferenced streets, towns and even the state.

References

1. Multiner: Consumo de energia elétrica cresce no Brasil e Belo Monte é garantia para essa demanda (2012),
   http://www.multiner.com.br/multiner/Default.aspx?TabId=117
2. Aneel: Atlas de Energia Elétrica do Brasil (2012), http://www.aneel.gov.br/arquivos/pdf/livro_atlas.pdf
3. Russel, S., Norvig, P.: Artificial Intelligence: A modern approach, 2nd edn. Pearson Education (2003)
4. Sapkota, P.: Modeling Diffusion Using an Agent-Based Approach. PhD thesis, University of Toledo (2010)
5. Wilensky, U.: NetLogo. Center for Connected Learning and Computer-Based Modeling, Northwestern University, Evanston, IL (1999), http://ccl.northwestern.edu/netlogo
6. Aneel: Aprenda a calcular o consumo de seu aparelho e economize energia (2011)
7. Braga, N.C.: O consumo da energia elétrica (EL015), Escrevendo sobre Tecnologia para as principais revistas do mundo desde 1966 (1966)
8. Gilbert, N., Troitzsch, K.G.: Simulation for the Social Scientist. Open University Press (2005)
9. Van Dyke Parunak, H., Savit, R., Riolo, R.L.: Agent-Based Modeling vs. Equation-Based Modeling: A Case Study and Users' Guide. In: Sichman, J.S., Conte, R., Gilbert, N. (eds.) MABS 1998. LNCS (LNAI), vol. 1534, pp. 10–25. Springer, Heidelberg (1998)
10. Tisue, S., Wilensky, U.: Netlogo: A simple environment for modeling complexity. In: International Conference on Complex Systems, Boston (2004)
11. Le, X.H.B., Kashif, A., Ploix, S., Dugdale, J., Di Mascolo, M., Abras, S.: Simulating inhabitant behaviour to manage energy at home. In: International Building Performance Simulation Association Conference, Moret-sur-Loing, France (2010)
12. Klein, L., Kavulya, G., Jazizadeh, F., Kwak, J., Becerik-Gerber, B., Tambe, M.: Towards optimization of building energy and occupant comfort using multi-agent simulation. In: International Symposium on Automation and Robotics in Construction (2011)
13. Reinhart, C.: Lightswitch 2002: A model for manual control of electric lighting and blinds. Solar Energy 77, 15–28 (1994)
14. Axelrod, R.: The complexity of cooperation: Agent-based models of competition and collaboration. Princeton Univ. Press, Princeton (1996)
15. Bermann, C.: Energia Para Quê E Para Quem No Brasil. Fase, Editora Livraria Física (2002)

Agent-Based Impact Analysis of Electric Vehicles on a Rural Medium Voltage Distribution Network Using Traffic Survey Data

Matthias Stifter, Stefan Übermasser, and Sawsan Henein

AIT Austrian Institute of Technology, Energy Department
Giefinggasse 2, 1210 Vienna, Austria
{matthias.stifter,stefan.uebermasser,sawsan.henein}@ait.ac.at
http://www.ait.ac.at/departments/energy/

Abstract. Based on trips of more than 10,000 cars, the impact of charging electric vehicles on a rural medium voltage network is analysed and presented. Traffic is simulated by micro-simulation where each of the electric vehicles is represented by an agent. The total demand for charging battery electric vehicles and plug-in hybrid vehicles for one day in summer and winter is determined. Two different charging scenarios (end-of-travel-day and opportunity charging) as well as temperature influence are compared. Results show that due to concurrency the impact on the voltage is significant in terms of increasing penetration levels, especially with the end-of-travel-day charging scenario.

Keywords: Electric Vehicles, Plugin Hybrid Vehicles, Battery Electric Vehicles, Multi-agent systems, Power System Analysis, Smart Grids.

1 Introduction

1.1 Sustainable Transportation and Energy System

Rising emissions of greenhouse gases (GHG) and recent efforts to stop this trend also affect the transportation sector, which is expected to be accountable for one-fifth of the EUs total CO2 emissions [1]. Electric vehicles (EV) will reduce GHG emissions and oil dependency in the transport sector only if powered by 'green' renewable energy. Therefore, combustion engine vehicles (CEV) are seen to be replaced more and more by EVs in the near future. Whilst CEVs provide long range and fast refueling at one of the many gas stations, battery electric vehicles (BEV) are limited in range and lack in charging infrastructure. For providing customer's familiar performance like CEVs combined with the environmental friendly BEV drive-train technology, plug-in hybrid electric vehicles (PHEV) are developed. Different studies show that the mean travel distances per day are below 50km, which apply for 95% of all trips [2]. For these trips the smaller and cheaper batteries in PHEVs seem adequate. In case of longer journeys the onboard combustion engine can be used. Different market penetration scenarios

J.M. Corchado et al. (Eds.): PAAMS 2013 Workshops, CCIS 365, pp. 405–416, 2013.

are visioning the future fleet of electric vehicles ([3],[4]), as well as standards and specifications of EV technology and charging infrastructure.

According to regulations, a network has to be operated between the allowed voltage limits, e.g. 10% of the nominal voltage, to ensure the save operation of the electric energy system. Problems are expected when higher penetration scenarios are becoming reality. This may include the negative impact on the voltages of simultaneously charging on the medium voltage (MV) and low voltage (LV) distribution networks. The rise of the voltage level due to distributed generation is identified as one of the major physical limitations of hosting and integrating renewable energy sources [5]. On the other hand the charging process will lower the voltages at the nodes, due to higher power consumption. That will affect the voltage range, which is defined as the spread of the highest and lowest actual voltage within the network.

A detailed knowledge of the highly dynamic impact of the energy demand caused by EVs – of not only *how much energy*, but of *where* and *when* – is needed to operate the network, both in terms of generation scheduling and reserving capacity for balancing. Also for network planning on the mid and long term, the information of, e.g., the placement of charging points will help to determine the reinforcement and construction needs of the network infrastructure.

With the capability of investigating the interaction between transportation simulation and energy systems on a timely and spatial base, it will be possible to develop smart solutions to integrate EVs and build up a sustainable energy system. Multi-agent based, distributed controlled charging is seen as a promising possibility to integrate EV. It will help to anticipate the variable nature of renewable energy sources such as wind or photovoltaic systems (PV).

1.2   Related Work

Micro-simulation based on agent systems is a common methodology used to investigate transport related questions in research. Recent works have coupled traffic with electric power system simulation to analyse various questions which arise with the electrification of the transport sector. Examples are the charging impact on the power system [6], [7], [8] or locating and routing to the nearest charging point [9].

In [10] the authors investigate the impact of different charging algorithms, e.g., Vehicle-to-Grid (V2G), by direct coupling of the presented simulation environment with charging control algorithms and with power system simulation. The dynamic coupling of the agent based charging control algorithms enables reacting to various grid conditions, such as voltage problems or congestion management.

2   Simulation Scenario and Environment

2.1   Traffic Data and EV Penetration

Based on population and vehicle data [11] a scenario was built for the rural region of 'Lungau' (consisting of 15 independent districts) in the state of 'Salzburg'

Table 1. Data of district "Lungau"

Description	Number
Population 2008	20835
Passenger vehicles Lungau 2008	10960
50% BEV/PHEV market-penetration	5749

(Austria). The scenario takes place around the year 2040, when an PHEV/BEV market penetration of about 50% is to be expected [3]. Table 1 provides an overview of the region's population and number of vehicles (note that no additional growth in number of passenger vehicles for 2040 has been considered).

Due to lack of accurate mobility data from this specific area the driving behaviour for 'Lungau' was generated based on over 1.6 million trips from Upper-Austria [11]. Fig. 1 shows the departing, arriving and number of simulated vehicles which are concurrently on the road during a 24 hours working day.

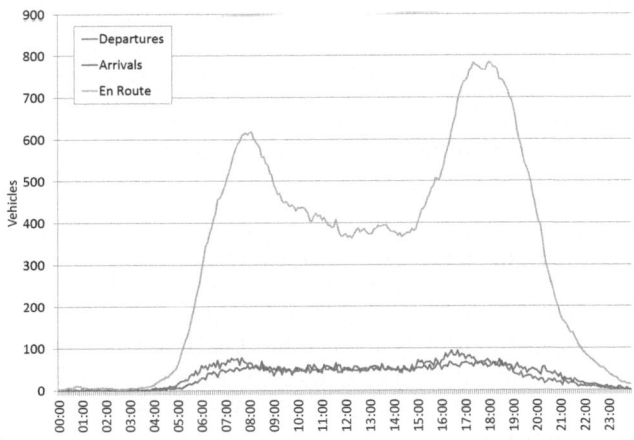

Fig. 1. Distribution of departing, arriving and en route simulated vehicles over one day

Traffic Simulation. Mobility data is provided often in form of origin/destination matrices (O/D matrix), which usually contain data of departing vehicles per hour (i.e. table 2).

For running simulations in MATSim [12] it is necessary to prepare a specific street network file and agent plans. The street network file can be generated with the tool OSMOSIS [13] and with data from open street map (OSM) [14]. Agent plans have to contain at least the information for the type of transportation (e.g., car), event times and the coordinates of the origin and destination locations.

Table 2. Example of an origin/destination matrix (O/D matrix)

Origin	Destination	Departure time [hh]					Cars
XY	YZ	00	01	...	22	23	Σ
		cars	cars	..	cars	cars	

For importing O/D matrices into MATSim it is necessary to prepare the data first. For the use case in this paper, agents with event sequences of 'home-work-home' and following departure and arrival distribution patterns from the survey in [11] were created. Based on statistical information such as population and vehicle portfolio [15], an O/D matrix covering the specific area was developed. For the number of agents per time-step individual agents are created for the sequence and departing and arrival times distributed according to the survey.

Based on geographic information each agent were given random coordinates around the centroid of a specific district (dependent on the information in the O/D matrix) for its origin (home) and a second pair of random coordinates representing its destination (work). With this method, most of the agents would not hit origin and destination coordinates with valid street coordinates. However, MATSim puts the agents on the nearest node in the street network.

The range of random coordinates for the work-location was chosen in a way that agents travel around 70 km on average per day. This number differs from the average day travel distance of 50km per day in [11], but is more realistic because of the wider geographic expansions of the investigated area compared to urban regions.

2.2   Simulation of the Charging Demand

BEV/PHEV Model. The specifications of the BEV represent the current market-ready average standard defined in [9]. Capacity was modelled after current vehicles which are available on the market. PHEV do not depend on energy from the battery alone. It is assumed that whilst the SOC of a PHEV is >0% energy for driving and for on-board devices is provided by the battery. In reality the combustion engine would take over before the battery is empty. Table 3 provides an overview of the specification of the vehicles which were modelled for the simulation.

The energy demand of the BEVs and PHEVs simulated in this study corresponds to measured data of BEV performances under different temperature conditions [16]. Energy consumption is modelled based on the trip distance and depends on the environmental temperature, taking also charging losses into account. Specific energy consumptions of individual EVs would strongly relate to the driving behaviour of each driver (or agent), but the model is valid for simulating a high number of EVs, which correspond to the statistical average of the measured data.

Table 3. Vehicle specifications

Vehicle	Battery [kWh]	Charging Specifications			Range [km][1]	Consumption [kWh/100km]	Losses [%][2]
		Amperage [A]	Voltage [V]	Phases			
BEV	27.5	16	230	3	130	21.15	22
PHEV	10.5	16	230	1	60	17.5	17.5

[1] at 20 °C temperature
[2] average charging losses

For simulating the worst case, when on-board consumption devices (like heating systems) are active, a cold winter day with temperatures down to $-14\,°C$ is chosen.

Electric Vehicle Simulation. The aim of the simulation tool called 'EVSim' is to simulate and determine the energy demand of EVs based on specified trips, derived from travel survey data or other sources. It models the discharging during driving and the charging with the various process states of connection/authentification/charging/disconnection with the charging points with different plug types. The main inputs for the simulation are: setup of the charging points and their locations; the configuration of the EV and battery types; the list of events for each agent (e.g. depart, drive, arrive, wait for free station and their respective parameters like distance). These events can be generated manually or via a format conversion from MATSim's [12] output of optimized agent plans. The battery model included in the EV model can be changed according to the needed accuracy and time scale of the simulation (e.g. temperature dependency, constant current / constant voltage charging sequence). The simulation of the energy demand for discharging during the driving phase is a linear approximation of the measured average consumption. An exact consumption model would include the driving behaviour and street parameters like velocity or height profiles. This could be achieved by dynamic coupling to a traffic simulation like MATSim and will be part of future research activities. EVSim is capable of performing offline and real-time simulation and provides an OPC interface which allows to connect and validate various charging control algorithms. A detailed description of the dynamic simulation capabilities and the co-simulation environment and applications can be found here [17].

Charging Strategies. Two charging strategies are applied to the simulations. The strategy 'end-of-travel-day' (EOTD) means that the BEV or PHEV can only charge at home, after having performed all trips. The vehicle starts recharging immediately after arrival at home until the SOC has reached 100% or until the next trip starts. In this simple model, PHEVs, which run out of battery power during the day, arrive at home with SOC 0%. This means that there is no on-board re-charging during the rest of the trip.

The 'opportunity charging' strategy permits additional charging possibilities during the trip, i.e. at work places. This assumes an available charging point infrastructure for the simulated agents and has to be configured for the various destination locations.

2.3   Electrical Network

Figure 2 shows the schematic layout of the medium voltage grid of the region of 'Lungau'. Nodes marked with black squares are considered in the simulation. The rest of the pictured grid is outside the defined scenario and will be therefore not examined.

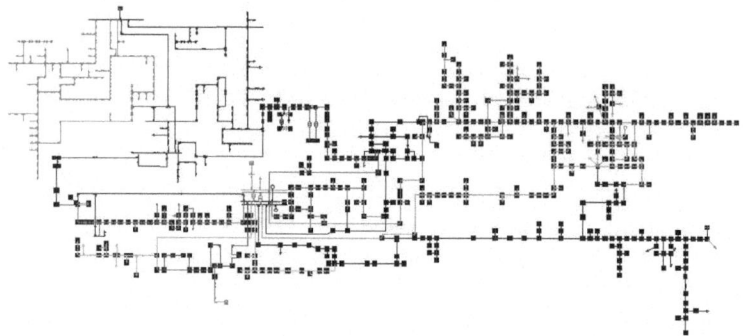

Fig. 2. Layout of the medium voltage grid topology

In order to analyse the impact of the integration of electric vehicles in the power system, a real medium voltage network was selected to be simulated with two different charging scenarios. It is a part of the distribution network operated by the distribution network operator 'Salzburg Netz', Austria. It consists of 408 km cables and overhead lines, 506 nodes, 325 loads (LV transformers) and 27 distributed generators, most of them are hydro power plants. EVs are charging at 260 LV transformer substations. The simulation tool PPS/SINCAL is chosen for this analysis. The impacts on voltage level and voltage range are the main focus of the analysis. A comparison between the two charging scenarios was made. For the allocation of BEVs/PHEVs to grid nodes the customer structure of the power grid was analysed. Each node containing household or agricultural profiles is allocated with BEVs/PHEVs, depending on the total share of these profiles.

2.4   Simulation Environment

To simulate the impact of the energy demand of electric vehicles on the electric energy system, the travel data and car activity has to be coupled to the power system simulation. Fig. 3 shows the static or loose coupling in principle. The traffic simulation based on the survey data is used for the agent based simulation of EV activity. The resulting energy demand for charging is used as a characteristic load profile representing the charging stations for the steady state power flow simulation.

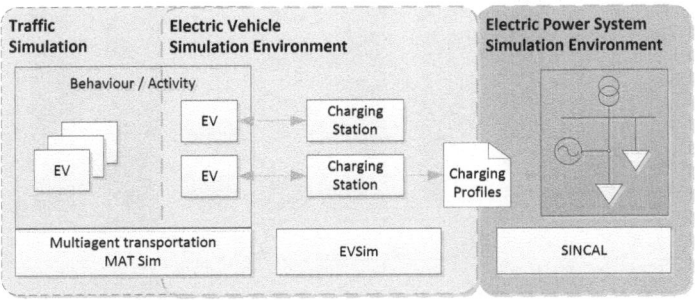

Fig. 3. Overview of the simulation environment, which connects agent-based transport simulation of electric vehicles with power system analysis

Since both renewable generation (such as hydro-power, wind and PV) and the demand depend on the weather, environmental influences have to be taken into account. Especially for power system operation, like scheduling of operation and support of balancing energy, the accurate estimation of the required energy is essential. In simulation real load and generation profiles (for the year 2006) were used with one minute resolution. Hourly temperature characteristics from the dates June, 18 and December, 19. represent summer and winter.

3   Simulation Results

3.1   EVs and Energy Demand

The simulation of the traffic provides a list of departure and arrival information as well as distances for each agent, which is used as an input for the EV model simulation. This simulation provides the energy demand for charging, according to the actual state-of-charge (SOC) of the individual agents.

Fig. 4 shows the classification into 0%, less and higher than 50% of the minimum level of the SOC during the day for all EVs. It shows that almost all of the PHEVs run out of battery power and are not capable of performing the trips without using their combustion engine. This applies especially in winter for the end-of-travel-day (EOTD) charging scenario and would not be expected when comparing the average day travel distance with the manufacturer's specified battery range. To prevent total discharge of the battery existing PHEV

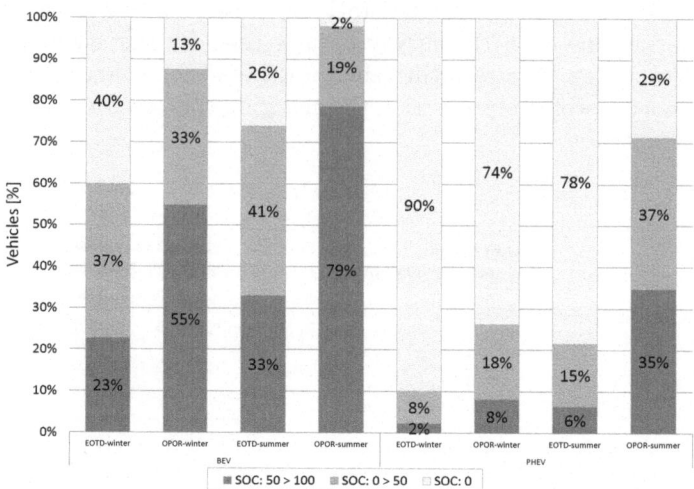

Fig. 4. Minimum SOC within one day for end-of-travel-day (EOTD) and the opportunity (OPOR) charging scenario. The SOC is classified into zero, less and higher than 50%. BEV would not be able to finish trips when the SOC of the battery is zero. With intermediate charging possibilities (opportunity charging scenario) most day trips are feasible with BEVs.

battery managements would use the combustion engine to keep the SOC e.g. between 20% and 30%.

The total amount of charging power during the simulated days for the 'opportunity charging' strategy is shown in Fig. 5. The additional demand in winter due to the temperature conditions corresponds to the filled area of the curve. In case of end-of-travel-day charging (not shown) the peak power demand would even exceed the peak of about 15 MW and accumulate naturally at the end of the day. This coincides with the peak of the household demand between 6 pm and 8 pm in the evening.

3.2   Impact on the Power System

The characteristic of the voltages for one winter day without EVs is shown in Fig. 6 on the left side. Due to distributed generation the voltages at some feeders are higher than the nominal voltage on the transformer (1.027 p.u.). The voltage range – defined as the spread between highest and lowest voltage in the network – is about 5% in average of the total 10% maximum allowed. On the right side of Fig. 6 the voltages for one day in winter when charging BEV (right upper side) and charging PHEV (right lower side) are shown, following the end-of-travel-day (EOTD) charging strategy. Fig. 7 shows the additional voltage drop of about 4% due to the additional demand for the worst case in winter for the (EOTD) charging scenario.

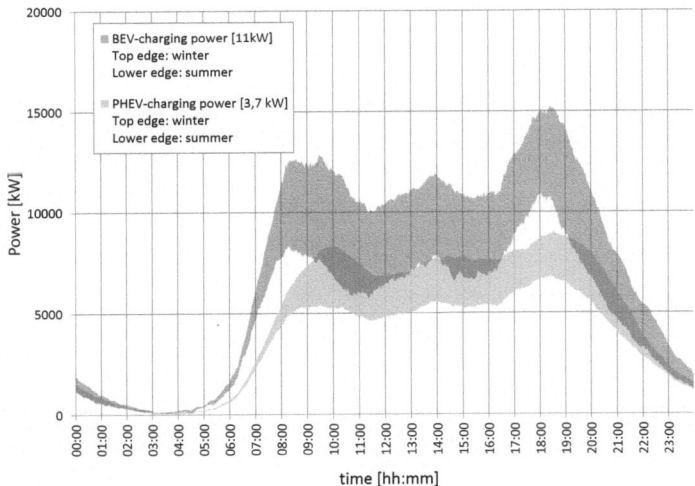

Fig. 5. Total amount of charging power needed for a winter and summer day for the 'opportunity charging' scenario for BEVs and PHEVs. The additional demand due to the temperature corresponds to the filled area.

Table 4. Simulation Results of Impact on Power System

Parameter	No EVs	BEVs	PHEVs
Additional voltage drop [%]	-	4	2
Highest voltage range [%]	5.66	8	6.3
Transformer peak power [MVA]	22.3	37.3	39.4

The impact of charging BEV and PHEV in winter is once more illustrated by the voltage range in Fig. 8. In the worst case, if the generation and the additional load due to charging are on different feeders, the voltage range will increase because the voltages are further apart. In the best case local generation would match the additional demand needed for charging and thus decrease the voltage range needed at least in that feeder.

Analysing the simulation results of the two charging scenarios summarised in Table 4 shows that the impact due to charging of the 50% PHEV penetration scenario is stressing the power system. Voltage levels for the PHEV scenario are within the allowed limits, opposed to the 50% BEV scenario where the allowed voltage levels may be violated, if uncontrolled charging takes place. Note that these penetration scenarios for 2040 are simulated with today's network state and do not take additional network reinforcement and construction into account.

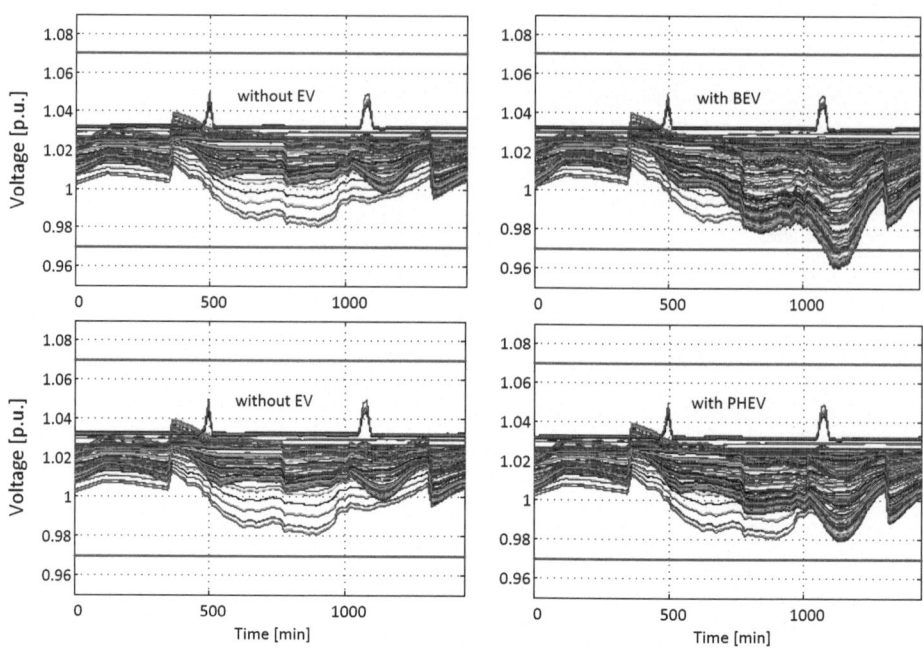

Fig. 6. Left side: Normal voltage level of the network nodes between the allowed limits (0.97 - 1.07 p.u.) during one winter day without charging any electric vehicles. Note the voltage levels above the transformer voltage of 1.027 due to distributed generation. Right side: Drop in voltages due to charging BEV (upper side) and PHEV (lower side), EOTD charging scenario.

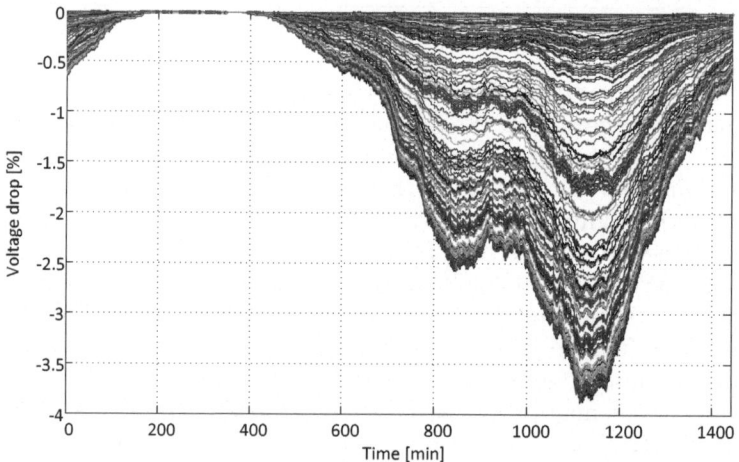

Fig. 7. Additional voltage drop of almost 4% (0.04 p.u.) when charging BEVs on a winter day for the end-of-travel-day (EOTD) charging scenario

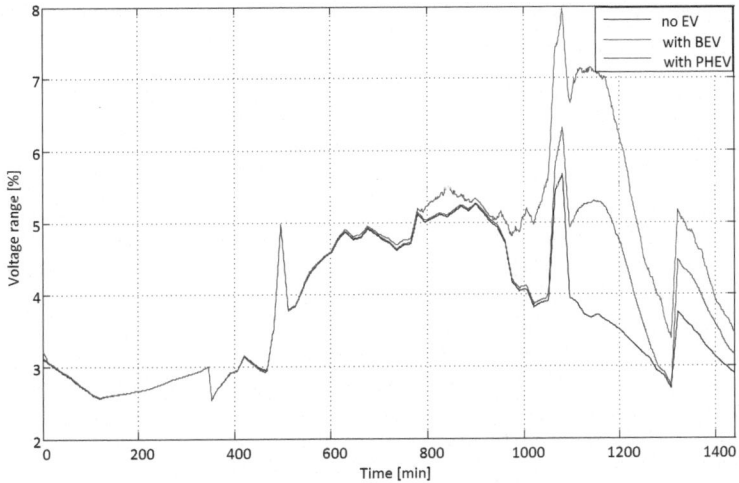

Fig. 8. Impact on the voltage range (spread between highest and lowest voltages in the network) for the different EV technologies in winter for the end-of-travel-day (EOTD) charging scenario. Note the voltage spikes in the range in up direction due to distributed generation.

4 Conclusion

Realistic simulations of the impact of EVs on the distribution network voltage levels have been demonstrated. These are based on traffic survey data and measured vehicle energy consumption data and take influences of temperature and losses into account.

Increasing the voltage range due to charging processes leads to less room for hosting renewable generation. The exact identification of the critical voltage levels of the network nodes make it possible to develop solutions to integrate EVs in the network operation and planning. With the help of agent-based micro simulation – to determine the energy demand of EVs in time and space – in combination with power system simulation it will be possible to investigate the feasibility of such solutions.

4.1 Outlook

The simulation will be extended to include 1,6 million trips for the whole region of Upper Austria to assess the impact on the MV network. The coupling of the EV demand with the power system simulation is file-based in a static manner and cannot take power system conditions into consideration. The presented simulation environment will be further developed to enable testing and validation of different controlled charging algorithms in combination with ancillary services, such as reducing charging power depending on the local voltage or vehicle to grid (V2G) scenarios. This will enable the possibility to validate such control algorithms in terms of dynamic system stability and implications.

Acknowledgments. This work is partly funded by the Austrian Climate and Energy Fund - Smart Grids ERA-Net Project 'G(e)oGreen'.

References

1. European Commission: Reducing emissions from transport - policies - climate action. Technical report, European Commission (2012)
2. Leitinger, C., Litzlbauer, M., Schuster, A., Simic, D., Hiller, G., Bäuml, T.: SMART-ELECTRIC-MOBILITY Speichereinsatz für regenerative elektrische Mobilität und Netzstabilität - Endbericht. Technical report, Vienna University of Technology - ESEA (2011)
3. Kloess, M., Müller, A.: Simulating the impact of policy, energy prices and technological progress on the passenger car fleet in Austria - A model based analysis 2010-2050. Technical report, TU-Vienna, Energy Economics Group (2011)
4. Pötscher, F., Winter, R., Lichtblau, G.: Elektromobilität in Österreich Szenario 2020-2050. Technical report, Umweltbundesamt (2010)
5. Stifter, M., Bletterie, B., Brunner, H., Burnier, D., Sawsan, H., Andren, F., Schwalbe, R., Abart, A., Nenning, R., Herb, F., Pointner, R.: DG DemoNet validation: Voltage control from simulation to field test. In: 2011 2nd IEEE PES International Conference and Exhibition on Innovative Smart Grid Technologies (ISGT Europe), pp. 1–8 (December 2011)
6. Galus, M., Waraich, R., Noembrini, F., Steurs, K., Georges, G., Boulouchos, K., Axhausen, K., Andersson, G.: Integrating power systems, transport systems and vehicle technology for electric mobility impact assessment and efficient control. IEEE Transactions on Smart Grid 3(2), 934–949 (2012)
7. Geske, M., Stotzer, M., Komarnicki, P., Styczynski, Z.: Modeling and simulation of electric car penetration in the distribution power system. In: 2010 Proceedings of the International Symposium on Modern Electric Power Systems, MEPS, pp. 1–6 (September 2010)
8. Soares, J., Canizes, B., Lobo, C., Vale, Z., Morais, H.: Electric vehicle scenario simulator tool for smart grid operators. Energies 5(6), 1881–1899 (2012)
9. Schuster, A., Bessler, S., Grønbæk, J.: Multimodal routing and energy scheduling for optimized charging of electric vehicles. e & i Elektrotechnik und Informationstechnik 129, 141–149 (2012)
10. Übermasser, S., Burnier de Castro, D., Kathan, J., Stifter, M.: A multi-agent based approach for simulating G2V and V2G charging strategies for large electric vehicle fleets. Submitted to CIRED 2013. 22nd International Conference and Exhibition on Electricity Distribution (June 2013)
11. Land Oberösterreich Verkehrserhebung Ergebnisse der Oö. Gemeinden
12. Multi-Agent Transportion SIMulation, http://matsim.org
13. OSMOSIS, http://wiki.openstreetmap.org/wiki/Osmosis
14. Open Street Map, http://wiki.openstreetmap.org
15. Statistics Austria, http://www.statistik.at/
16. ÖVK: Batterieelektrische Fahrzeuge in der Praxis - Kosten, Reichweite, Umwelt, Komfort. Technical report, Österreichischen Vereins für Kraftfahrzeugtechnik (ÖVK) (June 2012)
17. Stifter, M., Übermasser, S.: Dynamic simulation of power system interaction with large electric vehicle fleet activities. PowerTech IEEE Power & Energy Society. IEEE (June 2013)

Agent Technology and Wireless Sensor Networks for Monitoring Patients in Residences and Their Homes

Ricardo S. Alonso, Dante I. Tapia, Gabriel Villarrubia, and Juan F. De Paz

Departamento Informática y Automática Universidad de Salamanca
Plaza de la Merced s/n, 37008, Salamanca, Spain
{ralorin,dantetapia,gvg,fcofds}@usal.es

Abstract. This paper presents an intelligent multi-agent system aimed at improving healthcare and assistance to elderly and dependent people in geriatric residences and their homes. The system is based on the PANGEA and HERA platforms and integrates a set of autonomous reactive and deliberative agents designed to support the carers' activities and to guarantee that the patients are given the right care. The system makes use of Wireless Sensor Networks and a Real-Time Locating System for providing autonomous responses according to the environment status. A case study where the multi-agent system has been tested in several real environments is presented.

Keywords: multi-agent systems, deliberative agents, real-time locating systems, wireless sensor networks, health care.

1 Introduction

The importance of developing new and more reliable ways to provide care and support to people is underlined by the ageing of world population, especially in industrialized countries [1], and the creation of secure, unobtrusive and adaptable environments for monitoring and optimizing health care will become vital. Therefore, tomorrow health care institutions (public or private) will be equipped with intelligent systems capable of interacting with humans.

Research areas such as Ambient Intelligence (AmI) and Ambient Assisted Living (AAL) propose news way to interact between people and technology, where this last one is adapted to individuals and their context [2]. The objective of AmI and AAL systems is to develop intelligent and intuitive systems and interfaces capable to recognize and respond to the user's necessities in a ubiquitous way, providing capabilities for ubiquitous computation and communication, considering people in the center of the development, and creating technologically complex environments in different fields, such as medical, domestic or academic, among many others.

On the one hand, Agent Technology [3] have become increasingly relevant for developing distributed and dynamic intelligent environments and therefore fulfils the requirements and goals of Ambient Intelligence and Ambient Assisted Living. These intelligent systems aim to support people in several aspects of their daily life,

J.M. Corchado et al. (Eds.): PAAMS 2013 Workshops, CCIS 365, pp. 417–428, 2013.

predicting potential hazardous situations and delivering physical and cognitive support. In this sense, it is important to integrate intelligent and dynamic mechanisms to learn from past experiences and therefore provide users with better tools for supplying healthcare.

On the other hand, Wireless Sensor Networks (WSNs) allow us to obtain information about the environment and act on this, expanding users' capabilities and automating daily actions [4]. One of the most interesting applications for WSNs is Real-Time Locating Systems (RTLS). Although outdoor locating is well covered by systems such as the current GPS (Global Positioning System), indoor locating needs still more development, especially with respect to accuracy and low-cost and efficient infrastructures [5]. In this sense, the use of optimized locating techniques allows obtaining more accurate locations using even fewer sensors and with less computational requirements [5].

This paper presents an intelligent multi-agent system aimed at improving healthcare and assistance to elderly and dependent people in geriatric residences and their homes. The system is based on the PANGEA (Platform for Automatic coNstruction of orGanizations of intElligents Agents) [6] and HERA (Hardware-Embedded Reactive Agents) platforms designed and developed by the BISITE research group [7], as an experimental deployment in a real scenario. The system integrates a set of autonomous reactive and deliberative agents designed to support the carers' activities and to guarantee that the patients are given the right care in both the residence and their homes. The system is divided into two sub-systems: the first one is running in the geriatric residence and acts as a control center; and the second one is running at the patient's home and is always linked to the first one. The system incorporates autonomous agents that manage information gathered from a wireless sensor network and a real-time locating system to provide the system with innovative interaction schemas using mobile devices.

The next section describes the motivation and explains why there is a need for developing a new telemonitoring system. Then, the system's main features and components are briefly described, including its architecture, as well as the PANGEA and HERA platforms. Subsequently, the system deployment in a real scenario is depicted. Finally, the conclusions are presented.

2   Background and Problem Description

Ageing is a natural evolution among all living things, part of the life cycle, well known by everyone. This life cycle can stretch based on several surrounding factors, among them, food diet, living habits, social aspects, society, and medication supplements. Nowadays, there is an ever growing need to supply constant care and support to the elderly and the drive to find more effective ways to provide such care has become a major challenge for the scientific community. During the last three decades the number of Europeans over 60 years old has risen by about 50%. Today they represent more than 25% of the population and it is estimated that in 20 years this percentage will rise to one third of the population, meaning 100 millions of citizens [8]. In the USA, people over 65 years old are the fastest growing segment of the population [9] and it is expected that in 2020 they will represent about 1 of 6 citizens totaling 69 million by 2030. Furthermore, over 20% of people over 85 years old have a limited capacity for independent living, requiring continuous monitoring and daily care. Some estimations of the World Health Organization show that in 2025 there will be more than 1000 million people aged over 60 in the world, so if this trend continues, by 2050 will be double, with about the 80% concentrated in developed countries [1]. Life expectancy increase over time, societies, demographic trends, which demands governments worldwide to take proper measures towards ageing challenges. As the evolution theory indicates, made by natural selection and environmental adaptation are key for surviving, it is possible to transpose the same ideas into the care domain, where ICT is "naturally" be incorporated and blended inside care environments.

With the appearance of AmI and AAL based systems, one of the most benefited segments of population will be the elderly and people with disabilities [2]. It will improve important aspects of their life, especially health care. The elderly of the future will have potential for an autonomous and active lifestyle, including all aspects of a healthy and fulfilled life such as sports, nutrition, education, entertainment, travel and social interaction. AmI provides a framework for developing intelligent environments that can assist the elder in the daily life [9]. More specifically, ambient assisted living (AAL) focus on the positive, as well as the negative aspects of growing life spans and improving the existing private and professional networks and infrastructures, thus reducing the burden on caregivers and increasing the autonomy of the caretakers at the same time, while preserving the immense skills and experiences of the elderly cohort within our society. In particular, AAL can be used to improve the daily life in a geriatric residence or in the elder's home.

As can be observed in the revised works, sensing is a key factor in the development of AmI and AAL based systems. The data obtained from sensors provides the basis to make decisions about the actions that need to be taken by the caregivers or the automated intelligent system. Identification and location data, amongst others, play a prevalent role in most of the existing systems, and this kind of data is obtained by means of technology that is embedded, non-invasive and transparent for users. In this regard, users' locations given by Real-Time Locating Systems represent key context information to adapt systems to people's needs and preferences. Real-Time Locating Systems can be categorized by the kind of its wireless sensor infrastructure and by the locating techniques used to calculate the position of the tags (i.e., the locating engine). This way, there is a combination of several wireless technologies, such as RFID, Wi-Fi, UWB and ZigBee, and also a wide range of locating techniques that can be used to determine the position of the tags. Among the most widely used locating techniques we have signpost, fingerprinting, triangulation, trilateration and multilateration [10].

A widespread technology used in Real-Time Locating Systems is Radio Frequency IDentification (RFID) [11]. In this case, the RFID readers act as exciters transmitting continuously a radio frequency signal that is collected by the RFID tags, which in turn respond to the readers by sending their identification numbers. In these kinds of locating systems, each reader covers a certain zone through its radio frequency signal, known as reading field. When a tag passes through the reading field of the reader, it is said that the tag is in that zone. Locating systems based on Wireless Fidelity (Wi-Fi) take advantage of Wi-Fi WLANs (Wireless Local Area Networks) working in the 2.4GHz and 5.8GHz ISM (Industrial, Scientific and Medical) bands to calculate the positions of the mobile devices (i.e., tags) [12]. A wide range of locating techniques, then, can be used for processing the Wi-Fi signals and determining the position of the tags, including signpost, fingerprinting or trilateration. However, locating systems based on Wi-Fi present some problems such as the interferences with existing data transmissions and the high power consumption by the Wi-Fi tags. Ultra-Wide Band (UWB) is a technology which has been recently introduced to develop these kinds of systems. As it works at high frequencies (the band covers from 3.1GHz to 10.6 GHz in the USA) [13], it allows to achieve very accurate location estimations. However, at such frequencies the electromagnetic waves suffer a great attenuation by objects (e.g., walls) so its use in indoor RTLS systems presents important problems, especially due to reflection and multipath effects. ZigBee is another interesting technology to build RTLSs. The ZigBee standard is specially intended to implement Wireless Sensor Networks and, as Wi-Fi, can work in the 2.4GHz ISM band, but also can work on the 868–915MHz band. Different locating techniques based on RSSI and LQI can be used on ZigBee WSNs (e.g., signpost or trilateration). Moreover, it allows building networks or more than 65,000 nodes in star, cluster-tree and mesh topologies [10]. ZigBee is, indeed, the wireless technology selected for our research.

From this point of view, it is important to assist the caregiver and the caretaker in the daily routine which, commonly, is composed of a series of tasks. Lanzola et al. [14], for instance, presents a methodology that facilitates medical applications and proposes a generic computational model for its implementation. Such a model could be specialized to manage all kind of information and knowledge in a hospital environment. However, the method proposed by Lanzola et al. [14] is very abstract and does not take into account the possibility of modeling certain technologies common in hospital environments (as shown in this paper) as wireless or RFID. Others such as Decker and Li [15], propose a system to increase hospital efficiency using global planning and scheduling techniques. However, this system does not work on wireless devices and does not use location information or RFID technology.

As observed in this section, the elder of the future require innovative systems to improve different aspects of his life, and both technology and intelligent systems are key factors in this process. There exist different projects focused on improving the quality of life. However, they do not take into account the use of wireless devices with hardware-embedded reactive agents platforms running on them. This paper proposes an innovative solution based on agent technology, a set of wireless technologies and indoor real-time locating techniques.

3   System Overview

This section describes the main features of the multi-agent system proposed in this paper. It is an Ambient Intelligence based multi-agent system aimed at improving healthcare of dependent people at the geriatric residences and their own homes. An essential aspect in this system is the use of Wireless Sensor Networks (WSN) to provide the agents with automatic and real-time information of the environment and allow them to react upon it. This way, the system makes use of several WSNs in order to gather context information in an automatic and ubiquitous way. The system enables an extensive integration of WSNs and provides a greater simplicity of deployment, thus optimizing the reutilization of the available resources in such networks. The agents in the system are implemented using two different agent platforms, PANGEA (Platform for Automatic coNstruction of orGanizations of intElligents Agents) [6] and HERA (Hardware-Embedded Reactive Agents) [7].

On the one hand, PANGEA is an agent platform to develop open multi-agent systems, specifically those including organizational aspects such as virtual agent organizations. The platform allows the integral management of organizations and offers tools to the end user. Additionally, it includes a communication protocol based on the IRC standard, which facilitates implementation and remains robust even with a large number of connections. The dynamics of open environments is one of the reasons that have encouraged the use of Virtual Organizations of Agents (VOs) [6]. A VO is an open system designed for grouping; it allows for the collaboration of heterogeneous entities and provides a separation between the form and function that define their behavior.

On the other hand, HERA [7] is an evolution of SYLPH (Services laYers over Light PHysical devices) [16]. SYLPH has the ability to use dynamic and self-adaptable heterogeneous WSNs. In HERA, agents are directly embedded into wireless nodes. This way, through the integration of HERA and PANGEA there is no difference between a software and a hardware agent. That is, PANGEA provides a high-level management system, where organizational aspects are taken into account, regardless of whether the agent is a piece of code or a wireless sensor. PANGEA includes facilities for implementing VOs and suborganizations, following any topology and with the appropriate tools for managing the VO itself; it is a complete platform for the execution and management of VOs, and incorporates intelligent agents with advances capacities for learning and adaptation.

3.1   The PANGEA Agents Platform

PANGEA is a platform that can integrally create, manage and control VOs. PANGEA manages roles, norms and the organizations that facilitate the inclusion of organizational aspects. The services are also included completely separated from the agent, facilitating their flexibility and adaption. PANGEA incorporates a CBR-BDI reasoning mechanism available for the agents. The basic agent types defined in PANGEA are:

- *OrganizationManager*: the agent responsible for the actual management of organizations and suborganizations. It is responsible for verifying the entry and exit of agents, and for assigning roles. To carry out these tasks, it works with the OrganizationAgent, which is a specialized version of this agent.

- *InformationAgent*: the agent responsible for accessing the database containing all pertinent system information.
- *ServiceAgent*: the agent responsible for recording and controlling the operation of services offered by the agents. It works as the Directory Facilitator defined in the FIPA standar.
- *NormAgent*: the agent that ensures compliance with all the refined norms in the organization.
- *CommunicationAgent*: the agent responsible for controlling communication amongst agents, and for recording the interaction between agents and organizations.
- *SnifferAgent*: manages the message history and filters information by controlling communication initiated by queries.

We have created a service-oriented platform that can take maximum advantage of the distribution of resources. To this end, all services are implemented as Web Services. This makes it possible for the platform to include both a service provider agent and a consumer agent, thus emulating a client-server architecture. The provider agent (a general agent that provides a service) knows how to contact the web service, the rest of the agents know how to contact with the provider agent due to their communication with the ServiceAgent, which contains this information about services. Once the client agent's request has been received, the provider agent extracts the required parameters and establishes contact. Once received, the results are sent to the client agent. Using Web Services also allows the platform to introduce the SOA architecture (Service-Oriented Architecture) into MAS systems. SOA is an architectural style for building applications that use services available in a network such as the web [17]. It promotes loose coupling between software components so that they can be reused. Applications in SOA are built based on services. A service is an implementation of a well-defined functionality, and such services can then be consumed by clients in different applications or processes. SOA allows for the reuse of existing services and a level of flexibility that was not possible before.

Each suborganization or work unit is automatically provided with an OrganizationAgent by the platform during the creation of the suborganization. This OrganizationAgent is similar to the OrganizationManager, but is only responsible for controlling the suborganizationn, and can communicate with the OrganizationManager if needed. If another suborganization is created hierarchically within the previous suborganization, it will include a separate OrganizationAgent that communicates with the OrganizationAgent from the parent organization. These agents are distributed hierarchically in order to free the OrganizationManager of tasks. This allows each OrganizationAgent to be responsible for a suborganization although, to a certain extent, the OrganizationManager can always access information from all of the organizations. Each agent belongs to one suborganization and can only communicate with the OrganizationAgent from its own organization; this makes it possible to include large suborganizational structures without overloading the AgentManager. All of the OrganizationAgents from the same level can communicate with each other, unless a specific standard is created to prevent this.

3.2   The HERA Agents Platform Running on the Wireless Sensor Nodes

This section briefly describes the HERA (Hardware-Embedded Reactive Agents) platform [7] and the WSN-SOA platform on which it is based, SYLPH (Services laYers over Light PHysical devices) [16]. In HERA agents are directly embedded on the WSN nodes and their services can be invoked from other nodes in the same network or other network connected to the former one. HERA is an evolution of the SYLPH platform [16]. SYLPH follows a SOA model [17] for integrating heterogeneous WSNs in AmI-based systems. HERA takes a step ahead over SYLPH, embedding agents directly on the wireless nodes. SYLPH implements an organization based on a stack of layers. Each layer in one node communicates with its peer in another node through an established protocol. In addition, each layer offers specific functionalities to the immediately upper layer in the stack.

The SYLPH Message Layer (SML) offers the upper layers the possibility of sending asynchronous messages between two nodes through the SYLPH Services Protocol (SSP), the internetworking protocol of the SYLPH platform. The SYLPH Application Layer (SAL) allows different nodes to directly communicate with each other using SSDL (SYLPH Services Definition Language) requests and responses that will be delivered in encapsulated SML messages following the SSP. The SSDL is the IDL (Interface Definition Language) used by SYLPH. SSDL has been specifically designed to work with limited computational resources nodes [16]. Furthermore, there are other interlayer services offered by the SAL for registering services or finding services offered by other nodes. In fact, these interlayer services call other interlayer services offered by the SYLPH Services Directory Sub-layer (SSDS). Any node that stores and maintains services tables is called SYLPH Directory Node (SDN). In SYLPH, a node in a specific type of WSN (e.g., ZigBee) can directly communicate with a node in another type of WSN (e.g., Bluetooth). Therefore, several heterogeneous WSNs can be interconnected through a SYLPH Gateway. A SYLPH Gateway is a device with several hardware network interfaces, each of which is connected to a distinct WSN. The SYLPH Gateway stores routing tables for forwarding SSP packets amongst the different WSNs with which it is interconnected.

The HERA platform adds its own agents layer over the SYLPH stack. This way, HERA agents running on WSNs with different radio technology can communicate amongst them through one or more SYLPH Gateways [16]. The main components added by HERA to the SYLPH stack are the HERA Agents Layer (or just HERA) and the HERA Communication Language Emphasized to Simplicity (HERACLES). HERA agents are specifically intended to run on devices with reduced resources, similar as SYLPH was designed for. Each HERA agent is an intelligent piece of code running over the SAL. There must be almost one facilitator agent in every agent platform. This agent is the first created in the platform and acts as a directory for searching agents. In HERA, the equivalent of this agents are the HERA-SDNs (HERA Spanned Directory Nodes). HERA agents communicate amongst them through HERACLES, the agent communication language designed for being used under HERA.

4   Case Study

This section presents a real scenario where the system has been deployed to provide healthcare for elderly people. The scenario consists of a telemonitoring system for elderly at a geriatric residence where elderly can be monitored not only at the residence, but also at their own homes. This way, the daily life and the safety of the external patients are also improved, delaying or even avoiding the moment in which they need to move to residence. The name of the residence have been omitted due to confidentiality reasons.

The system includes an innovative indoor and outdoor Real-Time Locating System that features an outstanding precision, flexibility and automation integration [18] [19]. Moreover, the application includes home automation capabilities, so that a light sensor can make a lamp to be switched on or dimmed by means of the invocation or a certain service stored in a wireless actuator node connected to the relay or dimmer of the respective lamp. Agents in the system collaborate with context-aware agents that employ Wireless Sensor Networks and automation devices to provide automatic and real-time information about the environment, and allow users to interact with their surroundings, controlling and managing physical services (i.e., heating, lights, switches, etc.). All hardware is someway integrated with agents, providing automatic and real-time information about the environment that is processed by the agents to automate tasks and manage multiple services.

On the one hand, there is a locating infrastructure at the geriatric residence for positioning patients, medical personnel and assets within the building. The configuration used in the system (shown in Figure 1) consists of a ZigBee tag mounted on a bracelet worn on the users' wrist or ankle, several ZigBee readers installed over protected zones, and a central workstation where all the information is processed and stored. These readers are installed all over the facilities so that the system can detect when a user was trying to enter a forbidden area according to the user's permissions. The ZigBee network also allows obtaining information of the environment from different sensors, such as temperature sensors, light sensors, as well as smoke and gas detectors. Each ZigBee node includes an 8-bit RISC (Atmel ATmega 1281) microcontroller with 8KB of RAM, 4KB of EEPROM and 128KB of Flash memory and an IEEE 802.15.4/ZigBee 2.4GHz transceiver (Atmel AT86RF230). These devices have several communication ports (GPIO, ADC, I2C and UART through USB or DB-9 RS-232) to connect to distinct devices, including a wide range of sensors and actuators [18]. In addition, it can be used different locating techniques using these devices as readers and also as tags carried by patients and medical personnel. These devices are small enough to be carried by a patient, a caregiver or even an object, and provide a battery life of up to six months. The location of users is given as coordinated points obtained from the locating techniques provided by a locating engine [19]. All information obtained by means of these technologies is processed by the PANGEA agents. Depending on the system requirements, several interfaces can be executed. The interfaces show basic information about nurses and patients (name, tasks that must be accomplished, location inside the residence, etc.) and the building (specific room temperature, lights status, etc.). The system allows users to keep track of any tag in the system as well as receive distinct alerts in real-time coming from the system in any Web-based device, such as PC or a smartphone carried by doctors and nurses. Among the different alerts there are panic button alerts (when a user press a panic button on its tag or in a fixed device including such a button), forbidden area alerts (when a user enter into a forbidden area according to its permissions), as well as low-battery alerts (if some tag in the system should be recharged).

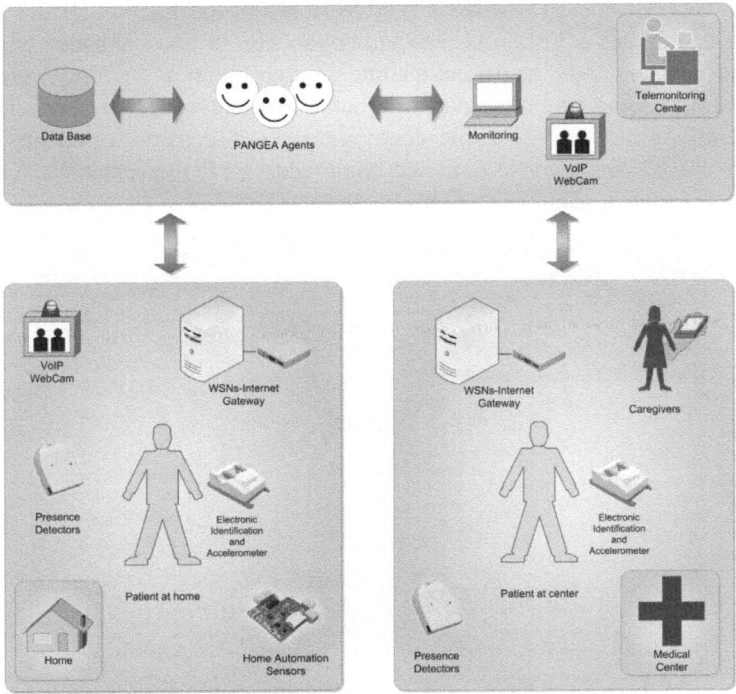

Fig. 1. Communication and infrastructure schema of the telemonitoring system

The ZigBee infrastructure has been deployed in a 600 m2 area within the residence where live dependent people with distinct dementias such as Alzheimer's disease. The locating infrastructure is intended to provide the real-time position of people (i.e., patients and medical personnel) and assets (i.e., wheelchairs and lifters) with an average accuracy of 2 meters within the monitored area. Figure 2 shows one of the Web-based interfaces of the telemonitoring system in the monitored area. The infrastructure deployed for the first pilot in the 600 m2 area includes 64 fixed ZigBee nodes [18] acting as readers and collecting nodes, 15 tags for residents and nurses, as well as a location server running in a local computer.

On the other hand, there is deployed a home automation in each patient's home for telemonitoring the environment where he or she lives from a remote control center installed in the own geriatric residence. Thus, there is a computer connected to a remote healthcare telemonitoring center (i.e. the geriatric residence) via Internet.

Alerts can be forwarded from the patients' homes to the caregivers in the remote center, allowing them to communicate with patients in order to check the possible incidences. These alerts can be, for instance, the detection of a patient's fall or a high smoke level in the patient's home. This computer acts as a ZigBee master node through a physical wireless interface (e.g., a ZigBee network adapter as a ZigBee USB dongle or a ZigBee node connected through the computer's USB port) [18]. If, for instance, the monitored patient falls over on the floor, his fall detector gets from its accelerometer a measurement higher than a previously specified threshold. This sensor (i.e. accelerometer) invokes a service stored in the Internet-HERA Gateway. Such service initiates a VoIP and webcam connection to be established between the telemonitoring center and the patient's home through Internet. This way, caregivers in the remote center can watch the patient's home and talk with him in order to verify the accident. As the telemonitoring center accesses directly to a patients database, caregivers can see his medical data and home address. If the accident is confirmed, the caregivers send an ambulance to his home.

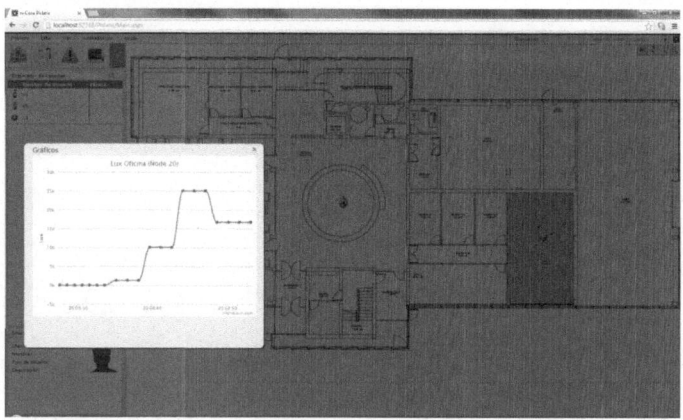

Fig. 2. Web-based interface for tracking people and assets

The home automation infrastructure for the remote telemonitoring of the elderly at their homes is formed by a ZigBee wireless sensor network fully integrated on the environment. For the pilot of the system, this network has been deployed in a typical bedroom in the own residence (simulating the patient's home), as shown in Figure 3.

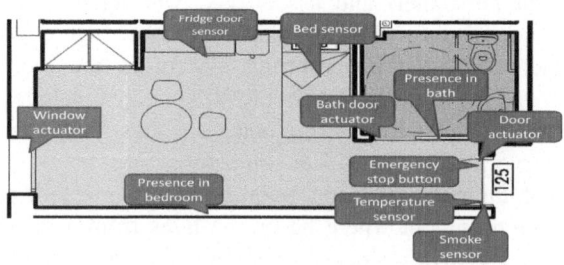

Fig. 3. Automation infrastructure deployed

The automation infrastructure is formed by 16 sensors and actuators distributed in 5 ZigBee nodes. The ZigBee nodes gather periodically the measurements from the sensors and forward this information to the remote center through one of the ZigBee nodes that acts as coordinator in the network and as gateway from the ZigBee network and the Internet.

5   Conclusions

In the future, health care for hospital patients, the elderly and people with other disabilities will require the use of new technologies that allow medical personnel to carry out their tasks more efficiently. In addition, the use of WSN and RTLS provides a high level of interaction among users and patients through the system and is fundamental in the construction of the intelligent environment.

The telemonitoring system presented in this paper improves security at home to dependents. It implements monitoring and alerting subsystems, as well as additional services to automatically react to emergency situations. The telemonitoring system's architecture goes a step ahead in designing systems for home care by offering features that make it easily adaptable to any pervasive environment. Unlike other telemonitoring systems, the presented system allows to integrate heterogeneous sensor networks from different technologies, even wired ones. So, it is possible to join multiple sensors in the same telemonitoring system using the technology that better fits each sensor's data characteristics. Furthermore, as result of the dynamic features of the PANGEA and HERA platforms, the presented system can be easily enhanced with new sensors without be redeployed and it can be adapted to new scenarios as even whole medical centers with many patients, whilst other approaches cannot. Finally, the system incorporates intuitive interfaces which facilitate usability and automatic adaptation to the user profile.

Acknowledgments. This project has been supported by the Spanish Ministry of Science and Technology project TIN 2009-13839-C03-03: Organizaciones Virtuales Adaptativas: Mecanismos, Arquitecturas y Herramientas (OVAMAH).

References

1. WHO: Global Age-friendly Cities: A Guide. World Health Organization (2007)
2. Emiliani, P.L., Stephanidis, C.: Universal access to ambient intelligence environments: Opportunities and challenges for people with disabilities. IBM Systems Journal (2005)
3. Wooldridge, M., Jennings, N.R.: Agent Theories, Architectures, and Languages: A Survey. In: Wooldridge, M.J., Jennings, N.R. (eds.) ECAI 1994 and ATAL 1994. LNCS, vol. 890, pp. 1–39. Springer, Heidelberg (1995)
4. Sarangapani, J.: Wireless Ad hoc and Sensor Networks: Protocols, Performance, and Control, 1st edn. CRC (2007)
5. Nerguizian, C., Despins, C., Affès, S.: Indoor Geolocation with Received Signal Strength Fingerprinting Technique and Neural Networks. In: de Souza, J.N., Dini, P., Lorenz, P. (eds.) ICT 2004. LNCS, vol. 3124, pp. 866–875. Springer, Heidelberg (2004)

6. Zato, C., Villarrubia, G., Sánchez, A., Barri, I., Rubión, E., Fernández, A., Rebate, C., Cabo, J.A., Álamos, T., Sanz, J., Seco, J., Bajo, J., Corchado, J.M.: PANGEA – Platform for Automatic coNstruction of orGanizations of intElligent Agents. In: Omatu, S., Paz Santana, J.F., González, S.R., Molina, J.M., Bernardos, A.M., Rodríguez, J.M.C. (eds.) Distributed Computing and Artificial Intelligence. AISC, vol. 151, pp. 229–240. Springer, Heidelberg (2012)
7. Alonso, R.S., Tapia, D.I., Bajo, J., García, O., De Paz, J.F., Corchado, J.M.: Implementing a hardware-embedded reactive agents platform based on a service-oriented architecture over heterogeneous wireless sensor networks. Ad Hoc Networks 11(1), 151–166 (2013) ISSN 1570-8705, 10.1016/j.adhoc.2012.04.013
8. Camarinha-Matos, L., Afsarmanesh, H.: Design of a Virtual Community Infrastructure for Elderly Care. In: Camarinha-Matos, L.M. (ed.) Proceedings of PRO-VE 2002, Sesimbra, Portugal (2002)
9. Kohn, L.T., Corrigan, J.M., Donaldson, J.: To Err is human: Building a Safer Health System. Committee on Quality of Health Care in America Institute of Medicine. National Academy Press, Washington, DC (1999)
10. Liu, H., Darabi, H., Banerjee, P., Liu, J.: Survey of Wireless Indoor Positioning Techniques and Systems. IEEE Trans. Syst. Man Cybern. Part C-Appl. Rev. 37, 1067–1080 (2007)
11. Tapia, D.I., De Paz, J.F., Rodríguez, S., Bajo, J., Corchado, J.M.: Multi-Agent System for Security Control on Industrial Environments. International Transactions on System Science and Applications Journal 4(3), 222–226 (2008)
12. Ding, B., Chen, L., Chen, D., Yuan, H.: Application of RTLS in Warehouse Management Based on RFID and Wi-Fi. In: 4th International Conference on Wireless Communications, Networking and Mobile Computing, WiCOM 2008, pp. 1–5 (2008)
13. Stelios, M.A., Nick, A.D., Effie, M.T., et al.: An indoor localization platform for ambient assisted living using UWB. In: Proceedings of the 6th International Conference on Advances in Mobile Computing and Multimedia, pp. 178–182. ACM, Linz (2008)
14. Lanzola, G., Gatti, L., Falasconi, S., Stefanelli, M.: A Framework for Building Cooperative Software Agents in Medical Applications. Artificial Intelligence in Medicine 16(3), 223–249 (1999)
15. Decker, K., Li, J.: Coordinated Hospital Patient Scheduling. In: Proceedings of the Third International Conference on Multi Agent Systems, Paris, France, pp. 104–111 (1998)
16. Corchado, J.M., Bajo, J., Tapia, D.I., Abraham, A.: Using Heterogeneous Wireless Sensor Networks in a Telemonitoring System for Healthcare. IEEE Transactions on Information Technology in Biomedicine. Special Issue: Affective and Pervasive Computing for Healthcare 5518, 663–670 (2009)
17. Cerami, E.: Web Services Essentials: Distributed Applications with XML-RPC, SOAP, UDDI & WSDL, 1st edn. O'Reilly Media, Inc. (2002)
18. Nebusens n-Core®: A Faster and Easier Way to Create Wireless Sensor Networks, http://www.n-core.info (accessed November 2012)
19. de Paz, J.F., Tapia, D.I., Alonso, R.S., Pinzón, C.I., Bajo, J., Corchado, J.M.: Mitigation of the ground reflection effect in real-time locating systems based on wireless sensor networks by using artificial neural networks. Knowl. Inf. Syst. 34, 193–217 (2013)

User-Centered Ubiquitous Multi-Agent Model for e-Health Web-Based Recommender Applications Development

Santiago Álvarez, Oscar Salazar, and Demetrio Ovalle

Universidad Nacional de Colombia – Sede Medellín - Facultad de Minas
{salvarezl,omsalazaro,dovalle}@unal.edu.co

Abstract. Despite recent progress in e-health system development, there are still significant problems in health service recommendation processes such as searching for healthcare specialists or medical appointments in hospitals and healthcare centers. Also, there are not so many e-health user-centered systems that provide assistance and good recommendations to users at any time in the location they are situated. The aim of this paper is to propose a model based on the integration of several approaches such as: ubiquitous computing, adaptive and recommender systems, web-based and user-centered multi-agent systems, and ontologies. In addition, an e-health web-based system prototype was built based on this model adopting mechanisms to search for information from anywhere and anytime, thus providing ubiquity characteristics. Finally, we present the validation of the U-MAS-HEALTH system by means of a case study.

Keywords: e-health, user-centered ubiquitous systems, multi-agent systems, recommender systems, adaptive systems, web-based applications, ontologies.

1   Introduction

Nowadays, it is very common to find out difficulties in health service recommendation processes such as searching for healthcare specialists or medical appointments in hospitals and healthcare centers. Thus, for instance, this frequently occurs when one patient decides to cancel an appointment with a healthcare specialist. Those appointments usually get lost due to the lack of an effective and efficient way that allows reassigning that appointment to another user who is already registered into the waiting list. Consequently, the allocation and canceling processes of appointments into the health services providers are becoming in arduous and repetitive tasks for employees. In addition, they must perform further relevant assignments that often neglect due to the fact that they must check over large databases to perform these two complex processes.

Another common problem that face the employees of health services providers as well as the users concerns the updating of the required documents for the renewal of the health service. This process consists to inform and remind the delivery of vital documents for users, such as transcripts, certificates of survival, identification copies, etc. In conclusion, the problem not only lies mainly in the substantial loss of medical

J.M. Corchado et al. (Eds.): PAAMS 2013 Workshops, CCIS 365, pp. 429–440, 2013.

appointments, but also on the time that hospital employees spend causing significant delays for both the hospital and other users.

In order to face these problems we propose a U-MAS-HEALTH model based on the integration of several approaches such as: ubiquitous computing, adaptive and recommender systems, web-based and user-centered multi-agent systems (MAS). In fact, the e-health system built based on this model is web-based and hence adopts mechanisms to search for information from anywhere and anytime, thus providing ubiquity characteristics [1]. In order to further potentiate this feature the implementation of the system was oriented not only to conventional computer desktops, but also increasing the scope to mobile devices with the Internet access such as smartphones, mobile phones, tablets, personal navigation devices, among others.

In addition to the above features, we also decided to implement two modules, one to automatically allow searching and selecting health specialists and other to select and allocate medical appointments both adapted to user preferences and limitations such as budget, location, service schedule, etc.

The rest of the paper is organized as follows: Section 2 outlines main concepts on ubiquitous systems, multi-agent systems development methodologies and main concepts involved in this research. Section 3 describes the ubiquitous multi-agent model proposed. Section 4 offers major results of system's validation. Finally, conclusions and future work are presented in Section 5.

2   Background

This section first provides main definitions about ubiquitous systems, MAS, recommender systems and ontologies. Then, a literature review through related works is presented to demonstrate the relevance of trends on ubiquitous, adaptive, user-centered, and multi-agent approaches for health web-based recommender system development.

2.1   Ubiquitous Systems

The ubiquitous computing was first defined by Mark Weiser in his article "The Computer for the 21st Century" [1] as a robust and transparent computing that allow users to access systems remotely. Ubiquitous systems also known as pervasive systems include systems that are in constantly communication through interconnected networks, the main and basic requirement of a ubiquitous system is the ability to provide enough level of privacy to the user anywhere and anytime [2].

As wireless technologies and telecommunication networks have gained strength, the ubiquitous systems are becoming more useful and necessary, searching for establishing a computing way that is present in objects that we use every day providing them with processing power and communication with other objects. In order to achieve interoperability among the different devices the ubiquitous computing must have a minimum level of intrusion, show an inherent proactiveness and dynamic adaptivity based on the current situation (context) and the user preferences according to the environment.

2.2   Multi-Agent Systems and Mobile Agents

The multi-agent systems (MAS) emerge from the distributed artificial intelligence (DAI) field and play a significant role, providing alternatives and tools for troubleshooting. These tools consist mainly of social organizations of agents with communication skills that exhibit characteristics of collaboration and cooperation to perform a complex task. In general, tasks are divided into subsets of tasks in order to assign among the different agents composing the system. This kind of systems promotes the acquisition and searching of information from remote servers. Furthermore, other system requirements such as adaptivity, proactiveness, reactiveness, decision making, among others can be perfectly tailored to the MAS characteristics.

There are different kinds of agents that can be associated with MAS. In this context a virtual agent is an entity that is able to act in its own environment and can create communications with other agents. Additionally, it is able to partially perceive its environment [3]. The intelligent agents have a set of functions that they perform and try to optimize in order to attain their goals.

Mobile agents [4] are processes that can move throughout a computer network, either Local Area Network (LAN) or WAN (Wide Area Network), migrating or cloning its code and state from a computer server to another. These agents can interact with heterogeneous devices, gathering information and then return to its origin with the data obtained. Mobile agents have gained wide acceptance in distributed systems due to their mobility. Since it is much more efficient an agent to mobilize up to a remote location and do a search, instead of bringing the information to be processed and filtered.

2.3   Ontologies

Ontology can be defined as a formal and explicit specification of a shared conceptualization of a domain. They provide a generalized understanding of a particular domain of interest [5]. Through the development of ontologies the comprehension of a domain can be done in a much more elaborate and organized way allowing a better acquisition of information and knowledge. In addition, the implementation of an agent-based platform developed under the FIPA (Foundation for Intelligent Physical Agents) standard allows the integration of ontologies [6]. This fact ensures the equal interpretation in the communication among two or more agents that use the same ontology [7].

2.4   Information and Recommender Systems

The recommender systems perform an outstanding task in current information systems, which are becoming more necessary promoting that the users receive the correct and precise information that they are looking for. If we add that the massive information sources such as the Internet give increasingly results, it becomes very useful to have this kind of systems to improve the filtering of information and thus provide the user with relevant information in a quickly and orderly manner.

The recommendations are generated from the opinions provided by other users on those items in previous searches or based on the user profile [8]. According to this choice there are two models for the selection of relevant information that can be presented to users: content-based systems and collaborative filtering recommender systems. The first one allows the suggestion about new products or services to user based on their similarity to the contents (description) of other products that he has previously tried [9], and has already chosen as relevant; hence the information is more focused on the user preferences. The second model uses the user assessments on certain elements of the total pool to predict ratings for the rest of the elements and recommends those with the most predicted rating [10].

2.5   Related Works

This section provides some of the works related to this research, which also use web-based approach but integrating issues like mobility of agents, adaptive agents, recommender systems, and ubiquitous systems.

A ubiquitous e-health multi-agent platform called PUMAS (Peer Ubiquitous MAS) was developed by Carrillo et al. (2005) whose main objective is to provide nomadic users (e.g. patients, healthcare professionals, doctors) with medical information adapted to different criteria (e.g., preferences, location) [11]. The system itself is composed of four additional multi-agent subsystems known as adaptation, information, communication, and connection. This system was designed for being used with mobile devices offering in this way ubiquitous features. The users make queries through query routing from mobile devices that the system provides. Even though PUMAS is a very robust system, however, it does not consider aspects of the social context and the environment, issues that are important when the system must adapt the queries made by the user.

R.Costa et al. (2007) propose VirtualECare being an a-health system developed in the field of home automation to allow building smart homes providing care for elders to improve their quality of life. Furthermore, VirtualECare uses a MAS approach not only to monitor their users, but also to be interconnected to other computing systems and devices running in different healthcare institutions, leisure centers, training facilities, or shops [12]. The system's architecture is a distributed schema whose components are unified through a network [13]. The system was implemented under the standards of the OSGi platform [14] thus providing modularity and real-time integration of components with different architectures. The system has a module for monitoring vital signs in real time that allows constant monitoring and gives the ability to communicate with the CallCareCenter. This entity is responsible for taking the necessary actions and can communicate with a hospital for an emergency report or to inform the patient about corrective actions to be taken. However, the system functionality shows possible delays when tries to communicate with hospital care centers. Also, it requires a constant human operation for performing health tasks.

Aiello et al. (2011) propose an agent-based signal processing in-node environment for real-time human activity monitoring based on wireless body sensor networks (WBSNs). Healthcare applications in which WBSNs could be greatly useful including early detection or prevention of diseases, elderly assistance at home, e-fitness, rehabilitation after surgeries, human biophysical/biochemical control, motion and gestures detection, cognitive and emotional recognition, medical assistance in disaster events, etc. An application of MAPS (Mobile Agent Platform for Sun SPOTs), for the development of a real-time WBSN-based system for human activity monitoring is described by authors. It is important to highlight that agent-oriented programming abstractions provided by MAPS allow effective and rapid prototyping of the sensor-side software. A comparison of MAPS with the AFME (Agent Factory Micro Edition) framework based on Sun SPOTs and the WBSN-specific framework SPINE based on TinyOS in the development of the monitoring system, performed by authors, has produced important considerations about the provided system efficiency and programming effectiveness [15]. From the system performance perspective, MAPS shows performances similar to those obtainable with AFME and SPINE that are suitable for fulfilling the real-time requirements of the monitoring system. From the programming effectiveness perspective, MAPS is more effective than AFME for WBSN applications as it is based on a FSM-based agent model that is more suitable than the AFME agent model for the development of lightweight WBSN-based components that are mostly reactive components. Moreover, with respect to SPINE, MAPS (and also AFME) is able to support peer-to-peer interactions among WBSN sensor nodes and proactive components.

3   Ubiquitous Multi-Agent Model Proposed

3.1   Development Methodology

There are different kinds of methodologies for modeling MAS, such as GAIA which is characterized for analyzing and designing agent-oriented systems. The main key concepts of GAIA are the following: roles, which are associated with responsibilities, permissions, activities, and protocols [16]. Another well-known MAS design methodology is MAS-CommonKADS proposed by Iglesias in his doctoral thesis [17] which integrates knowledge and software engineering along with object-oriented protocols. An integration of both methodologies was used in order to model the U-MAS-HEALTH system. The following is a brief description of each of these models: Role Model (GAIA): Allows the system designer to identify the expected functions of each of the entities that composes the system (goals, responsibilities, capabilities, and permissions). *Service Model (GAIA):* This model identifies all the services associated with each of the roles, its inputs, outputs, pre-conditions, and post-conditions. *Agent Model (GAIA and MAS-CommonKADS):* Describes the characteristics of each agent, specifying agent name, role, kind of agent, description, skills, services, activities, and goals. According to the GAIA methodology an agent can play several roles. *Task Model (MAS-CommonKADS):* This model describes all the tasks that agents can perform along with the objectives of each task, its decomposition, and troubleshooting

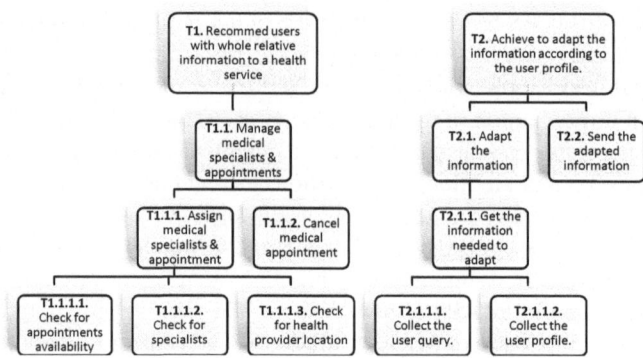

Fig. 1. Task diagram

methods to achieve each objective. Figure 1 shows part of the task diagram of U-MAS-HEALTH system corresponding to two of the main tasks.

Expertise Model (MAS-CommonKADS): Describes the ontologies (knowledge and its relationships) that agents need to achieve their goals. Figure 2 presents an example of Ontological Model for U-MAS-HEALTH.

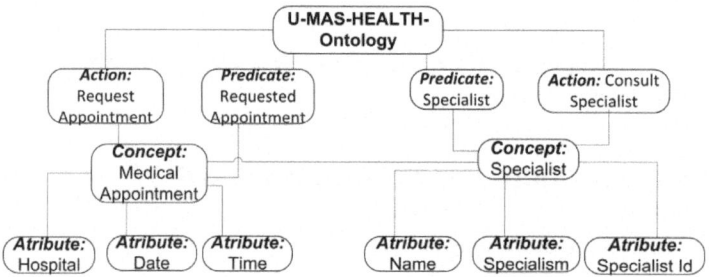

Fig. 2. Ontological model

Communication Model (MAS-CommonKADS): Describes main interactions among humans and software agents along with human factors involved for the development of these interfaces. *Organization Model (MAS-CommonKADS):* This model aims to describe the human organization in which the MAS is involved along with the software agent organization structure. *Coordination Model (MAS-CommonKADS):* Dynamic relationships among software agents are expressed through this model. For doing so, all the conversations among agents must be described: interactions, protocols, and capabilities required. Figure 3 shows the U-MAS-HEALTH sequence diagram that specifies main interactions among agents.

3.2   System Architecture

The design of the system architecture was conceived and developed using the design model of MAS-CommonKADS methodology which has three phases: network design which consists in describing the network topology and its structural components, agent design which consists in decompose each agent in subsystems, and finally, the design of the platform, which includes the necessary hardware and software features.

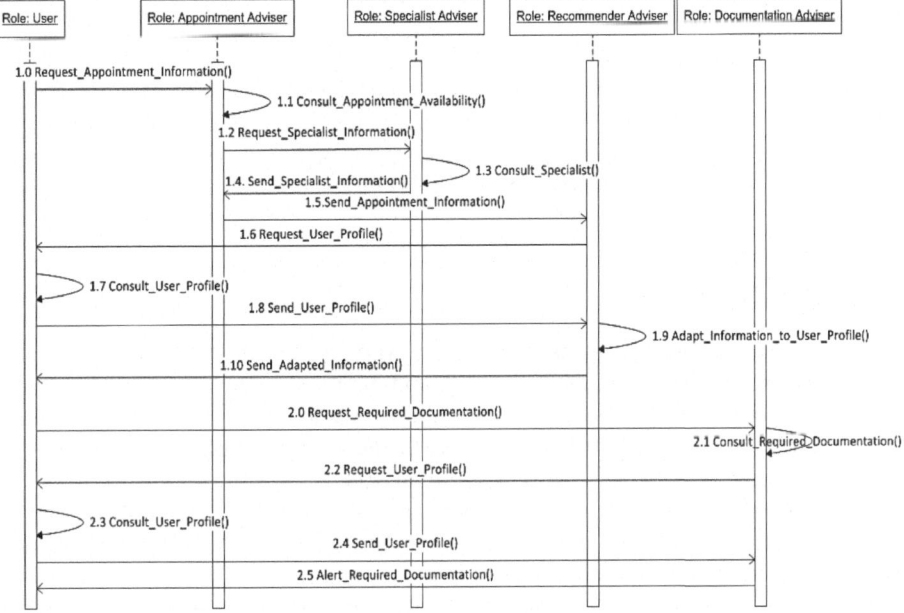

Fig. 3. Sequence diagram

Figure 4 shows the U-MAS-HEALTH architecture and the telecommunication requirements concerning the establishment of the network topology needed to implement it.

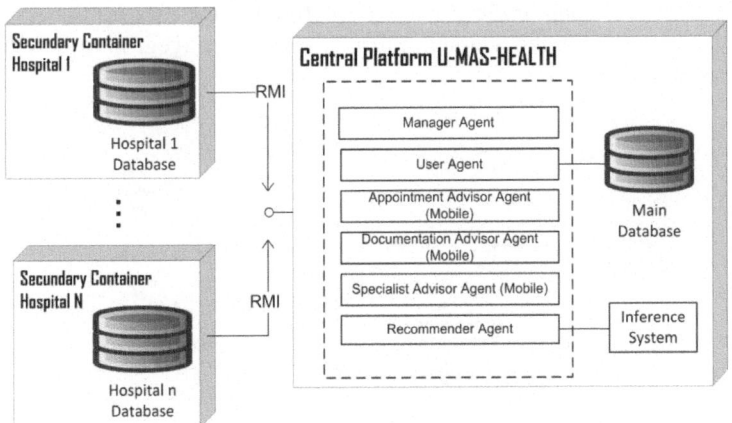

Fig. 4. U-MAS-HEALTH architecture

It shows the distribution of the system in different nodes as we had proposed in previous stages; the component in the right illustrates the central platform and the main container, where the system agents are created. In this same network node (central platform) the main database is located with the recorded information concerning user profiles. As we can see the user agent is the only one that has connection with the database.

The other two nodes represent each of the hospitals associated with the e-health system, which have their own databases that contain vital information of the system (reference information, documentation required and healthcare specialists). These network nodes will be visited by mobile agents previously created on the central platform, such as *Documentation Advisor Agent, Appointment Advisor Agent* and *Specialist Advisor Agent.*

3.3   Agent Description

The information agents belong to the common typologies such as deliberative agents, reactive and proactive agents, while network and interface agents are rather focused to the system operation. The five agents identified in the analysis phase are information agents while controlling agent becomes part of the interface agents because it is focused as a service between user interfaces and agents.

Documentation Advisor Agent: This agent has as a goal to check required documentation by the hospital and send alerts to the user if is necessary. It is representing with this behavior one kind of proactive agent because it takes decisions in order to satisfy the goals. *Appointment Advisor Agent:* This agent has to advise the user with whole the information related to a medical appointment. In addition, is the manager and responsible to inform about available medical appointments, allocation and cancellation of appointments. *Specialist Advisor Agent:* This agent has the objective of searching for specialists in any of medical branches. Its task is to provide the information to the User Agent about health provider location, medical facility, consultation fee, specialism, etc. *Recommender Agent:* This agent is of deliberative nature since it takes care of obtaining and adapting information according to the user profile (Figure 5). In addition, this agent gives the adapted information to user agent in an intelligent way through reasoning.

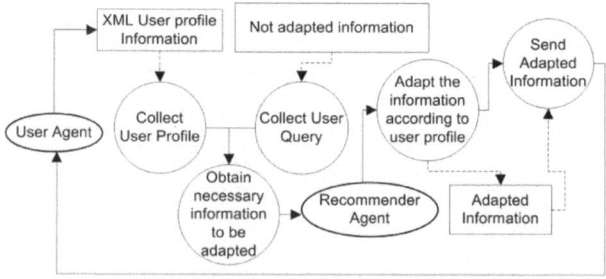

Fig. 5. Recommender agent inference model

The main goal is broken down in two tasks: The first one leads to a purely reactive task which is to deliver adapted information to the agent's request, the second task has reasoning mechanisms much more robust since it requires inference techniques for adapting the initial query information. It is important to highlight that in the model proposed, the recommendation is based on the XML user's profiles that describes the information of preferences, budget, the nearest hospital, preferred hospital, preferred specialist. *User Agent:* This agent directly represents the user within the U-MAS-HEALTH system. Besides, it is the responsible of setting communications with other agents. Also, the user agent manages the user profile, which enables the retrieval, creation and modification of profile's characteristics and preferences. *Manager Agent:* This agent is part of the interface agents because it manages the web platform. Also, it is focused between user interfaces and the agents serving as a bridge between the Web application and the agent platform.

The *User Agent*, *Appointment Advisor Agent* and *Specialist Advisor Agent* have as many instances as active users in the system. However, the other two agents (*Documentation Advisor Agent* and *Recommender Advisor Agent*) have a single instance in the system during the execution regardless of the number of active users on the system. Furthermore, it is significant to stand out that 3 of the agents above have mobility features: *Documentation Advisor Agent, Appointment Advisor Agent and Specialist Advisor Agent*. In this way, those 3 agents go through the Internet to different platforms located in other hospitals to consult their databases.

3.4   Platform Design

The U-MAS-HEALTH agent architecture was developed in JAVA, creating and managing the agents supported in the advantages of using JADE platform and FIPA-ACL performatives [18]. In addition, the integration was through ZK, a java web framework for building rich AJAX and mobile applications. ZK framework also allows web interfaces to link the java code of the agents. By using JDOM were handled the different XML user profiles. The local repository manager is stored in the MySQL database that is characterized to be stable, with high performance, and great flexibility. Finally, the ontology creation was performed by using Protégé.

4   Experiments and Results

In order to verify and validate the results of the suggested model, a ubiquitous e-health MAS prototype was built and a test was performed in which three hospitals were considered each having its own information repository. In addition, three users with their profiles were created to interact with the system as well as possible.

To validate the U-MAS-HEALTH system a comparison was made between the results given and the expected results for each of the users according to their needs, preferences and constraints. In spite of the test was performed with a few records in databases, the obtained results were satisfactory due to fact that all the recommendations were well tailored to the user and without mistakes. In addition, if the recommender agent had not been used (i.e. by using traditional software), the results provided by the system would have an average error rate of 40% (i.e. medical appointments that are not interesting to the user). On the other hand, by using the recommender agent, the average error rate was only 0.5%. Figure 6 shows the results got for the tests being performed for the module "Recommended specialists and selection of medical appointments".

The U-MAS-HEALTH system makes a good recommendation process since the specialists and medical appointments provided as results are well adapted to the user's profile. Thus, virtual users obtained adapted results from simulated hospital databases. In fact, the system exhibits relevant features and behaviors previously described such as proactivity, adaptivity, ubiquity and mobility as follows:

- **Proactivity:** the system is proactive because through the Documentation Advisor Agent the user can receive notifications and alerts about required documentation by the hospital or medical facility. The above is possible since this agent takes decisions to send the notifications without the user intervention.
- **Adaptivity:** the main goal of the system is to give adapted information according to the user's profile. So, the *Recommender Agent* satisfies this task thanks to the inference system that is incorporated in its internal architecture. This agent receives the whole information of the other agents and develops the respective adaptation in order to give to the user only the relevant information.

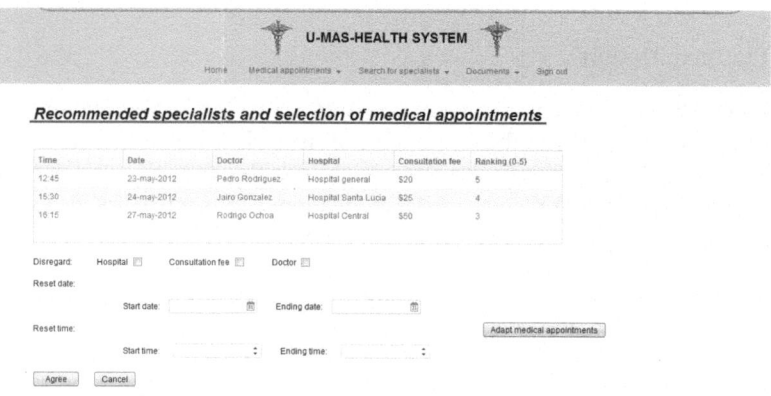

Fig. 6. U-MAS-HEALTH's web-based interface

- **Agent Mobility:** due to the fact that the information is not located in only one place and in the majority of cases each hospital has its own database, three agents (*Documentation Advisor Agent, Appointment Advisor Agent and Specialist Advisor Agent*) with the purpose of achieving their goals had to go through Internet to different platforms and databases in order to search and retrieve relevant information.
- **Ubiquity:** the ubiquity of the system was verified through the tests developed in which the system was accessed from different devices especially, mobile phones and tablets. Thus, the user has the possibility to access to diverse functionalities provided by U-MAS-HEALTH system from their mobile devices.

5   Conclusions and Future Work

The power of MAS-CommonKADS and GAIA methodologies throughout the assistance provided by AUML diagrams gives more flexibility to the agents interaction and the complexity of the MAS organizational structures. Indeed, the representation of all the aspects of the MAS based on models provided by both methodologies implies a better understanding by developers and actors giving the possibility of system upgrades in the short and long term.

This article shows the design and development of U-MAS-HEALTH that provides guidance and recommendations to the user on healthcare services by integrating features of several approaches such as: ubiquitous computing, web-based recommender systems, intelligent agents, and ontologies. The main features and characteristics exhibited by the U-MAS-HEALTH system are:

- It gives to the user the possibility to select the specialists in any branch of medicine, adapting in this way the searching to the user's preferences and constraints.
- It can be used as a support to the health services provider in the processes related to allocation and cancellation of medical appointments. In addition, it provides proactive features to these processes, mainly offering regular reminders about appointments.

The results from U-MAS-HEALTH system have been quite successful not only in the process of querying and retrieving information relevant to healthcare but also when adapting information to the user's profile. Furthermore, is important to emphasize that previously exposed features are represented in the system, so in this way it is demonstrated that the use of ubiquitous and adaptive MAS can be relevant and effective in order to provide a significant solution in health service recommendation processes.

As future work it is planned to perform the improvement of the recommendation system with more elaborated techniques, such as collaborative filtering where the previous recommendations made to other users who have similar profiles are taken into consideration. Also, it is envisaged to make the adaptation to several mobile device technologies in order to display the content correctly. Finally, another future work will be to integrate the U-MAS-HEALTH system with an expert system module to diagnose patient's diseases based on symptoms and recommended healthcare specialists who can be the most adequate to deal with the found diseases.

Acknowledgements. The research reported in this paper was funded in part by the DIME (Universidad Nacional de Colombia - Bureau of Research) project entitled "Mejoramiento de la capacidad académica, visibilidad, contacto e interacción con la comunidad nacional e internacional del grupo de investigación en inteligencia artificial de la Universidad Nacional de Colombia – Convocatoria Nacional 2011 - 2012 - Modalidad 2".with QUIPU code 202010010368.

References

1. Weiser, M.: The Computer for the 21st Century. Scientific American (1991)
2. Dehghantanha, A., Ramli, R.: A User-Centered Context-Sensitive Privacy Model in Pervasive Systems, Coll. of Technol. & Innovation, Asia Pacific Univ., Kualalumpor, Malaysia (2010)

3. Ferber, J.: MAS: An Introduction to Distributed Artificial Intelligence (1999)
4. Zhou, D., Gao, J.: Maintaining Approximate Minimum Steiner Tree and k-center for Mobile Agents in a Sensor Network. In: 2010 Proceedings IEEE, INFOCOM, March 14-19, pp. 1–5 (2010)
5. Uschold, M., Gruninger, M.: Ontologies: Principles, methods and applications. Knowledge Engineering Review 11(2), 93–155 (1996); Proceedings of the 10th International Conference on Computer Supported Cooperative Work in Design
6. FÍPA-IEEE: Foundation for Intelligent Physical Agents (2012), http://www.fipa.org/
7. Garcia, D.: Introducción al estándar FIPA. Universidad Complutense de Madrid (2000)
8. Chesani, F.: Recommendation Systems. Corso di laurea in Ingegneria Informatica, pp. 1–32 (2007)
9. Mizhquero, K., Barrera, J.: Análisis, Diseño e Implementación de un Sistema Adaptivo de Recomendación de Información Basado en Mashups. Tecnológica ESPOL-RTE (2009)
10. Sanjuán, O., Torres, E., Castán, H., Gonzalez, R., Pelayo, C., Rodriguez, L.: Viabilidad de la Aplicación de Sistemas de Recomendación a entornos de e-learning (2009)
11. Carrillo, A., Gensel, J., Villanova, M., Martin, H.: PUMAS: A Framework based on Ubiquitous Agents for Accessing Web Information Systems through Mobile Devices. In: 20th Symposium on Applied Computing (SAC 2005), pp. 1003–1008. ACM Press, New York (2005)
12. Costa, R., Neves, J., Novais, P., Machado, J., Lima, L., Alberto, C.: Intelligent Mixed Reality for the Creation of Ambient Assisted Living. In: Neves, J., Santos, M.F., Machado, J.M. (eds.) EPIA 2007. LNCS (LNAI), vol. 4874, pp. 323–331. Springer, Heidelberg (2007)
13. Costa, R., Novais, P., Lima, L., Carneiro, D., Samico, D., Oliveira, J., Machado, J., Neves, J.: VirtualECare: Intelligent Assisted Living. In: Weerasinghe, D. (ed.) eHealth 2008. LNICST, vol. 1, pp. 138–144. Springer, Heidelberg (2009)
14. OSGi Alliance: OSGi Service Platform Core Specification (2012), http://www.osgi.org/
15. Aiello, F., Bellifemine, F.L., Fortino, G., Galzarano, S., Gravina, R.: An agent-based signal processing in-node environment for real-time human activity monitoring based on wireless body sensor networks. Journal of Engineering Applications of Artificial Intelligence 24, 1147–1161 (2011)
16. Wooldridge, M., Jennings, N.R., Kinny, D.: A methodology for agent-oriented analysis and design. In: Proceedings of the Third Annual Conference on Autonomous Agents-AGENTS 1999, vol. 27, pp. 69–76 (1999)
17. Iglesias, C.: Definición de una Metodología para el Desarrollo de Sistemas Multiagentes. Universidad Politécnica de Madrid, España (1998)
18. Bellifemine, F., Poggi, A., Rimassa, G.: JADE – A FIPA-compliant agent framework. In: Proceedings of PAAM (1999)

Requirements for an Intelligent Ambient Assisted Living Application for Parkinson Patients

Millán Arroyo, Lucila Finkel, and Jorge J. Gomez-Sanz

Universidad Complutense de Madrid, Spain
{millan@cps,lfinkel@cps,jjgomez@fdi}.ucm.es

Abstract. Ambient Assisted Living is attracting the attention of researchers not only for dealing with aging, but also to improve the quality of living of people with other circumstances, like those of Parkinson patients. An Ambient Assisted Living system for a Parkinson patient has to consider the particularities of this disease. It mainly involves the alteration of the motor capabilities. There are few studies dealing with the problems of Parkinson Disease and how AAL can alleviate them. Some of these problems are centered in the patient and the disease itself, but others are derived by the patient's social context, i.e., the place the patient occupies in the society and how the patient relates to other people. The contribution of this paper consists in an enumeration of issues to consider when creating an AAL application for them and it is part of a research project called SociAAL.

Keywords: software requirements, Parkinson disease, ambient assisted living.

1   Introduction

People with disabilities caused from some pathology usually feel frustrated and depressed because they are not as independent as before. The interest in recovering the independency and, possibly, the incorporation of the person into the productive tissue of the society, would be a win-win situation for everyone. This is one of the goals for the research of Ambient Assisted Living (AAL), which takes advantage of different technologies, like Ambient Intelligence or Software agents, to assist the user and improve the quality of living.

AAL seems to mainly focus on the aging population issue, where several projects have been developed looking to address concrete areas: education, emergency attendance, mobility, or recreation, to mention some. More can be obtained from the calls in the AAL Joint Programme or AAL-JP (see http://www.aal-europe.eu). In the case of Parkinson Disease (PD), the subject has been regarded more lightly. Using as reference the 2012 catalogue of running/completed projects by the   AAL-JP only one project, the HELP project, is studying some aspects of PD, out of 90. HELP project aimed at providing body sensors (to monitor the patient status) and actuators (to supply medicines) that allowed remote health care attention.

J.M. Corchado et al. (Eds.): PAAMS 2013 Workshops, CCIS 365, pp. 441–452, 2013.

It is the hypothesis of this paper that current AAL development may not be fully compliant with the circumstances of a PD patient. Parkinson Disease (PD) patients may benefit from assistive solutions devised for other AAL users, like those looking for keeping the patient connected with the world. However, a PD patient has specific concerns. First, PD mainly affects motor capabilities in form of tremors and muscle rigidity. There are situations where the PD patient is unable to move, something that can happen while the patient is opening a door, and require external stimulus (e.g,. a noise or a light) to resume movements. This demands aids capable of detecting the blocking situation and means to break it. Second, despite these motor problems, a PD patient usually keeps cognitive capabilities almost fully intact until advanced stages of development of the disease. Unlike Alzheimer, the patient's memory, judgment, or reading/writing skills are not affected in most cases. This implies user interaction in the AAL system could be more advanced than the average case in neural diseases. Third, this disease impacts a wide range of ages. According to Parkinson Madrid association, there is a 30% of patients younger than 65. The age is important when conceiving what the AAL is going to do for the patient and how it is going to do it. Younger patients may not have strong feelings against technology and this may be a chance to overcome a possible rejection of the assistance.

In this paper, we collect statistical data, some preliminary results of interviews, and medical information that may be relevant for a developer to know in advance before designing an AAL system for a PD patient. This knowledge would be of the Domain Knowledge kind, which ought to be identified early, at the beginning of any development [20]. Collecting these requirements is not unusual, though, in the case of PD, we could not find similar works. The roadmap on AAL by AALLIANCE [22] does account AAL use cases, relevant services, and existing technologies. Parkinson is not even mentioned. There is a section for motor disabilities where problems like the temporal rigidity is not considered, nor tremors. The application of AAL to elderly people is studied in a similar way in [23], though, again, the case of neurological diseases and motor disabilities is not considered. The SOPRANO project also produced a recompilation of user requirements for AAL [29]. They assume elderly users paying attention to the following issues: social isolation, safety and security, forgetfulness, health exercises and routines, social inclusion, getting access to shops and services, checking up on care provision, and mobility inside and outside the home. There is no mention of neurological problems in the users, except the forgetfulness issue. The case of PD patients may benefit of developments for some of these cases, like social inclusion, or health exercises. Nevertheless, the case of a PD patient is not the case of just any elderly person.

The identification of PD specific requirements we make in this contribution is complemented with an initial assessment of what techniques could be relevant to each specific issue considering mainly the Multi-Agent Systems (MAS) perspective. The reason to focus on MAS is the kind of deployment we envision. We assume a non invasive solution based in ambient intelligence deployment, where sensors and actuators in the environment assist the patient. This kind of scenario can be regarded as an Ambient Intelligence (AmI) one, which is frequently approached using MAS technology [21]. So, rather than reviewing each possibly known technology related to a particular issue, in this paper we focus in the related research made in MAS about similar problems. This study will have to be completed in the future with a more comprehensive account of related research, not only MAS specific.

This study is made within the SociAAL (Social Ambient Assisted Living) project, coordinated by the Universidad Complutense de Madrid and with the participation of the Universidad de Murcia. The project aims at the affordable creation of customized software for people with concrete disabilities due to aging or PD. The contribution of this paper is related to SociAAL, since it is a preliminary study of the circumstances of PD patients together with some assessment of the relationship of these problems and some existing research areas. Demographic data has been obtained from the survey Edad-2008 [6], which is properly cited, while others have been deduced by the authors from the database provided by the INE (Statistical, National Institute). This study is not considering yet issues related with the anonymity or the privacy of the user, which we assume to be inherent to any AAL system, as registered in the different calls for the AAL-JP.

The methodology used to obtain this information has been initiating interviews with experts in the Parkinson Madrid association where an important number of the members of the project were present; then two people were consulting the literature and existing demographic studies to obtain existing information; the resulting report was evaluated by a third person looking for meaningful software requirements and enabling technologies; and now we are doing a field study to gather new information specific to the goals of SociAAL. This study will serve to deliver a first complete report of the situation of PD patients and the assistance they require.

This paper is organized as follows. Section 2 introduces the Parkinson disease. Section 3 introduces demographic information about the people with this disease. Section 4 focuses on the Parkinson patients and their concrete symptoms. Section 5 is dedicated to the caregivers. From section 3 to 5, there are subsections that introduce some discussion about the related technological solutions of the identified issues. Finally, we present some conclusions in light of what has been discussed.

2   What Is the Parkinson's Disease?

Parkinson's disease (PD), also called *idiopathic parkinsonism* or *paralysis agitans*, is a degenerative neurological illness associated with muscle stiffness, difficulty in walking, tremors and disorders in the coordination of movements [1].The disease can not be cured and treatment is applied only to improve the symptoms, in order to improve the patient's quality of life. Often, after an effective treatment in which the symptoms are controlled, the medication is no longer useful. Over time, the disease progresses and symptoms worsen. However, PD rarely causes death, so Parkinson's patients can live for many years, with important problems of dependence [1, 2].

The main problem that generates this disease is the progressive difficulty for the patient to carry on an autonomous everyday life. With time, he needs a caregiver, even for the most basic activities. As the disease progresses, the patient becomes more and more dependent [2, 3, 4].

Another problem of this disease is the difficulty of diagnosis. It is difficult to detect and diagnose because the criteria are basically clinical. When Parkinson's disease is finally diagnosed, it may be already relatively advanced [2,3]. In addition, protocols oriented to primary care physician are not common.

3   Age and Status of People with Parkinson Disease

The epidemiological incidence of PD is not high, but is increasing due to population aging. Due to the difficulties of diagnosis, at least in the early stages, detected cases are much less than the real ones. In Spain, they estimate that there are 116.000 people diagnosed, according to the survey Edad-2008 [6], which represents the 1.1% of the population over 60 years, according to the census of January 1, 2012. In Europe, more than 500,000 people suffer from this disease. Worldwide, it is estimated that 4 million people have PD [3].

It is a disease associated with aging; it mainly affects older people. 78% of people who had the disease in Spain in 1999 were 70 or older [5], but according to 2008 data [6], people over 70 years with PD were 85%, which is indicative of the strong pace of aging of this group. The mean age of people suffering from the disease in 2008 [6] was 78 years, and it rarely appears below the age of 60 (only 4.9% of patients in 2008). Nevertheless, when the disease appears below this age, it has a large negative social impact, since it prevents from having a working life and makes it very difficult to lead a life social. If the affected person also has dependents, the situation is even more dramatic.

Taking gender into consideration, there are more women (58% of female vs 42% of men), due to their increased survival rate among the elderly [6]. By marital status, married and widowed people predominate: 55% of them are married, 36% widowed, 8% singles and 1% divorced [5]. According to the same source, we know that 14% live alone, 43% in households of two people (usually with their partners) and 43% in households of three or more. A Parkinson's patient only could live alone in the initial phase of the disease, due to the strong dependence they develop. The incidence of loneliness in women is 3.3 times higher than in the case of men.

The percentage of married patients decreases with age: at 80 years old, 51% of the affected men are widowed, while in the case of women, 71% of the patients 80 or over are widowed, due to their longer life expectancy. Most of those affected (43%) live in households with two people [5], but there is a high percentage (20%) of affected women living alone compared to the 6% of men in equal circumstances.

3.1   Deduced Requirements and Related Research Lines

The studies remark the gender of patient and caregivers, but the relevance of this information is uncertain. Some researchers claim that **gender matters** in some tasks, like problem solving with software applications [12].

The patients are not alone, except in initial stages of the disease, where the patient is more independent. At some point, the person will live together, or visited frequently, by others, so the system should be **aware of the existence of other persons** in the house to take advantage of this fact. It should be expected having two people, the patient and his/her wife/husband or some daughter, according to the study. Sometimes, this number is increased with a visiting caregiver and/or relatives.

The age is certainly an issue when new technologies come into play. Elderly people are not always used to keyboards or touchable interfaces. This fact, together with a possible affectation of motor capabilities, may make difficult to interact with the PD patient. Pushing a button may be too much, and, sometimes, uttering words, difficult. Hence, being capable of **recognizing an intention** would be useful. Intention recognition is highly related to the Activities of Daily Living (ADL), for which there is abundant research and even a competition called EvAAL [24]. Also, there are MAS based implementation of intention recognition, like E-tools [25], which has been applied to make a wheelchair capabable of facilitating the navigation of an impaired user through complex installations, concretely, a hospital. Work in this line for PD has been made by Vanhooydonck et al [17]. The work shows an intelligent wheelchair that can learn from the user and deduce what he is going to do, i.e., recognizing the intention of the user to perform an action, so that the system completes it on behalf the user.

Also, it may be expensive to have monitors all around the house to interact with the user. So the system should be capable of using a variety of communication means, which means **all interfaces with the system will have be multi-modal**, to adapt to whatever mean is available. The interface itself, despite its modality, will have to be customized for the skills of the inhabitants of the house, possible **recognizing and adapting** to the skills of the interlocutor.

4   Concrete Needs of a Parkinson Patient

The main impact for the patient is that the disease makes him dependent on the caregiver. He will need more and more help as the disease progresses, even the most basic and everyday tasks. Obviously, the level of independence or dependence to perform these and other tasks varies depending on how the disease progresses, and the type of symptoms, that can be from very mild at first, practically not preventing individual autonomy, to the almost total loss of mobility in the most extreme situations, in which a patient cannot get out of bed [3, 4, 7].

Being in this situation or feeling that one is progressing towards it, generates fear and depression, besides other negative effects such as psychological distress and anxiety, sleep disturbances, sexual dysfunction or even psychotic symptoms [3]. The patient experiences a decrease in self-esteem as he feels he no longer has control over his own life. From the early stages, patients face serious difficulties in going out, so they seclude in their homes and lose social contacts. This loss of social relationships is both cause and effect of the psychological discomfort these people feel. Therefore, they experience the disease as something that limits and binds them. Often, they do not accept it and assume that the changes in their life imply stress and emotional exhaustion [3,4]. The insecurity they feel due to their disease is also related to the decrease of their social relationships, even coming to suffer 'sociophobia', or not wanting to go out or see anyone because of an excessive fear of symptoms and / or negative reactions from people.

According to the Hoen and Yahr classification [8], there are five stages in the disease. In the first one, symptoms are mild and appear on one side of the body without seriously hinder individual autonomy. It is likely that at this stage the disease has not yet been diagnosed, and discomfort had not been associated with Parkinson's. In the second stage, symptoms expand and become more intense, manifesting at both sides, but not impairing balance. Dependence for specific tasks begins to appear but is still moderate and does not entail an important loss of autonomy. Moderate dependence arises from slower movements and more insecurity: the patient needs more time to get dressed, have difficulties with laces and zippers, using the toilet, and getting in and out of bed. He needs help to perform certain tasks such as cutting meat and uses some specific devices to prevent him from spilling food or liquids when shaking. Also, he requires support for getting in and out of the tub and may experience alterations in writing or in the use of language.

In stages three and four the disease is advanced but not extreme. In the two first stages the individual is less dependent and does not feel so bad, but in these stages the situation worsens. The distinction between phase three and four is of degree. They have in common the presence of impaired balance and some characteristics such as the shortening of the steps, difficulties in turns, falls, and difficulty in starting and stopping movement as wells as problems in taking corners and going through doors. Patients experience fatigue and pain and communication difficulties. They are dependent for bathing, washing, getting in and out of the bath, eating or cooking. They may be independent for some tasks, but if they manage to dress themselves or go to the toilet, they are slowly and proceed with difficulty. They enter in and out of bed with help. They may incontinency problems and cannot stay alone. Finally, in stage five, patients stay in wheelchairs or permanently in bed, being totally dependent for all activities (they cannot stand alone, it is difficult to understand them, they have problems in swallowing and must be monitored to avoid drowning, etc) [3]. At this stage the person constantly depends of a caregiver and technology would not avoid the human attention.

4.1   Deduced Requirements and Related Research Lines

We have structured the requirements into two groups: the disease itself (monitoring and control) and external assistance to compensate the symptoms.

In the first group there would be those elements whose goals is to monitor the health of the user and/or suministrate the medicines. This part is sufficiently studied in works like HELP Project (Home-based Empowered Living for Parkinson's disease patients) from the Call 1 of the AAL-JP. HELP focuses in the creation of wearable sensors for the patient, automatic health monitoring devices, and medicine dispensers. Thought it is not PD specific, research works for **reminding activities** and **guiding in diary physical exercises** can be of relevance here too. Like other AALs, the system also must **deal with emergencies** of different nature (the patient falls or the patient does not move). The reaction of the system depends of the available means (are there robotic actuators available? Is there anyone else at home? Has the patient fallen or is he just lying on the sofa?). If no other option is available, the system ought to have **means to communicate with the nearest health center**. The **monitoring of the patient** of PD is well studied in the abovementioned project, and in the work of Cunningham et al. [15]. Cunningham et al. propose a direct test where the patient is proposed to click on a button in an interface. Observing how the user moves the mouse or types with the keyboard in especially prepared notebook, they can recognize the current status of the patient. MAS for monitoring have been used frequently too, as in Tocino et al. [26] where different uses of MAS for health monitoring are introduced.

In the second group, there are different elements in the AAL that intend to assist externally the user. It is the assistive technology, perhaps through **robotic actuators**, but not limited to them. For instance, about the stiffness of the person, which is very recurrent. The PD makes the person unable to move from a position, be it resting in the bed, sofa, or standing up. It is documented that walking stride can be improved with the provision of a different visual stimulus [13]. Hence, mediums to create those visual stimuli in the environment of the user would be meaningful. Nevertheless, there are no actuators compensating anything in the PD. The body equilibrium problems can be alleviated with different mechanical apparatus, as reviewed in [16]. These apparatus are not usually computerized, though they may have some automatisms, like the laser cane. Cunningham et al. [14] make another review attending to monitoring technologies and assistive technologies intended to assist with using devices or carrying out tasks. They focus mainly in the patient movements observation and the use of computer or devices for walking. MAS for controlling actuators are possible, though the interest now seems to be in the coordination of multiple robots using agent technology [27].

In the area of assistance for carrying out tasks, we have already mentioned the **intention recognition** feature before in section 3.1. This would influence positively the independency of the user and improve the self-esteem.

The variety of assistive technologies in the market, the different needs that each patient has in order to deal with the disease, the different activities a user may be involved into (new activities due to the disease and old ones that ought to be maintained), and the variety of budgets that a family with a PD patient may have, demand a very flexible AAL system. Ideally, it should be an **open system** where software developed by different people could interact without caring for who was the vendor of the specific hardware. A technology that may be useful for this endeavor is **software agents**. In this area there are standard protocols (see FIPA http://www.fipa.org), means to create and share ontologies to successfully interact, technologies to control unknown software behavior (like norms and laws to force agents not to deviate from the intended behavior), and means to define and obtain emergent behaviors as a result of the interaction of the individuals, to mention some. Also, the AAL must show **adaptiveness** to the different stages of the disease. It is not likely another system development can be made, so the same system must cope with the available means to adapt to the changes in the symptoms. Also, with the way the **multi-modality** is handled by the users, recognizing which is the best way to communicate. The adaptation can be requested and guided by some user, not necessarily the patient. The work from Burns et al. [18] show a prototype called *HomePUI* which allows the configuration of an AAL for three disease aspects: cognitive, physical, and chronic. Some of these authors, later on, progress towards changing automatically the interface features by collecting and updating **user profiles** [19]. We think both options could be available, in order to increase the feeling of the user having the control.

Among these extra future functionalities, there is one highlighted by the study and it is the need of **keeping the person in touch with the world**. Finding ways in which a person can interact with others despite the PD could be a great advance for the patient and would prevent reclusion and depressions.

Last, but not least, there is a problem with assistive technologies vendors. Making some vendor specific hardware interact with another can be indeed challenging. The key concept here is **interoperability**. This can be achieved through standards, platforms, or some middleware, like software agents. Related standards are OSGi, the more specific for health devices ISO EN 13606, the HL7, or the ISO 11073. There are not many platforms, though. We located only UniversAAL, which promises a flexible, and configurable middleware. Agents can be a mean to achieve this interoperability, too, but whether they can do it better, it is something to be proven, yet. Nevertheless, this **interoperability** is quite desirable since it would affect enormously the cost of the system. It would be possible to choose the best assistive technology with the available budget. Also, it would be possible to upgrade in the future.

Another factor that affects the cost of the PD AAL system is its management costs. **Self-management** research can aid in this aim. Self-management usually attends to four areas (though there is not a general agreement): self-heal, self-configuration, self-protection, and self-optimization. Being able to realize these features in the system, would require a greater initial investment, but, long term, it would be worth. Nehmer et al. [28] already apply these concepts to AAL, using these concepts as guideline to realize concrete solutions for the system.

5   Concrete Needs of a Caregiver

Most Parkinson's patients live in family homes and are cared by relatives. 90% of them require personal care, 66% of those are cared by relatives who live in the same household, 5% have an employed person living at home, and 35% receive care from people who are not residing in the home [6], mainly relatives.

Caregivers play a key role, from various points of view. First, they constitute an important economic support, since Parkinson would be a disease with a high social cost if it had to be publicly funded [3]. It is important to keep in mind that only a minority of diagnosed cases receive public aid. Second, they provide emotional support, especially as other social relations tend to weaken or disappear due to the disease. Family members offer encouragement, and they often seek information, resources and treatments [3, 7, 9].

The vast majority of caregivers are women (in 99% of cases) [5, 6]. If the patient is a male, the caregiver may be his own wife or daughter [3, 5, 6]. If the patient is a woman, usually her daughter becomes the principal caregiver, since their husbands do not assume that role or tend to hire external services if no related woman is available [3, 6]. However, although some households pay for help, it is not a total release of the responsibility of care.

If a family member has Parkinson, it is very likely that the organization of the household will experience some kind of imbalance. The disease generates tensions and problems of coexistence between the affected person and the caregiver (due to changes in behavior, stress, fear, increased workloads, etc.). In addition, the focus is put on the disease problems and other family problems tend to fade. [3] There are new difficulties in making work and household chores compatible with the care of the patient (sometimes it is necessary to leave work) and the caregiver' workload increases while the leisure time decreases, making it very difficult to have an independent life with her new role. It is also important to mention the economic burden posed by the disease, especially for lower income households. [3, 7, 9, 10]

It is very common to identify a syndrome called "caregiver burn", [11] a phenomenon that is not specific to Parkinson patient's caregivers, but generalizable to other situations of dependence. Due to the significant dependencies of these patients, and to the fact that the caregivers are usually elderly with some limitations to adequately fulfill their role, the "caregiver burn syndrome" has special emphasis on parkinsonism [9]. The caregiver tend to feel "burned" when the workload exceed her possibilities, either because the physical effort involved, or because the increased workload involves new tasks, or the feeling that they spend their lives caring for a sick without having her own life. If they have other tasks or occupations, the situation gets even more complicated.

This disease, therefore, not only constrains the patient's life but that of his family members who take care of him, especially wives or daughters. For this reason, the development of AAL technology will not only help the sick, but also improve the caregiver's life, because becoming more autonomous the patient, caregiver burden decreases too.

5.1   Deduced Requirements and Related Research Lines

The simple existence of an AAL system that succeeds even partially to increase the self-esteem of the patient or that serves to improve the independency of the patient, will mean work is relieved from the caregiver. This should improve the chances of a caregiver from suffering burn syndrome.

Again, the fact that most of the times the caregiver is a woman, may affect the way the system ought to interact. For instance, statistically, woman may prefer one mean of interaction over others, like preferring speech oriented interfaces instead of key boards or mousses.

As in the case of the patient, when the caregiver is a relative, there is a high risk that the person reduces the interaction with other people. Hence, aiding to keep **the social** relationships with others ought to be important as well in the case of the caregiver. If these relationships help to provide emotional support to them, it would be much better. Also, they need some leisure time. Therefore, the AAL system may also be capable of entertaining and assisting the caregiver in other activities, like shopping online the

450 M. Arroyo, L. Finkel, and J.J. Gomez-Sanz

weekly food. The system could even help the caregiver to bring some work to home and make the assistance to the patient compatible with the daily routines. As in the case of the patient, the number of services an AAL system could provide is uncountable.

So the reasons to look for an **open system** where the functionality can be improved along the time are reinforced. Bringing new services to the system that improve even more the quality of living of the persons attracts new challenges, like how to keep the backwards compatibility, i.e., ensure the system is still capable of doing what it did well in the past.

6 Concluding Remarks

Accounting the problems of a person with Parkinson Disease is an extensive task. Some of the problems are common to those of ageing, but others are more particular, like the stiffness. The capability of dealing with them depends on the potential of the intended AAL and the number of actuators available to them. We expect from those systems to be open ones where new sensors, actuators, and control software, are installed and un-installed. In principle, the paradigm that better suits this kind of problem is the software agents' one. For us, it seems intuitive to picture the AAL system as a community of cooperating agents that can accommodate their behavior to new-comer agents or deal with failures in existing devices. This cannot happen magically, of course, it has to be programmed. Some of these desirable behaviors have been studied for long in agent research, and we expect to incorporate them as needed without neglecting to study other areas.

This openness is very important also because it would permit to build affordable systems, where choosing different vendors could make their devices interoperate (perhaps using some of the standards for AAL which are being developed).Adaptability is equally relevant, to deal with the advance of the disease and aid in whatever is possible, may it be for the PD patient or for the caregiver.

The study acknowledges there is a part which has not been presented here referring to the anonymity or the privacy of the user. We assume these are essential features which we want to explore too, but after the general overview of the situation of a PD patient is better known in the project.

Another missing part of the study is the connection of PD AAL with generic AAL. Such link does exist, since PD is more common in elders. As stated in the introduction, AAL has focused mainly in the generic issues with aging, with some people working in concrete neurological diseases, like Parkinson.

Part of the evidences presented in this paper has been obtained from other demographic studies, though the concrete numbers are original of this report. When the data was directly obtained and no interpretation was made on our side, the numbers were accompanied by the corresponding citation.

Acknowledgements. This paper has been funded by the the project SociAAL (Social Ambient Assisted Living), supported by Spanish Ministry for Economy and Competitiveness, with grant TIN2011-28335-C02-01. We also acknowledge the Parkinson Madrid Association for supporting this project and advising in its inception.

References

1. Parkinson's disease,
   `http://en.wikipedia.org/wiki/Parkinson's_disease`
2. El parkinson, `http://www.parkinsonmadrid.org/el-parkinson/`
3. Dávila, P., Rubí, E., Mateo, A., et al.: La situación de los enfermos afectados por la enfermedad del parkinson, sus necesidades y sus demandas. Colección Estudios. Serie Dependencia. N° 12009, Imserso, Madrid
4. Martignoni, E., et al.: How parkinsonism influences life: the patients' point of view. Neurol. Sci. 32, 125–131 (2011)
5. Instituto Nacional de Estadística: Encuesta sobre discapacidades, deficiencias y estado de salud (EDDES 1999), Madrid (1999)
6. Instituto Nacional de Estadística: Encuesta sobre discapacidad, autonomía personal y situaciones de dependencia (EDAD 2008), Madrid (2008)
7. Anaut-Bravo, S., Méndez-Cano, J.: Relatives and caregivin to people affected with parkinson. Portularia XXI(1), 37–47 (2011)
8. Hoehn, M.M., Yahr, M.D.: Parkinsonism, onset, progression and mortality. Neurology 17, 427–442 (1967)
9. Kim, K.S., Kim, K.H., Kim, K.H., et al.: Subjective and objective caregiver burden in parkinson's disease. Journal of Korean Academy of Nursing 37(2), 242–248 (2007)
10. Davey, C., Wiles, R., Ashburn, A., Murphy, C.: Falling in parkinson disease: the impact on informal caregivers. Disability and Rehabilitation 26(23), 1360–1366 (2004)
11. Pérez Peñaranda, A.: El cuidador primario de familiares con dependencia. Universidad de Salamanca, Tesis doctoral. Fac. Medicina (2006)
12. Burnett, M., Beckwith, L., Wiedenbeck, S., Fleming, S., Cao, J., Park, T.H., Grigoreanu, V., Rector, K.: Gender pluralism in problem-solving software. Interacting with Computers 23(5), 450–460 (2011)
13. Lewis, G., Byblow, W.D., Walt, S.E.: Stride length regulation in Parkinson's disease: the use of extrinsic, visual cues. Brain 123(10), 2077–2090 (2000)
14. Cunningham, L.M., Nugent, C.D., Finlay, D.D., Moore, G., Craig, D.: A review of assistive technologies for people with Parkinson's disease. Technol. Health Care 17(3), 269–279 (2009)
15. Cunningham, L.M., Mason, S.S., Nugent, C.D., Moore, G.G., Finlay, D.D., Craig, D.: Home-Based Monitoring and Assessment of Parkinson's Disease. IEEE Transactions on Information Technology in Biomedicine 15(1), 47–53 (2011)
16. Constantinescu, R., Leonard, C., Deeley, C., Kurlan, R.: Assistive devices for gait in Parkinson's disease. Parkinsonism and Related Disorders 13, 133–138 (2007)
17. Vanhooydonck, D., Demeester, E., Hüntemann, A., Philips, J., Vanacker, G., Van Brussel, H., Nuttin, M.: Adaptable navigational assistance for intelligent wheelchairs by means of an implicit personalized user model. Robotics and Autonomous Systems 58(8), 963–977 (2010)
18. Burns, W.P., Nugent, C.D., McCullagh, P.J., Zheng, H., Finlay, D.D., Davies, R.J., Donnelly, M.P., Black, N.D.: Personalisation and configuration of assistive technologies. In: Annual International Conference of the IEEE Engineering in Medicine and Biology Society (2008)
19. Skillen, K.-L., Chen, L., Nugent, C.D., Donnelly, M.P., Burns, W., Solheim, I.: Ontological User Profile Modeling for Context-Aware Application Personalization. In: Bravo, J., López-de-Ipiña, D., Moya, F. (eds.) UCAmI 2012. LNCS, vol. 7656, pp. 261–268. Springer, Heidelberg (2012)

20. Zave, P., Jackson, M.: Four dark corners of requirements engineering. ACM Trans. Softw. Eng. Methodol. 6(1), 1–30 (1997)
21. Sadri, F.: Ambient intelligence: A survey. ACM Computing Surveys (CSUR) 43(4), 36 (2011)
22. Van Den Broek, G., Cavallo, F., Wehrmann, C.: AALIANCE Ambient Assisted Living Roadmap. Ambient Intelligence and Smart Environments, vol. 6. IOS Press (2010)
23. Kleinberger, T., Becker, M., Ras, E., Holzinger, A., Müller, P.: Ambient Intelligence in Assisted Living: Enable Elderly People to Handle Future Interfaces. In: Stephanidis, C. (ed.) UAHCI 2007, Part II. LNCS, vol. 4555, pp. 103–112. Springer, Heidelberg (2007)
24. Álvarez-García, J.A., Barsocchi, P., Chessa, S., Salvi, D.: Evaluation of localization and activity recognition systems for ambient assisted living: The experience of the 2012 EvAAL competition. JAISE 5(1), 119–132 (2013)
25. Barrué, C., Cortés, U., Martínez, A.B., Escoda, J., Annicchiarico, R., Caltagirone, C.: e-Tools: An agent coordination layer to support the mobility of persons with disabilities. In: Bramer, M. (ed.) Artificial Intelligence in Theory and Practice. IFIP, vol. 217, pp. 425–434. Springer, Boston (2006)
26. Tocino, A.V., Calvo Alcalde, A.I., Andrés Gutiérrez, J.J., Álvarez Navia, I., García Peñalvo, F.J., Castrejón, E.P.: MIMO: Multi-Agent System for Personal Health Monitoring. In: Handbook of Research on Developments in E-Health and Telemedicine, Hershey, pp. 827–850.
27. Fukuda, T., Takagawa, I., Hasegawa, Y.: From intelligent robot to multi-agent robotic system. In: International Conference on Integration of Knowledge Intensive Multi-Agent Systems, pp. 413–417 (2003)
28. Nehmer, J., Becker, M., Karshmer, A., Lamm, R.: Living assistance systems: an ambient intelligence approach. In: Proceedings of the 28th International Conference on Software Engineering (ICSE 2006), pp. 43–50. ACM (2006)
29. Müller, S., Santi, M., Sixsmith, A.: Eliciting user requirements for ambient assisted living, Results of the SOPRANO project. In: eChallenges 2008 Conference, pp. 81–88 (2008)

Mobile Phone-Based Fall Detectors: Ready for Real-World Scenarios?

Raul Igual, Carlos Medrano, Lourdes Martin, and Inmaculada Plaza

R&D&I EduQTech group - Electronics Engineering Department, Escuela Universitaria
Politecnica de Teruel, University of Zaragoza, Teruel (Spain)
{rigual,ctmedra,lourdes,inmap}@unizar.es

Abstract. Falls are a major health problem among the elderly. The consequences of a fall can be minimized by an early detection. In this sense, there is an emerging trend towards the development of agent systems based on mobile phones for fall detection. But when a mobile phone-based fall detector is used in a real-world scenario, the specific features of the phone can affect the performance of the system. This study aims to clarify the impact of two features: the accelerometer sampling frequency and the way the mobile phone is carried. In this experimental study, 5 participants have simulated different falls and activities of daily living. Using these data, the study shows that the sampling frequency affects the performance of the detection. In the same way, when a fall detector intended to be attached at the body is carried in an external accessory, the performance of the system decreases.

Keywords: Fall detection, mobile phones, real-world scenarios.

1 Introduction

Falls in the elderly are a common cause of mortality, morbidity, reduced functioning, and premature nursing home admissions [1]. Among many other factors, the severity of a fall depends on the amount of time the elder remains lying on the floor after falling [2]. Therefore, a quick detection and assistance is needed.

The evolution of mobile phones to integrated systems with computing power, communication resources and embedded sensors opens the door to new innovative research in fields such as ambient intelligence [3]. Modern mobile phones have the potential to act as intelligent agents [4]. In particular, the design of agent systems based on mobile phones for automatic fall detection is an emerging research area. The first system appeared in 2009: Sposaro et al. [5] presented a detector for the Android operating system that is available for download from the Google Play store. Since then, the number of mobile phone-based detectors has increased dramatically, each time with more features and enhanced algorithms. The system of Dai et al. [6] can be considered the first relevant work in this field. Following this trend, Lee et al. [7] compared the motion signals acquired by the built-in accelerometer of the phone to those recorded by an independent body-mounted accelerometer, showing better

J.M. Corchado et al. (Eds.): PAAMS 2013 Workshops, CCIS 365, pp. 453–459, 2013.
© Springer-Verlag Berlin Heidelberg 2013

results in the latter. Albert et al. [8] propose a system not only to detect a fall but also to automatically classify the type. In this sense, Martin et al. [9][10] describe a multi-agent system capable of detecting falls through the sensors embedded in a mobile phone. Other authors have also worked in this direction [11,12].

In all of these studies, the signals from the built-in accelerometer of the phones are used for fall detection. However, it should be noted that there is high variability within mobile phone models. When mobile phone-based fall detectors are used in real-world scenarios, there is a risk that the performance is affected by the specific device features. This risk is greater for sensor-dependent applications such as fall detectors. In this experimental study, we aim not only to identify some of these features but also to quantify them.

The rest of this paper is structured as follows: Section 2 examines the contributions of this work, section 3 describes the methodology used in the experiments, section 4 introduces the detection algorithm, section 5 explains the influence of the accelerometer sampling frequency, section 6 explores the idea of wearing the phones in handbags, and section 7 draws some initial conclusions and outlines areas that can be researched further.

2   Contributions

This study aims to clarify the impact on mobile phone-based fall detection of some factors that can compromise its performance in a real-world scenario. We put the focus on two:

- Accelerometer sampling frequency: The built-in accelerometer of the phones samples at different frequencies depending on the model in question. This study examines the degradation of the detection as the sampling frequency decreases. This is an important aspect when selecting the suitable smart phone for a real-world application.
- The way the mobile phone is carried: All previous research placed the mobile phone in a standardized position of the subject's body (waist, thigh, trunk, back, wrist, etc.). However, users may wish to carry the mobile phones in external accessories like handbags. To the best of our knowledge, this is the first study that examines the effect on fall detection of wearing the phone externally.

3   Subjects and Methods

Mobile phone-based fall detectors use the acceleration signals from the built-in accelerometers of the phones. Then, these signals can be classified as falls or activities of daily living (ADL). Therefore, to measure the performance of a detector, it is necessary to acquire acceleration data from both falls and ADL.

Since this is an experimental study, these data have been collected from 5 young volunteers (mean age 27.6, SD 8.5, 3 males, 2 females). All participants performed 4 different simulated falls: forward, backward, lateral left and lateral right. Fall types were selected to fit into the broader categories of typical fall events of older people [13,14]. They were completed on a soft mattress. The methodology of the simulations was the following: firstly, researchers gave oral information on the experiment including the preventive measures that should be adopted to avoid any risk, secondly a written consent was obtained from each participant; thirdly researches performed a practical demonstration of each fall type, fourthly subjects were required to be as natural as possible, using, if desired, common strategies to minimize the fall impact such as flexing their knees or putting their hands. Each fall type was repeated 4 times.

Subjects were also requested to simulate the most common types of ADL (table 1). Each ADL was repeated 3 times.

During the experiments, participants wore a mobile phone in both their pockets (left and right) and in two handbags. Thus a total of 64 fall records and 180 ADL records were collected from each participant. Half of them were acquired from the pockets and the other half from the handbags. After each simulation, the acceleration data were downloaded wirelessly from the mobile phones to a PC. The sampling frequency was 50 Hz. Each record contained a 6 second width time window around the highest peak of the acceleration magnitude.

Table 1. List of common ADL performed by the 5 volunteers

Most common types of Activities of Daily Living	
Sitting down on a soft chair	Getting up from a soft chair
Sitting down on a hard chair	Taking the lift (two floors, up)
Picking up something from the floor	Squatting and tying shoelaces
Lying down on a bed	Getting out of bed
Jogging	Walking
Walking downstairs	Walking upstairs
Getting into the car	Getting out of the car
Jump to pick something	

4   Fall Detection Algorithm

A low-complexity algorithm has been selected for fall detection. This algorithm has been tested with the data from the falls and ADL (section 3). It considers both an upper and a lower threshold. If the maximum value of the acceleration within a checking time window of 1 second around the peak, is higher than the upper threshold, the pattern recognition is triggered to check the minimum value. If this value is less than the lower threshold, a fall detection is reported [5].

This algorithm has been used to measure the impact on its performance of the two mentioned factors: the acceleration sampling frequency (section 5) and the way users carry the phones (section 6).

5   Frequency-Dependent Detection

The present section quantifies the effect on performance of the reduction of the accelerometer sampling frequency. The fall and ADL records from the pockets, initially sampled at 50 Hz, have been resampled to lower frequencies (50/4 Hz, 50/8 Hz, 50/16 Hz, 50/25 Hz). A total of 5 datasets have been obtained, one set for each frequency.

The performance of the detector is measured using ROC curve. A ROC curve plots the true-positive rate of detection, TPR, against the corresponding false-positive rate of error, FPR [15]. The formulae to calculate both rates are the following:

$$TPR = \frac{TP}{TP+FN} \tag{1}$$

$$FPR = \frac{FP}{FP+TN} \tag{2}$$

where TP is the number of falls labelled as falls, FN is the number of falls labelled as ADL, FP is the number of ADL labelled as falls and TN is the number of ADL labelled as ADL.

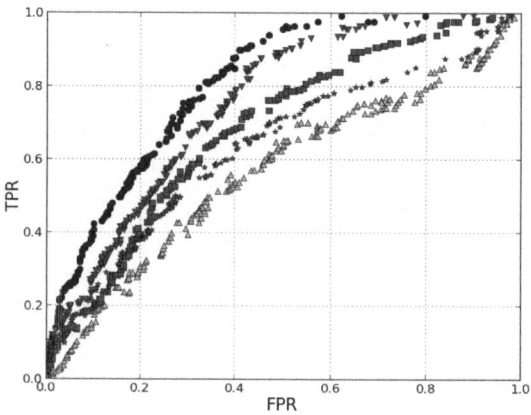

Fig. 1. Representation of ROC curves corresponding to the threshold based algorithm using different data sets: 50 Hz (blue circles), 50/4 Hz (red triangles down), 50/8 Hz (green squares), 50/16 Hz (magenta stars), 50/25 Hz (yellow triangles up)

A ROC curve of the algorithm of section 4 has been obtained for each one of the 5 datasets. Each set has been randomly divided in two equal parts: one for training and the other for testing. For each one of the 5 datasets, we have selected a set of threshold pairs from its training set in the following way. One of the thresholds is kept fixed while varying the other. In this way a ROC curve can be plotted. For several values of the fixed threshold, several ROC curves are obtained, whose envelope is taken as the final ROC. In other words, for a given FPR, the thresholds are adjusted to get the maximum TPR. Using these optimal thresholds, the ROC curve of each dataset (50, 50/4, 50/8, 50/16, 50/25) has been obtained with its testing set. The 5 curves are represented in figure 1.

Figure 1 clearly illustrates that the higher the sampling frequency the better the detection. Table 2 shows the area under the ROC curve for each dataset.

Table 2. Area under the ROC curve for each sampling frequency

	50 Hz	50/4 Hz	50/8 Hz	50/16 Hz	50/25 Hz
Area under the ROC curve	0.8363	0.7908	0.7129	0.6590	0.6086

According to the results of table 2, we can quantify the degradation in performance that occurs as the sampling frequency is varied. When the sampling frequency diminishes to 50/25 Hz, the area is decreased by 27% compared to the performance at 50 Hz. This decrease is higher when the frequency is less than 12.5 Hz.

6   External Handbag

Subjects may wish to carry the mobile phone not only in some parts of their bodies (waist, thigh, back, etc) [16-17], but also in external handbags. This study aims to quantify the loss in performance when a detector initially intended to be worn on the body is placed in a handbag.

For this purpose, we have used the data from both pockets and handbags, obtained as described in section 3, and the low-complexity algorithm introduced in section 4. This algorithm has been trained with half of the data from the pockets (thigh), simulating a body-worn detector. Then, it has been tested using either the other half of the data from the pockets or the data from the handbags. Figure 2 illustrates the ROC curve for each set of data.

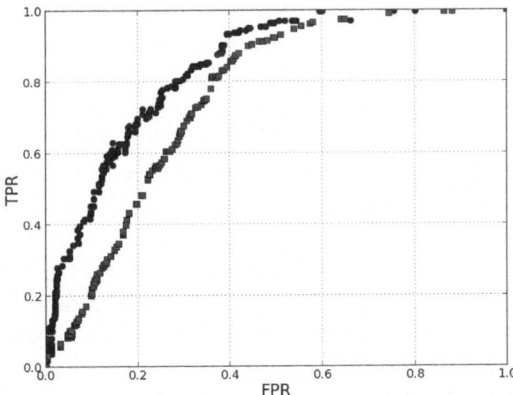

Fig. 2. ROC curves of the algorithm trained with the data from the pockets and tested with two different datasets: the rest of the data from the pockets (blue circles), the data from the handbags (red squares)

The performance of the algorithm is clearly worse when tested on the handbag data set compared to the performance on the pocket data set, the kind of data for which the detector was originally trained. Table 3 quantifies the difference by measuring the area under the ROC curves. It reaches 10%.

Table 3. Area under the ROC curve for both, the pocket-tested and the handbag-tested system

	Detector tested with data from the pockets	Detector tested with data from the handbags
Area under the ROC curve	0.8363	0.7559

7   Discussion and Conclusions

This study has proven that the acceleration sampling frequency influences the performance of a fall detector. The level of dependence is in part conditioned by the fall detection algorithm. As an example, a low-complexity algorithm has been used in this study. Other algorithms could have strengthened or weakened this dependence. This is not a minor problem in mobile phone-based fall detection. This implies that the same application can behave differently depending on the particular phone model in which it is run. Researches in this field must be very cautious when selecting the sampling frequency. Also, the features of the built-in accelerometers must be examined to ensure they can sample at the proper frequency.

Unlike dedicated fall detectors, mobile phone-based systems not only detect falls but also perform many other tasks, for example, making calls, sending SMS, running other applications, etc. In a real-world scenario, subjects may wish to use these functions as well as to carry the mobile phones in different places. In this way, handbags are proper accessories to keep these devices. This study investigates for the first time the effect of carrying the mobile phones in them. Results show that the performance of the system decreases when a traditional fall detector intended to be worn on the thigh is carried in a handbag. Therefore, studies in this field should consider using the phones as true "phones". Otherwise, their performance may decrease in a real-world scenario, leading probably to their rejection. To be accepted by their potential users, fall detectors should meet their needs and this inevitably includes usability aspects.

This study has still some limitations. For the analysis, we have considered a simple threshold-based fall detection algorithm. Further research should incoporate more sophisticated algorithms based on machine learning and investigate their performance when faced to real-world conditions.

In conclusion, future studies in mobile phone-based fall detection should also consider the specific features of phones since they could compromise the performance in a real-world scenario. In this study, we have shown the impact of two factors: the sampling frequency and the way the device is carried.

Acknowledgments. The authors wish to thank the 5 volunteers who participated in the study. This work was in part supported by the "European Social Fund" and the "Departamento de Ciencia, Tecnologia y Universidad del Gobierno de Aragon".

References

1. Rubenstein, L.Z., Josephson, K.R.: Falls and their prevention in elderly people: What does the evidence show? Med. Clin. North. Am. 90(5), 807–824 (2006)
2. Masud, T., Morris, R.O.: Epidemiology of falls. Age Ageing 30(4), 3–7 (2001)
3. Lane, N., Miluzzo, E., Lu, H., Peebles, D., Choudhury, T., Campbell, A.: A survey of mobile phone sensing. IEEE Commun. Magazine 48(9), 140–150 (2010)
4. O'Grady, M.J., O'Hare, G.M.P.: Mobile devices and intelligent agents - towards a new generation of applications and services. Information Sciences 171, 335–353 (2005)
5. Sposaro, F., Tyson, G.: iFall: An Android application for fall monitoring and response. In: Proc. IEEE Engineering in Medicine and Biology Society, EMBC, pp. 6119–6122 (2009)
6. Dai, J., Bai, X., Yang, Z., Shen, Z., Xuan, D.: Mobile phone-based pervasive fall detection. Personal Ubiquitous Comput. 14(7), 633–643 (2010)
7. Lee, R.Y.W., Carlisle, A.J.: Detection of falls using accelerometers and mobile phone technology. Age and Ageing, 1–7 (2011)
8. Albert, M.V., Kording, K., Herrmann, M., Jayaraman, A.: Fall classification by machine learning using mobile phones. PLoS ONE 7(5), e36556 (2012)
9. Martín, P., Sánchez, M., Álvarez, L., Alonso, V., Bajo, J.: Multi-Agent System for Detecting Elderly People Falls through Mobile Devices. In: Novais, P., Preuveneers, D., Corchado, J.M. (eds.) ISAmI 2011. AISC, vol. 92, pp. 93–99. Springer, Heidelberg (2011)
10. Sánchez, M., Martín, P., Álvarez, L., Alonso, V., Zato, C., Pedrero, A., Bajo, J.: A New Adaptive Algorithm for Detecting Falls through Mobile Devices. In: Corchado, J.M., Pérez, J.B., Hallenborg, K., Golinska, P., Corchuelo, R. (eds.) Trends in PAAMS. AISC, vol. 90, pp. 17–24. Springer, Heidelberg (2011)
11. Fang, S.H., Liang, Y.C., Chiu, K.M.: Developing a Mobile Phone-based Fall Detection Sys-tem on Android Platform. In: Proc. Computing, Communications and Applications, ComComAp, pp. 143–146 (2012)
12. Lopes, I.C., Vaidya, B., Rodrigues, J.: Towards an autonomous fall detection and alerting system on a mobile and pervasive environment. Telecommun. Syst. 1–12 (2011)
13. Noury, N., Rumeau, P., Bourke, A.K., OLaighin, G., Lundy, J.E.: A proposal for the clas-sication and evaluation of fall detectors. IRBM 29(6), 340–349 (2008)
14. O'Neill, T.W., et al.: Age and sex influences on fall characteristics. Ann. Rheum. Dis. 53, 773–775 (1994)
15. Fawcett, T.: ROC graphs: Notes and practical considerations for data mining researchers. Technical Report (2003), http://binf.gmu.edu/mmasso/ROC101.pdf (accessed December 2012)
16. Kangas, M., Konttila, A., Lindgren, P., Winblad, I., Jämsä, T.: Comparison of low-complexity fall detection algorithms for body attached accelerometers. Gait & Posture 28(2), 285–291 (2008)
17. Bourke, A., O'Brien, J., Lyons, G.: Evaluation of a threshold-based triaxial accelerometer fall detection algorithm. Gait & Posture 26(2), 194–199 (2007)

Defining and Transforming Models of Parkinson Patients in the Development of Assisted-Living Multi-agent Systems with INGENIAS

Iván García-Magariño

Departamento de Ingeniería Informática y Organización Industrial,
Facultad de Enseñanzas Técnicas,
Universidad a Distancia de Madrid,
Collado Villalba, Madrid, Spain
ivan.garcia-magarino@udima.es

Abstract. Some people suffer from the Parkinson disease and need assistance for living. Multi-agent Systems (MASs) can provide a suitable solution for their assistance. However, each patient has different circumstances, symptoms and skills that need assistance. This paper presents a model-driven approach for developing MASs customized for each patient. The current approach presents a metamodel for modeling Parkinson patients as models. In addition, this paper introduces a suite of model transformations that can transform a Parkinson patient model into an initial MAS model. This MAS model can be refined by designers and the programming code can be generated from this model. This approach applies the INGENIAS methodology for generating the MAS from a design model. Finally, a case study is presented as a proof of concept.

Keywords: Agent-oriented software engineering, assisted living, metamodel, model-driven engineering, multi-agent system, Parkinson disease.

1   Introduction

The Parkinson Disease (PD) is a degenerative disorder of the central nervous system. Although some factors can influence in the risks of suffering this diseases, such as smoking, there is a percentage of people with a certain gene that unavoidably suffer PD in the last years of their lives [8]. In these cases in which the most advanced medicine research cannot avoid the symptoms, patients need other kinds of assistance for getting along with their disease. The social environment including the family members usually becomes a pillar of support for overcoming the needs of patients [5]. However, in some cases there are not any member that can exclusively dedicate their life to take care of a patient. In these cases, the different familiar carers have to coordinate for taking care of the patient, and in some hours of the day the patient may not be able of having human company. For these cases, this work proposes a MAS as a solution for coordinating partial human carers and assisting patients in some skills.

J.M. Corchado et al. (Eds.): PAAMS 2013 Workshops, CCIS 365, pp. 460–471, 2013.

Although there is a set of symptoms that can appear in patients of PD, each patient usually only suffer a particular subset of these symptoms. In addition, each patient may only need assistance in a subset of skills of the global set of skills that need to be assisted in PD. For this reason, the development of a MAS needs to be customized according to the particular needs of each patient.

This work presents a Model-driven Engineering (MDE) approach for developing MASs customized for the particular needs of patients. MASs have been selected for addressing this issue because of some features of agents such as autonomy, social behavior, reactiveness and proactiveness. This approach includes a metamodel for defining a Modeling Language (ML), in which each model determines all the features of a patient including: their social environment with home members and other carers, their symptoms, the skills in which the patient needs assistance, and their economical circumstances. In addition, some Model Transformations (MTs) are defined to transform the models of the mentioned ML into initial MAS models, from which MASs can be developed after refining these. In particular, the remaining development of each MAS is recommended to follow the INGENIAS methodology, which was previously introduced in [10].

The remaining of the paper is organized as follows: the next section briefly introduces the background comparing some related works to the current one; section 3 presents the model-driven approach for developing and customizing MASs for PD patients, including a metamodel for determining patient models and MTs for transforming these models into initial MAS design models; ultimately, section 5 mentions the conclusions and future work.

2   Background

There are several MASs that have been developed for ambient assisted living for elderly people or people suffering a disease. For instance, Kaluza et al. [6] present a MAS that assists elderly people that is living on their own at home, in order to prolong their independence. This system can detect an emergency situation in real time. This system uses several sensors that receive abstract data, and these data are interpreted in several ways. The system detects domestic accidents with several facts, such as vertical acceleration or a frozen weird position for a long time. This MAS was tested in a nearly-realistic room with several movements. This MAS could be used for people who suffer PD, although it was not specifically designed for them. In addition, Nefti el al. [9] present a MAS for ambient assisted living for people suffering the dementia disease. In fact, this MAS keeps patients observed in an unobtrusive way, warn them of possible risks, and alert the local authority when a risk is ignored. Furthermore, Su [13] introduces a framework for e-health monotoring in wide areas such as metropolitan and national. This framework contains mobile agents conforming MASs. These MASs allow carers to monitor the patients with light-weight portable devices, without interfering their daily activities. This monitoring is aimed at patients in general without considering the particular needs of PD patients. In contrast to all these works, the current work is specifically aimed at PD patients, and uses a model-driven approach for customizing the development of each MAS for the particular circumstances of each patient.

There are several metamodels that have been defined for modeling patients in general. For example, Calvillo et al. [2] present a metamodel that is integrated in a healthcare system in which each patient can determine who can access their information such as demographic data, health, well-being and social conditions. This metamodel defines the information regarding each patient considering three main group of actors: people (e.g. nurses, relatives and friends), organizations and healthcare devices. In addition, Lopez et al. [7] have developed a framework for achieving semantical interoperability in health information systems. This framework uses the Model-driven Architecture (MDA) approach, defining the corresponding metamodels for the Computation-independent Models (CIM), Platform-independent Models (PIMs) and the Platform-specific Models (PSMs). Raghupathi et al. [11] apply the MDA approach for developing healthcare systems. Their metamodels are mainly focused on defining the models of the health clinics. In particular, a PIM is created for each clinic, and this is transformed to several PSMs. All these works present approaches for healthcare systems for patients in general, without including metamodeling concepts for some symptoms and assisted skills that are especially common in PD patients. Furthermore, none of these works relates their metamodels with the development of MASs, which can be especially useful for instance for the coordination between the patients and their carers. On the contrary, the current work presents a metamodel that takes into account all the common symptoms and assisted skills of PD patients, and provides a model-driven approach for developing assisted-living MASs for these patients.

Lastly, Gascueña et al. [4] use a model-driven approach for developing MASs, using the set of the Eclipse modeling tools. In particular, this work defines the Prometheus metamodel with the ECore language, and generates the corresponding graphical editor by means of the Graphical Modeling Framework. In addition, a metamodel is proposed for determining the security requirements in MASs [1]. This work uses a MDE approach for transforming high-abstraction models into code-specific models, so MASs can be constructed considering the security requirements. Another metamodel is specifically designed for designing robotic MASs with the Gaia methodology [12]. For instance, this metamodel can determine the environment of robotic agents, sub-organization of agents, interactions and certain kinds of roles. Nevertheless, these works do not define metamodels for domain-specific information as the current approach does for the circumstances of the PD patients.

3   Model-Driven Approach for Developing MASs for PD Patients

This work proposes a model-driven approach for developing and customizing a MAS for each PD patient with their particular social, economical and symptomatical circumstances. This approach includes a metamodel for modeling each

PD patient and their circumstances, and MTs for creating a initial MAS design model from each PD patient model. Subsection 3.1 presents the metamodel, whereas subsection 3.2 presents the MTs.

3.1   Metamodel for Modeling PD Patients

The metamodel has been defined following our previous guideline for defining metamodels with the ECore language by means of the Eclipse Modeling Framework (EMF) [3]. In particular, this metamodel uses an homogeneous representation of relationships with EReferences according to the kinds of relationships that are necessary for modeling PD patients.

This metamodel represents a ML that describes patient suffering PD. In particular, each model of this ML represents a patient with all the features concerning their illness, and their social and economical circumstances. Thus, the patient is the central concept of the model, and will be represented with the root element of the model. Figure 1 shows the excerpt of the metamodel that concerns the patient and all its surrounding concepts. As one can observe, the social environment of the patient is determined with the concepts habitat and human carer. The economical circumstances are represented with the allowance concept and the incoming attribute of the human carer and patient concepts. The features of the patient concerning their illness are represented with their symptoms and the skills that the patient needs assistance with the corresponding concepts. All these aspects of a patient influence in the MAS that can assist them, and consequently are taken into account in the metamodel.

The concept for symptoms is classified into two different kinds of symptoms, which are physical symptoms and psychological symptoms, as one can observe in Figure 2. This classification is determined by extending the symptom metamodeling concept. Each of these kinds is extended with concrete symptoms, which

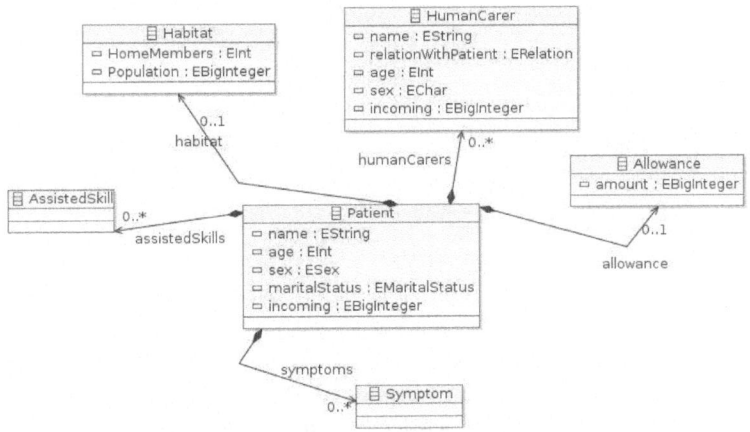

Fig. 1. Excerpt of the metamodel for modeling PD patients

are detailed in the same figure. In the future, developers can add more concrete symptoms adding the corresponding metamodeling concepts if necessary, without altering the structure of this metamodel. It is worth mentioning that the level of intensity of each physical symptom of a patient is determined with the level attribute from one to five.

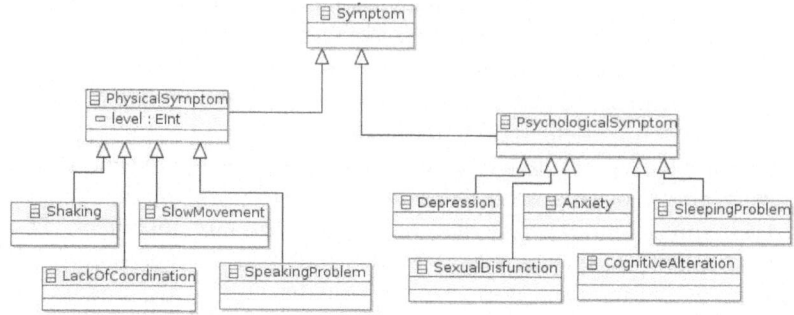

Fig. 2. Excerpt of the metamodel for modeling PD symptoms

The MASs for PD patients depend on their symptoms, mainly for designing the interface of communication between each patient and its customized MAS.

The presented metamodel can determine the particular skills in which a patient needs to be assisted. A PD patient may need assistance for eating, walking, having a shower, cooking, opening a door, sitting down, getting to bed, writing, reading or going to the toilet. As one can observe in Figure 3, each of these particular skills is represented with a metamodeling element that extends the assisted skill metamodeling element.

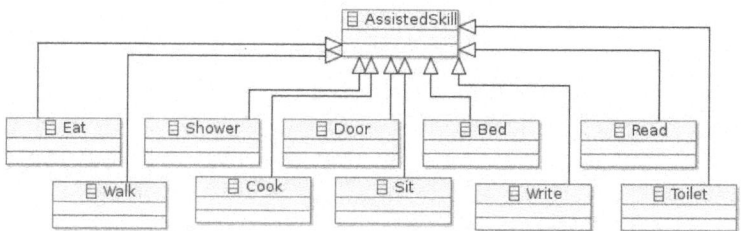

Fig. 3. Excerpt of the metamodel for skills of PD patients that need to be assisted

A MAS needs to be customized according to the skills in which each patient needs to be assisted. For instance, if the assisted actions of the patient only take place few times per day or only in a specific part of the day (e.g. having a shower or going to bed) and their human carers are partially available, the MAS can coordinate the human carers and the patient in order to allow that a patient is assisted in these actions. On the contrary, if the patient needs more assistance than the human carers can offer, then the MAS may need extra devices for assisting the patients without human assistance. In these cases, the necessary devices depend on the nature of the skills that are assisted.

Finally, the metamodel has some enumerations in order to determine possible values of some attributes, and these enumerations are specified in the part of the metamodel that is shown in Figure 4. An enumeration is defined for determining the relationship of the human carer with the patient. Another enumeration is aimed at indicating the marital status of the patient, and he last one indicates the sex of the patient or human carer.

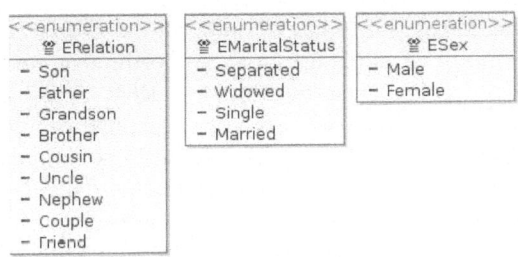

Fig. 4. Enumerations of the metamodel for determining characteristics of the human carers and patients

The relationship of the human carers of a patient are considered in order to distribute the workloads for assisting the patient, assigning greater workloads to the human carer with stronger relationship, if allowed by the specific circumstances. For instance, a husband or a wife of a patient usually is usually more devoted to assist the patient than one of their friends.

An editor has been automatically generated from the metamodel by means of EMF. This editor allows developers to define models that represent PD patients and their circumstances. In particular, section 4 presents an example of a patient model defined with this editor.

3.2   MTs for the Development of MAS for PD Patients

The architecture and behavior of an assisted-living MAS depend on many aspects regarding the patient. Thus, the information formalized in the proposed metamodel needs to be taken into account for customizing a MAS for a particular agent. However, the association between the specific metamodeling elements of the proposed metamodel and the elements of a particular Agent-oriented Software Engineering (AOSE) metamodel is not straightforward.

This approach proposes some MTs from the proposed metamodel for PD patients to the metamodel of the INGENIAS AOSE methodology that is defined with ECore. It is worth mentioning that the MTs are defined with the Atlas

Transformation Language (ATL), since this language is appropriate for transforming models that are instances of ECore metamodels.

The first group of MTs regards the coordination of the patient and human carers. The first MT of this group transforms each human carer element into a coordinator carer agent copying most of the attribute values, and creating the corresponding role and goals. In particular, a goal is created for coordinating the assistance of each skill that only needs to be assisted a few times per day. This coordination goal is to schedule a timetable in which all the patient needs are covered with the minimum effort from behalf of the human carers. The carer agent interacts with the human carer, generally in a mobile device. This agent updates the restrictions of a human carers, such as their job timetables. The second MT transforms the patient element into a coordinator patient agent that plays a role with the same goals than the coordinator carer agents. In summary, the coordinator carer agents and the coordinator patient agent interact with each other in order to guarantee that a patient is assisted when needing a human carer. The communication among carer agents and the coordinator patient agent is established by means of interactions composed of interaction units (i.e. messages). The coordinator patient agent delivers a timetable with the patient needs to all the carer agents. Each carer agent replies with their time availability. Finally, the coordinator patient agent fills the timetable with the carer agents, minimazing the effort from behalf of the corresponding human carers, and broadcast this filled timetable to all the carer agents. The carer agents show this timetable to the corresponding human carers.

Another group of MTs concern the creation of an adequate interface agent with a role and a goal, according to the physical symptoms. The interface agent is the responsible for an appropriate and fluid communication between the patient and the MAS. In particular, the interface agent receives the petitions of the patient and consequently makes requests to other agents in order to satisfy the patient petitions. For example, if the patient needs a human carer, then the interface agent indicates so to the coordinator patient agent, which can search for a human carer through the coordinator carer agents. The interface agent also provides some responses to the patient if convenient. Specifically, a MT creates an Interface agent with the ability of recognizing the human voice of the patient, if the patient has symptom of shaking and does not have the symptom of speaking problem. Conversely, if the patient has an speaking problem, another MT creates an interface agent with the keyboard communication. If the patient has both symptoms of shaking and speaking problem, the MTs compare their intensity levels in order to create the interface agent with keyboard communication, voice recognition or both kinds of communication.

There are some MTs that are aimed at creating a psychologist agent that imports certain modules for treating the particular psychological symptoms. Therefore a MT creates psychologist agent with a role and certain goals from a non-empty group of psychological symptoms in the input model. Each particular symptom will imply that a MT includes the appropriate task and goal for treating it. In particular if the patient suffers depression, the psychologist agent will perform a therapy with positive messages for avoiding depression. Each MT adds the corresponding internal application for each psychological problem. If the patient has several psychological problems, a MT creates a task that determines the therapy for the patient according to the dominant symptom of a patient each time a conversation takes place.

A suite of MTs add certain modeling elements to the MAS for assisting the skills that may not be able to be assisted by human carers because for instance these are necessary a high number of times per day. For example, if the patient needs assistance in writing and does not have a speaking problem, the interface agent includes the software for voice recognition, and a new writer agent is created. When the patient needs to write in a browser or a document, the interface agent sends a request to the writer agent, which performs the writing request. In a similar way, if the patient needs assistance to read, a reader agent will be created, which can read documents from a browser, a text editor or a Portable Document Format (PDF) reader. This agent also collaborates with the interface agent for reading aloud the responses of the MAS.

The assistance in certain skills such as eating, having a shower, walking, opening doors, cooking, sitting down and going to bed require specific hardware components, and depend on what the patient and their carers can afford according to their incoming. Generally, some skills that are not very frequent can be assisted with the human carers, such as going to bed, specially if the patient has any home member. In other skills that need frequent assistance, like opening the doors or walking, MTs can generate an agent that interacts with the assisting-living equipment for each assisted skill.

Finally, it is worth mentioning that the names of the created agents, roles, tasks and internal applications have the suffixes -A, -R, -T and -IA respectively, in order to avoid conflicts of names and clarify the design of the MAS.

4   Case Study of Modeling a Patient with PD

In this case study, a PD patient is modeled with the editor generated from the presented metamodel, as one can observe in Figure 5. This PD patient is called Manuel Pérez and its home has three members including himself. The other two members are two sons, called respectively Javier and Raúl. Both of them have jobs and act as human carers. The patient has also a nephew called Alonso García, who lives in the nearby and is also a human carer. The patient has mainly three physical symptoms, which are shaking, slow movement and lack of coordination. The level of the first symptom is three, while the level of the others is two. His psychological symptoms are depression and sleeping problem. Finally, he needs assistance for writing, cooking and having a shower.

The presented MTs were applied to the patient model to create an initial design in the INGENIAS ML for the development of a MAS for assisting his life. The agent diagram is shown in Figure 6. Firstly, one can observe the agents for coordinating the patient with his human carers. There are two roles for these agents, which are the coordinator patient role and the coordinator carer

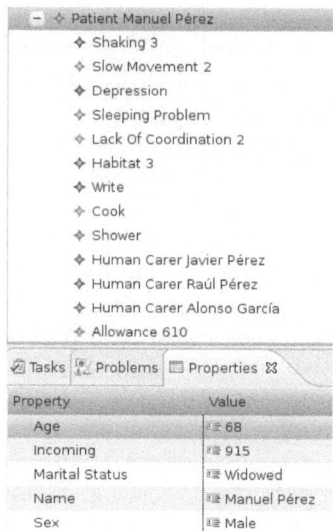

Fig. 5. Example of a PD patient model

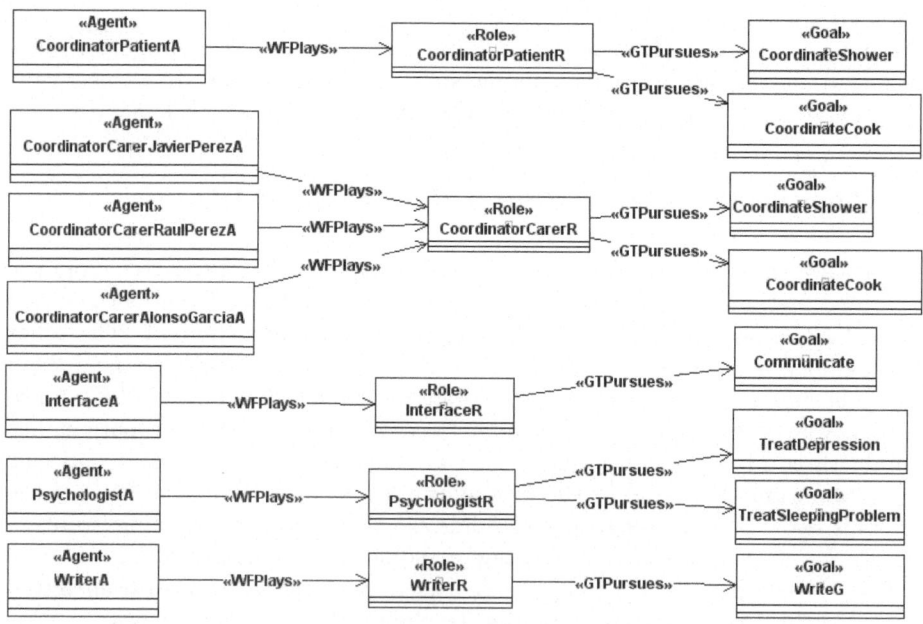

Fig. 6. Excerpt of the agents diagram of the generated MAS design

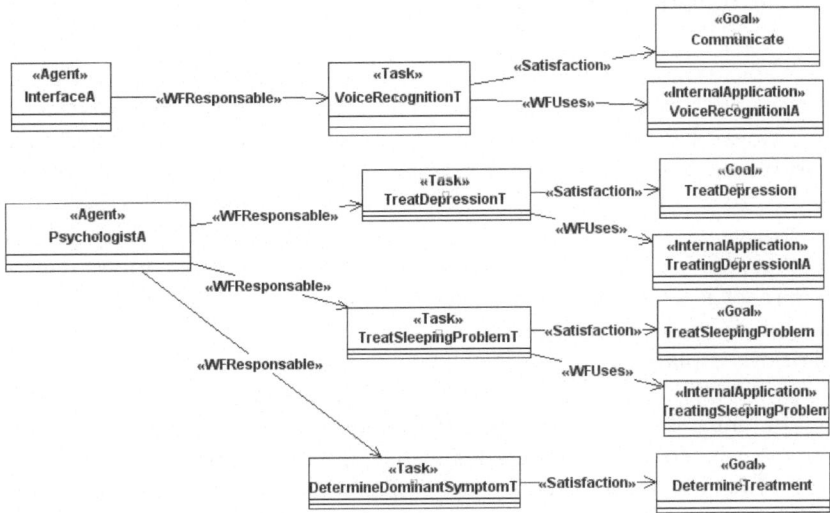

Fig. 7. Excerpt of the tasks and goals diagram of the generated MAS design

role. A MT creates an agent playing the former role since the system supports only one patient. Another MT is applied three times for creating three different agents that play the latter role, including the manes of the human carers in the coordinator carer agent names, in order to distinguish the three different agents. Both roles pursue the goals of coordinating the assistance of the patient skills that only need to be assisted a few times per day, which are to have a shower and to cook. Notice that the cook of the lunch and dinner can be done together if necessary. In addition, there is an interface agent that guarantees a fluid communication with the patient. The psychologist agent with its role pursues to treat the two different psychological symptoms, which are depression and sleeping problem. Finally, a writer agent is generated with its role and goal for writing in a browser or a document whenever the patient requests it so.

The MTs generated a tasks and goals diagram, and a relevant excerpt of this is presented in Figure 7. Since the patient needs assistance for writing according to the input model, a MT creates a task for voice recognition for the interface agent, and this task uses a specific internal application for this task. In a similar way, a task is generated for each psychological symptom for the psychologist agent. Each of these tasks uses an internal application that is specialized for treating the corresponding symptom. Since there is more than one psychological symptom in the input model, a task is generated for determining the dominant symptom in each conversation, so that the psychologist agent can determine the treatment in each conversation therapy with the patient.

After refining the aforementioned INGENIAS models, most of the software implementation can be generated from these models by means of the INGENIAS Development Kit (IDK).

5   Conclusions and Future Work

On the whole, this paper has presented a MDE approach for constructing MASs for assisting PD patients in their life. The first step is the definition a model that describes a PD patient, indicating the social, economical and symptomatical circumstances, by means of the proposed metamodel. Then, the proposed MTs are applied to obtain an initial MAS design model customized for the particular circumstances of the patient. At last, the INGENIAS methodology guides the process for refining the initial model design and generating a functional MAS. This approach is exemplified with a case study in order to test its usefulness and present its practical application.

This work is planned to be extended in several ways in the future. For now, the proposed MTs only generate modeling elements for agents, tasks, goals and interaction units. In the future, new MTs will be added to generate other modeling elements such as interaction definitions, interaction protocols, deployments and tests. In addition, this metamodel is planned to be evaluated and compared with other metamodels on the field of health by a group of postgraduate students. Moreover, an analysis study can be performed with a relevant group of PD patients in order to know whether the proposed metamodel can represent the circumstances of most PD patients. The metamodel can be improved as a consequence of this evaluation and study, including new elements for representing most of their circumstances. Furthermore, some new MASs will be developed with this approach for several PD patients with different circumstances in order to assess the current approach. This work is also planned to be further compared with similar works, measuring several parameters, such as development time, patients responses in surveys, and numbers and portions of assisted needs, to assess the actual value of the current contribution. Finally, the presented metamodel is planned to be mapped to the most common health standards, such as the ones proposed by the Health Level Seven (HL7) and Integrating the Healthcare Enterprise (IHE) organizations, in order to improve the interoperability of the presented approach and make it reusable in existing medical systems.

Acknowledgements. This work has been done in the context of the project *Social Ambient Assisting Living - Methods* (SociAAL), supported by Spanish Ministry for Economy and Competitiveness, with grant TIN2011-28335-C02-01. In addition, we acknowledge support from the *Programa de Creación y Consolidación de Grupos de Investigación de la Universidad a Distancia de Madrid,* with grant UI2011-3.

References

1. Beydoun, G., Low, G., Mouratidis, H., Henderson-Sellers, B.: A security-aware metamodel for multi-agent systems (MAS). Information and Software Technology 51(5), 832–845 (2009)

2. Calvillo, J., Román, I., Roa, L.: Empowering citizens with access control mechanisms to their personal health resources. International Journal of Medical Informatics 82(1), 58–72 (2013)
3. García-Magariño, I., Fuentes-Fernández, R., Gómez-Sanz, J.: Guideline for the definition of EMF metamodels using an Entity-Relationship approach. Information and Software Technology 51(8), 1217–1230 (2009)
4. Gascueña, J., Navarro, E., Fernández-Caballero, A.: Model-driven engineering techniques for the development of multi-agent systems. Engineering Applications of Artificial Intelligence 25(1), 159–173 (2012)
5. Jenkinson, C., Dummett, S., Kelly, L., Peters, M., Dawson, J., Morley, D., Fitzpatrick, R.: The development and validation of a quality of life measure for the carers of people with Parkinsons disease (the PDQ-Carer). Parkinsonism & Related Disorders 18(5), 483–487 (2012)
6. Kaluža, B., Mirchevska, V., Dovgan, E., Luštrek, M., Gams, M.: An agent-based approach to care in independent living. In: de Ruyter, B., Wichert, R., Keyson, D.V., Markopoulos, P., Streitz, N., Divitini, M., Georgantas, N., Mana Gomez, A. (eds.) AmI 2010. LNCS, vol. 6439, pp. 177–186. Springer, Heidelberg (2010)
7. Lopez, D., Blobel, B.: A development framework for semantically interoperable health information systems. International Journal of Medical Informatics 78(2), 83–103 (2009)
8. Miyake, Y., Tsuboi, Y., Koyanagi, M., Fujimoto, T., Shirasawa, S., Kiyohara, C., Tanaka, K., Fukushima, W., Sasaki, S., Yamada, T., et al.: LRRK2 Gly2385Arg polymorphism, cigarette smoking, and risk of sporadic Parkinson's disease: A case-control study in Japan. Journal of the Neurological Sciences 297(1-2), 15–18 (2010)
9. Nefti, S., Manzoor, U., Manzoor, S.: Cognitive agent based intelligent warning system to monitor patients suffering from dementia using ambient assisted living. In: 2010 International Conference on Information Society (i-Society), pp. 92–97. IEEE (2010)
10. Pavón, J., Gómez-Sanz, J.: Agent oriented software engineering with INGENIAS. In: Mařík, V., Müller, J.P., Pěchouček, M. (eds.) CEEMAS 2003. LNCS (LNAI), vol. 2691, pp. 394–403. Springer, Heidelberg (2003)
11. Raghupathi, W., Umar, A.: Exploring a model-driven architecture (MDA) approach to health care information systems development. International Journal of Medical Informatics 77(5), 305–314 (2008)
12. Silva, D., Braga, R., Reis, L., Oliveira, E.: Designing a meta-model for a generic robotic agent system using Gaia methodology. Information Sciences 195, 190–210 (2012)
13. Su, C.: Mobile multi-agent based, distributed information platform (MADIP) for wide-area e-health monitoring. Computers in Industry 59(1), 55–68 (2008)

Author Index